TOP
50

SPECIAL
ADVERTISING
SECTION

CONSULTING
FIRMS

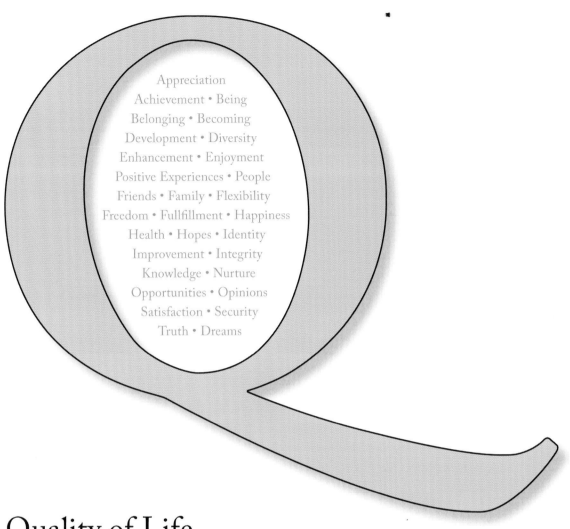

Appreciation
Achievement • Being
Belonging • Becoming
Development • Diversity
Enhancement • Enjoyment
Positive Experiences • People
Friends • Family • Flexibility
Freedom • Fullfillment • Happiness
Health • Hopes • Identity
Improvement • Integrity
Knowledge • Nurture
Opportunities • Opinions
Satisfaction • Security
Truth • Dreams

Quality of Life

What is your definition of QUALITY of life? At Gallup, you'll work in a culture that SUPPORTS you not just professionally, but personally. Whether your PASSION is building new business, managing consulting projects, or assisting executives, you'll have the OPPORTUNITY to do what you do BEST every day. We'll help you discover your TALENTS and build STRENGTHS.

How do we know that life is BETTER at Gallup? **A recent survey by Vault.com of 2,500 consultants ranks Gallup #1 for corporate culture and work-life balance, and as #2 for overall quality of life.**

At Gallup, we offer more than just a job — we offer you a FUTURE.

www.gallup.com/careers/

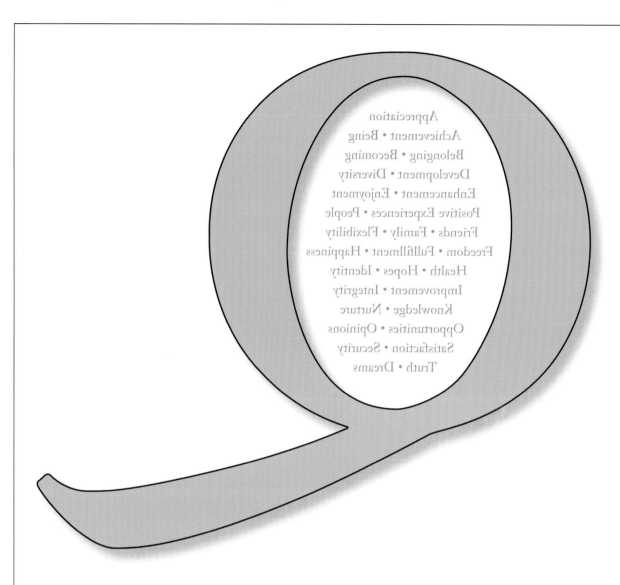

Quality of Life

By the way, did we mention that Gallup is made up of world-class teams? By bringing the BEST minds and the most TALENTED individuals together to address our clients' needs, we create a STRONGER, richer team enviroment.

We take great PRIDE in our global workforce and our inclusive culture, which embraces uniqueness and VALUES individuals for their strengths. Our corporate philosophies are founded on RESPECT for talent, personal GROWTH and development, pay for performance, and a high QUALITY of life.

www.gallup.com/careers/

Global Pharmaceutical and Biotech Consulting

TRINITY
PARTNERS

www.trinitypartners.com • careers@trinitypartners.com
www.trinitypharmasolutions.com • careers@trinitypharmasolutions.com

The media's watching Vault!
Here's a sampling of our coverage.

"The best place on the Web to prepare for a job search."
– *Fortune*

"[Vault guides] make for excellent starting points for job hunters and should be purchased by academic libraries for their career sections [and] university career centers."
– *Library Journal*

"The granddaddy of worker sites."
– *US News and World Report*

"A killer app."
– *The New York Times*

One of *Forbes*' 33 "Favorite Sites"
– *Forbes*

"To get the unvarnished scoop, check out Vault."
– *Smart Money Magazine*

"Vault has become the go-to source for career preparation."
– *Crain's New York*

"Vault has a wealth of information about major employers and job-searching strategies as well as comments from workers about their experiences at specific companies."
– *The Washington Post*

"For those hoping to climb the ladder of success, [Vault's] insights are priceless."
– *Money magazine*

"Vault [provides] the skinny on working conditions at all kinds of companies from current and former employees."
– *USA Today*

Join us on our way to becoming the world's No. 1

We at Deutsche Post World Net with the brands DHL, Deutsche Post and Postbank live for logistics. The excellent quality we deliver worldwide contributes to our customers' success. We're on our way to becoming the world's No. 1. Join us and help Deutsche Post World Net reach its targets with innovative ideas for Logistics, Mail and Financial services.

Inhouse Consulting is the internal top management consultancy of the Deutsche Post World Net. With a dynamic team of over 120 consultants and growing, we work at the heart of DHL – globally. We develop high-impact strategies for the important business challenges of today and tomorrow, working for top executives of all business divisions. Inhouse Consulting is key in enhancing the value of Deutsche Post World Net and DHL.

We thrive on global challenges, speed and change.

As our successful growth continues, our teams in the USA (Fort Lauderdale), Germany (Bonn) and Singapore are seeking graduates and high performing professionals to join us as:

Management Consultants

Your work involves strategic consulting, developing new business and product strategies, and guiding high-impact integration and optimization efforts. You will take on responsibilities quickly, with full exposure to top management. In addition, you will build up your own personal network and gain professional experience together with your skilled and motivated colleagues. You will benefit from our strong focus on teamwork and diversity, our great career prospects, and the fast-changing environment we work in.

You, as a successful candidate, offer outstanding academic records. Fluency in an additional foreign language and prior international experience is a plus. Good analytical and problem-solving skills, team spirit and an open mind are necessary attributes for your success.

Start building your career now. Join us!

For additional information see our website at www.ic.dpwn.com or contact our recruiting specialist.
Please send your application through our online application system at www.dhl-usa.com/careers

Deutsche Post World Net Business Consulting GmbH, Inhouse Consulting-US.
ATT: IC Recruitment • 1200 South Pine Island Road • Suite 210 • Plantation, FL 33324
Email: ic.recruiting@dhl.com

THE VAULT GUIDE TO THE **Top 50**
MANAGEMENT AND STRATEGY
CONSULTING
FIRMS
2008 EDITION

How many consulting job boards have you visited lately?
(Thought so.)

Use the Internet's most targeted job search tools for consulting professionals.

Vault Consulting Job Board

The most comprehensive and convenient job board for consulting professionals. Target your search by area of consulting, function, and experience level, and find the job openings that you want. No surfing required.

VaultMatch Resume Database

Vault takes match-making to the next level: post your resume and customize your search by area of consulting, experience and more. We'll match job listings with your interests and criteria and e-mail them directly to your inbox.

VAULT
> the most trusted name in career information™

THE VAULT GUIDE TO THE Top 50 MANAGEMENT AND STRATEGY CONSULTING FIRMS

2008 EDITION

NAOMI NEWMAN
and the staff of Vault

All information in this book is subject to change without notice. Vault makes no claims as to the accuracy and reliability of the information contained within and disclaims all warranties. No part of this book may be reproduced or transmitted in any form or by any means, electronic or mechanical, for any purpose, without the express written permission of Vault Inc.

Vault, the Vault logo, and "the most trusted name in career information™" are trademarks of Vault Inc.

For information about permission to reproduce selections from this book, contact Vault Inc., 150 W. 22nd St., 5th Floor, New York, NY 10011, (212) 366-4212.

Library of Congress CIP Data is available.

ISBN 13: 978-1-58131-491-5
ISBN 10: 1-58131-491-4

Printed in the United States of America

Acknowledgments

Thank you to all the Vault editorial, sales, graphics and IT staff for writing, selling, designing and programming the guide. Special thanks to Melissa Newman, Anu Rao, and Laurie Pasiuk for their writing and editorial support.

As always, the book is dedicated to the more than 3,600 consultants and 86 consulting firms who took time out of their busy schedules to distribute and complete our survey.

The best working with the best. Mars & Co.

Table of Contents

Visit the Vault Consulting Career Channel at www.vault.com/consulting - with insider firm
profiles, message boards, the Vault Consulting Job Board and more.

VAULT CAREER LIBRARY

ix

Your | Opportunity

smart business tools

best consultants

high profile clients

fast growth company

www.huronconsultinggroup.com

At Huron, We invest in you.

Huron
CONSULTING GROUP

THE BEST OF THE REST   383

Visit the Vault Consulting Career Channel at www.vault.com/consulting - with insider firm
profiles, message boards, the Vault Consulting Job Board and more.

VAULT CAREER LIBRARY   xi

Visit the Vault Consulting Career Channel at www.vault.com/consulting - with insider firm profiles, message boards, the Vault Consulting Job Board and more.

VAULT CAREER LIBRARY   xiii

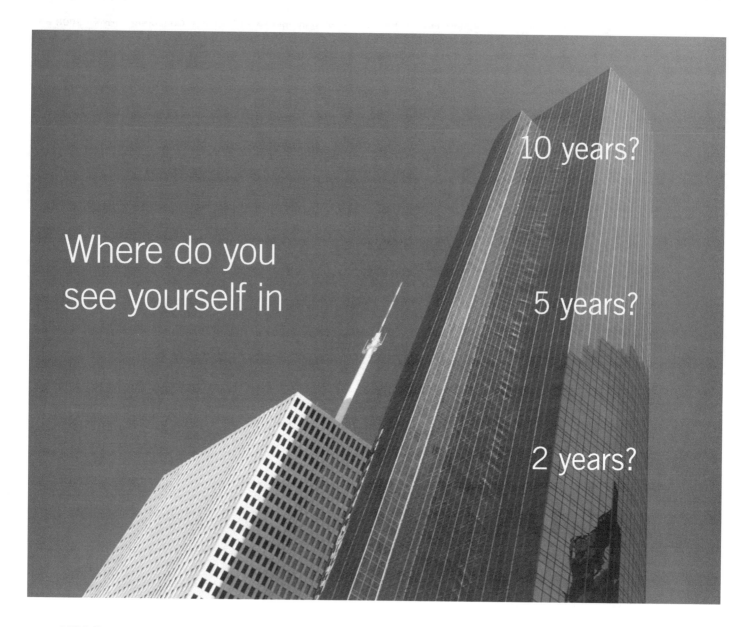

**Where do you
see yourself in**

10 years?

5 years?

2 years?

MBA Programme

**It's the question we will all hear at least once in
our career. With an MBA from London Business
School, it is a question that has no limitations.**

The London Business School MBA provides the
skills, opportunities and global connections for
you to achieve your career goals.

Our direct access to London's impressive finance
and consulting recruiter base, excellent relationships
with over 50 private equity firms and connections
with 100 major corporations ensure you have the
opportunities you need to satisfy your ambition.

Only the most talented are invited to attend our
global classroom, for a learning experience that
is both character forming and life changing.

Could this be you?

**To download a brochure on our MBA programme
visit www.london.edu/mba/ambition1/**

London Business School
Regent's Park
London NW1 4SA
United Kingdom
Tel +44 (0)20 7000 7505
Fax +44 (0)20 7000 7501
Email mba1@london.edu
www.london.edu/mba/ambition1/

London experience. World impact.

Introduction

The $300 billion management and strategy consulting industry showed healthy growth in 2007. North American firms are seeing opportunities abound, making it an exciting time to embark on a career in consulting. That's why we've surveyed 3,640 consultants to bring you the tenth edition of the *Vault Guide to the Top 50 Management and Strategy Consulting Firms*. Every year, we survey the best of the management and strategy firms, as well as those consulting firms with narrower focuses in fields like financial consulting and health care consulting.

The 86 profiles in this year's edition are based on detailed research and extensive feedback from current consultants—talking about everything from company culture to compensation, travel demands and diversity. And we cover everything from gigantic multinational consulting firms to boutique firms with fewer than 100 employees.

Check out the Top 50 rankings to see which firms have the golden touch of prestige, according to peer consultants. Consultants at prestigious firms tend to enjoy access to a high caliber of clients and projects, not to mention the fact that a recognizable and well-regarded name puts a sheen on any resume. Still, there are plenty of other great reasons to choose a consulting firm—specialty, training, perks—and you'll learn about all of them in the *Vault Guide to the Top 50 Management and Strategy Consulting Firms*.

The Editors
Vault, Inc.

Visit the Vault Consulting Career Channel at **www.vault.com/consulting** - with insider firm profiles, message boards, the Vault Consulting Job Board and more.

VAULT CAREER LIBRARY

1

A Guide to this Guide

If you're wondering how our entries are organized, read on. Here's a handy guide to the information you'll find packed into each firm profile in this book.

Firm Facts

Locations: A listing of the firm's offices, with the city (or cities) of its headquarters bolded. For firms with a relatively small number of offices, all cities are included. Countries for international offices are typically not specified unless the location is uncommon.

Practices Areas: Official departments that employ a significant portion of the firm's consultants. Practice areas are listed in alphabetical order, regardless of their size and prominence.

Uppers and Downers: Good points and bad points of the firm, as derived from consultant interviews and surveys, as well as other research. Uppers and downers are perceptions and are not based on statistics.

Employment Contact: The person, address or web site that the firm identifies as the best place to send resumes, or the appropriate contact to answer questions about the recruitment process. Sometimes more than one contact is given.

The Buzz

When it comes to other consulting firms, our respondents are full of opinions! We ask them to detail their views and observations about firms other than their own, and collect a sampling of these comments in The Buzz.

When selecting The Buzz, we include quotes most representative of the common perceptions of the firms held by other consultants, even if in our opinion the quotes do not accurately or completely describe the firm. Please keep in mind when reading The Buzz that it's often more fun for outsiders to trash, rather than praise, a competing consulting firm. Nonetheless, The Buzz can be a valuable means of gauging a firm's reputation in the consulting industry, or at least of detecting common misperceptions. We typically include two to four Buzz comments. In some instances we opt not to include The Buzz if we do not receive a diversity of comments.

The Stats

Employer Type: The firm's classification as a publicly traded company, privately held company or subsidiary.

Ticker Symbol: The stock ticker symbol for a public company, as well as the exchange on which the company's stock is traded.

Chairman, CEO, etc.: The name and title of the leader(s) of the firm, or of the firm's consulting business.

Employees: The total number of employees, including consultants and other staff, at a firm in all offices (unless otherwise specified). Some firms do not disclose this information; figures from the most recent consecutive years the information is available (if at all) are included.

Revenue: The gross sales (in U.S. dollars) the firm generated in the specified fiscal year(s). Some firms do not disclose this information; numbers from the most recent consecutive years the information is available (if at all) are included. In some cases, revenue is given in Euros (€).

The Profiles

The profiles are divided into three sections: The Scoop, Getting Hired and Our Survey Says.

The Scoop: The firm's history, clients, recent firm developments and other points of interest.

Getting Hired: Qualifications the firm looks for in new associates, tips on getting hired and other notable aspects of the hiring process.

Our Survey Says: Actual quotes from surveys and interviews with current consultants at the firm on topics such as firm culture, feedback, hours, travel requirements, pay, training and more. Profiles of some firms do not include an Our Survey Says section.

Best of the Rest

Even though the name of this book is the *Vault Guide to the Top 50 Management and Strategy Consulting Firms*, we didn't stop there, and added 36 other firms we thought notable and/or interesting enough for inclusion. These firms are listed in alphabetical order.

Visit the Vault Consulting Career Channel at **www.vault.com/consulting** - with insider firm profiles, message boards, the Vault Consulting Job Board and more.

 VAULT CAREER LIBRARY

3

TOP

THE VAULT
PRESTIGE
RANKINGS

CONSULTING

FIRMS

VAULT CAREER LIBRARY

Ranking Methodology

For the 2008 edition of the *Vault Guide to the Top 50 Management and Strategy Consulting Firms*, we selected a list of top consulting firms to include in the Vault survey. These consulting firms were selected because of their prominence in the consulting industry and their interest to consulting job seekers. This year, over 3,640 consultants responded to our survey.

The survey was distributed to the firms on Vault's list in the spring of 2007. In some cases, Vault contacted practicing consultants directly. Survey respondents were asked to do several things. They were asked to rate each consulting firm on the survey on a scale of 1 to 10 based on prestige, with 10 being the most prestigious. Consultants were unable to rate their own firm, and they were asked to rate only those firms with which they were familiar.

Vault collected the survey results and averaged the score for each company. The firms were then ranked, with the highest score being No. 1 down to No. 50.

We also asked survey respondents to give their perceptions of other consulting firms besides their own. A selection of those comments is featured on each firm profile as The Buzz.

Remember that Vault's Top 50 Management and Strategy Consulting Firms are chosen by practicing consultants at top consulting firms. Vault does not choose or influence the rankings. The rankings measure perceived prestige (as determined by consulting professionals) and not revenue, size or lifestyle.

Visit the Vault Consulting Career Channel at **www.vault.com/consulting** - with insider firm profiles, message boards, the Vault Consulting Job Board and more.

 **VAULT** CAREER LIBRARY

7

The 50 most prestigious consulting firms

2008 RANK	CONSULTING FIRM	PRESTIGE SCORE	2007 RANK	2006 RANK	2005 RANK	HEADQUARTERS/ LARGEST OFFICE
1	McKinsey & Company	8.427	1	1	1	New York, NY
2	The Boston Consulting Group	8.037	2	2	2	Boston, MA
3	Bain & Company	7.809	3	3	3	Boston, MA
4	Booz Allen Hamilton	6.600	4	4	4	McLean, VA
5	Monitor Group	6.392	5	5	6	Cambridge, MA
6	Mercer Management Consulting*	6.236	6	6	7	New York, NY
7	Mercer Oliver Wyman**	6.052	7	7	9	New York, NY
8	Deloitte Consulting LLP	5.856	10	15	8	New York, NY
9	Mercer Human Resource Consulting	5.742	8	8	10	New York, NY
10	The Parthenon Group	5.604	9	9	17	Boston, MA
11	IBM Global Services	5.564	13	13	12	Armonk, NY
12	Gartner, Inc.	5.492	16	17	5	Stamford, CT
13	L.E.K. Consulting	5.463	11	12	20	Boston, MA London
14	Accenture	5.403	15	20	13	New York, NY
15	A.T. Kearney	5.388	14	14	11	Chicago, IL
16	Katzenbach Partners LLC	5.336	19	18	43	New York, NY
17	Marakon Associates	5.252	12	10	18	New York, NY London
18	Towers Perrin	5.219	20	19	14	Stamford, CT
19	Mercer Delta Organizational Consulting†	5.193	NR	NR	NR	New York, NY
20	Roland Berger Strategy Consultants	4.935	17	11	15	New York, NY Munich
21	Cambridge Associates LLC	4.854	23	31	23	Boston, MA
22	Capgemini	4.845	27	30	21	New York, NY Paris
23	Hewitt Associates	4.827	18	16	22	Lincolnshire, IL
24	ZS Associates	4.816	28	24	31	Evanston, IL
25	Watson Wyatt Worldwide	4.776	21	25	24	Arlington, VA

NR = Not Ranked

*As of May 2007, Oliver Wyman—General Management Consulting

**As of May 2007, Oliver Wyman—Financial Services

†As of May 2007, Oliver Wyman—Delta Organizational Leadership Consulting

2008 RANK	CONSULTING FIRM	PRESTIGE SCORE	2007 RANK	2006 RANK	2005 RANK	HEADQUARTERS/ LARGEST OFFICE
26	AlixPartners	4.738	NR	NR	NR	Detroit, MI
27	NERA Economic Consulting	4.726	22	23	26	White Plains, NY
28	BearingPoint Inc.*	4.717	32	29	19	McLean, VA
29	Navigant Consulting, Inc.	4.694	31	45	39	Chicago, IL
30	CRA International, Inc.	4.638	24	21	30	Boston, MA
31	Gallup Consulting	4.597	40	27	16	Washington, DC
32	Lippincott	4.586	NR	NR	NR	New York, NY
33	PRTM	4.573	43	40	37	Mountain View, CA Waltham, MA
34	Giuliani Partners LLC	4.547	42	44	40	New York, NY
35	LECG	4.526	29	35	NR	Emeryville, CA
36	Kurt Salmon Associates	4.509	36	33	36	Atlanta, GA
37	Cornerstone Research	4.463	33	37	NR	Menlo Park, CA New York, NY
38	The Advisory Board Company	4.453	38	36	28	Washington, DC
39	Huron Consulting Group	4.448	46	NR	49	Chicago, IL
40	Arthur D. Little	4.352	30	32	27	Boston, MA Paris
41	Corporate Executive Board	4.337	34	43	35	Washington, DC
42	First Manhattan Consulting Group	4.291	35	34	45	New York, NY
43	Alvarez & Marsal	4.285	NR	NR	NR	New York, NY
44	Hay Group	4.261	NR	39	29	Philadelphia, PA
45	Diamond**	4.223	26	26	33	Chicago, IL
46	FTI Consulting, Inc.	4.206	50	NR	NR	Baltimore, MD
47	Analysis Group, Inc.	4.197	39	48	NR	Boston, MA
48	Mars & Co	4.176	25	28	32	Greenwich, CT
49	Aon Consulting Worldwide	3.994	NR	NR	46	Chicago, IL
50	Putnam Associates	3.961	47	41	34	Burlington, MA

*BearingPoint Inc. Management & Technology Consultants
**Diamond Management & Technology Consultants, Inc.

Visit the Vault Consulting Career Channel at www.vault.com/consulting - with insider firm profiles, message boards, the Vault Consulting Job Board and more.

VAULT CAREER LIBRARY

9

Practice Area Rankings

Methodology

Vault also asked consultants to rank the best firms in several areas of business focus. These areas are economic consulting, energy consulting, financial consulting, human resources consulting, operational consulting, and pharmaceutical and health care consulting. Consultants were allowed to vote for up to three firms as the best in each area.

The following charts indicate the rankings in each practice area, along with the total percentage of votes cast in favor of each firm. (As long as at least one consultant voted for more than one firm, no firm could get 100 percent of the votes; if every consultant had voted for the same three firms, for example, the maximum score would be 33.3 percent.)

Economic Consulting

RANK	FIRM	% OF VOTES	2007 RANK
1	McKinsey & Company	12.83	3
2	NERA Economic Consulting	12.15	1
3	CRA International, Inc.	9.13	2
4	Analysis Group, Inc.	7.02	6
5 (tie)	Bain & Company	6.11	8
5 (tie)	LECG	6.11	4
5 (tie)	Cornerstone Research	6.11	5
6	The Boston Consulting Group	5.81	7
7	Booz Allen Hamilton	3.55	9
8 (tie)	Monitor Group	2.42	NR
8 (tie)	Deloitte Consulting LLP	2.42	NR
9	L.E.K. Consulting	2.11	10
10	Navigant Consulting, Inc.	1.81	NR

Energy Consulting

RANK	FIRM	% OF VOTES	2007 RANK
1	McKinsey & Company	25.81	1
2	Booz Allen Hamilton	11.29	2
3	Bain & Company	7.26	4
4	The Boston Consulting Group	6.45	3
5	Accenture	6.32	5
6	Deloitte Consulting LLP	5.11	6
7	CRA International, Inc.	4.03	9
8	A.T. Kearney	3.23	6
9	BearingPoint Inc. Management & Technology Consultants	2.69	NR
10	NERA Economic Consulting	2.55	NR

Financial Consulting

RANK	FIRM	% OF VOTES	2007 RANK
1	McKinsey & Company	23.29	1
2	Bain & Company	10.71	4
3	Mercer Oliver Wyman*	9.15	3
4	The Boston Consulting Group	8.85	2
5	Deloitte Consulting LLP	7.59	6
6	Accenture	4.76	8
7	Booz Allen Hamilton	4.46	7
8	First Manhattan Consulting Group	4.09	5
9	Capgemini	2.16	NR
10	BearingPoint Inc. Management & Technology Consultants	1.93	NR

*As of May 2007, Oliver Wyman—Financial Services

Human Resources Consulting

RANK	FIRM	% OF VOTES	2007 RANK
1	Mercer Human Resource Consulting	33.40	1
2	Hewitt Associates	17.13	2
3	Towers Perrin	10.36	4
4	Watson Wyatt Worldwide	7.10	3
5	Deloitte Consulting LLP	4.85	6
6	Hay Group	4.65	5
7	McKinsey & Company	2.12	7
8	Accenture	2.06	8
9	Booz Allen Hamilton	1.33	NR
10	Aon Consulting Worldwide	1.26	9

Visit the Vault Consulting Career Channel at www.vault.com/consulting - with insider firm profiles, message boards, the Vault Consulting Job Board and more.

VAULT CAREER LIBRARY

11

Operational Consulting

RANK	FIRM	% OF VOTES	2007 RANK
1	Accenture	15.76	1
2	Deloitte Consulting LLP	12.65	5
3	A.T. Kearney	11.89	2
4	McKinsey & Company	11.11	3
5	Booz Allen Hamilton	10.49	4
6	IBM Global Services	7.38	6
7	Bain & Company	4.96	7
8	The Boston Consulting Group	4.85	8
9	BearingPoint Inc. Management & Technology Consultants	3.35	9
10	Capgemini	2.49	10

Pharmaceutical & Health Care Consulting

RANK	FIRM	% OF VOTES	2007 RANK
1	McKinsey & Company	18.55	1
2	ZS Associates	10.36	3
3	The Boston Consulting Group	9.14	2
4	Deloitte Consulting LLP	5.62	7
5	Bain & Company	4.67	4
6	IMS Health Incorporated	4.54	5
7 (tie)	Accenture	3.72	8
7 (tie)	The Advisory Board Company	3.72	NR
8	Booz Allen Hamilton	3.25	NR
9	Monitor Group	2.78	10
10	Capgemini	2.71	NR

Visit the Vault Consulting Career Channel at www.vault.com/consulting - with insider firm profiles, message boards, the Vault Consulting Job Board and more.

VAULT CAREER LIBRARY   13

Use the Internet's
MOST TARGETED
job search tools.

Vault Job Board

Target your search by industry, function, and experience level,
and find the job openings that you want.

VaultMatch Resume Database

Vault takes match-making to the next level: post your resume
and customize your search by industry, function, experience
and more. We'll match job listings with your interests and
criteria and e-mail them directly to your in-box.

> the most trusted name in career information™

TOP

THE VAULT
QUALITY
OF LIFE
RANKINGS

CONSULTING
FIRMS

Quality of Life Ranking Methodology

In addition to ranking other firms in terms of prestige, survey respondents were asked to rate their own firms in a variety of categories. On a scale of 1 to 10, with 10 being the highest and 1 the lowest, respondents evaluated their firms in the following quality of life areas:

- Overall satisfaction
- Compensation
- Work/life balance
- Hours in the office
- Formal training
- Interaction with clients
- Relationships with supervisors

- Firm culture
- Travel requirements
- Offices
- Diversity with respect to women
- Diversity with respect to minorities
- Diversity with respect to gays, lesbians, bisexuals and transgender individuals

Ranking the firms

A firm's score in each category is simply the average of these rankings. In compiling our quality of life rankings, we only ranked firms from whose consultants we received 10 or more responses for a particular question. Only consulting firms that distributed the Vault survey to their consultants were ranked. Firms that distributed the survey this year were:

- A.T. Kearney
- Accenture
- Alvarez & Marsal
- Arthur D. Little
- Bain & Company
- Bates White
- BearingPoint Inc. Management & Technology Consultants
- Booz Allen Hamilton
- The Boston Consulting Group
- The Brattle Group
- Celerant Consulting
- Cornerstone Research
- Dean & Company
- Deloitte Consulting LLP
- Diamond Management & Technology Consultants, Inc.
- Deutsche Post World Net Inhouse Consulting

- Easton Associates, LLC
- Fair Isaac Corporation
- First Consulting Group
- First Manhattan Consulting Group
- FTI Consulting, Inc.
- Gallup Consulting
- Greenwich Associates
- Health Advances
- Huron Consulting Group
- IBM Global Services
- IMS Health Incorporated
- Kaiser Associates
- Katzenbach Partners LLC
- Kurt Salmon Associates
- L.E.K. Consulting
- Marakon Associates
- Mercator Partners LLC
- Milliman, Inc.
- Mitchell Madison Group LLC

- Monitor Group
- Navigant Consulting, Inc.
- NERA Economic Consulting
- Novantas LLC
- OC&C Strategy Consultants
- Oliver Wyman*
- Opera Solutions
- PA Consulting Group
- Pearl Meyer & Partners
- PRTM
- Putnam Associates
- Roland Berger Strategy Consultants
- Simon-Kucher & Partners
- Stockamp & Associates, Inc.
- Strategos
- Trinity Partners, LLC
- Vantage Partners
- Vivaldi Partners
- ZS Associates

In May 2007, Mercer Management Consulting and Mercer Oliver Wyman combined to form Oliver Wyman. Prior to the merger, consultants from both firms had separately completed the Vault Management and Strategy Consulting Survey. As such, Mercer Management Consulting and Mercer Oliver Wyman appear in our rankings as separate consulting firms.

Visit the Vault Consulting Career Channel at **www.vault.com/consulting** - with insider firm profiles, message boards, the Vault Consulting Job Board and more.

V\ULT CAREER LIBRARY   **17**

The Best 20 Firms to Work For

Which are the best firms to work for? For some, this is a far more important consideration than prestige. To determine our Best 20 firms, we analyzed our initial list of 86 firms using a formula that weighted the most relevant categories for an overall quality of life ranking. Each firm's overall score was calculated using the following formula:

25 percent overall satisfaction

15 percent compensation

15 percent work/life balance

10 percent hours in the office

10 percent travel requirements

5 percent formal training

5 percent interaction with clients

5 percent relationships with supervisors

5 percent firm culture

5 percent overall diversity

Like our Top 50 rankings, our Best 20 is meant to reflect the subjective opinion of consultants. By its nature, the list is based on the perceptions of insiders—some of whom may be biased in favor (or against) their firm.

RANK	FIRM	SCORE
1	Trinity Partners, LLC	8.575
2	Bain & Company	8.530
3	Cornerstone Research	8.385
4	Gallup Consulting	8.247
5	Novantas LLC	8.224
6	Putnam Associates	8.194
7	Arthur D. Little	8.150
8	Marakon Associates	8.143
9	PRTM	8.132
10	The Boston Consulting Group	8.066
11	Milliman, Inc.	8.022
12	Health Advances	7.945
13	Mercer Oliver Wyman*	7.910
14	Bates White	7.903
15	Katzenbach Partners LLC	7.900
16	Monitor Group	7.870
17 (tie)	The Brattle Group	7.827
17 (tie)	Strategos	7.827
18	Diamond Management & Technology Consultants, Inc.	7.806
19	ZS Associates	7.805
20	Alvarez & Marsal	7.792

As of May 2007, Oliver Wyman—Financial Services

Overall Satisfaction

On a scale of 1 to 10, where 1 means very poor and 10 means excellent, how would you rate your overall satisfaction with your firm?

RANK	FIRM	SCORE
1	Bain & Company	9.354
2	Trinity Partners, LLC	9.333
3	Arthur D. Little	9.161
4	PRTM	9.100
5	Gallup Consulting	9.019
6	Katzenbach Partners LLC	9.018
7	Cornerstone Research	8.973
8	Monitor Group	8.958
9	Novantas LLC	8.950
10	Strategos	8.923
11	Marakon Associates	8.920
12	Putnam Associates	8.880
13	Milliman, Inc.	8.829
14	The Boston Consulting Group	8.774
15	Diamond Management & Technology Consultants, Inc.	8.720
16	Mercer Oliver Wyman*	8.663
17	Alvarez & Marsal	8.559
18 (tie)	Health Advances	8.533
18 (tie)	Opera Solutions	8.533
19	The Brattle Group	8.531
20	A.T. Kearney	8.519

*As of May 2007, Oliver Wyman—Financial Services

Visit the Vault Consulting Career Channel at www.vault.com/consulting - with insider firm profiles, message boards, the Vault Consulting Job Board and more.

VAULT CAREER LIBRARY

19

Work/Life Balance

On a scale of 1 to 10, where 1 is very poor and 10 is excellent, how would you rate your firm's efforts to promote a livable work/life balance?

RANK	FIRM	SCORE
1	Novantas LLC	8.725
2	Putnam Associates	8.720
3	Trinity Partners, LLC	8.692
4	Marakon Associates	8.560
5	Bain & Company	8.470
6	Gallup Consulting	8.463
7	Easton Associates, LLC	8.438
8	Fair Isaac Corporation	8.400
9	Arthur D. Little	8.375
10	Mercer Oliver Wyman*	8.193
11	Simon-Kucher & Partners	8.188
12 (tie)	Kurt Salmon Associates	8.182
12 (tie)	Mercer Human Resource Consulting	8.182
13	PRTM	8.143
14	Health Advances	8.107
15	Alvarez & Marsal	8.089
16	Booz Allen Hamilton	8.004
17	Navigant Consulting, Inc.	7.857
18	Diamond Management & Technology Consultants, Inc.	7.845
19	Mercer Management Consulting**	7.826
20	The Boston Consulting Group	7.825

*As of May 2007, Oliver Wyman—Financial Services
**As of May 2007, Oliver Wyman—General Management Consulting

Hours in the Office

On a scale of 1 to 10, where 1 means completely unsatisfied and 10 means extremely satisfied, please rank your satisfaction with the number of hours you spend in the office each week.

RANK	FIRM	SCORE
1	Gallup Consulting	8.604
2	Novantas LLC	8.150
3	Mercer Human Resource Consulting	8.000
4	Arthur D. Little	7.969
5	Alvarez & Marsal	7.921
6	Trinity Partners, LLC	7.917
7 (tie)	Fair Isaac Corporation	7.857
7 (tie)	Navigant Consulting, Inc.	7.857
8	Strategos	7.833
9	Easton Associates, LLC	7.813
10	Health Advances	7.733
11	Putnam Associates	7.708
12	Bain & Company	7.685
13	Marakon Associates	7.680
14	Booz Allen Hamilton	7.670
15	NERA Economic Consulting	7.632
16	Mercer Oliver Wyman*	7.610
17	Milliman, Inc.	7.500
18	Cornerstone Research	7.487
19	Simon-Kucher & Partners	7.452
20	PRTM	7.420

*As of May 2007, Oliver Wyman—Financial Services

Visit the Vault Consulting Career Channel at **www.vault.com/consulting** - with insider firm profiles, message boards, the Vault Consulting Job Board and more.

VAULT CAREER LIBRARY

21

Compensation

On a scale of 1 to 10, where 1 is far below average and 10 is far in excess of industry average, how would you rate your firm's compensation (including salary and bonus)?

RANK	FIRM	SCORE
1	First Manhattan Consulting Group	8.533
2	Mercer Oliver Wyman*	8.494
3	Mitchell Madison Group LLC	8.200
4	Milliman, Inc.	8.125
5	A.T. Kearney	8.074
6	The Boston Consulting Group	8.007
7	Bates White	7.932
8	Trinity Partners, LLC	7.923
9	Bain & Company	7.750
10	Cornerstone Research	7.742
11	Alvarez & Marsal	7.667
12	Mercer Management Consulting**	7.652
13	Marakon Associates	7.600
14	Opera Solutions	7.563
15	Diamond Management & Technology Consultants, Inc.	7.542
16 (tie)	L.E.K. Consulting	7.500
16 (tie)	Katzenbach Partners LLC	7.500
17	PRTM	7.370
18	Strategos	7.364
19	Novantas LLC	7.189
20	Gallup Consulting	7.076

*As of May 2007, Oliver Wyman—Financial Services
**As of May 2007, Oliver Wyman—General Management Consulting

Interaction with Clients

On a scale of 1 to 10, how satisfied are you with your opportunity to interact with your clients' top-level management?

RANK	FIRM	SCORE
1	Kaiser Associates	9.583
2	Trinity Partners, LLC	9.417
3	PRTM	9.354
4	First Manhattan Consulting Group	9.267
5	Katzenbach Partners LLC	9.151
6	Arthur D. Little	9.103
7	Bain & Company	9.019
8 (tie)	Marakon Associates	9.000
8 (tie)	IMS Health Incorporated	9.000
9	A.T. Kearney	8.962
10	Stockamp & Associates, Inc.	8.954
11	Opera Solutions	8.938
12	Milliman, Inc.	8.875
13	Strategos	8.833
14	Novantas LLC	8.821
15	Diamond Management & Technology Consultants, Inc.	8.800
16	Gallup Consulting	8.796
17	Health Advances	8.786
18	Monitor Group	8.783
19	Alvarez & Marsal	8.777
20	Mercer Management Consulting*	8.696

As of May 2007, Oliver Wyman—General Management Consulting

Visit the Vault Consulting Career Channel at **www.vault.com/consulting** - with insider firm profiles, message boards, the Vault Consulting Job Board and more.

V∧ULT CAREER LIBRARY   23

Relationships with Supervisors

On a scale of 1 to 10, where 1 means very poor and 10 means excellent, how would you rate your relationships with your superiors/supervisors?

RANK	FIRM	SCORE
1	PRTM	9.542
2	Arthur D. Little	9.433
3	Putnam Associates	9.400
4	Monitor Group	9.271
5	Novantas LLC	9.237
6	Bain & Company	9.233
7	Kaiser Associates	9.167
8	Gallup Consulting	9.130
9 (tie)	Cornerstone Research	9.000
9 (tie)	Navigant Consulting, Inc.	9.000
10	A.T. Kearney	8.889
11	Marakon Associates	8.833
12	Milliman, Inc.	8.824
13	Katzenbach Partners LLC	8.778
14	Deloitte Consulting LLP	8.774
15	L.E.K. Consulting	8.773
16 (tie)	Stockamp & Associates, Inc.	8.767
16 (tie)	Simon-Kucher & Partners	8.767
17	Diamond Management & Technology Consultants, Inc.	8.750
18	The Boston Consulting Group	8.712
19	Strategos	8.692
20	FTI Consulting, Inc.	8.686

Firm Culture

On a scale of 1 to 10, where 1 is not at all pleasant and 10 is extremely pleasant, assess your firm's culture.

RANK	FIRM	SCORE
1	Bain & Company	9.636
2	Novantas LLC	9.450
3	Katzenbach Partners LLC	9.429
4	Cornerstone Research	9.351
5	PRTM	9.320
6	Arthur D. Little	9.313
7	Monitor Group	9.277
8	Gallup Consulting	9.241
9	Trinity Partners, LLC	9.231
10	Marakon Associates	9.167
11	The Boston Consulting Group	9.067
12 (tie)	Putnam Associates	9.000
12 (tie)	Kaiser Associates	9.000
13	Strategos	8.923
14	Kurt Salmon Associates	8.909
15	IMS Health Incorporated	8.879
16	Simon-Kucher & Partners	8.844
17	Diamond Management & Technology Consultants, Inc.	8.821
18	The Brattle Group	8.807
19	ZS Associates	8.804
20	Deloitte Consulting LLP	8.803

Visit the Vault Consulting Career Channel at **www.vault.com/consulting** - with insider firm profiles, message boards, the Vault Consulting Job Board and more.

VAULT CAREER LIBRARY

25

Formal Training

On a scale of 1 to 10, with 1 being very poor and 10 being excellent, how would you rate your satisfaction with the training offered by your firm?

RANK	FIRM	SCORE
1	Bain & Company	9.573
2	Cornerstone Research	8.865
3	Marakon Associates	8.600
4	The Boston Consulting Group	8.535
5	Booz Allen Hamilton	8.327
6	ZS Associates	8.309
7	Accenture	8.291
8	Arthur D. Little	8.080
9	Deloitte Consulting LLP	7.771
10 (tie)	Mercer Management Consulting*	7.739
10 (tie)	Putnam Associates	7.739
11	L.E.K. Consulting	7.727
12	Stockamp & Associates, Inc.	7.674
13	Diamond Management & Technology Consultants, Inc.	7.654
14 (tie)	The Brattle Group	7.643
14 (tie)	Navigant Consulting, Inc.	7.643
15	Health Advances	7.621
16	PA Consulting Group	7.553
17	Bates White	7.547
18	Simon-Kucher & Partners	7.484
19	Novantas LLC	7.462
20	PRTM	7.380

As of May 2007, Oliver Wyman—General Management Consulting

Offices

On a scale of 1 to 10, with 1 being miserable and 10 being optimal, how would you rate your offices (your firm's offices, not your clients' offices)?

RANK	FIRM	SCORE
1	Gallup Consulting	9.500
2	Marakon Associates	9.280
3	Katzenbach Partners LLC	9.038
4	Cornerstone Research	8.972
5	Bain & Company	8.963
6	Mercer Management Consulting*	8.913
7	The Boston Consulting Group	8.830
8	PRTM	8.800
9	Arthur D. Little	8.786
10	Bates White	8.741
11	Diamond Management & Technology Consultants, Inc.	8.692
12	Monitor Group	8.625
13	Pearl Meyer & Partners	8.609
14	Accenture	8.481
15 (tie)	Putnam Associates	8.400
15 (tie)	Mitchell Madison Group LLC	8.400
16	Milliman, Inc.	8.317
17	A.T. Kearney	8.185
18	Kaiser Associates	8.083
19	Booz Allen Hamilton	8.068
20	L.E.K. Consulting	8.046

As of May 2007, Oliver Wyman—General Management Consulting

Visit the Vault Consulting Career Channel at **www.vault.com/consulting** - with insider firm profiles, message boards, the Vault Consulting Job Board and more.

VAULT CAREER LIBRARY   27

Travel Requirements

On a scale of 1 to 10, where 1 means excessive and 10 means minimal, how would you rate your firm's travel requirements?

RANK	FIRM	SCORE
1	Cornerstone Research	8.730
2	Putnam Associates	8.480
3	The Brattle Group	8.387
4 (tie)	ZS Associates	8.364
4 (tie)	L.E.K. Consulting	8.364
5	Bates White	8.346
6	NERA Economic Consulting	8.235
7	Trinity Partners, LLC	8.083
8	Pearl Meyer & Partners	8.053
9	Health Advances	8.040
10	IMS Health Incorporated	7.970
11	Dean & Company	7.632
12	Simon-Kucher & Partners	7.531
13	Milliman, Inc.	6.850
14	Booz Allen Hamilton	6.825
15	Bain & Company	6.701
16	Gallup Consulting	6.653
17	Easton Associates, LLC	6.600
18	Kaiser Associates	6.500
19	First Manhattan Consulting Group	6.438
20	Mercer Human Resource Consulting	6.364

TOP 50

THE VAULT
DIVERSITY
RANKINGS

CONSULTING FIRMS

Diversity Rankings: Top 20

Vault's survey asked consultants to rate their firm's diversity with respect to women, with respect to minorities and with respect to gays, lesbians, bisexuals and transgender individuals. When asking consultants to assess their firm's diversity in these categories, we asked them to think about hiring, promoting, mentoring and other programs.

The Best 20 Firms for Diversity

To determine an overall diversity score, we took the average of the scores firms received in each of the three diversity categories (women, minorities, and gays, lesbians, bisexuals and transgender individuals).

RANK	FIRM	SCORE
1	IMS Health Incorporated	9.140
2	Gallup Consulting	9.026
3	Katzenbach Partners LLC	8.998
4	Bain & Company	8.938
5	Cornerstone Research	8.882
6	Mitchell Madison Group LLC	8.828
7	Arthur D. Little	8.746
8	Milliman, Inc.	8.731
9	IBM Global Services	8.724
10	Booz Allen Hamilton	8.701
11	Deloitte Consulting LLP	8.687
12	Simon-Kucher & Partners	8.580
13	The Brattle Group	8.539
14	Bates White	8.481
15	Novantas LLC	8.478
16	Stockamp & Associates, Inc.	8.443
17	PRTM	8.415
18	The Boston Consulting Group	8.402
19	Kaiser Associates	8.350
20	Health Advances	8.258

Visit the Vault Consulting Career Channel at www.vault.com/consulting - with insider firm profiles, message boards, the Vault Consulting Job Board and more.

VAULT CAREER LIBRARY   31

Diversity—Women

On a scale of 1 to 10, where 1 means needs a lot of improvement and 10 means exemplary, how receptive is your firm to women in terms of hiring, promoting, mentoring and other programs?

RANK	FIRM	SCORE
1	Health Advances	9.667
2	Cornerstone Research	9.595
3	Easton Associates, LLC	9.429
4	IMS Health Incorporated	9.375
5	Gallup Consulting	9.340
6	Kaiser Associates	9.167
7	Milliman, Inc.	9.077
8	Bain & Company	9.065
9	Stockamp & Associates, Inc.	9.000
10	Katzenbach Partners LLC	8.982
11	Deloitte Consulting LLP	8.932
12	The Brattle Group	8.931
13	The Boston Consulting Group	8.808
14	Navigant Consulting, Inc.	8.769
15	NERA Economic Consulting	8.746
16	IBM Global Services	8.688
17	Booz Allen Hamilton	8.568
18	Arthur D. Little	8.517
19	Novantas LLC	8.425
20	Monitor Group	8.404

Diversity—Minorities

On a scale of 1 to 10, where 1 means needs a lot of improvement and 10 means exemplary, how receptive is your firm to minorities in terms of hiring, promoting, mentoring and other programs?

RANK	FIRM	SCORE
1	Arthur D. Little	9.346
2	Mitchell Madison Group LLC	9.214
3	Opera Solutions	9.000
4	IMS Health Incorporated	8.813
5	PRTM	8.809
6	Simon-Kucher & Partners	8.759
7	Booz Allen Hamilton	8.685
8	Gallup Consulting	8.566
9	IBM Global Services	8.556
10	Bain & Company	8.408
11	Milliman, Inc.	8.389
12	Bates White	8.326
13	Katzenbach Partners LLC	8.321
14	Deloitte Consulting LLP	8.286
15	Novantas LLC	8.231
16	ZS Associates	8.226
17	Accenture	8.216
18	Cornerstone Research	8.086
19	Kaiser Associates	8.083
20	Diamond Management & Technology Consultants, Inc.	8.041

Visit the Vault Consulting Career Channel at **www.vault.com/consulting** - with insider firm profiles, message boards, the Vault Consulting Job Board and more.

VAULT CAREER LIBRARY

33

Diversity—GLBT

On a scale of 1 to 10, where 1 means very poor and 10 means excellent, how would you rate your firm's commitment to diversity with respect to gays, lesbians, bisexuals and transgender individuals?

RANK	FIRM	SCORE
1	Mitchell Madison Group LLC	9.769
2	Katzenbach Partners LLC	9.691
3	Bain & Company	9.342
4	IMS Health Incorporated	9.233
5	Simon-Kucher & Partners	9.207
6	Gallup Consulting	9.174
7	Cornerstone Research	8.966
8	IBM Global Services	8.929
9	Bates White	8.905
10	Booz Allen Hamilton	8.852
11	Deloitte Consulting LLP	8.844
12	The Brattle Group	8.833
13 (tie)	Diamond Management & Technology Consultants, Inc.	8.781
13 (tie)	Stockamp & Associates, Inc.	8.781
14	Novantas LLC	8.778
15	Milliman, Inc.	8.727
16	PRTM	8.692
17	Monitor Group	8.649
18	The Boston Consulting Group	8.590
19	Mercer Oliver Wyman*	8.474
20	Mercer Management Consulting**	8.438

*As of May 2007, Oliver Wyman—Financial Services
**As of May 2007, Oliver Wyman—General Management Consulting

TOP

OVERVIEW OF THE
CONSULTING
INDUSTRY

CONSULTING
FIRMS

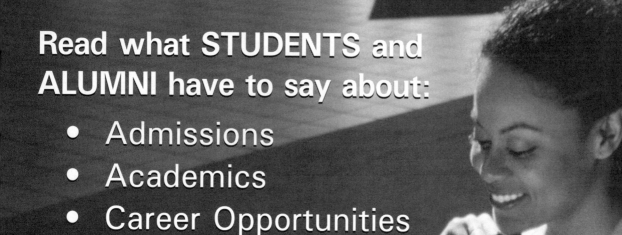

The State of Consulting

On a roll

In 2006, the consulting industry posted its second consecutive year of double-digit growth. Following a decade of market exuberance, the industry took a dive at the turn of the century. The stock market bust of 2000 and 2001 reverberated throughout the global economy, forcing companies to cut budgets and staff, and leaving them with little capital for "discretionary" services—factors that invariably stunted the consulting industry. After several years of layoffs and languishing profits, the industry began showing signs of recovery in 2004, and by 2005 strategy consulting was back in the saddle. In the U.S., consulting services generated about $156 billion in revenue in 2006, a 12 percent hike over the prior year. The U.S. accounts for more than half of the global consulting market, estimated to be worth $300 billion in 2007.

Though the industry is cheering another year of profitability and expansion, the pace of consulting is now different. Kennedy Information predicts a moderate annual growth rate of 5 to 10 percent through 2010—quite a contrast from the 20 to 25 percent annual rate of the last decade. At present, the industry's expansion rate is actually in step with overall economic growth: measured, yet stable. Since the end of the dot-com era, businesses have changed the way they operate, reorganizing priorities and becoming slightly more cautious in their spending, with a sense of realism tempering the favorable economic outlook. The good news for consulting firms is that companies are again confident enough to invest in improvements, such as upgrading IT systems, improving a product line or evaluating a potential merger—which will guarantee a steady stream of engagements.

Strategy shows its strength

Consulting firms have also been thrust back into action as businesses seek to raise cash, compete on a worldwide scale and comply with new government regulations. In 2006, a red-hot M&A market and continued globalization put "pure" strategy consulting back in the spotlight. Though demand for all types of consulting services is strong, strategy consulting is expected to outpace the growth of the overall management consulting market, according to a 2007 Kennedy Information report. Fee rates (which prior to 2007 were relatively flat, causing tighter margins and fierce pricing competition) are also expected to climb by over 5 percent in 2007, up from a 1.5- to 3-percent range in 2006, signaling that depressed profit margins may finally be bouncing back.

Greater expectations

Clients have also become much more sophisticated—and more cautious—consumers of consulting services. They now call for quantifiable results and a significant return on their investment. Clients are also demanding that consultants bring to the table specialized expertise, top qualifications and a proven track record in a particular industry. And with a larger number of consulting firms to choose from, clients have the luxury of selecting the one that fits their specific needs.

All shapes and sizes

As the market for specialty services has intensified, so has the competition. Added to the mix is a new crop of smaller, niche firms—in many cases launched by consultants laid off during the downsizing at the turn of the century. With clients currently obsessive about cutting costs and receiving customized services, such boutique firms are able to compete with the traditional blue-chips by running leaner, with a smaller staff, or by narrowing their focus. Often, niche firms can outprice larger, better-known strategy houses that offer everything from business advisory services to implementation to outsourcing. To compete with the majors, these petite players are often willing to accept less-glamorous projects—like implementation—to prove their skills, or take on one-off engagements based on a niche service.

Visit the Vault Consulting Career Channel at **www.vault.com/consulting** - with insider firm profiles, message boards, the Vault Consulting Job Board and more.

V∧ULT CAREER LIBRARY   37

Fine-tuning services

To adjust to current market conditions and more stringent client demands, consulting firms have had to repackage their services. Consultants are now positioning themselves as long-term partners in a client's success, rather than as short-term problem solvers. Though consultants still do crisis recovery work, today they also step in to increase efficiency, boost productivity and maximize technology resources, even for healthy companies. And as competition heats up, firms are recognizing that a large part of consulting is relationship-based. Several firms have beefed up their business development teams, specifically to strengthen client loyalty and ensure a steady flow of business.

Multisourcing is another way that consulting firms are adjusting to client demands. On multisourcing engagements, teams from different firms each take a portion of one large, complex project. In addition, the emphasis on value for money has fueled a pay-for-performance trend. Though not all firms accept this bargaining structure, smaller companies hungry for work may be more inclined to accede to such arrangements.

And they're back

As the noncompete agreements signed by accounting industry heavyweights Ernst & Young, KPMG and PricewaterhouseCoopers come to an end in 2007, the Big Four are causing a rumble as they reenter the consulting arena. Between 1999 and 2001, these firms separated their consulting divisions, after conflict of interest issues arose and the Securities and Exchange Commission clamped down on independence regulations. Now operating in full force, advisory services divisions in these firms showed strong growth in 2006: At Ernst & Young, revenue in assurance and advisory business services (which includes consulting and audit services) increased 11 percent, while PwC and KPMG saw consulting revenue rise over 10 percent. These firms are rapidly ramping up hiring to strengthen their business advisory services, as well as their financial and operations consulting divisions. PwC added more than 6,000 new consultants in 2006, and Ernst & Young plans to add over 3,000 entry-level associates in 2007.

The private equity party

Part of the growth in consulting demand has been driven by the M&A boom that began in 2004, as firms are increasingly serving hedge funds, asset managers and corporate acquisition specialists. Private equity surged in 2006, and private equity funds in the U.S. raised a record $184 billion in capital. With record-breaking market returns averaging 21.3 percent, it's easy for these funds to reel in more investors. And as these businesses expand, consultants are increasingly called in to do deal review, due diligence and postmerger integration.

The financial services sector as a whole has driven up demand for consulting, thanks to increased concerns regarding operational risk and new regulatory compliance. Major U.S. banks racing to meet Basel II requirements by 2008 are fueling growth in the sector's spending. And though most companies have by now caught up with 2002 Sarbanes-Oxley regulations, new regulatory requirements and changes to the existing Sarbox framework have continued to stimulate a need for consulting services in this area. The global financial services consulting market is valued at $41.2 billion in 2007, up from $38 billion in 2006.

More than just a fling

Business process outsourcing is also a driving force in the industry's growth, as clients hope to further boost profits and reduce costs. As multinationals take advantage of a globalized market, consultants are hired to help firms maneuver in foreign business environments, transform strategic operations and improve performance. The global BPO market is projected to reach $173 billion in 2007, and grow 11 percent annually through 2009. According to a survey by IDC Research, spending on U.S. outsourcing services is expected to climb at a compound annual rate of 7.1 percent through 2010. Although the number of outsourcing projects is up, deal value is down, indicating that megadeals—long-term, $1 billion-plus engagements—have fallen out of favor. And with the dizzying number of outsourcing service providers to choose from, it's truly a buyer's market; businesses are able to spread their risk by selecting separate consulting firms for each part of a project, based on a firm's area of expertise.

India has been the traditional outsourcing destination of choice, and its growth spurt isn't over yet. In 2006, Accenture increased staff in the country by 400 percent; IBM announced plans for 100,000 new jobs there by 2010; and Capgemini doubled the size of its consulting operations in the country in 2006. However, the Indian outsourcing market has matured and the rising costs of labor are pushing outsourcers elsewhere—like Singapore, Manila and Hong Kong. Thanks to a greater percentage of employable college graduates, the skills gap is narrowing in China and other Asia-Pacific countries, generating a boom in outsourcing activity there. IDC Research estimates that the value of the BPO market in Asia-Pacific will grow over $1 billion to $8.3 billion by the end of 2007.

Emergent economies

Europe is witnessing its own surge in outsourcing activity. As the number of Eastern European countries meeting European Union economic standards continues to rise, the region has become the second-fastest-growing outsourcing area after China. These countries benefit from close proximity to Western Europe and from a larger pool of workers with English and Western European language skills. Consulting firms have followed a growing list of banking, financial services and telecom clients who have opened offices in Poland, Romania, the Czech Republic and Hungary. As these countries look to the management expertise of well-established Western companies, strategy consulting is primed for takeoff in the region. According to the McKinsey Global Institute, outsourcing activity will triple in Eastern Europe by 2008, adding over 130,000 new jobs to the $4 billion market.

Steep staff shortage

Recruiting is a top concern, as consulting firms can't seem to hire fast enough to keep up with the demand for services. Overall, recruiting budgets are up, and teams are hitting campuses in droves to meet ambitious hiring targets. Kennedy Information projects that headcount at the junior-consultant level will more than quadruple in 2007. The push to reign in new staff is a bold mark of confidence, indicating that firms anticipate a healthy flow of future engagements. According to a 2007 *Wall Street Journal* article, firms are also ramping up intern hiring to cast a wider net for future graduate hires. At Bain & Company, for example, undergraduate hiring for summer internships in 2007 rose about 10 percent over 2006, and PwC plans to hire 1,800 interns in 2007, an increase of about 6 percent for the year.

In addition to bringing in new staff, firms are contending with a high rate of attrition—the result of a recent talent squeeze. The current demand for specialized skills has made it more costly for firms to retain talent, as consultants are lured away by other firms or private industry jobs with promises of higher compensation. In North America, the attrition rate at most consulting firms was 15 to 20 percent in 2006, but a number of firms have seen a staggering 20 to 35 percent loss, according to the "2007 Retention Report," published by Top-Consultant.com.

What's your specialty?

With clients looking for seasoned consultants to handle complex problems, recruiters are targeting MBA candidates with prior specialty consulting or industry experience. Applicants with a background in one of the hot industries, such as finance, banking, public sector or health care, will find plenty of choices available to them in this year's market.

Lifestyle compensation

Graduates looking for a consulting position in 2007 will find that salaries haven't increased as much as demand. In 2006, the average base salary rose 4 percent and annual bonuses increased 5 percent, with the highest bonuses paid out in health care and government consulting, according to Kennedy Information. Though raises were slightly higher than in 2005, pay scales haven't lived up to prerecession levels. Realizing that they are competing with the lucrative finance and banking industries for talent, consulting firms are finding other meaningful ways to compensate new hires. Some are offering a number of "lifestyle benefit" options—like flexible schedules, telecommuting or part-time career tracks—to win candidates who place a higher priority on work/life balance.

Visit the Vault Consulting Career Channel at www.vault.com/consulting - with insider firm profiles, message boards, the Vault Consulting Job Board and more.

VAULT CAREER LIBRARY   39

Candidates are also posed with many options in terms of what type of firm they'd like to join. Public firms can offer stability and equity-based incentives, such as stock options, though private firms might argue that their compensation is more competitive since profits aren't distributed to shareholders. And while the giant, long-established consulting firms frequently offer a higher base salary, smaller, niche consultancies may boast more flexible advantages like quicker career progression or profit sharing for all consultants, not just those at the partnership level.

Practice Areas

Operations and implementation

Operations consulting is the difference between devising a plan and putting that plan into action. In the 1990s, operations consulting centered around cutting costs and increasing efficiency. With clients now oriented toward growth, operations consulting focuses on innovation and customer interaction engagements. Operations consultants help clients rework processes to better respond to competition or changes in the market. While strategy involves marking out clear goals, operations consulting hones in on the practical means of reaching these goals, which might include allocating resources, shifting value chain priorities, evaluating benefits of outsourcing or examining customer service and distribution. Kennedy Information estimates that the $45 billion operational consulting market will grow at a compound annual rate of 7.1 percent through 2010.

Examples of typical operations and implementation engagements include:

• Outsourcing procurement functions for an international bank

• Mapping and designing workflow to increase production efficiency for a manufacturer

• Reengineering the infrastructure of a firm that has outgrown its former structure

Human resources consulting

Even with fine-tuned strategies and streamlined operations, businesses can fail without the right people in position to manage them. HR consulting addresses the issues of maximizing the value of staff and placing the right employees in roles that suit each individual. HR consulting firms are also hired for organizational restructuring, talent management, HR systems implementation, or benefits and compensation planning. In 2006, HR consulting services grew by 9 percent, reaching $18.4 billion. Partly driving the U.S. market's growth is the demand for benefits consulting, due to revisions in the U.S. Pension Protection Act and other recent legal changes.

An important subsection of HR consulting is HR outsourcing, where clients turn to firms to manage their internal human resources systems.

Examples of typical HR consulting engagements include:

• Conducting a benchmarking study to find opportunities to reduce headcount and costs

• Combining the HR functions of two recently merged corporations

• Determining the financial impact of adopting a new pension plan

Health care/pharmaceutical consulting

With a market worth $19 billion, health care consulting continues to be a core growth area in the U.S. consulting market. As the population of the United States and of other industrialized countries ages, and as scientists continue to make advances in genetic engineering, the health care industry thrives. In addition, pharmaceutical companies are increasingly concerned about cost structures, as patents for blockbuster drugs expire.

Plunkett Research reports that total U.S. health care expenditures are expected to rise from $2.17 trillion in 2006 to $2.88 trillion in 2010, with annual increases averaging about 7 percent. Furthermore, health spending in the U.S., now at 16 percent of GDP, accounts for a larger share of GDP than in any other major industrialized country. But an industry of that size is predictably overrun with companies all trying to get a piece of the pie. That's where health care and pharma consulting firms come in— helping clients like hospitals, HMOs and drug companies cope with a complicated maze of legislation, face competition with other health care providers, manage costs on vendors and equipment and implement new technology.

Examples of typical health care/pharma engagements include:

• Advising a pharmaceutical company on a drug licensing agreement

• Identifying acquisition targets for an expanding medical device manufacturer

• Implementing a plan to improve patient waiting time in a hospital emergency room

Economic consulting

Businesses in the U.S. are no longer isolated from economic changes in other parts of the world, so clients often turn to think tank-like economic consulting firms for a global perspective. These firms are typically loaded with economics PhDs and MBAs, as well as industry experts, and investigate economic factors to help clients resolve problems caused by competition, antitrust issues, public policy and regulations. Heavy on quantitative analysis, statistical studies and modeling services often play a key role in economic engagements. These consultancies are prized for their independence and ability to give candid counsel to clients affected by increasingly dynamic economic conditions.

Examples of typical economic consulting engagements include:

• Conducting due diligence for a client involved in an acquisition

• Preparing analysis for a firm involved in antitrust litigation

• Developing a pricing strategy for a multinational client

Financial consulting

According to Kennedy Information, in 2006, global spending on financial consulting services rose about 10 percent to $41.2 billion, and growth in the sector is predicted to remain strong over the long term. The market has gained momentum as companies seek consultants to help them deal with global competition, develop offshore establishments and seek new markets and customers. Other financial service areas driving the expansion are regulatory compliance, M&A, divestitures, private equity, and corporate planning and strategy.

Financial consulting firms tend toward two types of service offerings: Either they work with financial services firms to enhance their strategies and performance, or they have a specific financial model they use with clients to maximize their performance. In both cases, the focus is typically on boosting shareholder value.

Examples of typical financial consulting engagements include:

• Helping a financial services company develop new products to target a new customer segment

• Developing an exit strategy for a private equity firm

• Implementing an outsourcing initiative for a bank's IT functions

Visit the Vault Consulting Career Channel at **www.vault.com/consulting** - with insider firm profiles, message boards, the Vault Consulting Job Board and more.

V/\ULT CAREER LIBRARY   **41**

TOP

THE VAULT
50

50

CONSULTING
FIRMS

McKinsey & Company

55 East 52nd Street
New York, NY 10022
Phone: (212) 446-7000
Fax: (212) 446-8575
www.mckinsey.com

LOCATIONS

More than 80 offices in over 40 countries worldwide

PRACTICE AREAS

Functional Practices
Business Technology Office • Corporate Finance •
Marketing & Sales • Operations • Organization • Strategy
Industry Practices
Automotive & Assembly • Banking & Securities •
Chemicals • Consumer/Packaged Goods • Electric
Power/Natural Gas • High Tech • Insurance • Marketing •
Media & Entertainment • Metals & Mining • Nonprofit •
Payor/Provider • Petroleum • Pharmaceuticals & Medical
Products • Private Equity • Public Sector • Pulp & Paper •
Retail Strategy • Telecommunications • Travel & Logistics

THE STATS

Employer Type: Private Company
Managing Director: Ian Davis
2007 Employees: 14,000 (est.)
2006 Employees: 13,000 (est.)

RANKING RECAP

Practice Area
#1 - Economic Consulting
#1 - Energy Consulting
#1 - Financial Consulting
#1 - Pharmaceutical & Health Care Consulting
#4 - Operational Consulting
#7 - Human Resources Consulting

UPPERS

• "The people here are fantastic, intelligent and open to learning from each other"
• Prestige
• "You feel really valued and cared for"

DOWNERS

• "Hours are slightly worse than other consulting firms"
• "People are very smart and ambitious—it's difficult to stand out"
• "Secretive" culture

EMPLOYMENT CONTACT

www.mckinsey.com/careers

THE BUZZ
WHAT CONSULTANTS AT OTHER FIRMS ARE SAYING ABOUT THIS FIRM

• "The gift that keeps on giving"
• "Very 'I'm smarter than you'"
• "10,000 MBAs can't be wrong!"
• "Serious black suits"

THE SCOOP

The McKinsey mystique

Ask a layperson to name a management consulting firm, and chances are good that the name McKinsey will be the first you'll hear. For better or worse, McKinsey has come to represent the consulting industry in the popular lexicon. The firm has a mystique that arises from a rare combination of tradition, stability and, of course, high-profile consultants and alumni—many of whom write the books on strategy.

Tradition!

McKinsey's loyalty to tradition is evident in its continued adherence to a code of conduct established under Marvin Bower, the protégé of founder James O. McKinsey. McKinsey, a lawyer, CPA and University of Chicago management professor, is credited with the idea of tapping "management engineers" to help both struggling companies and thriving ones strengthen and grow their businesses. McKinsey's name endures, as does his legacy as a pioneer in the world of consulting. But Bower, who joined the firm in 1933, is credited with fleshing out the firm's culture. Under Bower's tenure as managing director from 1950 through 1967, the firm's revenue grew from $2 million to $20 million.

Bower's five-part code of conduct instructs McKinsey consultants to put client interests ahead of firm interests, serve clients in a superior manner and adhere to high ethical standards. Bower also encouraged consultants to be prepared to have differences of opinions with management at client firms, and to always give clients the unvarnished truth, however painful it might be.

Shhhh ... we're engaged

Another key element of the code, an insistence on strict confidentiality regarding all client engagements, continues to separate McKinsey from many of its peers. According to the firm, client confidence is "what we believe is professional behavior and the appropriate posture given our conviction that we supplement our clients' leadership, but never replace it." This stance is particularly notable in an era of self-promotion and press releases, but it certainly hasn't hurt McKinsey's marketing angle. In fact, many see the air of secrecy as an essential element in the firm's mystique.

This mystique—which leads insiders to refer to McKinsey simply as "The Firm"—also has lent McKinsey a reputation as the cool kid on the consulting block for ambitious MBAs. For more than a decade, the firm has been named the most desirable employer by U.S.-based MBAs in an annual survey by Universum Communications. (Its 12-year stint at the top of the list came to an end in May 2007, though, when Google claimed the No. 1 slot). This, too, is part of Bower's legacy. Early on, he recognized that demand for established talent would eventually outpace supply, and the firm became the first to recruit candidates fresh out of graduate school. Rather than relying solely on seasoned veterans wedded to a particular industry, McKinsey was able to mold its bright young recruits into savvy generalists, and rival firms soon followed suit.

McKinsey continues to seek "a firm of leaders who want the freedom to do what they think is right," as the firm puts it. The talent knocking down McKinsey's door includes Rhodes Scholars, law review editors, PhDs and even nuclear physicists. And alumni of the firm rarely have trouble landing the corner office when they leave. In February 2007, McKinsey alum and former Wharton School Vice Dean Jonathan Spector was named chief executive of the Conference Board. Other names in the news include Gerald Storch, named chairman and CEO of Toys "R" Us in February 2006; Jeremy Philips, appointed in January 2006 as head of Internet acquisition strategy for News Corp.; and Jim McNerney, named CEO of Boeing in 2005.

Everywhere at once

While New York was for many years home to McKinsey's managing director, the company doesn't claim any one office as its home base. In fact, the firm is operated as a decentralized partnership, led by a managing director who is elected every three years by a group of around 1,000 active directors and principals (roughly corresponding to senior and junior partners at other

Visit the Vault Consulting Career Channel at www.vault.com/consulting - with insider firm profiles, message boards, the Vault Consulting Job Board and more.

45

firms) who are considered McKinsey's owners and managers. As McKinsey explains it, the decentralized approach means that no one at the firm "owns" a particular client relationship; rather, the firm draws on its global network to find the "right minds for the right solutions" depending on the engagement.

Currently serving as managing director is Londoner Ian Davis, a 28-year veteran of the firm. An avid cricket player with an Oxford degree in policy, philosophy and economics, Davis replaced Rajat Gupta, who led McKinsey for its maximum of three, three-year terms. Davis' election was seen as a sign of a return to measured growth, as compared to the high-flying dot-com days under which Gupta served.

In fact, Davis was so low-profile he didn't even grant a press interview until he'd held the directorship for a year. When he did come out to the press, Davis reflected on the firm's progress over the past few years. During the dot-com boom, he told the *Financial Times* of London in July 2004, some of the firm's "basic values" were unintentionally compromised. Though he didn't elaborate, McKinsey critics are quick to associate the firm with the disgraced Enron, which was headed by former McKinsey consultant Jeff Skilling. Skilling had brought other McKinseyites onboard, and the firm's name was mentioned during the trials surrounding Enron's collapse. While no one has argued that McKinsey bore responsibility for Enron's shady dealings, *New Yorker* writer Malcolm Gladwell has accused the firm of "creat[ing] the blueprint for the Enron culture."

Practice, practice

McKinsey serves clients across industries and functions, but to put more focus on some, it has created practice areas in six functional areas (the business technology office, corporate finance, marketing and sales, operations, organization and strategy) and 18 industry practices, ranging from banking, high tech, pharmaceutical and private equity to health care, public sector, retail and telecommunications. While most of the firm's practice areas have remained consistent through the years, the business technology practice, or BTO, established in 1997, is a relative newcomer. The BTO helps clients align technology to the management of their businesses in the areas of IT governance, architecture and infrastructure.

Multinational McKinsey

Though McKinsey's revenue figures remain under wraps, the firm hasn't been shy about its global growth. McKinsey consultants work from more than 80 offices worldwide. This geographical growth is relatively recent; while the firm opened its first overseas office in London in 1959, it wasn't until the 1990s that McKinsey went truly global. During this period, the firm doubled its staff and opened 20 new offices in cities from Abu Dhabi to Rio de Janiero. These days, the firm reportedly derives more than 60 percent of its revenue from non-U.S. engagements, with China being one hot market: The firm has conducted more than 500 Chinese engagements over the last decade. In May 2005, Reuters reported that McKinsey was set to increase staff in Asia by 30 percent, with plans to add more than 700 employees in the region over the next two years. The firm has established a program aimed at hiring Chinese students, including English language training and overseas stints in the U.S. and Frankfurt. McKinsey's globe-trotting consultants have also worked with Singapore Airlines and the Singaporean government, the Colombian Coffee Federation, Czech oil group Unipetrol, and Turkey's Savings and Deposits Insurance Fund, to name just a few international clients.

Indian influencers

Recently, the firm's international reach has been keenly felt in India. McKinsey's influence on the subcontinent isn't simply limited to the clients it serves, which include the Indian government, the State Bank of India, liquor company Shaw Wallace, and engineering and construction firm Larsen & Toubro. McKinsey's presence in India has also helped raise a whole new generation of executives and entrepreneurs, with many McKinsey alumni going on to lead major corporations and projects of their own. Ex-Director Ashok Alexander went on to head the Bill & Melinda Gates Foundation in India, and fellow alumnus Pulak Prasad is a leader at Warburg Pincus. And some of the most influential drivers of the outsourcing trend in India have roots at McKinsey. Marc Vollenweider, a former partner at McKinsey in New Delhi and London, became a co-founder of Evalueserve Inc., a New Delhi-based provider of market research and data analysis for hedge funds and investment banks. Fellow McKinsey alum Neeraj

Bhargava founded Indian call center giant WNS Global Services, and former McKinsey associate Manoj S. Jain runs an influential outsourcing firm that taps talent from India and China. Rizwan Koita, from Bombay, left the firm at age 29 to found two thriving outsourcing services companies.

These prominent figures in outsourcing are true believers, thanks to McKinsey's early work in the field. Back in 1995, the firm began anticipating a world of "remote services" spurred by the new digital economy. Setting up a "knowledge center" in New Delhi, the firm employed its own offshore researchers to run numbers and do other tasks like assemble PowerPoint presentations from afar. The successful facility eventually became a model that McKinsey could showcase to clients who were curious about the potential of outsourcing.

An important book of interest to anyone trying to grasp the McKinsey approach to the global economy is an anthology, published by Harvard Business School Press in 2007 as part of the McKinsey Global Institute Anthology Series. The collection focuses on issues arising from the integration of global markets, according to three McKinsey publications—*Offshoring: Understanding the Emerging Global Labor Market*, *The Productivity Imperative: Wealth and Poverty in the Global Economy* and *Driving Growth: Breaking Down Barriers to Global Prosperity*.

Gloves off

Despite the firm's vow of silence, some of its engagements do make it to the press—unfortunately, it's often the more contentious cases that get buzzed about. A May 2006 *BusinessWeek* article highlighted documents related to McKinsey's consulting work for insurance giant Allstate that were used as the basis for *From Good Hands to Boxing Gloves*, a book penned by the plaintiff's lawyer David Berardinelli. The book purports to reveal the advice McKinsey gave to Allstate when the insurance company sought its help in reengineering its auto claims operations. Allstate had attempted to have the book's publication quashed, but a New Mexico state court rejected the effort.

The same court also ordered Allstate to make public copies of PowerPoint slides prepared for the insurer by McKinsey from 1992 through at least 1997. The slides reportedly advise Allstate to treat some claimants with "boxing gloves" rather than the "good hands" that form a critical part of Allstate's brand. "Rather than simply rushing to the scene of an accident and doling out cash, Allstate deploys a variety of systems set in place by McKinsey to make sure it pays the minimum necessary—and it plays hardball with those who seek more," in an attempt to save cash, *BusinessWeek* contends. The article reports that McKinsey has performed similar work for insurers USAA, State Farm and Fireman's Fund, though the latter argued in a letter to *BusinessWeek* that its handling of claims involved none of these hardball tactics. Of course, author Berardinelli has his own agenda, as an attorney seeking to pursue "bad faith" lawsuits on behalf of plaintiffs against Allstate. While McKinsey continued to remain mum about the affair, Allstate denied the book's allegations, arguing that any attempt at cost-saving was for the ultimate benefit of consumers.

Magazine empire Time Inc. made headlines with a series of dramatic layoffs over the holiday season in late 2006 and early 2007. A February 2007 *BusinessWeek* article about Time CEO Ann Moore suggested that McKinsey's advice may have influenced the shake up, noting that Time's massive size required a "thorough review" from the consultancy "and had to be completed in stages."

Not all of McKinsey's publicly leaked engagements make for juicy gossip fodder, however. According to Israeli publication *Globes*, McKinsey was tapped in March 2007 to advise American-Israeli Paper Mills Ltd. on the feasibility of building a new recycled paper production system, which could boost paper recycling in Israel by 50 percent. In June 2006, a *BusinessWeek* article outlined a "major screwup" at aircraft giant Airbus, whose top executive, Noel Forgeard, resigned following a series of embarrassing aircraft delivery delays. According to the article, Airbus execs asked McKinsey to step in and analyze the problem.

Read all about it

The firm's consultants regularly dispense wisdom on the pages of the influential *McKinsey Quarterly*. They also write periodically for publications such as the *Financial Times*, *The Wall Street Journal* and *BusinessWeek*. In January 2007, *The Wall Street Journal* reported on a McKinsey study mapping $140 trillion worth of financial assets around the globe, tracing the way

Visit the Vault Consulting Career Channel at **www.vault.com/consulting** - with insider firm profiles, message boards, the Vault Consulting Job Board and more.

 **VAULT** CAREER LIBRARY   **47**

money flows across international borders. The firm broke new ground in December 2006, when it compiled a list, published by the *Financial Times*, of the FT Non-Public 150. The list was the first to track nonpublicly traded companies, with the goal of stimulating debate about the impact of different ownership structures on corporate performance and health. In a July 2006 study, the firm analyzed productivity in the public sector, arguing that policymakers needed to help set standards for higher performance among federal programs, and calling for an independent entity to be created to track public-sector productivity levels.

According to the publication *The Lawyer*, in early 2007 New York City's Mayor Michael Bloomberg and New York Senator Charles Schumer received the results of a study commissioned from McKinsey on the city's financial services sector. Called "Sustaining New York's and the U.S.'s Global Financial Services Leadership," the report apparently took a grim view of New York's ranking among its peers, arguing that financial centers like London, Dubai, Frankfurt and Shanghai could overtake it in market share in the future. Reportedly, McKinsey blamed New York's shaky position on the effects of stringent securities regulation, such as the Sarbanes-Oxley Act.

McKinsey must-reads

In addition to reports and studies, McKinsey's consultants and former consultants have produced an impressive array of business best sellers in recent years. Perhaps the most well-known book to bear a McKinsey pedigree is Tom Peters' and Bob Waterman's *In Search of Excellence*, published in the 1980s (back when Peters and Waterman were relative unknowns at the firm) and since hailed as one of the most important business books of the century. More recently, in *The Origin of Wealth*, published by Harvard Business School Press in June 2006, McKinsey Senior Fellow Eric Beinhocker addresses basic questions about the subject of wealth, arguing that the latest work in economics is radically redefining the way the economy is understood. Under the principles of so-called "complexity economics," the economy has come to be seen as a dynamic system that is constantly evolving. Relating this idea to the question of the origin of wealth, Beinhocker proposes that the evolutionary processes of variation, selection and amplification are what drive growth in the economy over time. Also in 2006, McKinsey's David Fubini, Colin Price and Maurizio Zollo published *Mergers: Leadership, Performance, and Corporate Health*. The book identifies key leadership challenges faced by execs at companies undergoing a merger. The year 2005 saw the publication of the fourth edition of *Valuation: Measuring and Managing the Value of Companies*, by Tim Koller, Marc Goedhart and David Wessels.

Hot on nonprofit

McKinsey also lends its consulting talents to the pro bono world, with about half of its consultants taking on a pro bono engagement at some time during their careers. Clients have included museums, theaters, operas, festivals, multinational NGOs and development agencies, philanthropic organizations, schools, conservation organizations, land trusts, zoos and more. Since the firm says it considers "nonprofit work to be part of each consultant's career, but not any one person's exclusive focus," consultants aren't hired directly into the nonprofit arena. But associates and analysts with at least one year of McKinsey experience can apply to the firm's Community Fellows program, working exclusively on nonprofit projects for six to nine months. In one typical nonprofit engagement, McKinsey consultants worked with the $2.5 billion Annie E. Casey foundation to help it classify and share its internal knowledge. In 2001, the firm launched The McKinsey Institute on the Nonprofit Sector, appointing Senator Bill Bradley as chairman of its advisory board. The institute donated teams to assist with rebuilding following the devastating tsunami of 2005, and worked with former Presidents Bill Clinton and George H.W. Bush on establishing the Katrina Fund, devised to help ensure that resources were allocated efficiently in the wake of the hurricane.

Tackling the big picture

The McKinsey Global Institute, established in 1990, operates as an independent economic think tank within McKinsey, conducting research and developing positions on big-picture issues affecting businesses and governments worldwide. The institute, located near the White House, "combines the rigor of academia with the real-world experience of business," according to the firm, and its studies often garner broad media attention. A January 2007 institute report on the U.S. health care system found that America's system is much more costly than that of comparable nations for reasons many observers suspected but none had quantified: doctors get paid far more than their peers globally; the system encourages overconsumption of certain health services and procedures; and average costs per day for drugs and hospital stays are far higher than elsewhere. In a December 2006 report, MGI took up the issue of energy efficiency, arguing that by improving technologies already in place, worldwide energy demand could be cut in half by 2020. In June 2006, the institute released a study indicating that reforming India's financial system could lift millions out of poverty. Other hot issues for MGI researchers recently have included offshoring, demographics and China's talent market.

GETTING HIRED

Be an early bird

If you plan to try scaling Mount McKinsey, start planning early—it's a long expedition and the competition is fierce. For campus recruits, the process starts early, so students should be sure to check with their schools to see if campus visits are planned. All this information and more can be found on the firm's web site, where you'll find a wealth of information, including a discussion of roles, interview tips and practice cases.

Entry-level McKinseyites (those just out of undergrad or some master's programs) enter as business analysts. Traditionally designed as a two- to three-year program, the BA option then affords analysts the opportunity to go work in the field or return to school, after which many are invited back to serve as associates—the level at which candidates joining from graduate schools are most likely to join the firm.

What's in the case?

McKinsey's "exhausting" interview process varies slightly depending on the candidate's level, but all of them include plenty of case interview work. Sources report that the process may entail as much as 75 percent casework, along with 25 percent personal experience questions. Insiders say not to worry about "brainteaser" questions. One campus recruit reports going through two rounds: the first with two case interviews, the second with three case interviews and one quantitative test. "The first round was with an associate and an engagement manager and the second round was with three partners. They also asked some questions about why I wanted to join McKinsey, as well as general fit questions. The interviewers were very friendly and professional."

According to an associate, "I had two rounds of interviews (first round was two interviews, second was three). In each interview I did a case and talked about a personal achievement. The second round interviews were with partners and generally the cases were less structured. For both interviews the 'personal experience' component was left wide open; I was just asked, 'Tell me about an achievement you are proud of,' etc."

Show some structure

When it comes to acing the case, an insider advises, "I think that showing some structure in how you present is critical. You need to show that you can think through a problem in a logical way, and that you can communicate clearly (this is important for both the case and personal experience component)." A colleague agrees, "It is very important to be very structured in case analysis and not be afraid to express your opinion. The interviewers are more than willing to answer your questions." One source cautions, "It is important to get to know the on-campus team well; they have a lot of say in who gets hired," though the firm insists that the hiring decision comes down to a candidate's performance in an interview and is entirely merit-based.

Visit the Vault Consulting Career Channel at **www.vault.com/consulting** - with insider firm profiles, message boards, the Vault Consulting Job Board and more.

 **V**AULT CAREER LIBRARY   49

OUR SURVEY SAYS

Without peer

Befitting McKinsey's outsized reputation, consultants have strong opinions about "The Firm." McKinsey has a "great culture" with "great people," functioning as a "caring meritocracy," but at the same time maintaining a "high intensity," insiders say. And according to one insider, McKinsey is "more secretive than [its] two closest competitors, Bain and BCG." Still, a source says, "The people here are fantastic, intelligent and open to learning from each other," and "you will not find people or an environment like this anywhere." Another source compliments his co-workers when he says, "People are very smart and ambitious—it's difficult to stand out." But that doesn't mean staffers don't enjoy being part of such an exclusive crowd. "It is by far the nicest place I have ever worked, compared to corporate and investment banking. People are really supportive and have very interesting personalities," an insider declares.

Get to know the partners

That said, sources report varying experiences with their peers and supervisors. One consultant observes, "As I had been told before starting at McKinsey, your engagement manager can make or break your experience at the firm. Choose wisely." The firm is "very focused on developing people," another source says. While "most people" are "very down to earth," a colleague notes, there are the occasional bad apples—"in this sense, I think the great thing about the size of McKinsey is that you can work with lots of different people ... hopefully avoiding the bad characters." Another insider grumbles about a "highly political and clique-oriented culture around partners."

Insiders counsel that the way to have a positive experience with management is to be proactive in building relationships. A consultant discloses, "Partners are very supportive generally, but you have to find people you want to work with and follow them. Partners will not follow you around; if you don't talk to them they will not talk to you. Overall though, they have been very open and greatly supportive."

Just like shift work!

The image of the hard-charging McKinsey consultant is hard to shake, but believe it or not, sources report being reasonably satisfied with their work/life balance. In fact, says a source, "If balance is important to you, it is certainly something you can actively manage, and you will be supported by your superiors in doing so." Work hours average between 55 and 75 a week, sources say, but "hours are extremely variable by type of study, so you can manage it by choosing lifestyle-friendly projects if that is what you want to optimize for," an insider explains. "In terms of hours, that depends," recounts a junior staffer, "I've been on four studies so far. On three of those, I've had reasonable hours, leaving the client at 7 or 7:30 in the evening and then doing work from the hotel later on, if I choose to. But there are those studies where you're going to be working all night long, and those are really bad." A colleague reports that while days lasting from 8 a.m. to 10 p.m. aren't uncommon, weekend work is rare and, in fact, it "sort of [feels] like a four days on, three days off shift job." "It can be hard if you're on the road, but I've never gone into the office to work on a weekend in the year-and-a-half I've worked here," another consultant says.

Luxury liners

Still, "travel adds another 10 to 15 hours to your workweek," a source reports. Traveling more than 50 percent of the time is standard, insiders say, and a colleague notes that the constant Monday and Thursday trips can be "a real drag." Of course, it helps that travel is "very luxurious" at McKinsey, as one staffer describes it. A co-worker agrees, praising the "great meals, great travel and accommodations," and adding that travel offers an "excellent ability to leverage [our] global footprint and work internationally."

Talking allowed

There's "no shortage of training" at McKinsey, an insider says, noting that the "development and feedback culture are continuous forms of training, while the firm has a strategy of reinforcing training through formal weeklong modules in international locales."

In addition, says a source, McKinsey offers lower-level consultants "great exposure to senior management of large companies, with the ability to present to them or offer opinions during meetings. [It's] not a banking culture where analysts are not allowed to talk. Your opinions are highly valued." Says an analyst, "For our age, it's a pretty good amount of responsibility. I'll do one-on-one meetings with higher-ups at the client site. But you have to demonstrate that you're capable of handling the responsibility. They'll give you as much as you show you deserve."

Ask for feedback

Promotion at McKinsey, we're told, is part of a "very structured advancement process with thorough evaluation at each step," and managers are willing to let you know where you stand. Explains an associate, "The firm follows a strict up-or-out policy, and it's very difficult to make it from one step to another. However, you are given detailed feedback whenever you ask for it." The firm notes that making it from one level to the next requires developing new skills—which it clearly defines and communicates to staffers—and adds that it provides coaching and training to help consultants succeed.

Whether or not consultants decide to move up or leave after the first two years, insiders claim that the firm always keeps individual development in mind. "Even if you eventually go on to work in something else, McKinsey will give you as much help as possible in getting the best positions you can get. Within the firm, career development is even more focused. There are mentoring opportunities and other opportunities that help you focus on your career goals," an insider explains.

As for monetary feedback, consultants report raking in bonuses of up to 30 percent of compensation, along with a 12 percent contribution to their retirement funds. The "very good" health coverage includes no co-pay, says an insider. On top of that, "consultants accumulate a significant number of points to be used at airlines and hotels." Summer associates also claim to bring home good money, along with insurance coverage.

Minorities at McKinsey

With respect to minority diversity, the firm reportedly lacks equal representation in its ranks. "Our firm is 2 percent black across the globe. There are definitely visible amounts of Indians and Asians, but still heavily male white," an insider observes. The firm counters that it is indeed very diverse, with consultants speaking over 120 different languages and coming from 108 different citizenships, adding that less than 40 percent of firm members are white males. McKinsey has developed diversity initiatives "to increase the numbers, especially for women and blacks within the organization." A colleague confirms that McKinsey is "making a huge effort to recruit, mentor [and] retain more women—it's a big priority."

For minorities who do make it into the ranks, insiders say there is plenty of peer involvement. "There are definitely support groups and networking opportunities in place. Blacks have a conference every year in South Africa that is about developing the numbers, diversity at McKinsey and how to move up within the company," a manager notes. In addition, being "out" at McKinsey is no problem for GLBT staffers; in fact, they attend an event called GLAM (Gay and Lesbian at McKinsey) in Berlin on the company dime.

Charitably inclined

Community service for McKinsey takes many forms, including "charity drives every year," an insider says. "We have a large nonprofit practice, [in addition to] lots of pro bono work, either with fully-staffed teams or with folks working 'out of hide,'" a consultant notes.

Visit the Vault Consulting Career Channel at **www.vault.com/consulting** - with insider firm profiles, message boards, the Vault Consulting Job Board and more.

VAULT CAREER LIBRARY   **51**

2

The Boston Consulting Group

Exchange Place, 31st Floor
Boston, MA 02109
Phone: (617) 973-1200
Fax: (617) 973-1339
www.bcg.com

LOCATIONS

Boston, MA (HQ)
64 offices in 38 countries

PRACTICE AREAS

Branding
Corporate Development
E-Commerce
Globalization
Information Technology
Innovation
Intellectual Property
Marketing & Sales
Operations
Organization
Postmerger Integration
Strategy

THE STATS

Employer Type: Private Company
Chairman: Carl Stern
President & CEO: Hans-Paul Bürkner
2007 Employees: 3,800 (consulting staff only)
2006 Employees: 3,300 (consulting staff only)
2006 Revenue: $1.8 billion
2005 Revenue: $1.5 billion

THE BUZZ
WHAT CONSULTANTS AT OTHER FIRMS ARE SAYING ABOUT THIS FIRM

- "Excellent intellectual capital; cerebral"
- "Not diverse"
- "Well-rounded firm; amazing opportunities to work in a broad variety of areas"
- "Filled with people who take themselves too seriously"

RANKING RECAP

Practice Area
#3 - Pharmaceutical & Health Care Consulting
#4 - Energy Consulting
#4 - Financial Consulting
#6 - Economic Consulting
#8 - Operational Consulting

Quality of Life
#4 - Formal Training
#6 - Compensation
#7 - Offices
#10 - Best Firms to Work For
#11 - Firm Culture
#14 - Overall Satisfaction
#18 - Relationships with Supervisors
#20 - Work/Life Balance

Diversity
#13 - Diversity for Women
#18 - Best Firms for Diversity
#18 - Diversity for GLBT

UPPERS

- "Tons of responsibility from the beginning, not crunching numbers for the guy one level up"
- "Surprising number of non-MBAs (PhDs, JDs) who bring a very interesting perspective to discussions"
- "Really cool clients and cases"
- International staffing opportunities abound

DOWNERS

- "The culture can be competitive and one of always giving off the appearance of being busy"
- "We are growing too fast and working too hard to always retain the most talented"
- Confusing staffing procedure
- "Limited mentoring for minorities and support for new consultants specific to their needs"

EMPLOYMENT CONTACT

www.bcg.com/careers/careers_splash.jsp

THE SCOOP

Setting the tone

Since its founding in 1963, The Boston Consulting Group has been the driving force behind many of the concepts informing the management consulting field—and it hasn't showed signs of slowing down. In keeping with the legacy of its founder, former Bible salesman and Harvard Business School alumnus Bruce Henderson, the firm always seems to be on the leading edge. BCG consultants have come up with concepts that effectively capture the latest strategy and business trends, including trading up/trading down, the deconstruction of value chains, time-based competition and even disease management. Believing that young go-getters could be cultivated as top consulting generalists given the right training and rewards, Henderson also had an impact on the way talent is recruited in the industry, setting a precedent of aggressively recruiting top grads from HBS, Kellogg and the like. The firm also was the first strategy consultancy to set up shop in Tokyo, in 1966.

Way beyond Boston

Though the firm has retained the name of the city in which it was founded, BCG is anything but provincial. The firm's 3,300 consultants (up from 2,900 in 2005, following an aggressive push to hire new MBAs that year) operate out of 64 offices in 38 countries. As a private company, BCG only discloses its revenue annually. The firm does say that it has had double-digit growth in each of the past three years with growth in each of its regions. The firm's steady growth has been steered by equally solid leadership; CEO Hans-Paul Bürkner, who joined BCG in 1981 and became chief in 2003, is only the fifth CEO in BCG's history. Bürkner, who has a reputation as an accessible leader who doesn't mind sharing an office with junior colleagues, was named to the top spot on *Consulting Magazine*'s list of the top-25 most influential consultants in 2003.

BCG doesn't trumpet its engagements, but the firm says it derives most of its clients from the 500-largest corporations worldwide. BCG's clientele also includes nonprofit organizations and government agencies. The many industries BCG covers include consumer, energy, financial services, health care, industrial goods, media and entertainment, retail, technology and communications, and travel and tourism. In February 2007, hotel giant Best Western tapped BCG to help it develop a 10-year "road map" for its products, along with new customer-focused initiatives. Other clients have included Whirlpool, Verizon and Limited Brands.

A global-local clientele

Having blazed a trail for strategy consulting in Asia with its pioneering Tokyo office, BCG has established a solid presence in the region. The firm derives roughly half of its Asian business from local entities (as opposed to other consultancies that bring in more business from American firms conducting operations overseas). BCG's Asian clients include five of the region's biggest non-Japanese companies, three of the top-five business conglomerates in Korea and eight of the biggest local commercial banks in Hong Kong, Indonesia, Malaysia, Thailand and Korea. Even in India, where many of its rivals have cultivated offices geared toward development and offshoring, BCG's activities in the region mainly focus on pure management consulting. The firm employs consultants in Mumbai and New Delhi who work on traditional strategy engagements.

In addition, the firm enjoys a strong reputation as an employer of choice among European MBAs. In the past decade, BCG opened European offices in Athens, Barcelona, Berlin, Budapest, Cologne, Prague, Rome and Warsaw. Most recently, an office was opened in Kiev in spring 2007. Russia is another hot spot for the firm, with demand growing for strategy services from both aggressive local and new Western entrants, as well as powerful incumbents with a solid position built on Soviet-era assets, but needing reassessment to help realize their ambitious growth goals.

As for other spots on the globe, in the second half of 2006, BCG opened offices in Abu Dabhi and Dubai, giving the company a permanent presence in the Gulf region. Beyond the U.S., BCG has a strong presence in the Americas, with offices in Toronto, Mexico City, Monterrey, Buenos Aires, São Paulo and Santiago.

Visit the Vault Consulting Career Channel at www.vault.com/consulting - with insider firm profiles, message boards, the Vault Consulting Job Board and more.

VAULT CAREER LIBRARY

53

The best and the brightest

In addition to organizing around industries, BCG divides its services into functions, including branding, corporate development, e-commerce, globalization, information technology, innovation, intellectual property, marketing and sales, operations, organization, postmerger integration and strategy. The firm employs a stable of consultants with well-established reputations for advising CEOs, senior management and boards. In July 2007, BCG Senior Partners Steve Gunby (also chairman of BCG's America's region) and Sharon Marcil were named to *Consulting Magazine*'s Top 25 Consultants list. And BCG senior partners, Ron Nicol, based in Dallas, and Kaz Uchida in Tokyo, were named to the list in 2006. Well-known BCG alumni can be found in the top tiers of the business world (Pepsi CEO Indra Nooyi, Bath & Body Works CEO Neil Fiske, Boston Beer Co. founder Jim Koch), politics (former Prime Minister of Israel Benjamin Netanyahu, and former governor and presidential candidate Mitt Romney) and even entertainment (pop musician John Legend).

Coming out on top

Among *Fortune* magazine's list of the 100 Best Companies to Work For in 2007, BCG placed first among all small companies (those with between 1,000 and 2,500 U.S. employees), and eighth overall, improving on its 11th-place ranking in 2006. *Fortune* lauded the firm for its strong employee development and intensive investment in training, supportive culture and progressive benefits. The firm's attention to women in the workplace also captured *Fortune*'s attention, as the magazine noted a 25 percent increase in female hires since 2004, thanks to a BCG initiative. The firm's female-friendly stance also earned it kudos from *Working Mother* magazine, which placed the consultancy on its list of the 100 best companies in 2006. In the survey that determined its rankings, *Working Mother* paid particular attention to flexible scheduling and leave time, both of which BCG offers generously to new parents.

Cows, dogs, stars ... and disease management

BCG's reputation as an innovator of strategic ideas goes all the way back to the Summer of Love. In 1968, the firm introduced the BCG Growth-Share Matrix, which explains the relationship between a company's profitability and its market share using "star," "dog," "cash cow" and "question mark" icons in a four-quadrant layout. The now-classic model indicates that profitable businesses in mature markets (cash cows) provide the funding for high-growth ventures with large expected returns (stars), while low-growth and low-return ventures (dogs) should be divested as companies try to build low-return fast growers (question marks) into market leaders before they become dogs.

Another concept pioneered by the firm is that of disease management, referring to the use of business systems analysis and total quality management principles to control and prevent long-term diseases like diabetes and asthma. The concept arose from an engagement BCG had with German pharmaceutical manufacturer Boehringer Mannheim in the 1980s on new approaches to managing costs associated with diabetes. The firm has continued to produce regular studies and reports on the subject.

A latte buzz

BCG garnered buzz in the business world for another concept, the "new luxury," developed by its consultants in 2003. In *Trading Up*, BCG Senior Partner Michael J. Silverstein and ex-BCGer Neil Fiske deconstructed how new luxury brands—like high-end chocolates, high-thread count sheets and pricey lattes—managed to thrive even in a weakened U.S. economy. The book argues that items once seen as luxuries in earlier times (such as fancy coffee) have become commonplace, leading to the success of brands like Starbucks and Restoration Hardware, which sell goods at a premium and rake in higher profits. The best seller was followed by the May 2006 *Treasure Hunt*, on the consumer trend to bargain hunt at discount stores or "trade down," earning Silverstein a reputation as the go-to guy on the topic of consumer spending and the luxury marketplace.

Tough thinkers

Other influential thinkers on BCG's consulting roster include Senior Partner Jeanie Duck, whose 2001 best seller *The Change Monster: The Human Forces that Fuel or Foil Corporate Change* explores a new way of looking at change strategy for senior executives, and Partner Luc de Brabandere, whose most recent publication, *The Forgotten Half of Change: Achieving Greater Creativity-Through Changes in Perception*, published in 2005, addresses how leaders can transform their organizations by changing perceptions of reality. Another attention-getting book, *Hardball*, published in 2004, challenges some commonplace ideas of the business world. Co-authors George Stalk Jr., a BCG senior partner, and Rob Lachenauer, an ex-BCGer, took a tough line against what they saw as a touchy-feely business style prevalent among American corporations, arguing that firms that focus too much on "squishy" concepts like employee empowerment are doomed to fall behind more aggressive rivals that focus more on undercutting the competition. (The approach may not have panned out too well for former Home Depot CEO Robert Nardelli, however; *BusinessWeek* reported on Nardelli's adoption of the *Hardball* philosophy in 2006, but he was forced stepped down from the struggling retailer less than a year later, amid grumbling about his management.)

Investing in innovation

In January 2007, the firm released a book by BCG Senior Partners Jim Andrew and Hal Sirkin, entitled *Payback: Reaping the Rewards of Innovation*. Identifying "innovation intoxication" and "idea worship" as phenomena that can slow down even the best-intentioned companies, the authors argue that true innovation must lead to cash profits. Identifying the right type of innovation requires metrics, say the authors, who offer techniques to help companies reach a balance between the input needed for idea generation (time, money and people) and the output to be gained from the process ("payback" in cash, as well as indirect benefits). *BusinessWeek* named *Payback* one of the year's 10 best books on innovation.

Getting a grip on all of BCG's influential ideas is a daunting task, but a relatively recent book may help matters somewhat. Published in 2006, *The Boston Consulting Group on Strategy: Classic Concepts and New Perspectives*, is an updated anthology of the firm's strategy and management articles published in the Harvard Business Review and by the firm. The book is a must-read for anyone wanting a basic overview of BCG's pioneering philosophies.

Surveying and ranking

Aside from its best-selling books, BCG also frequently publishes studies and surveys that cover issues specific to certain industries (such as a February 2007 report on the outlook for the global steel industry), countries (the firm often analyzes business trends in India, as in a February 2007 report on the subcontinent's manufacturing sector) and consumer trends. A November 2006 study tracked consumers' attitudes toward spending in the retail sector as the holidays approached, while a September 2006 report analyzed the offshoring of R&D to India and China by major pharmaceutical companies. The firm made headlines in August 2006 with a survey indicating that rising gas prices were causing middle and lower-middle income Americans to "trade down" on shopping and leisure activities. For three years running, the firm has also helped *BusinessWeek* magazine produce an annual report ranking the world's most innovative companies: Apple, Google, Toyota, GE and Microsoft all placed in the top-five in 2007.

A common ground for strategy

BCG's Strategy Institute, established in 1998 to research and foster discussion on strategy for business and society, gathers insights from leaders in various academic disciplines and strives to distill them into coherent strategy ideas. The institute provides an opportunity for select academically-minded BCG consultants to explore interdisciplinary topics, such as the relevance of military historian Carl von Clausewitz's thinking to business strategy—or the power of metaphors to enhance strategic thinking. The entire firm can access articles and participate in discussion groups through its online Strategy Gallery. As the firm puts it, "Whether they be philosophers, neurobiologists, anthropologists, mathematicians or artists, when they approach the subject with open, inquiring minds, all may find common cause and a common vocabulary for talking about strategy."

Visit the Vault Consulting Career Channel at **www.vault.com/consulting** - with insider firm profiles, message boards, the Vault Consulting Job Board and more.

VAULT CAREER LIBRARY   55

Where charity and strategy meet

BCGers with a charitable bent enjoy many opportunities for social impact projects. At the global level, the firm recently refocused on three goals set out by the UN Millennium Project: fighting poverty and hunger, advancing children's well-being and improving global health. To address these challenges, the firm partnered with the World Food Programme, Save the Children and several organizations in the global health arena, such as the PATH Malaria Vaccine Initiative and the Roll Back Malaria Partnership. At the local level, each BCG office chooses the topics it wants to focus on, as well as partner organizations. Some examples of recent local initiatives include the Chicago office helping the local public school system transform its high schools, the Paris office working to encourage the hiring of disabled workers by French corporations and several Latin American offices assisting the nonprofit organization Endeavor by providing consulting services to entrepreneurs in emerging markets.

GETTING HIRED

Diversity is key

If you're looking for what defines the "ideal" BCG consultant, you won't hear it from the firm; on its web site, BCG argues that the industry "demands great diversity of experience, perspective, thinking style and expertise." Online, you can learn about the levels at which candidates with various educational and professional levels may enter the firm. Undergrads, recruited from top universities (you can find a search engine listing campus visits online), typically sign on as associates. Candidates with MBAs, typically drawn from the top-10 business schools in the country, usually start as consultants. And those with other advanced degrees may start as either associates or consultants, depending on the type of degree, work experience and other factors.

The firm tends to target "all the usual suspects—top-tier universities" for campus recruiting, an insider says. "Harvard and Penn are by far the two biggest feeder schools for North American offices," another source tells us. Regional offices, however, also draw from local schools. A consultant in Atlanta reports recruiting from Duke, Georgia Tech, Emory, UNC and Vanderbilt, while a Los Angeles-based BCGer says his office draws from Claremont McKenna, Pomona, Harvey Mudd and Caltech, among others. Another source reports that the firm also brings in "a small number of recruits from alternative channels, including law school, PhDs and lateral industry hires." Oh, and "SAT scores and GPA matter," an insider adds.

Casting a wide net

"All interviews are case interviews, but candidates are rated against their peers (undergrads and MBAs are not compared to each other)," a source says, noting, "We realize that most of the people we interview will not get an offer, so we try to make the process interesting and fun." Typically, undergrad and MBA recruits go through first-round interviews on campus, followed by second rounds at the office in question, staffers say. "Interviews consist of two to three standard 45-minute sessions, about 30 minutes of case study and 15 minutes of personal interviews each," a source reports. As one consultant puts it, "BCG casts a wide recruiting net, getting to know hundreds of candidates for each office. The firm places a premium on finding exceptionally bright, yet personal individuals. Thus, each office invests considerable time in getting to know candidates in advance of interviews. Ultimately, the selection process is extremely tight."

Frozen pizza, tree farms and everything in between

There's "no typical interview question" at BCG, an insider says; rather, "each case is unique to the interviewer, given their BCG experience. Thus, over the course of five case interviewers, candidates will be broadly tested and evaluated in terms of their conceptual, analytical and communication skills." Case interviews are described by another source as "extremely open-ended (on absolute basis and relative to peer firms)," with a "high burden on the candidate to effectively structure his approach to solving the problem." "BCG doesn't ask brainteasers," another consultant comments. "They ask business questions based on real cases and numbers. This makes the interview a bit more relaxing, because the problem is real and logical." According to a colleague, "We don't give the 'how many mailboxes are there in Omaha' question because it's not applicable to what we do."

Looking at a number of case question examples provided by insiders highlights their diversity—as well as the diversity of the engagements BCGers work on. "You are a frozen pizza maker, you want to grow, how do you do it?" "Our client is a major brewer with approximately 50 percent market share. Over the last several years, revenue has been flat/growing slightly, however profits have taken a serious dive. What would you recommend?" "How should I think about entering the European food packaging industry if I am a North American producer?" "An airline is trying to decide whether to continue to pull planes from the gates to do maintenance or to do some maintenance at the gate. What factors must you consider to make the best decision?" "You have been hired by a large power plant manufacturer to assist in determining a location for their new generation plant. The potential locations are town A, town B, and town C. Which location will maximize expected profits?" "A company has two options for managing a tree farm—the first option has fewer trees but takes longer to ramp up, the second option requires more trees but ramps up much faster. Which one should the company pursue? This requires some math (cost/benefit analysis) and some strategic thinking (what other factors might be important for this decision?)."

A summer to remember

BCG offers 10-week internships, and interested candidates are directed to the web site for more information. One former intern describes the experience as a "great opportunity to know the firm and convince myself that this was the place to be." It's a "realistic job preview, with actual case participation with true accountabilities," notes a colleague. In fact, "clients often do not know you are an intern," another source claims. According to an Atlanta BCGer who interned with the firm, there were "lots of fun events, including an Outward Bound adventure in the North Carolina mountains that allows the class to bond." A former intern in Chicago says, "There were many organized activities to ensure we met people at all levels in the office (partner lunches, Cubs game, sailing, golf). We also had many activities organized for just our intern class (scavenger hunt, dinners, go-carts)." An added bonus: BCG offers a "very high salary compared to other internships," reports a source. "I highly recommend it for anyone who is curious about the field," another happy ex-intern (and current consultant) enthuses. "Coming back was a no-brainer," a colleague agrees.

OUR SURVEY SAYS

Unique in their uniqueness

Several consultants agree that a defining characteristic of BCG is its "diverse culture." As one insider puts it, "When I think of BCG versus other firms, one unique element is the fact that at BCG there are multiple routes to success. When I think of the very senior partners in the firm, they are culturally very different people. This says to me that I can carve out my own path here without having to change who I am culturally. If I want to go party, there are folks to party with; if I want to go to the opera, there will be opera fans. And if I want to go home and watch TV, that's perfectly fine, too." A colleague agrees, "BCG embraces individuality and is very accepting of all cultures. None of that matters as long as you are intellectually curious and interested in solving problems." BCGers describe their peers as "open-minded," "laid-back," "fun," "warm," "cordial" and "collaborative." "We are all a bit nerdy, a bit weird (in a good way) and fun!" one consultant declares.

"BCG is a set of eclectic, very kind and generally very sincere people," one insider says. "The reason most people stay at BCG is because of the people. That said, the consulting culture itself can be a bit toxic—it's deadline-driven with often meaningless formatting work, and there's the frustration of working all night on something that doesn't get used." Others worry that there's "too much emphasis on critical feedback," and "sometimes the driven personalities create an atmosphere of expectation that can be stressful." "Sometimes," a source notes, "feedback is so sugarcoated that it's difficult to gauge your own performance." Not everyone feels that way, however. As one consultant says, "The support system here is amazing—I was recently having a tough time with my case, and so many people (from the most junior to the most senior) took time out to listen to how I was feeling and to help me deal with the situation. I don't know what I would have done without them."

Visit the Vault Consulting Career Channel at **www.vault.com/consulting** - with insider firm profiles, message boards, the Vault Consulting Job Board and more.

V**A**ULT CAREER LIBRARY   **57**

Staying in the zone

"Given that this is a professional services company where standard hours are on the higher side, work/life balance is good," says a consultant, who adds that "forethought and planning are well respected, and if you are up front about commitments, teams will usually try to honor them." The source continues, "In general, Monday through Thursday we have to be willing to prioritize work over personal life when work demands it, but generally the weekends are our own. 'Red zone' reports help keep principals and partners aware of the hours their teams are logging." Another source notes that "they actively track our hours and want us to average 60 a week. If it is continuously more, they will intervene. They seek to minimize attrition." It helps that there's "no face time required," adds a colleague, who says, "I can leave when I want to and work from home after dinner with family."

The firm "has generous policies when it comes to the little things," we're told, including "flying [business] class, staying in comfortable hotels, using limo services, using administrative staff to produce slides, providing every consultant with access to an administrative assistant, fully staffing support functions such as travel and IT so that any hassles can be off-loaded from the consultants, etc." The source adds that when it comes to work/life balance, these extras "really add up when it comes to daily quality of life. The bottom line: Look at the senior partners. The rate of divorce is much lower than average. It's obvious that most of the partners have healthy and happy family lives. This set of values is reflected in how the firm is run."

Relaxing on the beach

"Consultants also usually have one or more weeks 'on the beach' in between case engagements, which are essentially free vacation days to catch up on life," a consultant states, and depending on client needs, "BCG also helps moderate the workload by assigning employees to one case at a time, rather than assigning them to two cases at 50 percent each (which in reality usually equates to 200 percent of work)," another insider remarks. Still, "Client and senior-level demands require me to be online or watch my e-mail throughout evenings and on weekends," a staffer admits. And a colleague warns, "It depends on the project and mostly the manager. Certain managers are respectful, while others are hell to work for and are literally work machines."

The fact that "BCG is not a face time culture" means there are few complaints about working long hours just to "look busy" insiders say. That said, workweeks can be long: "The unpredictable nature of the job means that even if your total hours for the week are reasonable, you may have huge standard deviations within that. One night you'll work till 4 a.m. and the rest of the week you'll have normal 9-to-5 hours and the total for the week ends up looking fine," a consultant reports. Sources report working anywhere from 50 to 90 hours a week (though the latter is rare). "Work hours can be variable around projects and deliverables in projects. This is not a job for those who love routine—it's for those who love stimulation, challenge and learning," says a source.

High-class travel

Travel at BCG occurs "on an as-needed basis," an insider explains, adding, "If you don't have a meeting or need to see the client, you don't need to be there." "Mandatory travel is lower at BCG than at other firms due to its local staffing policies," a colleague notes. "If a metric of 'hotel stays per consultant' existed, BCG would be on the low end relative to all firms," opines an insider.

"When you travel, you usually come back Wednesday night, and stay at home either Thursday or Friday," a source explains, though others report a Monday through Thursday routine. And while consultants admit that travel does get tiring after a while, there are those who genuinely appreciate the opportunity to traverse the globe. One such insider boasts: "Travel with BCG is amazing. We stay in the best hotels and eat at the best restaurants in all the cities we visit." "For more junior employees, I think the travel is a plus—very rarely do senior team members travel without their teams. That means valuable exposure for junior team members, which promotes the flat culture," a staffer offers. According to another BCGer, "We use private aircraft for our larger clients. This makes travel very easy, quick and comfortable."

Should I stay or should I go?

For the road-weary among the bunch, "the staffing people are very receptive to comments and the need to mix local and travel cases," says an insider. "In the Chicago office, there is an intense effort to develop the local client base and minimize unnecessary travel. As a working mother, I prefer to travel as little as possible. I have been able to optimize my own staffing around my priorities, and have been able to do the vast majority of my work with local clients."

Likewise, the firm is open and flexible to accommodating requests for more travel. "If I wanted to travel more, I could easily do so," a consultant comments. "I receive e-mails almost weekly about staffing opportunities across the U.S., Europe, Asia, Latin America and the Middle East. Many of my peers who are associates have worked for months in Germany, Argentina, China, Mexico, etc., because they expressed an interest." This, says the source, is "in addition to the formalized ambassador programs in which [top-performing] BCG staff can spend a year working in another country."

It ain't I-banking

As for salary, a source confides, "I like how much I am making and the path forward looks even better." Of course, "We are undercompensated compared with our peers in investment banking," says a contact, who adds, "Our job is harder to get and we're more qualified, yet we get paid less. It speaks volumes about the experience, and most people would take a pay cut for this type of training and intellectual engagement." Another insider observes that the "general impression is that base salary is on par with other firms, if not slightly less, but the profit-sharing retirement fund and medical benefits far exceed other firms, and the bonus structure is at the least comparable, if not superior." "The profit sharing goes into a retirement vehicle; it has historically averaged 15 percent of all-in compensation (base salary plus bonus)," a source explains.

It's the little things

When it comes to benefits and perks, an insider appreciates how BCG "generally exhibits care to employees—little things like ordering in lunch for the whole office when it is snowing or pouring rain really have a big effect on office culture, happiness, etc." "After a very intense case, the principals have insisted that we take the following Monday and Tuesday off to recharge, and have even told the staffing coordinators [about this]. In addition, we've had some very nice postcase dinners and lunches," a colleague pipes in. Other "little things" include an entertainment area with "foosball, pool, table tennis and poker tables, a big-screen TV, an XBOX and a fridge with beer. It's great for breaks during the day or Friday evening poker games." Those rowdy Fridays, we're told, "are always filled with people egging each other on and trading insults as we play." Employees also enjoy the "passport lunch program, where a new associate/consultant can ask any management level person to lunch and the firm will pick up the tab." In some cities, there's free car service home after 8 p.m., and in New York, the firm pays moving expenses and broker's fees, sources tell us.

Major medical perks

But it's the bigger things that BCGers really appreciate, such as fully-funded health care coverage. "It costs $5 for me to visit any doctor and $2 for any prescription, and there are no deductibles. The assistants at my doctor's and dentist's offices always comment that I have the best health care benefits they've ever seen!" claims one source. And BCG's accommodations for new parents are legendary—they include at least 12 weeks of leave for moms, a week for dads and even a lactation room in the office. Of course, the "100 percent paid health care premiums for families is a big one—quite simply it is amazing," an insider comments. "My wife had severe complications during pregnancy in 2005 and we paid little to nothing. People often joke of the $5 baby at BCG; you pay one co-pay for first visit and everything is generally covered!" The firm also offers flexible schedules for new parents, and sometimes really goes above and beyond: "My manager has personally babysat my son when I needed to be at a client meeting and my nanny was sick. He actually drove to my house and picked up my son," marvels an insider.

Others cite the firm's flexibility as a top perk: "When a family member recently passed away, I assumed that I would have to use vacation days to attend the funeral as I have at other jobs. At BCG, there is such a high level of trust that people will not abuse the system, that I was told explicitly, 'That's not how we treat people here, especially in their times of need,'" an insider shares.

Visit the Vault Consulting Career Channel at **www.vault.com/consulting** - with insider firm profiles, message boards, the Vault Consulting Job Board and more.

VAULT CAREER LIBRARY   59

In addition, says a colleague, the firm offers "full sponsorship to go to two years of grad school, which includes full tuition, a $10K living stipend, a $10K interest-free loan and a laptop, and you remain an employee [for profit-sharing purposes]."

Plenty for wanderers

Those who like to travel and explore appreciate the firm's ambassador program, where consultants can apply to work from another international office for a year. In addition, says a source, "every year we go on a weekend retreat with our office. This year, we are going to Puerto Rico with our families for a weekend of team-building and relaxation as a gift for a great year of work." When it comes to retreats, "BCG really goes upscale on these things, and significant others are always invited," a consultant adds. And, there's a "generous expense policy when traveling extensively; for instance, instead of flying home one weekend, you can use the cash equivalent to fly a significant other to your client location and spend the weekend touring," a staffer notes. And though BCG sets expense guidelines, colleagues say the firm is liberal when it comes to food, drink and hotel expenses.

Hangin' with the partners

At BCG, "supervisors are very involved and serve as mentors," sources report. "BCG really adheres to the apprenticeship model and project leaders strive to help you develop and grow." An insider adds that the firm is "unique here in that our leverage ratio is so low (ratio of consultants to partners) that you get much greater access to them and build better relationships. By being staffed with predominantly partners out of your home office, you also build deeper relationships with partners and other co-workers." Says one newbie, "One of my closest friends in the office is a partner. This means a lot to me that someone so high level will take time to chat and hang out with someone who is entry level, like myself." In fact, a colleague states, "I hardly think of my supervisors as real supervisors in the traditional sense of the word. I think of them more as wiser consultants who give advice and guide me to help me optimize my output." A source chimes in, "The supervisors are one of the main things that keep me at BCG. If you aren't good at your job and enjoy it, most people won't get to a supervisory role, so these folks are the top dogs."

While some BCGers grumble about a lack of interaction with client top brass at first, many more report positive experiences. "Day one at the client, I had a meeting with the CFO of a Fortune 500 company. As a 22-year-old, that's incredible exposure," says one staffer. "Access to the client's top-level management is made easy by BCG's brand and history of insight and impact," a colleague suggests. "I frequently schedule meetings with C-level clients to talk about the broader context of what's going on at their company, rather than just specific engagement work. We strive for and often achieve the role of 'thought partner' for senior clients." A source adds, "The clients that we deal with are at the top ranks of their organizations. As a new associate, I've had the ability to interact with numerous CEOs, SVPs, and even mayors and political figures."

Connecting with training

Training at BCG is, in a word, "amazing!"—at least according to one consultant, who gushes, "I am convinced that BCG provides some of the best business training in the world. There are numerous formal and informal training sessions—so many I don't even have time to attend half of them. They assign at least two mentors to you as soon as you arrive to help answer your questions and support you. You constantly receive informal feedback and receive a formal project review/feedback at the end of each case. There are tons of online learning materials and trainings as well." Another insider notes that while "informal training is the most useful and occurs nearly constantly," BCG's "formal training is necessary but less effective." There's "a lot of formal training spread throughout the year," much of which is "monotonous." But others, like presentation coaching, are more "helpful," the source adds. "In general, one would learn more by working with a peer or superior for two hours than attending a two-hour training." In addition, a colleague reports, "We have a program called BCG Connect, where all associates meet up in a common place (this year Dallas), stay in the Four Seasons resort, eat and drink on the company and go to training during the day for four days." Still, a source advises, "Make sure you take as many finance classes as you can before you start. There is very little opportunity to learn that on the job."

Offices with personality

BCG's offices generally earn high marks, particularly the "spacious, modern" Los Angeles office with a "good location" and "great views," which reminds one insider of a "Mandarin Oriental hotel." In Toronto, the office is "bright, open and very nicely appointed," and benefits from "great IT support and production assistants." BCGers in Atlanta work out of the tallest building in the city: "It really is a beautiful building with great views. The individual offices are large and associates/consultants usually sit two to an office. Every office has a whiteboard and the overall office is very high tech," says a source. "We are growing in Texas and will need new space in short order; however, the leadership is planning for and addressing it," says a Dallas insider. The Boston office, featuring a "180-degree view of Boston Harbor from my desk," is "very inspiring," and a New York-based consultant reports that "people complain about the office a lot because other BCG offices are nicer, but it works great for me," adding that the firm "could use a little more space—but this is New York after all." However, a source adds, "there are offices without windows in this building, which is not pleasant at all." Another consultant sums up, "Each office has its own style," and remarks that "it's nice that each location reflects its office personality in the office space."

Where women take the initiative

You say you want a women's initiative? Just come to BCG, where it's front and center. "The women's initiative has so much focus here that it borders on being too much. Occasionally I feel like we're asked to focus too much on our gender," says one female BCGer, who adds, "However, I think BCG has done a fabulous job of reaching out to women to widen the applicant pool, and I feel respected and supported in the firm." The trend toward a bigger female population at the firm is definitely on the rise: "My class was 40 percent women and the class after me was 70 percent women," a newbie reports. But while the firm is "very receptive and very women-friendly," another insider says, there are "few women partners, and mostly male case teams can make it a bit tough, especially in client situations that are old boys' clubs."

BCG's family-friendly policies help the situation, another source notes: "BCG provides women who want fewer hours the opportunity to work at 50 percent capacity or less. They can continue to serve as consultants, work within one of the BCG practice areas (to build up internal research for BCG) or work in another nonclient-facing function (staffing, recruiting, etc.). Even in internal, nonclient roles or part-time roles, people are often promoted to the manager level."

It's easy being green

Like many of its peers, BCG is described as "exceptionally receptive" to minorities, but still has "room for improvement in absolute numbers." It's an "ideal place for minorities, but not good at communicating that message and actively going after minority recruits," an insider comments. Still, the firm is making an effort, a co-worker asserts: "We hold special recruiting events for diversity candidates. There is also a diversity network that holds seminars and an annual conference to discuss diversity issues." According to one consultant, this is just enough. "Being a minority myself, I hate when companies harp on the minority issue because it starts to feel like people value your race more than your intelligence and ability to contribute to the firm. BCG takes the best people, whether they are yellow, black or white. I guess you could say that once we're here, we're all BCG green." And there's plenty of diversity, in a broader sense, for another BCGer: "In our small office of around 90 consulting staff (partners, principles, project leaders, consultants and associates), we have nationals from 18 different countries, speak 25 different languages, and have lived and worked in more than 50 different countries. Not only is there a diversity of national and ethnic backgrounds, there is truly a diversity of ideas and personalities. There is really no set mold for a BCGer. They come from different socioeconomic backgrounds, practice different religions and have various political beliefs. I love the inclusive nature of BCG and feel that anyone would feel welcome and free to be themselves here."

BCG is "hyper-progressive" on GLBT issues, staffers say, and the firm has "an internal group" that "sets a great support structure for people to interact and discuss any issues." The firm is "extremely inclusive and open-minded," a consultant comments. Sources tell us that there are "senior leaders who are openly GLBT." A consultant in the San Francisco office notes, though, that it's "bizarre" that "not one employee falls into the category" there. "It would be totally acceptable, but we just don't make a concerted effort to hire."

Visit the Vault Consulting Career Channel at **www.vault.com/consulting** - with insider firm profiles, message boards, the Vault Consulting Job Board and more.

VAULT CAREER LIBRARY

61

Pro bono, low bono—it's all good

"Everyone I know at BCG is very passionate about giving back to the community," a consultant claims—and that spirit is a reflection of the firm's attitude toward social impact. Insiders tell us that around 5 percent of the firm's total consulting capacity is reserved for pro bono work. As a source explains, "We have begun to be more systematic and strategic about our social impact work. In particular, 'low bono' work in public education (U.S.) and global health (worldwide) has grown significantly in the past year. Many consultants are interested in the work; I think it's had a very positive impact on morale, even among those who haven't been involved in the specific cases. It just helps to know that your firm is doing good things, and not just random good things, but systematic, impactful good things." According to a colleague, "Each office has a well-defined pro bono platform (a set of topics and organizations it works with). Pro bono work is staffed like any other project and is taken seriously. Good performance on pro bono work helps your career as much as paid client work."

Out in the community, BCGers can be found working on plenty of projects, from building playgrounds to helping the Bill & Melinda Gates Foundation tackle disease in the developing world. "Each year, BCG has a Day of Care when the office shuts down and we all help out somewhere in the community," an insider reports. Consultants are proud to say that a recent airline mile drive for the Make-a-Wish Foundation resulted in the donation of more than 750,000 miles.

In 2007, BCG published a detailed report on its social impact activities—its second since 2004—which was distributed to all employees worldwide. The 84-page publication summarizes the firm's work with dozens of organizations around the globe and features profiles of select BCGers who played leadership roles. All BCGers who contributed to social impact initiatives are listed, reflecting the value BCG places on such work.

"BCG really adheres to the apprenticeship model, and project leaders strive to help you develop and grow."

– *Boston Consulting Group source*

Visit the Vault Consulting Career Channel at **www.vault.com/consulting** - with insider firm profiles, message boards, the Vault Consulting Job Board and more.

VAULT CAREER LIBRARY

63

3

Bain & Company

131 Dartmouth Street
Boston, MA 02116
Phone: (617) 572-2000
Fax: (617) 572-2427
www.bain.com

LOCATIONS

Boston, MA (HQ)
36 offices in 24 countries

PRACTICE AREAS

Change Management
Corporate Strategy
Cost & Supply Chain Management
Customer & Marketing Strategy
Growth Strategy
IT
Mergers & Acquisitions
Organization
Performance Improvement
Private Equity

THE STATS

Employer Type: Private Company
Chairman: Orit Gadiesh
Managing Director: Steve Ellis
2007 Employees: 3,700
2006 Employees: 3,200

RANKING RECAP

Practice Area
#2 - Financial Consulting
#3 - Energy Consulting
#5 - Economic Consulting (tie)
#5 - Pharmaceutical & Health Care Consulting
#7 - Operational Consulting

Quality of Life
#1 - Overall Satisfaction
#1 - Firm Culture
#1 - Formal Training
#2 - Best Firms to Work For
#5 - Work/Life Balance
#5 - Offices
#6 - Relationships with Supervisors
#7 - Interaction with Clients
#9 - Compensation
#12 - Hours in the Office
#15 - Travel Requirements

Diversity
#3 - Diversity for GLBT
#4 - Best Firms for Diversity
#8 - Diversity for Women
#10 - Diversity for Minorities

UPPERS

- "The people, the people, the people"
- "Incredibly powerful, no-BS culture"
- "I'm pushed out of my comfort zone—to a new industry or to a more senior role in the firm. It really keeps this job interesting"
- The opportunity to learn from the top minds in the industry

DOWNERS

- "It's a demanding place—there's no opportunity to slack"
- "Can be hard to stand out"
- "This is a tough place to work if you don't have thick skin and/or confidence"
- Rigid promotion cycles

THE BUZZ
WHAT CONSULTANTS AT OTHER FIRMS ARE SAYING ABOUT THIS FIRM

- "Thought leaders; they only hire rock stars"
- "Too cocky"
- "Family-friendly"
- "Cultish"

EMPLOYMENT CONTACT

www.bain.com/join

THE SCOOP

Big on prestige

Founded as a three-person operation working out of Bill Bain's Boston apartment in 1973, Bain & Company is a walking advertisement for its own strategy know-how. In over three decades, Bain has secured a place for itself among the elite of strategy consulting firms. This is no small feat for a not-so-huge firm—Bain has fewer consultants than its A-list peers, operating out of 36 offices worldwide. Like its rival McKinsey, Bain has cultivated an air of mystery by refusing to trumpet its engagements. The firm has taken some other iconoclastic stances over the years, including holding off on opening offices in New York City until 2000, and waiting to set up an official shop in the consulting market's latest hot spot, India, until mid-2006. Since its opening, the firm's New York office has grown to 250, while the India office now has over 70 employees.

In fact, Bain has always approached the market from a slightly different angle than many of its peers; while many large consultancies moved to integrate IT and outsourcing services into their offerings over the past decade, Bain stuck to its strategy guns (though it has added specialized capabilities like IT and supply-chain management to its offerings). Not that this approach has hurt Bain in the slightest: The firm's client roster of more than 3,600 has outperformed the market by four to one, and satisfied customers like Charles Schwab and Michael Dell have publicly praised its services.

Claiming a stake

Compared to its peers, Bain puts a greater emphasis on small- and midsized companies, with the rest of its business coming from Fortune 500, private equity and nonprofit clients. Big names associated with the firm have included diamond empire DeBeers, Starbucks, Kroger, Ford and Continental Airlines. One typical engagement had the firm advising on the integration of software companies Symantec and Veritas. Bain occasionally takes equity in lieu of fees and, in fact, reins in about 10 percent of its revenue from equity or "success" stakes. For example, the firm took an ownership stake in fruit processor Del Monte while working to revamp the company's strategy.

Money matters

The first consultancy of its kind to establish a private equity practice, Bain is well known among the money set, offering services like due diligence, IPO preparation, portfolio profit improvement and revenue enhancement, geared toward leveraged buyout and venture capital firms. However, Bain the consultancy shouldn't be confused with its venture capital wing, Bain Capital, founded in 1984 by four former Bain consultants—including former Massachusetts Governor and presidential candidate Mitt Romney. Today, Bain Capital manages over $50 billion in assets. The two companies are completely separate entities and have no insight into the other's client base. But, our sources say, it's not difficult for insiders to jump between the two companies.

A bridge to the nonprofit sector

Another innovation at Bain is the Bridgespan Group. Though it maintains a close relationship with the parent firm (Bain Managing Director Steve Ellis serves on its board, and employees attend Bain's global training sessions), the group, established in 2000, operates as independent, nonprofit organization. Nonprofit clients have included foundations such as the Bill & Melinda Gates Foundation and The Rockefeller Foundation, as well as local and national organizations such as Big Brothers Big Sisters of America, Bay Area Coalition for Equitable Schools and the National Council on Aging. For Bain consultants, Bridgespan offers the opportunity to get a taste of the nonprofit sector; consultants often pursue six-month rotations into Bridgespan. Bain encourages the rotation, noting that it gives Bridgespan clients a fresh perspective while providing Bain consultants with valuable experience in the nonprofit sector.

Visit the Vault Consulting Career Channel at **www.vault.com/consulting** - with insider firm profiles, message boards, the Vault Consulting Job Board and more.

65

Bain personalities

Bain is distinguished by its roster of high-profile alumni and its current leadership. Often described as a Renaissance woman, Chairman Orit Gadiesh has led the firm since 1993. Gadiesh, known for her flashy style—at least, in comparison to the usual boardroom look—joined Bain straight out of Harvard Business School, which she attended following a stint in the Israeli army. For the past few years, she has landed among *Forbes'* list of the 100 most powerful women in business. Gadiesh's colleague, Worldwide Managing Director Steve Ellis, has held his position since March 2005, when he was elected to replace John Donahoe, who left to lead eBay's business unit.

Bain isn't shy about pushing its consultants up the ladder, often announcing a sweeping series of promotions to its partnership ranks. In July 2006, for example, 28 consultants worldwide were tapped with the partnership wand—a record number for the firm in any given year since its founding. As for its alumni, former Bainies include eBay head Meg Whitman, American Express Chairman and CEO Ken Chenault, and Intuit Inc. founder Scott D. Cook.

Into India (finally)

In July 2006, Bain opened its first official consulting office in India, employing more than 20 staffers in New Delhi under the leadership of Managing Director Ashish Singh. This wouldn't be earth-shattering news for most consultancies these days, but it was the cause of much buzz for Bain, which had yet to set up shop on the subcontinent, aside from a small in-house capability servicing center in Guragaon. Though Bain has served clients in the region for over 10 years, typically from its Singapore office, the firm was seen as slow to gain traction in India compared to its competitors. Asked by India's *Economic Times* about the firm's strategy in late 2005, Bain Partner and worldwide IT practice head David Shpilberg insisted, "We are not entering India as an afterthought, our objective is not just to have an office here; our objective is to integrate India into the global look of how we serve our clients." A few months later, Ellis himself explained to the paper that his firm wasn't concerned about its relatively late arrival, adding, "We believe that there is an opportunity for us to grow the business here and we are successfully working with alternative ways of servicing certain parts of our business process and that's been very encouraging for us."

Meanwhile, over in Europe, business has been strong for Bain. In 2007, the firm brought its number of worldwide offices to 36, with the opening of offices in Kiev, Moscow, Helsinki and Frankfurt in Europe. Though the facility is the first Bain shop in Finland, the firm has been doing business with Finnish companies for more than a decade, and noted that the opening would help meet a growing demand for its services in the Nordic region. The firm has positioned itself for growth in the area, notably with its relocation of star consultant Chris Zook to its Amsterdam office in early 2006. The firm stated that Zook, a best-selling author and head of the firm's global strategy practice, would preside over an expansion of Bain's European capabilities. In addition, Chairman Gadiesh resides in Paris.

Over the past 10 years, Bain has maintained a strong presence in the Middle East. Clients have included government bodies as well as private equity firms, local businesses and multinational corporations. The work in this region has been historically managed from the Paris office, however Bain registered as a company in Dubai in 2005. Given the massive growth of the economy of the Gulf countries and the growing interest of the firm's clients in this region, the firm opened an office in Dubai in 2007 to support clients in the Middle East and countries of the Gulf Cooperation Council.

Zook's books

The prolific Bain author Chris Zook, educated at both Oxford and Harvard, made a name for himself with his "core" approach to business profitability, explained in his business books *Profit From the Core* and *Beyond the Core: Expand Your Market Without Abandoning Your Roots*. Building on these works, Zook's latest title, *Unstoppable: Finding Hidden Assets to Renew the Core and Fuel Profitable Growth* shows businesses how to find undervalued, unrecognized or underutilized assets that can serve as new foundations for growth. These books, which analyze how companies can profit from locating and focusing on their core business, are required reading for anyone studying up on the Bain approach. But they're just the tip of the bookshelf for Bain consultants, who have produced more than a few must-reads for execs and B-school busy bees.

The firm's most recent best seller was the 2006 *The Ultimate Question: Driving Good Profits and True Growth*, authored by Fred Reichheld, founder of the firm's loyalty practice. Reichheld, like Zook, is an alumnus of *Consulting Magazine*'s Top 25 Consultants roster. Dubbed the "high priest" of loyalty by *The Economist*, Reicheld argues in his latest book that companies must address the one question that will determine their future: "Would you recommend us to a friend or colleague?" Another Bain book worth checking out is the 2004 *Mastering the Merger: Four Critical Decisions That Make or Break the Deal*, by current and former Bain M&A practice area leaders David Harding and Sam Rovit (now CEO at Swift & Company). Examining shareholder returns of 1,700 companies over a span of 15 years, the authors concluded that companies deemed "frequent acquirers" outperform those with less M&A activity, but the most successful companies know how to start with small deals and ramp up, focusing on "overlap" mergers rather than a rapid expansion of business capabilities.

In addition to books, Bain consultants publish regular and one-off studies and surveys, and are often called upon by the business press. One regular publication is the Management Tools and Trends Survey, a biannual global survey on the usage, satisfaction and effectiveness of the 25 most popular management tools among a broad range of senior executives. Directed by Bain Partner Darrell Rigby, the survey, published since the mid-1990s, has been cited as a bellwether in *Forbes*, the *Financial Times*, *The Economist* and other business pages.

All-star lineup

In November 2006, Bain published its latest annual lineup of "brand growth all-stars," analyzing the performance of an array of 8,000 consumer brands in 100 categories from 1997 through 2005. According to Bain, brand leaders typically spend more on advertising than their category averages, and also tend to beat out their peers in introducing new products. Growth leaders generally are also less likely to cut prices, the firm noted. Bain named 17 companies to the all-star list, including Pepperidge Farm and Neutrogena.

Another Bain study, published in August 2006, found that a company's complexity is a key predictor of its performance. Looking at 75 companies across 12 industries globally, Bain found that the lower a firm's complexity (as defined by practices such as limiting the unnecessary proliferation of products), the more likely it is to experience revenue growth. In fact, firms with a more streamlined profile grew their revenue an average of 1.7 times faster than their competitors, the study found.

An award-winning employer

In 2007, Bain made its first-ever appearance on *Fortune* magazine's annual 100 Best Companies to Work For, coming in at No. 45 among a list of leading Fortune 500 companies. The publication applauded Bain's diversity, its percentage of female employees (nearly 50 percent), its telecommuting-friendly culture and its sabbatical program. Bain describes its working environment as "down-to-earth, friendly and approachable," and offers flexibility to meet its consultants' needs. A part-time (60 or 80 percent) work option is available in some offices to consultants who have been with Bain more than a year. In fact, Bain says that the majority of its female managers and VPs have worked part time at some point in their career, and men have been signing on for the option, too.

Train with Bain

Bain is big on training, starting all of its associate consultants off with two weeks of orientation in their local offices, followed by a 10-day global training event in Cape Cod. The firm doesn't skimp on locales for its training sessions, either, sending consultants to places like Cancun, Barcelona and Phuket for meetings. Global training, conducted by some of Bain's best managers and partners, is held every 12 to 18 months.

In the Northeast offices, Bain consultants may be assigned to more than one case at a time. A typical engagement team is made up of a partner, a manager and a number of consultants and associate consultants. The firm encourages its consultants to gain experience working with a range of industries, practice areas and project types before settling into one area of expertise. New consultants get to join case teams right away, performing research and data analysis and making presentations for the client.

Visit the Vault Consulting Career Channel at **www.vault.com/consulting** - with insider firm profiles, message boards, the Vault Consulting Job Board and more.

VAULT CAREER LIBRARY

67

Inspired to give back

In addition to their opportunities to work with Bridgespan, Bain consultants often take the time to help out in their communities. The firm is a founding sponsor of City Year, a program designed to give young people an opportunity to spend a year working to improve urban neighborhoods. Another Bain brainchild, Inspire—founded along with consultancy Monitor—is run by volunteer associate consultants and provides management consulting advice to nonprofit organizations with a youth-oriented, educational focus. Many of Bain's community efforts take place on the local level; Boston employees volunteer time to help out students at local Charlestown High School, while their colleagues in Los Angeles volunteer at local schools and organizations like the Los Angeles Museum of Contemporary Art.

GETTING HIRED

Getting into the Bain zone

Recent undergrads typically launch their career at Bain as associate consultants. ACs, according to the firm, are "a diverse group of highly qualified people with extremely broad backgrounds—from hard science to literature." Candidates with advanced degrees, including MBAs and most PhDs and JDs, join up as consultants. The firm notes that "demonstrated success in their field and the potential to quickly develop business acumen is important for PhDs, JDs and other special candidates." Experienced hires with "excellent academic backgrounds, records of success in their recent experiences, and relevant business and analytical experience" may enter as either ACs or consultants. The firm explains, "As new Bain employees, experienced hires have the same training, promotion and work opportunities that we offer to all of our professional staff."

Bain generally draws from the best and brightest, recruiting undergraduate candidates from Princeton, Harvard, Yale, Stanford, Wharton/Penn, MIT, Dartmouth, Duke and the like, in addition to MBAs from top business programs worldwide. However, a source says, "We are always looking for great talent, regardless of the institution."

Amazing summers

Most Bain offices offer summer internships for those in undergrad and B-school. Students and soon-to-be grads interested in opportunities at Bain should first visit the firm's web site, where they can look up procedures for their schools in an online index, and fill out an online application. The summer internship program at Bain garners rave reviews from participants. It was an "amazing 10 weeks." "Going into the internship, I would have said my likelihood of working in consulting full time was less than 10 percent," says another source. "Needless to say, I was not only blown away by the great fun I had and great relationships I built over the summer, but I realized how impressive Bain was and decided to stay on full time." "MBA summer internships at Bain are a blast. The firm is committed to promoting a fairly accurate view of what full-time life here is like, without sacrificing the social and fun aspects of your summer. There are no 100-hour weeks for summer interns. You are here to contribute positively to a case team, work reasonably hard (45 to 50 hours), and you spend the rest of your time getting to know the firm and its people," another insider states. Though the firm emphasizes that the internship experience focuses on professional activities, a source adds there are "tons of social events" for interns, including lunches galore, along with dinners and a boast cruise.

Two roads to Bain

Both intern and full-time AC candidates for the Northeast offices go through two rounds of two interviews. The firm states that the interview format for other North American offices and international offices can be different. Case interview questions generally consist of some mix of market sizing, business judgment and problem-solving questions." An AC adds that "we do 'test fit' interviews by assessing resumes and doing more informal screening." The firm adds that AC candidates can expect business problems that a nonbusiness major can understand, since only a limited understanding of business concepts is required.

As is the case with AC interviewing, MBA summer internship (summer associate) and full-time candidates go through the same interviewing process and screening. MBAs typically participate in two rounds of interviews. Round one involves two case interviews, while the second round includes two case interviews and one experience interview. The experience interview involves some combination of resume questions, a resume case and behavioral questions. MBA cases require some formal business training or knowledge and are generally based on Bain casework.

Indeed, it's impossible to escape the case interview process at Bain, we're told, with case questions popping up during all rounds of the interview process. "We try to make cases mirror our real work as much as possible, so we tend to share a considerable amount of data with the interviewee and then hope to have an engaging business discussion with them," says a consultant. Another insider reports, "We tend to stay away from brainteasers and other wildly abstract interview questions. We use general, CEO-level business case interviews most often." The source adds that the case interview "gives us a pretty good window into a candidate's ability to problem solve in our environment." And a colleague remarks, "Bain case interviews are fun—a cross between reading a great article in *The Wall Street Journal* and solving a puzzle."

To ace the case, an insider advises, "A structured approach is very important to make sure you lead your interviewer through every step of your analysis. Also, if you start down the wrong track, be receptive to real-time coaching by the interviewer, who typically will try to help you get back on track."

OUR SURVEY SAYS

Collegial, not collegiate

First things first: Several Bain consultants want the world to know that the firm is not simply an overgrown fraternity. "Bain's culture … is about a lot more than the 'frat' reputation we get," says an insider, who adds, "As a woman who doesn't drink, what I love about Bain is that we laugh a lot, we have amazing interests outside work and we are a friendly, social lot." A colleague adds, "Bain also has a bit of a reputation of having alcohol as a part of the culture. I'm not sure where this reputation comes from, because the large majority of events do not involve alcohol." As another puts it, "Other firms sometimes regard us as a fraternity, a label that Bain is actively trying to squelch. I personally don't mind; if given the choice between working in a fraternity and working in a library, I will choose the fraternity. In reality, Bain's culture is a mix of work [and] play."

When it comes to culture, Bain's got the competition beat, insiders insist. "I sincerely cannot imagine a firm with a better culture," raves one consultant. "This is as fun a place to work as you will find in the industry," says a colleague. "People work extremely hard, but they just don't take themselves—or their work—so seriously that they can't laugh about it." Another source agrees, "Bain is a truly collegial place. We are committed to an excellent work product, but we don't allow our team members to kill one another to get there." It's all about the people, says a co-worker: "Every single time I have worked late or gone the extra mile in my career, it has been because I didn't want to let down my team—not because I wanted to advance my own career. I love the people here. The hardest thing about leaving (if I ever do) will be leaving the people I work with every day."

Premium people

Bain newbies, especially, are impressed with the environment they find at the firm. An associate consultant just out of undergrad tells us, "There's a strong premium placed on developing a diverse skill set, participating in as wide a variety of projects as possible, getting involved in the company beyond cases, and getting as much out of the experience as possible. Also, personally, I think people are Bain's biggest asset. There's an impressive consistency across my colleagues in their humor, their fun attitude and their perspective." According to another recent hire, "I was nervous about leaving my academic career to pursue a career in consulting because of the change in type of people/culture of the workplace that I anticipated. Bain has been nothing like what I expected it could be, and the people/culture are my favorite part of the job."

Visit the Vault Consulting Career Channel at **www.vault.com/consulting** - with insider firm profiles, message boards, the Vault Consulting Job Board and more.

 CAREER LIBRARY

69

Working for the weekend

Bain's culture is also boosted by the efforts of the firm to secure a decent work/life balance for consultants, insiders say. "Managers go out of their way to ensure employees are having a fun and fulfilling experience," a consultant reports, adding, "People have ownership of their time and the flexibility to work on their own schedule—the concept of face time does not exist. I am continually surprised at how accommodating my superiors are to my personal requests regarding vacation and breaks. It makes the environment great." Agrees a colleague, "Bain really emphasizes work/life balance, and actively discourages us from stretching ourselves too thin, even in entry-level positions. For me, that's one of Bain's biggest selling points. The consulting lifestyle doesn't leave a huge amount of time outside the office during the week, but Bain ensures that we don't start to act like bankers and that we keep our weekends for ourselves."

Of course, staffers don't kid themselves about the challenges of a consulting lifestyle. "You arrive knowing you're going to work more than 40 hours per week," says an insider. "That said, there's flexibility. If I'm working over the weekend, there's a good chance it's because I left early on Friday, or to get ahead for the next week. They're open to taking off late afternoon to go to the gym and come back to work after." A colleague concurs, stating, "Consulting is a demanding industry, but I think Bain manages work/life balance better than any other top firms. Our local office-based staffing model allows people to be home more and we have a series of programs in place to monitor people's workload." As another source puts it, "I have several peers that have time-intensive activities they are involved in, including dance and improv comedy, and the work/staffing process allows them to pursue these with relative ease. I have the ability to manage my own time usually, so I can duck out of the office early on a weekday if I do some work that weekend, or vice versa." The firm emphasizes that while work/life balance is important, working at Bain is demanding, and hard work is definitely part of the job.

Overload alerts

Bain also has internal mechanisms in place to prevent burnout, we're told. "In general," says a West Coast consultant, "there is genuine concern when people are being overworked. For example, if I work over 60 hours two weeks in a row, it flags my staffing manager and my boss gets an inquiry about it. It won't necessarily stop it from happening again, but I like that it's a built-in safeguard. Further, if you are getting hammered for a few days straight and/or over the weekend, comp days do happen." "Bain tracks weekly hours and surveys each team monthly. The team scores are posted on the wall for everyone to see, so there is pressure to improve the work/life quality of a case if people are not happy," another source explains.

As for numbers, one associate consultant reports that "there have been some weeks where I have worked 75 hours and loved it, and there have been others where I have worked 45 hours and was bored. Bain does try to limit hours to an average of 60 per week, which feels sustainable over the long run." Another consultant, who reports an average of 55 to 60 hours per week, says, "My work hours have decreased substantially as I've gotten more senior. I also have much more control over when the hours arc, so if I want to go to the gym in the middle of the day, or leave the office at 6 and work from home, that's just fine."

As one consultant sees it, "Working at Bain is neither a sprint nor a marathon. Rather, it is more like an interval workout." The source elaborates, "When I am working to deliver results to a client, I am really cranking. However, when I have finished my job, I take as long a break as possible ... If I finish my work at noon, I leave at noon. If I am between tasks, I don't go into the office at all." And commenting on this no-face-time approach, a source notes, "At Bain, you are rewarded for results, not hours. Therefore, if you work excessive hours it is viewed as a potential sign of inefficiency as opposed to the sign of a diligent worker. Don't get me wrong, we work hard, but there is no credit for face time."

Closer to home

Travel at Bain really "depends on the case," says a consultant, who adds, "In New York, the majority of the teams do not travel, which is unique among consulting firms from my experience. But there are a handful of cases that require weekly travel. It is a mix." "My sense is that Bain has less demanding travel requirements than other consulting firms. My current case travels three days per week, but this is the first time in my two-plus years at the firm that I've had regular weekly travel. It varies," says a colleague. Comparisons aside, a staffer chimes in: "But don't take this to mean you will never travel—most of us are away from the office one to two days per week." "The basic assumption is work will be 'home office-based.' That said, travel certainly occurs when there is a client need to be on site," a consultant remarks.

Equity opportunities

Salaries at Bain are "right in line with the rest of the industry," says an insider. A colleague elaborates, "Bain remains competitive with other strategy consulting firms like McKinsey & Company and Boston Consulting Group. However, it doesn't often try to be a leader in compensation. Rather, Bain is very reactive to what the other firms do." For postundergrads who join the firm and stay on for a few years, the source adds, there's a "senior associate consultant (third-year) position that offers a 25-plus percent increase in salary and a 50-plus percent increase in annual bonus." One source wishes "that people's bonuses varied more based on their performance."

The firm's compensation structure supports equity opportunities. For example, in North America, many consultants participate in some form of profit sharing, beginning at the associate consultant level. Sources tell us that while ACs, consultants and managers are involved in profit sharing, "the value of the rewards increases as your seniority increases," so it's the managers and partners who reap the greatest rewards. For those at the manager level, profit sharing is boosted further based on utilization, and "once you reach manager, you get access to Bain's investment vehicles," a higher-up explains. "We get the opportunity to put in our own funds into [some of] the deals we diligence (and recommend!)—this gives us an impressive IRR that outperforms the private equity indices." Another manager notes that "managers are compensated out of the North American profit pool, in addition to salary and performance bonus." Other perks in North American offices include retirement plan contributions (percent of salary depending on tenure), paid cell phone, Internet and BlackBerry usage, as well as a gym membership rebate. The benefits vary for different offices around the globe.

Three's enough

By far, the most frequently cited perk of working at Bain comes from the firm's hyper-social culture. As one source puts it, "Any time you get a critical mass of Bainies together (more than three), you're going to have a great time!" Events include "bay parties (one section of the office will host a small themed party with food and drinks on a Friday afternoon)," as well as ice cream parties for birthdays, "one-off" events like "take your partner out to lunch," community service days, holiday parties and regular athletic events. "In addition to all the little things," says an associate consultant, "I've really enjoyed the firm's emphasis on fostering a global Bain community. All our trainings bring together people from all over the world, and I now have people to call in almost any city I find myself. Looking ahead to the fall, I'm particularly excited for the Bain World Cup, when each international office fields a soccer team and we all descend on Europe for a weekend of competition and partying." Other office-specific opportunities for travel include a "company off-site trip, which includes days off work and travel for all employees including admin, with their significant others to all-inclusive resorts in places like Playa del Carmen and Miami," says a consultant. If that's not enough, West Coast staffers also may enjoy the "Bain ski house every winter in Tahoe" and the "Bain summer house every summer in the Wine Country."

Other insiders see the opportunity to change things up in their careers as a noteworthy perk. "Your third year out of undergrad, you have the opportunity to do a six-month transfer to another office or to do a sabbatical at another firm. I worked for six months on a political campaign. Bain actively assisted me in finding the opportunity," says a source. Another insider appreciates the Take 2 program, which provides a two-month leave of absence opportunity for Bainies to pursue personal goals.

Taking a break for parenting

Bain goes the distance for new parents, insiders report. "Bain enables new parents to work part time, take leaves of absence and temporarily move from client-facing to administrative roles. Many firms say they have these policies, but Bain is the only place where I have seen them utilized by so many people! The VP and manager on my last case were working 80 percent and 60 percent time, and seemed to be making it work very well with their lives," says a consultant. In addition, says a colleague, the firm offers "two weeks' paid paternity leave (as nonprimary care giver) within the first 12 months after the birth of a child. Bain

Visit the Vault Consulting Career Channel at **www.vault.com/consulting** - with insider firm profiles, message boards, the Vault Consulting Job Board and more.

VAULT CAREER LIBRARY   71

has lots of parents with babies, which is great since people tend to be very understanding of my situation right now with an infant." In addition, the firm offers nanny services and has a nursing room in most offices.

Bays at Bain

Bain earns praise for its offices, which all feature "an open plan that really encourages discussion among colleagues across all levels," says a source. "One look at our space and you'll understand the Bain culture. It's a dynamic, fun, energetic atmosphere," a colleague cheers. According to another, "Consultants sit in bays of cubicles, which give us the opportunity to ask one another questions and have some interactions to break up the workday. We are given a bay budget to buy decorations, or basketball hoops in the case of my bay, which help to liven up the office. I love giving tours of our office because it is so unique and not at all like the *Office Space* stereotypes most people have of business offices." "Designed to encourage openness and communication, the home office in Boston is the most unique and nicely designed office space I have seen," a staffer notes. In New York—which recently got a new floor with a gym and lounge—"we have a foosball table that is actually used. I play normally about 20 to 30 minutes a day when I am in the office," a consultant tells us.

High bar for managers

Supervisors at Bain get above-average marks—in fact, they're expected to, says one manager: "Bain managers simply do not succeed if they cannot consistently lead and motivate teams. It's 100 percent mission critical to the job, so the bar that teams hold us to is very high. That said, the firm's management expects hard work and commitment in return for this effort." According to a junior colleague, "Every manager I've worked for has invested time in making the experience one that adds to my development. My current manager has pushed back against the partner to do so. It's been a major determinant of my job satisfaction." A source adds, "There is an open-door policy that permeates the entire firm. The partners are very approachable—and always attend the major social events (summer off-site, Christmas party, etc.)." According to an insider, consultants receive a "formal review every six months, plus an 'input' review at end of each case. Reviews are very important at Bain, and a lot of thought is put into completing feedback and delivering it. I always have a professional development talk with my supervisor (and with my direct reports) at beginning of each case, and check in frequently. Three-hundred-and-sixty-degree feedback is completed every six months (from direct reports, peers, supervisors)."

CEO interaction

Most consultants are also satisfied with their interaction with senior-level clients. "I met six or seven CEOs since working at Bain, and it was amazing how they sought out my opinion on strategies for their business. People who have worked at these companies for 20-plus years did not have the senior exposure I had," one consultant reports. "On my first case, I was making slides that went in front of the CEO of a $40 billion company," a colleague attests. Another co-worker is thrilled that he had "the opportunity to interact with very senior clients from about three months after starting my new position! This is a great way to make employees feel like their work is important." A manager in Dallas explains that some engagements will foster more client interaction than others: "The partner group works hand in hand with [the client] team. On smaller projects, there is total access to executive suite. On large projects with more partners, there is less access for the team."

Getting oriented on the Cape

Training at Bain starts out on a high note, with associate consultants spending a two-week orientation "with all the new hires from around the globe" in Cape Cod. New consultants spend their initial training week in Miami. "All at once, it was one of the most exciting, engaging and exhausting things I've ever done," an insider says. After that, consultants participate in one-week, global off-site training activities every 12 to 18 months in places like Barcelona, Cancun, Miami and San Francisco. "They have become like class reunions," a consultant reports. A colleague appreciates that staffers get to "socialize in a meaningful way with colleagues from around the world at the global training events. For example, I have one colleague that lives in Melbourne, Australia. I live in New York City. I consider her a close friend even though we only see each other once a year at global training events."

An insider notes that "Bain invests significantly in training, always sending Bain consulting staff to be trainers—training is never outsourced," and a colleague states, "The opportunity to be a trainer has been incredibly rewarding." On a day-to-day level, a consultant says, "We recognize this is an apprenticeship job. Thus many elements of the case/team process are about professional development over time. On a global scale, I firmly believe Bain formal training programs are best in class."

Supporting Bain women

Bain maintains a healthy gender balance, with one associate consultant reporting a group split evenly between women and men. Another consultant in the Toronto office says, however, "In our office we have signed on most women that we give an offer to, but we are still a male-dominated office." According to a female colleague, "Bain does absolutely everything possible to make it work for women. I'm not personally convinced that I want to do this job and raise my family at the same time, but I have no question that, should I choose to, Bain will bend over backward to support me."

The firm's Global Women in Leadership Summit, held every two years, was attended in 2007 by more than 100 Bain women from around the world, covering career planning, leadership, financial goals and other topics, like "work/life balance, connecting with clients, mentoring, managing dual-career families, getting promoted to partner or manager and career planning," an insider adds. The source describes the conference as a "fantastic initiative," where she "had a chance to develop close ties with a number of women at my level in other offices, as well as find two 'coaches'—a senior partner and a senior manager. My coaching team is committed to checking in on some of our specific career and personal goals on a quarterly basis." In addition, the consultant says, "In our office we have a very active women's program. Every month we have an event—one month just consulting staff, and the next month all women in the office. We've brought in or gone to see speakers (balancing career and life, image consulting, experience sharing), discussed articles, had lots of lively dinners, volunteered together and overall developed closer bonds among the women."

Minorities wanted

While Bain supports minorities through affinity groups such as Blacks at Bain, many insiders want to see more minority representation at the firm. As one source puts it, "It's frustrating that we don't get more minority applicants. I hope this will change as I firmly believe that Bain is a true meritocracy and that our culture, which is heavy on mentorship and light on politics, does well by minority Bainies." "This is an area I think we need to work harder on," agrees another, adding, "To be clear: It's not that there is anything even vaguely like discrimination or racism, we just don't seem able to attract minority candidates the way I wish we could." Another insider notes that the firm's "Hispanic/Latino outreach could also be better."

GLAD to be out at Bain

Bain's GLBT consultants get lots of support from the firm, insiders suggest. "Bain has very clear cultural norms about nondiscrimination, and also has a very visible group, BGLAD, which holds annual events and provides confidential support for gays, lesbians and bisexuals," says a source. A colleague notes that BGLAD "has been around for many, many years, and counts some very senior employees in its membership," adding, "After receiving my offer to join Bain, but before even starting, I was invited to San Francisco for BGLAD's annual conference. I have a very high opinion of BGLAD and have found many mentors through my participation in the group's events." According to another insider, the group also has "events open to straight consultants that have been a lot of fun the past. Furthermore, we have a variety of recruiting events at top schools to attract gays, lesbians and bisexuals."

Inspired to serve

As one insider puts it, "Being involved in the community is an important part of who we are as a firm, and I think it comes through in the variety of ways Bainies can get involved." "Bain holds community services days and charity auctions, and frequently devotes office space to Bain-sponsored groups like City Year and Big Brother Big Sister. We also have a mini-consultancy called Inspire (co-organized by Monitor), that is run by associate consultants and focuses on not-for-profits helping

Visit the Vault Consulting Career Channel at **www.vault.com/consulting** - with insider firm profiles, message boards, the Vault Consulting Job Board and more.

VAULT CAREER LIBRARY   73

children," another source explains. Other unique opportunities, according to staffers, include pro bono work, a "cooking challenge night at a local food shelter (use their facilities after hours, and donate money and excess food to the shelter)," and the chance for new MBA hires to participate in a paid Habitat for Humanity project somewhere around the world.

"People have ownership of their time and the flexibility to work on their own schedule—the concept of face time does not exist."

– *Bain consultant*

Visit the Vault Consulting Career Channel at **www.vault.com/consulting** - with insider firm profiles, message boards, the Vault Consulting Job Board and more.

VAULT CAREER LIBRARY

75

Booz Allen Hamilton

8283 Greensboro Drive
McLean, VA 22102
Phone: (703) 902-5000
Fax: (703) 902-3333
www.boozallen.com

LOCATIONS

McLean, VA (HQ)
More than 100 offices worldwide

PRACTICE AREAS

Change Management
Economic Business Analysis
Global Resilience
Institutional Strengthening & International Development
IT Strategy & Systems
Mergers & Restructurings
Operations
Organizations, People & Performance
Outsourcing Advisory Services
Product & Service Innovation
Program Management
Sales & Marketing
Strategy
Supply Chain Management
Transformation Life Cycle
Wargaming, Modeling & Strategic Simulation

THE STATS

Employer Type: Private Company
Chairman & CEO: Dr. Ralph W. Shrader
2007 Employees: 19,000
2006 Employees: 18,000
FY 2007 Sales: $4 billion
FY 2006 Sales: $3.6 billion

THE BUZZ
WHAT CONSULTANTS AT OTHER FIRMS ARE SAYING ABOUT THIS FIRM

- "Bright people and diverse work"
- "Always struggling between rebuilding and doing great stuff"
- "Great government business"
- "Losing steam"

RANKING RECAP

Practice Area
#2 - Energy Consulting
#5 - Operational Consulting
#7 - Economic Consulting
#7 - Financial Consulting
#8 - Pharmaceutical & Health Care Consulting
#9 - Human Resources Consulting

Quality of Life
#5 - Formal Training
#14 - Travel Requirements
#14 - Hours in the Office
#16 - Work/Life Balance
#19 - Offices

Diversity
#7 - Diversity for Minorities
#10 - Best Firms for Diversity
#10 - Diversity for GLBT
#17 - Diversity for Women

UPPERS

- "Very supportive during the first months on job"
- "The freedom to make your own path"
- Blue chip reputation
- "Great performance feedback system

DOWNERS

- "The frustration of supporting the government bureaucracy"
- "Very cliquish culture that is difficult to penetrate"
- Formal dress every day
- "Having 'scapegoat' be part of my client-support job description"

EMPLOYMENT CONTACT

www.boozallen.com/home/careers

THE SCOOP

Blazing a trail

Giant consulting firm Booz Allen Hamilton has become a major player in the private and public sector since its start in 1914. The founder, Northwestern grad Edwin Booz, is given credit for coming up with the idea that an outsider could analyze a business and find ways to make improvements and increase profit. Along with his partners, James Allen and Carl Hamilton, Booz began the firm in Chicago, working with Midwestern companies like Montgomery Ward, Goodyear Tire & Rubber and General Mills. In 1940, the firm was hired to help the U.S. Secretary of the Navy with World War II preparations, a project that marked the start of a longstanding relationship with the U.S. federal government. Since then, Booz Allen has had a hand in several notable private and public engagements throughout its years, such as advising on the breakup of Ma Bell and helping organize the National Football League in the 1960s.

Dual concentration

Today, based just outside of Washington, D.C., Booz Allen employs over 19,000 staff in offices all over the globe. The firm claims that what sets it apart from most consulting firms is its deep expertise in both strategy and technology work. Its services include business strategy, operations, organization and change, and information technology. Within the strategy practice, Booz Allen assists clients through corporate strategy and finance, business unit strategy, industry structure and dynamics, strategic leadership, enterprise resilience and strategic risk services. The firm serves clients in a broad range of industries, including automotive, chemicals, financial services, high tech, health care, media and transportation, as well as a wide range of government agencies.

Global spread

Booz Allen started expanding its operations overseas in 1953, when it landed its first international contract, an engagement to analyze and organize land-ownership records for the newly established Philippine government. In 1957, it opened its first international office in Zurich to serve European clients. The firm established an outpost in Düsseldorf in 1985 to reach businesses in Switzerland, Germany and Austria. Through the 1990s, Booz Allen gained a presence in Asia, opening offices in Seoul, Shanghai and Bangkok, as well as other far-flung locales, including Abu Dhabi, Bogota, Frankfurt, Mumbai and Pretoria. In 1999, the firm purchased Carta Corporate Advisors AB, a top Scandinavian consultancy, giving it a footprint in Sweden, Finland, Norway and Denmark. The firm doubled the size of its Tokyo operation in 2003 with the purchase of Gemini Consulting Japan. In 2004, Booz Allen once again broadened its capacity stateside, by enlarging its facilities in Fairfax, Va. The firm invested $133 million at that time and created 4,000 jobs, mostly centered around its government business.

Transformers

"Strategy-based transformation" is the term Booz Allen uses to describe its approach to solving problems for businesses. The firm's goal is to develop solutions for problems created by fundamental changes in a client's industry or company. To do this, it works with clients to develop strategies across four dimensions: improving quarterly performance, accelerating strategic innovation by approaching new markets and customers, innovating new ways to do business and enhance operations, and attracting and retaining the right employees. The firm also claims that its consultants do more than just strategize: They spend one-third to one-half of a project's time helping clients implement changes called for in the new strategy. The firm emphasizes client involvement throughout the whole transformation process, including client execs and staff on the consulting team.

Structural shift

Until 2006, the firm separated its business according to its clients—commercial and government. In January 2006, leadership announced a reorganization along four functions, assigning a new leader to each division. Dennis O. Doughty was named head

Visit the Vault Consulting Career Channel at www.vault.com/consulting - with insider firm profiles, message boards, the Vault Consulting Job Board and more.

 VAULT CAREER LIBRARY   77

of the Global Functional Capabilities group, which serves commercial and government clients through a number of capabilities, including strategy and operations, organization and change leadership, and IT. Global Government Markets, which focuses on government clients worldwide with an emphasis on defense, intelligence and homeland security, is led by Mark J. Gerencser. Daniel C. Lewis was tapped to head Global Commercial Markets, which assists commercial clients in a range of industries. And Klaus Mattern, formerly head of the global industry and strategic leadership practices, was chosen to lead Global Integrated Markets, serving emerging geographic markets along with public- and private-sector clients in what the firm calls "converging markets," such as global health and global transportation.

Chairman with a cause

Overseeing the four divisions is Chairman and CEO Ralph Shrader. A 30-year veteran of the firm, Shrader has served as chairman since 1999, and in 2005 was asked to extend his six-year term for four more years, until 2009. He is credited with leading the firm through the dot-com boom and bust of the late 1990s. Not only did Booz Allen make it through the economic downturn, but since Shrader's been in office, its sales have increased 80 percent and headcount has almost doubled. Looking to examples of enduring leaders like Mahatma Gandhi, Shrader claims his goals are to be consistent and to establish trust with those under him.

Around the firm, Shrader gained a reputation for getting involved with employee causes: He established a women's advisory board, participates in employee forums and actively promotes diversity. In 2007, B'nai B'rith presented Shrader with its Distinguished Achievement Award for his commitment to philanthropic leadership and diversity education and for fostering a culture that recognizes the need for tolerance and combating prejudice. The firm's Workforce Diversity Council has also given Shrader an award and, in 2003, he received the CEO Leadership Award from Diversity Best Practices for his commitment to a diverse and inclusive environment within the firm. In 1998, the Armed Forces Communications and Electronics Association established the Ralph Shrader Diversity Scholarship, given annually to students currently working toward a master's degree in a particular field. The scholarship, funded by Booz Allen, was established to honor Dr. Shrader's work to increase opportunities for women and minorities in the communications and electronics fields.

Public-sector popularity

As the ninth-ranked federal contractor in 2006, the firm continues to bring in deals that secure its status as a go-to agency for government work. In 2006, about $1.6 billion in revenue came from defense deals. In April 2006, Booz Allen bagged a contract with the Food and Drug Administration to conduct an evaluation of the postmarketing study commitment process—studies that are conducted after a drug has been approved for sale. In March 2007, the firm was one of nine awarded a portion of the $3 billion U.S. Agency for International Development Support for Economic Growth and Institutional Reform (SEGIR) contract. The goal of SEGIR is to reduce poverty, expand trade, promote open competitive markets, and spur economic growth and prosperity in developing and transition countries. That same month, Booz Allen was awarded a project to work with six other prime contractors on a $19.25 billion IDIQ contract with the Army's Communications Electronics Life Cycle Management Command. The U.S. Navy contracted Booz Allen in February 2007 to help the Director of Material Readiness and Logistics (OPNAV N4) with business process improvements. The $9.5 million deal is potentially worth $47 million if all options are exercised. The firm will provide support to command, control, communication, computer, intelligence, surveillance and reconnaissance systems.

Staff switchover

With Booz Allen's close ties to Washington agencies, it's no surprise that quite a few ex-government officials have joined the firm's ranks after leaving their federal posts. James Woolsey, former CIA director, is now a vice president at the firm, and Ron Turner, former associate for the CIA's homeland security division, former Army Deputy Chief of Staff for Intelligence Lt. Gen. Robert W. Noonan, and former Associate Director for the CIA's homeland security division Winston P. Wiley also came to Booz Allen after leaving their posts. In January 2007, Mike McConnell, a Booz Allen senior vice president and a retired Navy vice admiral, was chosen to succeed John Negroponte as the National Intelligence Director.

Helping out in the homeland

Since September 11, 2001, Booz has been deeply involved in assisting the government with strategic security initiatives, mainly with the Federal Transportation Authority and the Department of Homeland Security. The firm also developed the analytical risk methodology, one of the tools the government uses to evaluate threats and reduce risks. In 2006, the firm was awarded the multibillion-dollar, indefinite-delivery, indefinite-quantity EAGLE contract to provide a range of support services to the Department of Homeland Security. And in September 2005, the Department's Science and Technology Directorate awarded Booz Allen a five-year, $250 million contract for various forms of support to DHS technology programs. The firm also serves federal clients such as NASA, the Military Health System and the National Institute of Child Health and Human Development.

Civilian strategists

Though the firm's government deals get a lot more press than its private-sector contracts, Booz Allen does its share of work for commercial clients. In 2006, the firm was hired by fast-food chain Wendy's to help turn around slumping sales and, earlier that year, the College Board enlisted the firm to improve its test scanning methods, after it discovered that the scoring methods for the new SAT test contained errors. In 2005, Habitat for Humanity hired Booz Allen to create a five-year strategic plan that included updating the organization's vision and goals. The firm has also been involved on engagements with R.J. Reynolds Tobacco Holdings, Ford, MTV and Boeing.

This land is our land

As the U.S. National Park Service has recently faced a $5 billion maintenance backlog, it turned to Booz Allen to identify the steps necessary to repair the parks' infrastructures. Since 2002, the firm has been a partner with the Park Service, assisting with asset management and identifying ways to address the "wave of expiring systems" in public lands. Recently, the firm worked on the Golden Gate National Recreation Area, assessing the park's condition and pinpointing areas for improvement. It has also completed evaluation projects for Yosemite, Grand Canyon, Great Smoky Mountains and the Appalachian National Historic and Scenic Trail, as well as other land under the charge of the Department of the Interior and the Bureau of Land Management.

Examining avian flu

For a number of years, Booz Allen officers have been among the selected movers and shakers that converge for the annual World Economic Forum, held in Davos, Switzerland. In 2007, six Booz Allen leaders participated in the annual WEF meeting, where Dr. Shrader took part in a major panel discussion called Leading in a Networked World. The firm served as a partner in WEF's 2007 Forum on the Middle East. In 2006, Booz Allen presented a simulation of an influenza pandemic, which it conducted in cooperation with WEF. The study found that a widespread outbreak of avian flu would severely challenge governments and the private sector's ability to manage essential services, communicate vital information and stop the spread of the flu. More than 30 CEOs and senior executives from leading corporations, private- and public-sector institutions, and governments gathered in Davos to discuss the simulation and explore the implications of an outbreak. Shrader also spoke on the need to determine a corporate strategy to drive an organization's success.

Booz Allen is also a major sponsor of the annual Aspen Ideas Festival, which takes place in July and draws more than 200 leaders from around the world and across many disciplines to serve as panelists on topics ranging from arts and culture to global dynamics. In 2006, Booz Allen officers led discussions in the global dynamics and health tracks and participated in panels on energy, emerging economies and business ethics.

A bookish bunch

Booz Allen consultants are quite prolific, publishing a vast array of papers, studies and books. In 2007, Booz Allen Vice President Justin Pettit authored *Strategic Corporate Finance: Applications in Valuation and Capital Structure*, which turns principles of corporate finance theory into practical ideas for implementing them. "The New Demographics—Reshaping the World of Work and Retirement," a study on the problems confronting the U.K.'s pension schemes, was published in March 2007,

Visit the Vault Consulting Career Channel at www.vault.com/consulting - with insider firm profiles, message boards, the Vault Consulting Job Board and more.

VAULT CAREER LIBRARY   79

as was "Defining Incentives to Cut Carbon Emissions in the Aviation Sector—Inevitable Steps to Fight Climate Change," a greenhouse gas emissions study. The widely-cited title, *Results: Keep What's Good, Fix What's Wrong, and Unlock Great Performance*, was written by Booz Allen Senior Vice President Gary Neilson and former Senior Vice President Bruce Pasternack in 2005. Neilson was named to *Consulting Magazine*'s Top 25 Consultants list in 2006.

Quarterly, the firm publishes *strategy + business*, a magazine featuring hot topics such as health care, e-business, emerging markets and technology. An article in the March 2007 issue, "Lights, Water, Motion!" recommended a $40 trillion makeover for the world's urban infrastructure, recalling events like the 2006 drought in London, the blackout in New York City that same year, and various traffic and energy problems facing major cities. Another 2006 *strategy + business* article, entitled "Manufacturing Realities: Breaking the Boundaries of Conventional Practice," was written by several Booz Allen consultants and analyzed new ways to understand the costs, value and opportunities in manufacturing.

Noteworthy

The firm maintains a high profile through its frequent mention in business publications and newspapers, such as *Bloomberg Markets Magazine*, the *Harvard Business Review* and *The New York Times*. In March 2007, Reuters cited Vice President Edward Tse in an article about China's proposed unified income tax, and the *Financial Times* cited Adrian Foster in an article on the "Travel & Tourism Competitiveness Report," developed by the World Economic Forum in cooperation with Booz Allen. In February 2007, *The Wall Street Journal* noted the Booz Allen-Duke University offshoring study, "The Globalization of White Collar Work," and *Consulting Magazine* featured Senior Vice President Gerry Adolph in a discussion on the rising demand for M&A services.

Award-winning workplace

The firm has received plenty of notice for its policies to attract and retain women. In 2006, *Working Mother* chose Booz Allen as a 100 Best Company for the eighth year in a row. According to the publication, the firm does a good job promoting family-friendly policies, including flex-time, child care and telecommuting. A 2006 article in Harvard Business School's *Working Knowledge* mentioned the "ramp up, ramp down" flexible program, which provides a way for part-time consultants to separate a project into tasks and identify the parts that can be done from a remote location or by shorter office stints. The firm indicates that the policy is a way to maintain ties with women who are taking time off, providing an easier transition when they decide to return to consulting full time.

Fortune also named the firm one of the 100 Best Companies to Work for in 2007, for the third consecutive year, and in 2007, *BusinessWeek* included Booz Allen on its Best Places to Launch a Career list, for the opportunities the firm provides to entry-level employees in terms of compensation, advancement and training.

GETTING HIRED

ABCs of BAH

The Booz Allen web site is a helpful starting point for learning about the many career paths at the firm, whether you're straight out of B-school, or have top security clearance and a few years under your belt. For those in the early stages of a consulting career, there are job profiles to help students consider where they might best fit within the company. Many local offices participate in the summer associate program—a great way for students to get a foot in the door. An Atlanta manager states, "I hire summer interns. They usually do very well, and often are active on engagements if they're sharp. If they do well, we typically make a permanent offer." Recalls one associate, "We were in a cohort of about 30 interns who all supported intelligence community clients. We had weekly brown-bag [lunches] with senior employees, a BBQ at a partner's house and a field trip to the International Spy Museum. Almost all of us returned to the firm after graduation."

Campus recruiting efforts are divided according to the business division. "The public-sector side focuses on Carnegie Mellon, Virginia Tech, University of Maryland and Penn State. The private sector seems to focus on the top-10 U.S. business schools, and top-five European business schools." Included on the list of business schools are "Columbia, Harvard, MIT, Wharton, Duke, Chicago, Stanford and NYU." Other offices focus on local hiring for technical consulting positions. "We hire nationally for Lean Six Sigma, but locally recruit MBAs heavily from the University of Georgia, Georgia Tech and Emory," notes a source from Atlanta.

Like a marathon

According to insiders, "every hiring process is different," though in general sources claim it's a "very structured, well-organized" process. Most government candidates face "an intense series of 30-minute interviews, each with one to three staffers, including at least one senior manager." "I experienced the 'speed-dating interview.' All interviewees were in a room, each sitting at a different table. Interviewers came to each candidate and spent 30 minutes interviewing. This was repeated three times," a consultant shares. Interview day can seem like a test of endurance, according to a strategy consultant, who says, "I was brought in for a marathon, four-hour session with five different interviewers that lasted until nearly 7 p.m. in the evening." An insider tells us that MBA graduates in the final round "are taken to a 'sell dinner'—this is important for understanding how the firm works. But do remember it's another part of the interview and you're being assessed." And a colleague offers a valuable tip: "You'd better be very personable."

Take your time

A number of insiders report that interviews for strategy consultants are heavy on the cases, consisting of "four case study interviews with staff," often based on "market sizing, go-to-market strategies and building business cases." One source advises, "I used the Vault case studies guide to prepare from. Don't go to the interview without having practiced at least 50 of them because being practiced in structuring problems is the most critical thing. Remember to be very structured in your responses. Take one minute to think about the question and jot down how you'll answer—the interviewer won't mind and you'll be so much more prepared to answer." "I received a case about commercial space flight, and whether it was a profitable endeavor for a company considering entering the market," recalls a consultant. Another example of a typical case question is, "What would you do if the Minister of Armenia wanted to conduct a benchmark of a taxpayer agency's collection processes?"

Aside from cases, we're told, "people will ask about consulting skills—writing, verbal communication and analytical skills—and will want examples of when these skills were used," describes a manager.

OUR SURVEY SAYS

Appearances aside ...

To outsiders, the idea of Booz Allen might bring to mind formally-clad consultants working in a staunchly traditional big firm. But sources advise there's no reason to be put off by mistaken impressions. "On the outside, the culture appears to be very straight-laced and conservative, with business suits dominating the dress. But, once inside, it is clear that diversity rules and brilliant minds are having fun and working hard," boasts a consultant. Insiders rave that working with "intellectually charged and friendly, down-to-earth individuals" is what keeps them happy at Booz Allen. "It's a true meritocracy, with some of the brightest and most collegial folks around," a staffer claims. One senior consultant expresses that "people at the firm are very down to earth, while still being extremely smart. I was once told, 'We take our work seriously, but we don't take ourselves seriously.'"

Many consultants laud the "cooperative environment" among staff. Witnesses a colleague, "So far in my experience, the people have been the best thing about coming to Booz Allen. I am just amazed at the willingness of co-workers and employees to give their time to help others advance and learn in any way they can. I see no competition between co-workers here, the withholding

Visit the Vault Consulting Career Channel at **www.vault.com/consulting** - with insider firm profiles, message boards, the Vault Consulting Job Board and more.

VAULT CAREER LIBRARY   **81**

of information to get ahead, the backstabbing." One longtimer insists, "During my 30-year career with a Fortune 500 company, two small companies and the U.S. Department of State, I have never found as pleasant and collegial a work atmosphere as Booz Allen. Some of my closest friends are co-workers. The firm spends a lot of time trying to find people who are a good fit." Another source describes it as "a fraternal environment that is both competitive and collaborative."

No lone ranger types

With a firm the size of Booz Allen, it's no surprise that opinions on culture vary among insiders. "Snobs, snobs everywhere," a source grumbles. Of course, not everyone feels that way. "Some partners and principals are a bit old school and make life painful, but overall it's very collaborative and friendly," admits a Dallas source, and a New Yorker gushes, "I adore the people I work with. They are supportive and fun."

There are some consultants at the firm who aren't feeling the fraternal air. Some insist that their colleagues are "rather pretentious." One consultant describes it as "very clique-ish—either you belong or do not." A co-worker claims, "It's a very uptight culture. You never feel like you can let your hair down." But what's clear from insiders' remarks is that Booz Allen is an ideal firm for those who enjoy a "consensus-oriented" place that encourages group effort. "People who succeed have to be more collaborative; teamwork and management style is valued over individual performance," an insider states. And for many, it's that sense of collaboration that makes them appreciate their job. Says one associate, "I work with lots of very smart people who are very willing to share what they know. It's my favorite part of working at Booz Allen."

Brown-bagged dinners

Hours are all over the map for these consultants; as one analyst reports, "Officially, I probably bill about 50 hours per week. If you include all the unbillable and 'volunteer' administrative work, I'd add another 20." A senior colleague notes, "I work over 80 hours a week," and another consultant remarks, "I usually work about 14 hours a day when at client site. I have been on projects where the manager expected us to pack dinner while buying lunch so that the team could stay at client site late (11 p.m.)." With hours like these, some respondents claim that work/life balance can be hard to come by. "I can achieve a balance due to general flexibility of my job, except assignments that are on government client sites that require rigorous sign in and sign out—then I'm a virtual wage slave," frets a staffer. Others indicate that work/life balance is not so bad, comparatively. An insider points out, "My boyfriend works for Deloitte and our work/life balance is 10 times better than theirs, from what I can compare."

There are also quite a few consultants who attest to more sane weeks of around 45 to 50 hours. A source says, "I work 50 hours a week, but 10 of that, which is administrative or business development, is off the books due to the utilization formulas that are used to measure performance." And a colleague claims to work "on average, 48 hours," adding, "Slow times can be only 40; approaching a project milestone can be 70 to 80." Still, one source cautions, "If you are not billing 40 hours a week to a client, it is viewed as a very bad thing." "It depends on job manager's ability to handle scope. However, it's definitely not your 9-to-5 job," concludes an insider.

Flexible and family-friendly

Despite demanding hours and frequent weekend work, some consultants claim that their managers have made work/life balance possible. "Managers are incredibly understanding and don't want people to work on weekends or late into the evening. There are many events that provide opportunities to participate and learn without actually working," says an insider. Another associate explains, "It's surprisingly easy to manage work and life. However, it all depends on the managerial abilities of the job manager on each individual job." "I feel that my managers encourage me to maintain a healthy work/life balance. I tend to be a workaholic and they frequently check in with me to make sure I am not overwhelmed. And the social culture of our close-knit office also helps maintain a balance," a colleague suggests.

In addition to understanding managers, another boost to work/life balance comes from the fact that Booz Allen provides a generous amount of flexibility when it comes to scheduling. An associate says, "I am permitted to work from home when needed, and comp days are available if client work permits. It's extremely flexible," adding, "They allow me to work from home if necessary, take time off whenever I need to and never require me to work late or on weekends." And a satisfied parent recounts, "Work/life balance is an individual thing, between an employee and his significant others. For me, I can leave the office at about 5 p.m. each day, go home, have dinner with my family and then put the kids to bed before I jump back online. It works." Another analyst explains that managers "encourage working from home," adding, "It is a great place for working women with families. As long as you get your hours in, your schedule is up to you."

Seeking superpeople

Attaining work/life balance, though, seems to pose a whole new set of problems. "There is pressure for those who want to succeed to put in more time or effort. Those with a work/life balance are not usually the ones on the 'fast track,'" a consultant states. A manager confirms, explaining, "The firm would like everyone to be a superman or superwoman. In addition to the client work, everyone is encouraged to 'volunteer' their time on heavy-duty administrative and governance tasks." A colleague goes so far as to say, "It is a big no-no to plan a pregnancy in early years. Taking paternity leave is not easy—people are pressured to work (out-of-town assignments) until the very last day when the baby arrives. There are instances when people have missed the birth of their newborns because they could not get back home in time." According to one insider, the key to balance is establishing limits: "Yes, I have balance, but it is because I set boundaries. People who do not set boundaries find themselves working every weekend. We are always asked first before being assigned to a project. The people who can't say no are the ones who suffer."

Personable leadership

The majority of consultants rate their supervisors highly. "Supervisors are akin to mentors. Successful supervisors at Booz Allen cultivate a rich learning environment where the proverbial consulting slur, 'sink-or-swim,' rarely enters the mix," an insider recounts. "The firm is very personable, up to the top partners. Doors are open and people have made time to talk to me," claims one associate. A co-worker reports, "The relationship is perfect. I have the ability to engage [supervisors] when I need them, but they have a hands-off approach to letting business grow."

But Booz Allen also sees its share of personality clashes. Some insiders grumble about their managers, whom they describe as "good at winning contracts but bad at managing." Complains one source, "Partners form their own fiefdoms, so if you are not aligned with the right person your career growth can be affected." Relationships with supervisors usually depend on the particular project, according to one source who reveals, "Management style varies greatly across the functional teams, some being considerably more effective than others. Part of that is a result of senior management promotions being driven more by market performance than leadership potential."

Some stay put

Much like work/life balance and management at the firm, opinions on travel vary widely. Consultants working with corporate clients may end up traveling all the time, while government consultants tend to stick with local clients, according to staffers. Notes an insider, "The Dallas office requires full travel weekly with little work sold locally," while a San Diego source says, "I travel approximately three times a year." Those with out-of town clients admit they don't necessarily love the lifestyle: "Travel is difficult. The firm tries to manage to your needs (like the need to be home for an event), but it is probably the most challenging part of the job." Moans one associate, "Sometimes you just don't know where you will be the next day or the next hour."

Second-rate salary

A number of insiders voice discontent over compensation at the firm. "I don't feel as if Booz Allen pays its employees on a level equal to our competitors," declares an insider. Though the firm claims that all new strategy consulting hires just out of business school enter at the same base salary level, a government consultant rants, "It's very poor. Unless you negotiate hard and have insider godfathers, they undercut you by several tens of thousands of dollars—it is disrespectful to highly qualified people." "Compensation is a big issue at the firm right now," grumbles a source, who winces when telling of his salary, which he claims

Visit the Vault Consulting Career Channel at **www.vault.com/consulting** - with insider firm profiles, message boards, the Vault Consulting Job Board and more.

VAULT CAREER LIBRARY

83

is lower than that of a "level-A secretary" on his project. While across the board, commercial consultants receive a bonus, insiders disclose that for junior government consultants, bonus is in the form of a "year-end contribution to employee 401(k), equal to 10 percent of salary." Reportedly, those in upper-level management receive bonus in addition to salary, which ranges from 10 to 50 percent and up.

On the other hand, some employees feel that lower pay is a fair trade-off for the benefits of being at Booz Allen. "I could be paid more if I went somewhere else, but I might have to travel or work more hours, and I don't want to do that," an associate declares. A colleague echoes the sentiment: "I had other competitors offer me higher salaries, but the firm's 401(k) and education [benefits], as well as the opportunities available, more than made up for the slightly lower salary."

Technology Petting Zoo

Among employees, the firm rates high for its well-rounded training program, which consists of official training and informal mentoring. "We are expected to take 40 hours of internal training a year. We are also given training dollars for external training ($2,500 for certificates or $5,000 toward a degree), and (on my team, at least) you are expected to not let that go to waste." There is plenty of official training available, including web casts and a "great online program, the Technology Petting Zoo." Still, insiders agree "the informal training is better than the formal training." "Mentoring and on-the-job training is much more common and immediately useful. Job managers are highly supportive of the apprenticeship model we have in place," a source explains. Agrees a colleague, "Mentoring is encouraged and very available, [and is] completely controlled by the employee."

Country club perks

Insiders also admit that there are a number of nice perks that make the intense hours a bit more bearable. "Access to the company box for sporting and concert events, discounts at Tiffany's and 'leveraged' weekends," are a few favorites. One consultant mentions "a cell phone discount and gym membership discount," and sources based at headquarters rave about the "nice holiday party" described as "over the top." Those who stay long enough to reach upper management can look forward to loads of cushy extras, like "annual dues and an initiation fee for one country club and one college, lunch or health club, 100 percent medical for staff and family, a $5,000 donation to business school of which you are an alum every three years and $8,000 per year of financial advice and tax prep services."

Consultants who travel also get their fair share of extras while they're on the road. Boasts one insider, "I was away for most of 2006 and didn't spend a cent of my own money on food, accommodation, travel or the gym. While working in our home city after 7:30 p.m., you take a taxi home and your dinner is paid for." Confirms a colleague, "The company takes care of every detail from the moment we step out of our homes till we come back: cabs, flights, hotels, even laundry!"

Humdrum offices

Though many insiders describe their quarters as "boring" and "utilitarian," most are grateful that "Booz Allen doesn't believe in cubicles." An insider states, "Offices are shared and each person has his own space. It definitely boosts employee morale." The office setup still doesn't satisfy some, who claim that the shared spaces offer "no privacy." Insists a consultant, "Sharing an office with a co-worker who sits less than five feet away doesn't allow for any private time or any private conversations." A McLean-based employee complains of "no windows and a very small and dark [space]," and says he "can hear people's conversations through the walls—a very antisocial setting." One government staffer in Baltimore picks the place apart and glumly states, "There is no gym on premises. Or showers. It's sort of lame in the health-conscious 21st century." On the whole, the office surroundings might be a bigger deal to those working in government consulting, since they see the offices a lot more than their travel-bound commercial consulting counterparts.

Either way, satisfaction seems to be partly a matter of location, according to a lucky employee in Atlanta, who boasts, "I am entry level with my own office, great medicine supplies on site, coffee, tea and hot chocolate machine, vending and access to tons of restaurants—and a subway directly under the building."

Strong support for women

Insiders give positive marks to the firm's efforts in hiring and retaining women, though they admit the applicant pool is tilted toward males. The firm clarifies that on the commercial side, it hires nearly as many women out of B-school as men, however on the government side, the applicant pool is heavily weighted toward men. "It is a little depressing always being the only woman in meetings. However, I know that our hiring is in line with the resumes we are receiving. In our area, my company is not as well known, and we rely heavily on former military," a source mentions. A manager explains, "The firm is making a big effort to retain talented women after they have children by offering them part-time schedules and no travel." Despite the slightly uneven balance, female consultants seem to be happy with the direction of things. "As a woman, I have received tremendous support to ensure work/life balance and have been very pleased with recent women's mentoring initiatives, which ensure that women get appropriate and ongoing support in the firm," a manager explains.

Booz Allen earns kudos for its benefits for parents and options for moms who return to work. Says an insider, "Mothers are able to take six months' leave, including at least two months paid. There is additional flexibility offered to take internal [instead of consulting] roles." "The parental leave is offered to both women and men, and it even applies for adoption," a manager explains. In addition, staffers rave about "assistance with adoption costs" and "in-house day care—if you're lucky enough to get your child in."

Like a "United Colors of Benetton ad"

Most employees laud the firm's efforts at creating a diverse atmosphere. "I feel like I'm working in a United Colors of Benetton ad," says an insider. One consultant states, "The company has excellent policies, programs and training in place. Opportunities for minorities are good at the execution level but they will still find it hard to reach higher management levels." At the upper management levels, staffers point out that minority diversity is lacking. A manager claims, "It's getting better. There is much more commitment from top levels now to target minorities." With regard to other diversity, a source states, "This firm is pretty diverse, especially when it comes to employees with physical impairments. The firm goes the extra mile with hearing and visually impaired co-workers." Another insider reveals, "I am a lesbian and I feel extremely supported."

"We have a very active diversity initiative that encourages the hiring and development of all kinds of people—women, minorities, GLBTs, etc. There are diversity forums, for people from or interested in particular cultures—Latin America, African-American, Middle East, gay/lesbian/bisexual, etc.," an insider explains. In fact, several employees remark that there is too much emphasis on diversity. "The forums offered seem to be a separating rather than unifying culture," observes a colleague. Another consultant opines, "It seems out of control to me."

Booz Allen reaches out

Insiders attest to the whirlwind of activity centered on improving local communities at Booz Allen. A source states, "There is extensive community service involvement. I believe that the published stat is 70 percent of employees are involved in charity work." Employees claim that there is "almost always some kind of fund-raising or opportunity to participate going on." "One example is a program to help unemployed women reenter the workforce through computer training. We provide the facility, equipment and instructors," notes a source in McLean. An Ohio-based consultant records "Cleveland Foodbank, Rebuilding Together, Market Under Glass, Harvest for Hunger, Providence House Crisis Shelter, Animal Protective League and Adopt-a-School" as a partial list of organizations his office supports. "The office usually sponsors one or two families at Christmastime, providing food, presents and necessities to each member of the selected family. And there is a drive in the summer for school supplies for Title One schools, usually two of the neediest in the area," explains a Huntsville government consultant. A colleague in D.C. declares, "The opportunity to reach out to the community is one of my biggest draws to Booz Allen."

Visit the Vault Consulting Career Channel at **www.vault.com/consulting** - with insider firm profiles, message boards, the Vault Consulting Job Board and more.

VAULT CAREER LIBRARY   **85**

Two Canal Park
Cambridge, MA 02141
Phone: (617) 252-2000
Fax: (617) 252-2100
www.monitor.com

LOCATIONS

Cambridge, MA (HQ)
28 offices worldwide

PRACTICE AREAS

Competitive/Corporate Strategy
Corporate Finance
Economic Development
Executive/Leadership Development
Innovation Strategy
Marketing/Growth Strategy
Operational Strategy
Organizational Strategy
Public Sector Strategies
Regional Competitiveness

THE STATS

Employer Type: Private Company
Chairman: Mark Fuller
2006 Employees: 950
2005 Employees: 800

RANKING RECAP

Practice Area
#8 - Economic Consulting (tie)
#9 - Pharmaceutical & Health Care Consulting

Quality of Life
#4 - Relationships with Supervisors
#7 - Firm Culture
#8 - Overall Satisfaction
#12 - Offices
#16 - Best Firms to Work For
#18 - Interaction with Clients

Diversity
#17 - Diversity for GLBT
#20 - Diversity for Women

UPPERS

- "Meritocratic culture, great collaboration among consultants"
- "Major focus on mentorship"
- Global bonus pool
- "Great opportunities to interact with senior leadership"

DOWNERS

- "Lack of transparency in compensation/relative performance"
- Fast growth, but some processes and systems haven't yet caught up
- "Mediocre top-down communications"
- "Cambridge-centricity"

EMPLOYMENT CONTACT

www.monitor.com/join

THE BUZZ
WHAT CONSULTANTS AT OTHER FIRMS ARE SAYING ABOUT THIS FIRM

- "Creative; nontraditional"
- "Flies under the radar; way too introverted"
- "Cares about feelings"
- "Overly academic—nerd alert"

THE SCOOP

Brains from Cambridge

Founded in 1983 by a group of brainy strategists, including alumni and professors from Harvard Business School, Monitor Group is a case study in how to merge theory and practice. Drawing high-level strategies from academia and think tanks, the firm's group of companies applies these ideas to the private and public sector. The firm still gets a lot of academic firepower from its headquarters in Cambridge, Mass., a location that, presumably, allows many of its top thinkers easy access to the ivied halls of their alma mater.

The firm serves clients through a range of services—and the ability to integrate those services in a customized way for each client. Monitor's clients include leading major corporations, governments and philanthropic institutions. The group's 1,000-plus professionals are located in the Americas, Europe, Africa and Asia, and offer expertise in marketing/growth strategy, competitive and corporate strategy, organizational analysis, corporate finance, operational strategy, innovation and public-sector strategies, as well as capability building, and executive and leadership development. The firm's management consulting clients are spread over a variety of industries, including health care, telecommunications/computing, consumer products, financial services, raw materials, media and entertainment.

More than consulting

True to the "group" in its name, Monitor is actually structured as a closely integrated set of business units linked by shared ownership, management philosophy and assets, focusing on a wide variety of areas, from regional competitiveness to innovation to marketing. In fact, the company refuses to even define itself as a "consulting firm," arguing that its breadth of services makes it "much more than" that. Monitor's units are broadly divided into the strategy-oriented Action Company and private equity-oriented Monitor Merchant Banking. The Action Company's projects are vast and varied, covering corporate restructurings, mergers and acquisitions, growth strategies, and the assessment of new technologies and markets for clients. Of these engagements, more than half are categorized by the firm as "marketing/growth strategy" projects. With a team of about 950 consultants, the Action Company is able to draw on the resources of its related Monitor Group companies to support these wide-ranging engagements.

Other Monitor Group companies include Lattice Partners, which serves as the firm's center of excellence and innovation for organizational design and development of teams and individuals; Market2Customer, which specializes in marketing strategy; Monitor Innovation, which helps grow through innovation, combining technology, strategy and design expertise; and Global Business Network, a "scenario consultancy" that helps clients master the challenges arising from uncertainty. Monitor's client list includes Fortune 500 companies, international firms, state, national and international government agencies, and nonprofit organizations.

Fiercely financial

When Monitor was first formed, it specialized in strategy consulting as part of a portfolio of service offerings. Within five years, the group opened offices in Europe and Asia. Monitor branched out in the next decade, adding merchant banking activities to management consulting services. The group developed relationships with investors and set about raising capital to create its own principal equity fund. With over $2 billion under management today, the funds gave Monitor an entry into venture capital and financial advisory services.

On the money side of the firm, the Monitor Merchant Banking Group, made up of MAST, Monitor Clipper Partners, Monitor Ventures and Monitor Equity Advisors, has collectively invested more than $1.5 billion in a range of industries and holds equity in over 20 operating companies, with total revenue over $1 billion. The banking group draws on Monitor's advisory resources to provide strategic support to portfolio companies.

Visit the Vault Consulting Career Channel at www.vault.com/consulting - with insider firm profiles, message boards, the Vault Consulting Job Board and more.

VAULT CAREER LIBRARY

87

Across the globe

From the beginning, Monitor was designed to be a global firm, opening international offices within five years of its founding. It currently has 28 offices around the world. The Action Company derives about 40 percent of its business from North America; roughly the same amount comes from Europe, with the rest divided between Asia-Pacific, Latin America and Africa. But rather than working from an "office-based" model, the firm explains, it prefers to organize itself globally based on key assets, using global recruiting and project allocation, as well as a global profit pool. The firm's consultants move freely among Monitor Group's businesses, too, eschewing a traditional industry-based vertical model.

A force for good

One of the firm's most well-known founders is Michael Porter, a strategy heavyweight, who Accenture called one of the top-50 business intellectuals of our time. These days, Porter, who serves as a Bishop William Lawrence University Professor at Harvard, still takes an active role at Monitor. The firm also maintains an impressive stable of other "thought leaders" it calls on for ideas, including technology guru Bruce Chew; Chris Argyris, director and professor emeritus of organizational behavior at Harvard; Joseph Fuller, a Monitor Group founder who also serves as a director of the Phillips-Van Heusen Corporation; former University of Southern California Professor Bernie Jaworski; valuation expert Tom Copeland; and former Harvard Professor Michael Jensen. In June 2006, Richard Perle, former chairman of the Defense Policy Board and resident fellow at the American Enterprise Institute for Public Policy Research, signed on as a senior advisor.

In May 2007, Monitor acquired Doblin, an innovation strategy practice based in Chicago, which reinforces the firm's commitment to being a market leader in innovation. In March 2007, the firm added new personnel in support of the planned expansion of its "learning-to-action" solutions, focusing on "smart" online tools. Steven Forth, founder and CEO of Recombo Inc., was hired as VP of online action solutions, and David Egan, formerly senior VP and group publisher of Horizon House Publications Inc., was tapped as VP of sales, marketing and external partnership strategies in support of the eMonitor division. In September 2006, the firm brought onboard as consultants the entire former North American leadership team of the strategy firm Adventis Corporation. Adventis specialized in telecommunications, media and technology.

Close with the Qaddafis

The firm works with an array of business and government leaders, though it remains tight-lipped about its specific engagements. One of its more high-profile engagements has been its work with Libya's government. In 2002, Michael Porter was contacted by the country's ruling powers, the Qaddafi family, who asked for his help in modernizing the economy. Though Porter himself took a few years to become seriously involved, Monitor Group's work for the country has gained momentum in recent years, especially following the restoration of relations between the U.S. and Libya in 2006. The firm's presence has become so influential that a February 2007 profile in the *Harvard Crimson* noted that Porter is "becoming a household name" in Libya, where he works closely with Saif al-Islam Qaddafi (the son of the country's leader, Muammar). That month, Porter attended the ceremony for the launch of the Libyan Economic Development Board, designed to help facilitate business development in the country, from streamlining the registration process for small businesses to helping local entrepreneurs access professional training. The Monitor team also developed a three-month leadership program intended to develop a group of probusiness elite in Libya: So far, 150 have graduated from the program. In an interview with *BusinessWeek*, Porter cited the country's "broken decision-making process," noting that its leadership had realized that it needed to modernize its processes to participate in the global economy. Porter called the Libya project "symbolic," arguing, "This is a test case of how to create action. We are learning a lot that we could use in other parts of the world—in the Middle East and in other countries with a history of socialist practices."

Idea factory

Obviously, Monitor Group's intellectuals aren't shy about sharing their ideas. The firm's recent books include Porter's *Redefining Healthcare*, co-authored with Elizabeth Olmsted Teisberg (May 2006); *The Strategy and Tactics of Pricing*, written by Tom Nagle and John Hogan (November 2005); and Chairman Mark Fuller's discourse on turnaround in the Japanese economy, *Japan's Business Renaissance*, co-authored by John Beck (October 2005). In March 2007, the Global Business

Network announced its findings from a white paper, "Impacts of Climate Change," exploring the possible effects of sustained greenhouse gas emissions on ecosystems, economies, human settlements and political institutions over the next half century. A Monitor Group report conducted for South Carolina on the state's dropout rate—the worst in the nation—was released in August 2006. The report was underwritten by a foundation on behalf of local business groups.

Capitalists with a cause

Monitor Group insiders have said they value the firm for its socially conscious leanings, as well as its intellectual star power. For the past few years, the firm has teamed with the magazine *Fast Company* to offer the Social Capitalist Awards, honoring organizations that use "creativity, business smarts and hard work to invent a brighter future." The 2007 awards, recognizing 43 companies out of an initial list of 314 nominees and 133 applicants, were the result of 3,000 hours of work by eight Monitor Group consultants. The list regularly includes organizations devoted to growth in developing countries, improving schools, investing in local nonprofits, building affordable housing and more.

Monitor recently developed a partnership with Management Leadership for Tomorrow, which aims to increase the diversity of leadership in business by promoting business career tracks to college juniors of color. The firm has consulted (in partnership with New Profit Inc.) with MLT on its growth strategy and participates as faculty in its Career Prep program. The firm also announced a partnership with Teach for America in fall 2006. College graduates who receive an offer from Monitor and from TFA may defer their Monitor offer for two years, while receiving career support from Monitor during that time. The firm also recruits from among TFA's corps members and supports the organization's career placement activities. Through the program, Monitor supports the philosophy that teaching is a relevant skill for serving clients in a consulting capacity, and points out that a number of senior staff and partners were teachers or professors before coming to Monitor.

GETTING HIRED

Weeding through the Ivies

Like fellow top consulting houses in the U.S., Monitor likes candidates from "Ivy League schools, top liberal arts colleges, and top business schools around the country." Other universities and MBA programs of interest include Anderson, Amherst, Bates, Berkeley, Bowdoin, Colby, Darden, Georgetown, Kellogg, MIT, Northwestern, Sloan, Stanford, Tuck, Tufts, UVA, Wharton and Williams.

Q: How many golf balls are there in the U.S.? A: Who cares?

Those who land an interview will get a first chance to see, and experience, Monitor's values. "The interview process is a great example of our unique culture, with emphasis on learning and teamwork," explains a Cambridge source. "We test a lot against the characteristics that our firm values, such as courage, generosity, responsibility and empathy," a colleague adds. "Many of the questions in our first round are focused on evaluating the candidates against those characteristics."

Expect a first round to last about an hour, combining a written case study and traditional fit interview. "The candidate gets 15 minutes to read the case, and then we take about 20 minutes to talk with them about the three questions (both quantitative and qualitative) that we have asked them to consider," describes a Cambridge-based consultant. "The rest of the time is devoted to the traditional getting-to-know-you interview." Importantly, all scenarios are based on actual Monitor cases. According to a New York source, these "may have to do with sizing an opportunity, or walking through which of two distinct target segments a candidate might choose for the given company, and why." A Cambridge consultant assures you, "There are no 'How many cabs are there in Manhattan?' questions." "We try to get a real sense for the person—his interests and motivations, as well as his capabilities," adds a Boston vet. "We try to understand those capabilities as much as possible in the way they're tested in our daily work. I've been a consultant for 15-plus years, and not once has a client sat me down and asked me to calculate off the top of my head how many golf balls there are in the U.S. So we don't test recruits' capabilities that way, either."

Visit the Vault Consulting Career Channel at **www.vault.com/consulting** - with insider firm profiles, message boards, the Vault Consulting Job Board and more.

VAULT CAREER LIBRARY   89

Second time's a charm

The second round requires applicants to interview in a group. The process may last four hours, and is divided into three sections: group interaction tests, role-playing and assessments of cultural fit. The first section is a "noncompetitive group interview of three to six candidates"; as a Cambridge source explains, "Everyone is given the same case to read, and then a different question about that case. The group is given half an hour to read the case and begin solving their question." Each candidate then presents his or her question and answer, discussing the latter for 15 minutes. "In this part of the interview process, we learn how well candidates interact with others and perform in a team setting," explains a consultant. In this manner, offers a colleague in New York, "The company tests not only an individual's analytics, but his/her ability to clearly communicate and explain problems to others. The process tests whether or not individuals are naturally collaborative." A staffer in Cambridge underscores this point: "It is important to note that this group interview really is noncompetitive. There are groups where everyone gets an offer, and there are groups where no one gets an offer." And according to a New York source, "Most candidates actually inform us that they enjoy this interview a great deal."

Next up in the process is a 30-minute role-play exercise. "You have to work through some potentially tough business scenarios with your interviewer," a consultant in Cambridge explains. "The candidate is given a situation to read and then role-plays how they would handle it if they were the consultant," adds a New York source. The final, 30-minute section revolves around feedback: a New York source explains, "The candidate and interviewer discuss the day, how the candidate thinks he/she did in the group, how the interviewers felt the candidate did, etc. The conversation then shifts to a more standard fit/resume interview." In this final portion, the candidate is also able "to give feedback on the interview process."

OUR SURVEY SAYS

The Monitor meritocracy

A source describes Monitor culture thusly: "Monitor is a meritocracy, where the standouts receive disproportionate benefits in terms of project allocations, transfer opportunities and bonuses. Consultants are often laid-back yet driven, and intellectual yet pragmatic. My colleagues possess considerable mental horsepower without being arrogant or careless." Insiders report forging close-knit relationships among colleagues that transcend work-related issues; comments one source, "I know what my manager's two-year-old says when he watches football, how my first-year is planning to train for the Boston marathon and even stories about how one of the partners invented a legendary drinking game at Dartmouth." As a Cambridge insider believes, "What makes Monitor particularly rich in culture is not a feigned corporate image or stiff mantra, but that each individual consultant offers a rich, diverse and textured experience. We are a company of truly unique and inspired individuals. It's that inspiration that is the cornerstone of our culture." And what impresses this San Franciscan about Monitor culture is that it is a global phenomena, and not particular to one office: "The collegial environment and vibrant culture are truly some of the highlights of my career here—and having traveled to seven of our 30 offices, I am constantly surprised and elated that Monitor's culture permeates offices on a global basis."

Burrito-eating contests and karaoke parties

Insiders tell us that Monitor strives to provide its employees with both a productive and enjoyable atmosphere. "I think Monitor works hard to make sure that it is a fun, exciting and entertaining place to work," relates a source. "This takes the form of more academic lectures by key thought leaders in a variety of fields, to the annual karaoke contest." Seconds this insider, "From burrito-eating contests to karaoke parties for charity to nonprofit consulting, the firm comes together in a variety of meaningful ways that build firm culture and speak to our values as a company." However, such intra-office socializing is not all fun and burrito-games. As one source stresses, at Monitor such socializing is also critical to professional growth: "There's a lot of information that gets shared through informal, interpersonal networks rather than through formal channels, and this can impact the opportunities you get. It's important to be aware of this heading in to make the most of your time here and avoid frustration."

All work and no play makes Jack a dull consultant

Live to work, or work to live? "We bring a lot of care to what we do but are frank about the fact that life outside of work is much more important," a Cambridge source relates. In fact, a San Franciscan reports, Monitor management "does a good job of encouraging a strong work/life balance. Consultants are reprimanded for not having taken vacation, managers don't ask for work on the weekends and schedules are nearly infinitely flexible. When unstaffed, consultants are encouraged to take some time away from the office and to catch up on the things they have had to set aside during busy periods, such as doctors' visits, etc." Adds a New York-based colleague, "There is a strong effort from the senior levels to maintain the work/life balance manageably, and they will intervene on cases where they see consultants putting in long hours over extended periods of time." Similarly, notes a Boston source, "Work comes in cycles. When you have no work, the firm is very good at telling you to go home—no questions asked."

Say yes to flex

Monitor consultants are able to maintain balance in part due to the company's attitude toward client-facing work, as well as its flexibility. Asserts a source in Boston, "Monitor has zero face time. Your work and impact is what matters. You can do your work when and where you want." A Cambridge colleague confirms this, noting that Monitor is "flexible on working from home, and with employees working nonstandard hours." Indeed, adds another, "As long as the work is done you can figure out when you're going to do it. However, the demands of this job mean it's not 9 to 5 by any means, and the work side of the scale can definitely be a bit heavy at times. Still, I find managers to be very empathetic toward this, and most work hard to ensure that the entire team is finding that balance." A Toronto staffer reiterates, "The firm is focused on high-quality output delivered on time—how you fit the work in is up to you. For some, the workday starts at 11 a.m. and runs later into the night, for others it is an early-morning affair. I have found that this built-in flexibility has allowed me to accommodate those elements of family, friends and external commitments in a manner that is very manageable." A Cambridge source states, "Having the flexibility to work from home while I'm doing laundry, leave work early for choir practice and plan out my out workweek is crucial." And, in a testament to Monitor's flexible work policy as it relates to working mothers, a 10-year vet has this to say: "I have three children under age six. I have been able to customize my percentage [full-time employee] status to accommodate fluctuations in my work/personal demands. I am the envy of my friends who are working mothers."

60 is the new 40

Sustaining a healthy work/life balance has a lot to do with hours expectations, predictability and the necessity for weekend work; Monitor sources report working an average of about 60 hours per week. "Sixty hours seems quite reasonable," suggests a Cambridge source. "When we have longer weeks, it can get frustrating, but usually those periods don't last too long." "Hours are extremely variable," adds a New York-based consultant. "Mine have been excellent for the past four months, though they will become more onerous in the coming months." "I think my work hours are good," another East Coaster relates. "I generally know in advance when things are going to get busy and I can plan accordingly."

As for weekend work, a San Francisco consultant states, "Most of my weekend work consists of a few hours here and there—that is fairly common. Less than one weekend per month do I really have to work all day for one day or both days." A Chicago consultant points out that, naturally, weekend work varies "considerably based on the project/stage within the project. I try my best to avoid weekend work and can typically manage that, but weeknights are usually until 9 or 10 p.m." And there are some who choose to put in the time on the weekend, if it means more free time in the week. A New York source explains, "Usually I'm doing a few hours of work on Sundays, so as to avoid staying late on Fridays," while a Cambridge source cites a "need to regularly spend time on Sunday to get ahead. But I almost always have at least one day 100 percent off over a weekend, and occasionally need to work one day (or part of one day)."

As for average project length, sources estimate that mandates can run anywhere from four to six months, with the typical client relationship lasting two to three years. And as the firm employs a 50/50 staffing model, "It is very rare to be completely unstaffed," a San Franciscan explains. In the opinion of this source, "[The 50/50 model] helps keep work fresh since you are able to switch back and forth. I think this helps make the workload more manageable." Attests another, "While I only had

Visit the Vault Consulting Career Channel at www.vault.com/consulting - with insider firm profiles, message boards, the Vault Consulting Job Board and more.

VAULT CAREER LIBRARY

91

approximately one week of non-billable time last year, I had two to three months where I was 50 percent billable, which basically means you get to enjoy a great work/life balance while still having meaningful responsibilities in the office."

Happy noncampers

"The upside of Monitor's 50/50 model is that it means we typically don't go and camp out at the client four days a week—instead, we just travel when there is a meeting," a San Francisco source offers. "I love Monitor's view on travel: Unless there is a specific need for you to be at the client (i.e., major meeting), you can be much more productive in your own office," enthuses a Cambridge consultant. "I really have found it to be true, and feel that it truly allows you to have a life outside of work. I am able to sleep in my own bed more days than not, and I still feel like I am getting good, quality opportunities for client exposure and contact." Agrees a colleague, "Monitor prides itself on only traveling when it's really going to add value." And with regard to the 50/50 staffing model, this colleague points out, "It simply isn't professional or practical to serve one client while on site for another."

Though travel requirements can fluctuate widely, on average Monitor sources report being away from their home office about one to two days per week—a requirement that they describe as being "very manageable" and "very reasonable." "We travel less than the classic consulting groups," affirms a Boston source. And in the opinion of a Cambridge colleague, "The fact that we don't travel that much helps in building and maintaining our strong culture." The firm is also "quite responsive to consultants' preferences, so those who don't like to travel (especially new parents) are often placed in 'no fly zones' and assigned local cases (easier to do in offices with many local clients)," testifies a New York source. Adds a long-term staffer in Los Angeles, "Consultants typically have a large degree of influence on the travel/no-travel decision, particularly as tenure increases. For the past three years I have been working with a local client with minimal travel requirements. Allocation to work on a local client is based on my personal preference not to travel. Before, when I liked to travel, the firm accommodated accordingly."

Interestingly, an upside of Monitor's low-travel policy is that when they do travel, many consultants appreciate the change. "I actually enjoy time on the road, both for seeing the country/world and getting the reward benefits," a Cambridge source relates. Agrees a San Francisco staffer, "I, frankly, enjoy the amount of travel I get to do with the firm. We are not on the road constantly, so when I do travel, I frequently take advantage of opportunities to stay weekends, visit friends and family." "The travel enhances my work life," concurs an East Coaster. "Being in front of clients is important and I enjoy the energy of having impact in 1:1 settings with clients. I would get bored if I didn't have any client travel."

He's not heavy, he's my partner

Monitor consultants tell us that at their firm, exposure to clients and senior management is early, fluid and constant. Affirms a New York source, "The culture is very open to feedback, which leads to very relaxed, open relationships with supervisors. We are also given a lot of responsibility quickly, and often get to interact with quite senior clients at a very junior level. This is particularly true with relationship clients." Confirms a source based in New York, "As a second-year analyst, I have had the fantastic experience of participating in meetings with over 40 company presidents, each responsible for over $1 billion in revenue. Due to Monitor's strong teaching culture, I feel my managers invested a lot of time in grooming/preparing me to take on these opportunities." Others convey similar experiences, especially regarding mentorship. "Senior leadership is phenomenally available and very open to interaction, even with the most junior consultants," appraises this lower-level contact in San Francisco. "I have had excellent relationships with the senior members on my case teams," contributes a Cambridge colleague. "Everyone that I have worked with has been very interested in my personal development and in what they can do to help me achieve my goals." A co-worker adds, "I get significant exposure to my superiors and supervisors, including senior leadership of the firm. On the client side I also get good exposure to top-level management. As a case team leader I tend to be an active member in steering committee updates on our projects with senior management of the client."

A Cambridge source offers this praise: "I have been especially impressed with the emphasis on making those you manage real thought partners (rather than grunts/number crunchers) and constantly offering them 'stretch' opportunities to accelerate development." Even those who've been with Monitor for many years praise the level of attention their supervisors offer in ensuring that associates are developing in the ways they want to. "My supervisor is very committed to my growth and development, and I'm able to have very honest discussions with him about the firm, where it's going, where I am going, etc.," shares one 10-year veteran of the firm.

Paying the piper

Although Monitor's compensation package is competitive with other top-tier consultancies, satisfaction levels do differ. "I'm pleased with my compensation," offers a Cambridge correspondent. "I feel that strong performers at Monitor are paid quite well and above industry average, and that type of meritocracy appeals to me." Meanwhile, a colleague in Boston shrugs, "Compensation seems pretty standard for consulting (given what other friends are earning at comparable firms)." Another insider clarifies, "We pay our strong performers above industry average and our average/good performers slightly below industry average." On the West Coast, a San Franciscan comments: "Within Monitor there is a perception that, on average, our compensation lags behind the other top-three consulting firms. That said, outstanding performers are compensated disproportionately well." This East Coaster, meanwhile, cites a beef with Monitor's raise policy, explaining that "the biggest frustration isn't how much we get paid, which is slightly lower than our close competitors, but how slow the compensation cycle is. You don't get your first raise until you've been here for over 18 months."

Throw that dog a bonus

Bonuses, on the other hand, are viewed by most as exceptional, and "can be up to 100 percent of base salary." "Bonuses are very strong," agrees a New York source. "Monitor really believes in the notion of disproportionately rewarding strong performers. As someone who has done well at the firm, I do believe that with salary and base combined, I have received a pay package that equals or exceeds my peers at other top consulting firms. However, I do think that during and after the third year, there is a disparity between strong performers at Monitor and those at other top consulting firms." A partner also clarifies that "this year [2006] is an exception regarding bonuses for partners. We are not receiving bonuses. The nonpartners are getting paid their full bonuses, so they will have very good years."

Sweetening the deal

Among the firm's benefits are "high-quality health [coverage], participation in investment activities, company shares for strong performance and a 401(k) plan" (though, a Cambridge staffer qualifies that the plan "does not match contributions. I hope this is an area they correct in the near future"). The firm also gives its employees the gift of time, with "generous" paid leave, "a week off at the end of the year" and sabbatical options. Additionally, Monitor offers "one year of tuition reimbursement for previous summer MBAs," "great social events," as well as "in-house laundry drop-off and pickup, gym and locker room, Friday office parties, free food and beautiful offices around the world." Brags a Boston source, "In most locations, everyone sits in an office, rather than cubicles."

Dedicated to giving back

Monitor participates and encourages its employees to engage in a number of community service and charity activities, many of which are grassroots efforts initiated by the firm itself. In fact, one source informs us, "Monitor has a separate business unit focused solely on community involvement." A New York consultant relates, "Monitor really encourages consultants to spend some of their time putting our skills and ideas toward helping those who can't afford consultants." A Cambridge source elaborates: "[We have an] incredible nonprofit community, with Inspire (pro bono consulting run by junior consultants), the Monitor Institute (a practice within the firm that works exclusively with nonprofits), and New Profit Inc., an affiliated venture philanthropy fund for which we do occasional pro bono cases." "Overall," agrees this staffer, "I feel like people at Monitor are pretty involved in and passionate about giving back to their communities, and Monitor definitely supports those efforts."

Visit the Vault Consulting Career Channel at **www.vault.com/consulting** - with insider firm profiles, message boards, the Vault Consulting Job Board and more.

VAULT CAREER LIBRARY   93

Teach me a lesson

Sources report that Monitor provides a mix of training opportunities, the bulk of which are informal. "Like all consulting firms, the primary source of learning is going to be on the job," asserts a Toronto source. "Training at Monitor consists of a centralized program as well as a local program. The central program accounts for about 25 percent of training hours with the local programs accounting for the remaining 75 percent." Lists a Cambridge consultant, "We have specific training modules on consulting tradecraft, interpersonal dynamics (like feedback or productive interactions) and content (like enterprise economics or customer dynamics), and one gets invited to different types of training throughout one's career. We do not do an extended training when one first starts, and instead rely initially on informal training and on-the-job training. I valued this type of training more when I first started because sitting in a classroom being taught about something before I've had a chance to experience it is not the optimal way for me to learn." Adds a colleague in the same office, "Given that there is so much patented, proprietary content to learn (we have phenomenal things to share with clients), I really like the fact we have our senior consultants teaching the tradecraft to new or more junior colleagues—it lends itself well to real-life examples, analogues and sharing best practices." A Boston consultant observes: "There is a lot of attention paid to mentoring and development here. Most is unofficial. That's far and away the predominant method of training. And people generally feel good about the development they have, the progress they make and the way they're supported by the firm on that dimension. We have a lot of strengths in this firm, but formal training isn't one of them. We think it's only one way to learn and not necessarily the best way."

Working toward a balanced blend

Monitor prides itself on the continuous building of a rich and diverse employee base. As a Cambridge consultant remarks, "Diversity at our junior levels is good, but we currently struggle at the more senior levels. This is an area of focus for us, and senior leadership has a number of initiatives under way to enhance our diversity." A colleague in the same office feels that "Monitor is investing heavily to improve" the balance, while another observes that the firm pursues "recruiting and community-building efforts" via diversity networks. An early adopter in providing partner benefits, Monitor has a diversity arm devoted specifically to gay and lesbian workers: "We have a GLBT network that focuses on community-building and recruiting activities." Comments a San Francisco colleague, "Monitor's efforts in GLBT hiring are the most impressive of any of its minority recruiting processes."

With regard to gender diversity, "Monitor has excellent representation for women at the junior levels and even at the junior partner levels, but fairly miserable representation at the higher levels," a New York source states. Agrees this female staffer, "At the higher levels there are very few women, which is slightly discouraging when I think about my longer-term career." A Cambridge consultant has noted that "women outnumber men in the firm's most successful unit (marketing strategy), although not at the senior-leader level." And a longtime female veteran has this to say: "We could always do more mentoring, but we have good records of promotions and hiring. We do face retention challenges in moving to partner levels, but as a female partner with two young kids, I truly believe women have a lot of opportunities here."

"I think Monitor works hard to make sure that it is a fun, exciting and entertaining place to work."

– Monitor associate

Visit the Vault Consulting Career Channel at **www.vault.com/consulting** - with insider firm profiles, message boards, the Vault Consulting Job Board and more.

VAULT CAREER LIBRARY

95

6

Mercer Management Consulting*

1166 Avenue of the Americas
New York, NY 10036
Phone: (212) 345-8000
www.oliverwyman.com

LOCATIONS

New York, NY (HQ)
Over 40 offices worldwide

PRACTICE AREAS

Automotive
Aviation, Aerospace & Defense
Communications, Media & Technology
Energy
Financial Services
Health & Life Sciences
Industrial Products & Services
Retail & Consumer Products
Surface Transportation

THE STATS

Employer Type: Subsidiary of Marsh & McLennan
Companies, Inc., a Public Company
Ticker Symbol: MMC (NYSE)
President & CEO: John P. Drzik
2007 Employees: 2,500+
2006 Employees: 2,000 (Mercer Management Consulting &
Mercer Oliver Wyman)
2007 Revenue: $1.2 billion (Oliver Wyman Group)

*As of May 2007, Oliver Wyman—General Management
Consulting*

RANKING RECAP

Quality of Life
#6 - Offices
#10 - Formal Training (tie)
#12 - Compensation
#19 - Work/Life Balance
#20 - Interaction with Clients

Diversity
#20 - Diversity for GLBT

UPPERS

- "Incredible MBA admission rates—90 percent get into school of first choice"
- "Unpretentious"
- "Relaxed firm culture"
- No face time requirement

DOWNERS

- "A small firm trapped in the body of a medium-to-large firm"
- "Easy to get lost in a firm that is growing at such an exponential pace"
- "The people could use some polishing"
- Experiencing some growing pains

EMPLOYMENT CONTACT

www.oliverwyman.com

THE BUZZ
WHAT CONSULTANTS AT OTHER FIRMS ARE SAYING ABOUT THIS FIRM

- "Lots of growth in North America"
- "Geek shop"
- "Fun and flexible"
- "Indistinguishable"

THE SCOOP

A blending of brands

Oliver Wyman was created from the May 2007 combination of three brands: Mercer Management Consulting, specializing in general management consulting; Mercer Oliver Wyman, focused on financial services consulting; and Mercer Delta Organizational Consulting, the organization and leadership consulting group. The new firm creates a single management consultancy under the umbrella of Marsh & McLennan Companies, which includes Marsh Inc., the largest insurance broker in the world. Oliver Wyman is the keystone of Oliver Wyman Group, which also encompasses corporate siblings Lippincott (brand, image and identity consulting) and NERA Economic Consulting. Today, Oliver Wyman consists of over 2,500 employees working out of 43 offices in 16 countries. In 2006, Oliver Wyman Group's revenue reached $1.24 billion, placing it among the top-four strategy consulting firms.

Headquartered in New York City, Oliver Wyman's strategic services are based on industry and practice expertise. Its practices encompass automotive; aviation, defense and aerospace; communications, media and technology; energy; financial services (corporate and institutional banking, insurance, retail and business banking); industrial products and services; health and life sciences; retail and consumer products; and surface transportation. The firm specializes in business transformation; organization and leadership; finance and risk; marketing and sales; operations and technology; and strategy—all geared toward a clientele made up of Fortune 1000 CEOs and executives.

A logical link

Industry observers might have seen the 2007 brand realignment coming after John Drzik, president of Mercer Oliver Wyman, stepped into the leadership spotlight in 2006 and launched a strategy review of the business, announcing his intention to draw Mercer's consulting businesses closer together. In his role, Drzik encouraged all divisions to exchange resources and cultivate clients collaboratively.

Financial finesse

The newly launched Oliver Wyman takes on the individual functions of its formerly separate three firms. The financial services and risk practice, a core group, was borne out of Mercer Oliver Wyman, which started in 1984 as Oliver, Wyman & Company—a group of ex-Booz Allen Hamilton and Boston Consulting Group consultants. From the outset, the New York-based group carved out its niche as the only major consultancy focused solely on the financial services industry covering both strategy and risk. The firm expanded in the U.K. and Canada in the 1980s, and added offices in Continental Europe and Asia-Pacific in the 1990s. In 2003, Oliver, Wyman & Company was brought into the fold of the Marsh & McLennan Companies, and became Mercer Oliver Wyman. Over the years, the firm has strengthened its financial consulting capabilities by buying up smaller consulting businesses around the globe. Today, its financial services clients include more than 75 percent of the world's top-100 financial institutions.

Taking strategy global

Oliver Wyman's general consulting business, which provides consulting services to corporations in a wide range of industries, was built under the Mercer Management Consulting brand. The firm was conceived in 1992, when Marsh & McLennan merged two of its smaller acquisitions. Since then, the firm has expanded its consulting practice by acquiring smaller consulting businesses internationally. Clients include many of the global Fortune 100 enterprises in all industry sectors and government organizations.

Visit the Vault Consulting Career Channel at www.vault.com/consulting - with insider firm profiles, message boards, the Vault Consulting Job Board and more.

VAULT CAREER LIBRARY   97

Leading leaders

Oliver Wyman's Delta Organization & Leadership practice began as Delta Consulting Group, which was founded by leadership guru David Nadler in 1980, and acquired by Mercer Inc. in 2000. These days, the practice covers organizational design and transformation, enterprise leadership and board effectiveness. Though it never trumpets its engagements, the group has worked with quite a few high-profile names in the past, including Johnson & Johnson, Avon Products, Citigroup, Coca-Cola, UBS and Unilever.

Acquiring a gem

Throughout its history, a string of strategic acquisitions has served to widen Oliver Wyman's service portfolio, the most recent of which occurred in April 2007. The company announced the acquisition of CAVOK International, a Texas-based consulting firm. CAVOK specializes in airframe maintenance solutions and air carrier certification support. The purchase boosted Oliver Wyman's aviation, aerospace and defense practice, which serves air carriers, maintenance repair overhaul providers, and banks and lending institutions that support the industry.

In July 2006, the firm made headlines when it purchased the European, South American and Middle Eastern consulting practices of Diamond Management & Technology Consultants, Inc. Included in the deal were Diamond's operations in Paris, Munich, Madrid, Barcelona, Dubai and São Paulo. The $30 million buyout sought to stretch the firm's IT and telecom capabilities globally, and created the second-largest consultancy in Europe in that sector. About 150 new strategy and operations consultants were brought on as part of the acquisition. In an effort to consolidate Diamond's operations with its own in those regions, the firm opened its newest office in Dubai Internet City in November 2006.

From New York to the world

Though its headquarters are in New York, Oliver Wyman retains an international flavor, with a large portion of its staffers hailing from Europe. Along with the U.K. branch, the firm maintains a major European presence out of its Frankfurt offices. The firm also boasts an established foothold in Asia Pacific. In China, for example, it acquired a solid client base over its 15 years of doing management consulting work in the country. The Shanghai office was opened in 2001, but even before that the firm was serving state-owned companies and large multinationals in the country. Many of the firm's published briefs share its intellectual capital on doing business in China, earned through its years of experience in the region. A 2006 report covered how to succeed in M&A in China, and another 2006 publication discussed the challenges of business-to-business selling in the country.

Prophets of profit

Oliver Wyman's studies and reports are widely circulated in its sectors of expertise. In March 2007, the firm published a report on mortgage trends in Europe. At the World Economic Forum in Davos, Switzerland, in January 2007, the firm presented the 10th annual State of the Financial Services Industry study. The study valued the industry at a record $10.7 trillion, and projected continued growth in 2007 and less M&A activity for the year. A November 2006 paper focused on investment opportunities in China, finding that the country is expected to account for 10 percent of the total increase in personal financial assets between now and 2015, second only to the U.S.

Over the past six years, Oliver Wyman execs have published a number of weighty business books on boosting profit and value. Management guru Adrian Slywotzky was described by *IndustryWeek* magazine as promising "to be what Peter Drucker was to much of the 20th century." A 2006 article in *The New York Times* featured an interview with Slywotzky on the topic of business innovation. Slywotzky's most recent title, co-authored with Karl Wolf, is *The Upside: The 7 Strategies for Turning Big Threats into Growth Breakthroughs*. Released in May 2007, *BusinessWeek* called the book "a thoughtful consideration of how risk can be managed for the good." Slywotzky's 2002 book, *The Art of Profitability*, walks readers through 23 lessons on improving profitability without breaking relationships. Other titles written by Mercer consultants include *How Digital Is Your Business?*, *Value Nets*, *Profit Patterns*, *The Profit Zone*, *Value Migration* and *Grow to Be Great*.

Polishing people skills

The firm's leadership research is a mainstay of the organization and leadership practice, reflected in publications such as the May 2006 book *Head, Heart & Guts: How the World's Best Companies Develop Complete Leaders*, by leadership heavy hitters David L. Dotlich, Peter C. Cairo and Stephen H. Rhinesmith (the original founders of CDR International). As the title suggests, the authors argue that along with analytical skills, leaders must also come equipped with "heart" (defined as emotional intelligence), and "guts" (a willingness to take risks, backed up by strong values). Another recent book is the 2006 *Building Better Boards: A Blueprint for Effective Governance*, authored by David Nadler, along with Beverly A. Behan and Mark B. Nadler, which tackles the often contentious topic of how to get corporate board members to work as a team.

Oliver Wyman's prolific staff also pens shorter works, like journals and white papers, on relevant management and strategy topics. In January 2007, the firm published a study on the demand for home communications and entertainment services in Spanish households, jointly conducted with Banco Santander. Another Mercer study in 2007 investigated ways utility companies can update aging infrastructure.

GETTING HIRED

An interview in three acts

It seems logical that a top-tier firm would seek out recruits from top-tier schools, which Oliver Wyman certainly does—the Ivies, UVA and Stanford make up a bulk of the firm's "core" campus recruiting network, with Williams, Northwestern, Oxford and the University of Michigan making it into the apex as well.

Once recruiters select eligible undergrad applicants, Oliver Wyman's "very rigorous" three-round procedure commences. For the financial services track, round one is made up of a 30-minute case interview and a 30-minute resume interview. A consultant in the financial services track recounts, "The second round is a Super Saturday with five interviews (three cases, two behavioral)." For the general management track, rounds one and two consist of 30- to 45-minutes cases and resume interviews with a number of additional 30- to 45-minute segments in the final stage, where contenders discuss "two longer cases, plus an interview entirely dedicated to fit." Candidates in the general management consulting track also relocate from respective campuses to their Oliver Wyman office of choice for the last interview leg, and should expect at least one lengthy resume review squeezed into the process. Insiders cite "basic profit/loss, market-sizing, investment decision cases" and "niche industry growth strategy" problems as potential case puzzles for candidates to work through.

Assures a consultant, "Applicants are unlikely to face brainteasers or 'pressure interviews.' Interviewers generally project a laid-back but professional approach to the sessions and encourage applicants to be at ease. Doing so allows us to get a more realistic read on the work that someone would do and what the experience of working with that person would be like."

Flex those math muscles

Off-cycle hires in the general management consulting track say there's an initial 20-minute math test "given prior to interviews," followed by phone case interviews and two subsequent in-office sessions. Staffers describe the whole process as "fair, thorough and multileveled," and say that it normally lasts from two to four weeks. And whether offered a position or not, "every interviewee gets feedback on why it did/didn't work," a perk that one employee calls "unique in the industry."

Visit the Vault Consulting Career Channel at **www.vault.com/consulting** - with insider firm profiles, message boards, the Vault Consulting Job Board and more.

99

OUR SURVEY SAYS

The slipper fits

"The firm's culture is one of total openness," we're told, where "people are genuinely friends as well as colleagues," and "often go out together after work or on the weekends." And while the firm is highly entrepreneurial in nature, its bottom-up structure alleviates an otherwise overbearing top-down model; in other words, the firm is "not stuffy," comments a colleague, which allows for a "very close-knit" team. One insider calls the firm "collegial and noncompetitive," adding that "there's an impressive balance of the desire for excellence with down-to-earth people." Staffers also appreciate Oliver Wyman's merit-based atmosphere, which leaves room for individual recognition. Shares a director, "Everyone loves to talk about their colleagues' accomplishments," and insiders say the firm is filled with "incredibly accomplished people who are friendly, considerate and self-effacing." A consultant sums up his experience: "This really is a Cinderella firm. My experience here has been so wonderful, I can't complain about anything."

Rubbing elbows

Oliver Wyman isn't afraid to nudge consultants into conducting tête-à-têtes with senior-level clients. In fact, as one newer hire boasts, "I've had more cases where I met the CEO/COO/CFO than cases when I didn't, which tells you something about the exposure here at Oliver Wyman." A colleague asserts, "Considering my level, I have had the opportunity to attend numerous high-level meetings or conference calls with CEOs and CFOs of Fortune 500 companies. Did I contribute much? Absolutely not ... but it was a great experience nonetheless." Another staffer confirms, "Meritocracy is excellent, giving even junior consultants many management opportunities." This elevated client responsibility and exposure given to staffers is "unique," according to insiders, and with the firm's "excellent case managers almost across the board," more often than not, consultants end up meeting "with C-level execs and almost always have some contact with VP-level execs."

Junior employees say relations with their own management are also cozy. "We have fantastic directors and consultants that are continually training and mentoring first- and second-years," an insider raves. A co-worker elaborates: "Directors and consultants sit and work side by side. We share flights, cabs, cubicles and dinners. Because of the strong culture and youth of the firm, it is very easy to forge very strong relationships with people at all levels in the firm."

Be your own manager

At this firm, work hours heavily depend on the case at hand. "At times, hours can get pretty demanding, sometimes reaching 100-plus hours per week," remarks a source, but many also work a "relatively low number of hours here, due to long and relatively manageable cases." One insider attests to the case-based variable dictating his load schedule: "I'm working 50-hour weeks, but for six months this summer I worked 80-hour weeks regularly." Apparently, those 80-hour weeks are more the exception than the norm. "On occasion, consultants work until 9, 10, 11 p.m., but these are rarities. We leave at 5:30 or 6 as (if not more) often," assures one senior source.

Some consultants figure that the amount of hours worked is largely dependant on how individual consultants' manage their time. A staffer claims, "With work/life balance, work hours are what you make them. If you can work productively and quickly, there is no need to put in face time during late nights. When and if your tastes run more toward long, leisurely workdays or intense catching up on weekends, that is an option as well." A number of insiders say that achieving a manageable balance "is what you make it." One consultant, who says he makes time for personal travel, keeping in touch with pals and brushing up on his Spanish, comments, "I think that the firm does a good job of providing staff options for how to balance things, but the impetus is on the individual to figure out what the right balance is for you, and how best to achieve that balance."

And for those who are able to manage their workloads during the week, working weekends is not expected of most employees. "Having weekends free is a key aspect for me. There has only been one time in my 18 months with the firm when my manager specifically asked me to work a full day on the weekend," recalls a consultant.

The burnout blockade

Staffers do name Oliver Wyman's hour-uncertain intensity as an occasional hindrance in obtaining a satisfactory work/life balance, but most say the firm's management does its best to accommodate employee needs. "Consulting work is notoriously difficult to balance," shares a consultant, "but the firm makes a concerted effort to keep you from burning yourself out." Others agree that "managers are easy to approach and amenable to compromise regarding work/life balance," offering multiple incentives and alternative planning schedules to staffers with demanding lives outside the firm. Adds a source, "There are 'burnout reports' for people who are working too many hours, and case managers are admonished to either set more realistic expectations with the client or increase the size of the case team." For especially bushed colleagues, "it is not unheard of for a manager to authorize a midweek trip home to have a special dinner with his spouse or attend a child's school play," and the firm sometimes offers 10- or 11-month years for professionals.

The road frequently traveled

"If you like traveling, this is your firm," exclaims a source. And while travel varies case by case, most Oliver Wyman employees report spending four days on site with clients. "Travel is pretty much a constant," notes a colleague, especially since the firm staffs internationally—although we're told that staffers generally "have 'veto power' over international assignments. "Domestic travel is expected; global travel does take away from ability to build up 'home,'" but insiders do acknowledge the need for direct client interaction, and say that managers try to be "very sensitive to balancing work and life and minimizing unnecessary travel." "I've found a way to balance my cases, where if I need to travel a lot for one case, I've had a case that wasn't as travel-intensive afterwards," one second-year articulates, exemplifying the firm's accommodating style.

Still, colleagues admit that being constantly on the go can get old. "Traveling definitely wears you out after a while. I wish we would adopt a policy of traveling when we really need to, as opposed to traveling as the status quo," an insider says. But on the bright side, you probably won't be sent to Podunk, according to another source: "On the whole, the destinations are nice places to be (Washington, Boston, London, etc.) and the team environment typically makes it fun, but there's no question that it's a traveling lifestyle and if that's not for you then the firm's not for you."

Friday reunion

No matter where Oliver Wyman consultants may roam during the week, Fridays are sanctioned as in-office days, which seem to be welcomed by employees. While face time with clients is vital, sources say, "Fridays back in the office are important and valued by directors and consultants." "Travel makes coming home to the office on Fridays a great reunion. You typically travel with your teams back to [your home office] on Thursday evening. Friday happy hours in the lunchroom usually consist of amusing stories from the week," an insider shares.

School yourself

For the most part, consultants subscribe to a do-it-yourself instruction model at Oliver Wyman. "Other than an initial two weeks of training, other training is often organized by consultants on an ad hoc basis," an insider states. "We have a good mix of official and unofficial training," adds one director, but colleagues claim that the unofficial, on-the-job teaching is most valuable to their development. And, we're told, the formal approach is a fairly new one at the firm. "There is an effort made at official training, but more could be done," shares a source, though "it's improved dramatically in the last year or two." According to a co-worker, "Consulting truly is an apprenticeship model. No matter how much formal training one receives, 90 percent of real learning will be on the job."

Moneyspeak

At Oliver Wyman, the compensation is competitive, although the "compensation structure is confusing" and "highly dependent upon the promotion schedule," one source gripes. Another staffer adds that the "firm only tries to match other competitors, but doesn't match cost of living increases, which can be annoying" when working from expensive cities like Boston, New York and

Visit the Vault Consulting Career Channel at www.vault.com/consulting - with insider firm profiles, message boards, the Vault Consulting Job Board and more.

VAULT CAREER LIBRARY   101

San Francisco. Explains one consultant, "Most firms pay each employee level the same base salary and give performance-based bonuses. We do the opposite. We give base salary raises based on performance, so after a year you may be making a different base than the colleagues in your class."

But base pay quips aside, the salary is "very competitive, particularly for top performers who receive excellent bonuses," according to an insider. One source notes, "The bonus is flat for all employees—if declared at 50 percent, everyone gets 50 percent of salary. So this is highly equitable and promotes cooperation." "I would be surprised if any other consulting firm had higher levels of average compensation than Oliver Wyman," surmises a manager. In addition, a consultant explains that "for staffers who take case assignments in far-flung areas of the globe (as measured by number of time zones between case location and home office), a long-haul travel incentive payment of 20 to 35 percent of base is paid each month beyond the second month on such a case," as well as "a budget for personal travel and flights for spouses or friends to visit you"—all of which makes time away from home "a bit easier to manage." Travel per diems also help to kick in a little extra dough. "Don't forget expenses! I make money just by not being in New York," exclaims a colleague. And according to another insider, the firm offers a "through-the-ranks" bonus paid to those who delay business school to stay with the firm.

On top of bonus, the firm offers staffers a discounted stock investment plan with matching contributions, "great benefits coverage (health care, dependent care, legal, etc.)," paid paternity and maternity leave, and a retirement plan that "can be increased based on firm performance."

Jet-setting perks

Oliver Wyman consultants don't fight the firm's protracted benefits list. Not only does it grant small-scale perks like Friday drinks, a snack closet and sporting events tickets, but employees laud much heftier benefits. Traveling consultants seem to love the personal vacations between workweeks: "Because we have a flexible travel budget, we can essentially fly anywhere for the weekends within the budget. This means that I have been to Puerto Rico twice, skiing in Salt Lake City, home to Los Angeles several times, and to Boston and Minnesota to visit friends," boasts one insider. Another source notes that performance rewards can be nice, declaring, "Someone won a two-week leadership training course in Antarctica."

For the general management track, along with externship opportunities, MBA sponsorships and paid leave (40 percent of salary) for nonprofit fellowships, the firm allows employees to work a "10/11-month year (prorated salary for one to two months off)"—a sabbatical that sources say "does not adversely affect one's career and allows many employees to pursue interesting, satisfying 'second careers.'" For example, one consultant notes, "I spent three months skiing in my third year."

Foosball, anyone?

Oliver Wyman's offices don't offer as much in the way of perks, we're told. Boston employees label their laboring quarters as "comfortable" and "modern," with fun amenities like flat-screen TVs and a foosball table. "Hancock Tower is a great place," notes a source, while other staffers commend the spatial dimensions and professional atmosphere. The New York office is described as having a "minimalistic modern open layout"—though several interpret the minimalist sentiment as "starved for space," and one colleague there complains about the "truck driver stop-level washrooms." And in Dallas, "facilities are not as nice/progressive as those of my prior firm or of other firms," a director gripes.

The diversity rub

One higher-up says Oliver Wyman does "a great job with hiring, promoting [and] mentoring women, and they are not differentiated from men in that regard," but the firm runs into difficulty when it comes to retaining women through the senior levels. As a colleague states, "I think we try very hard to recruit women, but we deal with the same challenges that most firms face in attracting female talent." A New York-based consultant expresses the firm's need for more senior women: "We have good hiring and mentoring. But in practice, few women are promoted to director." "Many of the women that are attracted by our work/life balance philosophy eventually get sick of the travel, especially if they want to start a family," an insider acknowledges.

As far as racial and ethnic minorities at Oliver Wyman, insiders remark that just as with women, recruitment is tricky. Explains a source, "The numbers (specifically of American-born minorities) that we get are pretty low right from the beginning of the recruitment process and info sessions, even though the pull-through and retention rates are pretty good." Concerning sexual orientation, staffers say that there's a very "active and open gay community" at the firm, and assert that there's no shortage of "very diverse colleagues in terms of gays [and] lesbians."

Charitable moves

To help out its neighboring communities, some offices take part in numerous charity efforts, including those surrounding Hurricane Katrina relief, September 11th and others in the form of annual auctions, volunteer outings and "frequent drives for food, clothing, school supplies and toiletries." The Boston office "has a charity auction each year that raises over $50,000 for Boston Cares, a citywide charity organization that helps homeless, impoverished and other groups across the city." And in Dallas, consultants participate in marathons and triathlon events "to raise money and awareness for MS and MS research," sources say. On a more global scale, "recently, staff have completed three- to six-month [paid] fellowships with microlending firms in Malawi and AIDS awareness groups in Ethiopia," we're told, with "pro bono consulting projects on an office-by-office basis." Through all its community and charity efforts, colleagues tout Oliver Wyman as "extremely active, both as a firm and through the efforts of individuals within the firm."

As of May 2007, Oliver Wyman—General Management Consulting

Visit the Vault Consulting Career Channel at **www.vault.com/consulting** - with insider firm profiles, message boards, the Vault Consulting Job Board and more.

V/\ULT CAREER LIBRARY   103

Mercer Oliver Wyman*

1166 Avenue of the Americas
New York, NY 10036
Phone: (212) 345-8000
www.oliverwyman.com

LOCATIONS

New York, NY (HQ)
Over 40 offices worldwide

PRACTICE AREAS

Automotive
Aviation, Aerospace & Defense
Communications, Media & Technology
Energy
Financial Services
Health & Life Sciences
Industrial Products & Services
Retail & Consumer Products
Surface Transportation

THE STATS

Employer Type: Subsidiary of Marsh & McLennan
  Companies, Inc., a Public Company
Ticker Symbol: MMC (NYSE)
President & CEO: John P. Drzik
2007 Employees: 2,500+
2006 Employees: 2,000 (Mercer Management Consulting &
  Mercer Oliver Wyman)
2007 Revenue: $1.2 billion (Oliver Wyman Group)

As of May 2007, Oliver Wyman—Financial Services
**See p.96 for a full profile on Oliver Wyman*

RANKING RECAP

Practice Area
#3 - Financial Consulting

Quality of Life
#2 - Compensation
#10 - Work/Life Balance
#13 - Best Firms to Work For
#16 - Overall Satisfaction
#16 - Hours in the Office

Diversity
#19 - Diversity for GLBT

UPPERS

- "Incredible MBA admission rates—90 percent get into school of first choice"
- "Unpretentious"
- "Relaxed firm culture"
- No face time requirement

DOWNERS

- "A small firm trapped in the body of a medium-to-large firm"
- "Easy to get lost in a firm that is growing at such an exponential pace"
- "The people could use some polishing"
- Experiencing some growing pains

EMPLOYMENT CONTACT

www.oliverwyman.com

THE BUZZ
WHAT CONSULTANTS AT OTHER FIRMS ARE SAYING ABOUT THIS FIRM

- "Lots of growth in North America"
- "Geek shop"
- "Fun and flexible"
- "Indistinguishable"

"I've had more cases where I met the CEO/COO/CFO than cases when I didn't, which tells you something about the exposure here at Oliver Wyman."

- Oliver Wyman insider

Visit the Vault Consulting Career Channel at **www.vault.com/consulting** - with insider firm profiles, message boards, the Vault Consulting Job Board and more.

VAULT CAREER LIBRARY   105

Deloitte Consulting LLP

1633 Broadway, 35th Floor
New York, NY 10019
Phone: (212) 492-4500
Fax: (212) 492-4743
www.deloitte.com

LOCATIONS

New York, NY (HQ)
Offices in every major business market across the US, along with access to audit, tax, consulting and financial advisory professionals in nearly 150 countries through the member firms of Deloitte Touche Tohmatsu (DTT)

PRACTICE AREAS

Enterprise Applications
Extended Business Services
Human Capital
Strategy & Operations
Business IT Strategy • Corporate Strategy • Customer & Market Strategy • Financial Management • Mergers & Acquisitions • Performance Improvement • Supply Chain & Operations
Technology Integration

THE STATS

Employer Type: Subsidiary of Deloitte & Touche USA LLP, US Member Firm of Deloitte Touche Tohmatsu
Chairman & CEO: Doug Lattner
Global Consulting Managing Partner: Ainar D. Aijala Jr.
2006 Employees: 43,000 (DTT Member Firm Consulting & Advisory)
2005 Employees: 39,000 (DTT Member Firm Consulting & Advisory)
2006 Revenue: $7.7 billion (DTT Member Firm Consulting & Advisory)
2005 Revenue: $7.1 billion (DTT Member Firm Consulting & Advisory)

THE BUZZ
WHAT CONSULTANTS AT OTHER FIRMS ARE SAYING ABOUT THIS FIRM

- "Stable, good growth and reputation"
- "Just too big"
- "Excellent for minorities"
- "Rigid and bureaucratic"

RANKING RECAP

Practice Area
#2 - Operational Consulting
#4 - Pharmaceutical & Health Care Consulting
#5 - Financial Consulting
#5 - Human Resources Consulting
#6 - Energy Consulting
#8 - Economic Consulting (tie)

Quality of Life
#9 - Formal Training
#14 - Relationships with Supervisors
#20 - Firm Culture

Diversity
#11 - Best Firms for Diversity
#11 - Diversity for GLBT
#11 - Diversity for Women
#14 - Diversity for Minorities

UPPERS

- "We work like a well-oiled machine"
- "The firm treats everyone as you would hope a company would treat its people"
- Assistance paying for grad school
- "A premium placed on work/life balance"

DOWNERS

- "Performance evaluations, project assignments and raises are determined in a fraternity-style environment, instead of by genuine merit"
- Less than competitive salary
- "No ability to transfer to other international offices"
- "You have to be flawless or you are just average"

EMPLOYMENT CONTACT

careers.deloitte.com

THE SCOOP

Bucking the trend

Created in 1995, Deloitte Consulting LLP is the consulting entity within the professional services firm, Deloitte & Touche USA LLP. Deloitte was the only firm of the Big Four that retained its consulting arm in the wake of the accounting scandal associated with Andersen and Enron. But it wasn't intended to be that way. After Enron's collapse forced the other big accounting players to break off their consulting practices to avoid a conflict of interest, Deloitte & Touche USA considered rebranding its consulting practice as Braxton. However, due to several factors, including the market slump in 2002, all plans for Braxton were scrapped, and instead, Deloitte Consulting remained a subsidiary of Deloitte & Touche USA. Though the past few years weren't exactly smooth going, Deloitte Consulting seems to have successfully come through its organizational turmoil unscathed. In 2007, Deloitte & Touche USA was named to *Fortune* magazine's list of the 100 Best Companies to Work for the eighth time.

Category of one

When Deloitte & Touche USA decided to keep its consulting business together with its other functions, it became a category of one. Analysts were initially skeptical, but the firm has driven double-digit growth every year since 2004. The result? The Deloitte U.S. entities are able to put together multidisciplinary teams with a broad array of talent—covering strategy, technology and human capital, as well as financial advice, risk management and tax planning. Deloitte Consulting divides its expertise into five service areas: enterprise applications, human capital, extended business services, strategy and operations, and technology integration. Deloitte Consulting's clients are in industries such as consumer business, health care, financial services, manufacturing, public sector, energy, real estate, telecom, media and technology.

Names of note

After CEO Doug McCracken announced his retirement after the split-off plans were terminated, Doug Lattner was chosen to lead Deloitte Consulting in 2003. Lattner, former global energy practice leader, was immediately confronted with the challenging task of getting things in order and determining which service areas would serve which clients. It's his reportedly "mild-mannered" leadership approach, along with his track record with clients, that earned him a place on *Consulting Magazine*'s Top 25 Most Influential Consultants in 2005.

Other Deloitte Consulting professionals have won recognition for their experience and accomplishments both in and out of the consulting arena. Principal Lee Ditmar was honored as one of *Consulting Magazine*'s Top 25 Most Influential Consultants list in 2006, and ranked among *Treasury & Risk Management* magazine's 2006 list of the 100 most influential people in finance. Tonie Leatherberry, another principal, also earned a spot on *Consulting Magazine*'s Top 25 list in 2006. Leatherberry is a specialist in human capital, governance and compliance. Principal Ainar D. Aijala Jr., recently named global managing partner for consulting, was appointed chairman of the board of directors of the global Junior Achievement organization in April 2006.

The Deloitte U.S. entities also attract well-known industry specialists. In October 2006, Tom Ridge, former two-term governor of Pennsylvania and first U.S. Secretary of Homeland Security, began serving as a senior advisor to the Deloitte U.S. entities state government industry group. John Hagel, a prolific author and a leading specialist on technology, innovation and strategy, joined Deloitte Consulting in May 2007 to serve as co-chairman of a new center for strategy and technology. Donald Ogilvie, former president and chief executive officer of the American Bankers Association, began serving in September 2006 as an independent senior advisor to Deloitte U.S. entities' banking and finance industry group.

Strategy and systems

A number of public-sector departments have called upon Deloitte Consulting's strategy and tech implementation services in recent years. In October 2006, Deloitte Consulting's specialists in education and public-sector service were chosen by the U.S. government to help address a growing concern about migrant students falling through the safety net. The project involved

Visit the Vault Consulting Career Channel at **www.vault.com/consulting** - with insider firm profiles, message boards, the Vault Consulting Job Board and more.

VAULT CAREER LIBRARY

107

developing a migrant student information exchange, linking students and state migrant education programs, and improving data collection, accuracy and timeliness of the information. In 2006, Deloitte & Touche LLP signed a General Services Administration contract, in partnership with the Department of Homeland Security Strategic Sourcing Acquisition Systems program office, to support DHS/SSAS strategic sourcing initiatives. Under the agreement, Deloitte Consulting will consult with program offices, program management and various projects and business functions within the scope of the program. The firm also secured an indefinite-delivery/indefinite-quantity contract to support the implementation of the Department of the Navy Financial Improvement Plan in 2004.

Bringing value back

Deloitte Consulting's engagements often revolve around helping clients find ways to increase shareholder value or return to financial health. Recently, the firm helped a technology company in its efforts to boost its share price. The services involved supporting three multibillion-dollar strategic divestitures simultaneously, a $450 million global cost reduction program and the restructuring of the company's shared services. Another client, a major Southeast U.S. health system suffering from profitability woes, called on Deloitte Consulting for transformational reorganization. Consultants helped the client develop and implement clinical, operational and financial initiatives in an effort to reverse a three-year tide of heavy losses and return the system to financial stability.

In praise of pricing

A recent health care engagement served by Deloitte Consulting's customer and market strategy service line professionals involved a diagnostic products provider that was confronting pricing and margin pressures because of globalization. In addition, this client was facing the dreaded "commoditization" of its technology, making it difficult to differentiate its product and demand higher prices from customers. Deloitte Consulting's mission was to help the client identify opportunities for improvement that had the largest potential impact. Using transactional pricing analyses, consultants helped the client identify six opportunities with projected benefits to the bottom line.

Megamergers

M&A is one of the Deloitte U.S. entities' key areas of specialization. More than 2,000 of their M&A professionals have been involved in helping clients worldwide in complex M&A deals over the last several years. Supporting one of the largest bank mergers in history, professionals from several of the Deloitte U.S. entities helped the client combine mission-critical operating systems, directed activities of 2,000 IT operations and completed integration of the two technical environments. Professionals from several of the Deloitte U.S. entities also helped a global medical device manufacturer, close its "merged" books, after having acquired the target only three months earlier.

Fighting disease, digitally

Deloitte Consulting has attracted attention for the way it integrates research and strategy with tech innovations. The prenatal and newborn screening system that the firm helped develop with the state of California made headlines in 2005, winning a Best of California award from the Center for Digital Government. Deloitte Consulting worked with the state of Pennsylvania to help it design and build the Pennsylvania National Electronic Disease Surveillance System, a secure web-based tool used by medical and public health professionals in disease reporting, surveillance and case management. The system—the first fully integrated disease surveillance system in the U.S.—won the Davies Award sponsored by the Healthcare Information and Management Systems Society in 2005.

Sharing information

Deloitte Research, a part of Deloitte Services LP, produces a steady stream of reports, surveys and commentaries that deal with a broad range of current issues. Recent topics include strategic planning, talent management, international sourcing, the global economy, and industry-specific issues. In addition, Deloitte Research is home to Michael E. Raynor, co-author with Clayton M. Christensen, of the best-selling *The Innovator's Solution*. Raynor also authored a recently released business book, *The Strategy Paradox*.

Specialists from the Deloitte U.S. entities sound off through a series of *Deloitte Insight* podcasts, which listeners can subscribe to or download by topic of interest. One example, *Adopting the Value Habit (And Unleashing More Value for Your Stakeholders)*, is a podcast featuring Bob Dalton, a Deloitte Consulting principal, and Brent Wortman, a Deloitte Inc., partner in Canada, discussing the challenges of creating value within a company through vision and strategy.

Notable and nice

Deloitte & Touche USA and its people often receive awards for their support of women and minorities in the industry. Continuing a 12-year winning streak, *Working Mother* magazine named Deloitte & Touche USA one of the 100 Best companies for Working Mothers. Deloitte & Touche USA won a spot on *LATINA Style* magazine's 2006 list of 50 Best Companies for Latinas in 2006. DTT member firm Deloitte Canada, Deloitte Inc., was ranked in 2007 one of the 50 Best Companies to Work For in Canada, according to a study by Hewitt Associates, and also made *Canadian Business* magazine's list of the Best Workplaces in Canada—in both 2006 and in 2007. And, DTT member firm Deloitte United Kingdom, Deloitte MCS Ltd., was named in 2006 as one of *The Times* top-50 Where Women Want to Work employers.

Deloitte & Touche USA reports that women make up 19.3 percent of its partners, principals and directors, a few points ahead of its competitors. *The Women's Initiative* blog, hosted by Cathy Benko, a principal at Deloitte Consulting, provides a forum for women to share ideas and experiences about the workplace.

Socially aware

Deloitte makes a point of giving back to communities in many ways. The firm is heavily involved with Junior Achievement Worldwide, ranked as the organization's fourth-largest volunteer. In addition, the firm launched a $1 million Excellence through Ethics scholarship initiative to promote ethics education among young people.

GETTING HIRED

Scouring the top 25

Deloitte Consulting has widespread campus recruiting efforts in place at many of the top-25 MBA programs, including Kellogg, Harvard, Columbia, Stern, Wharton, UCLA, INSEAD and London School of Economics. An insider says, "Deloitte Consulting does a great job interviewing on campus. It is a one-day interview process; all required decision makers assemble on campus and complete two rounds of interviews.

The campus interview process tends to be fairly quick, according to an analyst: "Deloitte Consulting's interview and hiring process is one of the fastest. I had a first-round behavioral interview on campus and waited that night for my second-round/final call. That same week, I went to the Philadelphia office and had two back-to-back interviews. One was behavioral with a short logic case, and the next was the typical consulting case. I knew I had an offer within two weeks."

At minimum, candidates will encounter at least three interviews. "The hiring process was friendly and efficient. I got to know my interviewers and learned a lot from the interview itself, including how honest and straightforward the people at Deloitte Consulting are. At the EYO (Explore Your Offer) Day, I met principals at Deloitte Consulting who I could tell cared very much about their staff and were supportive and encouraging of staff development," a business analyst recounts. "Relative to other firms, Deloitte Consulting has a similar format, but perhaps less rigorous. I had one interview on campus, one interview in office and that is it. Nothing out of the ordinary, although I have heard that they are starting to ask brainteasers—more market sizing or estimating though—and nonstandard cases," explains a colleague.

Visit the Vault Consulting Career Channel at **www.vault.com/consulting** - with insider firm profiles, message boards, the Vault Consulting Job Board and more.

VAULT CAREER LIBRARY   109

Seeking "softer qualities"

According to sources, an example of a case question is, "Analyze trash company: Here are brief stats. Now estimate revenue, costs and profits, and identify revenue growth opportunities. Estimate the impact of the opportunities identified." One source states, "My case interview was about finding the right price point for a luxury pet food. It was more theoretical versus actually cranking out the numbers, which I thought was much more useful in terms of having a discussion about the concepts at play." Though case questions are used, they aren't the sole basis for making hiring decisions. "In general, the hiring process seems to be based on matching prior skill sets and experiences with current or imminent market opportunities. Also, we tend to hire on the softer qualities, such as: how engaging is this person; how articulate is this person; would I want to work with this person around the clock, and so on," a manager explains.

OUR SURVEY SAYS

No bullies allowed

No matter which office you mention, colleagues cheer the welcoming team spirit that pervades the firm. "One of Deloitte Consulting's big strengths is culture. People are very collegial, embrace diversity and try to build relationships beyond work," declares one insider. A big buzzword among these folks is "collaboration"—everyone claims Deloitte Consulting is full of it. "The culture is one of collaboration, for certain," a source says, and another Deloitte Consulting consultant confirms, "My firm fosters a very interactive, collaborative culture that encourages individual and collective success." A manager states, "I believe Deloitte Consulting has one of the best cultures of any management consulting firm. It is open, honest and very collegial." While the culture is described as "pleasant" and "supportive," insiders explain that doesn't necessarily mean there isn't a serious side to Deloitte Consulting. "This is a nice culture, but should not be mistaken for being unwilling to make the tough decisions. What it means is that jerks are kept to a minimum and bullying behavior is not acceptable, regardless of whether you are a 'star' or not," an associate explains.

BFF

To hear these respondents talk about their co-workers, you'd think they were referring to old buddies from summer camp. "Coming in as an analyst, I expected my peers to be smart, motivated and diverse professionals. They met and exceeded my expectations; some of my colleagues are now also my best friends. The network I have here will stay with me for the rest of my life," a newbie beams. Says a colleague, "I came and remain at Deloitte Consulting because of the people and culture. I have been here almost three years and some of my closest friends are also my colleagues." One cohort goes Hallmark on us when reflecting on the bonding that takes place on an engagement: "It can be hard to say goodbye to team members when the project is over."

Deloitte Consulting's friendliness also is a plus when it comes to charting your career. Says a happy staffer, "From analysts through top-tier partners, it is by far the most comfortable work environment I know of among my friends who joined consulting and banking following undergrad. The social networking events held practically every Friday, in and outside the office, enable you the option to network into groups that do work you'd like to be involved in," adding, "Every new person you meet at Deloitte Consulting is happy to refer you to an upper level they know in the area you're seeking. Because Deloitte Consulting, the firm, can only truly succeed with the success, development and investment of its junior practitioners who begin their paths of developing long-term client relationships from the bottom up."

Better than banking

Deloitte Consulting insiders admit to working hard, but say that the average 50- to 60-hour weeks are not too difficult. "So long as the work is interesting and impactful to developing our firm's qualifications and strategic positioning in the marketplace, and so long as there is palpable value realized by the client, then I don't really mind having bursts of time where I work extremely long days," relates a source. A second-year consultant admits, "Hours are not nearly as much as banking, and the firm requires less face time once you get rolling." Insiders claim that hours depend on the group and the project, ranging "from 40 hours a week to 70, with other nonclient work on top of that." Hours also vary by service area or industry group, we're told. Says a staffer, "I do M&A work and, given the current market conditions, all M&A practitioners across all firms and investment banks and legal firms are working a lot of hours." One staffer in the government industry group admits to having a lighter workload: "Federal projects tend to have lower hours than commercial projects. I'm in the federal practice, and have been staffed solely on federal projects for two years now."

Doing the firm's work

In addition to billable hours, many Deloitte Consulting professionals take on some additional roles within the firm, such as running the analyst program for the five Bay Area offices. Says one staffer, "Some of my hours at Deloitte Consulting are spent on internal projects that I choose to be involved in. Sometimes these activities require large time commitments, but I prefer to have that over not being involved in my office community."

Like hours, the length of projects also fluctuates widely. "Average engagements are not supposed to be more than six months, and typically because of the business analyst rotational program, we are true to the six-month policy. I have been ... a rare case and have spent close to a year on two projects. This is rare for a business analyst," a source explains. For most consultants, engagements tend to last under one year, and generally "range from a few weeks, to three to eight months."

Life on the outside

Sources say that weekend work isn't required, and that overall flexibility with work hours contributes to a pretty satisfying work/life balance. "After-hours and weekend work is often voluntary. Managers do not force their resources to monitor e-mail and do work in the evenings or weekends, but most do in an effort to differentiate themselves," explains an insider. A colleague declares, "Balance is very reasonable. I am all for working hard and getting a lot done, but then getting out and having a life. While there are times that this gets pushed [aside], overall, the expectations have been reasonable."

Consultants say they are able to make up for rough weeks by taking some personal time off when needed. "Hours are entirely manageable—more often than not, if you have a really high-burn project four days a week that maxes out above 45 hours, the lead on your project will encourage you to work half a day Friday, or take the day off and manage your personal life. As long as you charge the client the true hours you're working, nothing more and nothing less, the firm is happy with your output and supports whatever you need to do to manage your work/life balance," a respondent insists. Another factor that helps maintain balance is the ability to work remotely, according to an employee: "Working from home is quite usual—the lower work hours allow me to pursue other things that are important to me."

Tripping

Though insiders claim that balance is good overall, the one thing that can throw it out of whack is extensive travel. A consultant says, "It is nice to be with the client, but I am always exhausted from the travel and it's hard to build a culture or relationships in the local office when you're there one day a week or less. Many people work from home or client site on Friday." Urges a colleague, "So long as staffing takes place regionally, the travel will have a less negative impact on one's health. Being out of town and on site at a client allows folks to truly focus on work and the client quite intensively Monday through Thursday. At times, I very much enjoy compartmentalizing my work that way, but this can be extremely challenging to cram quality into a weekend." Long term, some insiders think travel on such a scale just isn't doable. "The travel can be fun and exciting at times, but for the most part, it just wears me out and makes me less likely to stay with consulting for the long term," admits a manager.

Insiders are quick to add that Deloitte Consulting has policies to mitigate the negatives of being on the road. "My first year in the firm, I spent over 100 nights in a hotel. Travel is a fundamental part of the job, but programs such as '3-4-5' (three nights on the road, four days at the client, fifth day—Friday—in the home office) help to minimize the negative aspects of travel," assures a source. Some consultants make the best of their away location by making it a base for personal travel. "Traveling can

Visit the Vault Consulting Career Channel at **www.vault.com/consulting** - with insider firm profiles, message boards, the Vault Consulting Job Board and more.

VAULT CAREER LIBRARY   **111**

make it difficult to keep up with friends and family. However, I can also take advantage of alternative travel to visit friends and relatives I would not otherwise see," shares a staffer. Boasts a colleague, "I get free plane tickets for the weekend or alternative travel … and flight miles. This year I got two first-class tickets to Greece, plus a hotel."

A few lucky insiders are in the enviable position of staying put for work, and employees note that travel is totally dependent on the project. One manager claims that "approximately 30 percent of the work is local." "I have been with Deloitte Consulting three years and have traveled for one project (two months) from New York to Houston. All of my projects have been local, but mostly because I live in New York and there are plenty of local client engagements, especially if you are interested in financial services. Peers across the country tend to travel much more than I do." A consultant remarks that employees in the "Bay Area office can basically stay local if they want," and while the majority of consultants expect to travel most days of the week, one Philly-based consultant notes that "the company makes an effort to staff people as locally as possible." The fact of the matter, says one straight-faced insider, is that "this is what anyone who wants to do consulting has signed up for."

Laudable leadership

Most staffers report enjoying great relationships with the higher-ups at Deloitte Consulting, who are said to be involved and accessible. "My mentors in the partnership are the main reason I stay at Deloitte Consulting—I am given a broad range of opportunities and learning experiences. I feel that they truly care about me and my development," says a senior consultant. Of course, not every supervisor gets rave reviews, but overall, consultants are positive about the interaction among all levels of staff at the firm. One source boasts, "I have very good relationships. My firm really believes in investing in people and the power of mentoring," while another notes, "[It's] not hierarchical at all. Everyone is very approachable."

Consultants also explain that there are ample opportunities to get in front of clients—usually early on in your career. "I have been in front of two C-suites on two projects. I'm batting 1,000 since joining Deloitte Consulting, and as a first-year analyst I think that statistic speaks for itself," mentions a newbie. Another insider confirms, "I'm always amazed with how quickly, on a new assignment, I'm thrown in front of high-level clients. Managers help us get up to speed and trust us very quickly." Naturally, staffers are only entrusted with client contact after proving themselves: "The level of client interaction you are afforded is based on the partners' comfort level with you and how well you can prove your competence," says a senior consultant.

Training is treasured

Though respondents tend to agree that most training is conducted on the job and through mentoring, insiders also suggest that there has been "much more emphasis on training and building skills over the past couple of years." Reports a manager, "We are leaning toward on-the-ground project training. The firm has been weak in the past couple years in offering valuable formal training, but has recently made some advances in establishing common training, which is so helpful to get everyone on the same playing field, and really makes a difference when you're trying to staff a job. You want everyone to have the same standards in the quality of their work product and, often, this may be achieved through formal, standardized training."

There are already multiple official training options for consultants to choose from. A source recalls, "The majority of training is on the job, however, the initial business analyst training (week one and week two) and consultant milestone training (for newly promoted consultants) are outstanding. Further, there are formal local office training opportunities (increasing in frequency, but varying by office) and hundreds of computer-based training courses." A colleague says, "The training opportunities are infinite. There are online and classroom trainings related to industries, service lines, skill sets—everything." Even with hundreds of classes to choose from, most respondents seem satisfied with the freedom to glean knowledge from their colleagues. An insider states, "Just being comfortable enough to ask upper levels uncomfortable questions is a huge weight lifted off your shoulders, as a junior practitioner constantly looking for answers internally."

"Deloitte Consulting's main weaknesses"

One of the few things some insiders aren't completely happy with at Deloitte Consulting is compensation. Some feel a bit slighted by slumping salaries and sparse bonuses. "The firm must do a better job of paying its top people on a scale [comparable] to that of other leading firms. While some form of 'discount' is appropriate in exchange for the culture and work/life considerations, the best of the best should be compensated on par with the best talent at competing firms," a manager claims. Expresses a colleague, "This is one of Deloitte Consulting's main weaknesses. Despite a big 'retention initiative,' great financial results and discussion of a war for talent, compensation remains well below other consulting firms. [It's] one of the main reasons that people leave the firm. After sufficient experience, industry just becomes more attractive, based on hours, work/life balance and pay." And while those at the senior consultant level and above receive a bonus, below that there is none. A consultant explains, "I think that there is dissatisfaction mostly due to the fact that we don't receive bonuses at the lower staff levels, and that our salaries are not at all comparable to banking salaries (which they shouldn't be, because we don't work nearly as much as bankers)." Deloitte Consulting seems to be aware of the grumbling, and notes that it has been steadily improving its retention rates over the past five years.

Strong on benefits

Compensation concerns notwithstanding, Deloitte Consulting professionals say benefits—like "23 days of vacation," health insurance and 401(k)—are top notch at the firm. And benefits for parents win especially high marks from insiders. "Deloitte Consulting works to accommodate local staffing for new parents and offers a variety of special support, emergency child care, lactation support and other services." There are also occasional niceties that everyone appreciates, like "team dinners or practice dinners and an annual holiday party." According to a source, a big perk is the opportunity to hang out casually with co-workers: "From a social aspect, Deloitte Consulting showers us with events. There are more social outings and events per week than I can ever dream to attend." Another employee claims that "the best perk at this company is the travel and expense account." Other travel-related perks enjoyed are "frequent flyer miles and hotel points," which associates get to keep for personal use, and the opportunity for a few talented soccer players to travel to the Deloitte international soccer tournament. In May 2007, three first-year U.S. business analysts traveled to the Czech Republic to participate in the 2007 Deloitte Prague Cup, where the American team placed in the top 10. (Before that year, no American team had ever even scored a goal.)

Insiders also boast about "graduate school tuition assistance" and various means of support for those who leave Deloitte Consulting to pursue an MBA degree. "The firm hosts a graduate school symposium conference for consultants applying to business school to meet admissions directors from all the top-15 MBA programs," says an analyst.

Aiming for more minorities

When it comes to support for minorities, insiders applaud Deloitte Consulting's efforts, while admitting that there is still work to be done. "Deloitte Consulting as a whole is a very diverse firm. I have worked with people from all different countries and personal and ethnic backgrounds. I do feel that Deloitte Consulting could do a better job targeting Hispanics and African-Americans," an associate suggests. "We're getting there," says a source, who adds that "it has been tough selling to minority recruits since 2002, when I joined the firm." Recruiting programs and special internal groups are set up to address hiring and supporting minorities at Deloitte Consulting. "The firm is an active participant in the INROADS internship program. We have specific recruiting activities targeting the National Black MBA Association and National Society of Hispanic MBA affinity groups," an insider comments. And Deloitte Consulting is continually working to improve diversity. According to one senior manager, "The firm is focusing a lot of energy in this area these days. There are more mentoring programs being put in place and I think we are starting to catch up to our Women's Initiative (WIN), but we still have room to do better."

Set up to WIN

Though the distribution of genders isn't totally equal throughout Deloitte Consulting, the consensus is that the firm is heading in the right direction when it comes to promoting and retaining women. "The firm is very supportive of women, and WIN provides great opportunities for [them]. I believe Deloitte Consulting sets the standard when it comes to supporting women in consulting," states a manager. An East Coast source remarks, "There is outstanding representation of women within the leadership ranks, and incoming women have several support networks to help integrate them into the organization." A few insiders acknowledge that it's an area that Deloitte Consulting still should try to improve. "We have some amazing mentoring programs for high-talent

Visit the Vault Consulting Career Channel at **www.vault.com/consulting** - with insider firm profiles, message boards, the Vault Consulting Job Board and more.

VAULT CAREER LIBRARY **113**

women, though we still don't have as many females in leadership roles as we probably should," concedes a senior analyst. A colleague adds, "We do a good job trumpeting the cause for women, but I think we still struggle with travel and providing meaningful promotion paths if you have to choose to stop traveling. The firm does well in addressing these needs."

Celebrating diversity

With respect to gays and lesbians at Deloitte Consulting, insiders give the firm high marks for its openness and acceptance of all. A source comments, "We have lots of diversity with gays, lesbians and bisexuals, and a specific business resource group devoted to them." Deloitte Consulting also encourages an open attitude through various support groups and special events. "Deloitte & Touche USA has diversity months dedicated to every minority you can think of. They do spotlights of individuals from those minority groups and post the spotlight around the office (kitchen, conference room, etc.). We also have the GLOBE club dedicated to gays, lesbians and bisexuals. Deloitte & Touche USA is a leader when it comes to celebrating diversity in the workplace," boasts an associate. "I am a member of our gay and lesbian affinity group, and am out at work with my co-workers and clients. My partner and our daughters are encouraged to attend all events," recounts a staffer.

A positive IMPACT

Deloitte & Touche USA's IMPACT day is nearly legendary to staffers: On one day each year, every person in the Deloitte U.S. entities takes off from work and spends that day volunteering in their communities. For example, in 2006, volunteers held career-building workshops for high school students at a school in Boston's Chinatown neighborhood. In San Diego, over 300 volunteers from the Deloitte U.S. entities helped build a new playground at a YMCA.

But not as well known is Deloitte Consulting's involvement with pro bono consulting efforts. "There is a ton of passion among Deloitte Consulting practitioners for pro bono consulting. Within the next year, and as early as this summer, I believe we will see Deloitte Consulting performing significant pro bono projects. Deloitte Consulting is committed to maintaining strong relationships with numerous charities, foundations and nonprofits," relates an insider. A colleague confirms that "there is a formal pro bono program being developed, and it will likely be implemented before 2007 is over."

Deloitte Consulting professionals assert there are plenty of firm-sponsored ways to plunge into charitable endeavors, such as "involvement with Junior Achievement, 'school-to-work day' and United Way." Comments a manager, "Regions have dedicated community involvement councils. Deloitte & Touche USA has also piloted a community service time program in five different offices, allowing staff to receive 'credit' for their volunteering hours/efforts on behalf of the firm." One analyst states, "We hold clothing drives and soap drives, where employees donate amenities collected from hotels while traveling," and another source lists "helping out with local schools, homeless organizations and rehabilitation centers," as opportunities for getting involved. "Deloitte Consulting is heavily committed to all forms of community involvement, from philanthropy to volunteerism to board involvement to pro bono consulting. This was a big draw for me, and I've definitely been able to maintain my involvement with the community while working full time," declares a giving Bostonian.

"I believe Deloitte Consulting sets the standard when it comes to supporting women in consulting."

– Deloitte Consulting manager

Visit the Vault Consulting Career Channel at **www.vault.com/consulting** - with insider firm profiles, message boards, the Vault Consulting Job Board and more.

VAULT CAREER LIBRARY   115

Mercer Human Resource Consulting

1166 Avenue of the Americas
New York, NY 10036
Phone: (212) 345-7000
Fax: (212) 345-7414
www.mercerhr.com

LOCATIONS

New York, NY (HQ)
Offices in 42 countries

PRACTICE AREAS

Communication
Global Investments
Health & Benefits Consulting
Human Capital Advisory Services
Information Product Solutions
Investment Consulting
Mercer HR Services
Mergers & Acquisitions
Retirement Consulting

THE STATS

Employer Type: Subsidiary of Marsh & McLennan
 Companies, Inc., a Public Company
Ticker Symbol: MMC (NYSE)
Chairman & CEO: M. Michele Burns
2007 Employees: 16,500
2006 Employees: 16,500
2006 Revenue: $3 billion
2005 Revenue: $2.7 billion

RANKING RECAP

Practice Area
#1 - Human Resources Consulting

Quality of Life
#3 - Hours in the Office
#12 - Work/Life Balance (tie)
#20 - Travel Requirements

UPPERS

- "Very well-known and respected firm"
- "Lots of people around the world to learn from"
- "Company gives me support and room to expand"
- Flexibility

DOWNERS

- "There is quite a bit of disconnect between offices"
- Too much administrative work—takes time away from working with clients
- "Not valued as highly as management consulting"
- "Bigger can be worse for some things, e.g., speed to market, accountability"

EMPLOYMENT CONTACT

www.mercerhr.com/joiningmercer.jhtml

THE BUZZ
WHAT CONSULTANTS AT OTHER FIRMS ARE SAYING ABOUT THIS FIRM

- "Specialists who are good at what they do"
- "Losing good people. Has had four presidents in two years"
- "Fair, effective, family-friendly"
- "Riding the Mercer name"

THE SCOOP

Huge in HR

The largest human resources consultancy of its kind, Mercer Human Resource Consulting knows a thing or two about the complexities and challenges of managing a workforce. A subsidiary of the $12 billion Marsh & McLennan Companies, Mercer HR employs nearly 17,000 people in 42 countries.

The firm has specialized in the HR niche for a long time, going back to 1937, when it was formed as the employee benefits department of Marsh & McLennan. The company took the name William M. Mercer when its parent company acquired the Canadian consultancy William M. Mercer Limited in 1959, and Mercer, in turn, became a wholly owned subsidiary of MMC in 1975. In 2002, the human resources division was rebranded as Mercer Human Resource Consulting.

Earning their keep

Mercer HR's giant corporate parent, MMC, divides its consulting businesses between Mercer HR and Oliver Wyman, with Mercer HR contributing about 70 percent of the total consulting revenue. In 2006, growth initiatives the parent company had put in place for the division 18 months prior began to pay off, and Mercer HR posted revenue of $3 billion, up 8 percent from the previous year.

Mercer HR's menu of services includes communication consulting, to help clients with effective employee communication; health and benefits services; human capital services, such as performance measurement, broad-based rewards, executive pay and sales force effectiveness; international consulting; investment consulting—working with pension funds, foundations, endowments and other investors in more than 35 countries; HR administration and outsourcing services; mergers and acquisitions; and retirement consulting.

The CEO shuffle

It's a good thing Mercer is so seasoned in the world of HR—the firm has seen a lot of movement in its executive suites over the past year. In September 2006, M. Michele Burns, who served as CFO of MMC, was named chairman and CEO of Mercer HR, replacing the retiring Michael Caulfield. Before joining MMC in March 2006, Burns served as chief restructuring officer at Mirant Corporation and chief financial officer at Delta Air Lines, and before then she was a consultant with Arthur Andersen for 18 years. She currently serves as a director on the boards of Wal-Mart Stores and Cisco Systems. Caulfield served a relatively brief stint as CEO, having taken over the reins from Brian Storms, who vacated the position in 2005 to become chairman and CEO of Marsh Inc., the risk and insurance subsidiary of MMC. In January 2007, the firm created a new position—chief operating officer of the consulting business—naming Thomas L. Elliott III to the role. Elliott formerly served as president of Unisys' global commercial services unit, and as an executive VP at BearingPoint. That same month, the firm named Cara Williams, a former chief administrative officer, as its global COO for the investment consulting group. And in February 2007, Robert A. Yungk, a former exec with Tenet Healthcare, joined the firm as president and global head of the health and benefits division, succeeding the retiring Bernard Morency.

Ordering out for HR

As the outsourcing of HR services has grown in popularity in recent years, Mercer HR has stepped in to fill the demand. In January 2004, the firm acquired Synhrgy HR Technologies, a provider of HR technology and outsourcing services to Fortune 1000 companies, with more than 375 employees. The practice, which was renamed Mercer HR Services, joined with sister company Putnam's defined contribution administration business in June of that year to create a cohesive, full-service human resources outsourcing organization. The acquisition extended the firm's capabilities in the U.S. to include retirement, health and group administration, employee relations, absence management, payroll customer support, compliance and data management. Another service, known as "co-sourcing," involves working more directly with clients on less automatable tasks, like

Visit the Vault Consulting Career Channel at **www.vault.com/consulting** - with insider firm profiles, message boards, the Vault Consulting Job Board and more.

VAULT CAREER LIBRARY   **117**

compensation planning. These days, the HR services division employs more than 4,100 staffers in service centers located in Melbourne, Toronto, Dublin and London, while another 1,600 staffers work in four U.S. service centers. In March 2007, the division announced its participation in a business transformation outsourcing contract, working alongside IBM to deliver health and benefits, pension plan and other HR administrative services to American Airlines.

Mercer HR has continued to grow its business through strategic acquisitions. In September 2006, the firm acquired HRPartnering Pty Ltd, a specialist talent management business in Australia with 15 employees. And in July of that year, the firm purchased Pendia Associates, a 55-employee, Switzerland-based firm specializing in retirement and investment consulting and pensions administration services.

Asian operations

Mercer HR has cultivated a strong foothold in the East, with more than 2,000 employees working out of 31 offices in the Asia-Pacific region. In April 2006, Mercer HR Services established a global operations center in Noida, India, and announced its intention to invest $50 million in India over the next three years. In January 2007, the firm named Rajan Srikanth as head of the Asia region and leader of its human capital advisory services group in Asia. Based in Chennai, India, Srikanth joined Mercer from Accenture, where he was an executive partner. And in February 2007, the firm created a new position—Asia business leader of Mercer HR Services—to meet a growing demand for benefits outsourcing in the region. The firm appointed Mercer HR vet Rosaline Chow Koo to the role.

Tracking the trends

Mercer HR consultants keep busy with a range of reports and research of interest to employers and employees alike. The firm publishes a headline-grabbing annual cost-of-living survey, ranking the world's major cities. (Moscow earned the dubious honor of most expensive city in 2006.) Billed as the world's most comprehensive cost-of-living survey, the report aims to help multinational companies and governments determine compensation allowances for their expatriate employees. A January 2007 study tracked salary and cost-of-living trends in various regions in Australia and New Zealand. And in October 2006, the firm published a survey showing that more women were being sent on international assignments than ever before, but that female employees are less likely to be accompanied by their partners than their male counterparts. The firm also produces a "Spotlight on Benefits" report, analyzing the benefits programs of more than 1,025 employers, and for 20 years it has conducted one of the most comprehensive surveys of employer-sponsored health plans in the U.S., as well as a highly visible annual analysis of CEO pay trends. In addition, the firm's investment consulting division publishes an array of regular performance surveys tracking results for corporate, public and foundation/endowment plans targeted toward specific audiences.

Top of the HR heap

Mercer HR often earns honors for its achievements in the HR industry. The firm was given the Consulting Firm of the Year for Change Management award from *China STAFF*, a bilingual journal dedicated to HR management in China and Hong Kong, in both 2005 and 2006. And in 2006, the firm's investment consulting division was named European Investment Consultant of the Year by *Financial News*. That same year, Mercer HR was named Benefits Consultant of the Year in the annual Global Pensions Awards for the second consecutive year, by a panel of 20 judges made up of pension funds and consultants globally.

GETTING HIRED

Getting in on the ground floor

On Mercer HR's web site, job seekers can search a list of openings around the world, and get detailed information on campus recruiting and internship opportunities. The firm says it's looking for candidates who have graduated from advanced degree programs in math, statistics, economics, business, HR management or actuarial science. The firm also offers a summer internship program, typically available to students entering their junior or senior year of college, but some opportunities may also exist for rising sophomores or MBA candidates. A former intern reports that "interns are treated pretty well during their time with the firm (beach passes, good pay, a 'buddy' and a supervisor are assigned to mentor you)." In addition, "interns are expected to attend all training sessions" on topics related to consulting, and are expected to make a final presentation at the end of the summer. The source adds that it's fairly common for interns to receive full-time offers.

Candidates who pass the campus recruiting hurdle can expect one on-campus interview and a second round of multiple interviews in the office. "Whenever possible, we try to limit to one round of in-office interviews," says a source, who adds, "We'll sometimes give cases to assess analytical skills if we are unsure." A junior hire describes the process as "not a very hard interview," noting that "enthusiasm and having a good personality are most important … The first round is quite conversational—who are you and why are you interested in Mercer? The second round is an all-day event where consultants ask slightly tougher questions—but it's nothing a few hours of preparation can't handle."

Patience is a virtue

More than one insider comments on the unusual amount of time Mercer HR's hiring process can take. One consultant, who went through "12 interviews over six months," quips, "Mercer can only make a decision by committee!" Another source reports, "The hiring process was quite long and I met with at least four different managers before the decision was made to hire me."

OUR SURVEY SAYS

Time of transition

Asked about their firm's corporate culture, several Mercer HR consultants say the company is in a "major transitional phase," with a period of higher turnover and greater focus on the bottom line. Aside from all this, though, insiders give the firm's culture high marks. As one source puts it, "The depth and breadth of practice consultants are huge and a wonderful plus. You are most definitely working with the best and the brightest and, in most cases, the nicest. It's a very convivial atmosphere, [with a] focus on team success. The consultants do excellent work consistently—you are proud to be a Mercer employee." The "friendly, upbeat" culture benefits from "lots of social gatherings," another contact says. However, a colleague notes that while "Mercer has a lot of very bright people," the firm "tends to be overly cautious and lacking in innovation. Talented consultants win profitable client projects, but Kafkaesque bureaucracy or operational inefficiencies often jeopardize delivery. After a while, the talented consultants become less enthusiastic and more cynical—or they move on."

You work, they flex

Work/life balance at Mercer is helped along by the firm's "hands-off management style," says a source, who adds, "As long as you are working hard and meeting goals, they rarely question your process." In fact, another consultant says, the firm is "very open-minded about changes for employees; there's lots of telecommuting, part time, etc. I have been working part time from home for eight years (before high-speed Internet access!)."

This flexibility extends to Mercer HR consultants' career paths, says an insider: "Mercer has a very positive attitude toward flexible working and work/life balance. Consultants have a lot of freedom and independence to work on different types of projects and to learn and develop new skills. There is a fair amount of global mobility within human capital advisory services or information product solutions. But retirement and health consultants are less mobile." A co-worker agrees that the firm is "very open to all kinds of career paths," "provides new opportunities for people who want them" and is "responsive to employees who want to do other things."

Visit the Vault Consulting Career Channel at **www.vault.com/consulting** - with insider firm profiles, message boards, the Vault Consulting Job Board and more.

VAULT CAREER LIBRARY

119

Choose your own adventure

"Because we don't have to travel as much as other consulting firms, I would say we generally have a better work/life balance," a source says. Another consultant characterizes Mercer HR's travel requirements as "average for the industry; you can choose roles with little or a lot of travel." As one employee reports, "My travel is mostly within a 40-mile radius of my office." "It is really up to the individual to assess travel requirements," another insider avers. Work hours hover between 50 and 60 per week, we're told.

Benefit blues

Compensation at Mercer HR has seen better days, some insiders claim. "Due to issues with MMC and sibling organizations, salary increases and bonuses have been below par," a consultant reports, adding, "Performance ratings were 'adjusted' to reflect what was available in the compensation pool." In addition, another source explains that benefits "have been decimated in recent years—the pension plan was gutted, our ESPP plan discount was essentially turned into a savings account, the stock investment plan match was changed to be performance-based, and my health insurance premiums and co-pays have probably increased by 400 percent since I joined the company." Still, the source reports, "I have received greater than a 10 percent pay increase every year I have been at Mercer, and in about six years of service, my pay is now 300 percent higher than when I started … My story is not typical, but there are good opportunities for star performers at Mercer." Another consultant reports having gone for two years without a raise.

Other benefits include stock options for the higher ranks, some educational benefits and a good 401(k). New parents are offered standard family and medical leave, insiders report. And Mercer HR's offices get relatively high marks: "The office in Hoboken is modern and has a great view, but the main office in New York tends to be a bit dated and cramped." Community service opportunities abound, with several events held each year, "including an all-day event on September 11, which is a tribute to the 300-plus employees we lost in the World Trade Center attacks," says a consultant. Others report participation in charity races and support for local school districts.

Disconnected training, fair diversity

When it comes to training, a consultant worries, "There is some disconnect here. Mercer really leaves this to the individual with excessive resources available. This would be much easier if it was streamlined and administered in a more regimented fashion." Another insider says that "most training is through town hall seminars and informal means." But the "new online training system is very good," says a colleague, noting, "I've been in the business 19 years and still found it useful." As for management relations, one source reports, "I feel like the support I get internally is pretty good in most areas, and not too intrusive compared to my prior employers."

When it comes to diversity, Mercer HR's heart is in the right place, insiders suggest. "I believe, on the whole, the company respects women," one consultant tells us, though "I would like to see more female leaders." Another insider states that there are "many women at the junior level (I'd say 60 to 70 percent), but fewer women at the senior level (20 to 30 percent). This is strange, since HR consulting is considered a female-friendly field." And regarding its minority presence, according to one consultant, it "seems like we've got pretty good representation among minorities here—myself included."

"Consultants have a lot of freedom and independence to work on different types of projects and to learn and develop new skills."

– Mercer HR Consulting insider

Visit the Vault Consulting Career Channel at **www.vault.com/consulting** - with insider firm profiles, message boards, the Vault Consulting Job Board and more.

VAULT CAREER LIBRARY

121

The Parthenon Group

VAULT TOP 50

10

PRESTIGE RANKING

200 State Street, 14th Floor
Boston, MA 02109
Phone: (617) 478-2550
Fax: (617) 478-2555
www.parthenon.com

LOCATIONS

Boston, MA (HQ)
San Francisco, CA
London

PRACTICE AREAS

Corporate & Business Unit Strategy
Education Center of Excellence
Innovation & Growth
Merger & Acquisition
Private Equity
Profit Improvement

THE STATS

Employer Type: Private Company
CEO: Bill Achtmeyer
2006 Employees: 150+
2005 Employees: 150

UPPERS

- Risk-based fee structure can lead to big bucks
- Equity investment opportunities

DOWNERS

- Long hours
- Low on diversity

EMPLOYMENT CONTACT

Eileen McBride
The Parthenon Group
200 State Street, 14th Floor
Boston, MA 02109
E-mail: recruiting@parthenon.com

See additional recruiting contacts on the firm's site

THE BUZZ
WHAT CONSULTANTS AT OTHER FIRMS ARE SAYING ABOUT THIS FIRM

- "Elite but small, good for development"
- "Think they are hot"
- "Gaining prestige, hard workers"
- "Locker room culture"

THE SCOOP

Small and selective

Founded by two former Bain consultants, John Rutherford and Bill Achtmeyer, The Parthenon Group is a Boston-based boutique consulting firm. The firm initially started in 1991 as both a strategy and venture capital company, but in 2000, the founding partners decided to split up the company's practices. Rutherford took over Parthenon Capital, a private equity firm, while Achtmeyer assumed leadership over the strategy side of the business. The two are now legally separate entities, but still maintain a loose association; in fact, The Parthenon Group is an advisor to Parthenon Capital. Today the firm serves emerging growth companies as well as Fortune 1000 clients like Ford Motor Company, Anheuser Busch, Thomson and the recently revived Indian Motorcycle Company.

Will you be mine?

The way the firm describes its client relationships sounds a lot like a marriage: It boasts often exclusive relationships with clients, and aims for close, lifelong partnerships. Parthenon also admits to being choosy about whom it wants to work with. Clients reportedly come through a tight referral network of CEOs. The firm emphasizes personalized service and states that its mission is "to be the strategic advisor of choice for CEOs and business leaders worldwide." Expansion isn't necessarily a part of that goal—the firm has never had more than 150 staffers from the beginning.

High-profile advice

Parthenon usually keeps its engagements under tight wraps, but it couldn't help but attract attention for its participation in the HP-Compaq merger battle in 2002. The firm prepared a report, which Walter Hewlett, son of HP founder Bill Hewlett, used in an attempt to halt the $23.5 billion deal. Parthenon's premerger research found that the deal wouldn't be in the shareholders' best interest and that HP would benefit more by increasing its printing and imaging market share. It compared the proposed merger to past failed technology megamergers. Despite the advice (and a notorious proxy battle), the shareholders voted to move ahead with the merger.

Generalists plus

Parthenon claims to be a generalist firm, but over the years has developed specialties in several industries, such as consumer products and retail, manufacturing, health care and financial services. Much of its work is aimed at improving the bottom line and creating value by advising CEOs on competitive strategy. It has also developed intellectual capital in education, macroeconomic econometrics and company value creation, and through its Education Center for Excellence, the firm helps schools and training organizations address issues like district reform or optimizing profit. Parthenon publicizes its knowledge through reports, accessible online, called the *Parthenon Perspective*. One recent study focused on the importance of the size of sales territories and sales forces critical to sales success.

Willing to risk

Parthenon's payment philosophy is not too common among consultancies. It was the first to offer "at-risk" advisory services when it allowed clients to pay for services in equity instead of cash. The firm established its alternative payment practices back in 1992, during the venture capital boom, when it began accepting equity for payment. According to Parthenon, it usually cashes in its equity after about three years, and consults with the client about when to sell, so as not to upset the market for the stock.

This unique practice doesn't always work in Parthenon's favor, however. In 1999, a health care provider client the firm was working with failed, and Parthenon lost $1 million. Observers note the potential for the firm to run into conflicts of interest by being in advisory situations with clients, but Parthenon insists that this is one of the ways it demonstrates a personal commitment to achieving results for a client.

Visit the Vault Consulting Career Channel at www.vault.com/consulting - with insider firm profiles, message boards, the Vault Consulting Job Board and more.

VAULT CAREER LIBRARY   123

GETTING HIRED

An elite boutique

As a boutique firm, Parthenon aims for "controlled growth," the firm says, and according to insiders, this means one thing: Hiring is extremely selective. The elite batch hails from schools like Harvard, Dartmouth, MIT, Stanford, INSEAD and the London Business School. Those still in school may be able to get in via Parthenon's 10-week summer program, offered to undergrads and MBA students. The program includes a week of training in Parthenon's methods and, the firm notes, many interns receive offers at the end of their stint to return after graduation.

On Parthenon's web site, there's a wealth of information about the firm's roles, culture and compensation structure, and you can also find contact information for sending resumes. Insiders describe the hiring process as "standard," with phone and in-person interviews emphasizing both business savvy and fit.

Parthenon boasts often exclusive relationships with clients, and aims for close, lifelong partnerships. Parthenon also admits to being choosy about whom it wants to work with.

Visit the Vault Consulting Career Channel at **www.vault.com/consulting** - with insider firm profiles, message boards, the Vault Consulting Job Board and more.

VAULT CAREER LIBRARY

125

11

IBM Global Services

New Orchard Road
Armonk, NY 10504
Phone: (914) 499-1900
Fax: (914) 765-7382
www.ibm.com/consulting/careers

LOCATIONS

Armonk, NY (HQ)
More than 300 offices in 160 countries

PRACTICE AREAS

Application Services
  Application Integration Services
  Application Management Services
Business Consulting Services
  Customer Relationship Management
  Financial Management
  Human Capital Management
  Strategy & Change
  Supply Chain & Procurement

THE STATS

Employer Type: Division of IBM
Ticker Symbol: IBM (NYSE)
Managing Partner: Ginni Rometty
2007 Employees: 190,000
2006 Employees: 190,000
2006 Revenue: $48.3 billion
2005 Revenue: $47.4 billion

RANKING RECAP

Practice Area
#6 - Operational Consulting

Diversity
#8 - Diversity for GLBT
#9 - Best Firms for Diversity
#9 - Diversity for Minorities
#16 - Diversity for Women

UPPERS

- Opportunities to transfer to other divisions of the company
- "Sort of like being your own boss"
- Face clients from day one
- "You can live anywhere and occasionally work from home"

DOWNERS

- "The Blueocracy"
- "Penny-wise, pound-foolish approach"
- "Many of the work relationships are virtual ones"
- Size of the company

EMPLOYMENT CONTACT

www.ibm.com/consulting/careers

THE BUZZ
WHAT CONSULTANTS AT OTHER FIRMS ARE SAYING ABOUT THIS FIRM

- "Anything and everything"
- "Still very IT-focused, despite efforts to move away from it"
- "Cool people, cool projects"
- "Army-like, no creativity"

THE SCOOP

Big Blue, at your service

While many of the consulting industry's traditional management and strategy firms have scrambled in recent years to incorporate IT into their practice areas, IBM has entered the industry from the opposite door. Though Big Blue will always be associated with computers, the company's business model over the past decade has trended toward services. These days, the Global Services division, including business consulting and IT implementation, contributes more than half of IBM's total revenue—$48.3 billion out of $91.4 billion in 2006—and employs more than 190,000 people worldwide.

IBM's high-tech roots and resources allow it to offer clients integrated engagements that can span from strategy, to IT design, to implementation and outsourcing. Under its business consulting arm, IBM's services include financial management, customer relationship management, human capital management, strategy and change, and supply chain and procurement.

PwC joins the fold

With an entrenched reputation as a corporation of computer geeks, IBM has had to work extra hard to establish itself in the consulting arena. The firm's services division got a major boost in 2002 with IBM's acquisition of PricewaterhouseCoopers Consulting, which added some 30,000 employees in 52 countries to the 30,000 IBM consultants already onboard. The acquisition came about after an unsuccessful attempt by PricewaterhouseCoopers to take PwC Consulting public in 2002.

Having created the largest consulting services organization worldwide through the PwC deal, IBM execs began tirelessly promoting the company's services capabilities. Global Services division President Virginia "Ginni" Rometty led an aggressive push into the consulting world, pursuing former PwC clients through a "win-back" program. In 2002, IBM's direction toward services became even clearer when the firm named Sam Palmisano its CEO. As former head of IBM Global Services, Palmisano wasn't shy about the division's continued plans for growth. Meanwhile, a series of smaller consulting and services acquisitions solidified IBM's position.

Establishing Services

By the time IBM decided to unload its personal computing business, in a deal that closed in early 2005, it was clear that major changes were afoot at Big Blue. The firm announced a major Global Services reorganization later in 2005, and the realigned group was tasked with focusing more on "high-value" skills in line with those offered by IBM's original Business Consulting Services division, which had been formed after the PwC purchase. The natural choice to head the group in its new iteration was Ginni Rometty, who now holds the title of managing partner. IBM continued taking steps to move itself away from a "commodity" model, focused on selling parts and technologies, and into a "services" model, selling the brainpower of its consultants and other resident experts. The move paid off; in 2006, three of the firm's consultants, Bridget Van Kralingen, William Pulleyblank and Mary Sue Rogers, were named to *Consulting Magazine*'s top-25 list—more than any other consulting firm.

IBM has continued to realign the division, offering new and rebranded services. In February 2007, it announced a new set of software and business consulting services under IBM's global Information on Demand initiative. Included in these new services is a software suite from FileNet, a company acquired by IBM in October 2006, geared toward content management, as well as consulting services to help implement the software. As part of the new services, IBM dedicated more than 1,000 consultants to the FileNet implementation cause. Another new offering, introduced in November 2006—the IBM Loss Analysis and Warning Solution—uses advanced analytics to help property and casualty insurers ferret out illegal and unethical activities by policyholders, service providers and employees. In October 2006, the firm announced a suite of new industry models and consulting services aimed at the financial markets. And IBM added a new practice to its management consulting roster in June 2006, devoted to helping clients get the most out of their research and development spending. Under the IBM Global Business

Visit the Vault Consulting Career Channel at www.vault.com/consulting - with insider firm profiles, message boards, the Vault Consulting Job Board and more.

VAULT CAREER LIBRARY   127

Services umbrella, the R&D consulting practice leverages resources from the firm's research, management, technology and intellectual property experts.

IBM innovates

The business consulting division also offers a number of innovation and research services. The IBM Institute for Business Value provides clients with strategic insights and recommendations, while the Center for Business Optimization uses advanced analytical methods to tackle large amounts of data to solve complex business problems. The firm's "component business methodology" service aims to identify the "basic building blocks" of a business to gather insights, and its On Demand Innovation Services combines IBM's research and business consulting capabilities. Finally, the firm's continuous improvement business process outsourcing, or IBM Daksh, is an outsourcing model based on Six Sigma and reengineering approaches, designed to help businesses improve year-over-year.

In addition to its purchase of FileNet, IBM has been on a bit of a spending spree lately, buying up small software providers such as New Jersey-based Palisades Technology Partners, which specializes in technologies and services for the mortgage lending industry, and MRO Software, a provider of asset and service management software and consulting services. Analysts have noted that these types of acquisitions will only boost Global Services' revenue in the long run, as customers who invest in new software typically also agree to purchase service contracts for installation and maintenance.

Truly global services

IBM consultants can be found taking on engagements around the world. Outside of the U.S., India is IBM's largest country organization, employing more than 43,000 people in 14 cities. Addressing the largest-ever gathering of IBM employees in India, in June 2006, CEO Palmisano declared that the firm expects to nearly triple its investment in India over the next three years, to nearly $6 billion. When it comes to outsourcing, the firm has declared that it doesn't see the Big Six outsourcers as a competitive threat as it gears up in India; rather, IBM is keeping its eye on homegrown Indian shops like Wipro and Infosys.

In November 2006, the firm announced a major initiative to help support innovation in China. Under the program, IBM planned to work with the Chinese Ministry of Education to develop a services science curriculum in universities, work with the Ministry of Health on a pilot program using IT to improve regional medical services, and provide services to a variety of businesses. IBM has 8,300 employees in China. In November 2006, the firm announced its plans to establish a global delivery center in Chengdu, complementing its other Chinese centers in Shenzen, Dalian and Shanghai.

Meanwhile, the firm has continued to strengthen its foothold in Europe. In October 2006, it opened a subsidiary office in the Ukraine, where it works with major telecom and banking providers. In September 2006, IBM announced initiatives to support entrepreneurship in Ireland, including a venture capital center in Dublin aimed at helping Irish startups. Also that month, Global Services was selected to provide and implement a new IT system for the steadily growing Prague airport. In July 2006, the firm announced that it was working with the government of Slovakia to transform its procurement systems as part of a broader push into e-government in the country. Other major clients in Europe have included Portugal's Banco BPI and broadcast network Retevision, brewing giant Carlsberg and Austrian insurance company Wiener Staedtische Group.

On to outsourcing

Through more than 30 global delivery centers worldwide, IBM has positioned itself to quickly jump on clients' outsourcing needs. In March 2007, the firm announced a $217 million outsourcing agreement to manage and transform human resources services for American Airlines. IBM plans to team up with Mercer HR Services on the project. In another outsourcing contract, signed with the Childrens Hospital Los Angeles in December 2006, the firm was tapped to manage and support the hospital's financial, HR, materials management and grants-tracking systems. And in November of that year, cosmetics giant Avon Products selected IBM to provide a portfolio of specialized HR services.

Global Services consultants work with clients in just about every industry you can think of. Airlines often tap the firm for its "on-demand" approach. JetBlue Airways, Air Canada, British Airways and others have engaged the firm to design self-serve check-in kiosks. The group also continues the grand old IBM tradition of technological innovation. In October 2006, Global Services announced that it was partnering with a number of organizations, including Heineken, shipping firm Safmarine and the University of Amsterdam, along with customs departments in the U.S. and the U.K., to create a "beer living lab." The project aims to track cargo container shipments of the Dutch brew from Europe to the U.S. using satellite and cellular technology. As part of a larger goal of transforming e-customs, IBM hopes to promote a solution that can facilitate international trade by creating less of a need for physical customs inspections at borders.

In with the feds

Over in the public sector, IBM keeps a lower profile than competitors Accenture and Booz Allen, but it still has managed to score some impressive government deals. In October 2006, the U.S. Department of Veterans Affairs inked a $16 million IT transformation deal with IBM, including the creation of a standardized, interoperable, secure IT environment. Another recent government contract was with the Defense Information Systems Agency, which hooked Global Services in mid-2006 to provide net-centric collaboration services that allow for real-time sharing of information across the Defense Department.

Jamming for ideas

IBM Chairman and CEO Samuel Palmisano has proved to be a big advocate for innovation. In November 2006, the firm announced that it would invest $100 million over the next two years to pursue business ideas generated by "the largest online brainstorming session ever," known as InnovationJam. The InnovationJam event, consisting of two 72-hour sessions, brought together more than 150,000 participants from 104 countries, including IBM employees, their family members, universities, business partners and clients. Of the 46,000 ideas posted by these participants, 10 solid business ideas were chosen, including health care payment systems using "smart" cards, simplified and prepackaged Web 2.0 services for small and midsized businesses, advanced, real-time translation services and more.

Reports and rewards

Like other consulting firms, Global Services keeps its name in the news with plenty of reports and surveys. In March 2007, the firm's Institute for Business Value released a study on business in China, noting that in order for multinational companies to succeed there, they will need to focus increasingly on mass markets, rather than limiting themselves to a handful of top-tier cities. In February 2007, the firm unveiled a report on "navigating the new media divide," offering steps companies can take to maneuver around the tensions between traditional media content owners and their more newfangled distribution counterparts. That same month, the Institute for Business Value released a report on how telecom companies can tap into the market for digital content. An earlier, November 2006 report examined the attitudes of consumers toward their banks.

In December 2006, IBM won two MITX awards, recognizing achievement in interactive technologies, for Best User Experience and Best Consumer Goods Experience. The awards honored IBM's design and development of a new web site feature for its client L.L. Bean. The previous month, IBM was ranked by Gartner Dataquest as the world's leading consulting and systems integration provider for the fourth consecutive year.

Sam's family

IBM has established a reputation as a solid employer, especially for consultants with families. For 18 consecutive years, *Working Mother* magazine has included IBM among the top-10 on its list of the 100 Best Companies for Working Mothers. The publication honored the firm yet again in 2006, naming Palmisano a "family champion" in recognition of his dedication to innovative programs for women.

In March 2007, the firm announced a new, multimillion-dollar personal finance and education benefit for employees in the U.S., aimed at easing the transition from its traditional retirement benefits to a new 401(k) program. IBM MoneySmart includes

Visit the Vault Consulting Career Channel at **www.vault.com/consulting** - with insider firm profiles, message boards, the Vault Consulting Job Board and more.

129

personal financial planning sessions, educational seminars and online tools to help employees manage their retirement assets. The firm said it planned to fully fund the program for the next two years, after which it would review the benefit based on affordability and employee satisfaction.

Education and hope

As a high-profile company, IBM also makes sure to invest in community service. Education tops the list of the firm's pet causes, and it has invested $75 million worldwide in a school reform program known as Reinventing Education. Another educational effort is the firm's commitment to EX.I.T.E. (EXploring Interests in Technology and Engineering) camps for middle school-aged girls, a program it has sponsored since 1999. The camps, taking place around the globe, are meant to inspire interest in math, science and technology among young girls. EX.I.T.E. campers work in teams with IBM employee volunteers on projects that touch on innovations in medicine, health care, agriculture, entertainment, consumer goods, environmental preservation, and rescue and relief efforts. Through another initiative, Hope and Harmony for Humanity, the firm works to bring computer technology access and education to low-income and remote Native American reservations across the U.S.

GETTING HIRED

Big Blue's got it covered

IBM's recruiters practically canvas the country, showing up at schools all over the U.S. Wharton, Harvard, Chicago, University of Texas, Emory, Michigan and Tulane are among the campuses where the firm scouts. A complete recruiting calendar can be found on the firm's web site. Students don't have to wait for a recruiter to come to campus, however. The firm also offers a listing of opportunities for both recent grads and experienced professionals on its web site.

The interview process is fairly standard, with a combination of behavioral and technical questions. Relates a staffer, "I had two or three rounds of interviews. For campus recruiting, there is an on-campus interview and then an office visit. For an experienced hire, there will be an additional interview, which would be the initial phone screen." A manager goes through the routine: "College recruiting is generally conducted with pairs of interviewers in the first round, followed by an IT aptitude test. Then there are office interviews with executives." Most insiders claim the interview process isn't too painful. "The interviewers really put us at ease. They were very kind and forthcoming about the company. It was enjoyable to meet them," a consultant shares. A colleague agrees, stating, "The process is very selective but very pleasant."

"Tell me" questions

Details of the interview process vary slightly, depending on where a candidate interviews. A manager in the Midwest states, "We ask relevant questions in the following categories: technical/functional skills, creative problem solving, interpersonal competencies, drive to achieve/leadership and verbal communication." Other sources note that interview questions aren't as clear cut, and "range from general experiences to very specific skill questions." One consultant, who had three interviews and was not asked to take a test, advises, "Expect the 'tell me' questions—about yourself, how did you manage tasks and projects, and how would you deal with team issues." Another source recounts an example of a case question: "You have a small regional bank that wants to go toward Internet services and close branches. What areas would you look at to determine if this approach would be viable?"

Let your personality shine

When it comes down to getting hired, insiders say that even the most astute answers to technical questions won't guarantee you an offer. A consultant expains, "Most interviewers look at the candidates and ask, 'Would I want to work with this person, are they flexible, can they learn and will they do whatever it takes to complete an assignment on time?'" Another source ruminates on his own hiring: "I felt the interview was geared more toward seeing how I would fit into the corporate culture, rather than toward my specific work experience. I considered that a positive aspect of the interview process."

OUR SURVEY SAYS

Love the ones you're with

Insiders at IBM hold different opinions about the firm's culture—understandable, due to its mammoth size. But no matter who you talk to, it's clear that the culture has come a long way from the pre-1990s, when its image conveyed a firm full of stodgy blue suits. "It's not the firm I remember as a child," a consultant proudly declares. On the whole, staffers claim the firm is full of "great people" who are "very smart, committed and fun." Exclaims a source, "Ours a very large firm, so our culture continues to evolve with the introduction of new people, new ideas and new culture, which is readily explored and embraced." Another associate points out, "The culture depends on the business unit or tower you are in. Some are, out of necessity, very systems- and technology-oriented—like the software group—and others are more focused on the customer, like the sales and distribution group in the industrial division." Colleagues mention that, overall, the firm is a sociable place where people enjoy working together. "The culture is lively. There are a million little groups for things ranging from happy hours to running clubs to volunteer work. The people are friendly, intelligent and fun. And the dress code is very laid-back," notes one analyst. In short, boasts a manager, "It is an extremely people-friendly environment. People care about each other and are always interested in learning more about one another and enjoying their co-workers in a nonwork environment (i.e., happy hour)."

One thing's for certain—the supportive attitudes of colleagues at IBM win praise from insiders. "The best things about the firm are the teamwork and sense of camaraderie. Everyone is willing to offer help or assistance, and to make you feel part of the team," a junior staffer affirms. Reportedly, the huge size of the firm doesn't keep these folks from feeling like a close-knit group. "Although the company is very large, I work on projects with a relatively small group of people. I have found them all to be intelligent, dedicated and cordial, usually developing good team camaraderie," states an insider. A co-worker explains that "on each project you work with new people, and that gives you the opportunity to help create a new culture within your team," while a co-worker adds, "Everyone at IBM is like a family—we all take care of each other."

Not the place for codependence

Employees also have positive things to report about their managers at the firm. "Supervisors and managers are down to earth. They make employees feel at home and are very welcoming," a consultant reports. Another insider confirms, "My partner is tops—both my internal reporting partner and my project partner. I would not leave them by choice. They are what make it such a great place to work."

But for those who need hand-holding, IBM probably isn't the place—most of the time, consultants work without much direct supervision. "Most people do not micromanage. The culture is generally pleasant, though contact with your high-level managers is quite limited," reports an associate. One colleague alleges, "I have only seen my manager once a year and she never calls me unless there is some administrative, performance measurement due date coming up." "I have had many managers over the years and only met a few of them. I have not had the opportunity to meet too many executives on my engagements, but the few I have, I had very good relationships with and often still speak with on a personal level," attests another source.

Time with teammates

A number of sources say that workweeks generally average a sustainable 50 hours, but of course that's "depending on the project and travel requirements." "There are some times where working may demand 80 hours per week, but probably 30 weeks we work an average of 45 to 50 hours per week only," details a consultant, speaking for the majority. One insider gets positively sappy about spending long hours with co-workers: "I rarely work over 55 hours a week and even when those times do happen, your teammates are so lovable that you don't mind being around them for prolonged periods of time."

Visit the Vault Consulting Career Channel at www.vault.com/consulting - with insider firm profiles, message boards, the Vault Consulting Job Board and more.

VAULT CAREER LIBRARY   131

The unwritten rule

Hours like these wouldn't normally warrant complaints, but some staffers get snarky about the amount of time it takes to actually meet the firm's billable-hour requirement. "It's a sweatshop," claims a consultant, stating, "Billable utilization rules all else. You can't go to class, be sick or attend your mother's funeral unless you make up the time. Of course, this isn't the written policy, just the realistic one if you want to get a decent performance rating. In essence, many more hours over 40 are required." Another source whines, "I spend, on average, 50 to 60 productive hours [working per week], not to mention the unproductive time of travel, eating and sleeping."

One source gives more insight into why those non-billable hours are a point of contention: "When you end up on an project with low or no billability, your manager tells you, 'Oh it'll be okay, we take that into account during the performance review.' However in reality, if you don't meet the target for utilization, you won't earn more than the 'average' review." A colleague further enlightens us: "In general, we have over 50 tasks to perform for the company over the course of a year. Some of these tasks are minor and only take a few minutes. A number of them are major and can take up to a week's work to complete." "It would be good if IBM recognized all the hours dedicated to the firm, not only the billable hours," suggests an analyst.

Balance at Big Blue

Due to positives like the work-from-home policy and a travel schedule that guarantees consultants are home on weekends, most staffers report that there's an even balance between the job and life outside. "I am able to balance work and life. There are times when I am giving the majority of my time to work to meet the client expectations. This is balanced out, though, during the downtime of the project," a source relates. Says another well-balanced source, "I am actively involved in my church and the community, and am able to negotiate a healthy work/life balance." One insider claims, "I think IBM has the best work/life balance of any company I have ever worked for. I travel most of the year. If I need to be at home for any reason, IBM allows me to work from home for that week or as long as needed. They work with us whenever needed. IBM bends over backward to help its employees in any way it can." Another associate who's found his equilibrium qualifies that balance exists "mostly because I make it a priority," adding, "I've been lucky enough to meet other consultants who help me to make it a priority. I know others, however, who have not been so lucky."

No matter how they feel about current work/life balance, insiders profess that over the years, the idea of work/life balance has come a long way from where it started. Declares a staffer, "It depends on client needs. IBM does focus on balance but sometimes it just doesn't work. It's better than it was five years ago when people were asked to cancel vacations. Another source indicates, "Generally there is a balance. There are only rare times when we're told we can't take vacation or time off—proposals, go-live dates or critical project milestones."

Bringing it on home

Even with policies that point to better balance, any consultant at this firm will tell you that a high level of commitment is simply part of life at IBM. "Although I now keep myself to 40 hours, that time is still stretched over seven days and even if it is not physically working, it is always mentally there. Our jobs aren't '9 to 5 and don't bring it home.' Our obligation and dedication to the client does not stop at 5. You can't check that at the door on your way out." A colleague seconds the motion: "You have to be 100 percent flexible for the client. That means showing up at 6 a.m. if that's what they want, or working until 10 p.m. if that's what they want." Another insider admits, "It's a daily struggle. My work is never done, so I have to make myself stop at the end of each day," while a first-year staffer adds, "As a new consultant, there is a pressure for excellent performance. This takes a lot of preparation, self-study and hard work that in turn makes balancing work and life a little harder to achieve."

But a number of insiders claim that bringing work home with them is part of what helps them maintain balance. "We are encouraged to work from home when we can. I like this because I feel that I get more done because I don't have to sit in traffic for two hours each day. I can start working right away," a source remarks. Relates one manager, "If I need to be at home a day during the week, I can work from home the entire week. Or, I can come home from the client site early and work around my schedule." "Work-from-home is an accepted practice and it helps greatly in maintaining the work/life balance," admits a co-worker.

User-friendly travel? Depends on the traveler

The majority of IBM consultants expect not to spend much time at home. Reports an insider, "Part of the employment agreement is that, as a consultant, you are willing to travel." A colleague affirms, "Frequent travel (80 to 100 percent) is a part of the consulting industry and is not excessive compared to other consulting firms." Another accepting consultant avows, "I have no problems with travel, it is part of the cost of doing business. If you can't travel, don't take the job." "The consulting practice has a goal of having staff work on a '5-4-3' basis, so that a person is only away from home three nights a week," an analyst relates. With that in mind, these road warriors seem pleased with the support that the firm offers to lighten the load. "IBM provides specific benefits to mobile consultants, such as legal assistance, health and fitness support, family counseling, financial/retirement planning, etc. Most of these services are provided at no additional cost," a manager explains. Another source adds that "IBM is good about covering expenses ranging from dry cleaning to car rental, meals, gas and even personal cell phone use. But again, this depends on the degree of travel, the area and the client."

While some consultants rave about the opportunity to travel, others maintain that extensive travel is to blame for the poor balance between work and personal life. "On most projects, we are only required to be away from home four nights a week. However, being away from home so much makes family and personal commitments difficult," notes an associate. One respondent claims that there's "too much travel—look at the employee turnover in the last six months as proof, and take a survey of the people who quit and ask what are the top-three reasons for quitting." One weary voyager says the minimum 70 percent travel requirement is "especially difficult for those with partners and/or kids. And typically, this is a nonnegotiable area for client-facing staff."

Luck of the draw

According to respondents, the amount of time IBM consultants spend traveling depends partly on the luck of the staffing draw. Says a manager, "Some folks are required to travel 100 percent. Sometimes you are lucky and get assigned to a local project. I know some consultants that have never traveled in eight years and others that travel all the time." "The travel requirements depend on the industry and specialty," reports a colleague, adding, "A person that does financial services and lives in New York will have limited travel. That person would have a lot of travel if they lived in Houston. IBM's practice is national and international, so there is a likelihood of a lot of travel." Another source interjects, "IBM requires that you are willing to travel. However, I am a consultant for the public sector, so travel is minimal because our clients are mostly in the D.C. area. This is not the case with the private sector, however."

Deferred enrichment

Reportedly, the firm has a strong training program, comprised of both on-the job and official training—mostly online—which insiders say is "generally excellent." "There is some type of training going on every week or month. Employees are encouraged to recertify and, furthermore, their education is paid by my company," adds an employee. "The training is generally available if one makes a case for how it can be applied and how it fits with your long-term plans. The official policy is 'just in time' training, where you get trained before you go to a project where you will apply that particular training. That is generally unworkable and does not promote depth of knowledge, so management approves training where appropriate," a senior consultant explains.

The downside, insiders indicate, is that while there is certainly no lack of available training, there just isn't enough time to pursue it. "The online and classroom training that is offered by the firm is satisfactory, but since there is no time allotted to training, I have not been able to participate," one staffer relates. A co-worker claims, "IBM has a wide variety of training offerings but actually penalizes you if you take it. Your chargeability expectations are so high that you either do not take vacation or training." And another colleague mentions a similar experience: "Training is easily available and some is mandatory—on our own time. However, it seems rather difficult to get time away to go to training classes, especially when you are assigned to a client." Even

Visit the Vault Consulting Career Channel at www.vault.com/consulting - with insider firm profiles, message boards, the Vault Consulting Job Board and more.

VAULT CAREER LIBRARY   133

if official training is hard to squeeze in, there's still plenty of learning going on, assures a source: "I've learned more through informal mentoring and on-the-job training, but that's how most adults learn."

Raising concerns

There is quite a bit of grumbling going on about compensation at IBM. Rants one source, "Our compensation and bonus structure is absolutely horrible. It has to be the industry worst." "Actually, it would be good to give people raises," a manager advises, admitting, "I know some folks who haven't seen a raise in three years." Another insider echoes the sentiment: "Raises are miserly; though IBM advertises up to a 12 percent range, even if you receive an above-average performance rating, you are not likely to get more than a 6 percent raise—typically 3 percent. Raises are also based on your entire division's performance. Therefore, even though you may be stellar, if your entire team is not wonderful, you lose out." "Bonuses are a joke, and after taxes it comes out to getting two paychecks within one pay period," moans another staffer.

Sources also claim that when it comes to compensation, there's not enough communication from management. Relates an associate, "IBM does a miserable job regarding variable pay due to bad or no communication of how measurements are determined and what an individual can contribute to achieve targets. Every year the official announcement to the public is that we had a great year, but the consultants receive the message that the targets were not achieved and therefore the bonus payment will be low. This leaves a very bitter taste in the mouth of all consultants, especially if this is happening four years in a row." Declares another source, "Promises are great, however promises have been like that since 2001 and I have not seen a real fulfillment of promises. However, the company said that this year will be different—that they actually will do something for us. I really want to see it."

Pay isn't paramount

There are insiders who contend that the positive aspects for the firm make up for disappointing compensation. One manager puts it in perspective: "In general, IBM is a great firm to work for if your main goal is to learn, experience top-of-the-line technology and work on amazing projects. If your goal is to make money, look for another firm." "IBM does not dish out huge raises or bonuses. If you are looking for a flexible work environment and job security, this is the place to be," declares another. A colleague chimes in, "I have been offered a lot more money to go to another firm. I refused the offer several times just because IBM is so good to me. The money is important. However, being happy with your company and wanting to come to work is far more important."

Paid to stay healthy

Across the board, consultants say, IBM offers "good health benefits and a good company match on the 410(k) plan." And according to sources, it pays (literally) to stay fit. "You are given a $150 rebate for not smoking and a $150 rebate for living a healthy lifestyle," a colleague notes. "This year I will be exercising four times per week and will receive $150," confirms an insider. Mentions another appreciative employee, "IBM offers discounts on a lot of things from photo development to Cingular Wireless services, to H&R Block tax refunds, to computers and flat-screen TVs. You also get to keep your hotel points and airline points, though not you car rental points." Staffers also praise the parental benefits offered, including "$2,500 for adoption and two weeks off paid, with manager's permission."

And while IBM isn't known for fancy fringe benefits, there are added perks like "thank you awards," an insider says: "There is the occasional surprise award for a job well done." Boasts one source, "They flew me to Puerto Rico as a top performer for a weekend," while another co-worker adds, "One day, out of the blue, my company gave me $5,000. There are also some project managers that are generous with nice dinners and tickets to sporting events."

Women in charge

When it comes to gender diversity, insiders deem IBM to be top notch. "There are great women role models at high levels of corporate headquarters to emulate. [The firm is] very involved and helpful, and reaches out with events, web sites and web casts targeted specifically to women," one consultant indicates. Another source adds, "The top executive in the consulting practice is a woman and there are many women in various leadership positions." "I am a woman, I work for a woman and my managing partner is a woman. I have never felt at a disadvantage working for IBM because I am a woman," declares a colleague.

Insiders also recognize that the firm makes an effort to retain women who need to cut back on travel for family reasons. Acknowledges a staffer, "Many women are recruited, but they still have a harder time staying with the profession than men do. The work/life issues are harder for them. IBM has moved several women to roles such as outsourcing and internal projects that allow them to maintain their careers without the heavy travel."

"Diversity is everywhere"

Colleagues maintain that IBM is also strong on minority diversity. "You couldn't ask for a more culturally diverse company," asserts a senior consultant. "I think it is a very diverse environment—it is fantastic. Every project is as diverse as it can be: women, men, Asians, Latinos, Caucasians, Europeans, Africans and others," an insider details. According to an associate, "A look at a typical consulting team will demonstrate that diversity is everywhere," though one insider suggests that "African-Americans are not represented as much as they could be."

Support groups for all

Sources also give shining reports of the firm's efforts toward gay and lesbian diversity. Insists a senior employee, "[The firm is] very receptive. Being gay in IBM is a nonissue. It's the most gay-friendly place I've worked, and I've worked for many of the Beltway bandits." Another analyst mentions that GLBT diversity "is brought out in orientation. IBM has respect for everyone, and makes sure that everyone fits in." "Same-sex couples are eligible for partner benefits. I am not in this category, but am proud of IBM being on the cutting edge of recognizing civil rights of all Americans," shares an insider.

Sources indicate that it's impossible to work at IBM and not find a support group to fit an individual interest or affiliation. "From a corporate standpoint, IBM encourages networking within our groups; for example, there is a women's networking group, and soon there will be a Hispanic networking group, which I plan to join," mentions one associate. Another source verifies, "We have many networks called communities of interest—I believe there more than 100—from the telecom industry community to gay and lesbian to women in business."

No coffee in cubicle-land

A few insiders in Ohio are pretty satisfied with their surroundings. Notes a consultant, "It's very well designed for mobile and anchored employees, and has great technology." More often, however, sources recount tales of no-frills office locations. One Boston source moans, "The offices for mobile consultants could improve in privacy, area, ergonomics, phone devices and natural light." A colleague in D.C. complains, "They took away our coffee and all the other good things. The office is practically a ghost town." And a Maryland source glumly says, "It's cubicle-land with minimal windows and lots of fluorescent lighting. Generally it's not maintained well with supplies," and adds that there's no coffee to be found there, while a colleague pitifully appeals: "This is petty, but bring back the filtered water and the coffee."

But, in general, the offices aren't a big sticking point for staffers, since "the primary locations for work are client and home." "I have never been to an IBM office aside from new-hire orientation," mentions an Oklahoma-based employee. "The consulting staff is mostly on a 'work-at-home' status so that we seldom go into the office, even when not assigned to a project."

Charity work comes naturally

Consultants at IBM may be stationed all over the place, but that doesn't prevent them from coming together to contribute to local causes. Insiders say efforts include "teaching in schools, judging science fairs, helping out with career fairs, installing computers in schools and Habitat for Humanity." "There is an entire group dedicated to sending out e-mails looking for volunteers to go to soup kitchens, provide canned goods or go to women's shelters," notes a source, adding, "There is also an established system for

Visit the Vault Consulting Career Channel at **www.vault.com/consulting** - with insider firm profiles, message boards, the Vault Consulting Job Board and more.

VAULT CAREER LIBRARY   135

donating obsolete software to NGOs and other charitable groups." One staffer relates, "We get extra points for [community service work], which usually comes naturally to those who come to work with IBM. I ran the Employee United Way Campaign this last year for our sector and won a desktop computer with all the bells and whistles to be given to my charity of choice for bringing my team in at 100 percent." A colleague notes, "It is 'unofficially' required that employees participate in such events. I have been involved in tutoring as well as clothing drives in Philadelphia organized by the company."

One of the firm's many charitable programs focuses on boosting technology in underserved schools. Explains an insider, "My company has a program that offers schools computers. The employees can buy computers for qualified schools. The employee pays 20 percent and the company matches 80 percent of the price. I donated three computers two year ago to my children's school, and last year was able to completely equip their computer lab with new computers. Every student in this small private school wrote a thank-you note for the new computers."

"The best things about the firm are the teamwork and sense of camaraderie. Everyone is willing to offer help or assistance, and to make you feel part of the team."

– IBM Global Services staffer

Visit the Vault Consulting Career Channel at **www.vault.com/consulting** - with insider firm profiles, message boards, the Vault Consulting Job Board and more.

VAULT CAREER LIBRARY   137

Gartner, Inc.

56 Top Gallant Road
Stamford, CT 06902
Phone: (203) 964-0096
www.gartner.com

LOCATIONS

Stamford, CT (HQ)
Operations in 75 countries

PRACTICE AREAS

Gartner Consulting
   Benchmarking Solutions
   IT Measurement & Management
   Market & Business Strategy
   Public Sector Solutions
   Strategic Sourcing
Gartner Events
Gartner Research (includes Gartner Executive Programs)

THE STATS

Employer Type: Public Company
Ticker Symbol: IT (NYSE)
Chairman & CEO: Gene Hall
2007 Employees: 3,800
2006 Employees: 3,700
2006 Revenue: $1.06 billion
2005 Revenue: $989 million

UPPERS

- "Brightest people I've ever worked with"
- Consultants are not constantly on the road
- "Relatively low utilization target compared to the industry"

DOWNERS

- "Not a lot of synergy between the lines of business (research, events, sales and consulting)"
- "It used to run like a smaller consulting firm with a big name, but is starting to operate more like a Big Five"
- Internal systems and processes aren't as efficient as they should be

EMPLOYMENT CONTACT

www.gartner.com/gartner_careers/careers.jsp

THE BUZZ
WHAT CONSULTANTS AT OTHER FIRMS ARE SAYING ABOUT THIS FIRM

- "Research guru"
- "Consulting services are underdeveloped"
- "Family-oriented"
- "Prima donna analysts"

THE SCOOP

Not just research

Gartner's business comprises three practice areas: Gartner Research (which includes Gartner Executive Programs), Gartner Consulting and Gartner Events. Since it came into existence, the firm has been associated with its well-known research division that points toward trends and identifies industry front-runners. Though not as high profile as its research practice, Gartner's consulting division brings in a fair share of the firm's overall revenue—almost 28 percent in 2006. Under the consulting umbrella, Gartner serves clients through benchmarking solutions, IT measurement and management, market and business strategy, public-sector solutions and strategic sourcing. Today, Gartner employs 3,800 people and operates out of 75 countries. On its long list of clients (numbering 60,000) are 65 percent of the Fortune 1000 and 80 percent of the Global 500 companies.

From private to public—twice

Headquartered in Stamford, Conn., Gartner was founded in 1979 by Gideon Gartner, an ex-IBM staffer and former tech securities analyst. Gartner originally started the firm to advise companies on buying and selling their IT equipment. In its early years, the company, known as Gartner Group, gained a reputation for giving the inside scoop on IBM's products and services. After a period of rapid growth, the firm went public in 1986 and was ranked by *BusinessWeek* as one of the best small companies in America. In 1988, the firm was purchased by British advertising giant Saatchi and Saatchi, but Gartner gained control again in 1990 through a leveraged buyout. In 1993, the firm's profits soared and it went public again, listing its stock on the Nasdaq. Gartner remained with the firm until that year, when he sold his equity position and completely severed ties with the company. The firm was transferred to the New York Stock Exchange in 1998, and is traded today under the symbol IT.

Keeping pace with globalization

Gartner has definitely made the move toward more global operations in the past few years. In September 2005, the firm established a wholly owned foreign enterprise (WOFE) in Beijing to boost its presence in China. The WOFE expanded possibilities for the firm to serve companies and international businesses in the country. Like a number of its IT clients, the firm has also expanded in other hot up-and-coming countries, such as Romania and Poland. However, in Latin America, Gartner made the move to cut its consulting services in 2004 to refocus on IT services, executive programs and events in the region.

Befriending an enemy

Since going public in 1993, the firm has acquired more than 30 companies to bolster its service offerings. The most buzzed-about acquisition was in 2005, when the firm purchased archrival META group, an IT research and technology firm with 52 worldwide locations. The $168 million deal added the energy and utilities, insurance and government sectors to the firm's portfolio of industries served. Gartner also explained that, as part of the merger, the expanded company's analysts would conduct rigorous review processes to try to smooth out conflicting positions between Gartner and formerly competing META analysts. Among other notable buys was Dataquest, Gartner's market research arm, in 1995, and Real Decisions, in 1993, which became Gartner Measurement, now folded into Gartner Research.

$1 billion and growing

In the past few years, Gartner's financial performance has remained solid. In 2005, overall revenue grew over 10 percent to $989 million, and in 2006 the firm passed the $1 billion revenue mark, a 7 percent increase over the prior year. The consulting division posted $305 million in revenue, up slightly from $301 million in 2005. Gartner's research division also grew 9 percent in 2006, posting $571 million in revenue.

Visit the Vault Consulting Career Channel at www.vault.com/consulting - with insider firm profiles, message boards, the Vault Consulting Job Board and more.

VAULT CAREER LIBRARY 139

Seeing the future

Gartner keeps its name in client view through its widely published forecasts and analysis of hot topics, often in the IT industry. Each year, the firm puts out *Gartner Predicts*, a blog covering areas like wireless telecommunications, regulatory compliance and security software. The firm keeps close tabs the IT market as a whole—a topic relevant to most of its clients. In December 2006, Gartner published 10 key predictions for IT organizations in 2007 and beyond. One of the most talked-about items on the list was the prediction that Vista will be the last major release of Microsoft Windows. Gartner estimates that the next generation of operating environments will be "more modular and will be updated incrementally." The firm also predicts that by 2010, 60 percent of the worldwide cellular population will be trackable, thanks to "follow-me Internet" technology, and that through 2011, businesses will waste a total of $100 billion buying the wrong networking technologies and services.

Trendspotting

Outsourcing is another hot topic consistently on the firm's radar. Gartner indicates that the number of jobs sent offshore now is only a drop in the bucket compared to the number of jobs that will be outsourced in the future. It also estimates that 30 percent of all IT jobs in developed countries will be offshored by 2015. Spending on offshore research and development and engineering will increase by a whopping 860 percent, to $12 billion in 2010, according to the firm. Aside from running numbers and analyzing outsourcing statistics, Gartner hosts the annual Outsourcing Summit, where academics and business leaders speak about outsourcing best practices and pitfalls.

Measuring up

Gartner consultants' work is often intertwined with Gartner research, enabling them to offer a variety of services that focus on outsourcing and IT management. For clients who want to know how their spending and best practices stack up in relation to their peers, the firm utilizes its extensive research to offer benchmarking, a service within the consulting division that draws on 5,800 environments a year—the largest IT performance repository in the industry. Financial services providers, pharmaceutical manufacturers and IT companies are examples of the clients that call on the firm's benchmarking services. Recently, a state government agency hired Gartner to conduct an independent assessment of cost efficiency in several internal technology areas. Because the agency was a repeat client, Gartner drew up a trending report from an analysis of current and past operations. Consultants also compared the agency to other organizations of similar size and characteristics. Based on its analysis, the firm provided a comparison of the client's costs, staffing and service, feedback on the its position relative to the IT marketplace and recommendations to increase efficiency of the client's infrastructure services.

Web-wise

Gartner's experts take advantage of blogging to chat about business happenings and express opinions. Though the blogs might offer outtakes on topics Gartner covers for clients, the firm stresses that its blogs are strictly commentary and should not be considered official research. Since 2002, the firm has been blogging about current events like the blackout of 2003 and the expansion of the European Union, as well as pertinent business topics. Today, the firm hosts blogs on customer relationship management, the media industry and the high-performance workplace, among other topics. The blogs' creative design and usability earned Gartner the prestigious Webby People's Voice Award for Best Business Blog in 2006, dubbed the Oscars of the Internet by *The New York Times*.

GETTING HIRED

Are you experienced?

Gartner's short and sweet careers web page gives basic information about the firm and links to online application databases for various regions. There's no information about campus recruiting, though insiders say the firm draws from top schools. That said,

"What we are bringing in are experienced consultants, not MBAs right off the bus," a source tells us, adding, "There's a little gray hair and a lot of experience." According to a colleague, "We are a senior-leveraged consultancy, so most of our consultants have industry experience. We do get junior-level hires from graduate programs or some undergraduate programs, but really that's the exception. It depends on the person." "We are typically looking for about five years of related experience beyond advanced degrees. And most people have advanced degrees," another source chimes in.

Even though experienced hires are favored, insiders say that doesn't mean you'll be stuck in one area of specialization once you join Gartner: "Everyone comes in having some area of capability and specialization already, but you're not going to be pigeonholed early on. We expect people to have core capabilities where we do business, and from there is always an opportunity to apply those and go into new situations, so your experiences are also broad."

A cross-sectional approach

Following a successful prescreen by HR, we're told, "each consultant needs to prepare a case study that we give them ahead of time. Candidates prepare a presentation based on the topic of the case study. This is for everyone, independent of level, but obviously we take into account capabilities according to your seniority and we would expect more from a manager-level hire than from a consultant level." The consultant continues, "The first thing we do is a group presentation. Then there are extensive rounds of interviews in the same day. There is also lunch with a senior partner. Interviews are across the board—you'll meet with a junior person, because we also want the opinion of a junior person. Then you'll meet with subject matter experts. We are trying to get a cross section of opinions. At the end of the day, we have a meeting where everyone gets together to talk about the candidates." As another source sums up, "The process in our office is to do a phone screening, bring them in for three interviews and a case study, and then an offer is made."

OUR SURVEY SAYS

Wearing many hats

You'll find "a bunch of type A players" at Gartner, a source says, yet the atmosphere still manages to be "collegial." An entrepreneurial culture pervades the burgeoning consulting arm, explains an insider: "We are in high-growth mode, so that makes us very attractive for people who want to wear multiple hats." Several sources praise the intelligence and savvy of their colleagues: "People are driven and very smart … There is a lot of respect for each other, since you know everyone is coming in from very diverse backgrounds," says a staffer, who adds that teamwork and cooperation are also Gartner hallmarks. One Arlington-based consultant declares his office's culture to be "the best" among the firm's locations, with around 150 people "who represent all core lines of Gartner businesses," leading to "real synergy."

Another hallmark of the firm is its collaboration with clients, says a source. "We are not an ivory tower consultancy. Everybody at every level is getting their hands dirty with clients. That's what I like about this job—working directly with clients. If I was ever in a position where I couldn't do that, I wouldn't be happy." Consultants also enjoy the autonomy Gartner offers, an insider tells us, though this "has its pros and cons. For junior resources who are looking to be in a highly structured environment with well-defined, discrete roles, doing repetitive tasks—that's not Gartner's environment … We give a lot more responsibility to junior people and, frankly, it's a great environment."

Hey, buddy

"Gartner is becoming much more social" as the firm grows, says one consultant. In fact, a source adds, there are signs the firm is maturing: "When we have events in our region, it's getting to be more family-oriented and families attend it. Instead of a golf outing, this time it's going to be a family picnic." Gartner also makes newcomers feel welcome through its "people first" department, an insider explains. "That department checks up and figures out which office the person is joining, then they find people at their peer level and they are assigned as that person's buddy. The buddy initiates contact with the newcomer before

Visit the Vault Consulting Career Channel at **www.vault.com/consulting** - with insider firm profiles, message boards, the Vault Consulting Job Board and more.

VAULT CAREER LIBRARY   **141**

they come into the office to give them information on the dress code, etc., and tries to assimilate them into the office. They introduce them around to everyone."

Strategy shift

Work/life balance at Gartner is "probably as good as it could be in this industry," says an insider, who adds, "We are all professionals and we do what it takes to get the job done, but when you have the time available and you can take it, you take it … Nobody is watching the clock—it gives you a lot of independence and flexibility." "I think we are getting better at work/life balance," another source says, as "we are transforming to a more long-term strategic advisor to clients, rather than a 'come in and hit or miss.' Two years ago, we had lots of engagements and lots of clients. But juggling engagements in that way could lead to a 50- to 80-hour week, since everything could blow up at once. We have been shifting to larger deals, with more density on engagements, and aiming for no more than two projects per consultant. It's the whole 'people first' thing—it is that we realize we have to invest in associates, and help them grow and thrive." A colleague comments, "Most people struggle with work/life balance not because of Gartner, but because they are very focused on their clients and providing value."

Shutting down for the weekend

Hours average between 50 and 60 per week for most Gartner consultants. "Sometimes you have to work on weekends," says a source, "but for the most part, my policy has been that on Friday evening I shut down for the weekend. I might turn on my laptop Sunday night to check e-mail and get prepped. Only if there is a deadline project and it's a tight schedule and there's lots to be done—then I might work on the weekend."

Insiders tell us that the firm keeps an eye out for balance. "The first few months I joined, my utilization was through the roof. My regional leader actually sat me down and said, 'You need to chill out, we don't want you to burn out. Stop taking on half a dozen projects and killing yourself, because at the end of the day I want you alive.'" Another consultant praises the firm's "solid resource management function," noting, "We have people watching out for resources that are getting overutilized—reports being run to make sure resources are not being overtaxed—and we try to do load-balancing across the resource pool. Does it work perfectly? No. But as far as consulting goes, it works pretty well."

Some for all

And as consultants know, balance often hinges on how much travel is required. At Gartner, this is highly variable, with staff in the Washington area rarely asked to leave the Beltway, and others traveling on a project-by-project basis. An insider notes that while "there's an attempt by Gartner to have people work closer to their home offices," the firm also wants to make sure it has "the right resources on the right projects, so for that reason you may have to travel a lot." According to another consultant, "Travel is project-driven. There will be times when I won't travel for three months, and it's dependent on where the client is. There is some amount of travel for all, and for the most part I would say the average is two or three days every two or three weeks. The other good part about it is we have the flexibility of working from home. So on the office days, we don't absolutely have to come into the office."

Project durations also vary, though sources suggest that the trend at Gartner is leaning toward longer engagements. An insider notes, "We are shifting from shorter duration engagements to longer, deeper-density gigs. The 'time away from home' will only increase as this trend continues." As for project teams, a consultant explains, "Typical project teams are three to four people," adding, "but that can scale up. They're made up of some junior and senior people, and there's a VP oversight role for quality assurance."

Your money or your life

When you ask Gartner consultants about compensation, the term "trade-off" frequently pops up. "I think I would not necessarily say we are the highest-paid consultants, but I suppose there is a slight trade-off. We have some form of a life. We aren't spending all our time in different hotels and different airports. Life is much easier and people have some form of relationships with their families," says a consultant. A co-worker agrees: "As far as pay goes, I think we're low. We're getting better. However, if you look at the pay against the work/life balance that we have, I think it's pretty good. A lot of people are starting to make that trade-off."

Regardless of how they stack up against their peers, Gartnerites generally seem satisfied with their salaries, though one consultant grumbles about a widely varying range and low raises. "Considering how much we bill to our clients, it doesn't seem to be represented in our salary," he sighs. Bonuses, according to another insider, are "improving significantly," and becoming "much more individual performance-based." A co-worker explains, "Every level has a base salary and a bonus associated with that base salary. It's different for every level and the percentages get higher, the higher the level. Over the past two years, I have received a higher-than-expected bonus."

Time after time

Gartner isn't known for fluffy perks, but one that stands out is the firm's "personal time" policy. An insider explains, "Once you get to a certain level of tenure, you can get six to seven weeks a year of personal time. It's hard to use it, but it's nice." Agrees a colleague, "Around us, there's a good deal of vacation that you can have—of course, that runs directly against your utilization, so that can be an issue for some people. But if you work really hard, then you can have a chunk of time off, get recharged and get back in the game. From what I've seen, people are allowed to have that time … I've seen the firm be very good to people who have had to take personal time off." Other benefits include a stock purchase program, a "401(k) that vests monthly," and "good health coverage."

Taking time to train

A consultant reports, "We have both formal and on-the-job training, so it's balanced. We have formal training when you come onboard—there is an extensive new-hire training program, which takes several days. Then we have Gartner University, which keeps you trained over the duration of your career on various skills. We also take advantage of semiformal lunch-and-learns, which are extensively used to make sure people stay on top of capabilities."

And there are other approaches to learning at the firm, an insider explains. "We are developing more solutions and certifications. We don't deliver out-of-the-box solutions, but there is a standardized approach or framework you can use, or core templates—we are developing ways to leverage work done in the past. We are investing as a company in a knowledge management system that we can use and access, though it's not actually a training program. We do have special interest groups, with roundtables and ways to reach out to other folks who have the same area of strength or interest."

But one staffer voices his dissenting opinion: "I personally think Gartner needs to improve on training. There is a certain amount of training that happens on the job, so you're learning as you go on a project. We do have regular training sessions, where you are on a conference call and you might walk through a process, but it isn't like there are formalized times set aside for training." Another insider agrees, stating, "Training is valued by the firm and supported; however, we do not have a culture where training is exercised by the associates." One reason for this, suggests another, is that "the delivery schedule [of training offerings] is very unpredictable." Reports a colleague, "It's a flexible work model, so most people have the time to take advantage of the formal training opportunities. What they do with their free time, however, is up to them."

Maximum mentors

Another way Gartner consultants grow is through their higher-ups. "The level of coaching and mentoring I am able to get here is the best thing about working here. I also am able to get into stretch roles at this point, so it's something I really like," says a source. Through a formal program, "someone who is a level above you is assigned to you, and is responsible for helping with career planning, as well as getting staffed on engagements and plotting near-term, current-year performance management activities. They serve as an advocate for the individual both now and in a three- to five-year approach." A colleague adds, "We have annual and midterm reviews, and also independent development plans, in addition to performance reviews. We lay out the career paths we'd like to take. We can describe our objectives and we can manage it personally, but the company makes sure it

Visit the Vault Consulting Career Channel at **www.vault.com/consulting** - with insider firm profiles, message boards, the Vault Consulting Job Board and more.

VAULT CAREER LIBRARY   **143**

provides the environment where you can really follow that plan. The nice thing is, even if I choose a delivery path, for example, I can at any time cross over to another area, so it's very flexible."

Insiders praise the open-door policy to be found among Gartner's management. "We have titles, but I consider Gartner to be flat, so the title really doesn't matter—it's about your capabilities and what you bring to the table for any project," says a source. According to a colleague, "As a senior consultant, your thoughts and views will be heard. Due consideration will be given to you. I can sit in a meeting with a senior director, we can be hashing out something and I can refute him/her, and I'll never be told not to say anything."

In addition, says a consultant, "The ability to interact with clients is pretty good, and it's only heading more and more in that direction. If you look at where Gartner was three or four years ago, the work might have been more behind-the-scenes analysis, where you worked with clients and on more specialized engagements. Now we are looking at clients who are going through big change initiatives and we have leveraged the brand to guide clients through bigger programs. We have moved from a one-off approach to a client-centric approach, so when you do that there is a lot more face time and visibility with clients."

Women on top—or not

Calling Gartner "naturally diverse," one insider comments, "There are women in leadership roles and we've had presidents of consulting in the past who were women, and directors and VPs across the board who were women. I know that there were breakouts at our consulting meeting for the women at Gartner. I don't know how formal that is or what the association is, but there are definitely groups for women." Others disagree, however, with one consultant reporting, "There are very few women in executive positions within my business unit; diversity is not a strong part of our culture," and another source chiming in, "Most of the women in our business hold administrative roles and there is limited female leadership." Says a female insider, "We are heavily focused on technology, so there is always a tilt toward the other gender, but in my office in Virginia, we are pretty diverse from a gender perspective."

"I think we have gotten better lately in terms of diversity," a source adds, specifying that minority hiring has improved as well. But another insider notes that "we could use a little more" minority diversity, and "there aren't any formal programs that I'm aware of." Gays and lesbians are welcomed at Gartner, with benefits offered to same-sex domestic partners.

Watch your region

Community efforts at Gartner are "office- and region-dependent," and "the larger offices have more of this happening," says a source, who adds, "We do have something known as Gartner Matches, so if you decide to give money to a charity, then Gartner will match your charity donation almost dollar for dollar to a certain level." As far as active participation in community events, a colleague adds, "This year, we had a number of events to support the American Cancer Society."

"We have people watching out for resources that are getting overutilized— reports being run to make sure resources are not being overtaxed—and we try to do load-balancing across the resource pool."

– Gartner consultant

Visit the Vault Consulting Career Channel at **www.vault.com/consulting** - with insider firm profiles, message boards, the Vault Consulting Job Board and more.

VAULT CAREER LIBRARY   **145**

L.E.K. Consulting

28 State Street, 16th Floor
Boston, MA 02109
Phone: (617) 951-9500
Fax: (617) 951-9392
www.lek.com

LOCATIONS

Boston, MA (US HQ)
London (Worldwide HQ)
17 offices around the world

PRACTICE AREAS

Finance
Marketing & Sales
Operations
Organization
Strategy
Transaction Management

THE STATS

Employer Type: Private Company
Co-Founder & Chairman: Iain Evans
2007 Employees: 700+
2006 Employees: 650

RANKING RECAP

Practice Area
#9 - Economic Consulting

Quality of Life
#4 - Travel Requirements (tie)
#11 - Formal Training
#15 - Relationships with Supervisors
#16 - Compensation (tie)
#20 - Offices

UPPERS

- "Good about recognizing, rewarding and challenging top performers"
- "The firm is rather young, which gives it an energetic and fun environment"
- Limited travel
- "Opportunity for personal and professional development at a fast pace"

DOWNERS

- "Our cases are shorter in length, so there's not much time for rework or coasting"
- "Too much private equity due diligence"
- Going through the growing pains of setting up standard processes and communication channels
- "You feel like an interchangeable part"

EMPLOYMENT CONTACT

www.lek.com/careers

THE BUZZ
WHAT CONSULTANTS AT OTHER FIRMS ARE SAYING ABOUT THIS FIRM

- "Gaining presence; strong brand among private equity/buyout circles"
- "All due diligence, all the time"
- "Strong on 'pure' strategy"
- "Workaholic culture"

THE SCOOP

Bain branch-off

L.E.K. is a London-based strategy consulting firm, serving clients from 17 offices in Europe, North America, Australia and Asia. Initially a small venture, LEK Partnership was launched by three ex-Bainies in 1983, serving British businesses. Ten years later, the firm merged with U.S. consulting company The Alcar Group to form L.E.K. Consulting. The global firm now employs over 700 staff and serves clients in a broad range of industries, including travel and leisure, energy, life sciences, retail and consumer products, health care services, financial services, media and entertainment and private equity. Its clients run from smaller startup companies to Fortune 500 companies and government agencies, as well as a number of the Eurotop 300. L.E.K. is proud to say that its clients keep coming back—90 percent of its work is from repeat customers or referrals.

Centered on strategy

L.E.K. divides its services into six practices: finance, strategy, marketing and sales, organization, operation and transaction services. Its core service—and the largest chunk of its business—is the strategy practice, offering corporate strategy, growth, business unit strategy, industry dynamics, regulatory and policy, strategic planning processes and financial strategy. Though the firm offers a breadth of strategy consulting, it claims extensive experience in M&A advisory work and shareholder value consulting. In the M&A sector, the firm was recently recognized by *Acquisitions Monthly*, winning the 2006 Due Diligence Advisor of the Year award.

Keeping score

The firm's own series of publications address issues that influence shareholder value. For 12 consecutive years, L.E.K. has collaborated with *The Wall Street Journal* to produce the Shareholder Scoreboard. The annual Scoreboard comprises the WSJ 1000, by analyzing shareholder returns for the largest companies, categorized by market capitalization as listed in the Dow Jones U.S. Total Market Index. The firm also ranks businesses in the Asia-Pacific region, by publishing similar scorecards with *The National Business Review* of New Zealand, *The Australian* and *The Bangkok Post*. L.E.K.'s quarterly newsletter, *Shareholder Value Insights*, covers strategy issues that establish competitive advantage and foster growth.

A variety of internal publications and newspapers, such as the *Financial Times* and *The Washington Post*, regularly feature the insights and research of L.E.K. consultants. The firm's *Executive Insights* newsletter is an industry-specific publication that discusses trends and provides insight for corporate leaders. The February 2007 issue, entitled "How to Succeed in China's Multi-Layered Retail Environment," explored four major challenges to successful retailing in China. In 2006, VP Stuart Jackson published *Where Value Hides, A New Way to Uncover Profitable Growth for Your Business*. The book advocates that the key to building value and improving a company's strategic market position is to identify the right market segments in which to focus efforts. L.E.K. also presents at and sponsors many industry events, such as the Association for Strategic Planning conference in 2007 and the Wharton Healthcare Business Conference in 2007.

The leisure market

In November 2006, L.E.K. hosted a master class called Winning in Asia's Tourism & Leisure Sector: Choosing Wisely and Getting the Most Value from your Investments. As incomes have risen and businesses have expanded in the region, tourism has rapidly picked up speed, making opportunities for investment more attractive. At the conference, the firm's experts made presentations on how to identify the most promising investments in the Asian tourism market and how to manage those investments in the future. L.E.K. has established a track record in the region through its own investment there—the firm maintains offices in Tokyo, Beijing, Shanghai, Singapore and Bangkok.

Visit the Vault Consulting Career Channel at **www.vault.com/consulting** - with insider firm profiles, message boards, the Vault Consulting Job Board and more.

VAULT CAREER LIBRARY   147

Pirates beware

As the issue of copyright theft has garnered quite a bit of attention recently, L.E.K. has gotten involved in the debate with its studies on film piracy. The firm originally conducted research on the issue for the Motion Picture Association of America in 2005. The study concluded that in 2005, major U.S. studios lost $1.4 billion, while worldwide studios lost $6.1 billion, due to bootlegging, illegal copying and Internet piracy. The survey, which covered 22 countries, marked the first time that the potential loss from copyright theft had been formally quantified. The study was picked up by *The Wall Street Journal* in 2006 and subsequently by the *Los Angeles Times*, *Irish Independent* and *The Australian*, among other publications. The MPAA had commissioned the study in hopes of gaining support from governments to crack down on bandits.

Big on biotech

Over the course of its 25-year history, L.E.K. has built a strong biotechnology practice. In fact, the firm claims to have the largest practice dedicated to biotechnology among established strategy consultancies. The firm has worked with over 250 life sciences and biotech companies, including Amgen, Biogen, Celera and Vertex Pharmaceuticals. Institutions like the National Center for Genome Resources in New Mexico and the Melbourne-based Garvan Institute have also enlisted L.E.K. consultants to conduct research. In 2006, the Ministry of Research, Science and Technology, along with New Zealand Trade and Enterprise and NZBio, New Zealand's national biotechnology industry group, commissioned L.E.K. to compile "The New Zealand Biotechnology Industry Growth Report." The report gave a complete analysis of the industry, by measuring the performance of the biotech sector and exploring New Zealand's successes and future capabilities.

L.E.K. also sponsors and sends its experts to speak at biotech and drug industry conferences. In 2006, one of the firm's vice presidents was a panelist at the GTC Bio 2nd Modern Drug Discovery & Development Summit in Philadelphia, and the Drug Discovery Technology and Development World Congress in Boston. The firm also sponsored the Bio 2006 conference, the Wharton Healthcare Business Conference and the PureTech Ventures Innovation Meeting.

Biotech benefactors

The firm doesn't limit its involvement in the biotechnology world solely to strategy projects; it has been active in supporting numerous events for charitable causes, particularly related to medical research. In 2007, L.E.K. was a sponsor at Gilda's Club New York City gala, benefiting cancer research and survivors, and at the Mathew Forbes Romer Foundation Awards Ceremony, which supported research of children's genetic brain diseases. L.E.K. also showed its colors by sponsoring the Children's Brain Tumor Foundation benefit and the Special Olympics Bio-Ball Tournament, both in 2006.

GETTING HIRED

Sizing up the market

L.E.K. may recruit from the very top of the East Coast business school pile—Harvard, Princeton, Columbia, Dartmouth, etc.—but it also opens its undergrad scouting arms to a broader U.S. pool, including West Coast hopefuls at Stanford, UC Berkeley and UCLA, with Brigham Young and Northwestern thrown into the mix as well. At the MBA level, the firm targets schools like Harvard Business School, Sloan, Kellogg, Wharton, Stanford and the University of Michigan, along with Ivy League graduate institutions, for potential consultants.

The L.E.K. two-step

Current L.E.K. employees describe the interview procedure as a "typical case interview process"; one consultant elaborates that the "interview process typically consists of two rounds: two interviews during the first round" and "three interviews during the next round." The course of action for first-round campus interviews depends on timing. If the firm recruits on cycle, interviewees get face time, but if off cycle, candidates will find a mix of phone interviews and in-person interviews. As far as the who's who of the L.E.K. interrogation squad, one consultant says first-round interviewers range "from associate consultant to manager level," while managers and VPs conduct successive interviews.

Candidates are posed with both case and fit questions, but we're told that "most of the interviews are case-based," mainly focusing on market-sizing and business strategy questions. "Interviewees are gauged on analytical ability, business and problem-solving logic, fit with the firm, communication and demonstrated leadership/management," one senior associate consultant reports. Another seasoned employee adds that there's "an emphasis on quant." So L.E.K. contestants had better be ready to play because, as an insider states, "If you're not quant-strong, you'll have problems."

OUR SURVEY SAYS

Culture vultures

L.E.K. consultants don't shy away from praising fellow officemates; one source describes the working climate as "young, dynamic and entrepreneurial," and another adds that "co-workers are genuinely nice and have positive attitudes, which helps make the work environment fun and makes you feel part of a team." In such a close-knit, friendly culture, staffers feel comfortable extending colleague relationships beyond office quarters, "with frequent social events, and a good base of people that like to go out together." One associate, agreeing that staffers are "generally friendly and fun to be around," doesn't want people to get the wrong idea about life at L.E.K. While colleagues are fun to party with, it's not all about the party. "The culture is all about getting the work done, no matter how long it takes or how difficult it is."

Open range

L.E.K.'s spirit of camaraderie is also demonstrated by its "open-door policy." One consultant attests to the firm's literal take on the phrase: "Only the partners have offices and they are glass; the doors are truly open. All of them are easy to approach and the office head knows the names of everyone in the office, from the most junior associates on up." And L.E.K. certainly doesn't let new consultants stagnate; multiple first-years discuss the firm's accelerated responsibility shifts, with hefty pushes toward upper-level and client interaction after only a six-month tenure with the firm. "Junior-level employees are given ample opportunities to take ownership of project modules, so there is a high level of responsibility," one source relays. Another contact acknowledges that "L.E.K. has a lot of faith in its consultants. If you're good, the firm will have no problem leaving you alone in the room with a CEO."

New consultants are also provided with "great learning opportunities for personal growth," one first-year declares, through gaining access to senior partners and staff. And post-MBA consultants entering the firm are offered chances "to work directly with Fortune 100 CEOs and board members" within the first 12 months, another employee says. Because of L.E.K.'s open and trusting management, staffers say they gain confidence at much earlier stages than they would at other firms. As one confides, "From what I have heard about other firms, and my experience at L.E.K., I'm not sure there could be a better situation for interaction with clients, as well as with the top-level partners at L.E.K."

Hours and after hours

Though long hours are definitely par for the course, many L.E.K. insiders feel that it's easy to burn out. "Hours can be tough, because we do a lot of short-timeline cases for private equity and hedge fund clients," shares one consultant; our insiders hit anywhere from 50 to 90 hours on the workweek clock, with 50 hours set as the firm minimum, and the firm average hovering around 60. Another insider reports, "The pace can be quite intense, and at times rather stressful." And staffers claim they have "no time on the beach between cases, so the long hours begin to compound after awhile." But as one employee says, "It is not always an easy job. The good news is that, although we often work late during the week, we rarely work on weekends."

It's a relief that work-filled weekends don't seem to plague L.E.K. consultants. Even when a Sunday session is in order, "it is rare that it requires coming into the office," a source replies. And while insiders may grumble about long, unpredictable weekday

Visit the Vault Consulting Career Channel at **www.vault.com/consulting** - with insider firm profiles, message boards, the Vault Consulting Job Board and more.

 149

hours and trouble scheduling weekly activities, one colleague speaks for many when he says L.E.K "consultants and managers recognize that there is life outside of work, and are willing to work around personal commitments." Another co-worker goes even further, saying that "there is a big push from the top level at our firm to reduce the number of late nights worked." According to consultants, senior managers take extra steps just to figure out whether working late "is necessary to make a deadline. Since it is coming from the top down," a first-year explains, "it feels that work/life balance is more than just lip service." At the end of the day, L.E.K. consultants commend their firm for attempting to bridge a gap often ignored; an employee says that L.E.K.'s "work/life balance is among the best in the industry. The pursuit of career goals does not impede the pursuit of personal goals."

Homebodies

Staffers also feel fortunate to work within a relatively travel-free zone; says one consultant, "When you start to consider a career in consulting, travel seems exciting, but living out of a suitcase gets old fast. With L.E.K., I rarely travel, so I get to live a fairly normal social life." At this firm, business trips center mostly around client presentations and rarely spill over onto a second day, and most respondents cite the lack of travel as one stressor they can happily duck past. The absence of travel also contributes to a positive work environment for many consultants. According to one, L.E.K. is a "very tight and fun culture, especially because we are all in the office together, as opposed to at a client site."

Switching gears

Word has it that L.E.K. is making monumental changes to its formal training procedure. Where more informal, on-the-job instruction reigned in the past, the firm has gone beyond fine-tuning to what some employees might call an overhaul. "There were revisions of the entire curriculum over the past year and the hiring of a full-time training manager to write curriculum and manage the process," a consultant tells us. With L.E.K.'s professional development program gaining momentum, another source remarks that "the firm has invested quite a bit in taking it to the next level."

But adding steel to the firm's training boots hasn't compromised L.E.K.'s dynamism. Even though winds are changing, one consultant says there's still "a grassroots feel" to the process, and most staffers report that "a large portion of training happens on the job." Formality may be present at some stages—one staffer reports being in London for three days of training—but respondents say they gain the sharpest and most valuable knowledge through colleagues, informally and on-the-job. As one associate consultant sums up, "Efforts are being made to improve official training, but unofficial is what's valuable."

Sharing is caring

Staffers at L.E.K don't complain too much about base salary levels—starting compensation is "fairly competitive"—but the firm's profit-sharing perk seems to furrow a few brows. One insider tells us, "We have a firmwide profit share based on how well the firm did in the previous year," and according to consultants, the plan isn't all it's cracked up to be. "For the last two years, profit share has been 20 percent of salary plus performance bonus," says a colleague, and "a lot of your bonus (more than half) is profit share, and therefore not personal performance-based."

While profit sharing is great in theory, some consultants wish they could see more profit filling their own pockets. "Profit share is nice," admits a source, "but L.E.K. should really shift more of its compensation toward personal performance."

Did somebody say beer trolley?

Despite some money grievances, insiders do feel that L.E.K. offers significant perks. "There is no up-or-out policy for promotion, which I believe many consulting companies have," a senior associate consultant tells us, which provides relief to staffers. And promotion rewards are plenty, it seems. Hardworking employees receive "two weeks of extra vacation time upon promotion to consultant or manager, if you have been at the firm for at least 18 months," we're told. And one associate mentions "a swap program where associates can swap to one of our international offices for six months," which he considers "a great opportunity that I think is somewhat unique."

Employee perks also manifest themselves in the form of happy hours, holiday parties, celebratory team dinners, golf and spa outings, and annual practice retreats. But that's not all: Colleagues benefit from a multitude of material goodies as well. Several consultants mention receiving a present from Tiffany's as a holiday gift, and one new staffer deeply appreciates "the beer trolley that comes around every Friday afternoon providing free beer for everyone around 5 p.m."

A room with a view

While L.E.K. consultants do not claim to work in luxury, insiders are pleased with office locale. As one L.A.-based source shares, "We are located in downtown Westwood, which is the best place to work in L.A. because it is close to where most people want to live. Plus," he adds, "there are lots of restaurants and shops within walking distance of the office, which is quite rare in L.A." The beach views may be hard to beat, but "L.E.K. really needs to update the furniture and facilities," a colleague remarks. Across the country, Boston staffers savor their "excellent views of Faneuil Hall/Quincy Market," commuting convenience and prime after-work social scene, but grumble about the office's rapid expansion—"it's hard for office space to keep up," sources say.

Passing the baton

Not only do employees benefit from the firm's bounty, but surrounding communities get some, too. "L.E.K. encourages and sponsors a number of community charities" and "is working on a pro bono consulting project," a senior associate explains. The project is run through the organization INSPIRE, which unites pre-MBA consultants to help out small nonprofit organizations. In addition, says a Boston consultant, "L.E.K. also sponsors a number of other events, such as the Special Olympics, the 'Bio-ball' event and the Pan-Mass Challenge." In the Los Angeles office, L.E.K. lends a hand by organizing "holiday toy drives, cooking dinner for the homeless and participating in 5K runs for charity," among other deeds. Charitable giving seems to be organized locally, since "each office has a community service committee that sponsors community service events like tutoring and charity donations, etc."

The diversity divide

Though one insider at L.E.K. tells of "an even split between men and women at the lower levels of the firm," most recognize the proportion's tendency to taper and nearly vanish at the manager and partner level. But receptivity apparently isn't the problem; as a staffer reports, "We are very receptive, we just don't get a lot of candidates. It's really a self-selection problem." Many consultants note a somewhat concerted effort to attract qualified women to the firm, but we're told that L.E.K. is "more applicant-driven than firm-driven."

When it comes to racial and ethnic diversity, consultants offer up the same observations: "We are receptive, we just don't get many hires," a colleague says. And with regard to sexual orientation, staffers again demonstrate tolerance. "As a gay male," an insider shares, "I feel that the company is very open and respectful," and adds that "it is really a nonissue being openly gay here at L.E.K." These sentiments reverberate around the L.E.K. halls, with another consultant emphasizing, "I think the firm is very receptive to diversity with respect to sexuality."

Visit the Vault Consulting Career Channel at **www.vault.com/consulting** - with insider firm profiles, message boards, the Vault Consulting Job Board and more.

 **151**

14 Accenture

1345 Avenue of the Americas
New York, NY 10105
Phone: (917) 452-4400
Fax: (917) 527-5387
www.accenture.com

LOCATIONS

Offices and operations in more than 150 cities in 49 countries

PRACTICE AREAS

Management Consulting
Customer Relationship Management • Finance & Performance Management • Human Performance • Strategy • Supply Chain Management

Outsourcing
Application Outsourcing • Business Process Outsourcing (BPO) • Infrastructure Outsourcing

Systems Integration & Technology
Complex Solution Architecture • Enterprise Architecture • Enterprise Solutions • Information Management Services • Infrastructure Consulting Services • Integration • IT Strategy & Transformation • Microsoft Solutions • Mobile Solutions • Research & Development • Service-Oriented Architecture

Operating Groups
Communications & High Tech • Financial Services • Government • Products • Resources

THE STATS

Employer Type: Public Company
Chairman & CEO: William D. Green
Ticker Symbol: ACN (NYSE)
2007 Employees: 152,000+
2006 Employees: 143,000
2006 Revenue: $16.65 billion
2005 Revenue: $15.55 billion

RANKING RECAP

Practice Area
#1 - Operational Consulting
#5 - Energy Consulting
#6 - Financial Consulting
#7 - Pharmaceutical & Healt Care Consulting (tie)
#8 - Human Resources Consulting

Quality of Life
#7 - Formal Training
#14 - Offices

Diversity
#17 - Diversity for Minorities

UPPERS

• "Opportunities to see the world"
• "A great place to learn how to manage large projects"
• Extensive support system
• "Ability to grow professionally"

DOWNERS

• "The culture has become less 'glamorous' and more 'ho-hum'"
• Below-average compensation
• "Red tape"
• "Still working through what it takes to make partner since going public"

EMPLOYMENT CONTACT

careers3.accenture.com

THE BUZZ
WHAT CONSULTANTS AT OTHER FIRMS ARE SAYING ABOUT THIS FIRM

• "Technically sound"
• "The McDonald's of consultants"
• "Great training and discipline"
• "Long implementation projects"

THE SCOOP

Banking on strategy

In the past, Accenture might have been known for its origin as the consulting arm of Arthur Andersen, however it's the firm's sheer size and impressive earnings record that define it today. Accenture is one of the world's largest consulting firms, counting over 152,000 employees located in 150 cities worldwide. The past few years have seen impressive earnings, and 2006 was no exception: Revenue grew 14 percent to $16.65 billion, proving that Accenture has been able to nail its own strategy for success.

The firm delivers its solutions to clients through three major service areas: consulting, technology and outsourcing. Strategy consulting is still the backbone of its business, offering change management, customer relationship management, enterprise performance management, finance management, human resources performance, service management, strategy, supply chain management and workforce performance. In 2006, consulting services pulled in $9.9 billion, almost 60 percent of total revenue. The outsourcing group is quickly catching up, however, contributing $6.75 billion that year, a 14 percent increase over 2005. Accenture organizes its capabilities into five operating groups: communications and high tech, financial services, government, products and resources. The communications and high tech group traditionally contributes the most revenue—in 2006, the group brought in $4.1 billion in revenue—while the products division posted $4 billion in revenue. Accenture boasts 91 of the Fortune Global 100 and nearly two-thirds of the Fortune Global 500 as clients, many of them long term.

That's some brand name

Accenture, established in 1989 as Andersen Consulting was formed when a group of partners from the consulting division of the various Arthur Andersen firms around the world established a new organization focused on consulting and technology services related to managing large-scale systems integration and enhancing business processes. Andersen Consulting was established as a separate business unit under Andersen Worldwide Société Coopérative (AWSC), a Swiss administrative entity. Though Andersen Consulting had reportedly sought a split since 1998, independence was finally granted on January 1, 2001, after a drawn out negotiating process and a $1.2 billion payment to Andersen. The new name was initially scoffed at ("Accenture" being a blend of the phrase "accent on the future,") by industry observers, and even inspired a mock web site that satirized the "nonsense name" trend of consulting firms at the time. Now reportedly worth $6.7 billion and ranked as the 49th most valuable global brand by *BusinessWeek* in 2006, the moniker has earned its credibility. Accenture also ranked No. 1 in information technology services on *Fortune*'s 2006 Most Admired Companies list.

Banner year

In 2006, the firm counted its fifth consecutive year of record revenue. It was also the first year that the Americas region raked in more than the EMEA (Europe, the Middle East, Africa) region. Revenue from the Americas was $7.7 billion, up 15 percent from 2005. Asia is Accenture's third geographic region of focus, which accounted for $1.2 billion for 2006. The firm wowed Wall Street when its share price hit an all-time high of $36.67 on December 21, 2006. Accenture also chalked up $20.4 billion in new business and brought on 43,000 new hires in 2006, attaining a 13 percent employee growth rate for the year.

Bleak days

In its first few years, Accenture faced skepticism from critics who doubted it had the clout to survive on its own. It also came onto the scene during a distressed economic climate, due to the stock bubble burst in 2001. Determined to prove skeptics wrong, in July 2001, then-CEO Joe Forehand took the firm public in a $17 billion IPO, just before the market rebound. A second public offering in May 2002 raised an additional $93 million in capital. Accenture's technology venture unit was a bust, however, and had to be sold in March 2002 after it failed to generate revenue.

The firm followed most of its competitors by slashing staff between 2001 and 2003, amidst a sinking post-September 11 economy. But instead of cutting all ties with laid-off employees, the firm proposed a voluntary flex leave—a six- to 12-month

Visit the Vault Consulting Career Channel at **www.vault.com/consulting** - with insider firm profiles, message boards, the Vault Consulting Job Board and more.

VAULT CAREER LIBRARY   153

sabbatical with benefits and 20 percent of current pay, and guaranteed a job upon return. The slump persisted through 2002, but by 2003, the firm got its revenue back on track and hired 20,000 new employees in the next year.

Changing hands

Joe Forehand, who served as CEO and chairman from 1999 to 2004, was by most accounts responsible for leading the firm's split from Andersen, rebranding and launching a successful IPO, as well as guiding the firm through the downturn. A popular favorite among employee ranks, Forehand was named Most Influential Consultant of the year by *Consulting Magazine* in 2001. In September 2004, William Green took over as CEO, and later as chairman, upon Forehand's retirement in 2006. Green, an outdoorsman and self-proclaimed Jimi Hendrix fan, is a 29-year veteran of the firm. In a 2004 *BusinessWeek* article, Green stated that he intended to make Accenture the "must have" advisor to corporate America and, in some cases, to guarantee results for clients by foregoing the firm's pay if certain performance metrics aren't met.

Dodgy digs?

When Accenture incorporated in 2001, it became the first professional services firm to register in Bermuda. The beachy vacation spot is favorable to businesses, since it levies no income or capital gains taxes and has relatively lax corporate regulations. The firm has faced criticism from those who believe that companies based in offshore tax havens shouldn't be able to win federal contracts. In July 2002, legislators attempted to pass a law to that effect, but it was blocked in Congress. Accenture lobbied Congress aggressively, arguing it had never been incorporated in the U.S. (as Arthur Andersen had been), and therefore hadn't moved offshore to dodge paying its due. It also affirmed that tax advantages were only one factor in choosing a location: With more than half of its 2,500 partners as non-U.S. citizens, Accenture claims Bermuda is a neutral location in which to base its global business.

Fair enough

Accenture pulls in a plethora of public-sector contracts, competing with traditional government go-tos like BearingPoint and Lockheed Martin. One notable deal was inked in June 2004, when a group of consulting firms led by Accenture won a 10-year U.S. border security contract worth up to $10 billion. Accenture's Smart Border Alliance (made up of Raytheon, the Titan Corporation and SRA International) was chosen by the U.S. Department of Homeland Security to develop US-VISIT, a system for tracking the whereabouts of foreign visitors to the U.S. The system would use biometric information obtained at 400 entry points and maintained in a central database. Again, the deal met with scrutiny from politicians voicing objections to awarding such a lucrative contract to a non-U.S. firm. However, since the firm met the criteria of procurement (it has 25,000 U.S. employees and pays federal taxes), the DHS argued there was nothing unfair about giving the contract to the most competitive bidder—in this case, Accenture.

Public-sector pros

In September 2006, the Department of Justice chose Accenture to develop, operate and maintain an integrated debt collection system for the department and its affiliates, including the U.S. Attorneys Offices. The new system will streamline communication and reporting between organizations and provide tighter financial controls. If all contract options are exercised, the multiyear deal could be worth $54 million. The firm scored another defense contract that same month, when the DHS awarded it a five-year deal to work on the Enterprise Acquisition Gateway for Leading Edge Solutions (EAGLE) program. EAGLE is the Department's vehicle for acquiring information technology services. Accenture was handed two portions of the EAGLE deal, involving software development and management support services.

The firm signed yet another five-year deal in March 2006: a $79 million contract with the U.S. Air Force to design, build and operate its new Defense Enterprise Accounting Management System. The project is aimed at remodeling the Air Force's finance and accounting methods. Also that month, the firm won a three-year, $179 million contract extension with the U.S. Department of Education to continue operating and maintaining the Office of Federal Student Aid's Direct Loan and Pell Grant origination and disbursement processing system, which Accenture developed. Recently, NASA launched a new Accenture-devised financial system, which supports the agency's $16.5 billion budget and 18,000-person workforce. The firm has been involved with the project since 2000, designing, configuring and testing NASA's SAP Core Financial platform.

Tangle in Texas

Though government work keeps the cash flowing in, it's not without its headaches, as Accenture knows from it's recent project in Texas. The firm came under fire by public officials in the Lone Star State for its project revamping enrollment in state aid programs. In 2005, Texas Health and Human Services Commission awarded Accenture a contract worth $840 million to update IT systems. Part of the engagement involved developing a user-friendly system to enable Texans to apply for Medicaid, food stamps and other programs in person, through the Internet, over the phone and by fax or mail. The project came under scrutiny, however, when in November 2006, Texas State Comptroller Carole Strayhorn issued a report accusing the firm of using the contract to boost profits. The report cited department layoffs and increasing privatization of the state's welfare system as unwanted results. It also claimed that the job was to blame for 20,000 needy children being dropped from Texas' Children's Health Insurance Program (CHIP). According to Accenture, the Texas Health and Human Services Commission noted that CHIP enrollment numbers had begun declining in November 2005, before the firm even started the job, due to more stringent eligibility requirements and an improved state economy. The contract's supporters questioned the timing of Strayhorn's report, having been released just before the comptroller entered the governor's race later in the year.

In other states, Accenture has been busy with a stream of human services and finance projects. In October 2006, the firm was awarded a $28 million, five-year deal with the California Public Employees' Retirement System, the U.S.'s largest public pension fund. The project involves upgrading the fund's IT system with a new web-based approach.

Bulking up in the wings

Accenture has strengthened its global presence with a host of engagements worldwide. The firm was tapped by the Greater Toronto Area in October 2006 to design and implement a smart card system for public transit in the region. The 10-year contract is worth $250 million CDN, and will be the largest transit payment system in Canada. And, across the channel, New Look, a large womenswear and footwear retailer in the U.K., awarded Accenture a 10-year, £23 million contract extension in April 2006. The firm will develop, manage and maintain New Look's U.K. and European core trading, supply chain and retail operations systems. In Februrary 2006, Alliance & Leicester plc, the seventh-largest U.K. bank, brought the firm onboard to overhaul its core IT systems by implementing its proprietary banking solution, Alnova Financial Solutions™. Accenture will replace the bank's key legacy systems with Alnova over the next three years, and will provide application development and maintenance services.

Walking away

Accenture also made the bold move of offloading one of its problematic outsourcing engagements in September 2006, after it reportedly ran into extensive delays and cost overruns. In 2004, the U.K.'s National Health Service awarded the firm a $23.5 billion contract to revamp its IT infrastructure. The project, called the "NHS computer upgrade from hell" by the *British Observer*, involved designing a network to connect 30,000 doctors with 300 hospitals and fully streamlining patient care by the year 2014. Two years behind and $11.5 billion over budget, the project was widely criticized by taxpayers and politicians. The firm attributed some of the delays to Isoft, one of the NHS subcontractors that supplied software. The two parties reached an agreement in 2006: Accenture bailed and Computer Sciences Corporation took over the remainder of the contract. The cancellation didn't seem to have too devastating an effect on the bottom line, however; though Accenture took a $450 million pretax profit hit in the second quarter of 2006, there was no impact on earnings per share for the quarter.

Visit the Vault Consulting Career Channel at **www.vault.com/consulting** - with insider firm profiles, message boards, the Vault Consulting Job Board and more.

VAULT CAREER LIBRARY   **155**

Outsourcing machine

As the fastest growing sector, outsourcing is making up an increasingly larger chunk of Accenture's business. In the past, CEO Green has stated that outsourcing should bring in 50 percent of the firm's total revenue, and the firm isn't far off that mark—in 2006, 42 percent of revenue came from outsourcing engagements, and Accenture has been the top pick for large BPO deals from companies like Halliburton, BP North America and the London Stock Exchange. In January 2007, the firm scored a 10-year, €100 million BPO contract with AIG Europe SA, a property and casualty insurer. Accenture's Bucharest service center will provide an IT platform and other support services for AIG Entrepreneur, the AIG unit specializing in insurance for small and medium businesses. Erste Bank group, Austria's second-largest bank, outsourced its procurement operations to Accenture in July 2006. The firm will supply a procurement platform and will run the bank's procure-to-pay functions, including order processing, payables and procurement contract management. And in March of that year, XM Canada, the country's largest satellite radio provider, signed an $11.5 million, three-year deal for Accenture to provide application outsourcing services to support its customer care and business platform.

Closer to home, in October 2006, the firm inked a five-year agreement with the Confederated Tribes of the Umatilla Indian Reservation (CTUIR) in Oregon to help manage Cayuse Technologies, LLC, a newly established American Indian enterprise. Cayuse Technologies will provide companies with services such as software development, call center, help desk, image and document processing, storage and retrieval, and finance and accounting support.

The HR niche

Lately, Accenture has been a rising star in the human resources outsourcing market as well, thanks to winning one of the largest HR BPO deals to date. The firm snagged a seven-year deal with Unilever in June 2006 to take over HR functions for over 200,000 of its employees in 100 countries—a contract reportedly worth over $1 billion. In April 2006, the firm also bagged a seven-year contract with paper products giant Kimberly-Clark, to perform a range of HR services, like payroll administration, workforce reporting and employee data management. And in February 2005, Accenture was tapped by BT to provide HR services in a $575 million deal. According to the "2006 Worldwide HRO Market" report published by IDC, the firm is the top HR outsourcing service provider based on its contracts, wide reach and capability.

A year of acquisitions

Accenture continues to expand its capabilities through strategic buys; as a matter of fact, 2006 was an acquisition heyday. In September, Accenture bought Navisys, a privately held life insurance software firm. The deal was expected to increase Accenture's presence in the industry, as it takes on more than 50 of NaviSys' clients. In July, the firm completed its acquisition of Random Walk Computing Inc., a technology consulting firm specializing in trading system applications, risk management systems and other technologies for banks and financial services providers. And in May 2006, Accenture purchased Pecaso Limited, a tech consulting firm specializing in SAP human capital management services. That same month, the firm pumped up its strategy capabilities by snapping up Hagberg Consulting Group, a strategic consulting company that specializes in the assessment of organizational culture and its alignment with corporate strategy.

BPO is another practice area getting a boost from acquisitions. In July 2006, Accenture purchased two specialist companies, Ohio-based Advantium and U.K. firm Meridan Informed Purchasing. The two niche players use sophisticated processes and proprietary software to analyze clients' procurement and payables data to prevent, detect and recover lost profits or erroneous payments. In April 2006, the firm acquired finance BPO specialist Savista Corp. After the purchase, Accenture formed a new BPO unit to serve middle-market companies, and named Savista CEO Jeff Bizzack to the CEO chair of its Accenture BPO Services division.

Indiacentric

Accenture's leadership is clear about its plans in India: By the end of 2007, the firm will have more employees in India than any other region, including the U.S., when it adds 8,000 hires to its existing staff of 27,000 there. The firm describes the subcontinent as "a critical part of the Accenture world." Accenture also opened a new delivery center in Guragaon in September 2006—the firm's tenth outpost in India. The center will offer applications, infrastructure outsourcing and systems integration services. To attract talent, the company offers a variety of incentives for prospective hires and emphasizes progressive policies that encourage women to apply. The women-friendly firm offers extras like day care centers and home office setups. Its plan seems to be working: According to *The Hindu Business Line*, as of March 2005, about 25 percent of Accenture's employees in India were women.

Accenting the globe

Accenture is also set to reinforce its ranks in other emerging spots through global delivery centers, which distribute work to 52,000 staffers worldwide. The company plans to hire up to 30,000 new workers from China, India and the Philippines over the next three years with the intent to raise productivity in their software development and other offshore projects. The firm opened its first Japanese delivery center in Hokkaido in August 2006. Accenture already has a strong footprint in Eastern Europe, with centers in Prague, Bratislava and Riga. In January 2007, it opened its second center in the Czech Republic in Brno, to provide technology services including application maintenance and development, as well as system integration, and offer services in multiple European languages. A delivery center focusing on BPO for finance, HR and procurement was opened in Bucharest in July 2006. In May of that year, Warsaw became the site of another office, which will provide BPO services in finance, accounting, supply chain management and HR. Currently, the center employs almost 600 staff.

Though India has been the center of attention when it comes to outsourcing, China is proving to be another hot growth area. Accenture has been helping to revamp systems for state-owned businesses and has assisted with IT projects for the country's four major telecom carriers. Recently, Accenture built a new core banking system for Minsheng Bank, and worked with the Shenzhen State Tax Bureau to help implement a more efficient IT system. Accenture also implemented a new generation trading platform for the Shanghai Stock Exchange in 2004.

Persuasive research

Since Green stepped in as CEO, he has advocated an aggressive approach to research and development, emphasizing the goal for the firm to be the first to come up with innovations for clients. With that aim, Accenture has established R&D labs worldwide. In September 2006, a tech lab in Bangalore become the firm's fourth, with others in Palo Alto, Chicago and Sophia Antipolis, France. Some of the firm's efforts revolve around "intelligent devices," or non-PC-oriented electronic devices. One program, Online Health Services, seeks to automate processes that assist chronic care patients in hospitals. It provides around-the-clock monitoring and intervention through wireless health devices and advanced analytics. Another innovation, predictive monitoring, identifies and addresses equipment failures before they occur—in kitchen appliances, automobiles and machinery. In February 2006, the firm's brainpower was called upon by French insurer MMA, to test the viability of digital pen and paper technology in the industrial risk underwriting process. Digital pens, which can store time-stamped content, would allow agents to speed up the underwriting process, which currently requires them to repeatedly handwrite data on paper forms.

Another buzzed-about invention out of the Sophia Antipolis lab is a mirror designed to show you a picture of your future self, released in May 2006. A computer builds a profile of a person's lifestyle, using cameras that film your everyday life at home. The webcams feed those images into a software program, which then translates how that behavior will affect a person's weight and appearance in the long term. If the computer feels a person is overeating or couch-lounging too much, it will calculate how many pounds to add to the image of the person standing in front of the mirror. The main purpose of the persuasive mirror is to give the user a concrete visual of the effects of overindulgence, and to determine how body image might be used to bring about positive change.

In print and on the web

Accenture regularly publishes its research, surveys and studies on a range of topics to interest clients in every industry. *Outlook* is the firm's journal focusing on high-performance business strategies. The February 2007 issue featured an article on how

Visit the Vault Consulting Career Channel at **www.vault.com/consulting** - with insider firm profiles, message boards, the Vault Consulting Job Board and more.

VAULT CAREER LIBRARY   157

companies can stay ahead of the curve by shaking things up when times are good, rather than in the middle of crisis. A January 2007 survey focused on discovering the top concerns of 900 business executives as their businesses become more global. It turns out that what these execs worry about more than anything else is how to maintain a common corporate culture.

Consultants also frequently author popular books on management and other business topics. Accenture exec Donald Vanthournout, along with fellow Accenture consultants, wrote *Return on Learning: Training for High Performance at Accenture*, released in July 2006. The book tells the story of how Accenture transformed its well-regarded corporate training program in the middle of an economic bust. Accenture's folks also voice their opinions through blogs and podcasts. *The Trivergence* blog, penned by Andy Zimmerman, explores how consumers and industries are adapting to a digital device age. Ed Gottsman, of Accenture Technology Labs, writes about surprising, often unwelcome ways that technology is used all over the world in the firm's tech blog. And Accenture's downloadable podcast series features an assortment of subject matter experts speaking about relevant industry topics and strategies.

World citizens

The firm devotes a lot of energy to corporate citizenship through the initiatives of consultants and executives. Much of its corporate giving centers around education. In 2007, the firm introduced a scholarship program for junior and community college students. CEO Green takes a personal interest in junior colleges, having attended Dean College, a two-year school, before proceeding to a four-year university to finish his bachelor's degree. In addition to scholarship funds, recipients at the junior-year undergraduate level are eligible for summer internships at Accenture. The firm awarded 20 scholarships of $5,000 each in 2007. In September 2006, the firm provided scholarships to 10 American Indian students through its American Indian Scholarship Fund, established in 2004. The program benefits the highest-achieving American Indian and Alaska Native students seeking degrees and careers in technology, professional and business fields.

Accenture also publicizes its involvement in worthy causes in the *Corporate Citizenship Review*, which covers the firm's charity and pro bono work, partnerships and employee volunteering, as well diversity programs. In 2006, the firm pledged $62,000 in cash and $538,000 in consulting services to the Louisiana Association of Nonprofit Organizations, to support the launch of the New Orleans Nonprofit Central resource cooperative. The cooperative will provide basic operations and technology services to nonprofits in the New Orleans region devastated by Hurricane Katrina. The firm's consultants are also active in the Volunteer Service Overseas program. VSO regularly sends staffers on three- to 12-month assignments as teachers or business planners in impoverished countries.

Female focus

Accenture also focuses on its recognition and support women in the workplace. In 2005, *Working Mother* magazine ranked Accenture one of the top-100 companies for working mothers for the fourth year in a row. Annually, Accenture offices worldwide plan events to commemorate International Women's Day. In 2006, events in 20 countries included discussions with prominent women like Dr. Mae Jemison, the first African-American woman in space, and Dina Dublon, former chief financial officer of JPMorgan Chase. In 2006, the company earned the Minority Corporate Counsel Association's Employer of Choice Award, recognizing its commitment to an inclusive workplace, particularly within the legal services area.

GETTING HIRED

Casting a wide net

Accenture's recruiters can be found conducting career fairs and on-campus interviews at dozens of colleges all over the country. "Recruiting is based on the needs of the geographic area for which the office resides. Overall, the recruiting process focuses on Tier 1 schools in and around the metropolitan areas in which the demand exists," tells one source. Wharton, Kellogg, Cornell, Notre Dame, Indiana University and University of Michigan are just a few of the schools where the firm holds on-campus interviews. But Accenture doesn't like to limit its applicants to just a few schools, according to an insider who notes, "Any school is a possibility, we just don't get to campus at every college."

"Are you normal?"

"The [hiring] process is rigorous and focuses on sought-after behavior profiles. It works," a manager states. Sources admit that the interview process "varies drastically," but typically consists of three rounds. According to one manager, "The first round asks: Are you normal? Are you interested in consulting?" "The screening process usually lasts about 20 minutes and ensures that you meet five key categories," another source adds. The second round is usually more behavioral, to find out "how you react to fast-paced environments, difficult situations and complex/convoluted problems." For the final round on site, a source claims that interviewers seek to find out: "Are you normal (double check)? How do you function in a new environment? Are you definitely interested in the firm (as shown by questions/intelligent conversation)?" "The third interview is a bit more about your track record and ways of working—and also about selling Accenture to the candidate to make sure it is a mutual fit," a staffer comments.

Fire away

Though a few case questions may be thrown into the mix, more often the third round of interviews is about "giving examples" and answering situational questions. A source advises, "Be prepared for traditional, structured interviews (devise how many golf balls could fit into a football arena), and be prepared for them to ask you nothing at all." One common question asked is the following: "Summarize a challenging group situation that you faced and what you did to resolve it." In addition to forming logical answers to analytical questions, respondents tell us that "the interviewee is expected to wow interviewer with depth of questions posed." "I always encourage candidates to ask lots of questions, especially at the last interview to ensure that it is a fit for them," mentions an associate.

OUR SURVEY SAYS

All for one and one for all

Insiders say that what sets Accenture apart is the "extroverted and team-based" culture. Explains an analyst, "Our culture is highly collaborative and team oriented, which is a positive environment in which to work, even if it can sometimes slow down decision making." Another colleague specifies that "the corporate culture is very intense, and it varies by project—some are good, others are not. You bond tightly to others on your projects as you share long hours and challenging work. Overall, it is good." "The thing I like most about our culture is the energy and the team atmosphere," shares another source. Most consultants don't seem to mind extended togetherness, since most of them really get along with their co-workers. One staffer professes, "I would hang out with 99 percent of the people I encounter on projects—they are open to new things, are friendly and love to travel and explore the world." As far as managers at the firm, consultants call them "supportive and dedicated to mentoring." "I consider many of these people friends and role models, personally as well as professionally," avows a consultant.

Others insist that the Accenture culture is better defined as hardworking. "Our company's culture is all about high performance. You have to have a drive to succeed," mentions a consultant. Another source agrees, "Overall a great culture with a strong work ethic, but a little too caught up in the 'old way' of working long hours to get ahead (rather than working smarter)." Like it or not, this focus on performance "breeds innovation and stretching yourself beyond what you thought was possible," according to one manager.

Personality change

No matter how they define it, some insiders mourn the loss of the former Accenture culture, saying there's been a definite shift since the firm went public. One source regrets that "the firm has had a complete identity crisis since it has gone public. The

Visit the Vault Consulting Career Channel at **www.vault.com/consulting** - with insider firm profiles, message boards, the Vault Consulting Job Board and more.

VAULT CAREER LIBRARY   **159**

focus on the individual has completely gone away." A colleague concurs, stating, "Today, there is some residual of the old culture, but as we have expanded with an offshore body shop model, the people element has been drastically reduced." An analyst chimes in, noting that the change from "type A personalities has slowly shifted toward the 'get-it-done-and-go-home' crowd."

Decent exposure

Insiders boast that consulting roles at the firm provide a lot of client contact. "I have had access to people I never would have in a nonconsultant role," says an analyst. Those opportunities come early on, according to another source, who comments, "I've had great opportunities working with C-level executives my first month out of college, and working closely with clients' upper management on a regular basis." Staffers also claim to appreciate the variety that comes with working for a firm with such a wide range of practices: "It is like getting a different job every 12 to 18 months without having to switch companies," an insider notes.

Tolerable hours

A weekly average of 50 hours seems to be the norm for most consultants at Accenture, though sources maintain that hours "vary greatly by project." One associate details the cycle: "Usually, it's 40 hours per week at the start, gradually ramping to 60 hours a week where it stays for most of the project—and going to 80-plus hours a week for the last month or so," continuing, "Some projects are real death marches, quickly going to 80 hours per week and staying there for the entire project (up to a year). This really depends on the client and the project leadership." Most consultants claim that the hours over time are "reasonable," with a "typical day starting at 8 a.m. and finishing between 8 and 10 p.m." Declares one consultant, "In my career, I have never had to work crazy hours for an extended period of time. There have been periods of two or three weeks where I had to work a lot, but it is not that often."

"Always working, never living"

"If traveling is a problem, you shouldn't work for Accenture," a source bluntly states, with many insiders bemoaning the fact that "consulting employees can and will travel for years at a time." An associate acknowledges, "Accenture is very up front to prospective recruits, so travel requirements should not be a surprise." Despite being well informed about the necessity of travel, insiders claim is not an easy lifestyle. "Its very hard to get all of your necessary personal items completed on Friday through Sunday. Sometimes, the projects are not flexible with your travel schedule, so you have to set aside paid time off months in advance to make sure it's communicated properly." And, all those trips mean that the consultants who want camaraderie have to miss out getting to know their colleagues. An insider shares, "I don't know anyone in my home office. Haven't been to the office in seven months." Another manager puts it this way: "The impact of travel on my work life means that I am always working and never living."

Travel is not all doom and gloom, admits an insider, stating, "Being away from your home five days a week does not lend itself to a stable social life, however, in my case, I've found silver linings to the clouds. For example, Accenture's flex-trip option lets me travel to cities (other than my home base) on weekends. And as an after-work musician, the benefits of playing in various metro cities have outweighed the costs of my skewed home life." Concedes another colleague, "Travel is something that people get used to and can be managed by getting comfortable with the trade-offs." Nevertheless, a source qualifies, "There are a lot of flexible arrangements that can be made to reduce this travel, but I'm not convinced that they don't significantly reduce your growth/earning potential."

The work/life seesaw

Respondents agree that work/life balance "leaves much to be desired" at the firm. "Having a life while working at Accenture is very challenging. The demands of the project and client require that you consistently put in long hours. A simple example of the impact this company has had on my life is that I had set a small goal for myself over a year ago to be able to take a class one day a week, and today I have made zero progress on that goal," indicates an associate. An insider explains, "The number of weekends worked isn't what hurts the work/life balance. It's the near-100 percent travel—the total time away from home." "Accenture will work people until they quit," states a manager, while another source tells us, "I have received advice that if I plan on being successful in this firm, I should plan on checking e-mail and taking phone calls every weekend."

Other consultants hold to the notion that "work/life balance is the responsibility of the individual." "You must work to make your personal life a priority, but co-workers are generally respectful to your decisions," a manager explains. Admits a colleague, "I also think this has a lot to do with me, not the firm. It took a long time for me to realize where and when to draw my personal boundaries." Another source claims, "Personally, my work/life balance has seesawed for the past five years. At times, when it's teetered on the edge of falling, I've been able to take a step back."

The firm reportedly "provides many options and alternatives" to help consultants with balancing work and life, as evidenced by one consultant who returned to work after becoming a parent: "After having my son, I took 15 months off. When I returned to Accenture, I was able to come back in a client-facing role, while working three days a week and limiting my travel to day trips and occasional overnights. I was promoted to senior executive (partner) last year while continuing to work part time."

"The topic of the month"

"Compensation is always the topic of the month," declares an insider. Generally, sources indicate that "Accenture pay is under the market at all levels." One consultant gripes, "Accenture does not pay bonuses. For managers and higher, they provide a reward called variable pay, which is actually part of your salary compensation. However it is the biggest joke among employees because the payout (if a payout occurs at all) is insulting." The firm also offers profit sharing, though a consultant whines, "They call it profit sharing, but it is exactly 3 percent of your salary, regardless of the amount of profit the firm makes—I would not call this profit sharing." Reportedly, raises aren't too bad, though: "It's a good percentage increase year on year, averaging 15 percent," a source states. But is there hope on the horizon? One insider says, "It's not great pay for the hours and travel. They say they are working to increase it." Another senior associate assures, "The firm has been making progress on compensating the top 20 to 30 percent of folks and we have improved in this area since I joined."

However, much to staffers' dismay, the firm doesn't have the generous hand it used to have when it comes to doling out perks. "We don't offer them anymore: The Christmas/holiday party has been scaled back from a black-tie to informal event, the sporting event tickets are long gone and spending for local philanthropic events is also gone," grumbles a manager. A few sources mention that parental leave benefits at the firm fall a little short. "Accenture could do a better job on maternity leave. It only pays for eight weeks in the U.S.," notes one insider.

Despite budget cuts, consultants say there are still some nice extras, like "discounts on just about anything (cars, phone service, gyms, etc.) and concierge service through LifeWorks to manage requests." For staffers who get their friends hired, the firm gives a "referral bonus of $5,000 to $7,000 per successful referral."

Cheers for chairs

"Hooray for the Herman Miller Aeron chair," exclaims a source who's thrilled with the firm's facilities in Chicago. Staffers claim that "depending on the city, the offices are really, really contemporary and nice." Still, a New York consultant states, "Offices are pretty good and nice, but they are too open. The openness means that we are distracted by our peers." Ironically, an insider claims it's too cold in Florida, complaining, "The office temperature is poorly managed with some areas being freezing while others roast. The facility management doesn't care about our requests." But some consultants mention that it doesn't matter what the offices are like. "I spend the majority of my time at a client office so the quality of our offices isn't really important to me," says a staffer.

Visit the Vault Consulting Career Channel at www.vault.com/consulting - with insider firm profiles, message boards, the Vault Consulting Job Board and more.

 VAULT CAREER LIBRARY   161

Top-notch training

Where Accenture really shines, insiders say, is in its "excellent training opportunities." "Accenture offers and encourages a great deal of official training. However, you will receive a tremendous amount of unofficial training just by working with the other great employees of Accenture," says a source. Though there is reportedly "lots of informal mentoring," we're told that "most training has been classroom-based and has been very effective." An associate points out that "if Accenture doesn't offer a course, they will send you to an outside vendor." Consultants say "the only problem is finding time" to cram in all those courses. "On the other hand, when there is time, Accenture's structured core training is quite comprehensive and appropriate for its workforces and levels," acknowledges a staffer.

Accenturites are also excited about the firm's unique benefits that encourage consultants to pursue outside interests—for example, the "Future Leave Program, which allows professionals to plan a leave of absence for a few months to accomplish personal objectives." Another tells of "the Accenture Development Partners, a program in which consultants can decide to perform an approved consulting project for a nonprofit, NGO or government for three to six months in an underdeveloped region at a reduced salary."

Mentors for women

The firm's attention to gender diversity wins praise from insiders. Expresses one source, "There is a constant focus on retaining and advancing women in the workplace." A manager reports, "One example is the Great Place to Work for Women mentor program, in which individual women in the strategy practice are matched with women mentors. There are over 40 people participating in the program, and the pairs meet either in person or by phone on a monthly basis to discuss a question of the month." Of course, there is always room for improvement; according to one source, "Our firm is focused on retaining women, but there are no obvious solutions, so they struggle to get women to stay to make it to the executive ranks." Notes one associate, "Accenture could do more to encourage keeping female employees in the company after they've had children. They don't have as many part-time opportunities."

Minorities at the top

Staffers say that while Accenture can be classified as "a very diverse firm," minority representation is not quite as broad as it should be. "This has been a real focus over the past five to 10 years, and I believe we have very focused hiring and great retention programs, such as flexible work programs and mentoring focused on minorities. My North American leadership team consists of five senior executives, and includes a woman and a minority senior executive," states a manager. Another insider declares, "Programs seem to be in place, but perception is reality and there is not an obvious presence of minority leaders." "There is a long way to go at the very top levels and somewhat at middle levels, but lower levels seem fairly diverse," a source consents.

In addition, "Accenture has a gay and lesbian social network that seems very open and positive. I know many employees that feel very comfortable in sharing their homosexual identities in the office," an insider tells. Compared to peers in the industry, another colleague indicates that the firm isn't doing too badly in this regard: "Accenture's GLBT group does exist. Unfortunately, it's not as widely known as other initiatives. But then again, who am I kidding? The consulting world was spawned from a homophobic mass of good ole' boys, so I don't expect to see the GLBT organization lit up in neon." And on the whole, insiders label the firm "open and receptive."

"Enormous" efforts

Insiders assert that at Accenture, "community involvement initiatives are enormous across the world," and each office decides which organizations to support, we're told. "Each employee is expected to be heavily involved in firm community activities. They play a significant role in promotion decisions," a manager notes. A colleague reports, "We sponsor several city events throughout the year and are very involved in giving back to the community in monetary donations and volunteer hours."

"The Accenture Foundation supports a number of charities, and we also sponsor both diversity scholarships and scholarships for the dependents of employees. We have a wonderful relationship with Junior Achievement, we have a mentoring/tutoring program in New York known as N-Power and we also run an annual charity drive," explains a senior staffer. A Tampa-based associate says his office pitches in with "several community activities like United Way, beach cleanups, March of Dimes fund-raisers and Junior Achievement." A consultant on the West Coast tells us, "We are involved in many charities that are too numerous to list. Some examples include: United Way, Junior Achievement, Toys For Tots, Guide Dogs of America, National American Indian Museum and L.A. Works Day."

Visit the Vault Consulting Career Channel at **www.vault.com/consulting** - with insider firm profiles, message boards, the Vault Consulting Job Board and more.

VAULT CAREER LIBRARY   163

15 A.T. Kearney

VAULT TOP 50

PRESTIGE RANKING

222 West Adams Street
Chicago, IL 60606
Phone: (312) 648-0111
www.atkearney.com

LOCATIONS

Chicago, IL (HQ)
Offices in 32 countries

PRACTICE AREAS

Enterprise Services Transformation
Growth Strategies
Innovation & Complexity Management
IT Strategies
Merger Strategies
Strategic Supply Management
Supply Chain Management
Supply Management Services

THE STATS

Employer Type: Private Company
Managing Officer & Chairman: Paul A. Laudicina
2006 Employees: 2,500
2005 Employees: 3,000
2006 Revenue: $750 million*
2005 Revenue: $798 million

*A.T. Kearney sold its A.T. Kearney Executive Search business following its management buyout from EDS in early 2006, and EDS retained the firm's maintenance, repair and outsourcing operations. Therefore, revenue from these discontinued operations is not reflected in the 2006 figure.

RANKING RECAP

Practice Area
#3 - Operational Consulting
#8 - Energy Consulting

Quality of Life
#5 - Compensation
#9 - Interaction with Clients
#10 - Relationships with Supervisors
#17 - Offices
#20 - Overall Satisfaction

UPPERS

- "Open culture; no sharp elbows here"
- High level of responsibility for junior consultants
- "Personal life is respected"
- "Newly partner owned, with the corresponding excitement and enthusiasm"

DOWNERS

- Upward feedback needs to be improved
- "Performance management too lax"
- "Work variety tilted toward cost minimization as opposed to growth"
- "Access to executive management is limited, as the firm really does 'work in the trenches'"

EMPLOYMENT CONTACT

www.atkearney.com

THE BUZZ
WHAT CONSULTANTS AT OTHER FIRMS ARE SAYING ABOUT THIS FIRM

- "Finally shaking off its recent troubles"
- "Past its prime; hurt by EDS"
- "Operations supply chain experts"
- "Major talent loss recently"

THE SCOOP

The sprawl

Before 1939, the name A.T. Kearney wasn't known as the superlative strategy service provider it is today—only as Andrew Thomas Kearney, one of James O. McKinsey's initial sharpshooters for his 1926 Chicago consultancy startup. Thirteen years later, Kearney packed up and bid McKinsey adieu, ready to flex his acquired consulting muscles by founding a firm of his own. Originally debuting with manufacturing and operations as key focus areas, A.T. Kearney grew to be more than just a man; in 1946, Kearney's brainchild company officially adopted his namesake.

Until 1961, A.T. Kearney called only Chicago home, but the firm spawned another U.S. branch that year and its first European office three years later in Düsseldorf. Now practicing in areas such as supply chain management, enterprise services transformation and merger strategies, A.T. Kearney has emerged as a frontrunner in the consulting industry, with offices in 32 countries, more than 2,500 employees and over 70 clients in the Fortune 500 category. With outposts throughout Europe, North America, South America, Asia and Africa, the firm is always on the lookout for new opportunities. In June 2006, A.T. Kearney announced it would set up a base at the Dubai International Financial Centre to aid the United Arab Emirates' economy—an area that is now growing exponentially. The firm predicts a possible 60 percent increase in the UAE's GDP by 2010.

Blood brothers

A.T. Kearney lost its 56-yearlong autonomy in 1995 when it became a subsidiary loop on EDS' giant belt. The prominent Texas-rooted IT company came into A.T. Kearney's life at a crucial point, and vice versa; both businesses needed the fusion, whether for securing a brawny empire (EDS) or gaining access to the world's foremost movers and shakers (A.T. Kearney).

During its earliest days, the relationship's alchemy seemed ideal. EDS profited from A.T. Kearney's valuable assets, using them to market outsourcing services, thereby beefing up the tech company's income. And A.T. Kearney saw success from the get-go, too, with revenue bursting its $320 million seams, spilling over to the sum of $1 billion by 1998. The early years of the union carried an air of optimism, even in the face of noticeable cultural disparities: EDS, a public giant, prospered with its multiyear deals and bottom-line drive for achievement, while its new acquisition nurtured a problem-solving, relationship-focused technique—a facet EDS promised to preserve when the two businesses locked hands.

Bad blood

But despite how the saying goes, these opposites did not attract for long. In addition to A.T. Kearney's staggering revenue after 1998 (tremors from EDS' struggle)—from $1 billion, to $857 million, to $806 million in consecutive years—litigations surfaced, A.T. Kearney reluctantly relocated to EDS' home base in Plano and the employee divide continued to widen, pushing both teams further into their respective corners. According to *BusinessWeek*, EDS insiders griped about the haughtiness generated from their smaller counterpart, especially considering their meager $1 billion portion in EDS' $21 billion annual sales pie. On the other side, A.T. Kearney consultants worried about giving up their intimate board affiliations on account of EDS' dominant structure, and disliked tossing clients back and forth with the parent company.

All troubles—financial and cultural—culminated in early 2005, when gossip about an A.T. Kearney buyout circulated in the business sphere. When Massachusetts-based Monitor Group, a big-shot global strategy and management consulting firm, threw down a bid, EDS thought negotiations would wrap up shortly—until the firm withdrew at the last minute. November 2005 brought a settlement with A.T. Kearney itself, and a management buyout was confirmed and completed by January 2006. At the transaction's end, over 170 A.T. Kearney officers hailing from 26 nations had tipped their hats as new investors, allowing the firm to reemerge as independently owned after 10 turbulent years.

Visit the Vault Consulting Career Channel at www.vault.com/consulting - with insider firm profiles, message boards, the Vault Consulting Job Board and more.

VAULT CAREER LIBRARY

165

The A.T. age

The winds changed rapidly once A.T. Kearney was released back into the wild to fend for itself. Officers assembled an 11-member board of directors to reign as chief authority moving forward, with its constituents representing the firm's cross-continental spread. Said then-Chief Executive Henner Klein, "Becoming a privately owned firm again as we begin our 80th year creates an opportunity to rededicate ourselves to the values Tom Kearney believed in." As for the firm's fresh, new direction, Henner boasted "putting clients first, exceeding their expectations, delivering tangible and sustainable results and fostering commitment and passion among our people are the things we will stand for as an independent firm."

Since going stag, A.T. Kearney has unveiled a slew of new developments. Along with installing a board of directors, the firm disclosed the formation of an executive committee and a management advisory council in March 2006, the latter to oversee the board of directors and executive committee, comprising 15 A.T. Kearney executives from all corners of the firm.

Lauded leaders

In July 2006, after a 180-shareholder vote, Paul A. Laudicina accepted a three-term appointment as A.T. Kearney's chairman of the board and managing officer. Already settled as the firm's Global Business Policy Council vice president and managing director, the new election also placed Laudicina into the council's chairman role, customarily reserved for the company's chief executive. Established in 1992, the GBPC serves as a business aid for CEOs and other head-honchos to track global political, economic, demographic and technological shifts and trends. Developing analytical goods and meeting in vital strategy hubs worldwide, only the corporate elite can gain membership to the council.

March 2007 brought about another GBPC leadership shift, naming 10-year faculty member Martin Walker as senior director to serve as council head. As he joins the firm's highest ranks, Walker's credentials go unquestioned; along with possessing editor-in-chief emeritus status at United Press International, his views regarding politics and current affairs have earned him publication in *The New York Times* and *The Washington Post*, not to mention frequent guest spots on CNN, Fox News, PBS, NBC and BBC. Before his time with UPI, Walker spent over 25 years as an assistant editor at *The Guardian*, while also contributing to the paper as a columnist, reporter and foreign correspondent. In addition, Walker has penned more than 12 books—on the list are *The Cold War: A History* and *Europe in the New Century: Visions of an Emerging Superpower*.

The fine print

Among its services, A.T. Kearney publishes a horde of surveys and studies each year to help track industry trends, effects and goings-on worldwide. The Global Services Location Index, for instance, measures advantages gained from offshore services locations, using people skills, availability, business environment and financial appeal as the litmus test. Published most recently in March 2007, the index's fourth annual study showed a dwindle in cost benefits for setting up shop overseas, but with India and China still leading the outsourcing pack. The current index showed a few surprising shifts, which may be due to key markets steadily emerging. And with countries fighting to launch themselves as prime services locations, the GSLI added 10 new nations to its coverage in 2007—Sri Lanka, Pakistan, Uruguay, Morocco, Senegal, Mauritius, the Ukraine and the three Baltic States.

In its sixth year, the A.T. Kearney/Foreign Policy Globalization Index compiles information about globalization and its impact, experimenting with 12 variables divided four ways—political engagement, technological connectivity, economic integration and person-to-person contact—and representing 62 countries. Also in the A.T. Kearney publishing basket is a corporate sustainability study conducted in partnership with the Institute for Supply Management, which assesses sustainability initiatives and commitments taken on by consulting firms in an effort to understand how these practices and strategies affect business.

GETTING HIRED

Crème de la MBA crème

Like most big-time consultancies, A.T. Kearney begins its search for new consultants at some of the country's highest-ranked undergraduate and graduate business schools, including the University of Chicago, Columbia, Duke, Harvard Business School, University of Michigan, MIT and Wharton.

Most MBAs whose resumes pass the grade face two rounds of a "rigorous interview process" before winning a job with A.T. Kearney, says one consultant. The first round usually consists of one 45-minute business case interview and one 45-minute behavioral interview with an associate, manager or principal to make sure candidates' personalities will mesh with the company. The final round, says another insider, "is composed of a one-hour case preparation followed by a 20-minute presentation to 'clients,' a role played by consultants, a 45-minute case interview with a principal and a 45-minute fit interview with a partner."

On a case-by-case basis

With two case interviews in the first round of interviews and two in the second, wannabe consultants better know their stuff. A manager from New York says most of the cases during the interview rounds involve "broad-based profit improvement needs at a global company" and that the best interviewees are those who can "disaggregate the problem into the component pieces and solve each piece logically." A Harvard Business School graduate and alumnus of A.T. Kearney's interview process adds that "case questions are unique to each individual interviewer and tend to be based on actual past consulting experience." Don't worry, there are "no brainteasers" here, assures an insider from Washington, D.C. Want a preview of the kinds of cases interviewers might be presenting? "See the casebook on our web site," advises a Chicagoan.

OUR SURVEY SAYS

Happy on their own

While still making changes and adjusting to its newfound independence after 10 years under EDS, many of A.T. Kearney's professionals say the management buyout has had a positive affect on the company's culture, how employees act with each other and clients and on in-house policies like training and benefits programs. "Our '80-year-old startup' firm is delivering on its promises as it recaptures the identity Tom Kearney built 80 years ago," says one consultant, while another insider says the firm has become "a completely different place."

Today's A.T. Kearney isn't just different from the A.T. Kearney of old—its people-oriented culture also sets it apart from many of its competitors. "The culture is unique in the consulting industry," says one associate. "I feel like the partners and principals are genuinely committed to me being successful and interested in the work I do." Another insider adds that A.T. Kearney is "the least stressful place I have ever worked. I would not easily trade this for other cultures."

Teamwork, teamwork, teamwork

A.T. Kearney is all about people, so introverts beware. "The firm's culture is a 'perpetual B-school study group,'" says one consultant, adding that A.T. Kearney's team focus can be "misery for lone wolves." Another insider says her "team members often volunteer to help me in all aspects. For example, fellow analysts will aid me with my PowerPoint and Excel questions; associates will help me understand and synthesize primary and secondary research, and managers and principals will also sit down and work with me." When there are problems, "even the most senior people are highly accessible," an associate exclaims. Another source adds, "There is strong internal support from all levels to be successful in project work."

Visit the Vault Consulting Career Channel at **www.vault.com/consulting** - with insider firm profiles, message boards, the Vault Consulting Job Board and more.

VAULT CAREER LIBRARY   **167**

Newcomers to A.T. Kearney's consulting ranks are never left out in the cold and often play an active role in client relationships. One associate, who received his undergraduate degree in 2003, says he was "leading meetings and developing personal relationships with the vice presidents of Fortune 200 companies." Partners take the lead, but are "easily accessible" and work "on the job with junior staff."

The hang-ups

That all-hands-on-deck approach to consulting, however, means that everyone has to work hard at A.T. Kearney, which translates into long hours and lots of time on the road. One consultant says "60 to 70 hours is probably typical, although it can vary somewhat, both up and down, depending on the client," but even that is "very balanced, given the nature of our industry," adds a manager. "The reality," adds another insider, "is that on some projects people have to work 80 to 100 hours per week," but in general, staffers are able to keep hours at a manageable level and avoid weekend work.

Many consultants rack up their hours on the road: "Travel is often four days a week," says a Chicago-based staffer. "Usually our working style demands that we spend time with our clients to ensure the successful implementation of our recommendations." A.T. Kearney "promotes traveling for its consultants in order to be face-to-face with the client every week," explains another consultant, enabling the firm to "help clients in a tangible way." Not everyone finds travel such a drag. "As long as you can travel comfortably and be home when you need to be home," says one associate, "the travel is not a detriment to work life, but an asset that allows you to build a solid foundation with the client and your team." Those in the New York office, especially, don't find travel to be too overbearing, since the firm has plenty of local clients in the metro area. One manager based in New York says he's made it "four straight years with mostly local work."

Finding a balance

The bottom line is, maintaining a good balance is an individual's prerogative: "In any consulting firm, if you personally do not make life out of work a priority, it won't become one," says one source. Such is the case at A.T. Kearney. Says one manger, "While work is demanding, the culture is flexible and not cutthroat, and allows people to balance their own needs with business demands." "As long as you produce good work and develop a strong relationship with the client," advises another insider, "you are given the trust and leeway to work the Monday through Thursday schedule around your personal life."

More generally, "the firm recognizes the need for balance," says one consultant, who adds that things are looking up for the overworked. "You will always have consultants who 'live and breathe' their careers, however those are becoming less and less. This transition has happened over time with the retirement of partners with the old-school mentality as well as the promotion of younger partners with families." The firm also "has programs that allow for extended leaves of absence and ample vacation (four weeks after three years)" that help consultants achieve balance.

A focus on training

Since 2006, there has been a renewed focus on both official and unofficial training at A.T. Kearney. "In the past, training virtually disappeared; however, since the [management buyout] it has become a key priority to the firm," says a manager from New York. Today, consultants have access to "onboard training, quarterly feedback from teams, ongoing career development and progression planning with mentors," outlines one insider, while for younger professionals, "we have more skill-development training," explains one consultant in Chicago. "Training content and topics are developed based on consultant feedback and requests," says one source, and there is "participation from A.T. Kearney's CEO and other top leaders," says another.

The one complaint: "Training is OK when you have the time to take it, which is rare," according to a source. A manager adds, "I find that the firm offers more training than I have time to attend, but the firm is clearly committed to training, since much of it is often presented by vice presidents and principal practitioners."

Pay day and perks

Pay is another area of focus in the post-EDS days. "Only recently has our compensation risen to meet the market, however, now it seems quite competitive with respect to my peers at other firms," remarks one insider. Staffers are pleased that A.T. Kearney has been "very transparent since the 2006 buyout from EDS," we're told, and "has been fair in its promise to benchmark compensation across peer group firms and adjust accordingly," adds one manager. An analyst shares, "A.T. Kearney recently did a compensation survey and communicated that it would be top-three in the industry in terms of competitive compensation. They conducted the survey in 2006, and the firm did exactly what it promised."

In addition to their salaries, A.T. Kearney consultants can expect healthy bonuses, a 401(k) matching program and a profit-sharing program. The firm's "scholars program pays full tuition for consultants to return to top business schools and earn their MBA," says an insider.

Family focus

For young moms and dads working at A.T. Kearney, "there is paid maternity and paternity leave and [the] option to get unpaid leave," an associate explains. New dads get "two to six weeks paid time off," one source says, which is "allowed for new hires as well." Another insider adds that "new parents can work out a part-time program," and that "many will work locally." Even though local placements for new parents "is not an official policy, the company will accommodate requirements to not be on the road," adds the insider.

A crack in the glass ceiling?

A number of staffers say the firm could do more to hire and keep women, minorities and lesbians, gays and bisexuals—especially at senior levels. While "generally supportive of women," it is "still not as common to see a woman in the higher ranks," says one insider. For now, though, A.T. Kearney has developed a number of in-house support networks for minority employees, such as the Active Woman's Network, managed by "one of the firm's top female partners," as well as "active" networks for African-Americans, Hispanics and South Asians. Another consultant adds that A.T. Kearney has "a strong GLBT diversity group with a sizable budget and a good network across the firm."

Giving back

A.T. Kearney also has a thriving community service initiative in all of its offices. Says one manager in Atlanta, "We not only encourage it, we have provided training to junior consultants on how to get involved in nonprofits. We also provide pro bono work on a regular basis in the markets in which we operate." The source goes on to explain that "as part of our people-care and development efforts, we have a community service team that identifies opportunities to contribute to the local community." Charitable activities undertaken by consultants include adopt-a-school programs, food and clothing drives, toiletry collections and women's shelter donations. Staffers are particularly involved in Junior Achievement, March of Dimes, Children's Hospital, Boys and Girls Clubs and United Way. In Chicago, community service gets heated when consultants enter into "a blood drive competition with the local McKinsey office." And in New York, consultants are currently "working on a pro bono project with New York State for Governor Spitzer." A source notes that "most consultants are involved with at least one initiative."

Visit the Vault Consulting Career Channel at **www.vault.com/consulting** - with insider firm profiles, message boards, the Vault Consulting Job Board and more.

VAULT CAREER LIBRARY   169

VAULT TOP 50

16

PRESTIGE
RANKING

Katzenbach Partners LLC

381 Park Avenue South
New York, NY 10016
Phone: (212) 213-5505
Fax: (212) 213-5024
www.katzenbach.com

LOCATIONS

New York, NY (HQ)
Chicago, IL
Houston, TX
San Francisco, CA

PRACTICE AREAS

Business Transformation
Culture Change & Merger Integration
Dynamic Strategy Development
Front Line Productivity Improvement
Organizationwide Pride & Motivation

THE STATS

Employer Type: Private Company
Managing Partner: Niko Canner
2007 Employees: 182
2006 Employees: 152
2007 Revenue: $60 million
2006 Revenue: $50 million

RANKING RECAP

Quality of Life
#3 - Firm Culture
#3 - Offices
#5 - Interaction with Clients
#6 - Overall Satisfaction
#13 - Relationships with Supervisors
#15 - Best Firms to Work For
#16 - Compensation (tie)

Diversity
#2 - Diversity for GLBT
#3 - Best Firms for Diversity
#10 - Diversity for Women
#13 - Diversity for Minorities

UPPERS

- "The firm is flexible and individually-focused when it comes to creating your personal career path here"
- "Opportunity to be part of such a 'lab' of learning"
- Friday lunches
- "Everyone here is fun, smart and quirky in good ways"

DOWNERS

- "Weak international presence is a bit disappointing"
- "Pay at higher levels is not at the levels of competing firms"
- "Struggling with work/life balance on many teams"
- "The firm is going through lots of growing pains and they cannot figure out who they are and what they want to be"

THE BUZZ
WHAT CONSULTANTS AT OTHER FIRMS ARE SAYING ABOUT THIS FIRM

- "Dynamic, growing, smart, modern"
- "Softer consulting, a little fluffy"
- "Gay-friendly"
- "Take themselves a bit seriously"

EMPLOYMENT CONTACT

Kristen Clemmer
Director of Recruiting
Katzenbach Partners LLC
381 Park Avenue South
New York, NY 10016

www.katzenbach.com/Careers/tabid/56/default.aspx

THE SCOOP

An elemental approach

What started out as a three-man business plan in 1998 has become one of the biggest U.S. names in consulting. Today, Katzenbach Partners is reportedly growing at more than 30 percent per year, with more than 180 professionals working in offices in New York City, Houston, Chicago and San Francisco. It counts among its happy customers megaclients like Pfizer, Aetna and Reliant Energy. Nonprofit organizations and small- to large-sized businesses around the globe also come to Katzenbach Partners for its management consulting services. The firm focuses most of its energy on the financial services, telecom, pharmaceutical, energy, managed care and enterprise software industries.

Katzenbach Partners has broken down its consulting services into what it considers the "core elements" that a company needs to achieve breakthrough organizational performance. These elements include having a good business strategy, which can mean knowing not only in what direction to take the company, but also how to deal with merger integration or how much to charge for a product. The firm's consultants also work with companies to help them get the most out of their formal organization (i.e., strategies, structures and programs) and informal organization (i.e., culture, networks and flexible work groups). In addition, Katzenbach Partners helps clients with leadership and capability development, which includes skills development and team building, and improving motivation and pride among employees. Companies also go to Katzenbach Partners for advice on performance improvement initiatives and change management techniques for dealing with issues like restructuring or mergers and acquisitions.

Keeping up with Katzenbach

The firm's namesake founder, Jon Katzenbach, is a 35-year veteran of McKinsey & Company, even coming in second in a 1988 election to become McKinsey's managing director. Consultant to the consultants, Katzenbach has advised some of the biggest of big names: J. Paul Getty, Lou Noto of Mobil, General Electric's Jim Rogers and David Rockefeller.

With a background like that, when Katzenbach talks, executives listen. And executives are just who Katzenbach wants to talk to. The best way consultants can add value to a client's company, Katzenbach maintains, is by enabling leaders to make the right decisions and take the right actions. "The CEO determines the culture," Katzenbach told *BusinessWeek* in April 2006. "If the CEO is determined to [improve] the surfacing of ideas and determined to make critical choices, then the chances of an [organization's] figuring that out are much, much greater." How do you become one of those consultants who can get inside CEOs heads? By being able to combine both analytic and people skills, and by relating to and instilling confidence in many different kinds of people.

Changing with the times

To meet the changing demands its clients face in a global business environment, Katzenbach Partners has developed a few "breakout ideas" to help its clients adjust and compete. The Empathy Engine is one such idea—an innovative approach for how companies can achieve a high level of customer service and sustain it for the long haul. The Empathy Engine represents a shift away from a hierarchical concept of customer service toward a more holistic approach that integrates senior leadership, management, the frontline and customers. According to the firm "Empathy Engine companies" realize distinctive competitive advantages based on customer relationships that cannot easily be replicated. The result: increased market share and shareholder value.

CHINA 2024: A New Generation of Leaders is another breakout idea initiated by the firm, which promises to provide a window into an evolving business culture. Katzenbach Partners is monitoring the development and potential of 115 Chinese MBA graduates. Hailing from the best business schools in China and the U.S., the firm will survey the group every year and check in with each candidate every four years with in-depth interviews until 2024. "They are the first professionally-trained managers in

Visit the Vault Consulting Career Channel at www.vault.com/consulting - with insider firm profiles, message boards, the Vault Consulting Job Board and more.

VAULT CAREER LIBRARY   171

China," Stacy Palestrant, executive director of the study, told the *Financial Times* in June 2006. "We will watch through their eyes the changes in China as they enter the workforce."

The firm also has a partnership with Marshall Goldsmith, which *Forbes* ranked as one of the top-five most respected executive coaching consultancies. The recently created Marshall Goldsmith Partners works with clients to help leaders change the one or two most important behaviors that directly impact their company's performance. Katzenbach Partners is so confident in this product that it only asks for payment when clients can demonstrate a measurable change in their targeted behavior.

Giving back

Katzenbach Partners isn't just out there for large corporations like Pfizer or Aetna. It has also developed its own practice for the nonprofit world. In 2005, the firm set up a nonprofit advisory board to seek out opportunities in the sector, drawing on the experience and interests of Katzenbach Partners employees who have experience with volunteer or philanthropic work. One of the firm's most recent pro bono initiatives is for Acumen Fund, a nonprofit venture fund that recently launched a 10-member fellows program. The fellows will be sent to Africa and South Asia to monitor Acumen Fund's investments in the emerging world.

GETTING HIRED

Katzenbach on campus

Katzenbach Partners' campus recruiting list reflects the discriminating nature of its hiring process. The firm draws candidates from all of the Ivy Leagues, as well as Rice, Duke, Wellesley, Berkeley and the University of Chicago. Candidates who don't attend one of these schools still have a shot of landing an interview—"the firm does recruiting on the campuses of top undergrad and graduate institutions, and maintains an open recruiting policy for people outside of those schools," says a senior consultant. These applicants are invited to submit a resume through the online system.

Excessive interviews

When it comes to new hires, insiders report that the firm is particularly selective. Says one consultant, "It is hard to get a job here, no matter if you are interviewing for a consulting role or an assistant role." Katzenbach Partners' "thoughtfully intense" hiring process differs slightly, depending on the interviewers. Most candidates face at least two rounds of three or four interviews, although one source relates, "I had 12 rigorous interviews—mostly case questions." Admits a manager, "We require an excessive number of interviews, regardless of what position you are interviewing for."

The real challenge comes after the first on-campus interviews, reports a source: "All candidates who make it to second rounds are then sent to New York where they typically have three one-on-one interviews, one written case and one group case. While the process is incredibly tough, the candidates who make it through the gauntlet are usually the ones who have the most fun throughout the day." Asserts a manager, "It's a very competitive process. At least two interviews in the first round and four to six in the second round. They were probably the hardest case interviews I did."

Beware the simple questions

Sources acknowledge that it's not easy to prepare for the kind of case questions typically asked during these interviews. "Our interviews are intellectually challenging and quite unconventional sometimes. A final-round candidate recently told me at the end of a great interview that he had never seen or imagined anything like this, even with all the prep work he'd done about Katzenbach," an insider declares. Associates tell us the firm "hardly ever uses brainteasers in undergrad and grad," and a consultant notes, "We don't use pure market-sizing cases in grad interviews." Elaborates a co-worker, "Case questions at the first round tend to be out-of-the-box, yet still informed by your typical frameworks. Second-round cases are definitely more intense. Expect more in-depth cases that delve into strategic, organizational and quantitative aspects, most of which are taken from our actual client work." The source adds this hint: "Candidates should be warned of questions that seem simplistic—they are often the most complex." According to an insider, one type of case question a candidate might be given is, "How do you think your strategic recommendation would affect the (fill in the blank: sales force, sourcing, marketing, finance operations relationship) of the company?"

Sources state that the intense questions are all meant to "probe very deeply for fit with the organizational culture." An associate explains, "Much of the process seeks out good fit candidates, meaning those that are interested in firm-building, growth and collaboration, rather than just attracted to the high selectivity of the firm or people who just want any consulting job." Aside from fitting in, one source declares, "Candidates must be well rounded with an exceptional EQ as well as IQ."

OUR SURVEY SAYS

Katzenbach family values

Insiders attest that Katzenbach Partners is a "tight-knit community," full of colleagues that one source describes as "intelligent, intellectually engaged and have the right mix of humility and humor." "The firm is truly what it aspires to be. It's a quirky, warm, nonhierarchical and open, and a uniquely collaborative place to work," boasts a staffer. Another insider raves, "The firm culture is extraordinary—very collegial, merit driven and, most importantly, offers a shared sense of enterprise. People are really motivated to build a distinctive firm, and while that creates a higher-than-normal sense of idealism, it also generates extraordinary energy." Consultants also couldn't be more thrilled about who they work with. "The firm attracts people that are seriously smart, very laid-back and a ton of fun to hang out with." It's common for colleagues to become personal friends, according to a source: "At a recent birthday party, I realized that over a third of the people I invited were people from Katzenbach." "And despite our growth, I'm proud to say it still feels like my family," affirms another insider.

Building a distinct culture is also important to this group; a manager explains, "The culture is deeply intellectual but (thankfully) easygoing and fun. We spend inordinate amounts of time thinking about and discussing our culture, explaining our culture to outsiders and worrying about how we're going to keep it as we grow, but these are probably good things. It means that it's worth something to most people and it's certainly the thing that sets us apart from other firms more than anything else." Praises another happy staffer, "The culture is an open and engaging one, and the firm tries to promote it by sponsoring events to Broadway shows in New York or rodeo concerts in Houston. The setup of the offices (with open pods) enables flow of conversation among everyone from partners to first-years to firm services. It's very different than the banking environment I came from with its office and closed-door mentality."

Joking with Jon

Reportedly, the collegial feeling among consultants carries over into relationships with managers and partners at the firm. "It feels very rewarding as a first-year to be on a first-name basis with the partners in the firm and to be able to joke around with Jon Katzenbach in the office," boasts one consultant. Another colleague is pleased that "managers are incredibly open and provide great support, especially for younger consultants." Sources also say it's not uncommon to develop friendships with supervisors at the firm. "I find that my managers have become some of my closest friends at Katzenbach. This ability to bond with senior people—not just at a professional but also a personal level—is one of the things I value most about my time at the firm," recounts a colleague.

The firm also offers "considerable access to senior clients starting from early in your career." "As someone who is just out of business school, I'm surprised that I've met and interacted with the CEO of every client I've worked with," shares one associate. Echoes a co-worker, "I haven't heard of anywhere else that lets junior people develop relationships like these with senior clients."

Visit the Vault Consulting Career Channel at **www.vault.com/consulting** - with insider firm profiles, message boards, the Vault Consulting Job Board and more.

VAULT CAREER LIBRARY   **173**

Work, eat, sleep, repeat

The "rigorous travel requirement" at Katzenbach Partners definitely takes its toll. Explains a manager, "There's a lot of travel here. We're still a small firm trying to build a national footprint, and that means our people travel a good deal." Asserts one analyst, "If you're on a traveling project, especially in far-fetched locations, you're pretty much working, eating and sleeping." Insiders seem less than thrilled that sporadic travel is an unavoidable part of the job. "Staffing attempts to respond to requests for travel or nontravel projects, but it's never worked out in my favor. I've traveled every week for eight of the past 10 months, and it's a total grind." "I experience back and shoulder problems because of carrying bags a lot," states a road-weary colleague, while an associate cautions, "Building out new offices in 2007 means it's getting worse before it gets better."

Texas transplants

Once you hit the road, it may be a while before you see home again, according to an insider who claims, "Projects tend to be long term … and if you are on a traveling project, that means you'll be on the road for a long time. Many New Yorkers have been working out of the Texas office for months, owing to the amount of work there." Those staffers on long-term client location get creative with ways to make being away more fun. Explains one source, "Last summer we organized a road trip/river rafting trip for all of our Houston-based and Houston-staffed consultants and had a fantastic time exploring the town of the oldest dance halls in Texas! The trip helped to give everyone a much-deserved break from work and travel. So we are trying, which in many ways is a great first step."

Admittedly, travel at Katzenbach Partners is no cakewalk, but staffers concede that "the firm really strives to do everything it can to make things easier." Observes a source, "There's an enormous support network when you're traveling. In some ways, I feel like I get more 'how are you doing' e-mails while traveling than I do when I'm staffed in my home office." Co-workers are pleased with the sense of camaraderie that comes from traveling with a team. "The travel itself can be a pain, but there's a certain bonding that comes with it—something like the intensity of working on a play, and getting to know people in the context of that very specific, limited time and intensive moment. Also, many folks at Katzenbach have a hearty respect for good, local cuisine, which makes being away from home a bit more palatable," an insider comments.

Crunching for all the right reasons

Hours for Katzenbach Partners consultants are cyclical, ranging from 60 to 70 hours a week, while projects tend to be in the four- to six-month range. Remarks an insider, "I'm working like crazy these days, but was leaving the office at 5:30 or 6 p.m. every day on my last project. Luckily, because there's really no such thing as face time here, it is totally fine to go home at 5:30 if you don't have work to do. No one will look at you askance or think less of you for it." Another colleague appreciates that hours aren't spent on busywork, claiming, "I work 70-plus hours per week, but in my role I've created doing work I love. I never feel like there is arbitrary creation of work. When we crunch, it is because something important and meaningful is at stake." Associates also mention that "hours in Texas tend to be longer than in New York," but a source adds, "That has changed recently, as our office has moved from the startup phase to become a more established regional office."

Trickle-down effect

With intense travel and demanding hours, it's no wonder insiders say balance is a struggle. "Work/life balance is talked about a great deal but really is not honored. Expect to work very hard. It starts with the partners and trickles down," advises a consultant. One senior staffer concedes, "Some projects are great, but there are more than a few that are all-consuming, and some partners are better than others at encouraging the right trade-offs."

Reportedly, those in charge are aware of the strain consultants feel, since "work/life balance is a topic that gets considerable airtime at the firm." Explains one manger, "In general, we try hard to at least have serious dialogues at the team level about work/life balance, and Jon Katzenbach had dialogues with groups of 10 to 20 firm members that touched every individual in the firm over the course of last year." But another staffer offers a different slant: "Conversations about work/life balance are a nice attempt, but are ultimately meaningless. It's impossible to maintain any kind of life balance when you're on the road four to five nights a week and working a large numbers of weekends. I have been here 18 months and have had to reschedule every single vacation so far."

What's it to you?

On the contrary, attaining balance is an achievable feat for some individuals. "There are certain elements of work/life balance that are great. The firm gives everyone four weeks of vacation. Managers tend to be flexible about outside commitments if you need to come in late or leave early," an analyst comments. Another source explains, "I think that the most important thing the firm does is allow you to define what work/life balance means to you. For some people, this means never working on weekends. For others, it means having the flexibility to take a few hours off in the middle of the day to attend to personal commitments." One principal admits that attaining personal balance "requires clear boundary setting and negotiation with managers."

Second-year salary jump

The firm's compensation is another thing that insiders seem particularly pleased with. "Comparatively speaking (and based on knowledge from my friends at other firms), compensation at Katzenbach is excellent. More impressive is the jump from a first-year to second-year associate—your base jumps $10,000 and your baseline bonus jumps—up $9,000," details one staffer. In addition to base salary, consultants receive "a generous profit-sharing package, usually 10 to 15 percent, based on the firm's profitability." "Because we don't have a 'two years and out' kind of model for undergrads, quite a lot of undergrads end up with MBA-level comp packages a few years in," a partner explains. Another newbie boasts, "I think that we're perhaps the most well-compensated consultants in the industry."

Props for perks

Katzenbach Partners staffers declare that "insurance coverage and medical benefits are pretty awesome," and the health care plan "even covers acupuncture and other alternative remedies." The firm's interest-free loan program for new MBA hires is also popular. "This is to help with whatever costs they are going to incur post-school, but it seems that most will be using it for whatever fabulous vacation they hope to take before joining full time ... which we think is great," a source points out. In addition, insiders rave about the "liberal and very trusting expense policy, the yearly off-site at the Ritz in Miami and monthly 'Katzenbach-on-the-town' events." A Houston-based consultant reports, "This year we got to go a resort in Costa Rica because we hit our revenue targets in our office," and a cohort adds, "Airline miles and Amex points mean that vacation is pretty much free."

Who needs luxurious perks? These consultants claim that it's the "smaller perks that add up," such as "a stocked Odwalla fridge in the office," "medicine in the cabinet" and paid cell phone bills. A firm favorite also seems to be the free Friday lunch, which an analyst describes as "a weekly tradition of eating a catered lunch together in the office, like the big quirky family that we are." If Fridays aren't enough, the firm promotes hanging out together with the 'buddy budget,' to encourage bonding among different members of the firm"—the source nots that it's "$100 to use each month for 12 to 18 months."

The dawn of a new age

There is some official training at Katzenbach Partners in the form of "monthly class trainings and mini-MBA workshops," however most sources rely on informal training to get up to speed. Consultants don't seem to mind learning informally, according to one insider who states, "Much of what we learn is client interaction and project management skills. These are tough to teach in a classroom, so we generally learn on the job." According to a manager, "This is an area where we still need to improve, but I think that we are headed in the right direction." One insider states that the training program is indeed expanding, and explains, "We're just moving from the Stone Age to the Bronze Age, and hopefully are going to go Mach 3 to the Industrial Age this year. We've finally put someone in place whose job is to manage our training efforts."

Visit the Vault Consulting Career Channel at www.vault.com/consulting - with insider firm profiles, message boards, the Vault Consulting Job Board and more.

VAULT CAREER LIBRARY   175

"Uplifting" office design

The Katzenbach Partners office spaces inspire nothing short of adoration from insiders. "Walking into work is an uplifting experience," claims a source, while another consultant exclaims, "Light! Air! Open spaces! Good design! I'm a fan. And we've worked with the same architect at each of our offices to get a consistent feel." One insider pronounces the Houston office design "wonderful," stating, "I love the open office concept and the pod concept. My favorite time of day is 'recess,' a time when the entire office decides to take a break and socialize." And a colleague in New York says, "The open plan, the abundance of greenery and the unusually luxurious ladies bathroom make our offices a truly pleasant and attractive place to work." "It always amazes everyone who walks in! Quite the source of pride—and it's mirrored in all of our offices," agrees another staffer.

Of course, having little division between working spaces might have its drawbacks, according to one analyst who mentions, "It's nicely appointed, but while the open floorplan promotes teamwork, it makes it difficult to concentrate." Still, it seems that no one really seems to mind the distraction of their co-workers. Declares a source, "[There's] so much common space that things tend to get a bit messy easily, but I love these offices—so big, friendly and open. I can never return to a cubicle again."

Lacking female leadership

Insiders are waiting for the firm to name its first female partner. According to one source, it "feels like that'll be a big symbolic win for the firm, but it's probably a few years out still." Despite the fact that there seems to be a "lack of female role models at the senior levels," insiders assert Katzenbach Partners is "incredibly receptive to women on all terms." "There is great diversity at all levels with respect to women, except at the partner level," confirms one director. Another consultant assures us, though, that "the presence of strong women at this firm is astounding."

"As with women, there are no minority partners," observes one associate. While a few insiders proclaim Katzenbach Partners to be the "most open-minded place ever," others disagree. An insider argues, "The firm is run by seven white men. They elected no partners in 2006. There are two black consultants and six Latino consultants. There are lots of Indian consultants. Seniority in the firm is 'pale, male and Yale.'" Though the firm reports that its principal group is split evenly between men and women, "we are in need of more Latino and black candidates in order to create a more diverse workforce," asserts a manager.

Though representation might not be equal, the firm is receptive to hiring and promoting minorities, sources say. "I think the firm tries really hard to give equal opportunities to everyone, regardless of gender, race or sexual orientation; whether it is hiring, promoting or retaining talent, it is all a matter of fit and merit," explains a source.

"Great to be gay at Katzenbach"

When it comes to GLBT diversity, insiders agree that the firm is "off the charts in terms of acceptance." Declares a consultant, "It's great to be gay at Katzenbach. The firm is one of the sponsors of the Out for Undergraduate Business Conference and makes an effort to reach out to the GLBT community. It's refreshing to work in a place where my sexuality is celebrated and accepted, not simply tolerated." "Same-sex significant others routinely come to firm events, the firm represents at GLBT events nationally and same-sex partner benefits are fully equivalent to married couples," a source tells us.

Inspired to give back

Katzenbach Partners' community service opportunities revolve mostly around pro bono consulting work. Says a source, "We are involved in the Inspire Consortium, which is a nonprofit group that consults to nonprofits in the youth and education arena. It allows junior consultants to run engagements and experience project management roles earlier in their careers, while donating their consulting services to nonprofits in the area."

Pro bono work aside, associates also get involved locally to help various groups. "We have a nonprofit advisory board, and firm members are encouraged to take initiative with respect to areas of interest. Two undergrads enlisted us in New York City's annual AIDS walk and even organized a silent auction to raise money, where firm members at all levels donated creative prizes," a source relates. In Houston, consultants have volunteered at the "local AIDS clinic, Houston Police Department and KIPP school." "Basically, no good idea for community involvement is rejected," states a manager.

Visit the Vault Consulting Career Channel at **www.vault.com/consulting** - with insider firm profiles, message boards, the Vault Consulting Job Board and more.

VAULT CAREER LIBRARY   **177**

17

Marakon Associates

245 Park Avenue, 44th Floor
New York, NY 10167
Phone: (212) 377-5000
Fax: (212) 377-6000
www.marakon.com

LOCATIONS

New York, NY (HQ)
London (Europe HQ)
Chicago, IL
San Francisco, CA
Singapore
Tokyo
Zurich

PRACTICE AREAS

Execution
Growth Through Acquisition
Leadership & Organization
Organic Growth
Productivity
Strategic Risk Management
Strategy

THE STATS

Employer Type: Private Company
CEO: Brian Burwell
2007 Employees: 300
2006 Employees: 300+

RANKING RECAP

Quality of Life
#2 - Offices
#3 - Formal Training
#4 - Work/Life Balance
#8 - Best Firms to Work For
#8 - Interaction with Clients (tie)
#10 - Firm Culture
#11 - Relationships with Supervisors
#11 - Overall Satisfaction
#13 - Hours in the Office
#13 - Compensation

UPPERS

• "Changing face of the company provides a lot of leadership opportunities"
• Rewarded meritocracy
• "Unparalleled exposure to senior clients"
• "A lot of care given to each individual, whether it be career development or work/life balance"

DOWNERS

• Fewer choices for client assignments
• "Still an unrecognized name outside of consulting"
• "Promotions can be slower at the firm for some consultants"
• "Limited overseas/interoffice transfer opportunities"

EMPLOYMENT CONTACT

www.marakon.com/careers

THE BUZZ
WHAT CONSULTANTS AT OTHER FIRMS ARE SAYING ABOUT THIS FIRM

• "Very good firm with an underrated lifestyle"
• "Retreating to their core competencies"
• "Financial wizards"
• "No real brand identity"

THE SCOOP

Among the elite

Look up the definition of "boutique" strategy consulting, and it may begin with Marakon. Employing just around 300 people in seven offices worldwide, the firm, founded in 1978, has developed a powerful reputation among both the business school and corporate crowds. Marakon has assembled a list of rave reviews from clients and other outsiders that rival those of a best-selling novel: Barclays Chairman Matthew W. Barrett calls the firm's consultants "original thinkers with a challenging point of view," and according to *Fortune*, Marakon ranks "among the half-dozen firms that form the elite in strategy consulting."

The firm owes its classy reputation to the business savvy of its founders, three Wells Fargo bank executives and a University of Washington finance professor, who first opened the firm on the West Coast before moving its headquarters to New York. Marakon's initial focus was financial strategy, covering topics like portfolio management and capital investment planning. Value was the watchword, as the firm helped clients gain it—and identify where they were losing it—by applying new performance measures like "economic profit."

Finding the value

Soon, clients also wanted the firm's advice on forward-looking investments, so in the late 1980s the firm broadened its practice to tie strategic planning to capital investment planning. The term "value-based management" was developed to describe these services. By the 1990s, Marakon had begun factoring in components like resource allocation, performance management and executive compensation in its strategic planning. Rebranding its approach as "managing for value," Marakon began to emphasize the need for a company's corporate strategy and organizational structure to be tied in to increasing value.

Today, Marakon organizes its services around seven core areas of expertise: strategy, execution, organic growth, growth through acquisition, productivity, leadership and organization, and strategic risk management. The firm works with members of the top management teams at companies in a variety of industries, including aircraft, banking, food, insurance, luxury goods, manufacturing, mining, oil and gas, paper, pharmaceuticals and telecommunications. Its blue-chip client roster has included Alcan, Barclays, Boeing, BP, Cadbury Schweppes, Cardinal Health, Dow Jones, Gillette, Nordstrom, Roche and Xerox.

From Asia to Zurich

Marakon's Chicago office, established in 1996, employs around 30 people; thanks to its "smallish" size, the firm notes, the office places a lot of emphasis on a fun, supportive culture. Established in 1998, the San Francisco office, with about 30 professionals, is equally sociable. In Marakon's office overlooking Trafalgar Square in London, the "close-knit" staff hails from all over Europe. And in the Singapore facility, opened in 2001, consultants hail from around Asia as well as the U.S. and Europe. Most recently, in 2006, the firm opened an office in Zurich—its first in continental Europe—though it promises more in select cities in coming years.

Back to the money

In a nod to its financial roots, in January 2007 the firm announced its merger with financial advisory firm Integrated Finance Limited to form a new company, Trinsum Group. With an aim of bridging the gap between management consulting and investment banking, Trinsum will serve the management of large corporations on strategy, execution, risk management, mergers and acquisitions, and related matters, while also offering a range of investment vehicles. Marakon continues to operate under its own name as the strategy consulting arm of the business. Jim McTaggart, Marakon co-chair and co-founder, was named CEO of the new venture. In addition to McTaggart, the Trinsum management team includes IFL co-founders Roberto Mendoza and Peter Hancock; Robert Merton, who won a Nobel Prize for his work on options pricing, serves as the firm's chief science officer. McTaggart was named to *Consulting Magazine*'s list of the Top 25 Consultants in 2004.

Visit the Vault Consulting Career Channel at **www.vault.com/consulting** - with insider firm profiles, message boards, the Vault Consulting Job Board and more.

VAULT CAREER LIBRARY   179

Changing chiefs

Marakon announced in May 2006 that Brian Burwell, a managing partner from its San Francisco office, would be taking over the lead position from CEO Ken Favaro, who stepped down to devote more time to promoting a new book. Favaro remained with Marakon as a managing partner and co-chairman. Burwell, a Stanford MBA who joined Marakon in 1979, previously worked with the Federal Reserve Bank of San Francisco and with a research group at the University of California. In July 2006, Michael Kennedy, former CFO of MasterCard International's consulting arm, MasterCard Global Advisors, joined the firm as CFO and partner.

Marakon derives additional intellectual power from its board of advisors, formed in 2002. The group consists of eminent business leaders, including Chris Jones, former CEO of J. Walter Thompson; William Stavropolous, chairman emeritus of the Dow Chemical Company; Sir John Sunderland, chairman of Cadbury Schweppes; Arthur Martinez, former chairman and CEO of Sears Roebuck; Sir Brian Pitman, former chairman and CEO of Lloyds TSB Group; and Frank Zarb, former chairman and CEO of the National Association of Securities Dealers and the Nasdaq Stock Market.

Leading the leaders

Marakon's ideas are widely circulated in the media, and its consultants are often called upon for comment in the business press. Leadership is an abiding interest of the firm, as evidenced by its recent publications. In January 2007, Marakon published *The Three Tensions: Winning the Struggle to Perform Without Compromise*, by Co-Chairman Favaro and former Managing Partner Dominic Dodd. Outlining three fundamental tensions every leader faces, the book discusses how to overcome these challenges, drawing on research and in-depth discussions with execs in the field. To assess a company's performance, the authors devised a "batting average" metric, calculating how often a business achieves its competing objectives at the same time. The ideas put forth in the book have been the subject of articles in *The Wall Street Journal*, the *Harvard Business Review* and *Financial Executive* magazine, among others.

Born free

Marakon is big on flexibility for its consultants, pledging to offer them "freedom to choose." Consultants have a say in how and where they will work, what type of work they will do and how much they will work. As for the "how and where," Marakon specifies that consultants are expected to spend two days a week at their home office and no more than three days a week at the client site. The firm offers flexible part-time arrangements and telecommuting options where appropriate, and the possibility of extended international assignments for those with the travel itch. Marakon consultants also have a lot of input when it comes to how they want to work, and have the ability to customize a part-time working model in client-facing or firm-building roles, or even opt to work just 10 months out of the year. The firm prorates consultants' pay based on these choices.

During the first two years of their careers, Marakonites work on a range of issues across a variety of industries. After that, they have the option of focusing on one or more of the firm's seven core areas of expertise. The firm takes pride in its professional development program, which includes core training on the principles and frameworks needed to tackle complex business problems, and "skills-focused" training on the tools needed to be an effective advisor. New hires receive more than 180 hours of formal instruction within their first 15 months at the firm. Consultants at Marakon also are assigned a coach on day one of their career at Marakon to provide support, guidance and structure. Monthly meetings are held with coaches, who are ultimately accountable for their advisees' career development. Marakon's case teams, made up of four to six people, give themselves regular "pulse checks" and plenty of feedback to assess progress, and take time to destress with social events.

Lift every voice

Back in the office, Marakonites participate in a "lively and uncommon" work environment, according to the firm, enjoying regular events such as charity auctions and karaoke. The firm's global C/AC conference, its largest annual meeting, takes place in the late summer, giving consultants from all of Marakon's offices a chance to exchange information and get updates on the firm's developments. An annual global women's conference involves practice sharing, training and networking for women across each of Marakon's offices and also includes discussions with accomplished female executives and alumni. Previous topics for the women's conference have included Making Change Happen, Influence and Communication: Achieving Impact and Women Making Rain.

According to the firm, more than 90 percent of its consultants have gotten involved in community service initiatives or pro bono projects. In Chicago, Marakonites have worked on a pro bono basis with the Kellogg School of Management and with community organizations such as the Greater Chicago Food Depository. In London, the firm's Marakon in the Community program has included initiatives like student mentoring and helping organizations such as the National Science Museum and the Dyslexia Institute.

GETTING HIRED

Make it fit

Aside from a few MBA alumni referrals, Marakon focuses its narrow recruiting energy on big-shot institutions, including Northwestern, Duke and the University of Pennsylvania for undergrads, and Wharton, Kellogg, Columbia and the University of Chicago for MBA all-stars. In the interrogation room, candidates endure two rounds, consisting of 40-minute fit and case interviews in the first, and multiple sessions with managers and partners in the second. "The final-round interview is different from other firms," says a consultant. "Interviewees are given a packet of information for a fictitious client (e.g., XYZ company) and are asked to present their findings after an hour of poring through the data." Other employees inform about the last leg's thorough intensity, noting "a very unique combination of interviews, including a timed quantitative assessment, a research report comprehension and a client interview role play." In addition, applicants occasionally field brainteasers during the first few minutes of the fit portion, just to further size up analytical faculty.

At Marakon, size does matter. "Given the small-firm culture, fit is a big part of the hiring process," shares a staffer. A colleague adds that it's difficult to fight attrition at the firm, "so we have to try and make sure the candidate will fit into our culture and succeed." Ultimately, Marakon strives to model both consulting capability and cultural comfort, "as opposed to just getting really smart people at the expense of bad fit," we're told. Sources say that a prepared candidate will learn about Marakon and understand how it differs from its competition.

OUR SURVEY SAYS

The buddy system

With a recruiting process built on cultural fit, it's no wonder that Marakon consultants stick together. Insiders report a "very open and fun culture," where support and socialization are plentiful. One associate comments that there's "a great focus on development; everyone takes an interest in your success, from your firm-assigned coach, to your manager and partner, to more senior consultants and peers." The firm's small size lends itself to co-worker bonds, fostering familiarity and connectivity across the office and even across branches.

Employees say Marakon's intelligent, dynamic and challenging environment helps create an extended family feel, where teamwork reigns. "We have a fabulous culture," gushes a new hire. "I am good friends with so many people I work with, and honestly I feel the culture is one of the best aspects of working at Marakon."

Munching with the pros

Tracking down a senior staffer at Marakon isn't as hard as it may seem. According to one partner, "A great advantage of working at Marakon is the chance to work directly with the firm's most senior leaders, including the founder, the chairman and the CEO." Junior associates report working side-by-side with supervisors, who also work in project teams and dole out training and

Visit the Vault Consulting Career Channel at **www.vault.com/consulting** - with insider firm profiles, message boards, the Vault Consulting Job Board and more.

VAULT CAREER LIBRARY   181

feedback when necessary. "Having a small firm means great interactions with senior people, both on your team and otherwise," an associate consultant shares, noting lunches and wine-tasting events with senior partners and the CEO as especially memorable events. Others agree that "partners and managers are easily approachable," including managing partners and the CEO, who make a few office rounds per year.

Early client exposure has Marakonites chatting, too. Sources speak of unparalleled opportunities at the firm, winning chances to converse with senior-level clients much earlier than other firms would allow. "After one year," relates an associate, "I was already presenting material to the head of a $5 billion industrial manufacturing company. Another colleague follows with a similar story, having "met with a CEO of a $3 billion pharma business in the first couple of months at the firm" and managing a CFO affiliation after only nine months. "If you have the capabilities, Marakon gives great opportunities to interact with clients," insiders say.

Don't toss the timesheet

According to a consultant, "Marakon steadily manages to stick to its 60-hour workweek targets," which sources say isn't just lip service. Consultants are instructed to turn in time reports each week to monitor hours, and "if hours exceed 60 hours, partners and managers on the given projects are immediately called to discuss how hours can improve quickly," a source explains. Due to this close supervision, consultants report a satisfying work/life balance at Marakon, where senior-level employees are quick to initiate open dialogues to prevent consultant burnout. "The firm also allows for a great deal of flexibility and allows people to manage their own time," a co-worker adds. Another agrees that "the firm is very cognizant of what is normal and 'too much' stretch. When there's too much, they throw a lot of solutions toward the consultant to help them work it out." After long workweeks, managers have also been known to throw in compensation days, just to help the firm's laborers destress and stay balanced.

While weekend work arises occasionally, associates note that personal priorities and needs are respected. "Having worked at another consulting firm," an insider relates, "I can honestly say that Marakon has made it clear that it is continually striving to find the right balance between work and life."

Travel with ease

A Tuesday through Thursday travel model keeps Marakonites sane, we're told, which "makes the work manageable and provides for both a great team experience and a great office culture." Spending only two nights away from the office helps consultants maintain work/life equilibrium, and insiders remark that "management takes special effort to see that people rarely exceed that" trekking schedule. Having consultants in the office every Monday and Friday adds to the camaraderie felt across the firm, along with the "flexibility to travel at any times that are convenient for us," a source states—or, for some, the ability to decline travel work.

While insiders report frequent travel (necessary for 75 percent of projects) perks are not uncommon. As one consultant notes, "Traveling around the country on weekends to visit friends and family on the company dime" isn't too bad, since consultants are lucky enough to keep all hotel/airline points accumulated while out globe-trotting. In addition, for every six to eight weeks, co-workers receive one voyage-free week to recoup. Many Marakonites cite the excitement associated with going to new places and getting away from the office for a few days, while still enjoying weekends at home. Despite an accommodating travel model, an associate still warns that "if you want a pet, you may not want this job!"

You say formal, I say informal

One first-year consultant reports that Marakon's training module is "as thorough as you could possibly want." Expounding on that summation, other consultants chime in to cite the extensive 180-hour instruction that newbies receive within their first couple years, along with daily coaching from superiors, "drawing on a lot of experience and expertise" to help out with client assignments. Time investment in official training is important to the firm, and it makes sure guidance is readily available at all stages of progression, from a consultant's first day to a "significant amount of formal training scattered throughout the year" for all employees.

"Formal training is a good way to get peer groups together," asserts a manager, "but ultimately, you learn more on the job." In addition to its formal instruction, Marakon recognizes the invaluable wisdom received from on-the-job encounters. While cracking cases with more seasoned consultants, junior colleagues learn the ropes on a natural level—especially since "the firm actively expects its more senior people to mentor." Insiders say their project team colleagues are prime candidates for model behavior. As one source states, "The culture is very open and willing to help."

Cocktails and casual dress

Among its cornucopia of added perks, Marakonites most appreciate the firm's two-month unpaid sabbatical option, allowing employees a chance to relax, pursue alternative interests and, in one insider's case, get married and enjoy a honeymoon. Another plus is that the "firm is small enough that we can be flexible and make individual arrangements given a person's situation and preferences," which includes maternity and paternity leave for expecting consultants. And with three- to four-week vacation allotments, depending on tenure, consultants say they have time to unwind.

With regard to more social bonuses, Marakon has "all the perks a company could offer," including cocktail parties, bar nights, casual office dress, family day, global conferences, community service, a year-end holiday party and other frequent firm activities.

Raking it in

At Marakon, outstanding performance brings swift rewards. "What makes the compensation so exceptional," a source explains, "is the rate at which it grows. Due to Marakon's commitment to being a meritocracy, good performers are rewarded quickly." Each year, the firm aims to secure its competitive edge with top consulting firms, while keeping staffer salary up to par; according to an insider, Marakon "retroactively pays employees when it makes adjustments." And though the firm "often lags peers a bit in adjusting compensation, i.e., we are not typically the trendsetter in higher wages," colleagues promoted from associate consultant to consultant say "the level of pay is truly outstanding relative to your peers."

Since joining forces with its newly-formed parent, Trinsum Group, consultants receive restricted stock options in the company, which start at 10 percent of base compensation and grow annually, depending on company performance. Employees can also benefit from profit sharing "when the firm exceeds its annual financial plan," and sources report "a lot more upside potential with our equity stake than is available in your typical consulting firm."

An A-plus office

"The firm is known for having beautiful office space," sources indicate, "both from a location and aesthetic perspective." Chicago branchers boast of their huge offices and cubicles, expansive desk space, free food and—perhaps most appreciated—a pingpong table in the kitchen, whose "lively matches and tournaments create a fun environment." In New York, Marakon spans a Midtown building's top floor, with picaresque views, kitty-corner convenience to Grand Central Station and award-winning style worthy of an *Architectural Digest* feature, while the San Francisco branch enjoys "a balcony overlooking the Financial District." Regardless of locale, "Marakon's office space is A-plus in every region," a partner comments.

Digging in

Throughout the year, Marakon's community service group plans events to keep active in its surrounding neighborhoods. With a hand in Habitat for Humanity, holiday gift drives, clothing drives, charity donations and auctions, school renovations, inner-city tax preparation programs and pro bono consulting to nonprofits, employees aren't standing idly by—they're doing what they can to remain a strong presence in the communities in which they work and live. In addition to the aforementioned causes, "there is a host of other events that are organized by consultants and associate consultants, which also get strong participation," an insider

Visit the Vault Consulting Career Channel at **www.vault.com/consulting** - with insider firm profiles, message boards, the Vault Consulting Job Board and more.

VAULT CAREER LIBRARY   **183**

comments. Each Marakon office uses a community service-specific budget to organize local activities, which generally take place six times per year.

Closing the gaps

As one manager states, retaining women at the firm is a "key agenda item right now," since consultants admit that Marakon is "very good at recruiting and mentoring junior levels, but not as good at keeping women" in the ranks. Reasons for female attrition could be a result of "the lack of role models due to senior women departure," which a staffer says "leaves a huge gap in our partner ranks, and it's hard to fill that gap." The recent push for more females at the firm "is creating a great pipeline of future women leaders," though, and Marakon has instituted a women-specific diversity initiative. And while support for female colleagues goes unquestioned at the firm—"I personally have felt very well supported," one associate adds—women tend to "find [a consulting career] unsustainable and leave on their own volition," consultants say.

Also a work in progress is Marakon's focus on attracting racial and ethnic minorities. Though receptive to minority recruitment, insiders note that the firm "still finds it very challenging to attract minorities." A manager remarks that minority recruitment is "a recognized issue and people have the right intentions, but it's not as explicit a focus of the firm as women's diversity issues are, meaning, it's not on our talent agenda while women's diversity is."

Just as welcome in the Marakon ranks are GLBT consultants. Insiders attest to a "very open environment" where colleagues from associate consultant to managing partner are openly gay. "Diversity of sexual orientation is included in our definition of diversity," a senior employee comments, and though Marakonites say the firm hasn't established any particular initiatives on this front, "I think everyone is quite open-minded and welcoming about it," another appends.

"A great advantage of working at Marakon is the chance to work directly with the firm's most senior leaders, including the founder, the chairman and the CEO."

– Marakon source

Visit the Vault Consulting Career Channel at **www.vault.com/consulting** - with insider firm
profiles, message boards, the Vault Consulting Job Board and more.

VAULT CAREER LIBRARY

185

Towers Perrin

One Stamford Plaza
263 Tresser Boulevard
Stamford, CT 06901
Phone: (203) 326-5400
www.towersperrin.com

LOCATIONS

Stamford, CT (World HQ)
Offices and business partner locations in the US, Canada, Europe, Asia, Latin America, South Africa, Australia and New Zealand

PRACTICE AREAS

Actuarial Services
Change Implementation
Communication
Employee Benefits
Enterprise Risk Management
HR Delivery Services
HR Program Design & Management
HR & Workforce Strategy
Insurance & Financial Services
Legacy Pension Solutions
Organization & Employee Research
Reinsurance Intermediary Services
Self-Insurance & Captives

THE STATS

Employer Type: Private Company
Chairman & CEO: Mark V. Mactas
2006 Employees: 5,484
2005 Employees: 5,171
2006 Revenue: $1.42 billion
2005 Revenue: $1.4 billion

RANKING RECAP

Practice Area
#3 - Human Resources Consulting

UPPERS

- "Name recognition"
- You set the pace of your career
- Strong training for junior employees

DOWNERS

- Telecommuting is discouraged
- Infrastructure improvements are needed
- "Work/life balance takes some effort since there are so many good work opportunities"

EMPLOYMENT CONTACT

careers.towers.com

THE BUZZ
WHAT CONSULTANTS AT OTHER FIRMS ARE SAYING ABOUT THIS FIRM

- "Impressive client base"
- "Once well known, less visible now"
- "Diverse"
- "Boilerplate"

THE SCOOP

A knack for HR

Towers Perrin is one of the world's largest niche consulting firms, operating with over 5,400 employees out of offices and business partner locations in the United States, Canada, Europe, Asia, Latin America, South Africa, Australia and New Zealand. The firm built its 74-year reputation on human resources and benefits consulting, though it also offers reinsurance and financial risk management services. Towers Perrin's main thrust is helping companies manage employees through benefits policies, compensation, change management and other employee-focused areas. The reinsurance business offers reinsurance strategy and program review, claims management and program administration, catastrophe exposure management, contract negotiation and placement, and market security issues consulting. The firm also provides risk consulting through its business, Tillinghast, which offers consulting, actuarial services and software solutions to insurance and financial services companies, and advises on risk financing and self insurance.

The first pension planner

Known as Towers, Perrin, Forster & Crosby, the firm started out in Philadelphia in 1934, offering life insurance and reinsurance. One of the firm's founders, H. Forster, is often called "the father of pension planning," having developed the first pension plan for Union Carbide in 1917. As New Deal federal legislation on Social Security and minimum wage came into effect in the 1930s, the employee consulting business picked up speed and the firm grew quickly. In the 1940s, Towers Perrin expanded with offices in Chicago and New York, and the pension division published its first *TPF&C Pension Tax Manual*, today a standard U.S. Internal Revenue Service reference on pension tax law. Over the next two decades, the firm expanded internationally, establishing offices in Montreal, Brussels and London.

Towers Perrin started to develop an HR consulting niche in the 1960s, and over the next 30 years, focused on expanding those services. In 1979, it developed the Human Resource Information Systems to support employers' complex HR needs. After several mergers and smaller company acquisitions, in 1987, the firm declared Towers Perrin to be the "umbrella name" for all of its businesses.

The power of partnerships

Towers Perrin's ever-expanding alliance network provides a gateway to new and emerging markets around the globe. In June 2006, the firm joined Greco International, a Vienna-based actuarial and benefits consulting firm. The well-established company will open the door to the Central European market, including Hungary, the Czech Republic, Slovakia and Slovenia. That same month, the firm also ventured into the Polish market when it allied with HRK Partners and Trio Management, leading Polish HR consultancies. In October 2005, Towers Perrin signed a similar agreement with Cerebrus Consultants, an Indian HR advisory firm, which made its compensation and benefits services available to clients with operations in Pakistan, Bangladesh and Sri Lanka, as well as in India.

Small-size additions

A string of recent acquisitions—mostly companies of fewer than 250 employees—have also bolstered the firm's size and strength. In March 2007, Towers Perrin acquired Chicago-based ISR, an employee research and consulting firm with 200 staffers. ISR's main feature is the arsenal of employee and leadership opinion surveys it has collected over the years; the company has built up a database of surveys of over 35 million employees in 105 countries. In February 2007, the firm purchased MGMC, Inc., a Connecticut-based firm that provides compensation surveys and advisory services to the financial services industry. Established in 2002, MGMC has 15 employees offices in London and Darien, Conn. Its main clients are investment and commercial banks and securities firms executives. Towers Perrin also shored up its enterprise risk management practice in June 2006 by purchasing financial risk consultancy Risk Capital Management Partners LLC. Risk Capital assists clients in

Visit the Vault Consulting Career Channel at **www.vault.com/consulting** - with insider firm profiles, message boards, the Vault Consulting Job Board and more.

VAULT CAREER LIBRARY   187

financial services, energy, utilities and mining industries with identifying and managing enterprise risk. In July 2005, Towers Perrin bought German pensions consultancy Rauser AG, adding over 130 employees. And in October 2004, the Tillinghast business was strengthened with the acquisition of the staff of EPIC Consulting.

Outsourcing player

For many years Towers Perrin provided outsourced benefit administration services to many of its clients. The firm beefed up its outsourcing offerings in March 2005, when it teamed up with EDS. Together the companies launched ExcellerateHRO, a human resources outsourcing business that combines the administration solutions business with EDS' payroll and HR outsourcing practice. With big-name clients like Bank of America and 7-Eleven hiring the firm during its first year, the company got off to an impressive start. In 2006, ExcellerateHRO was selected as a leader in The Global Outsourcing 100, a list of the top outsourcing service providers established by the International Association of Outsourcing Professionals. Of the world's outsourcing providers, 65 were designated leaders on the list, reflecting their status as the more established companies. In March 2007, ExcellerateHRO also began offering on-demand employment background and drug screening, thanks to an agreement signed in March 2007 with HireRight, an employment screening company.

Staff surveys

Towers Perrin's surveys and research studies keep track of the current hot topics, as well as opinions and attitudes of employees all over the world. A January 2007 *Wall Street Journal* article featured the firm's 2007 study of the pension plans of 79 Fortune 100 companies. The study found that after years of being underfunded, defined benefit pension plans were actually in the black. According to estimates, companies had 102.4 percent of the assets needed to pay pensions indefinitely. Another 2007 survey on benefit strategy, entitled From Responsibility to Action: Making Benefit Change Work, found that Americans are fairly unsatisfied with the benefits provided by their employers. Of 2,380 employees polled, the majority felt that their health care and retirement plans are not meeting their needs, and that employers should be doing more to subsidize benefits. And a study conducted in 2006, the 2007 Health Care Cost Survey, found that health care costs for U.S. employers are projected to rise by 6 percent in 2007, an average of $518 per employee. The increase is expected to put pressure on businesses and employees, since both will have to increase spending to make up for the difference.

Annually, Towers Perrin puts out the "HR Service Delivery Report," which analyzes the service delivery and HR technology strategies and tactics of 325 large and small organizations in North America. The firm also hosts an annual forum, where HR execs and business leaders discuss issues like strategy, communication and new developments in HR software.

Overpaid?

The firm's research on executive compensation garnered attention in April 2006, when *The New York Times* featured an article on "gilded paychecks" for execs. The *Times* article suggested that some companies overpay underperforming CEOs. Adding ammo to the argument was a 2006 study conducted by the Corporate Library—"Pay for Failure: The Compensation Committees Responsible"—which singled out companies whose shareholder returns had been negative for five years, but whose top execs had been paid over $15 million over the last two years. Companies such as AT&T, BellSouth, Hewlett-Packard, Home Depot and Wal-Mart were among those mentioned. The over-the-top salary is set, according to the article, with guidance from HR consultancies such as Towers Perrin, Hewitt Associates and Watson Wyatt. But since these firms offer strategy in addition to salary consulting, the article makes the case that this creates conflict of interest for HR firms. As the media increases awareness of this issue, HR consulting firms can expect regulatory agencies to demand more accountability, particularly the Securities and Exchange Commission. In response to these concerns, Towers Perrin asserts that it has established formal policies to ensure the objectivity and independence of its advice in its consulting engagements.

In a tiff over torts

The high cost of litigation in the U.S. is a controversial topic, so it's no surprise that the annual Tillinghast study on the cost of torts in America usually sparks hot debate in the media. In March 2006, *The Wall Street Journal* quoted the most recent study's estimates, which put the dollar value of the torts system at $260 billion in 2004, and projected the figure would hit $315 billion by 2007. The *Journal* reported that critics refuted the findings, arguing that the "startling toll" was a "flawed" figure, since it lumped in minor things like payments from insurers for fender benders, to the total cost of torts. But the *Journal* also noted that the figures are a useful snapshot of the general expenses insurers pay for through the legal system each year. The study annually draws criticism from attorney advocacy groups, such as the Association of Trial Lawyers of America, who disagree with the basis used to come up with the figures. But despite the controversy surrounding it, media watchdogs and citizen groups who argue that taxpayers bear the costs—estimated at $886 annually per average American—continue to use the Tillinghast studies as a defense for tort reform.

GETTING HIRED

Don't forget the soft skills

Towers Perrin claims that candidates who have the best chance of getting in are those with an analytical and quantitative bent. But that's not all—the firm also emphasizes the importance of teamwork, sharp communication and having "an understanding of human behavior and motivation." In other words, it takes interpersonal skills, in addition to a talent for running the numbers, to be a fit here. Interested candidates can explore the firm's web site, which details "key skills" needed for the job and particulars on the hiring process.

The firm visits a number of campuses for recruiting events, covering more than 50 schools in the U.S., Canada and the U.K. Candidates who don't attend one of the universities on the recruiting schedule are invited to apply via the online application system. As far as the interviewing process goes, Towers Perrin uses all kinds of "selection tools" to determine whether candidates are a match. Aside from an office visit and traditional behavioral interview, the process might include a problem-solving interview, case study, group exercise, written exercise or hypothetical situation interview. The firm claims that after the interviews, it doesn't keep candidates waiting long. If interested, it promises to "issue the job offer as quickly as possible."

OUR SURVEY SAYS

Top-notch team

Insiders cheer about the committed and collegial corporate culture at Towers Perrin. "We have an amazing group of very intelligent, committed individuals … We are a bunch of hard driving, high achievers who work collaboratively to help our clients be successful," remarks a consultant. And though the atmosphere is said to be collegial, it's no less industrious: "The culture rewards high performance, so those less committed to the profession may view this as too intense," an associate states.

Being a large organization, naturally, the personality of each office varies somewhat, though a consultant claims that overall, "the people here are generally of a high quality and good to work with." One respondent says, "The culture can be largely dependent on the office you work in. I work in a great office. The work is interesting and diverse." Explains a colleague, "The vast majority of employees are self-motivated high achievers. [There are] lots of talented consultants to learn from and work with." The staffer adds, "Plus, we have great clients with lots of interesting work opportunities."

Move over, up-or-out

There's no doubt that serious devotion to the job is expected and rewarded. That being said, sources admit that the firm still makes room for those who prefer to be on the "slow track" career-wise. An insider explains, "The career path is determined by

Visit the Vault Consulting Career Channel at **www.vault.com/consulting** - with insider firm profiles, message boards, the Vault Consulting Job Board and more.

189

an individual's motivation. Up-or-out takes a back seat to do-the-work-you-can-and-want-to-do. Those who want to move up the ladder quickly do, and those who don't, don't have to." "People work at their own pace. You are either on the fast track or you are not," a source concurs. And while employees won't be forced to leave, insiders note that those who don't want to move up may tend to get stuck. An analyst states, "[It's] not strictly an up-or-out policy, but those that don't move up can get pigeonholed into a role."

Though criteria for getting ahead are clearly established at Towers Perrin, insiders explain that promotion is a personalized matter. "Career paths are well established and each consultant is mentored through the advancement process. Advancement is individualized and can range from one to five years," verifies an associate. According to sources, this firm is big on finding the right fit for employees as they progress. "The promotion policy is based on matching skills with positions; they focus on using each employee's individual strengths. There is consistency in talking about and rewarding high performance and extra effort," states a principal. A manager states, "To be promoted you must show skill growth and take on greater responsibility. We are very open about the promotion process and what needs to be done to be promoted, and no, it's not strictly up-or-out. Depending upon the specialty, it can take 10 or more years to become a principal (partner)."

Working toward balance

"Work/life balance takes some effort since there are so many good work opportunities," a source remarks. A handful of employees report that it is possible to balance a career at Towers Perrin with personal life, but it is up to the individual to structure his own schedule in a balanced way. "Workload is dictated largely by an employee's ability to manage his/her time wisely and not necessarily by the volume of projects for which a person is responsible," a manager notes. Some insiders assert they are able to achieve balance because of the flexibility allowed in arranging their own work hours. "By being treated as a professional, there is an understanding of meeting deadlines and deliverables, but it is not dictated how this is done, giving the freedom to arrange schedules as necessary to meet both home and work obligations," a consultant insists. A co-worker suggests that "there are busy times and slower times. Improved staffing would improve work/life balance, but I am able to work from home regularly, which helps out a lot. The company has also been very open to reduced-hour schedules when appropriate for employees.

On the flip side, other consultants claim they don't have much leeway when it comes to arranging their workload. Declares a staffer, "Flexible time or telecommuting is not encouraged by the firm. The firm is aware that work/life balance is an issue, but little support is provided to employees." Some reconcile this discrepancy by asserting that the ability to keep a steady equilibrium varies with each employee's circumstance. A source states, "The balance partly depends on what's happening with individual clients. Many of my colleagues are working reduced hours to be more involved with their families."

"The career path is determined by an individual's motivation. Up-or-out takes a backseat to do-the-work-you-can-and-want-to-do."

– Towers Perrin insider

Visit the Vault Consulting Career Channel at **www.vault.com/consulting** - with insider firm profiles, message boards, the Vault Consulting Job Board and more.

VAULT CAREER LIBRARY   191

Mercer Delta Organizational Consulting*

1166 Avenue of the Americas
New York, NY 10036
Phone: (212) 345-8000
www.oliverwyman.com

LOCATIONS

New York, NY (HQ)
Over 40 offices worldwide

PRACTICE AREAS

Automotive
Aviation, Aerospace & Defense
Communications, Media & Technology
Energy
Financial Services
Health & Life Sciences
Industrial Products & Services
Retail & Consumer Products
Surface Transportation

THE STATS

Employer Type: Subsidiary of Marsh & McLennan
Companies, Inc., a Public Company
Ticker Symbol: MMC (NYSE)
President & CEO: John P. Drzik
2007 Employees: 2,500+
2007 Revenue: $1.2 billion (Oliver Wyman Group)

*As of May 2007, Oliver Wyman—Delta Organizational Leadership
Consulting
**See p.96 for a full profile on Oliver Wyman

UPPERS

- "Incredible MBA admission rates—90 percent get into school of first choice"
- "Unpretentious"
- "Relaxed firm culture"
- No face time requirement

DOWNERS

- "A small firm trapped in the body of a medium-to-large firm"
- "Easy to get lost in a firm that is growing at such an exponential pace"
- "The people could use some polishing"
- Experiencing some growing pains

EMPLOYMENT CONTACT

www.oliverwyman.com

THE BUZZ
WHAT CONSULTANTS AT OTHER FIRMS ARE SAYING ABOUT THIS FIRM

- "Lots of growth in North America"
- "Geek shop"
- "Fun and flexible"
- "Indistinguishable"

"With work/life balance, work hours are what you make of them. If you can work productively and quickly, there is no need to put in face time during late nights."

– *Oliver Wyman employee*

Visit the Vault Consulting Career Channel at **www.vault.com/consulting** - with insider firm profiles, message boards, the Vault Consulting Job Board and more.

VAULT CAREER LIBRARY   193

Roland Berger Strategy Consultants

230 Park Avenue
Suite 112
New York, NY 10022
Phone: (212) 651-9660
Fax: (212) 756-8750
www.rolandberger.com

LOCATIONS

New York, NY (US HQ)
Munich (HQ)
33 offices worldwide

PRACTICE AREAS

Corporate Development
Information Management
Marketing & Sales
Operations Strategy
Restructuring & Corporate Finance

THE STATS

Employer Type: Private Company
Chief Executive Officer: Dr. Burkhard Schwenker
2007 Employees: 1,700
2006 Employees: 1,700

UPPERS

- "Dynamic, entrepreneurial culture with very talented people"
- "Amazing" teamwork; small teams
- "Fast career development opportunities"

DOWNERS

- Lots of long-distance travel
- "Small size (in the US) means ups/downs in project frequency/intensity or client travel needs"
- Extremely long hours

EMPLOYMENT CONTACT

Ms. Diane Greyerbiehl
Roland Berger Strategy Consultants LLC
2401 West Big Beaver Road
Suite 500
Troy, MI 48084
Phone: (248) 729-5178
Fax: (248) 649-1794

www.rolandberger.com/career/en/html/fs3.html

THE BUZZ
WHAT CONSULTANTS AT OTHER FIRMS ARE SAYING ABOUT THIS FIRM

- "The European McKinsey"
- "Not right for North America"
- "Cool boutique"
- "Lost their cutting edge"

THE SCOOP

A powerhouse from Deutschland

With more than 1,700 consultants in 33 offices worldwide, Roland Berger is one of the largest strategy firms in Europe—and cuts an imposing figure on the international stage, too. Based in Munich, the firm serves 30 percent of the Global 1000 and more than 40 percent of the leading companies in Europe. Roland Berger has boasted a growth rate of more than 17 percent per year since its founding in 1967.

The firm arranges its services by function, offering corporate strategy and organization, information management, marketing and sales, operations strategy, restructuring and corporate finance. Its industry competence centers include: automotive, energy and chemicals, consumer goods and retail, engineered products and high tech, financial services, infocom, pharma and health care, public services and transportation.

A one-man show

The consultancy's success probably came as no surprise to founder Roland Berger, an ambitious, influential businessman who, at age 30, started a one-man firm, Roland Berger International Marketing Consultants, in 1967. By 1973, the consultancy had merged with its first client, becoming the third-largest strategy firm in Germany. Deutsche Bank, impressed with the firm's growth, purchased a majority stake in 1987, but left the decision-making power in Berger's hands. A few years later, Berger and his partners orchestrated a buyout of the bank's shares.

Berger ascending

As his company rose, so did the influence of Roland Berger himself. Well known as a confidant of Germany's political elite, Berger has helped shape the country's direction in recent years. This hasn't always sat well with Germans, who are inclined to be suspicious of the convergence of business and politics. Nevertheless, Berger's championing of causes such as privatization has led to changes in the country: The firm has been involved in the privatization of a number of local, state and federal utilities and services. But while Berger was chummy with former German Chancellor Gerhard Schroeder, he has been seen as less closely aligned with the country's current leadership. A May 2006 article on Consultant-News.com noted that "the last German election could have been characterized as the battle of the strategy consultants," as current Chancellor Angela Merkel's victorious CDU party tends to be more associated with McKinsey.

In July 2003, Berger moved over to chair the company's supervisory board, putting control in the hands of an executive committee made up of Burkhard Schwenker, António Bernardo and Martin Wittig, and in 2004 added Vincent Mercier and Dirk Reiter. In October 2004, the firm unanimously elected Schwenker as its CEO. Schwenker, who joined the firm in 1989, was reelected as chief in December 2006. Roland Berger's partners—numbering around 130 at the end of 2006—serve as shareholders in the firm. Berger still remains very much involved, having retained all of his enthusiasm for the industry; he told a German student paper in February 2007, "I enjoy consulting as much now as I did 40 years ago."

Crossing borders

Though Roland Berger enjoyed a rapid rise in Germany, it took a while for the firm to move into the American market, with its first U.S. office opening in New York in 1995, and the second in Detroit in 1998. Though the company hasn't made any official statements, insiders have reported that Roland Berger plans to boost its U.S. hiring in the near future. China is another growth area for the firm, which has offices in Beijing, Shanghai and Hong Kong. Having worked in the Middle East since the late 1990s, the firm opened its first office in the Arab states, in Bahrain, in April 2006.

Visit the Vault Consulting Career Channel at **www.vault.com/consulting** - with insider firm profiles, message boards, the Vault Consulting Job Board and more.

VAULT CAREER LIBRARY   195

Buzz in the East

The Eastern and Central European markets have been the focus of much Roland Berger activity recently, with the firm declaring that "growth is the buzzword" for the region. In September 2003, the consultancy opened an office in Zagreb, Croatia, an area it tapped for its growth potential. In an interview with a Russian business journal in October 2006, Roland Berger Partner Uwe Kumm said the firm's business had doubled annually in the region since 1988. In Warsaw, where Roland Berger has a centrally-located office in the Metropolitan building, the firm has seen year-over-year growth of 70 percent, even though it entered the Polish consulting market "relatively late" in the game. The firm has set up four competency centers (specializing in financial services, energy and chemicals, infocom and automotive) in the region, and is actively looking to train junior consultants to work in offices in Romania, Poland, Russia and other countries in the area.

Roland Berger brings in scores of awards in Europe. In July 2007, German business publication *Manager Magazin* presented a ranking of management consultancies' reputations, with Roland Berger coming in first. Clients particularly cited the firm's restructuring services. And in the 2006 annual Lünendonk rankings of the top-25 German management consultancies, Roland Berger came in at No. 2 for the second consecutive year.

Think first, act later

The firm also wins praise for its executive magazine, *think:act*, launched in 2004. The magazine has an annual circulation of about 11,000, produced in English, German, Russian, Chinese and Polish. The firm says it avoids "self-praise" in the publication, instead allowing the range of topics—of interest to international execs—speak for themselves. In 2006, the publication received the Mercury Award, selected as the "best consulting magazine" in a competition involving 940 corporate publications from 15 countries hosted by the International Academy of Communications Arts and Sciences in New York.

Roland Berger produces plenty of other reading materials, including studies and surveys relevant to the many industries it serves. A February 2007 report found automotive suppliers around the world anticipating a tough year for business, while a January 2007 study tracked restructuring trends in Germany. Also in January, the firm produced the CEE 2016 study, analyzing challenges ahead for businesses in Central Europe. And in August 2006, Roland Berger published a survey of over 200 European pharmaceutical execs on sales issues.

The top in the EU

The firm hosts an annual Best of European Business event in Brussels, naming top companies from European countries in three categories: growth, "Europeanness" (defined as "making the best of Europe's opportunities"), and cross-border mergers and acquisitions. At the March 2007 gala, the firm produced what it deemed "the most comprehensive European executive survey ever," querying more than 400 execs on the business climate of the EU. One of the survey's notable findings was that Europe's top decision makers want to see greater leadership in the region on the topic of global climate change.

A strategic partner of the World Economic Forum held annually in Davos, Switzerland, Roland Berger also serves as lead partner of the Forum of Young Global Leaders, a group that brings together talented young entrepreneurs, scientists, cultural leaders, artists and NGO members. The forum aims to develop and implement a "vision" for 2030, with the aim of shaking up traditional approaches. Each global leader, selected by a committee chaired by Jordan's Queen Rania, serves a three-year term on the forum.

Molding young minds

In 2007, Roland Berger said it planned to hire 150 new consultants and 120 interns in German-speaking countries, and an even larger number of staff in international offices. The firm is big on cultivating homegrown talent, producing several events each year aimed at attracting and recruiting young minds. The firm's "start2007" recruiting workshop, aimed at students and recent grads, took place in Munich in January 2007. Participants from Germany, Austria and Switzerland worked in small groups to develop solutions for a real-life client project involving the consumer goods industry. The participants got to present their findings in a mock forum, allowing them to try out and practice their consulting chops. Similar recruiting events have been held for students and recent grads with backgrounds in engineering and the natural sciences. The firm also invests time in prestigious events for MBA students at leading European business schools, such as the Roland Berger International Case Competition, conducted at IESE Business School in Barcelona. In an effort to bring more women into the fold, in 2002 Roland Berger launched the FORWARD initiative (For Women-Attracting, Retaining, Developing) to encourage greater female participation in the firm. Events have included small conferences where young women interested in consulting can meet with established professionals.

Roland Berger shouldn't have too much trouble attracting the talent it seeks, since it has earned high marks for its employment policies. In June 2005, the firm became the first consultancy to earn a Work and Family certificate from the nonprofit Hertie Foundation, in recognition of its family-friendly initiatives. These include flexible working hours for consultants, as well as telecommuting options and day care assistance. The certificate was awarded after an intensive audit by the foundation, which will monitor the firm's work/life efforts in coming years. In addition, sabbaticals are "part of corporate culture" at Roland Berger, an Austrian publication reported in 2006. Training is also a priority for the firm, with opportunities ranging from "kickoff seminars" at exclusive European locations for newbies, to ongoing events for more seasoned consultants. Roland Berger reports that about 10 percent of its incoming new-hire pool can expect to make it to partner, with the average tenure of a Roland Berger consultant at around four or five years.

Roland Berger also encourages its consultants to continue their education and provides support for PhD and MBA programs. The firm is tapped in to the academic world through the Roland Berger Strategy Consultants Academic Network, which pairs consultants with thinkers at 15 universities. The firm also sponsors the Roland Berger Chair for E-Business and Information Technology at French business school INSEAD and the Internet-based Information Systems chair at Munich's Technische Universität.

From Dutch dance to Polish opera

Roland Berger's community efforts are wide-ranging, including participation in a volunteer day involving activities such as building playgrounds, and sponsoring antiviolence seminars for young people in Europe. The firm is involved in the arts and culture, too. Through a strategic partnership with Dutch dance company Nederlands Dans Theater, in the fall of 2006, young professionals with three to five years of work experience were given the opportunity to explore the world of consulting through a series of workshops held in the dance company's dressing rooms. The partnership is seen as a win-win for both parties, with Roland Berger getting to cultivate new consulting talent, and the dance company benefiting from free strategy advice. The firm has a similar partnership with the Bavarian State Opera. Under an initiative called Counterparts, the firm also supports culture and education in Central and Eastern Europe. In 2006, it sponsored a production of *The Magic Flute* by the Polish National Opera. Other projects have included an upgrading of public libraries in Dubrovnik, and the sponsorship of an art exhibition in Zagreb.

GETTING HIRED

Cozying up to Roland

To join Roland Berger's international clan, good analytical and conceptual abilities, along with creativity, team spirit and strong communication skills, are a must, the firm says. While university majors "are of secondary importance only," Roland Berger adds, scores should be stellar. Work and international experiences are also helpful.

For many Roland Berger offices, including those in the U.S., consulting hopefuls can hop online to fill out an application. The firm says applicants can expect to hear back within two weeks. Roland Berger hopefuls are advised to plan ahead—for entry-level positions just out of undergrad (typically junior consultants or consultants), students should begin applying up to nine months before finishing their schooling. The lead time is shorter for summer associates and interns, at around three months. Generally, internships are offered to undergrads, while summer associate positions go to MBAs. In the U.S., a source says, the firm has been drawing from the University of Chicago, Michigan, Wharton and Stern. "The firm is very selective in its hiring

Visit the Vault Consulting Career Channel at www.vault.com/consulting - with insider firm profiles, message boards, the Vault Consulting Job Board and more.

VAULT CAREER LIBRARY   197

practices," an insider says, adding, "The U.S. practice has less than 50 people and all the U.S. partners are involved during the final round of interviews."

Another consultant elaborates: "The hiring process consists of three temporally separate sessions for a total of three distinct interviews. Each interview is managed by one single partner or project manager. Generally, in the first meeting, you will be subject to a couple of interviews conducted by two project managers." In the second meeting, the source adds, a partner may be involved, followed by a meeting with a managing director. Expect questions on a "business case, quantitative analysis and market sizing."

Wild case weekends

Once they make it to the interview stage, applicants can expect to face a "GMAT-style admissions test," another insider says. There are also "at least four case interviews and the 'case weekend'—a weekend in a hotel in which candidates are supposed to solve a real case, simulating the company's environment." A staffer shares a case example: "You're with Boeing's CEO and he asks you whether the company should purchase large-capacity airplanes or invest in smaller planes. What do you say?"

OUR SURVEY SAYS

Peer to peer

Perhaps defying the stereotype of a giant German corporation, Roland Berger boasts a rather warm culture, insiders suggest. It's a place where "peers are more than just peers, they are real friends" who "will not only help you thrive on new concepts and acquire extensive corporate knowledge, but also guide you in personal issues and be keen to support you in any case needed," says a source.

The "flat hierarchy" at Roland Berger offers consultants "a lot of empowerment," one staffer says. Indeed, colleagues agree that the firm boasts an "entrepreneurial culture." In the U.S., an insider tells us, "Team sizes are small, work pressure is intense and it's always a very dynamic environment, as the firm is striving to grow its U.S. presence in several industry/function practices." Specifically, the source says, teams are made up of three to five people in total, so "if you want to join a firm to 'get lost' in a sea of consultants (with team sizes of 25 to 40)," and specialize in limited industries, Roland Berger may not be for you. Still, says a consultant, "Sometimes you find yourself working alone and don't feel really part of a team," adding, "Some seniors are in conflict with the newcomers and try to maintain their own 'gardens.'"

Your passport, please

Several sources cite the "very international" feel of the firm, where "cross-country and cross-continent teams are very common on all projects." "Client interaction, project staffing (and even services) are always managed globally. The firm has a very 'open' culture, yet strong values and tradition, especially due to its Western European heritage," remarks another staffer. Of course, this globe-spanning tradition means lots of globe-trotting for consultants, who can expect international travel on a fairly regular basis. With few offices in the U.S., coast-to-coast travel also isn't uncommon, insiders say.

Consultants suggest that work/life balance comes largely at the whim of managers. "Management promotes strong work/life balance whenever client interests are not jeopardized," claims one source, but a colleague grumbles, "In order to do some personal activities, I must sometimes sleep less than four hours a day." Another insider claims that striking a balance is "really hard," as "time slots not fully taken by clients are filled with commercial initiatives." Workweeks average between 50 and 75 hours, we're told, and "when not assigned to clients," there's a "strong focus on knowledge development," a source reports. According to a co-worker, "A majority of our training is 'unofficial'; however, we also have an excellent official training program."

Language learning

Compensation at Roland Berger is described as "in line with the market," with bonuses of 20 to more than 100 percent of salary, depending on seniority. The firm also reportedly offers 401(k) matching. One insider sees travel as the firm's top perk: "The greatest thing here is to travel for trainings in Europe, at least once a year." There's also the option to transfer to an international office for a limited time period. A consultant notes, "we have social events about once a quarter to bring the team and occasionally our families together. We also have an outstanding end-of-the-year party for the employees and their spouses." Other perks include a "top-notch" dental and health plan, generous vacation for maternity and paternity leave, and even language training for consultants' spouses.

Visit the Vault Consulting Career Channel at **www.vault.com/consulting** - with insider firm profiles, message boards, the Vault Consulting Job Board and more.

VAULT CAREER LIBRARY   199

Cambridge Associates LLC

100 Summer Street
Boston, MA 02110
Phone: (617) 457-7500
Fax: (617) 457-7501
www.cambridgeassociates.com

LOCATIONS

Boston, MA (HQ)
Arlington, VA
Dallas, TX
Menlo Park, CA
London
Singapore

PRACTICE AREAS

Advisory Services
Alternative Assets Benchmarking
Asset Allocation & Investment Policy Development
Financial Planning Advisory Services
Financial Policy Databases & Research
Governance Consulting
Internet Services
Manager Search & Evaluation
Performance Measurement & Reporting Services
Planned Giving Services
Strategic Financial Advisory Services

THE STATS

Employer Type: Private Company
President & CEO: Sandra A. Urie
2007 Employees: 800
2006 Employees: 700+

UPPER

• Very young company culture

DOWNER

• Long hours

EMPLOYMENT CONTACT

E-mail: resumes@cambridgeassociates.com

THE BUZZ
WHAT CONSULTANTS AT OTHER FIRMS ARE SAYING ABOUT THIS FIRM

• "Great work, great people"
• "Unnecessarily pretentious"
• "Solid"
• "Too small"

THE SCOOP

Need advice? Get it here

Since 1973, Cambridge Associates has been in the business of giving financial advice to more than 750 institutional clients worldwide, including colleges and universities, foundations, nonprofits, private clients and pension, agency and government funds. A third of Cambridge Associates' clients have less than $100 million in assets. The firm delivers investment consulting, independent research and performance monitoring services from six worldwide locations, specializing in asset allocation and investment advice, manager search and evaluation, performance measurement and reporting services, and capital markets research.

Hailing from Harvard

Co-founders and former Harvard roommates James Bailey and Hunter Lewis founded Cambridge Associates after they conducted a comprehensive review of how Harvard University invested its endowment fund. Together, they gathered information on asset classes, investment managers and institutional investors' best practices. Within six years, Harvard's endowment became the largest in the country, beating out even the oil-funded University of Texas.

Meeting with such success, the two decided to continue their research on an ongoing basis under the umbrella of a private firm. Soon afterward, Bailey's and Lewis' Cambridge Associates was working with a dozen other universities to help them garner more and better information on investment issues for their own endowment funds. These 12 universities remain loyal Cambridge Associates clients to this day.

For nearly a decade, Cambridge Associates' client list was made up exclusively of universities and nonprofits, such as foundations, museums, libraries, and performing arts and religious organizations. In 1982, private clients were added to the mix at the behest of one of the board members of a Cambridge Associates nonprofit client. Now, the firm selectively works with large institutional investors, including pension, agency and government funds. As a sign of approval, most of CA's business today comes from client referral, the majority of which are nonprofits like the Conrad Hilton Foundation and the Knight Foundation.

New leadership

In 2001, Cambridge Associates' Chief Operating Officer Sandra Urie was appointed president and chief executive officer of the firm. Urie joined up in 1985, fresh out of the Yale School of Management because she felt the firm "married my nonprofit roots and emerging interest in investments," as she told *Foundation & Endowment Money Management* in March 2006, a year after she was honored at the National Council for Research on Women's Women Who Make a Difference awards dinner. Before becoming head of Cambridge Associates, Urie specialized in the firm's financial planning practice, assisting colleges, museums and independent schools with long-range financial planning.

A little of this and a little of that

In the *Foundation & Endowment Money Management* interview, Urie stated her belief that it is in CA's best interest to research everything that is fair game for endowments to invest in. That's because CA believes its clients will get the most for their money by diversifying their investments, buying into such areas as traditional and clean energy, real estate, distressed debt, and even hedge funds and venture capital. Asset allocation, the company says, is a key factor in portfolio performance, much more so than security selection, market timing or other factors. Therefore, every new client relationship begins with developing an asset allocation that meets the client's goals, risk tolerance and constraints.

In the last few years, Cambridge Associates has seen a huge surge in demand for its Cambridge Capital Advisory Service, which helps clients create and monitor customized portfolios. Urie chalks up the increased demand for the service—tailored for private clients, endowments with alternative asset programs and endowments seeking total fund oversight—to the difficulty her clients

Visit the Vault Consulting Career Channel at **www.vault.com/consulting** - with insider firm profiles, message boards, the Vault Consulting Job Board and more.

V\ULT CAREER LIBRARY   **201**

are having recruiting and retaining qualified investment staff. Add to that the increasingly tangled web of regulations imposed by the U.S. Securities Exchange Commission, under which more and more companies are looking for more transparency and financial oversight, and it seems CA has found itself in the right place at the right time.

Doing their homework

The advice Cambridge Associates' professionals dole out is based on years of research conducted by a group of research professionals the firm has hired to conduct thorough and objective research on capital markets, in addition to the collection of investment strategies pursued by fund managers. The firm's research consultants scattered throughout the U.S., London and Singapore are divided into four research concentrations—hedge funds, venture capital/private equity, marketable managers and publications—and manage a number of proprietary databases such as CA's investment manager database, the alternative assets investment manager database, and its investment office organization and compensation database.

The researchers also maintain proprietary indices that trace more than 2,000 venture capital and private equity funds. And in whatever time is leftover, CA's researchers manage to publish more than 100 research reports annually, exclusively for their clients, and provide benchmark statistics for evaluating returns on venture capital funds, funds-of-funds, real estate and other alternatives to public stocks.

GETTING HIRED

East Coast groove

To apply for a position at Cambridge Associates, resumes (indicating desired position and office locations) can be submitted via the firm's web site. The company even lets you go old school, if you wish to fax or mail your resume to your Cambridge office of choice. All submissions will be kept on file for a year.

The firm recruits at "almost all" of the NESCAC (New England Small College Athletic Conference) schools, and up and down the Eastern Seaboard from A to Z—or, from American University to Washington and Lee. Graduates join up in the entry-level positions of consulting associate, performance measurement or research associate, while MBA candidates are eligible for generalist consultant, specialist consultant and research consultant positions. The firm also recruits at such big-name B-schools like Harvard Business School, Dartmouth's Tuck School of Business, MIT's Sloan School of Management, Wharton, Berkeley's Haas and UV's Darden, and internationally at INSEAD and the London Business School.

Q&A

Sources tell us that the firm "basically brings in 20 to 30 people at a time" during each hiring cycle; according to one associate, the "initial interview is very informal," though "second rounds are a little more intense" and involve "a small case study." In the experience of this staffer, the process was "very short": He was "interviewed by three current employees and that's it." Expect what one source terms "very basic personality interview questions." According to an insider, it can't hurt to stress your "high attention to detail" and job-completion skills. A consultant recalls being asked to define "three things affecting the market at the moment," as well as being "given one of the reports that Cambridge Associates produced" and asked to fill out a test based on the graphs and data included.

As a sign of approval, most of Cambridge Associates' business today comes from client referral, the majority of which are nonprofits like the Conrad Hilton Foundation and the Knight Foundation.

Cambridge Associates LLC

Visit the Vault Consulting Career Channel at **www.vault.com/consulting** - with insider firm profiles, message boards, the Vault Consulting Job Board and more.

VAULT CAREER LIBRARY

203

Capgemini

750 Seventh Avenue
Suite 1800
New York, NY 10019
Phone: (212) 314-8000
Fax: (212) 314-8001
www.us.capgemini.com

LOCATIONS

New York, NY (US HQ)
Paris (HQ)
Offices in 32 countries

PRACTICE AREAS

Consulting Services
  Customer Relationship Management
  Finance & Employee Transformation
  Supply Chain
  Transformation Consulting
Outsourcing Services
Technology Services

THE STATS

Employer Type: Public Company
Ticker Symbol: CAP.PA (Paris Bourse)
Chairman: Serge Kampf
CEO: Paul Hermelin
2007 Employees: 78,000
2006 Employees: 68,000
2006 Revenue: €7.7 billion
2005 Revenue: €6.95 billion

RANKING RECAP

Practice Area
#9 - Financial Consulting
#10 - Operational Consulting
#10 - Pharmaceutical & Health Care Consulting

UPPERS

- "Good training"
- "Plenty of opportunities to work with high-profile clients"

DOWNERS

- "Limited growth potential for nontechnical roles"
- Subpar compensation

EMPLOYMENT CONTACT

www.us.capgemini.com/careers

THE BUZZ
WHAT CONSULTANTS AT OTHER FIRMS ARE SAYING ABOUT THIS FIRM

- "International"
- "Never the same after the Cap merger with Ernst & Young"
- "Real integration"
- "Big, clumsy"

THE SCOOP

Identity crisis

In 1967, Frenchman Serge Kampf founded a small Paris-based enterprise management and data processing company, known as Sogeti. When Sogeti bought European firm CAP in 1973, followed by Gemini Computer Systems in 1975, it came to be called Cap Gemini Sogeti. After a string of different owners, further acquisitions (over 10) and name changes (seven, to be exact), this consulting firm has finally settled on an identity: Capgemini. Today, the firm offers consulting, technology and outsourcing as well as local professional services through its subsidiary, Sogeti. Its 78,000 employees serve clients in a host of industries, including financial services, health care, life sciences, telecom and utilities. The consulting practice of Capgemini is divided into six areas: relationship management, finance and employee transformation, supply chain, global sourcing, operational research and transformation consulting services. Capgemini is truly a global firm, with an established a presence in 30 countries.

Postmerger malaise

Though it's been around a while, the latest version of the firm came about as a result of a name change in 2004. After Cap Gemini acquired Ernst & Young Consulting in 2000, it took on the moniker Cap Gemini Ernst & Young and conducted a $72 million branding campaign to establish the new identity. The merger was a shaky one, with the first few years resulting in revenue losses and layoffs. In 2004, CFO William Bitan stepped down after the firm posted a $24.6 million operating loss for the first half of the year, though the firm had been expecting a profit.

Not for sale

By that time, spending had started to pick up for the consulting industry as a whole, but the firm showed few signs of improvement. By 2004, industry observers began to predict that only a buyout would be able to right the ship, and HP and Atos Origin were names tossed around as possible bidders. But late in the year, the firm issued statements denying any intent to sell, and announced a turnaround plan in early 2005. The full-scale recovery program involved resizing operations in North America, refocusing on fewer market segments and changing management, with the intent to achieve "accountability, affordability and efficiency."

The firm disposed of its health care consulting practice in April 2005, selling it off to Accenture for $175 million. Capgemini retained its health care outsourcing and public-sector health clients, however. The following October, the firm revamped its project and consulting line of business, appointing Salil Parekh to lead the group. Firm leadership predicted a $100 million savings through cutting costs, reducing IT spending and making use of offshore locations when possible.

Shaping up

A shift in management was integral to the firm's recovery plan. In June 2005, Capgemini transformed its operating model to a geographically-oriented profit and loss model, naming four area directors to head up U.S. regions. Former CFO of the North American strategic business unit, Tim Crichfield, was named head of consulting and technology services in the Midwest; Lanny Cohen, formerly market segment and sales leader for the telecom media and entertainment group, was appointed to lead the Eastern region; Bill Campbell, formerly North American geographic sales leader, was named director of the Southern region; and Kevin Poole, formerly supply chain leader for North American consulting services, was tapped to head up the Western area. Fifteen-year consulting veteran Chell Smith was given the responsibility of overseeing the entire U.S. division. Smith has developed a reputation in the industry as a champion of women's issues and a big supporter of work/life balance through flexible schedules.

Visit the Vault Consulting Career Channel at **www.vault.com/consulting** - with insider firm profiles, message boards, the Vault Consulting Job Board and more.

205

Back in black

In 2005, the firm finally returned to positive net income, posting €141 million in income and €6.9 billion in revenue. Major contracts in outsourcing were responsible for the boost: North American business benefited from a seven-year contract with Bombardier; an outsourcing partnership in collaboration with HP; a contract with Limited Brands to overhaul the company's IT systems at stores such as Victoria's Secret and Express; and an $8.9 million contract to design, implement and maintain a new Oracle-based financial management system at Washington's National Gallery of Art.

In 2006, results looked even better, as net profit doubled and revenue grew 10.7 percent, to €7.7 billion. The consulting services group showed the most improvement, up five points over the prior year, thanks to improved workforce utilization. Though cost-cutting and restructuring kicked off the recovery, the firm's growth was mostly fueled by projects conducted from its low-cost global sourcing locations, particularly India and China.

Doing something right

Capgemini has turned its attention to opportunities in outsourcing, and understandably so—in 2005, outsourcing accounted 38 percent of its revenue. The firm has dubbed its global delivery strategy "rightshoring," meaning a combination of onshore, near-shore and far-shore locations into one integrated, seamless service. This approach has attracted attention in the field: In May 2006, Capgemini was ranked among the world's top-five outsourcing providers by the International Association of Outsourcing Professionals. The ranking was based on 18 criteria, including the number of employees devoted to outsourcing, the number of professional certifications and track record of management.

Key contracts

In 2006, the outsourcing practice continued to rake in contracts. In December, the firm signed a seven-year deal with food packaging company TetraPak to take over a range of finance and accounting services. Swedish firm SKF, a ball bearings and seals supplier, awarded it another seven-year outsourcing deal in October. Capgemini will provide multilingual finance and accounting services from its dedicated BPO center in Krakow. The firm's Swedish office bagged a five-year deal with Nordea, a Nordic financial services group, in July. Another major contract, valued at over $500 million, was awarded by GM in February. Capgemini was hired to assist GM's information, systems and services organization, by supporting some of the program's key strategic elements, including the management of enterprisewide application integration, which provides enterprise-level strategic planning, architecture, program management and verification/validation services. And in January, the firm inked a contract with Zurich Financial Services, one of the world's largest insurance companies. The multiyear agreement put Capgemini in charge of Zurich's finance and accounting processes from its service center in Krakow.

All eyes on India

Capgemini has sharpened its focus on India, beefing up new hires in the country and, recently, acquiring Kanbay International, an Indian financial IT services firm. Revenue from the country has grown 80 percent annually over the past few years. In 2006, CEO Hermelin announced intentions to employ 10,000 in India by the end of 2007, but the purchase of Kanbay International, in December 2006, boosted the number of staff in the region to 13,250, surpassing Hermelin's goal ahead of schedule. The $1.25 billion acquisition also made India the second-largest country in the Capgemini group. The firm also expanded its BPO capabilities in India when it acquired a 51 percent stake in Unilever India Shared Services Limited (Indigo), announced in September 2006. As part of the acquisition, Capgemini and the Unilever Group entered into a seven-year agreement to deliver finance and accounting services to Unilever companies, which are Indigo's current customers. The deal also gave the firm a presence in Chennai. At the time, the firm already operated centers in Bangalore and Mumbai, as well as a 500-person office in Kolkota, opened in March 2006.

And while India is the center of attention, other regions have popped up on the firm's outsourcing map. Capgemini's centers in Krakow, Katowice, Warsaw and Wroclaw together employ 1,500 staff and are dedicated to finance and accounting services. At its facility in Guangzhou, China, the firm employs 1,000 and serves a range of global BPO clients. Aside from finance and accounting, the firm aims to develop other BPO services from these locations, such as procurement, HR and the latest addition, knowledge process outsourcing.

Winning over the Brits

Capgemini has drummed up plenty of business in U.K. lately. In October 2006, the firm was contracted to help develop an electronic dispensary system for U.K. chain Lloydspharmacy. The system, known as CoMPaSS (Complete Medication and Patient Support System), will be installed at all Lloydspharmacy branches and is meant to streamline the 110 million prescriptions dispensed each year. The pharmacy also awarded Capgemini a five-year contract to manage and support the IT for the system. In April 2006, the firm won an extension through 2014 for an IT and support services contract with Her Majesty's Revenue & Customs, known as Aspire. The buzzed-about deal, originally awarded in 2003, is valued at £3 billion and is considered one of the largest outsourcing deals to date. In January 2006, the Swansea Council of Wales announced the signing of the first phase of a project to launch the biggest e-government program in the country. The program aims to modernize the way the government operates and provides service to users. Capgemini was given the job of designing and building the new IT systems, as well as running them on an outsourced basis for 10 years. Earlier, in March 2005, Capgemini inked a five-year, £20 million contract with British Energy, the U.K.'s largest energy producer.

On paper and on screen

Capgemini's consultants often publish research and white papers related to their clients' industries, most of which can be found online. Collaborate with Capgemini, the firm's North American e-newsletter, offers opinions on technology and business trends, written by the firm's experts. A recent issue examined the transformation of the economy into an invisible asset marketplace where "service-centric companies" have become increasingly popular. Annually, experts put out the "European Energy Markets Observatory" report, which tracks progress in deregulation of the electricity and gas market in 25 European countries.

In January 2006, the firm partnered with Intel and Micro Industries to unveil Retail Media Networks, a joint initiative to "influence buying behavior in real time." The networks provide point-of-decision media screens that give consumers product information, directions for finding products in the store, product news, promotions and services, in addition to paid advertising, customizable for retail locations. The networks are being used by several large retailers to give consumers a more user-friendly shopping experience and to impact buying decisions.

GETTING HIRED

Making a good impression

Capgemini's campus recruiting is "fairly regimented," according to sources. Each office draws applicants from universities in the surrounding area, and candidates typically go through two rounds of interviewing. According to a staffer, "The first [round] is behavioral and the second is more functional." Throughout the hiring process, Capgemini also tries to get to know candidates' personalities in a more relaxed environment, explains one insider. "There are also numerous recruiting events (info sessions, happy hours, etc.) where you will be informally judged. Your impact, positive or negative, is noticed."

It's a surprise

It's anyone's guess as to what types of questions will be asked in an interview. "Case questions are not used on any consistent basis," says one consultant. "Interviewees for the transformation consulting or technology strategy group are more likely to get them (because of their strategic focus) but there is no consistency in the questions," he adds.

Visit the Vault Consulting Career Channel at **www.vault.com/consulting** - with insider firm profiles, message boards, the Vault Consulting Job Board and more.

 VAULT CAREER LIBRARY   207

OUR SURVEY SAYS

More like a 9-to-5er

Capgemini reportedly offers employees more of a consistent and regular schedule than one might expect of a consulting firm. Says an insider, "My firm is not really the 'work hard, play hard' type of organization that I was looking for. Some of my colleagues seem more like regular 9-to-5 industry professionals than consultants." Staffers say that "hours vary" per week, but overall it is easy to maintain a tolerable schedule and a healthy work/life balance. "Capgemini works very hard to promote work/life balance, and creates incentive for projects to be managed and sold at rates and with scope commensurate with a 40- to 45-hour workweek. Obviously, as one nears deliverable dates you may be asked to put in some extra time," a source reports. In addition, most employees don't have to work on the weekends, though advancing along the career path might require putting in more hours than normal. As one insider who's on the track attests, "I don't need to work extra on the weekdays or work on the weekends, but I am trying to be involved in things other than my normal day-to-day client delivery work."

Set your expectations skyward

It's a given that consultants at Capgemini will spend a lot of time on the road. "Don't join Capgemini unless you are OK with traveling 100 percent of the time," reveals one manager, adding that it's "a 3-4-5 schedule. That doesn't mean that you will travel that much, but it does properly set your expectations." The source continues, "And though we are regionally based, I have not found that to matter too much. I have been traveling out of region for most of the time I have been with the firm." An analyst notes that "it's pretty much what you would expect from any consulting gig." Suggests a colleague, "People that are surprised by this are the ones that really didn't know what they were getting into."

Be on your best behavior

Insiders claim that one of Capgemini's strengths is "good training." However, they also indicate that the path to advancement is not quite as clear as it could be. "Promotion relies on being calibrated during a closed 'unminuted' meeting by your peers. So if you ever fall out with someone, you are stuck." In addition, we're told, there's "no formal feedback from the process, so [there is] no knowledge of why you were not promoted."

Disappointing bonuses

Compensation also draws complaints from staffers. "Compensation, particularly bonuses, is a joke. The average range is now between 4 and 6 percent. I could do better working in the industry," an associate grumbles. Another employee confirms, "Our compensation is fairly poor compared to the industry average, particularly around bonuses."

Staffers relate that the firm's involvement with charitable endeavors varies between offices. "Community involvement is handled on an office-by-office basis. Typical activities are things like Ronald McDonald House and United Way," a consultant shares.

"Capgemini works very hard to promote work/life balance, and creates incentive for projects to be managed and sold at rates and with scope commensurate with a 40- to 45-hour workweek."

– *Capgemini staffer*

Visit the Vault Consulting Career Channel at **www.vault.com/consulting** - with insider firm profiles, message boards, the Vault Consulting Job Board and more.

VAULT CAREER LIBRARY

209

Hewitt Associates

100 Half Day Road
Lincolnshire, IL 60069
Phone: (847) 295-5000
Fax: (847) 295-7634
www.hewitt.com

LOCATIONS

Lincolnshire, IL (HQ)
Offices in 35 countries

PRACTICE AREAS

Actuarial
Compensation & Rewards
Federal Consulting
Health Care
HR Efficiency & Effectiveness
International HR
Organizational Change
Retirement
Talent Management

THE STATS

Employer Type: Public Company
Ticker Symbol: HEW (NYSE)
Chairman & CEO: Russell Fradin
2007 Employees: 24,000
2006 Employees: 22,000
2006 Revenue: $2.8 billion
2005 Revenue: $2.8 billion

RANKING RECAP

Practice Area
#2 - Human Resources Consulting

UPPER

• Big name in BPO

DOWNER

• Getting over some recent financial hurdles

EMPLOYMENT CONTACT

hewittassociates.com/Intl/NA/en-US/WorkingHere

THE BUZZ
WHAT CONSULTANTS AT OTHER FIRMS ARE SAYING ABOUT THIS FIRM

• "Leader in their sector"
• "Low hiring standards"
• "Diverse and family-friendly"
• "Glory days are gone"

THE SCOOP

Bringing the benefits

Founded in 1940, Hewitt Associates is a trailblazer in the human resources field. The firm was established by Ted Hewitt as a modest insurance outfit in Lake Forest, Ill. While helping his first client, Parker Pen, with an insurance-related matter, Hewitt realized that what the office supplier really needed was a well-structured employee benefits package. From that point on, Hewitt Associates embarked on a mission to augment its actuarial work with two types of services: outsourcing and consulting.

Among its many firsts, Hewitt Associates went on to launch the first noncontributory employee savings and pension plan to be registered with the IRS (in the 1940s), became the first consultancy to measure ongoing investment performance for defined benefit plans (in the 1950s), and created the widely used Total Compensation Measurement methodology to assess the value of employers' pay packages (in the 1970s). The firm's business continues to be divided among consulting (including health management consulting, retirement and financial management consulting, and talent and organization consulting) and outsourcing (handling administration of benefits, payroll and broader BPO for client companies).

During its early years, the firm expanded its business in the U.S., opening offices in Minneapolis, New York City, Milwaukee, Los Angeles and Dayton. Its first international office opened in Toronto in 1976, followed by branches in Paris and St. Albany, just outside of London, in 1985. Outsourcing has globalized the firm even further; according to India's *Economic Times* in April 2006, nearly 20 percent of Hewitt's total workforce is based in India. Today, the firm's 24,000 staffers work out of 35 countries.

Exulting in BPO

Outsourcing accounts for more than two-thirds of the firm's revenue, and the company is the sixth-largest diversified outsourcing company in the U.S., according to *Fortune*. Hewitt boasts 2,500 clients, including more than half of the Fortune 500 and more than a third of the Fortune Global 500. Marquee clients include Alcoa, Blue Cross and Blue Shield, Capital One, MeadWestcavo and Sun Microsystems. Nearly 95 percent of the firm's clients have been with Hewitt for more than five years.

Hewitt's steady growth in outsourcing is due in part to its 2004 acquisition of HR business process outsourcing firm Exult, Inc., a deal which effectively redefined the HR BPO industry. Thanks to the acquisition, Hewitt now enjoys a global market share of 35 percent in HR outsourcing, with 42 BPO service centers devoted to HR services in 15 locations, including the U.S., Brazil, Canada, the U.K. and India.

Too much too soon?

But the firm's aggressive expansion hit a few bumps in 2006. When Hewitt CEO Dale C. Gifford announced his retirement in June, the head of Hewitt's outsourcing business, Bryan J. Doyle, also made an exit to pursue other opportunities, while another sales exec, Michael Salvino, left for Accenture's outsourcing business. In a July 2006 article, *Crain's Chicago Business* saw the exits as an "exodus," making the case that Hewitt was suffering the pangs of "too much outsourcing too fast." Following the Exult acquisition, the article argued, Hewitt may have been forced to invest too much up front in setting up BPO contracts, many of which aren't expected to break even until 2008. The article also noted that "the din of takeover chatter" surrounding Hewitt had grown louder, naming IBM, Accenture and Fidelity Investments as possible suitors.

Though the takeover rumors had subsided by the time the firm's 2006 financial results were released, Hewitt was forced to admit that the year had been challenging, reflecting some disappointments in the profitability of certain BPO contracts. In 2006, the firm's global revenue was nearly $2.8 billion, down 2 percent from the previous year. For the next year, the firm said, it planned to focus on growing its benefits outsourcing and consulting businesses, while "redefining" its approach to HR BPO.

Visit the Vault Consulting Career Channel at www.vault.com/consulting - with insider firm profiles, message boards, the Vault Consulting Job Board and more.

VAULT CAREER LIBRARY   211

Movement in the ranks

In September 2006, Russell P. Fradin took over the role of chairman and CEO. Fradin most recently served as president and CEO of The Bisys Group, Inc., a provider of outsourcing solutions for the financial services sector, and before that, he was an executive at ADP. Fradin is also a McKinsey man, having spent 18 years as a consultant at the firm. His compensation raised some eyebrows in the media, when it was reported that he had pulled in a cool $2.4 million in less than a year on the job. In January 2007, the firm created a new position—senior VP of corporate development and strategy. Matthew C. Levin, formerly an exec with HIS Inc., was named to the role, which emphasizes mergers, acquisitions and partnership opportunities along with strategic and growth initiatives for consulting and outsourcing. In July 2006, the firm announced the launch of a health care consulting practice in the U.K., to be led by James Kenrick.

International expansion

In March 2007, the firm expanded its operations in Italy with the acquisition of Adelaide Consulting, a Rome-based company specializing in benefits and compensation services. In October 2006, Hewitt announced the launch of mobility services, a type of outsourcing service, in Shanghai. The firm provides HR outsourcing and consulting services in 11 markets in the Asia-Pacific region, including Australia, India, Japan, China, Korea, Malaysia, Singapore, New Zealand and Thailand. Europe has been another big BPO growth area for the firm. In March 2006, the firm announced the opening of a new HR outsourcing center in Krakow, Poland, employing approximately 300 associates.

Executive pay blues

As a provider of executive compensation advice, Hewitt, like some of its HR consulting peers, has found itself the target of criticism. An April 2006 *New York Times* article disclosed the firm's role as executive compensation consultant for unpopular Verizon CEO Ivan Seidenberg, who was seen as a prime example of the overpaid, underperforming CEO. Making matters worse, at the same time, the paper noted, Hewitt was performing other services for the telecom giant, including running its employee benefits program. In addition to expressing outrage over Seidenberg's inflated pay package ($19.4 million in 2005), critics were quick to call Hewitt's dual roles for Verizon a conflict of interest. Verizon took on a new compensation consultant, Pearl Meyer & Partners, in the fall of 2006.

Through the brouhaha, Hewitt maintained that it has "strict policies in place to ensure the independence and objectivity of all our consultants," but the *Times* article, along with follow-ups on the topic of executive pay in other mainstream media, caught the attention of the public. A March 2007 article in *The Wall Street Journal* looked at the growing ambitions of legislators to put a check on executive pay. The article noted that Rep. Barney Frank, newly appointed chair of the House Financial Services Committee, was introducing legislation to give shareholders a veto on outsized executive compensation packages. According to the article, legislators and other "mainstream activists" are gaining traction in their push to curb executive pay and rein in conflicts of interest. Based on a letter drafted by an assistant treasurer for the state of Connecticut in October 2006, the *Journal* reported, Morgan Stanley dropped Hewitt as its compensation advisor because the financial giant also engages the consultancy for advice on its pensions. Experts predict that, with an increasingly dissatisfied and empowered shareholder culture, it's only a matter of time before firms like Hewitt (as well as competitors Towers Perrin, Watson Wyatt and Mercer HR) are forced to separate their executive compensation and other consulting roles.

Tracking trends

Hewitt is a widely-tapped source for words of wisdom about trends in HR, including compensation and outsourcing, with its consultants often called upon to provide quotes and stats for top business publications. In a study published in February 2007, Hewitt found that employees typically don't take advantage of their flexible spending accounts, leaving an average of $100 to $200 on the table each year. Another study of large U.S. companies published that month reported that many planned to reevaluate their retirement programs. A January 2007 survey suggested that companies are potentially losing millions of dollars in payroll expenses and employee productivity by not tracking and managing employees' time away from work. In another January 2007 release, Hewitt announced the availability of data it had compiled from a "microcosm of the U.S. labor market"—

more than 1,000 large companies and 20 million employees—to help establish a human capital metric it deems the "talent quotient." According to the firm, tracking this metric can help firms quantify the financial impact that pivotal employees make on their business results. Hewitt argues that for the average Fortune 500 company, a 10-point increase in a company's TQ score adds approximately $70 to $160 million to its bottom line over the next few years. Hewitt also regularly releases lists of interest to HR professionals, such as rankings of the best employers in regions such as Latin America and Central and Eastern Europe.

Practicing what it preaches, Hewitt has been lauded for its own HR excellence, with family-friendly perks like maternity and paternity leave packages, unpaid leave options, flexible schedules and an overnight dependent care plan. For six years and counting, the firm has made *Computerworld*'s list of the best work environments in the U.S. for IT employees.

Service with a smile

Hewitt says that it takes its community relationships "every bit as seriously as our client relationships," initiating service projects around the world. Its efforts include community partnerships, pro bono work, grants, thought leadership and old-fashioned "sweat equity." Through the Hewitt Associates Foundation, associates nominate nonprofits in the U.S., with a focus on those that provide essential services to the poor. Both the company and its associates sustain the foundation. The firm also maintains partnerships with and supports the American Red Cross, Court-Appointed Special Advocates, Habitat for Humanity, i.c. stars, the American Cancer Society, the Juvenile Diabetes Research Foundation and the AIDS Foundation.

In the realm of education, the firm's "signature" community service program is the Hewitt Career Center, first established at Waukegan High School in Illinois, where students have access to technology tools for career navigation, a dedicated career counseling staff and partnerships with employers for career inspiration. The firm's other education-focused projects include participation in America Scores, an after-school program for at-risk youth, the Diversity Pipeline Alliance, aimed at steering minorities toward business careers, Junior Achievement, the Ruby Bridges Foundation and the United Negro College Fund. In honor of the firm's founder, Ted Hewitt, the company matches contributions from U.S. associates to secondary and college educational institutions up to $500.

GETTING HIRED

Just follow the script

Hewitt Associates online career page lists its current schedule of recruitment events and locations. Job openings in the firm's U.S., U.K. and Asia-Pacific divisions are also posted, and the firm encourages applicants to submit application materials online. Don't fret that your resume will fall into the "Yeah, Whatever, Black Hole"; Hewitt assures that "within three business days of submitting the form, you'll receive an acknowledgement e-mail with an ID and password," enabling you to edit your information, and that they do regularly review all online materials. Resumes enter a firmwide database, are checked against all open positions in the firm for suitability and remain active for one year. The firm will contact likely applicants directly.

According to one source, once you score an interview, you will be "meeting with four people, for 45 minutes each." Expect mostly "behavioral questions," with interviewers "only going into technical questions if it comes up somehow." It is a fairly standard process: "The interviewers will have a script of behavior questions that they will follow exactly, and they make a decision later that day." Such scripted questions and prompts, an insider tells us, will run along the lines of: "Give an example of a time you were given a task to accomplish and were given little or no instruction"; "Describe a time when you had to learn new information or a new technology and quickly apply it to your role"; and "What are some important components of client relationships?"

Be prepared for interviewers to focus on such hiring criteria as "adaptability/flexibility, appreciating and valuing differences, client knowledge and responsiveness, client relationships, coaching and feedback, communication, continuous improvement, creativity and innovation, customer service and delivery, employee relations, financial management, industry and market

Visit the Vault Consulting Career Channel at **www.vault.com/consulting** - with insider firm profiles, message boards, the Vault Consulting Job Board and more.

VAULT CAREER LIBRARY   213

knowledge, learning agility, organizational perspective, problem solving/decision making, project planning and execution, teamwork and technical/functional skills." Whew!

Practicing what it preaches, Hewitt has been lauded for its own HR excellence, with family-friendly perks like maternity and paternity leave packages, unpaid leave options, flexible schedules and an overnight dependent care program.

Visit the Vault Consulting Career Channel at **www.vault.com/consulting** - with insider firm profiles, message boards, the Vault Consulting Job Board and more.

VAULT CAREER LIBRARY

215

24 ZS Associates

1800 Sherman Avenue, 7th Floor
Evanston, IL 60201
Phone: (888) 972-4173
Fax: (888) 972-7329
www.zsassociates.com

LOCATIONS

Evanston, IL (HQ)
15 offices worldwide

PRACTICE AREAS

Analytical Data Warehousing
Call Planning & Team Selling
Compensation Design & Administration
Customer Relationship Management
Go-to-Market Strategy
Marketing Mix Optimization
Marketing Research
Market Segmentation & Targeting
Mergers & Integration
Sales Force Design
Sales Forecasting
Sales & Marketing Effectiveness
Territory Design
Value Proposition Development

THE STATS

Employer Type: Private Company
Managing Director: Jaideep Bajaj
2007 Employees: 1,000
2006 Employees: 825

RANKING RECAP

Practice Area
#2 - Pharmaceutical & Health Care Consulting

Quality of Life
#4 - Travel Requirements (tie)
#6 - Formal Training
#19 - Best Firms to Work For
#19 - Firm Culture

Diversity
#16 - Diversity for Minorities

UPPERS

• "Sleeping in my own bed every night"
• No competition between co-workers
• "The company is very learning-oriented and encourages personal development and growth"
• "I can wear a polo shirt, jeans, flip-flops and headphones"

DOWNERS

• "Some of the younger people in our firm take ZS' laid-back culture a bit too far"
• "There's no one to limit your workload but yourself"
• "Benefits could be better"
• "The extremely high standards we are held to that cause high levels of stress"

EMPLOYMENT CONTACT

E-mail: careers@zsassociates.com

See specific application details and recruiting contacts in the careers section of the firm's web site

THE BUZZ
WHAT CONSULTANTS AT OTHER FIRMS ARE SAYING ABOUT THIS FIRM

• "Specialist with a good brand"
• "Formula drive, narrow thinking"
• "Up and coming; smaller but fun"
• "Too niche"

THE SCOOP

Sales savvy

ZS Associates was the brainchild of two professors at Kellogg School of Management who were both doing research on sales force sizing and effectiveness. Andris Zoltners and Prabhakant Sinha decided to transform their academic endeavor into profit, formally launching a business in 1983. From the get-go, ZS associates aimed to apply rigorous operations research techniques to sales force and territory sizing decisions. The firm took off from there, and now boasts 15 offices and over 1,000 consultants around the world. ZS is organized around 10 industry verticals: consumer products, energy, financial, high tech, industrial products, medical products, media and entertainment, pharmaceuticals, telecommunications and transportation. Its consulting services are all aimed at strategic and tactical ways to optimize sales.

Pharma-focused

Though the firm has a diverse client list, it has a keen interest in the pharmaceutical and biotech industry, likely due to its founders' original work in drug marketing research. ZS is often tapped to help drug companies develop a marketing strategy or integrate two sales forces during a merger. Some of the projects involve analyzing data on customers and sales staff, optimizing the territory with the ideal number of salespeople per physician, determining the best way to pitch a product to medical staff, analyzing the success of sales pitches and allocating budgets for marketing and sales purposes. One of the firm's focuses is determining prescribing behavior of physicians. ZS developed a resource for pharmaceutical companies called PhysPulse, which tracks a product launch. The online system is designed to evaluate why physicians prescribe certain medications, and how they respond to a new product when it hits the market.

Multinational markets

With international clients selling products across borders, it makes sense that ZS would look toward global expansion in emerging areas. The firm established a Tokyo office in 2003, and opened its first Indian office in Pune, in 2004. The firm serves global clients from that location, and ultimately hopes to employ more than 200 staffers there. The outsourcing work in the Indian outpost accounts for over $50 million of the firm's revenue. In November 2005, *India Business Insight* and the *Financial Times* noted the India expansion as an example of companies that have begun moving strategy work (not just IT services) from Europe and North America to India.

Marking your territory

Part of the ZS' analytical strength lies in its proprietary software tools that help sales managers aim for the optimal territory division. Its first product, MAPS®, launched in 1983, was the first PC-based mapping system for sales territory design. Using MAPS, clients can model, view, analyze and change territory alignments based on sales results in each area. In 2001, ZS introduced eMAPS®, a program that helps sales managers view territories from an Internet connection. The tool also can show hypothetical analysis of territories based on changing the design. A custom mapping product, MapPix®, offers mapping services and produces large-format maps to draw out territory designs or show customer and market demographics. The firm also offers SmartAlign, another tool for analyzing territories.

Founders Zoltners and Sinha have earned notoriety for their work on sales territory analysis. They were awarded the 2004 Marketing Science Practice Prize by the Institute for Operations Research and the Management Sciences (INFORMS) for their work entitled "Sales Territory Design: 30 Years of Modeling and Implementation." Their research explains the evolution of the sales territory alignment system they pioneered and implemented in the firm's consulting work. The presentation laid out case studies detailing the quantitative and qualitative impact of their work in maximizing profit for clients. It's no wonder the two founders know what they're doing: They claim to have worked on 1,500 sales projects, with half-a-million salespeople in 39 different countries.

Visit the Vault Consulting Career Channel at www.vault.com/consulting - with insider firm profiles, message boards, the Vault Consulting Job Board and more.

VAULT CAREER LIBRARY   217

What's my incentive?

ZS knows that compensation is the best way to motivate an employee to sell, so it develops tools of all kinds to help companies determine the best way to pay their sales force. And if managers aren't satisfied with that one, they can look to Prism™, a program intended to help managers determine compensation for the sales force through a system that allows two-way communication with sales teams and management. The web-based tool collects data on incentive compensation goals, payout history, motivational tools and a variety of other elements. A recent title in the ZS Sales Force Series, *The Complete Guide to Sales Force Incentive Compensation: How to Design and Implement Plans That Work*, published in August 2006, lays out examples and strategies for companies to motivate their sales force, drive results and increase their bottom line.

Strategic software

The firm's software development team, based in Evanston, Ill., is constantly coming up with innovative tools for consultants to use with clients. One recently developed application, dubbed Jawlensky, computes the optimal customer-level call plans. Call plans are what a sales rep uses to determine what customer to visit, when to call on them and how often to see them. Jawlensky takes input from sales reps on things like call capacity, current relationships and customer access, to come up with a precise call plan for covering a multitude of customers. Porpoise is another tool invented by the development team, designed to help sales reps avoid overlapping visits to the same customer. The software shows a team of sales reps when each individual member is calling on a customer, so they can better coordinate efforts.

Globe-trotting gurus

ZS representatives are a busy bunch, combining client engagements with a load of international conference appearances through the year. In 2007, the founders and principals presented at the Senior Sales Executive conference in New York, the Pharma Latin America conference in Cancun, Pharma Forecasting Excellence conference in Monaco and the World at Work Conference and Exhibition in Orlando. ZS execs also get the word out about sales strategy through their management strategy books, such as the October 2006 title, *Forecasting for the Pharmaceutical Industry—Models for New Product and In-Market Forecasting and How to Use Them* and *Sales Force Design for Strategic Advantage*, published in 2004.

Still in the classroom

When Zoltners and Sinha started the firm, they still kept teaching on their radar. In fact, the two remain visible thought leaders in the industry by teaching over 500 executives in courses each year. Zoltners is still a professor at the Kellogg School of Management, while Sinha teaches through Kellogg's executive education program and at the Indian School of Business in Hyderabad. Sales execs all over the world can attend classes led by the two experts, such as the New Strategy for Sales Force Effectiveness class taught in Beijing, in addition to sales force effectiveness workshops held all over the U.S. The partners also regularly give instruction on sales force performance at London Business School's Executive Education Programme.

GETTING HIRED

Helpful hints

Prospective ZSers should head straight to the firm's web site, which boasts a detailed careers section with campus recruiting schedules, position descriptions and much more. The Recruiting Hints section offers everything from interview tips to a "self-assessment" to help candidates gauge whether the firm—and a career in consulting—is the right path for them. As listed on the site, ZS recruits from the nation's top schools, and those clustered around its regional offices. So while the Chicago office draws from institutions such as Kellogg and Northwestern, the San Francisco office looks to schools like Stanford and Berkley. Grades are important, too: "In general, we do not recruit candidates with a GPA of less than 3.5."

"For undergraduates," an insider reports, "the process begins with a set of on-campus interviews. One is behavioral and one is a case interview. For candidates who appear to be a good fit, this is followed by an on-site interview day, consisting of another behavioral interview, an analytic interview, a case study, an informative demo (an associate walks you through a sample project) and lunch. Definitely attend the career fair and/or information session/company presentation in preparation for your interview." During the interview process, a source says, the firm looks for some "key competencies." Unsurprisingly, these include analytical ability, problem-solving skills, motivation, dedication to quality, communication skills, creativity and teamwork.

It's showtime

Similarly, for grad students, "There are usually two interviews in the first round (a case and a fit interview), followed by multiple interviews in the final round held at offices or on campus. The cases and format used in the MBA final round are particularly interesting and challenging, as they involve a panel discussion on a case on which the candidate has to present. It is a great opportunity to showcase your fact-gathering, problem-solving, time-management and communication/presentation skills in one hour." Another insider recalls a "presentation case where you were given a bunch of written materials and a case to review, had to create a presentation in about 45 minutes, and then present to a panel of two to three people as if they were your clients." He adds, "I found out that night that I had an offer. While the process was stressful, it was great to get such immediate gratification." The source also advises potential candidates to "be prepared to do math and to interpret data."

During the interview process, a consultant notes, "You meet approximately 15 ZSers from start to finish." Sources tell us that "cases vary depending on the position we are recruiting for," and that "all cases focus on assessing problem-solving skills, analytical ability and communication skills." A staffer offers the following example: "Given the data, what would be your recommendation for an incentive compensation system? What are the potential flaws in the data provided?"

A summer to remember

ZS offers a limited number of internships for undergrads and for MBA students between their first and second years. As the firm points out on its site, internships are limited to students at the institutions where ZS recruits. One source reports, "I had an excellent experience as a summer intern. I had the opportunity to work on both a client project and an internal project … I was given the same level of responsibility and client contact that a full-time consultant would have received. The internal project gave me the opportunity to interact/interview many other employees across all levels and offices, which gave me a good sense for the people and culture of the firm." A colleague adds, "The summer was structured very well, with concise but sufficient training followed by a variety of projects. As an intern, I was valued as highly as a full-time associate." Calling it the "best summer of my life," another former intern tells us, "Princeton is a great place to be in the summer. And, if they get offers, interns get their choice of offices afterwards."

OUR SURVEY SAYS

In the lab

ZS is described by insiders as a laid-back sort of place, full of "tremendously bright and funny" people, with a "relaxed and friendly" culture and minimal politics. As one source puts it, "The culture is very academic. I like to compare it to an undergrad computer lab around finals. Everyone is working hard to meet deadlines, but at the same time, chatting with friends and taking breaks to get a drink or snack." And with a "collaborative, rather than competitive" culture, adds another source, "we all win by sharing knowledge and helping each other out."

It helps that "the firm is effective at planning and holding events that reinforce the firm's culture and create a personal and collaborative atmosphere," another consultant reports. "They also promote a very healthy collaboratively competitive atmosphere through team competitions and group activities." And since "offices are kept to a max of 150 people to ensure an optimal relationship mix," ZS still maintains a "small company feel in an organization that is rapidly growing," an insider says.

Visit the Vault Consulting Career Channel at www.vault.com/consulting - with insider firm profiles, message boards, the Vault Consulting Job Board and more.

VAULT CAREER LIBRARY   219

Catching their Zs

Work/life balance is possible at ZS, a source says, as "the structure and delivery model of the firm makes scheduling very flexible—both day to day in the office and from a travel standpoint. The firm leadership recognizes the importance of balance and develops this mindset in the workforce." "It is very common for all levels within our company to leave by 6 or 7 p.m. to have dinner with their families or go to the gym, and then get online for another two hours of work from home," a source reports. According to another insider, "I have to proactively manage my time so that I achieve the balance that I desire. I occasionally have to make personal sacrifices, but find that I am able to keep a reasonable work/life balance (reasonable for consulting). This becomes easier over time. I have found that I have more control over my schedule as my career progresses." As this consultant puts it, "The concept of work/life balance is not clear in consulting. However, at ZS, we are allowed to voice our commitments, and team members will make every effort to work around it to let us attend to them. In consulting, schedules are unpredictable and ZS allows me to keep my commitments."

Though the "hours can be a little crazy" at times, one consultant observes, "Some people also contribute to their own long hours, taking on more than they can swallow or trying to impress (which will work, if you do a good job)"—even though at ZS, "face time is less valued than quality work." Nevertheless, a colleague agrees, "The firm culture does a great job of finding those who aren't good at saying no and loading them with work." When it comes to hours, "There are highs and lows," observes a consultant, who adds, "I've worked five 100-plus weeks successively, and I've had a couple of 40-hour weeks, too. There are always a million things to do and you can always have more worked poured on you. The onus is on you on where to draw the line between 'need to have' and 'nice to have.'" "As with other consulting firms, hours fluctuate with client demands and deliverables. On average, I work 60 hours per week, with a max (so far) of 105 and a minimum of 45," a colleague reports. As one insider sees it, "Although our hours are pretty good, they could be better. Sometimes we work hard, rather than smart, and don't push back against clients enough. We value our responsiveness, but sometimes this becomes ridiculous, especially since turning things around overnight only creates that expectation in the future." Project length ranges from less than three months to more than a year, and "when on a shorter project, it is likely [you will] be put on another short project with the same client after that one finishes," a source says.

Intelligent travel

Fortunately for most ZSers, "Most clients are a short drive away," and "since we are typically only on site for meetings, much of the travel is day trips," offers a source. Explains another, "There is generally more travel for people at the consultant level and above, but at the associate level (undergraduate), out of town travel is very rare. Also, it varies by office; offices where most of the work is outside of health care have their people travel and be on site more." "I don't travel any more than a midlevel executive would at one of my clients," says another insider, who adds, "We have an 'intelligent travel' policy which means we travel to meet with the client when necessary, but we don't live at the client site. That kind of 'face time' isn't necessary, and the clients don't want it. ZS' approach results in a better lifestyle for its consultants, and lower costs for its clients." "I love that we don't travel a whole lot, although there are opportunities if that's what someone wants. Still, business travel is truly overrated based on what I have experienced, so I'm glad I don't have to do it often," another insider reports.

Racing toward partnership

"We tend to be behind in compensation [compared to] our peer consulting firms," one insider frets, noting, "Most firms have raised their salaries to match McKinsey and BCG, and ZS has not." But unlike at bigger firms, a colleague points out, "The opportunities for an accelerated career path to partnership are great at ZS, and are based on performance, so the opportunities for higher compensation are also great." "Partners own shares in the company and receive profit distributions," and there are bonuses for all, insiders report. The firm contributes a matching 3 percent to a 401(k), which is vested over six years.

For new moms and dads, an insider explains, "Individuals have different needs. Therefore, the company discusses options with each individual depending on their situation. Examples have included part-time programs (e.g., four days a week) and temporary changes in roles (consulting staff may decide to take on administrative responsibilities for some time, including recruiting, staffing, training, etc.)." A colleague notes, "There's a formal maternity policy, and it's understood that new dads will take time off after delivery. The firm sends a wonderful package of baby gifts, and there's a feature in our biweekly newsletter. We have many moms that prefer to be at home, and have made arrangements for them to work part time in administrative roles, oftentimes from home."

Crazy bowling and more

Many insiders cite ZS' devotion to socializing as a major perk. "I appreciate that my firm maintains a busy social calendar and attempts to boost company morale," says a source. "At one point in 2006, I felt that my track would benefit from some additional team-building and social activities. I was encouraged by my track managers to plan such an event—we designed T-shirts and rolled them out at a fantastic Crazy Bowling event—all on the company dime!" Back in the office, there's free Snapple, plus "fun monthly celebrations like poker tournaments, kickball tournaments, office picnics, 'back to school' lunch day, Cinco de Mayo and Bastille Day celebrations. Little things to get excited about each month," a source says. Others appreciate the firm's annual office retreats to places like Monterey and Yosemite, along with a flexible attitude toward time off: "Individuals who are planning a major international vacation are often able to take up to a month off, particularly if they are traveling half a world away," reports a consultant. A colleague notes, "My managers have been great about rewarding team members with 'comp days'—days off not counted toward our vacation balances—after particularly demanding projects."

According to an insider, "The managers and principals at ZS have all worked in the trenches, so they know what it's like to be an associate or a consultant. There's great empathy throughout the organization for various roles—each has its own challenges, so there are no 'us' versus 'them' issues." A colleague agrees, "We're part of a matrixed organization, so we interact with a variety of different partners and managers, depending on the engagement. I've found that though the partners tend to each have their own style in management, they all make a strong effort to maintain consistency in delivery. All the partners are involved in project delivery, so they remain close to the action and are typically excellent sounding boards (and at times, contributors) for project deliverables." In addition, says a source, "Our company is really flat. On my first two projects at ZS, I was sitting in meetings with the partners of the firm, discussing aspects of the project."

When it comes to client interaction, a consultant reports, "We have great relationships with people at all levels of our clients' organizations—from top management down to individual sales reps." "Exposure to client management will vary widely with company size, but I have been satisfied with the level of management that we are interacting with, anywhere from directors to the executive team (CFO, CEO), depending on the project content," says a colleague.

More space, please

Offices at ZS vary by region. A source notes that "our Princeton office could really use some renovation. It's probably too small for the number of people here. All of our others offices are incredible." In New York, an insider frets, "We need more office space. Currently we don't have common meeting space in the office because of the unprecedented growth." But everything's cool in California: "We have a great location in San Mateo on the top floor of a 15-story building with a beautiful view of the bay—most people sit in offices, not cubicles," says a consultant. And in Chicago, "Our offices are in great shape. It's common for clients to request meeting at our office instead of their own facilities because of our office space (and the fact that we're in downtown Chicago)," a source raves. Though one insider complains about poor ergonomics, another source declares that overall, "Offices are clean, organized, ample and well run. They are well equipped, technically. There is a lot of consistency across offices as well. They're definitely not flashy or fancy. We prefer to save costs in this area and invest instead in our people."

Transferring knowledge

Training at ZS is a "nice combination" of formal and informal, a source says. "Formal new employee orientation occurs three times a year. Local training happens one to two times per month, ranging from one-hour 'brown-bag lunches' to full-day training sessions. We also have a formal mentoring program for new employees." During the new employee orientation, a source says, "you become indoctrinated in the ZS way, get to know up to 100-plus other new hires from all of our offices and participate in training sessions to begin to understand the work you will likely do." In addition, a colleague notes, "we have a 'just-in-time'

Visit the Vault Consulting Career Channel at **www.vault.com/consulting** - with insider firm profiles, message boards, the Vault Consulting Job Board and more.

VAULT CAREER LIBRARY   221

training program, which is outstanding. People can request training when they need it (e.g., I just got staffed to a new project and I don't have any experience with the particular practice area), and our training department will arrange for it." Furthermore, "each position has a monthly meeting by office, and a significant portion of these meetings is dedicated to transferring knowledge, training and building skills," the source notes. A colleague adds, "One advantage is that official training is generally created and conducted internally, so it can be customized to the level and needs of the audience." According to another insider, "Our training curriculum is part of the review process, so it behooves us to make sure that we're taking advantage of the training that is offered if we have the time."

Strides for women

"Women are well represented at all levels at ZS," one source declares, adding, "The firm has made great strides in this area, and a very significant number (close to half, if not more) of promoted principals in the past few years have been women. Several recently promoted managers were also women." Another insider reports, "While women are a minority, I do not feel that this is due to lack of opportunities for women. As a woman, I have found no problems with my career progress." There is a "small number of women hired from MBAs," says another source, who comments, "We have several women who are partners, however they either do not have kids, or if they do, their spouses typically stay at home. One of the female partners whose husband also works as a partner for this firm has a part-time arrangement. Let's see how it works!" "ZS does not have any special programs for women," an insider chimes in. "However, there are so many women in the firm that women do not feel at all disadvantaged by their sex. Promoting and mentoring women happens informally by example of the women who hold leadership roles within the company."

The firm's efforts when it comes to recruiting minorities are proceeding slowly, insiders suggest, but it's not for lack of trying. "I can count the number of African-American consulting staff across the two largest North American offices on one hand, maybe a few fingers onto hand two. I feel strongly that it is not a purposeful bias, but one that stems from the schools and programs from which we recruit," explains a source. Aside from a noticeable lack of African-Americans, "ZS has an incredibly diverse collection of cultures and backgrounds," says a staffer. "Our people speak more than 70 different languages and our hiring practices bring in the best from around the world."

As for gays and lesbians at the firm, an insider remarks, "The firm provides domestic partner benefits. If one chose to be 'out' at the firm they would be treated with respect and their partners welcomed at company events. Also, all the firm's offices are located in or very close to urban, gay-friendly areas (New York, Chicago, San Francisco, London, Paris). However, there is no gay affinity group that I am aware of similar to those that exist at other major consulting firms."

Having a heart

At ZS, community service "starts at the employee level," from toy drives to fund-raising walks, a consultant tells us. "If anyone in the firm has a good idea for charitable work, they are often open to it and will help fund the cause," says an insider. The American Heart Association is a big beneficiary, with employees raising thousands of dollars for the nonprofit through the annual Heart Walk and other events.

"The culture is very academic. I like to compare it to an undergrad computer lab around finals. Everyone is working hard to meet deadlines, but at the same time, chatting with friends and taking breaks to get a drink or snack."

– ZS Associates insider

Visit the Vault Consulting Career Channel at **www.vault.com/consulting** - with insider firm profiles, message boards, the Vault Consulting Job Board and more.

VAULT CAREER LIBRARY

223

Watson Wyatt Worldwide

901 North Glebe Road
Arlington, VA 22203
Phone: (703) 258-8000
Fax: (703) 258-8585
www.watsonwyatt.com

LOCATIONS

Arlington, VA (HQ)
93 offices in 30 countries worldwide

PRACTICE AREAS

Communication
Compensation
Data Services
Government Consulting
Group Benefits & Health Care
Human Capital/Organization Effectiveness
Insurance & Financial Services
Investment Consulting
Mergers & Acquisitions
Multinational Consulting
Retirement
Sales Effectiveness
Technology & Administration Solutions

THE STATS

Employer Type: Public Company
Ticker Symbol: WW (NYSE)
Chairman, President & CEO: John J. Haley
2007 Employees: 6,000
2006 Employees: 6,000
2007 Revenue: $1.4 billion (est.)
2006 Revenue: $1.27 billion

RANING RECAP

Practice Area
#4 - Human Resources Consulting

UPPERS

- Excellent gender diversity
- Flexibility

DOWNERS

- Required to account for even non-billable time
- "The firm doesn't provide necessary tools that consultants need—like a laptop or BlackBerry for younger associates"

EMPLOYMENT CONTACT

www.watsonwyatt.com/careers

THE BUZZ
WHAT CONSULTANTS AT OTHER FIRMS ARE SAYING ABOUT THIS FIRM

- "Great surveys"
- "Striving, aggressive in the marketplace"
- "Family-friendly"
- "Old school"

THE SCOOP

Brilliant idea, Watson

Watson Wyatt Worldwide is a global human resources consulting firm that originated in 1878. The Watson in the name refers to the founder, Reuben Watson, an English apprentice who offered his financial services to friendly societies—the precursor to modern employee benefit plans. After earning its stripes as a U.K. government advisor on social insurance programs, the firm expanded by building a solid customer base in Europe. In 1995, the company, known as R. Watson & Sons, joined The Wyatt Company, an established American benefits and insurance consulting firm. For 10 years, the two operated as separate groups, serving different geographic markets: Watson Wyatt & Company focused on the Americas and Asia-Pacific, while Watson Wyatt Partners dealt with the European market. In August 2005, the two finally merged and became Watson Wyatt Worldwide. Today, the firm is able to serve global clients through the combined strength of 93 offices in 30 countries. Watson Wyatt still serves its original client from back in 1878, the Manchester Unity Friendly Society.

Headquartered in Arlington, Va., Watson Wyatt offers an array of consulting services that help companies manage their most valuable asset: employees. The firm organizes its practices around four areas of specialization: employee benefits, human capital strategies, technology solutions, and insurance and financial services. Typical projects involve managing the cost of employee benefits plans, advising clients on their pension plans and investment strategies, and developing compensation plans to attract and retain employees.

Balance sheet boost

Watson Wyatt executives were hoping that the 2005 merger would strengthen the firm's bottom line, and results show it has done just that. After disappointing revenue figures in 2004, the firm pulled off a turnaround in 2005, posting 5 percent revenue growth. The following year was even more encouraging, as Watson Wyatt earned $1.27 billion in revenue, a 9 percent increase over 2005. The benefits consulting practice accounted for the largest chunk of that figure—$726 million—making up 54 percent of total revenue in 2006. Out of the firm's practices, the insurance financial services and investment consulting groups showed the most impressive revenue growth, with an increase of 18 percent and 12 percent, respectively.

International footprints

As the name suggests, Watson Wyatt has made an effort to expand its presence worldwide over the past few years. In February 2007, the firm acquired Watson Wyatt Brans & Co., its longtime alliance partner in the Netherlands. And in March 2006, the Frankfurt office was added to its German investment consulting group. A Shanghai outpost specializing in insurance and financial consulting was established in February 2006. The firm also boosted its South American presence with two additions in May 2005: a human capital consulting practice in Santiago, Chile, and a dedicated benefits research center in Montevideo, Uruguay. In 2004, the firm acquired KPMG's Irish Pension and Actuarial Group. The purchase gave Watson Wyatt the second-place spot behind the leader in the Irish market, Mercer Human Resource Consulting, which it maintains to this day.

When it comes to getting a foot in India, Watson Wyatt was already ahead of the curve, having opened an office in Mumbai in 1996, before most of its competitors had entered the region. The country remains a target growth area for the firm, and it already boasts a growing list of clients there, including banks and insurance companies. In 2005, the firm announced plans to build a valuation center based in India, set to launch in 2007. The location will serve Watson Wyatt's European clients with its pension valuation services. The firm had already been serving some European clients from its other regional office in Gurgaon.

Trimming the fat

In addition to expansion, the company has also sold off some divisions. Watson Wyatt New Zealand was sold to competitor Mercer Human Resource Consulting in August 2005. In 2004, the firm spun off its small insurance and financial services practice in Boston, before two partners eventually bought out the entire Boston practice in March and changed the name to Spring

Visit the Vault Consulting Career Channel at www.vault.com/consulting - with insider firm profiles, message boards, the Vault Consulting Job Board and more.

 VAULT CAREER LIBRARY   225

Consulting Group LLP. Earlier in 2004, the firm consolidated its practices in Malaysia and Singapore to combine resources for clients in the Asia-Pacific region.

Happy employees = happy shareholders

The firm's numerous surveys on HR practices worldwide have added to the large body of knowledge on the way employment policy affects a company's value. In 1999, Watson Wyatt published the first Human Capital Index study, which examined the correlation between HR practices and shareholder value. According to the firm, although the index surveys more than 2,000 companies worldwide, it reveals specific human capital practices related to shareholder value that ring true all over the world. For example, the 2005 study showed that firms could increase return to shareholders by implementing rewards for employees, such as stock ownership and paying above the market. It also illustrated that firms that clearly communicate company strategy and financial data to employees have a higher shareholder value than those that keep those things under wraps.

Pension pros

As the pension reform debate in the U.S. has escalated in the past few years, Watson Wyatt has taken an active role in public discussion. The Pension Protection Act of 2006 (H.R.4), signed in August 2006, completely reworked the pension law, requiring defined benefit and contribution plan sponsors to make major revisions. In response, Watson Wyatt published an executive summary of the act, meant to guide sponsors in making decisions when the changes take effect in 2008. The firm's consultants have also authored a number of white papers and studies on pensions, including a January 2007 technical paper, "Building Blocks: Managing Pension Funds in a Liability-Driven Investment World," and the "Global 2007 Pension Assets Study," a research report on asset and liability trends in the 11 major pensions markets over the past 10 years. In addition, Watson Wyatt published the eighth edition of its authoritative reference work, *Fundamentals of Private Pensions*, in 2005.

Benefits best practices

Watson Wyatt regularly conducts its own benchmarking studies and surveys to identify the most and least effective strategies for attracting and retaining employees. The Strategic Rewards survey measures the things that are most important in an employee's decision to stay at (or leave) a company. The most recent survey, conducted in 2007, showed that employees and employers have conflicting opinions about the things that matter most when it comes to recruiting, motivating and keeping talent. Realities of "Executive Compensation—2006/2007 Report on Executive Pay and Stock Options" compares overall executive compensation. And Watson Wyatt's WorkUSA® annual survey allows over 12,000 U.S. workers of all levels to rate their senior management on qualities like trust, confidence and behaving in line with a company's values.

Not only does the firm study the best methods of keeping staffers satisfied, but it also seems to do a good job of keeping its own employees happy. In 2007, Watson Wyatt was named for the first time to *Forbes*' list of the 400 Best Big Companies in America. In 2006, *The Washington Post* placed it in the Post 200, a list of top firms with headquarters in the Washington D.C. area, and in 2005, for the fifth year in a row, London's *Sunday Times* included Watson Wyatt in its 100 Best Companies to Work For, determined by random employee survey responses on issues such as pay and benefits.

Quoted and noted

Watson Wyatt executives, considered authorities on HR issues, are frequently quoted in U.S. publications, including *The Wall Street Journal*, *The New York Times* and *The Washington Post*, as well as industry journals such as *Pensions & Investments* and *Human Resource Executive*. The firm also puts out a slew of its own journals and magazines, which provide updates on current trends and issues related to human resources. The *Insider*, a monthly newsletter, compiles current regulations, policy and research about benefits, retirement and other issues, and the HR Finance Alert analyzes HR issues relating to the financial side of companies. "The Global Investment Review" is an annual report covering topical pensions and investment issues in Europe, and Strategy at Work is the firm's online publication.

GETTING HIRED

Explore the possibilities

Watson Wyatt has an active recruiting program at a long list of universities, including Cornell, University of North Carolina, University of Virginia, Penn State, Fairfield University, Boston College, University of Texas at Austin, University of California, Berkeley, and Yale. An updated recruiting calendar is maintained on the career page of the firm's web site. Watson Wyatt also has an internship program for college students who want to explore what it's like to work on actual projects. The firm says interns get a change to dive right in, tackling benefits pricing, financial modeling, incentive plan benchmarking or investment studies. Interns can join the retirement group, health care, investment or compensation practice. Opportunities for interns and new graduates can all be found online, by checking out the careers area of the web site, under the Graduates & Interns section.

What it takes

The firm doesn't beat around the bush when listing the qualities it's looking for in a consultant: superior analytical skills and interpersonal abilities are key, as are project management skills, self-motivation and the ability to multitask. Especially sought are candidates with a degree in an analytical field, such as math, statistics or management. The firm also posts employee testimonials on its site, with firsthand accounts of what it's like to be an actuarial analyst or compensation consultant at Watson Wyatt. Candidates whose resumes make the cut can expect several rounds of interviews with managers and consultants. One insider reveals that the process consists of "four interviews, both group and individual," with "no test questions."

Lifelong training

There are abundant opportunities at Watson Wyatt for official training, through the firm's development and mentoring programs. New hires start by attending orientation, and then receive a "navigator" (buddy) and a mentor to help them get acquainted with life at the firm. For ongoing formal training, the firm offers opportunities to gain internal continuing education credits, receive executive coaching and sales training, and pursue individual courses. In addition, there is annual national training for different career levels, professional seminars on specialized topics and technical instruction in software and statistics.

OUR SURVEY SAYS

Welcome to the family

Insiders say the best thing about Watson Wyatt's culture is, by far, their colleagues. "The people are collaborative and collegial; they are positive and fun to work with. They are very focused on keeping our clients happy and having fun while doing it," boasts a longtime employee. An analyst appreciates the "high integrity and values, trust and flexibility" at the firm. Sources also insist that their co-workers are easy to talk to and are especially welcoming toward newbies. One consultant explains, "We work with many very engaging and intelligent people. There are enough of us 'old schoolers' left around to keep the atmosphere friendly and open. We keep pressure on those who want to work with closed doors and discourage drop-in questions, which helps to bring our newer associates into the family quickly."

Questionable balance

Sources hold varying opinions about the ability to maintain work/life balance at this firm. A few staffers claim that it's possible, thanks to reasonable hours and being able to independently manage your own schedule. "Work/life balance is a matter of perspective. Being able to juggle the demands of home life with work responsibilities is an art. Some days one side gets more attention than the other. Knowing when to push back and refocus is necessary," says one manager. Other insiders contest that work/life balance is merely an idea that isn't taken seriously at the firm. Gripes a source, "Our 'powers that be' give a lot of lip

Visit the Vault Consulting Career Channel at www.vault.com/consulting - with insider firm profiles, message boards, the Vault Consulting Job Board and more.

VAULT CAREER LIBRARY   227

service to the cause, but the reality is if you do not average 50 or more hours per week, it will cost you—either money or career advances, or both." Others insist that while balance is achievable, it should not come at the expense of your career: "The firm is very flexible and encourages work/life balance. However, it's the high-performing consultants who advance. Generally poor consultants are counseled out."

40 is the new 70

Respondents are conflicted when it comes to opportunities for advancement at the firm. "Watson Wyatt tries to promote from within, but it's really more focused on making the right hires whether inside or outside the firm. Consultants can advance based on their own initiatives," attests a manager. But a colleague insists that if you don't move up quickly, you never will, claiming, "There is a lack of opportunity for those who do not manage to get onto an immediate fast track. Age discrimination is becoming a big thing. If you are over 40 and not at a top level yet, your career is dead."

Balanced at the bottom

The firm earns high marks from respondents for its hiring and retention of women, although sources claim that at the higher levels, the number of women shrinks. "We hire more women than men and advance them equally through the initial phases of their career," a consultant relates. The source adds, however, that women "tend to 'top out' at the senior consultant level. We did promote several a few years ago, but that appears to have been a short-term response to pressure and has not continued."

"There are enough of us 'old schoolers' left around to keep the atmosphere friendly and open. We keep pressure on those who want to work with closed doors and discourage drop-in questions, which helps to bring our newer associates into the family quickly."

– *Watson Wyatt consultant*

Visit the Vault Consulting Career Channel at **www.vault.com/consulting** - with insider firm profiles, message boards, the Vault Consulting Job Board and more.

VAULT CAREER LIBRARY

229

2000 Town Center
Suite 2400
Southfield, MI 48075
Phone: (248) 358-4420
Fax: (248) 358-1969
www.alixpartners.com

LOCATIONS

Detroit, MI (HQ)
Chicago, IL
Dallas, TX
Los Angeles, CA
New York, NY
San Francisco, CA
Düsseldorf
London
Milan
Munich
Paris
Shanghai
Tokyo

PRACTICE AREAS

Corporate Turnaround & Restructuring
Financial Advisory Services
IT Transformation Services
Litigation Consulting Services
Litigation Technology Services
Performance Improvement

THE STATS

Employer Type: Private Company
CEO: Michael Grindfors
2007 Employees: 650
2006 Employees: 550

UPPERS

- "High-impact situations"
- Merit-based compensation
- Vacation time is respected

DOWNERS

- "Hyper-growth beginning to impact culture"
- "Egos flair, leadership ducks"
- Minimal work/life balance

EMPLOYMENT CONTACT

E-mail: careers@alixpartners.com

THE BUZZ
WHAT CONSULTANTS AT OTHER FIRMS ARE SAYING ABOUT THIS FIRM

- "Very diverse and professional"
- "Highly compensated but overworked"
- "Top-three restructuring firm"
- "Senior people do junior work"

THE SCOOP

Turning the beat around

Founded in 1981 by Wharton alum Jay Alix, AlixPartners takes credit for inventing the concept of the "turnaround"—helping troubled companies get back on their feet. Among its innovations in the field, Alix's firm pioneered the concept of a chief restructuring officer (a professional appointed at the executive levels of a troubled firm who drives the turnaround process), as well as the idea of success fees (aligning consultants' compensation with the results they help clients achieve).

Despite the big splash the firm made by focusing on this niche, Jay Alix & Associates PC, as it was known for its first 20 years, remained relatively small for many years. By 1989, the firm employed only 12 people, though it continued to win notable clients. Working for creditors of struggling car company DeLorean in 1984, the firm managed to recover millions of dollars in hidden assets, in a process that largely involved sorting through reams of case documents. For another early client, Phoenix Steel Corp., the firm took over as president and COO.

As Alix grew his business, he focused on making the company a people-oriented organization, hiring well-rounded, seasoned professionals and administering psychological tests in the interview process to ensure cultural fit with the firm. He also insisted on "institutionalizing" the firm, guaranteeing a consistent level of service for clients regardless of their size or location. By the early 1990s, the company began to see more rapid growth, doubling its staff and serving marquee clients like Unisys, Phar-Mor and General Motors' National Car Rental subsidiary. In the 1990s, the firm also developed its IT and performance improvement practices.

Quest for profits

Of course, sometimes all troubled companies (or anyone else, for that matter) need is a daring investor to come along with a healthy injection of cash. In 1995, Alix teamed up with Dan Lufkin, co-founder of legendary New York investment firm Donaldson, Lufkin & Jenrette, to form private equity firm Questor. Since then, Questor has invested more than $1.2 in underperforming and distressed companies targeted for turnaround. Having made some successful investments, Questor is currently "harvesting its second fund," according to the firm.

Partners in growth

In 2002, the firm rebranded and changed its name to AlixPartners, appropriately reflecting, Alix said, the company's ethos of partnership. AlixPartners got aggressive about its growth at the dawn of the 21st century, launching a "fast" European expansion that saw the opening of offices in London, Munich, Milan and Düsseldorf within 18 months. The firm's first West Coast office was opened in Los Angeles in 2003; San Francisco and Tokyo followed in 2005, followed by Paris in 2006 and Shanghai in early 2007. In 2005, the firm also established relationships with corporate turnaround firms in Brazil and Australia. Meanwhile, the bankruptcies of companies like WorldCom and Kmart (where AlixPartners installed managing directors temporarily in executive positions) and Enron (from which the firm tried to recoup funds lost by investors) created a hefty demand for the company's turnaround services.

Sharing the wealth

In August 2006, AlixPartners underwent a major recapitalization, giving investment firm Hellman & Friedman a significant stake in the company. The firm's 78 managing directors at the time, along with the rest of its employees, also gained a considerable equity stake, giving them a majority interest in the $800 million company. (Though the private company's finances are kept under wraps, revenue reportedly was grown by over 30 percent annually for the past decade.) Founder Jay Alix transferred a substantial portion of his interest, but remained the largest individual shareholder, taking on a co-chairman role along with Hellman & Friedman's Philip Hammarskjold. The move fulfilled Alix's "long-held objective of an orderly succession from an

Visit the Vault Consulting Career Channel at www.vault.com/consulting - with insider firm profiles, message boards, the Vault Consulting Job Board and more.

VAULT CAREER LIBRARY   231

entrepreneurial firm to a self-perpetuating institution," while rewarding long-term employees and setting up an attractive equity prospect to help the firm attract new talent.

Star directors

In February 2007, the firm created some new executive positions to help manage its global growth. The new positions of co-president were filled by two managing directors, Stefano Aversa and Peter Fitzsimmons, who were tapped to lead the firm's European/Asian operations and U.S. operations, respectively. In September 2006, the firm brought more fire power to its roster of managing directors, hiring Philip Toy, who formerly led Mercer Management Consulting's supply chain practice; Matthew Katz, who led the organizational design and merchandise management practice for Kurt Salmon Associates; and Alan B. Lee, a former partner in the middle-market advisory services practice of PricewaterhouseCoopers. And in January 2007, the firm promoted 12 of its consultants to managing director.

AlixPartners is led by a group of directors who, as the firm puts it, have done plenty of time in the trenches. Part of AlixPartners' philosophy, in fact, is to use "seasoned, senior people to help solve our clients' challenges, rather than freshly-minted MBAs," as Co-President Aversa has put it. Current CEO Michael Grindfors is formerly president of Puma USA, as well as a managing director in Goldman Sachs' investment banking division and a former senior VP with The Boston Consulting Group.

Healthy clients, too

Though the firm made its mark in the corporate turnaround game, more recently AlixPartners has declared its ambition to invest more heavily in corporate consulting and litigation advisory services. In fact, AlixPartners doesn't want to be associated solely with troubled clients—the firm notes that in 2006, more than half its revenue came from "healthy" companies. In its business performance improvement area, AlixPartners works in what it calls a "roll-up-the-sleeves style," helping management identify areas for improvement through a proprietary assessment process called QuickStrike[SM], then helping to implement the necessary changes. Other services include IT transformation services, claims and estate management, litigation consulting, litigation technology and financial advisory services.

Helping rev the engine

Still, companies in distress have remained a hot area for AlixPartners, which was tapped to work on two of the three-largest corporate bankruptcies in the U.S. in 2006. In May 2006, auto giant General Motors announced that it would be restructuring its finances, retaining AlixPartners to help with a range of accounting and financial reporting services. In January of that year, the firm announced that client Atkins Nutritionals emerged from a fast-track Chapter 11 bankruptcy after just five months. The diet promoter unveiled a new strategy, slimming down the number of products it sells while boosting on-time deliveries. The trend continued and the firm worked on a number of major cases through 2007, including restructurings at Calpine Corporation, Dana Corporation and Bally Total Fitness.

Meet the new boss

AlixPartners continues to send its own directors into the breach at client firms when needed (Alix himself has taken on the roles of CEO, COO and CFO for troubled client companies). In January 2007, Managing Director James Bonsall was named interim president and COO of manufacturer Tecumseh Products Company. In June 2007, another managing director, Eric Simonsen, was named interim CFO of Nokia Siemens Network, in addition to his role as global head of restructuring for the joint venture company. And sometimes, AlixPartners draws its specialists directly from the turnaround trenches. For example, in January 2007 the firm appointed Holly Felder Etlin as a managing director, following her successful stint as chief restructuring officer and acting CEO of Tanner & Halley, a luxury destination club that Etlin helped steer out of troubled financial waters.

Surveying the terrain

Reflecting its ambitions in the area of working with healthy companies, AlixPartners also publishes studies and surveys analyzing the marketplace. In 2007, the firm launched its Brand Power Index[SM], a survey of U.S. consumers' views on name brands, slated to be published biennially. The report aims to elucidate consumers' brand preferences, covering areas such as cars, fashion and consumer electronics. The firm's annual Consumer Sentiment Index[SM], meanwhile, tracks consumers' opinions about companies in 13 retail categories. The report is headed by Frederick A. Crawford, who published a similar study at his former companies, Ernst & Young and Capgemini, and turned his research into a best-selling business book, *The Myth of Excellence*. In November 2006, the firm released the results of a study it had conducted with Cleveland, Ohio-based Cleveland Clinic, outlining the top-10 medical innovations for 2007. The list, which AlixPartners helped compile on a pro bono basis, highlights technologies the clinic predicts will have an impact on health care in the next year. And John Hoffecker, a managing director and co-lead of the firm's performance improvement practice, publishes an automotive original equipment manufacturer and supplier benchmarking study every year.

In 2006, AlixPartners' David Lovett and Laura Barlow, along with Stuart Slatter, published the book *Leading Corporate Turnaround: How Leaders Fix Troubled Companies*, highlighting how even CEOs of untroubled companies can improve results by adopting the leadership strategies of turnaround specialists.

GETTING HIRED

Seeking senior hires

Newbies need not apply: AlixPartners looks for MBA grads with a few years of experience—and that's for entry-level positions at the firm. Notes an insider, "We hire only midcareer professionals, including a number of nonconsultants," while a source specifies that the firm "only hires professionals with five to 10 or more years experience." Since there's no campus recruiting, candidates have the best chance of getting in by way of connections with current employees. "It's a very referral-based recruiting process," says an associate.

Battery of tests

Seasoned consultants who score an interview can expect "rigorous intelligence and psychological testing if they pass the interviews." One staffer recounts, "There is a single day of interviews, with five 45 to 50 minute interviews. If you pass that, there are special IQ and personality tests to evaluate raw intellectual capacity and fit with firm culture. Occasionally," he continues, there is a "follow-up on interviews for those with highly specialized or unusual backgrounds, or for those who had one or two negative appraisals during the interview process." A director adds, "Depending on interviewers, quick case studies might be given," noting that "chemistry is a big factor."

OUR SURVEY SAYS

Keeping it real

Associates laud the "very strong peer group" and "excellent culture" at AlixPartners. "There are great people—really smart, but really 'real'," a source comments. Assures a colleague, "It's truly an 'up,' people-first environment (well beyond the usual, *Dilbert*-esque words that all firms mouth)." Sources also praise the "warm and caring" atmosphere that distinguishes the firm. "This is the most truly friendly culture I've ever worked in," an insider raves.

In addition to friendly peers, insiders give high marks to the firm's approachable management. "All senior personnel are accessible to anyone at any time, but you should have a good reason for reaching out. [They are] open to and want to hear

Visit the Vault Consulting Career Channel at www.vault.com/consulting - with insider firm profiles, message boards, the Vault Consulting Job Board and more.

VAULT CAREER LIBRARY   233

consultants' perspectives," explains a source. And a co-worker calls the firm "a very flat organization. Even most senior people work directly with clients to drive impact."

"More modern model"

Staffers suggest that the recent booming state of business has prompted some changes—among them, bringing out a more "entrepreneurial" side to AlixPartners. "There is a high level of autonomy," mentions a manager. But one consultant is not completely onboard with the new direction of the firm, stating, "I much preferred the older, more collaborative environment." Others view the adjustments as an inevitable part of expansion, however. Claims an associate, "[There are the] usual growing pains of moving from a one-time regional company focused on corporate restructuring to a big, international one now doing consulting as well." Despite the internal shifts, employees still seem enthusiastic about the firm overall. An analyst exclaims, "Joining AlixPartners has been the best professional decision of my career. This is a new, more modern model than a traditional consulting firm."

Travel—like it or not

One consultant points out, "Traveling or living with the client is part of our work style and is OK." And while not every consultant at AlixPartners is in a constant state of motion, most find themselves on the road a fair amount. "I don't personally have to travel that much, but in many of our service lines, it is imperative to be at the client," a director explains. Comments a co-worker, "I travel 80 to 100 percent of the time when active on client assignments; 20 to 60 percent when developing clients."

But even though they recognize travel as a necessity, that doesn't always make it easier. One source claims that being away is one of the most challenging parts of the job: "I tend to work longer hours when on the road, so that I can keep my weekends and evenings free when I'm at home. The worst part of travel is the long periods spent alone in generic hotel rooms. Our firm does a good job of making travel palatable, but the travel requirement is a significant negative to the consulting profession in general."

When staffers are able to work in the office, they generally expect to work in the 60-hour range each week, with some fluctuation depending on the project. "When on assignment and away from home, I often work 60-plus hours a week. When not on assignment or at home, closer to 45 hours a week," a consultant shares.

The client comes first

The majority of insiders insist that a heavy travel schedule means work/life balance plays second fiddle to the needs of the client. "There's not really any work/life balance," one associate reveals, adding, "Client demands always take priority, and work needs to be done wherever the client is located. That demands constant travel. We're usually engaged on high-priority projects. That demands a continual sense of urgency." And while a colleague admits that "our leadership encourages us to keep work/life balance in mind and is very protective of our personal time (e.g., vacations)," he adds, "we all are heavily tilted toward work over life."

Another consultant asserts that there is the opportunity to attend to personal tasks during the occasional downtime: "Because we are typically involved in complex and often urgent situations, there are peaks of work. But it is possible to organize yourself to relax after the company is stabilized." "I'm allowed to work from home occasionally and encouraged to take necessary time to deal with family or personal issues," points out a co-worker.

Already trained

Because associates don't come to the firm completely green, AlixPartners doesn't put a lot of effort into an official training program. Although a few insiders claim there are "opportunities to do both formal and informal" training, the consensus is that "most training is picked up along the way." One consultant gives some glimpse into the future: "There is mostly unofficial training, though there have been recent attempts at improvement."

All about the Benjamins

Sources give positive reports of the way AlixPartners determines compensation and bonuses. "We get a very small equity share in the business. Bonus is partially tied to hours worked—in effect an overtime benefit; unique in the industry," says a manager. Another consultant reveals, "Bonus is based on judgment of the overall performance and not linked to predefined formulas," and "it's 20 to 30 percent higher than industry average," boasts another.

As for perks, AlixPartners offers basic benefits, like "full health coverage and [airline travel] club membership for MDs." "Vacations are pretty much sacrosanct," mentions a staffer. One consultant enjoys the "car service to and from the airport," while another appreciates the "nice offices and free coffee." For most employees, though, the extra perks aren't the real draw at this firm: "It's all about the pay," an insider states frankly.

Everyone seems to agree that AlixPartners offices are worth writing home about. "We have absolutely first-class office space in every city in which we're located," notes a director. A colleague confirms that "all offices are in premier locations and are very well maintained." "We have the nicest offices on the planet," brags another source.

Receptive to women

According to associates, the firm is "more receptive to women than most in this industry." But even with an open attitude, gender balance is not quite achieved. "We are very receptive to hiring qualified women, but the very demanding travel/lifestyle is typically a nonstarter for the experienced (10-plus years post-MBA) women we interview," a source explains. Having said that, in its turnaround practice, the firm employs a number of senior women, including Lisa Donahue (co-lead of the restructuring practice who was recently selected as the 2007 International Women's Insolvency & Restructuring Confederation Woman of the Year in Restructuring) Becky Roof, Laura Barlow and Holly Etlin.

When it comes to other types of diversity, AlixPartners doesn't have an official policy. "We are completely race indifferent when it comes to hiring qualified personnel," mentions a consultant. Another colleague declares, "[It's] completely sexual preference-indifferent, but [there is] clearly an expectation of professional, discrete behavior regarding sexual preferences, whether straight or otherwise."

AlixPartners also doesn't have an official program for community service efforts, though insiders report that the firm does encourage involvement on a local or individual level. According to one consultant, "We are encouraged to be active in community and the firm provides some matching funds." "We have numerous sponsorship and charity programs that we support in every part of the world," relates a Detroit source.

Visit the Vault Consulting Career Channel at **www.vault.com/consulting** - with insider firm profiles, message boards, the Vault Consulting Job Board and more.

VAULT CAREER LIBRARY   235

NERA Economic Consulting

50 Main Street, 14th Floor
White Plains, NY 10606
Phone: (914) 448-4000
Fax: (914) 448-4040
www.nera.com

LOCATIONS

White Plains, NY (HQ)
22 offices worldwide

PRACTICE AREAS

Antitrust & Competition Policy • Commercial Litigation &
Damages • Communications • Employment & Labor
Economics • Energy • Environment • Financial Risk
Management • Healthcare • Intellectual Property • Market
Design • Mass Torts/Product Liability • Postal Services •
Regulation/Public Policy/Survey Design • Securities &
Finance • Transfer Pricing • Transport • Valuation • Water

THE STATS

Employer Type: Subsidiary of Marsh & McLennan
  Companies, Inc., a Public Company
Ticker Symbol: MMC (NYSE)
President: Dr. Andrew S. Carron
2007 Employees: 600
2006 Employees: 550
2006 Revenue: $1.2 billion (Oliver Wyman Group)

THE BUZZ
WHAT CONSULTANTS AT OTHER FIRMS ARE SAYING ABOUT THIS FIRM

- "Best in economic consulting"
- "Eat what you kill"
- "Serious, sharp"
- "Emphasis on senior consultants over junior
  consultants"

RANKING RECAP

Practice Area
#2 - Economic Consulting
#10 - Energy Consulting

Quality of Life
#6 - Travel Requirements
#15 - Hours in the Office

Diversity
#15 - Diversity for Women

UPPERS

- "NERA makes an effort to make its employees
  happy"
- No barriers to rising from entry level to the very
  top
- "The job allows me to use my brain all the time"
- "A great first job out of college that leaves all
  doors open"

DOWNERS

- No interaction between practice area groups
- "People here are exceedingly dorky"
- "Most days are like study hall, quietly working in
  silence on fairly academic topics"
- "The firm is not glamorous. Cocktails are served
  in paper cups—when they are served at all"

EMPLOYMENT CONTACT

Recruiting Team
NERA Economic Consulting
50 Main Street
White Plains, NY 10606
Fax: (914) 448-4148
E-mail: recruitingteam@nera.com

Additional contacts by country available at:
www.nera.com

THE SCOOP

Economic advisors

NERA Economic Consulting is the small but well-known economic consulting arm of the Oliver Wyman Group, which is in turn owned by giant insurance broker Marsh & McLennan Companies. Acquired in 1983 by Marsh & McLennan, a firm with over $12 billion in revenue, NERA has access to the global network of the MMC group. It provides economic analysis and advice to corporations, governments, law firms, regulatory agencies, trade associations and international agencies. The firm operates out of 22 offices in North and South America, Europe, Asia and Australia, and employs over 600 consultants. It has 11 U.S. offices, including a headquarters White Plains, New York. Headed by Dr. Andrew Carron, NERA is best known for its litigation support and regulatory advisory consulting.

Initially founded as a think tank in 1961, Dr. Jules Joskow, a former City College economics professor, and Dr. Irwin Stelzer, an acclaimed economist, started doing consulting work to take time off from academia. Their company was named NERA, or National Economic Research Associates, and provided econometric analysis to businesses. After a few years of success, the founders realized they'd found their marketplace niche. Today, the firm specializes in industrial and financial economics, and applies its analysis to a number of practice areas, including antitrust and competition, securities, intellectual property, mass torts and product liability, environment, transfer pricing and labor consulting. Typical projects for NERA might involve predicting the impact of a merger, forecasting claims resulting from mass tort litigation or applying game theory to power auctions.

Can I get a witness?

NERA's services are frequently called upon in the courtroom to assist clients defending antitrust, competition or product liability lawsuits. In many cases, consultants can be found on the witness stand, giving expert testimony in big-stakes lawsuits involving tobacco, automobile or medical device claims. In addition to taking the stand, consultants also provide statistical analysis of damages, preparation of testimony, and preparation of deposition and cross-examination strategy for opposing expert witnesses. Because the firm's research and testimony is often used in court decisions, NERA has earned recognition for being independent and unbiased when it comes to in-depth economic analysis.

Litigation savvy

For clients involved in litigation, the firm also provides dispute resolution and avoidance, analysis of economic impact testimony and other strategies for companies facing litigation or calculating damages. For instance, a client might hire NERA to quantify the value of product liability or defend a patent. An example of the kind of case where NERA's analysis comes into play is Daiichi Pharmaceutical Co., Ltd., et al. v. Apotex, Inc. et al. A U.S. patent disclosed a method of treating certain ear infections with a solution, sold by Daiichi under the brand name FLOXIN® Otic. Apotex contended that the patent was invalid due to obviousness and other reasons, and announced its intention to introduce a generic equivalent before the patent expired. Retained by Daiichi, NERA analyzed FLOXIN Otic's performance in the marketplace and concluded that the formula described in the patent had been a commercial success. NERA experts testified on Daiichi's behalf and explained NERA's research and analysis to the court. Citing NERA's analysis, in August 2006, the judge ruled in favor of Daiichi, stating that the patent was indeed valid since FLOXIN Otic was a commercial success, and that Apotex would infringe the patent if it introduced a generic version of the drug before the patent's expiration.

Class action stats

For over a decade, the firm has been tracking case filings and settlements in shareholder class action suits. Semiannually, the firm publishes a report on class action settlement trends. The 2007 study, entitled "Recent Trends in Shareholder Class Action Litigation: Filings Plummet, Settlements Soar," found that average class-action settlements paid by corporations to shareholder plaintiffs rose by 37 percent in 2006. The increase was due to several outsized "megasettlements," exceeding $100 million each.

Visit the Vault Consulting Career Channel at www.vault.com/consulting - with insider firm profiles, message boards, the Vault Consulting Job Board and more.

VAULT CAREER LIBRARY   237

NERA has also been following trends in asbestos claim filings in the U.S. A 2007 paper, "Where Are Mesothelioma Claims Heading?" written by two vice presidents and a senior consultant, examined statistics from the National Cancer Institute of the National Institutes of Health as well as data from the Manville Trust, which was formed to settle asbestos personal injury claims resulting from exposure to products mined or manufactured by the Johns-Manville Corporation. Mesothelioma claims are of particular importance to defendants, since they are the most serious and expensive asbestos-related cases. NERA's research concluded that mesothelioma claims are on the decline, and that corporations will likely face fewer asbestos injury claims than had been previously predicted.

Passing the baton

After 18 years serving as president, Dr. Richard Rapp stepped down in December 2005, and was replaced by Dr. Andrew Carron, former chair of the firm's securities and finance practice. Carron's focus is in securities and financial economics, particularly in fixed income instruments, derivatives and risk management. Carron holds a BA in economics from Harvard University, an MA in philosophy and a PhD in economics from Yale University.

Settling in Shanghai

In December 2006, NERA opened its newest office in Shanghai, which focuses on transfer pricing services. Yasunobu Suzuki, a vice president and transfer pricing expert, was chosen to head the new location. After establishing an office in Tokyo in 2002, the firm has gradually been boosting its Asian presence, and already boasts a list of local clients in the country, including Toho Titanium Company and Sumitomo Chemical Company, and multinationals like Samsung and Sony.

An authoritative pen

Among NERA's ranks are some of the brightest minds in economics today—most hold PhDs in economics and are former academics or notable experts in their field. Industry publications such as *Gas Actual*, *Tax Planning International* and the *Journal of Regulatory Economics* often feature NERA experts' articles on current topics in various industries. Other research the firm conducts is used to assist governments in economic planning for issues with wide-ranging effects. A recent NERA report, "The European Equities Post-Trading Industry: Assessing the Impact of Market and Regulatory Changes," was published by the *City of London* in February 2007, as part of the research contributing the ongoing debate about posttrade clearing and settlement services in the European Union. And the Welsh office of The Association of the British Pharmaceutical Industry commissioned a study in 2006 on the current and future burden of two long-term illnesses, entitled "CHD and Diabetes in Wales: Meeting the Challenges."

Quite a few of NERA's consultants also distribute their knowledge through newsletters and studies. The firm's *Antitrust Insights* is a bimonthly journal featuring current antitrust topics. In the December 2006 issue, one of the firm's VPs discussed using and designing surveys to define relevant markets. *Global Antitrust Weekly*, *Perspectives in Telecommunications* and *Energy Regulation Insights* are just a few of the firm's other regularly published works. The entire inventory of publications can be accessed online, through NERA's eLibrary.

GETTING HIRED

Are you "pretty smart"?

If you're a microeconomically-minded type, NERA may have a paycheck for you. The firm's web site provides information for both undergrads looking to join the firm as researchers, and PhDs who want to try their hand at consulting. The firm also provides a list of campus recruiting events online, and can also be found recruiting at annual AEA/ASSA events. According to an insider, "In-person interviews are fairly relaxed. We look primarily for demonstrated quantitative skills and apparent skill at interpersonal interactions. A good attitude and ability to work on a team is a plus. Mostly, you just have to be pretty smart to work here."

A research associate describes his recruiting experience: "I dropped off my resume at my school's career fair, and later was asked to submit a cover letter, a writing sample and two recommendation letters. I heard back when I was selected for an interview at the office location I applied to. Went to the office, had about 10 30-minute, one-on-one interviews with the people in the office. I was asked a lot about the coursework and academic background that I had from school. There were no case interviews or questions that required specific knowledge about economics, but rather behavioral and personal questions were asked." Another researcher reports attending a "Super Day with five to eight candidates," adding that while on-campus interviews are "standard," with a focus on the resume, "Super Day is much more personalized. It's enough to impress one VP or consultant so that he/she wants you for his/her group ... Out of six interviews you will get one to two senior researchers to talk to. You will be asked about your senior thesis, large research paper, etc., and examined quite thoughtfully on it, so you better think about it hard. You might get one to two case studies, but since it's economic consulting, it's not necessary." A more experienced recruit grumbles, "As someone hired with a couple years of experience, I still had to submit a writing sample, cover letter, resume and two letters of recommendation. I thought that was a little ridiculous for someone with experience. I spent one day interviewing with the firm—six separate interviews and lunch."

Evaluating the Ivies

Though NERA is reportedly light on cases, insiders provide us with some examples: "Ivy league graduates earn $80,000 per year more than graduates of other colleges. Does this mean that Ivy League schools give a better education? If you disagree, how would you design a study to determine whether an Ivy League education is as good as, say, a major state school like Penn State?"; "Imagine Apple is suing a company for infringing on its iPod patents. How would you go about calculating damages (what kinds of information would you want to know and what types of data might be helpful)?" One source explains that the case question "depends on the practice area—for IP, you could get a scenario about patent infringement and how you would approach calculating damages; for securities, you could get a question asking you how to go about damages calculation for stock fraud, what else you would have to control for, etc."

The firm offers some summer intern opportunities; one former intern tells us, "The work is obviously far more interesting as a regular employee than as an intern, but you do get an idea of how interesting working here can be."

OUR SURVEY SAYS

Neo-academic NERA

Academics and their kindred spirits will find themselves right at home at NERA, otherwise known as the "nerdiest place you can work and not be in IT," according to one insider. "Working with several people at NERA is like going to office hours of good professors," another source comments. A colleague chimes in, "NERA has a neo-academic feel. We are very interested in theoretical economic issues, both for the sake of the work and because we enjoy economics." "Because there are many former academics here, people have a somewhat liberal bent, meaning they are pretty accepting of you as you are. On the other hand, all those PhDs can be pretty snobbish about it, often without a lot of real knowledge to back up their superior attitude," one consultant scoffs.

Some insiders tell us they've noticed the culture at NERA evolving recently. "The New York office has grown a lot in size over the past couple of years, so the vast majority of employees are now people recently out of college. I think that's changed the culture a lot since I got here. It's made the culture less academic and more pleasant, socially. Seniors, virtually all PhDs, remain dorky, but they are by-and-large pleasant and accessible. Overall, the work environment is quiet and (usually) low-intensity," says one source. Another insider notes that while "NERA is self-contained (with respect to the corporate parent Marsh & McLennan), and functions in between an academic atmosphere and a corporate office," the parent company recently "has exerted more influence over all of the consulting companies and it is too early to tell how this will change the culture."

Visit the Vault Consulting Career Channel at www.vault.com/consulting - with insider firm profiles, message boards, the Vault Consulting Job Board and more.

VAULT CAREER LIBRARY   239

Laid-back in the city

Still, a fundamental characteristic of NERA is its "friendly" culture, where "the work atmosphere is pretty laid-back, especially for New York City," and there are "basically no office politics," insiders say. According to a consultant, "The researchers also have a strong (but welcoming) social bond, whether it be office birthday parties, Thanksgiving parties (with homemade sweet potato pie), outside work events or the basketball and softball teams. People are both nice and (with very few exceptions) smart, making work quite enjoyable!" And hard workers can benefit from the firm's "true meritocracy," says a source, adding, "I know a lot of firms claim that they promote this structure—but at NERA, one can work really hard and advance very quickly, both in terms of position and salary (six month evaluations; 50 percent salary increase in under two years)."

Work/life balance at NERA really "depends on what office you're working in, "reports a source, who says that "people live in the office" in New York, but it's "more balanced" at other locations. Different respondents report wildly varying experiences, with working under some supervisors compared to "investment banking" and others as "very accommodating." And schedules can be "cyclical," an insider reports, noting, "There are weeks when I leave every night at 6. Then there are the weeks where I work past 10 every night and come in for a full day on Sunday."

"Glorious" schedules

For one insider who reports working 40 to 45 hours weekly "in slow times," NERA offers "probably one of the best bang-for-your-buck jobs available." "I work 9 to 6 every day. It's glorious," exults another source. Overall, the hours are "very good for a consulting firm," reports a colleague, adding, "Weekend work is generally rare, and occurs only near deadlines. One insider sums up, "It's not an I-bank, but it's no nonprofit, either. When project deadlines approach, things can ramp up, but that means 65 hours instead of 50. It also depends on your group/boss. I don't think anybody would complain that they don't have a life. Not having to travel is a bonus, too."

Indeed, travel is minimal to nil for the majority of NERAites, where "junior-level employees seldom travel, and if they do, it's only for a few days and is so rare as to be exciting," an insider observes. "At the researcher level, we travel about once per year," says one insider. A consultant reports traveling a bit more often, though only "when it is needed in order to meet with clients, to participate in seminars or presentations, or to work with people in other offices." A more senior-level insider reports that "travel is typically to interesting places, international destinations or occasional client visits, typically in major cities," and is usually "short trips." Overall, it's a "great environment if you're looking for a consulting job that does not require a lot of travel," an insider sums up.

At NERA,"there is no 'beach' time, says an insider, who explains, "Everyone is always busy doing their own work or checking other people's work." Projects can range anywhere from two weeks to seven years, so it's "meaningless to speak of an average," another says. "Generally, we carry three to five projects at a time," a consultant tells us. According to a colleague, "We generally work on cases in spurts since we are so litigation-centric. If there is a hearing coming up, chances are we will be working on the case. If the case is stagnant, we will do nothing."

Your money or your life

As for compensation, an insider says, "Very few firms pay this well for the hours demanded, at least in terms of base salary. Bonuses are small, but the additional change is nice still. A good employee can expect to be making in the six digits three-and-a-half years out of undergrad, at least in the securities practice." A colleague agrees, "The salary the first few years is probably on the low side for the industry, but growth potential and speed seem to be better than other firms." As another consultant puts it, "If you only want to make money, do finance. If you want to enjoy your job and have time to enjoy the money you have, work at NERA."

NERA does offer year-end bonuses, though they "vary widely by group," says a source. A colleague explains, "If you personally bring in an engagement, you are going to receive a share of the profit in that engagement, regardless of your level of seniority (even the most junior people can potentially get it). Vice presidents and senior vice presidents routinely have a profit share." Another insider adds, "The firm has 401(k) and stock plans, and gives you the opportunity to purchase MMC stock (blech) at a crappy discount (5 percent)." In addition, a colleague reports, there's a "better-than-average health plan. Benefits will not lapse if the employee leaves the firm for up to five years and returns."

"Endearing" Christmas gifts

Aside from that, a source says, "If perks make you feel special, don't come to NERA. We get free breakfast every Friday, free lunch Mondays, free dinner if you're working—nothing extraordinary. Casual Friday (jeans, polos, or T-shirts if you're daring) is universally loved." But others report more substantive perks, including full reimbursement for "any additional academic training such as a master's in economics, MBA or CFA exams," "ice cream sundae celebrations," and "free entry to museums and other cultural institutions." For researchers, there are monthly outings such as booze cruises and comedy club trips, and the "Christmas gift is endearing in that it's always very bad (an mp3 player that could fit 10 songs was a standout)," a source tells us.

In keeping with NERA's academic flavor, insiders describe their relationships with supervisors (or "seniors," as they're known at the firm) as "very collegial," and similar to those they had "with professors in college (most seniors are PhDs with some teaching background)," and "like mentors, good teachers and interested in our success, advancement and training." "My supervisor is very good, but I got lucky," says another insider. "You are assigned to a supervisor when you arrive, so it's pretty much luck of the draw here. Client interaction is somewhat limited at the researcher level, but if you develop a relationship with one, your supervisor will often feel comfortable letting you explain analysis to them, as it might not be cost effective for the supervisor to do it at $550 an hour." Another source tells us, "Seniors do not give junior people enough client responsibility early on. This is a weaker part of NERA." According to a colleague, "There isn't a ton of client interaction—this is economic consulting, not management consulting. We work with lawyers who you probably don't want to deal with much anyway."

Into the fire

As for training, one source observes that "NERA has long advocated a type of throw-you-right-into-the-fire type of training. There is very little formal training, but everything you need to know you can learn on the job. There is a very steep learning curve. That being said, you can learn as much (or as little as you would like). You just have to be really proactive." A colleague agrees, "The work varies so much on a case-by-case basis that it's difficult to have a uniform training process. I was worthless for my first six months, then I started to pick things up. Seems like most people are this way." A few formal opportunities exist, sources say, with events like lunchtime lectures. "Training about economics and finance is great. Training about managerial skills is not very effective," an insider remarks.

NERA's offices get satisfactory reviews from insiders. But a New York-based consultant reports, "At the moment, my office is good, but this year we are supposed to move to a space that is less than half of what we currently have (part of the reorganization plan of our parent company). In all likelihood, all people at my level will lose their offices and will end up in open cubes." Other New Yorkers have similar concerns, with one insisting that the reorganization plan "looks awful," and fretting, "If it goes through, people will likely be less able to work, and it may be tougher to recruit people because we will have to get them to look past the poor office design." In Washington, D.C., NERA's space is said to resemble "a law office (marble, dark wood, art on the wall)." A D.C. consultant complains, "Our office does not have as wide a variety of beverages/snacks/options for dinner (or lunch) as our Manhattan office."

Female economists

The D.C. and New York City offices also are split when it comes to gender balance, insiders suggest. "I think that in the New York office, female vice presidents and senior vice presidents greatly outnumber men," says one insider. But down in D.C., a consultant reports, "The firm seems very receptive to full inclusion of women, however, my particular office has very few female seniors. Though having more female seniors would certainly change the office for the better, the current male seniors are doing what they can to help make do with this imperfect situation." In any case, the firm's securities and finance practice is headed by a woman, and another consultant observes, "I continue to be surprised by how many women there are at NERA, compared to

Visit the Vault Consulting Career Channel at **www.vault.com/consulting** - with insider firm profiles, message boards, the Vault Consulting Job Board and more.

VAULT CAREER LIBRARY   241

how many there are in your average economics department." In addition, "many moms elect to work a four-day week, even when their kids are in grade school," a source says.

When it comes to diversity, one insider describes the firm as "fairly homogenous. I'd like more diversity." "I think that the firm is welcoming of every minority. I think the only thing missing to achieve a perfect score is specific outreach (such as participating in career fairs directed at African-Americans)," says a colleague. "We have a very diverse set of colleagues, but most are foreign-born. African-Americans are underrepresented, but we do not have many apply," another insider says.

"Comfortably out" at NERA

While the firm reportedly hires "openly gay professionals for client-facing positions with no hesitation," as one insider puts it, those who are out at NERA express interest in more firm visibility. "Our parent company, MMC needs to support the creation of a companywide GLBT group. MMC also needs to add transgenders to its nondiscrimination policy," says a source. A colleague echoes, "On a firmwide level, MMC could do a whole lot more to promote GLBT recruiting efforts and GLBT groups. Within NERA, though, I'm comfortably out to my supervisors and friends and haven't noticed any homophobia. I also have gay friends within the firm, which is very nice."

Community service at NERA is said to be "very ad hoc, though our parent company offers a grant program where, if you volunteer with a nonprofit, you can apply for a grant," a source says. Most NERAites report that MMC handles the more high-profile side of do-gooding at the firm, such as matching donations for Hurricane Katrina victims, but there's plenty going on among the economic consulting set, too. "I have been doing an ongoing pro bono project for six years. There are no negative ramifications for the lost 'billable' hours," a consultant reports. And "NERA sponsors functions for the New York Lawyers for The Public Interest," says a source, adding, "Researchers and analysts have tutored public school students at lunchtime."

"At NERA, one can work really hard and advance very quickly, both in terms of position and salary."

– *NERA associate*

Visit the Vault Consulting Career Channel at **www.vault.com/consulting** - with insider firm profiles, message boards, the Vault Consulting Job Board and more.

VAULT CAREER LIBRARY   **243**

BearingPoint Inc. Management & Technology Consultants

1676 International Drive
McLean, VA 22102
Phone: (703) 747-3000
Fax: (703) 747-8500
www.bearingpoint.com

LOCATIONS

McLean, VA (HQ)
Operates in 60 countries

PRACTICE AREAS

Asset Management
Customer Relationship Management
Enterprise Performance Management
Enterprise Resource Planning
Enterprise Risk Management
Enterprise Strategy & Transformation
Finance Advisory
Growth & Innovation
Human Capital Management
Information Management
IT Strategy & Transformation
Managed Services
Merger Integration
Operational Excellence
Oracle Supply Chain Management
SAP Systems Integration
Technology Infrastructure

THE STATS

Employer Type: Public Company
Ticker Symbol: BE (NYSE)
Chairman: Roderick C. McGeary
CEO: Harry L. You
2007 Employees: 17,000
2006 Employees: 17,000
2006 Revenue: $3.44 billion
2005 Revenue: $3.39 billion

THE BUZZ
WHAT CONSULTANTS AT OTHER FIRMS ARE SAYING ABOUT THIS FIRM

- "Strong in the government sector"
- "In big trouble; poor morale"
- "Implementation-focused"
- "BoringPoint"

RANKING RECAP

Practice Area
#9 - Energy Consulting
#9 - Operational Consulting
#10 - Financial Consulting

UPPERS

- "The remote work arrangement"
- A lot of vacation time
- "It is quite easy to differentiate oneself and gain recognition from supervisors"
- "Easy to expand beyond one's job description— no one tells you that you can't do something"

DOWNERS

- "Still wrestling with effects of poor PR due to delayed filings"
- "Difficulty navigating the career paths and options"
- "Severe disorganization within the firm; no clear focus, strategy or agenda"
- "Pay is about 80 percent of industry scale"

EMPLOYMENT CONTACT

bearingpoint.com/careers

THE SCOOP

High-tech roots

BearingPoint, based near Washington, D.C., has become a powerful player in the consulting arena in a relatively short period of time. This is partly thanks to the firm's strong roots; spun off from Big Five accounting company KPMG in 1999, BearingPoint (then known as KPMG Consulting) got a boost from a $1 billion investment from Cisco Systems. In 2002, the firm made its final break from KPMG with the selection of its new name, designed to reflect the concept of "setting direction to an end point."

BearingPoint's location—near both the Beltway and the East Coast's high-tech corridor—reflects the firm's own direction. The consultancy is known for its IT savvy, serving both government and private-sector clients with systems implementations and more. In the private sector, BearingPoint's clients include more than 700 of the Global 2000, including all of the Fortune 100's software, electronics and pharmaceutical companies, as well as nine of the top-10 global wireless carriers and the top-10 banking and finance companies in the U.S. These days, however, the company derives the majority of its business from the public sector. The firm employs more than 17,000 staffers in 60 countries.

Clerical complications

A publicly traded company, BearingPoint has struggled through a few messy financial years, marked by earnings restatements, unhappy shareholders and an inquisitive Securities and Exchange Commission. In 2002 and 2003, a series of layoffs, restructurings and bonus reductions dampened employee morale, while a series of earnings restatements left shareholders grumbling. BearingPoint's financial picture was complicated by its many acquisitions, most notably its May 2002 acquisition and hiring of most of Andersen's global consulting operations, a deal worth $150 million.

The years 2004 and 2005 brought additional financial fretting, including clerical complications that led to further earnings restatements. By 2005, it was clear that the firm's annual report was going to be some time coming. Making matters worse, in October 2005, the firm reported that the SEC, which had been looking into BearingPoint's earlier earnings restatements, had decided to launch a formal investigation of the matter. And in December 2005, the firm had to enter a $15.5 million settlement agreement with the Department of Justice over allegations of "potential understatement of travel credits to government contracts."

Hey, You

All of this drama was accompanied by plenty of shuffling in the executive levels, beginning with the high-profile departures of BearingPoint CEO Randolph Blazer and CFO Robert S. Falcone, in late 2004. Neither exec gave a reason for leaving, but the firm didn't remain rudderless for long. In March 2005, Harry L. You, a former CFO for Oracle and, before that, for BearingPoint rival Accenture, stepped up to take the lead. You's appointment heralded a new era for BearingPoint; calling its previous financial bumbling "embarrassing and inexcusable," he announced that the firm's "first order of business" would be to "reestablish financial credibility and consistency with an unswerving commitment to transparency in disclosure and rigorous financial processes."

You brought onboard a fresh new C-level crew, including a new executive VP of finance and chief accounting officer, a new corporate controller and a new director of investor relations, to name just a few. Most recently, in January 2007, Ed Harbach was tapped to serve as BearingPoint's president and chief operating officer. A former managing partner and chief information officer for Accenture, Harbach brought more than 28 years of tech industry experience to the firm (along with valuable ties to You, a former Accenture colleague). Meanwhile, former COO Rich Roberts was moved aside to serve as chairman of BearingPoint's global public services unit.

In October 2006, the firm brought on another chief financial officer, Judy Ethell, who had formerly been serving as BearingPoint's chief accounting officer, and charged her with righting the fiscal ship. Ethell took over the CFO duties from CEO You, who presumably had been working overtime in both positions. As CFO, Ethell was responsible for cleaning up the firm's

Visit the Vault Consulting Career Channel at **www.vault.com/consulting** - with insider firm profiles, message boards, the Vault Consulting Job Board and more.

VAULT CAREER LIBRARY   245

financial reporting and auditing procedures, and her success over the 15-month project made her the "clear choice for the job," You said. The firm also got a new chief compliance officer in July 2006, naming Russ Berland, formerly with Hewlett-Packard, "responsible for reinforcing the culture of integrity at BearingPoint."

Coming clean

BearingPoint continued to clean up its act later in 2006, coming to agreements with some holders of outstanding debentures, amending its credit facility and filing overdue paperwork with the SEC. In November 2006, the firm finally filed its audited 2005 financial statements with the SEC. "In many ways, today's filing puts the past behind us and we are now moving full speed ahead at completing our 2005 Form 10-Qs and 2006 filings," You said. In its 2005 statement, BearingPoint reported revenue of $3.4 billion, roughly equal to that of 2004. But the firm's losses for the year grew, from $546 million in 2004 to $721 million. One contributing factor in the losses was a snag in the firm's contract with Hawaiian Telecom Communications. Because of delays (BearingPoint and HT are at odds over who's to blame), the contract cost the firm over $113 million over the course of the fiscal year.

During 2005, the report indicated, the firm derived nearly 30 percent of its income from U.S. federal government clients. About 31 percent of revenue came from outside of North America, and BearingPoint received the bulk of its revenue from the public-services sector ($1.3 billion in 2005), with commercial services coming in second ($664 million) and financial services rounding out the picture (at $380 million).

Global plans

The long-anticipated report also gave a glimpse into the firm's strategy for the near future. Beginning in 2007, BearingPoint said, "We intend to begin transitioning our business to a more integrated, global delivery model. This transition will begin by more closely aligning our senior personnel worldwide who have significant industry-specific expertise with our existing public services, commercial services and financial services industry groups. Our nonmanaging director employees will then be assigned, as needed, across all of our industry-specific operations. We expect this change to improve our utilization and provide added training for our professional personnel." The firm also indicated that it planned to continue concentrating its sales efforts on its more profitable large client accounts. And as for those finances, in July 2007, BearingPoint announced it expects to be caught up with its SEC filings by late 2007.

Keeping consultants

Along with its financial challenges, BearingPoint also has suffered a bit of a brain drain in recent years, with a voluntary attrition rate for consultants approaching 28 percent at the end of 2006. In its annual filing for 2005, the firm admitted that a comprehensive review showed that it "must become more efficient and coordinated in our efforts to recruit, train and utilize our professional services staff," noting that BearingPoint has had trouble transitioning consultants out of completed projects into new engagements and forecasting demand for services. To tackle the problem, the firm said, it is focusing on updating and improving its systems worldwide, aligning senior personnel more closely with industry groups and strengthening training programs.

Despite these challenges, in 2006, BearingPoint was named among *BusinessWeek*'s first-ever ranking of the best places to launch a career. The firm reportedly hired more than 1,800 entry-level staffers in 2005, at an average salary of $45,000 to $49,999. Employee retention programs introduced in 2005 included streamlining the management structure; reducing excess management layers while focusing on retaining managing directors; revising compensation to raise the variable component (such as bonuses) while reducing the fixed percentage of salary; encouraging stock ownership by nonmanaging directors; and using better metrics for employee evaluations, rewards and advancement.

Speedy delivery

In recent years, BearingPoint has turned to a near- and offshoring delivery model for many of its IT services, investing in global development centers worldwide, from China and India to Hattiesburg, Miss. In its latest annual filing, the firm announced that it plans to create another delivery center in Eastern Europe to serve its European customers. In China, BearingPoint has an Asian hub in Shanghai, along with offices in Beijing and Guangzhou. In 2006, the firm announced plans to boost its Indian headcount to 1,000 over the next two years, with an emphasis on a senior-level team in the region set to focus on ERP, SAP and enterprise application services. The firm's new global development center in Bangalore has capacity for 600 staffers; another global development center in Chennai is a partnership with Covansys.

Saving the world, one country at a time

BearingPoint has developed a close relationship with the U.S. Agency for International Development, which often engages the firm to help countries looking to overhaul and modernize their technical and economic infrastructures. In November 2006, the firm scored two contracts from USAID to support labor mobility and tax systems in Bosnia-Herzegovina. In October of that year, USAID granted the firm a contract to implement a sustainable business enhancement program for Jordan. Another USAID contract signed that month was geared toward helping Serbia strengthen its financial infrastructure.

BearingPoint is becoming well known for its international work in war-torn areas, including Iraq, Afghanistan and Sudan. In Iraq, the firm reportedly has been working with the U.S. government to reorganize the country's financial sectors, including its oil industry (to the tune of more than $2 million a year, according to *The New York Times*). Some critics raised eyebrows when noting that BearingPoint was also tapped to advise the government over legislation affecting the oil sector. The firm has also been working with USAID in Afghanistan on a variety of projects "to support the rapid transition of Afghanistan to a more stable and productive state through the promotion of democracy, rule of law and sustainable economic and social development that is responsive to citizens' needs."

Involved with the Feds

Closer to home, BearingPoint is involved with just about every government agency you can think of. In December 2006, the firm was awarded a $5.9 million contract by the Navy as part of a one-year project to transition to the new Navy-Marine Corps Intranet. One month earlier, the firm completed its implementation and deployment of a portion of the Department of Health and Human Services' Unified Financial Management System, the cornerstone of a departmentwide effort to transform financial management at HHS. When completed, the UFMS is expected to be the largest civilian financial management system in the world. BearingPoint's contract to help the Department of Navy roll out the world's largest electronic records management solution was reupped in September 2006, a contract worth $8 million. Another engagement, with the Centers for Disease Control's Financial Management Office, was renewed in May 2006. And in April of that year, the firm was selected for an IT contract with the National Institutes of Health, valued at up to $35.9 million.

BearingPoint also has been working with the U.S. government on a competitive contract to help deliver new highly secure identity cards for personnel from nearly 40 agencies. These types of solutions, often involving biometric data embedded in ID cards, are increasingly sought-after among government clients. In October 2006, the firm announced the successful development and delivery of an e-passport for the government of Ireland. The project was completed under a tight deadline, meeting new U.S. requirements for a visa waiver program involving biometric passports for participating countries, such as Ireland, with large numbers of visitors to the U.S. each year.

Updating HR stateside

The firm also continues to rack up contracts on the state level. In September 2006, BearingPoint announced a $28 million, two-year contract with the state of North Carolina to implement its new human resources and payroll modernization project, replacing a 30-year-old system with an online model. And in March 2006, the firm was awarded a $69 million contact to implement a new payroll and personnel system for the state of California. Working with SAP Public Services, BearingPoint is tasked with replacing yet another obsolete, 30-year-old system with a state-of-the-art solution.

Visit the Vault Consulting Career Channel at **www.vault.com/consulting** - with insider firm profiles, message boards, the Vault Consulting Job Board and more.

VAULT CAREER LIBRARY   247

The search is on

In February 2006, BearingPoint got noticed in the tech world when it announced a partnership with search engine empire Google. BearingPoint's new search solutions practice group, established to deliver search solutions to major enterprise clients, offers customized search technology tailored to specific business environments in industries such as pharmaceuticals, banking, brokerage, high tech and aerospace. By delivering integration assistance, along with techy solutions like application plug-ins, BearingPoint expects to cash in on the heavy demand for enterprise search solutions—Google's enterprise business more than doubled in 2005.

Intellectual capital

BearingPoint is recognized for having some of the brightest minds in the consulting field. Christopher Formant, head of the firm's global financial services division, was named to *Consulting Magazine*'s list of the Top 25 Most Influential Consultants for 2006. The consultancy also keeps its profile up in the leadership arena with its Institute for Executive Insight. Founded in 2005, the institute aims to provide C-level execs with packaged information, such as research and reports, as well as an information-sharing forum. BearingPoint also collaborates with the George Washington University's school for public policy on the GW Center for Innovation in Public Service. In November 2006, the center released a report detailing how government agencies can improve their talent acquisition and retention. The study outlined basic needs to be met by federal HR managers, including recognizing employees as critical assets, strategically planning for staffing and skills, prioritizing human capital costs for sustained investment, and engaging staffers through communication and collaborative channels.

GETTING HIRED

Sweeping the country

An insider tells us that the firm recruits from "the usual suspects of top MBA schools and undergrad schools." In addition to top B-schools such as Yale and Wharton, BearingPoint recruits and holds on-campus interviews at a list of 30 "target schools" in each region, including Boston University, Louisiana State University, Rice and Santa Clara University. The firm encourages candidates who aren't at one of the listed schools to attend an event at any campus in the area. Interested candidates can check out the firm's complete recruiting events calendar, maintained on the careers page of its web site.

No standard routine

Sources reveal that each office determines its own hiring and interview process, so there's no one set routine for all candidates. Generally, staffers say the process consists of interviews with three or four managers. "I had a phone interview, face to face with the team, and a final interview with a managing director," relates a consultant. Another colleague recalls, "I was hired after one interview, with an immediate offer. I don't think this is the norm. When I hire now, we bring candidates in for a series of interviews with two to four people."

Consultants also report encountering different types of questions during the course of interviews, and insiders mention that not all interviews include case questions or logic tests. Says a consultant, "Besides the standard interview questions, they focused a lot on assessing my leadership abilities. I did not take any tests." A co-worker comments, "After the screening process was complete, I met with the person who would be my new boss. He asked questions like, 'Where do you see yourself in five years?' and 'Have you had any testing experience?'—just to see how I handled them and to see what my communication is like." According to another employee, the interview was all about past work experience: "I had one phone screening with an HR rep, followed by an on-site visit consisting of three back-to-back interviews with senior consultants to managers from my group. Each interview was 30 to 60 minutes long. All were resume-based, with a few very basic behavioral questions mixed in."

Another manager on the East Coast reports using a more thorough interview approach, consisting of "critical behavior questioning, case study, skills match and experience match." An insider says that one such behavioral question might be the following: "You are working on an important assignment and the deadline is closing. You have made a mistake but you are not sure if it will affect the project or not. How do you handle and resolve your mistake?"

OUR SURVEY SAYS

Putting the pieces in place

Sources claim that the culture at Bearing Point is a hard to pin down. Explains one staffer, "My firm's culture is a mosaic of multiple companies' cultures, as numerous acquisitions have taken place in recent years." And the fact that consultants don't stay in one place and don't always work with the same people means that the culture can vary as much as the engagements. "I think it depends a lot on the project, if you're on a big project with the right people, then the culture is really there. But if it's a small one, then you barely remember who pays your salary," claims an insider. An analyst points out, "If you are in the right practice and around the right people, this is a great place to work, with exciting engagement opportunities and lots of flexibility when it comes to developing a career." Though there's no one way to define BearingPoint's culture, on the whole, insiders seem optimistic that after few years of postmerger bumps, things are looking up. "It's been improving significantly in past years— moving more to teamwork and transparency," tells one longtimer.

Peer pleasure

But no matter how insiders feel about the overarching culture of the firm, the majority are highly complimentary of their co-workers. "The company struggles with establishing a culture because so many employees work off site with clients. That said, there is a lot of camaraderie among the staff," a manager points out. Notes a consultant, "It's very laid-back, with great people. Every project has been a lot of fun," and a colleague boasts, "I have met some highly intelligent people that are a joy to work with. I feel like I have a lot of support, and a lot of people who want me to succeed." One new hire says, "Overall, the culture is inviting and everyone I have met are great colleagues and friends, except for a few bad apples."

On friendly terms

BearingPointers also benefit from favorable relationships with management. "My relationship with my supervisor and internal clients is what keeps me at my firm," attests one source. "My performance manager is the most professional manager and leader I have had in my career. He is supportive, very accessible and, most importantly, knows how to manage to help me succeed," raves an associate, while a colleague praises, "I can't say enough good things about my supervisor."

There are also those insiders who acknowledge that since supervisors are "unique by project," experiences aren't always necessarily positive. Explains one insider, "For my first one-and-a-half years I had terrible superiors, but I've been transferred now and these are great. It's basically just the hand you're dealt: If you get a good group, you'll go far and fast; if not, you'll stagnate."

Working for balance

Some BearingPoint insiders cite the "work-at-home" policy as a huge plus that allows for a positive work/life balance. "BearingPoint is very flexible, allowing its employees to work at home often. I believe this experience is shared by most of the employees in the company," states one source. An analyst agrees, explaining, "While I tend to work a lot, it's balanced time because much of my work time is at home. The firm is very open to remote employees, and we can work pretty much wherever we want. As a former freelancer, I appreciate this from a corporation." The policy seems to be especially appreciated by those with families. According to one consultant, "My firm enables me to work from home and take comp time to spend time with my young children." With such leeway in terms of where they work, most staffers believe that work/life balance "seems to working fine."

Visit the Vault Consulting Career Channel at **www.vault.com/consulting** - with insider firm profiles, message boards, the Vault Consulting Job Board and more.

 249

And while location flexibility helps consultants manage their time, many sources claim that with weekly hours in the 55 to 60 range, work/life balance is just not attainable. "I don't know any consulting firm where you can balance work and life adequately. Many of the weekends are worked to help with flexibility during the week," an associate claims. A colleague remarks, "I work approximately 55 hours a week and, in peak weeks, it can be up to 90 or more." A manager in New York asserts, "It's very difficult in this business [to balance work and life] due to delivery demands. Also, we have a 'do-what-it-takes' culture, which is frequently demanded of us." Some employees are able to cut back their schedule permanently to achieve better balance. Relates a consultant, "I have a unique situation in that I am part time. This opportunity was given to me after I submitted my resignation. I don't believe that work/life balance can be achieved as a full-time employee." An Atlanta-based insider declares, "Achieving a work/life balance can be difficult at BearingPoint. Hours are often long and can be unpredictable, making planning for social activities outside of work difficult."

If you don't like traveling …

At BearingPoint, attitudes about travel trend toward acceptance—a practical outlook when faced with BearingPoint's demanding travel requirements. These insiders no doubt grumble about constant travel required, but at the same time admit that it is a necessary part of the job. "In consulting you have to travel. Can't complain about that. If you don't like traveling, get into a different industry," a source frankly states. One staffer announces, "Let's face it, it is consulting. Expectations are to travel four days a week. Depending upon the project, one can work out arrangements to work from home occasionally." According to a colleague, even those employees without families have a hard time finding balance when travel is frequent: "Travel is a demanding work life that is hard to balance. We also believe that if you are single without kids it is 'easy,' which is completely untrue and unfair, as singles have pressures in work/life balance too."

Other BearingPointers choose to see the upside of life on the road. "I have always enjoyed the excitement of being in new places, meeting new clients and tackling new problems. I have traveled throughout the world. It certainly, at times, gets a little tough. That's when some personal time off comes in handy," says one positive spirit. A co-worker elaborates, "It is both a good thing and can be a bad thing at times. It's good in the sense that you could be traveling to a fabulous city like San Diego and getting to experience it with all expenses paid. The bad part: being away from home five days a week." "There are benefits of traveling as well. Household bills are less expensive because you are never there, and there isn't as much wear and tear on your car or any gas expense," points out a practical analyst.

More, please

Compensation at BearingPoint isn't giving anyone cause to celebrate. Says one comparison shopper, "Our salary is below market rate, other firms (Deloitte, Accenture, Capgemini, etc.) compensate better." One source complains, "BearingPoint goes to great lengths to let us know that the future will be really great, yet never can seem to address base compensation issues where they lag seriously behind the market." As for raises, a senior consultant moans, "3 percent raises are not enough, especially when there are no exceptions for promotions."

Barely a bonus

With respect to compensation beyond base salary, insiders report that managers and above might receive a bonus around 10 percent, but it's "firm-driven and not aligned to individual productivity"—in other words, bonus isn't guaranteed. One smug associate remarks, "There is no concept of bonus in BearingPoint. I do remember our CEO handing out $50 to the employees when BE was rated highly by an external firm. Yes, that $50 to $30 after tax took care of my home mortgage." According to insiders, the firm is coming around to the fact that it needs to do better where compensation is concerned. "The company is improving to a point that bonuses are becoming standard and much higher for high performers," a staffer explains. Another source remains optimistic: "I do expect a healthy bonus this year. And there are other opportunities in the firm to make additional compensation, such as special recognition bonuses for generating new ideas or products."

Training wheels

BearingPoint is reportedly "dramatically improving focus on training this year," say insiders. Currently, the firm offers both informal and formal training, though a source mentions, "I wish we put a higher priority on formal training." Most of the training is left up to individual initiative, explains a staffer: "The company provides training resources and expects employees to develop their own training program." This sort of reliance doesn't seem to be having the intended results, though. One insider reports that training is "almost always unofficial, and it seems to take an act of G-d to get vendor-based training on marketable skills." Another consultant is disappointed that "mentoring is minimal (observed) but dependent on the manager." "This is an area where the firm is also improving," says a manager. "We've added training at Yale University, which everyone is excited about."

The firm's core official training program is on the intranet, which draws a few complaints. "Most training is done online, which can be tedious," says a consultant. And a co-worker comments, "The online training is really nice, but the content is pretty stale and I think that part of learning is the ability to interact with others. We don't do much of that here and I think that's one downside to the virtual organization we have."

Perks, for some

A handful of consultants appreciate the benefits, basic though they may be, at the firm. In addition to basic health care benefits, "we get the standard offerings for maternity leave and well-baby care as part of the health benefits plan." Beyond that, perks vary by the office. One New York insider suggests, "There are no 'perks' in this firm. This term is not applicable for BE." But an Atlanta employee disagrees, noting, "There are many work events. Sometimes these events allow you to leave early and enjoy cocktails and network with other employees. Other times they may include a sports event or local outing to an entertaining site." A source in McLean highlights the opportunity to "take classes through Yale" as a nice extra. Points out another associate, "The miles, points, etc., are yours to keep," while a colleague agrees, adding, "The travel perks are nice (per diem, miles, points), but they come at a high cost."

A California source mentions that BearingPoint has a policy of rewarding employees for outstanding work: "We have the ability to win awards for doing good work or creative work, such as the Annual Innovation Awards of $25,000. Six are given to individuals or teams each year for work they did or creative ideas they came up with."

No "cube to call home"

BearingPointers have a wide range of views about their offices, since each one is different. "The actual office is very nice, but I hate being located in Tyson's Corner—horrible traffic, megamalls, etc.," groans one McLean-based associate. A Denver insider mentions that in his digs, "There is some lack of facilities and newer technology, as well as messy quarters." And a shortage of space is an issue for Atlanta employees, according to a staffer: "Space is limited in many offices. I haven't had a cube to call home in the past two years. You are constantly moving around and there isn't much opportunity for privacy." And on the subject of this musical chairs office-space setup, an analyst in Manhattan states, "The hoteling system means you need a home office to do your work most of the time. Not even directors have permanent offices," another Manhattanite shares, while a colleague notes, "The new New York office space is great." Seemingly those happiest with their "high tech and modern" space are consultants in Palo Alto. Remarks an associate, "The offices make me feel good about my job and my career."

Room to improve

Sources insist that BearingPoint could also stand to improve its support for minority diversity. Notes an insider, "There are minorities here, but very few in management." A manager confirms, "Overall, it seems pretty 'white,' but I don't know the reason for this and how it is different at different locations." Another source opines, "I think it varies by individual managing director. Most seem very open to diversity, but there are a few that seem to be less accepting of other cultures." One director succinctly sums it up: "We need to do a much better job on diversity."

Visit the Vault Consulting Career Channel at **www.vault.com/consulting** - with insider firm profiles, message boards, the Vault Consulting Job Board and more.

VAULT CAREER LIBRARY   251

Try not to bump your head on the way up

Overall, we're told, BearingPoint is reportedly receptive to hiring and promoting women, but the prevailing attitude among insiders is that it "could be far more progressive." A senior employee explains, "Women seem to make it to manager level and then hit the glass ceiling around here. This is an old accounting/auditing firm, turned consulting. We are improving on this front, but it still needs work." Echoes a colleague, "I think we do a good job of hiring women and promoting them up to a certain point (just before the partner/managing director level). I'm not aware of any mentoring programs." One Denver staffer notes a recent positive trend: "There were a lot of women executives hired recently. [They were] very well received."

Birdies for the Brave

Employees give the firm high marks for its level of involvement in community efforts. "We definitely encourage community involvement across many different areas," a director says. Explains an insider, "Each office has a local connectivity team that organizes community involvement—blood drives, clothing drives, tutoring, volunteering with local charities, etc." "We are a founding partner of Phil Mickelson's Birdies for the Brave Program. We also donated $150,000 to the Pentagon Memorial Fund. My firm is a good corporate citizen and cares about our communities and clients," a consultant in Florida is proud to say. And since there's no centralized firm effort, it's up to consultants to find causes to which they'd like to contribute. "Charities vary. Sometimes it's an employee going through a very difficult time. Once, it was a woman who worked at the restaurant in our building who had two small children and a husband who just had a bad accident," a staffer explains.

At BearingPoint, "I feel like I have a lot of support and a lot of people who want me to succeed."

– BearingPoint source

Visit the Vault Consulting Career Channel at **www.vault.com/consulting** - with insider firm profiles, message boards, the Vault Consulting Job Board and more.

VAULT CAREER LIBRARY   253

29

Navigant Consulting, Inc.

615 North Wabash Avenue
Chicago, IL 60611
Phone: (312) 573-5600
Fax: (312) 573-5678
www.navigantconsulting.com

LOCATIONS

Chicago, IL (HQ)
Offices in 42 cities

PRACTICE AREAS

Construction
Corporate Finance
Discovery Services
Disputes
Energy
Financial Services
Government Contractor Services
Healthcare
Insurance/Reinsurance Services
Investigations

THE STATS

Employer Type: Public Company
Ticker Symbol: NCI (NYSE)
Chairman & CEO: William M. Goodyear
2006 Employees: 2,300
2005 Employees: 2,000
2006 Revenue: $681.7 million
2005 Revenue: $575 million

RANKING RECAP

Practice Area
#10 - Economic Consulting

Quality of Life
#7 - Hours in the Office (tie)
#9 - Relationships with Supervisors (tie)
#14 - Formal Training (tie)
#17 - Work/Life Balance

Diversity
#14 - Diversity for Women

UPPERS

- "The people here are young and a lot of fun"
- Management is flexible and supportive of work/life balance
- "The firm is good at recognizing its top performers"

DOWNERS

- "Sometimes I feel the work I am doing doesn't truly help anyone"
- Lack of back-office and "virtual technology"
- "The downtime in between projects"

EMPLOYMENT CONTACT

Go to the careers section of the firm's web site

THE BUZZ
WHAT CONSULTANTS AT OTHER FIRMS ARE SAYING ABOUT THIS FIRM

- "Strong up-and-comer"
- "They do the work no one else wants to do"
- "A player in their specialties"
- "Losing staff and losing the confidence of the stock market"

THE SCOOP

A good place to start

Ranked as one of the 2006 Best Places to Launch a Career by *BusinessWeek*, Navigant Consulting is one strategy consulting firm to check out, especially if your business is running into a little trouble. The Chicago, Ill.-based consultancy specializes in helping companies navigate through regulatory or structural change by providing litigation, financial, health care, energy and operational consulting services to government agencies, legal counsel and large companies. It also focuses on markets undergoing substantial regulatory or structural change, including the construction, energy, financial services, insurance/reinsurance services, health care, corporate claims and public-sector industries.

To serve clients in these areas, Navigant divides its services into two main client channels: disputes, investigative and regulatory advisory services, and business, financial and operations advisory services. The former unit serves clients such as corporate counsels, law firms, corporate boards and special committees, which face the challenges of dispute, litigation, forensic investigations, discovery and regulatory compliance. The latter serves businesses in the health care, energy, financial and insurance industries, facing strategic, operational and technical management issues.

Acquisition after acquisition

Before it was Navigant Consulting, the firm was known as the Metzler Group, which went public in 1996. During its first three years as a publicly traded firm, Metzler acquired a number of consulting firms, including Peterson Consulting and the Barrington Consulting Group. In 1999, the new-and-improved Metzler Group changed its name to Navigant Consulting.

But the acquisitions didn't stop there. The firm has acquired 16 firms since 2002, and today employs more than 1,800 consultants working in 42 cities, including global offices in London, Toronto, Hong Kong and Shanghai. Revenue increased to $681.7 million in fiscal 2006, up from $575 million in 2005. In fact, revenue for the first six months of 2005 alone increased 21 percent, to $274.1 million from $155.2 million just two years prior. That kind of growth earned Navigant a place on *Fortune*'s list of the 100 Fastest Growing Companies in 2005.

Bulking up its disputes unit

In 2006, Navigant acquired Precept Programme Management, one of the U.K.'s top independent dispute advisory and program management consulting firms specializing in the construction industry for approximately $50 million. Until the merger, the firm had been assisting British law firms and public- and private-sector clients with their dispute and program management challenges in the U.K., as well as in European, Middle Eastern, African and Asian markets. According to Navigant's global construction practice leader, David Tortorello, in March 2006, "This acquisition further positions us as the leader in large international infrastructure dispute matters worldwide."

Earlier in 2006, Navigant also acquired Toronto-based corporate investigations consultancy the Inkster Group. Led by Norman Inkster, a former commissioner of the Royal Canadian Mounted Police and former president of Interpol, the firm specialized in corporate investigations, fraud prevention, business intelligence and the safeguarding of assets.

In good with Goodyear

At Navigant's helm is William Goodyear, who has served as chairman and chief executive since May 2000 and was named one of *Consulting Magazine*'s Top 25 Most Influential Consultants in 2004. Before joining Navigant, Goodyear served as president of Bank of America's Global Private Bank.

Visit the Vault Consulting Career Channel at **www.vault.com/consulting** - with insider firm profiles, message boards, the Vault Consulting Job Board and more.

V/\ULT CAREER LIBRARY 255

GETTING HIRED

Dancing the two-step

Navigant's hiring process is a relatively straightforward, two-step process. As a consultant in Los Angeles tells us, "Our firm recruits at countless universities. We have about 40 offices nationwide, and recruiting is done mainly on a regional/local basis." Reports a source in Southern California, "The Los Angeles office recruits at USC, UCLA, Claremont McKenna and Berkeley"; in Washington D.C., "UVA, Georgetown, William and Mary, UNC and Wake Forest" are favored schools. The Chicago office is partial to "Notre Dame, Michigan, Indiana and Illinois," while "the Princeton office recruits from Lehigh University, Villanova and Rutgers."

Applicants will usually face "two interviews, one on campus and one in the office," with the office-based portion consisting of roughly "three in-house interviews, followed by a lunch with a couple of consultants." As a staffer describes them, NCI interviews are "very much behavioral, to see if the candidate will fit in with the culture/attitude of the firm." And yippee skippee: Navigant puts "more focus on personality and undergraduate training than on-the-spot cases/brainteasers." You heard right, grins a staffer in Chicago—"no cases, tests, etc. All situational questions." A firm that doesn't want to know how many pingpong balls fit into a Boeing 747? How refreshing!

OUR SURVEY SAYS

That's what I like, that's what I like about you

Ask Navigant staffers what they appreciate most about their firm, and they are likely to say ,"The people!"—with an exclamation point. A Los Angeles associate loves "how 'chill' everyone is," while a colleague adds a handful more adjectives: "The people are outstanding—supportive, encouraging, helpful, friendly and inspiring." A source in D.C. observes, "Larger offices tend to be more corporate in feel and politics. The smaller offices and practice groups have more camaraderie and less internal competition for projects." But across offices, cooperation and collaboration are the binding tenets. A staffer in the Los Angeles feels that "people at NCI are extremely open and willing to share information and collaborate to help a team member accomplish their goal."

In addition to great colleagues, staffers appreciate "the opportunity to work on some really interesting cases," as well as their "exposure to many different industries and projects." Comments one source in Southern California, "I have been able to gain technical, marketable skills that I know will be valued throughout my future career. I have learned an extraordinary amount in the short time that I have been a consultant here in L.A." Another correspondent notes that the "internal mobility program is good for those who decide to work in a different group," and that at Navigant, you have the "ability to pick and choose cases that are of interest to you, and are in line with your career goals."

As for what they are not so keen on, this D.C. source believes that NCI "managers are mainly ex-Big Four (Big Five), and thus come with an accountant's rigid mindset about change (i.e., in compensation, benefits, dress code)." New associates might find that "there is a lot of document review work in litigation consulting for entry-level staff." Hmm, what's worse: document review or nothing to do? A D.C. rookie acknowledges that while "there is sometimes a lack of work for recent new hires in the very beginning, this unbillable time can be spent doing training or practice development. [Unbillable time] is also taken into consideration during the year-end evaluation and not counted against the consultant."

Oh, get a life!

According to insiders, Navigant management is flexible and downright encouraging when it comes to achieving work/life balance. Asserts one Chicago staffer, "NCI is very flexible. Even when I am very busy and have tight deadlines, directors make sure that I have adequate time to workout and have a life." A newer associate in Los Angeles comments, "I am able to balance work and life at NCI. My managers are extremely willing to accommodate my personal needs—after a particularly demanding project, my managers recognize the effort I put in, and usually reward me with additional hours off. My managers are also extremely supportive of my training needs, and accommodate these needs by enabling me to study at home on many occasions." And a source in the same office remarks, "It kind of goes back to the culture—everyone sticks out for one another. So if you have plans and your project starts getting ramped up, the other people on your project will gladly cover for you."

Still, a Dallas consultant points out that sure, "Managers are very understanding of granting time off for vacation, even in the middle of a project, but they will not hesitate to call you while you're on it." But this D.C. staffer feels that it is up to the individual consultant to draw boundaries: "The firm allows you to balance your life. No one is going to force you to leave to spend time with your family, as there is always some work to do. Since we work on a project basis, the firm is often good about giving one or two days off after the completion of a big project or deadline." Still he concedes, "I don't have children. If I did, it would be difficult to manage work and family."

A typical workweek, insiders tell us, is hard to predict. Shrugs one source, "Some weeks I'll work in excess of 70 hours and barely 40 others." Adds another, "Although deadline days tend to be pretty rough, subsequent days are really relaxed and no one will say anything if you come in late or leave early, knowing you were there late the night before." As for project duration, a source in Dallas feels that "smaller projects are generally three months, whereas larger projects could be a year. I do not work on just one project at a time; they are intermittent." In general, states this consultant, "Most of the projects that I have worked on have allowed me to maintain a personal schedule outside of work and leave the office at a decent time."

There's no place like home

"Travel depends on your practice area and your office location," explains a D.C.-based source. "My office and my specific practice area does not require much travel. However, others in different groups within the office and elsewhere in the country can travel extensively." A source in the same office adds that "the amount traveled really depends on the client, as well as the consultant's desires. I personally have not traveled at all, but have worked with others who travel 100 percent. I do work away from the home office, but it is at a local client site." In Los Angeles, a staffer agrees that travel really varies, but nevertheless feels that at NCI it is "quite minimal in comparison to other firms."

One consultant describes his routine: "I am currently working on an engagement that has meant traveling four days a week. I have managed to stay in touch with my home office and go in on Friday to work on other projects or catch up on my own work. The traveling has not impacted my work life too much, other than the fact that I am not there as often as I might like." A Dallas source feels that "as I'm not married, it's not too bad," but does point out that "since we do not bill for travel hours, I feel pressure to work 40 billable hours on top of my travel time." A senior-level consultant explains that "a consultant is allowed to be very vocal on whether or not he/she would like to travel. I choose to stay on the road, and the company accommodates that. Others request not to travel and are not invited on major travel projects, if possible." And, adds a colleague, "NCI is good about rolling you off of projects if you've been traveling for an extended period of time." For some, traveling isn't onerous at all: "I love traveling," says one senior consultant, simply. "When you are on the road, you can work as hard as you need to without distractions, so that when you are home it is enjoyable. Traveling allows me to leave work at work much easier than when I am working at my office down the street."

What's the 401?

"Compensation seems to be higher than that offered by other competing firms in the area," guesses one D.C. source. "The firm is good at recognizing its top performers." According to this insider, "There's a 401(k) that's matched 100 percent for up to 3 percent of your paycheck and vests immediately. There's also an employee stock purchase plan that allows you to allocate 15 percent of your paycheck toward acquisition of company stocks priced at a 15 percent discount on the final day of each quarter." Rounding out the compensation package, NCI offers "profit sharing and incentive bonuses (referral, overtime, etc.)." One newbie reports receiving "a one-year, interest-free loan of $3,000 when I started"; another adds that the firm dangled "a retention bonus if I stayed for an established period of time." Still, a road-weary source complains that he "does not feel compensated for traveling more than other employees."

Visit the Vault Consulting Career Channel at **www.vault.com/consulting** - with insider firm profiles, message boards, the Vault Consulting Job Board and more.

V**AULT** CAREER LIBRARY   **257**

Nonetheless, all air miles and hotel points from traveling do go toward the consultants' own use. Additionally, Navigant funds "gym and cell phone" costs, various "happy hours and group bonding at fun hotels and restaurants," and offers employees a "continuing education reimbursement and potential advanced degree grant." Explains one happy source, "Our tuition grant program provides employees seeking further education with a $50,000 grant to support them in these endeavors." Many staffers appreciate the firm's "formalized flexible work arrangements program that enables employees to balance their personal and professional needs." And there's good news for families: NCI offers "extensive maternity and paternity leave policies" for new parents, and "will also help offset the costs of adoption, too."

Supervisor exposé

"The supervisors are ridiculously approachable and very down to earth. A great bunch to work for," marvels an L.A. source. This D.C. staffer agrees, stating, "The people at NCI are phenomenal! They are reasonable and do a great job of being accessible and approachable. I would have no hesitation approaching even the most senior management in my office." Another associate is unequivocally gushing: "My supervisors have been absolutely supportive of me. Many have acted as mentors and friends, and truly encourage my own professional development. I have felt so lucky to work with the people that I do. I respect and value the opinions of my peers, and I am inspired by many of my supervisors' rapid career advancement and accomplishments."

In terms of client contact, however, standpoints differ. A D.C.-based associate reports: "Of my peers, I know of no other company to offer my staff level more exposure to client management. Most lower-level (inexperienced) consultants don't get the opportunity to interact with the clients so often. However, I was appointed as point of contact to the counsel we were working with on my last assignment, and I am currently working directly with the client and its top-level management on my recent assignment. This has provided good insight into how to best represent the firm and to establish good client relationships." Still, this insider has had the opposite experience, noting that "unfortunately, there's barely any client interaction at the consultant level"—though he qualifies this observation, saying, "But that makes sense, given the type of consulting we do."

Sweet charity

A D.C. source believes that Navigant is "starting to push it more" with regard to community and charitable involvement: "We certainly sponsor charitable events, and we're now trying to get some pro bono projects going." The D.C. office takes part in "community service projects, a 10K Charity Run, the March of Dimes and blood drives," we're told. A Los Angeles correspondent notes, "On a local level, we have taken on pro bono consulting efforts, as well as Reading to Kids." In Chicago, Navigant "highly encourages community involvement; we have done pro bono consulting and participated in a tax assistance program, and organized 5K runs and other events throughout the year in conjunction with law firms/legal societies." Not to be left behind, the Princeton office "volunteers at local soup kitchens and charities." A consultant notes that the firm has also "established a foundation called Lending a Hand, in which employees can submit a request for funds for nonprofit causes of their choice."

Knowledge exchange

You never stop learning—in life and at NCI. "There are constant training opportunities," confirms one Los Angeles correspondent, and a D.C. source adds, "Most of one's training will occur on the job throughout one's various assignments, although there are opportunities for official training programs as well." Due to the "opportunities to work directly with upper-level managers and directors" and the firm's "great mentoring program," a pleased associate reports that "people more senior than you are always teaching you something new." As an added bonus, "NCI is willing to pay for all certification prep and tests (i.e., CPA, CFA, etc.)" But for some associates, the only drawback to the firm's educational offerings is that there is just "no time to take them."

Steps in the right direction

A female staffer in California feels that Navigant offers a great deal of gender diversity. "NCI has female leaders at the corporate level—our president, human capital officer and several executive directors and business leaders are all women. In L.A., the majority of people I work with are women." Across the nation, however, this D.C. insider is not so sure: "We do not have many high-ranking women in the firm, but we have many entry-level and middle-level women." The firm hopes to increase the percentage of women in its highest ranks via its women's leadership initiative, we're told, which "offers quarterly creative programming for the female professionals in the office" and "reaches out to women across the firm to address issues pertaining to working mothers, mentoring, etc." Other sources report that "seminars and conferences are offered throughout the year to women within the firm," and note that "NCI is currently working to improve upon and provide even more programs in the future."

Visit the Vault Consulting Career Channel at **www.vault.com/consulting** - with insider firm profiles, message boards, the Vault Consulting Job Board and more.

259

CRA International, Inc.

John Hancock Tower
200 Clarendon Street, T-33
Boston, MA 02116
Phone: (617) 425-3000
Fax: (617) 425-3132
www.crai.com

LOCATIONS

Boston, MA (HQ)
23 offices worldwide

PRACTICE AREAS

Antitrust Economics • Auctions & E-Commerce • Business Strategy • Capital Projects • Commercial Litigation • Corporate Investigation & Fraud Management • Damages • Employment & Labor Litigation • Environmental • European Competition Policy • Finance & Accounting • Forensic Accounting • Forensic Computing • Intellectual Property • International Trade • Market Analysis • Mergers & Acquisitions • Product Liability • Survey Research • Tax Litigation • Technology Management • Transfer Pricing

THE STATS

Employer Type: Public Company
Ticker Symbol: CRAI (Nasdaq)
Chairman: Rowland T. Moriarty
President & CEO: James C. Burrows
2007 Employees: 733
2006 Employees: 667
2006 Revenue: $350 million
2005 Revenue: $296 million

RANKING RECAP

Practice Area
#3 - Economic Consulting
#7 - Energy Consulting

UPPERS

- "No prima donnas"
- Academic atmosphere
- "There is a sense of real teamwork"

DOWNERS

- "Increasing implementation of processes (these are needed, being a publicly traded firm) that are somewhat irksome!"
- Some "pressure cooker" work
- Minimal training opportunities

EMPLOYMENT CONTACT

www.crai.com/careers

THE BUZZ
WHAT CONSULTANTS AT OTHER FIRMS ARE SAYING ABOUT THIS FIRM

- "Classy, well respected for economic consulting"
- "Emphasis on senior, not junior, consultants"
- "Always underrated"
- "Small, regional"

THE SCOOP

International advisors

Founded in Boston in 1965, CRA, formerly known as Charles River Associates, has grown into an international powerhouse with an emphasis on economic and legal issues. Following a successful IPO in 1998, the firm has grown by leaps and bounds, and its public profile has been raised through a number of well-known engagements. CRA's 733 consultants have advised on such cases as the Justice Department's antitrust action against Microsoft Corp., the 2005 merger of Sprint and Nextel, provided expertise in a dispute between credit card giants Visa and MasterCard, and completed an economic and transfer pricing analysis for Hallmark Marketing Corporation, which had been engaged in a dispute with the New York Division of Taxation.

In 2006, the firm's revenue increased by more than 18 percent to $350 million, fueled in part by strong growth among the chemicals and petroleum, competition and finance practices. Internationally, the firm has continued to thrive, with overseas engagements contributing 24 percent to the firm's total business, thanks to increased activity in the Middle East and expansion in London. The firm has drawn a steady stream of business from the Middle East since 2002, when it acquired Arthur D. Little's energy consulting practice in the U.K.

Buying and growing

In fact, much of CRA's growth in recent years has come from strategic acquisitions. In May 2006, the firm announced its acquisition of The Ballentine Barbera Group LLC, a consulting firm specializing in transfer pricing services, for about $22.7 million. The move, which added 35 staffers, reflected CRA's plan to add businesses that complement its core capabilities while expanding its American and European reach, the firm's execs said. Through the Ballentine Barbera acquisition, CRA began offering transfer pricing services in the Netherlands in December 2006. In April 2005, the firm acquired Lee & Allen Consulting Ltd., a London-based consulting firm offering financial dispute resolution and forensic accounting services to the corporate, legal and regulatory markets. Also in 2005, CRA completed the acquisition of the former Lexecon Ltd. consulting firm, a U.K.-based company specializing in economic consulting.

CRA's clients hail from every major industry, including aerospace and defense, chemicals, consumer products, energy and utilities, financial services, health care, technology, manufacturing, petroleum, pharmaceuticals, telecommunications and media, transportation and government contracting. The firm's broad wingspan means CRA is less vulnerable to ups and downs in some of the more volatile markets it serves, such as its Middle Eastern business.

From telecom to climate change

CRA's work often takes the form of analyses and reports that help clients make significant business decisions. In March 2007, the firm published a report analyzing the effect of the acquisition of South African telecom firm Business Connexion by its rival, Telkom. In a similar project in early 2007, the firm was engaged by Singapore's Pacific Internet to report on the impact of a proposed acquisition of another firm, Connect. CRA has also been working with the Australian government to provide advice on climate change and energy. In August 2006, CRA teamed up with international management consulting firm UMS Group Inc. to provide consulting services to coal generator DPL Inc., including a performance analysis of DPL's coal plants.

Executive maneuvers

In October 2006, CRA announced five newly created executive positions. Fred Baird, who heads up the firm's Europe and Middle East practices, was appointed to the role of chief corporate development officer; Arnie Lowenstein, group vice president of business consulting, was named chief strategy officer; and three other consultants were appointed to lead the finance, litigation and applied economics group, as well as the strategy and business consulting platforms.

Visit the Vault Consulting Career Channel at www.vault.com/consulting - with insider firm profiles, message boards, the Vault Consulting Job Board and more.

VAULT CAREER LIBRARY   261

Navigation aids

CRA's experts can often be found in the mainstream business press, quoted in publications such as *The Wall Street Journal* (in a January 2007 article on climate change legislation), *The New York Times* (in a December 2006 article on carbon emissions) and others. The firm also generates plenty of its own research, including a 2007 report on trademarks in transactions and 2006 reports on antitrust damages and cartels. In a book published in 2007, *Terra Incognita: A Navigation Aid for Energy Leaders*, CRA consultants Chris Ross and Lane Sloan summarized lessons learned from execs in the energy sector.

GETTING HIRED

Financial focus

CRA offers an online tool through which consulting hopefuls can upload resumes and cover letters (required), as well as transcripts and other supporting documents (not always necessary). To join the firm at the ground-floor analyst level, candidates "should hold a good undergraduate degree in a science-, engineering- or technology-related subject," and "have strong quantitative and analytic, presentation and communication skills," the firm says. Associates should come equipped with degrees in finance, accounting or business economics, plus one to two years of work experience. CRA International draws from a variety of schools across the country, including Cornell, Middlebury College, Carnegie Mellon University, Bowdoin College, University of Pennsylvania, Swarthmore, Northwestern, UT Austin, Rice, USC, UCLA and Stanford.

Patience, patience

Since "our work environment requires teamwork and team players," a source says, "all current consultants must agree to potential hires." Typically, the interview process includes "two sets of interviews (on campus and local office) with a total of eight individuals," says another insider. But one consultant reports, "It's a long interview process, but they were generous enough to pack it all in one day. It could be grueling, but it's better than making several trips. I interviewed with all the senior staff members and many of the questions were general interview questions."

After that, prepare to sit back and wait, an insider says: "Patience is a virtue because total process time from first interview to offer letter was four months (and that is considered 'quick' by CRA experience)."

OUR SURVEY SAYS

Check your politics at the door

CRA, according to insiders, is a place where "politics are not tolerated." It's a "democratic meritocracy" that's "supportive without forcing conformity." As one consultant puts it, "CRA does not have the cutthroat, eat-what-you-kill mentality of most management consulting houses. There is a sense of real teamwork and collaboration, rather than teamwork being a code word for 'how I get you to do the work that I'll take credit for.'" "Even if it is consulting (fast-paced, dynamic, etc.), it has a distinctive academic feel," says a source. "It feels like a mixture of academics and business," a colleague agrees.

Flex-time

At CRA, an insider declares, "I am the master of my ship. CRA doesn't care where I'm sitting as long as the work gets done. So some days I'll work from home or a coffee shop with a wireless connection, and I'm never asked 'where were you?' the next day." But while "senior staff has a great deal of flexibility in personal scheduling," a source says, "junior staff is expected to work as needed and to pitch in on other projects that have tight deadlines." And "work on time-critical, complex litigation and similar projects can develop into a pressure-cooker environment with inadequate project management," an insider reports. Still, participating in these high-pressure projects can be good for exposure: "All members on my engagement team are routinely exposed to senior client executives," an insider reports.

According to one CRA staffer, the "best aspect of CRA from a lifestyle perspective is that I have broad discretion over when and how long I travel. Thus, I have the ability to block out weeks on the calendar at home and work, which rarely collapses. Plus, clients seem to dig that we aren't in their hair all the time." While some insiders report traveling only a handful of days per year, however, others explain that this "varies by practice an engagement." "I have been on engagements that have not required any travel and on projects that needed me to be on site three to four days a week," a source comments.

Perks at the top

Compensation at CRA is described by one consultant as "comparable to, if not better than, any consulting firm out there," and there's "profit sharing for everybody," we're told. Top brass may receive "very generous perks," from equity in clients to fully paid health care, but an insider regrets that "salaries for junior staff are not negotiable."

Training at CRA is said to be on the upswing, as it's "an area where the firm leadership has made a strong commitment this year," says a consultant. In addition, the firm reportedly coordinates corporate giving through individual offices.

Visit the Vault Consulting Career Channel at **www.vault.com/consulting** - with insider firm profiles, message boards, the Vault Consulting Job Board and more.

   263

Gallup Consulting

The Gallup Building
901 F Street, NW
Wasington, DC 20004
Phone: (202) 715-3030
Fax: (202) 715-3041
www.gallupconsulting.com

LOCATIONS

Washington, DC (HQ)
43 offices in 20 countries

PRACTICE AREAS

Brand Management
Customer Engagement
Employee Engagement
Executive Performance Coaching
Marketing Research
Performance Evaluation & Development
Performance Reward & Compensation
Performance Strategy
Sales Force Effectiveness
Strengths Development
Succession Management
Talent-Based Hiring

THE STATS

Employer Type: Private Company, Division of The Gallup
Organization
Chairman, President & CEO: James K. Clifton
2007 Employees: 2,000+
2006 Employees: 2,000+

RANKING RECAP

Quality of Life
#1 - Hours in the Office
#1 - Offices
#4 - Best Firms to Work For
#5 - Overall Satisfaction
#6 - Work/Life Balance
#8 - Relationships with Supervisors
#8 - Firm Culture
#16 - Interaction with Clients
#16 - Travel Requirements
#20 - Compensation

Diversity
#2 - Best Firms for Diversity
#5 - Diversity for Women
#6 - Diversity for GLBT
#8 - Diversity for Minorities

UPPERS

- "Freedom to come and go as I please"
- "You are free to say yes or no to any projects you want"
- On-site child care center
- "The people are generally not prone to political nonsense"

DOWNERS

- "It can be hard to break in to groups where people have been with the organization for 15 to 20 years and you are on year one"
- "The only way one can 'give yourself a raise' is to work more hours"
- "Systems are too slow to change"
- Lack of internal mechanisms for collaboration

EMPLOYMENT CONTACT

www.gallup.com/careers

THE BUZZ
WHAT CONSULTANTS AT OTHER FIRMS ARE SAYING ABOUT THIS FIRM

- "The pollsters' polling and research firm"
- "Weird recruiting process"
- "Better work/life balance"
- "Lacks strategic focus"

THE SCOOP

We know how you feel

If anyone knows how people feel about their jobs and their businesses, it's Gallup Consulting, which draws on the resources and experience of its parent company, The Gallup Organization. Famous for its Gallup opinion polls, The Gallup Organization has a deep research background in behavioral studies, employing more than 2,000 people in more than 40 offices around the world who work as advisers to companies, government agencies, school systems and nonprofit organizations. But even though Gallup Consulting may be less well known than its parent company's polls, most of The Gallup Organization's revenue comes from consulting services, which focus on a few key industries, including automotive, business services, education, financial services, government, health care, hospitality, manufacturing and retail.

People power

Gallup Consulting isn't your average consulting firm. Instead of advising clients on immediate problems, like how to reduce costs or rework their processes and systems, Gallup focuses on people and how it can strengthen their skills to boost their employers' bottom line. Gallup consultants work with company leaders to find ways to build employees' and customers' emotional engagement with the company.

Because of its focus on "organic growth" by taking a people-centric approach, Gallup's specialty services sound a little different from the rest of the hard-line business consulting crew: performance strategy, customer engagement, employee engagement, strengths development, talent-based hiring, performance evaluation and development, succession management, performance reward and compensation, executive performance coaching, sales force effectiveness, brand management and marketing research.

The "emotional economy"

Gallup Consulting's starting point is that people are emotional first and rational second. That's why employees and customers have to be emotionally engaged in order for a company to reach its fullest potential—something the best-run companies have come to understand. At all levels, every employee contributes in some degree to sales growth, profit and, for publicly traded companies, even the share price. Those companies that choose to ignore the so-called emotional economy get stung in the end, Gallup's consultants warn.

The Gallup Path—Gallup Consulting's trademark consulting strategy—uses bits and pieces from The Gallup Organization's background in management sciences, economics and psychology, to figure out what role human nature places in driving business outcomes. The company claims its theory is the first to prove and track the connectedness of managers to employees, employees to customers and customers to financial outcomes. A January 2006 Gallup study, for example, found that happy employees are measurably more capable of dealing with workplace relationships, stress and change, and are generally more productive than their unhappy counterparts. For each of its clients, Gallup Consulting aims to spur organic growth by zeroing in on linkages among employees, supervisors and customers, and on how they can be strengthened to help the company reach its financial goals.

A longstanding tradition

The Gallup Organization has had its finger on the pulse of American business since 1935, when Dr. George Gallup left his job with New York City's Young & Rubicam advertising agency to found the American Institute of Public Opinion, later the Gallup Organization. By the time Gallup died in 1984, the business had built an industry off of Gallup's original polling techniques, which provided insight for industries and organizations around the world.

In 1988, Gallup's sons, Alec and George Jr., merged the company with Lincoln, Neb.-based Selection Research, Incorporated, which used structured psychological interviews for finding employees that "fit" into new positions. Both brothers stayed on with

Visit the Vault Consulting Career Channel at www.vault.com/consulting - with insider firm profiles, message boards, the Vault Consulting Job Board and more.

VAULT CAREER LIBRARY   265

the new company, which retained the Gallup name. Together, Gallup and SRI grew the company tenfold over the next 10 years, as it expanded further into professional services like consulting.

During the business boom of the late 1990s, more and more corporations became interested in using Gallup's polling services and consulting advice for evaluating how their employees felt about their bosses. Rather than conducting largely ineffective in-house employee surveys, executives started asking Gallup to study their employees' attitudes, which they recognized took a toll on the company's overall productivity. The research Gallup conducted at this time developed into a system of 12 key measurements—called Q12—that revealed what people needed to stay engaged in the workplace. In 2000, The Gallup Organization wrapped up everything it had learned over the previous 65 years and rolled it into a single unique concept: the Gallup Path.

Now in paperback

Gallup's approach to consulting passed a major popularity test in 1999, when its management book on employee engagement—*First, Break All the Rules*—became an almost-immediate best seller in the U.S. and abroad, as did its second book, *Now, Discover Your Strengths*. Both books are still regularly included in business top-10 book lists in the U.S. The firm's other management books include *Follow This Path* (2002), *Discover Your Sales Strengths* (2003), *Animals, Inc.* (2004) and its latest best seller, *How Full Is Your Bucket* (2004), which argues that even the briefest interactions can affect relationships, productivity, health and longevity. Most recently, Gallup Press has published *Vital Friends: The People You Can't Afford to Live Without* (2006), which encourages friendships at work, and *12: The Elements of Great Managing* (2006), the sequel to *First, Break All the Rules*. Gallup also publishes the Gallup Management Journal, an online magazine that highlights the issues most critical to companies today.

GETTING HIRED

4.0-plus

Graduates who have set their sights on working for Gallup after graduation better start applying well in advance—insiders warn the interview process "can take anywhere from four to 12 months to find the right fit." Gallup recruits from "top undergrad and business schools," we're told, and a staffer notes, "We have a lot of grads coming out of Georgetown MBA, as an example." But even with a successful academic track record from a top school, Gallup is "a very tough organization to get in to." "The firm is highly selective and proud of it," a source echoes. Advises one associate, "Gallup essentially uses psychological profiling to find candidates likely to succeed in a role. Forget about blowing them away with your experience and education alone!"

It's all about talent

The focus of the entire lengthy hiring process is clearly individual talent. "We are a talent-based selection firm. So we look for people with the strengths to fit a particular role," an insider explains. The "rigorous and time consuming" interview process starts with a visit to the web site, where candidates complete an online assessment to evaluate individual potential. "Every role starts with taking a talent assessment. This scientific assessment determines if candidates have the basic talent to do and be happy in the role," an insider comments. The initial assessment stage consists of at least "three psychometric interviews." Mentions a consultant, "After this screen for talent, there are phone interviews that are behavioral in nature and again focus on talent and strengths." An insider clarifies, "We have one to four in-depth psychological profiling interviews, depending on the position. Then, in-person interviews with two to eight individuals."

The real determining factor seems to be the live phone assessments. According to a source, "If you get that far, you come in for an in-person interview where you will talk to a number of different folks in the office or role. This part is really just to ensure that you like the people and you match up to the information on the assessments. It seems like you will pretty much be offered a job if you come for the in-person interview." Notes a staffer, "If you make it past the phone interviews you are basically in, as long as you are a culture/personality fit for the department."

A scientific approach

Despite the intense tests and scrupulous questioning, insiders indicate that the process is a positive one that seems fair and impartial. A manager explains, "The firm uses Gallup science to find the most qualified talent." "It's like nothing else I've ever experienced, it was rigorous and challenging, but fun and insightful at the same time," one source exclaims. Confirms another colleague, "It's an excellent process—objective and focused on measurable talent."

OUR SURVEY SAYS

Flexible and supportive

Judging by the glowing remarks insiders make about the firm's culture, it's evident that Gallup is a place where people relish coming to work. "If you fit into the culture (and you can tell within the first six months), it is the best place in the world to work. There is great accountability and high talent levels," raves one source. A colleague boasts that "great flexibility, marvelous support, employee ownership, opportunity to invent and reinvent myself are all pluses here." "Gallup's strengths-based culture makes it an extremely positive environment," claims a manager. Several sources comment on the "culture of praise and recognition" that rewards individual effort. "It is a hardworking, pay-for-performance culture that is also very fun to be a part of for motivated individuals," reports another staffer.

"The Gallup Kool-Aid"

Gallup reportedly offers a friendly and social environment that is best described as "family-like." "Having a best friend at work is encouraged, and even intra-office relationships are not discouraged," notes an insider. An analyst raves, "The people are really phenomenal—both dedicated workers and also very real about life not being work. It is fun to be around these people." Attests a happy staffer, "I have many best friends at work. I choose to socialize with people I work with. I don't try to run away from my co-workers at the end of the day. I have had numerous job offers over the years, many with higher base salary offers, but there is nowhere else where I would rather work."

Sources also claim that while it's a collegial place, Gallup is not just about group-think. "The culture embraces others and allows for difference of opinion without being detrimental," mentions one insider, while another source confirms, "It allows for individual diversity in thought and person." According to one consultant, the only downer about working at this firm is "the peculiar looks you get from friends and relatives when it becomes obvious that you've drunk the Gallup Kool-Aid."

You'll get a go-to

When it comes to management, Gallup puts its own twist on the concept. "Here we don't have managers—we have 'go-tos.' A go-to is really just a person you can go to for development, for questions or to be your advocate. There is no one micromanaging you." Assures a colleague, "it's a very mentoring relationship as opposed to authoritative," and sources seem satisfied with the way the system works. "Mine is terrific. She is my mentor and my friend and takes time to listen to me and help me, and we just enjoy being around each other," gushes a consultant. Another insider attests, "Supervisors are around mostly for support and to remove barriers to get things done. My supervisor is great."

Earn as you go

Most respondents praise Gallup's unique compensation system, which also has its own moniker. One insider details, "On top of your base salary you earn 'formax,' which is a percentage of the total revenue of any project you work on. Formax is paid out monthly, and is $3,500 to $4,500 per year for a $1 million project. Proclaims a staffer, "It is great. We have a pay-for-performance system, such that you can take on more account work and you get paid more. You can control the amount you make to a large extent." "This is the only consulting firm I know of where entry-level consultants are paid off the revenue of their client base," a manager notes.

Visit the Vault Consulting Career Channel at **www.vault.com/consulting** - with insider firm profiles, message boards, the Vault Consulting Job Board and more.

VAULT CAREER LIBRARY   267

Some consultants acknowledge there are downsides to being compensated for actual hours worked. Explains an insider, "The negative side is with a loose structure, the good people are working well over 40 hours a week, while others struggle to make 40 hours a week," while another states that formax "is the only bonus." "The only bad thing is that there are no holidays, sick time or vacation, so any time that is taken still has to average to 40 hours a week. You can take as much vacation as you want as long as you get all your work done and average 40 hours weekly," explains a D.C. source. Several insiders say the pay scheme detracts from company culture. According to one, "Everyone is always so busy working and making money there is not enough time to build team and friendships like you would like."

Despite the drawbacks, most consultants say they are thrilled with the level of independence such a system affords. "I set my own schedule. Within limits, I can earn as much or as little as I choose. No one makes me take an assignment or a project," a respondent asserts. A manager concurs, stating, "Work hours are up to you. If you want to make more money, you work on more accounts. It is the best system and is fair."

Overachievers encouraged

Gallup's pay-for-performance system encourages working as much as you can handle, which often results in long hours. "A typical day is 12 hours long," a source shares, and others indicate that typical weeks range from 55 to 60 hours. Even aside from monetary rewards, the hours don't seem to burden these folks—insiders express that the worker bees at Gallup tend to be go-getters anyway. "Gallup does a good job of promoting balance. On the other hand, our hiring tool selects for overachievers, and we are compensated largely on productivity, so there is always incentive to work harder," suggests one consultant.

Work when you want

Considering the arduous hours, work/life balance at Gallup comes in the form of flexibility with regard to work scheduling. "Although the work is extremely demanding and the hours are very, very long, we have flexible scheduling options that allow us to juggle personal demands more easily than if we worked strictly 8 to 5," comments an insider. A manager makes it look easy, claiming, "There is absolutely balance. I choose to work on the weekends, and work as much as I do because our culture is all pay for performance. You can easily balance your personal life and work life in this type of environment. Every employee knows what needs to be done and finds a way to achieve it."

Sources say that, in general, the firm is respectful of personal obligations, though many still feel a push and pull between family and work. A source remarks, "It is difficult because client needs come first and often we are working nights and weekends, even though our families need us—it is a constant struggle." Still others maintain that no one's forcing you to put in those extra hours. "The firm selects high achievers. I could work less if I chose. The nice thing is that I can leave for my kid's events in the middle of the day without a problem. I answer to my clients, not to a boss," an insider asserts.

Free agents

The firm's focus on independence in choosing projects and scheduling also applies to travel, which sources say is more of a choice than an obligation. "You get to choose which parts of the country you want to work on. Everyone is like a free agent, and you get to refuse or accept projects that you would like to work on," says a staffer. A colleague relates, "I choose accounts so I do not have to travel, but most consultants in my role travel every week."

Compared to most firms, insiders say the travel requirements at Gallup aren't too overwhelming. "It's largely driven by the person and the role. Certainly there's less travel than for an average consulting firm, but to more varied destinations, as associates could be working with quite a few different clients at any one time," a manager remarks. A colleague adds that "travel will increase the longer you are with the company. As an associate consultant I travel about once a month." He continues, "When traveling, you are still expected to be in touch with your regular clients and workload, which can be difficult, particularly at the beginning before they deem that you travel enough to warrant a laptop."

Unstructured training

Staffers claim that when it comes to learning, "most is through informal mentoring and on-the-job training," but a few insiders mention that more formal training would be appreciated. "It could improve. For the first six months, it's somewhat sink or swim," a consultant reports, while a colleague notes, "We offer a lot of client training but not enough onboard training." One respondent justifies the gaps in training by measuring the toll it would take on the bottom line: "We really do not have a lot of time for training due to client demand and our compensation—it really does not always seem a wise investment of time if it influences the paycheck too much. You really have to prioritize if you want to get training."

Women raise the roof

Insiders affirm that the door is wide open for women to step into leadership roles at Gallup. "As a feminist, I am very sensitive to the glass ceiling and women's issues. I specifically chose this firm because of the number of women in real leadership positions and the endless opportunities for women in leadership and strategic planning," a consultant asserts. A source points out that "the dean of Gallup University is a woman, and the COO of the whole organization is a woman. Women play a prominent role in this organization." And employees are proud to say that there is at least an equal number of women at Gallup Consulting, if not more. Reports a staffer, "A number of the top execs are women, and more than half of the top consultants are female."

Consultants also note that the firm is open to minority diversity, even if there is not yet equal representation. Gallup is "very open and inclusive, but the major office is in Omaha, so that tends to tilt the pool there heavily," suggests an insider. Another source notes, "I've noticed that there don't seem to be a lot of minorities in the company, but those that are here seem to have the same opportunities as everyone else." One manager remarks, "Our focus on screening for innate talents opens the doors for a lot of minority employees." And while it is respected, Gallup doesn't have special programs in place to promote diversity hiring, says a director: "Our hiring is based on talent and fit, not race. If the person is qualified to do the job they will get hired."

"A safe place to be out"

When it comes to GLBT diversity, insiders report that welcoming attitudes prevail. "As an alliance member, I was sensitive to a firm's stance on gender and orientation issues. This firm could be held up as a guide for others in this area," a consultant states. One gay employee mentions, "There are other gay people here, which is nice. It's a safe place to be out. Benefits are extended to domestic partners, even though state law doesn't require it." "I know of a few homosexual employees in our office and have not seen any discrimination against them. Their partners have been welcomed at company functions," says a colleague.

Fab facilities

Gallup sources located in the headquarters office are understandably pleased about their cushy office—"all consultants have large offices (doors and everything) with nice furniture, and there are beautiful common areas." In addition, consultants can keep fit, thanks to a fully equipped gym with "free personal trainers." Another consultant who's happy to be there gushes, "It's fantastic! I love going to the office, being at the office and showing my friends my office." Notably, parents enjoy the chance to bring their kids to work: "We have a world-class child care center on the corporate campus, which enables a family-friendly environment," a consultant says. As for other Gallup locations, insiders seem equally impressed. "My office space is wonderful; materials and equipment are excellent, clients are mostly local, facilities are posh," a St. Paul source boasts. A source from the Gallup office in Omaha states, "We have beautiful facilities" located on riverfront property, while a Chicagoan remarks, "Our firm has the nicest offices of any firm I know of. Everything is new, technology is great and everyone gets an office."

"Fried chicken Fridays"

Gallup's benefits are fairly standard, but the perks are a strong point, insiders tell us. The Omaha office provides "an excellent day care center on site, for which employees pay about $650 per child per month," and D.C. insiders love "Fried chicken Fridays," where lunch is offered, compliments of the CEO. A satisfied recipient adds, "Our CEO buys the whole office lunch every Friday and often takes everyone out to lunch on days when few people show up to the office, such as the day before Fourth

Visit the Vault Consulting Career Channel at **www.vault.com/consulting** - with insider firm profiles, message boards, the Vault Consulting Job Board and more.

VAULT CAREER LIBRARY 269

of July or the day before Christmas Eve." "We have frequent office events and outings, and share these with other offices in our region," notes a Detroit staffer. And when it comes to taking time off, the firm is characteristically flexible. "There's no vacation policy. If you need a vacation, take one. Just get your work done," a source states.

Building better communities

Gallup gets high marks for its commitment to charitable causes. "There are multiple ways of being involved and it is highly encouraged. If you believe in a cause, you can gain support here." Each office has a "community builders" program that allows employees to decide which organizations to support. "They meet once a month to hear local charities tell about their work and vote to donate money or time to each group," says an associate. A Chicago-based analyst remarks, "I think this year my city center raised $10,000 for local charities. My firm is also a major contributor to the Thurgood Marshall Foundation." Reports another Midwestern insider, "We help by filling packets of food for children in low-income areas to take home on weekends when they do not have access to in-school meal programs." A consultant in Omaha mentions that his colleagues pitch in with the "Ronald McDonald House, Special Olympics events, food shelters, community mental health programs and services for the developmentally disabled."

"The culture embraces others and allows for difference of opinion without being detrimental."

– Gallup Consulting insider

Visit the Vault Consulting Career Channel at **www.vault.com/consulting** - with insider firm
profiles, message boards, the Vault Consulting Job Board and more.

VAULT CAREER LIBRARY   271

32 Lippincott

499 Park Avenue
New York, NY 10022
Phone: (212) 521-0000
Fax: (212) 308-8952
www.lippincott.com

LOCATIONS

New York, NY (HQ)
Boston, MA
Dubai
Hong Kong
London
Paris

PRACTICE AREAS

Brand Environments
Brand Identity
Brand Management
Brand Science
Brand Strategy
Interactive Communications
Naming
Packaging Design
Sensory Branding

THE STATS

Employer Type: Subsidiary of Marsh & McLennan
  Companies, Inc., a Public Company
Ticker Symbol: MMC (NYSE)
Chairman & CEO: Ken Roberts
2006 Revenue: $1.2 billion (Oliver Wyman Group)

UPPERS

• Creative atmosphere
• Exposure to different industries

DOWNERS

• Focused on a small niche
• More brand strategy and design work than
  traditional management consulting

EMPLOYMENT CONTACT

E-mail: careers@lm.mmc.com

THE SCOOP

Mmm, mmm, good design

Lippincott's branding wizards can take credit for some of the most recognizable corporate identities in the world, from the red and white Campbell's soup can to General Mills' big "G." Formed by J. Gordon Lippincott and Walter P. Margulies in 1943, the firm is credited with revolutionizing the way consumers think about corporate identity. Through the decades, the firm has honed the art of branding and, in fact, turned it into a science, using a range of analytical approaches to help clients strengthen and develop corporate identities.

When the firm got its start, the economy was gearing up for a period of postwar prosperity, including an avalanche of new brands—and new ads to support them. With an explosion of choices for consumers, along with new media like TV, the time was right for a branding expert to come along and counsel clients on the best ways to stand out. Beginning with a focus on industrial design, Lippincott (then known as Lippincott & Margulies) branched into package design and the larger concept of "brand identity."

Brand anthropology

Taking a different approach to design than its contemporaries, the firm deployed mixed teams of experts, including engineers, artists, interior decorators and merchandising specialists, to create brands for clients. A 1965 *TIME Magazine* profile of the firm found Lippincott employing 130 people, among them psychologists, sociologists and anthropologists.

Among its early clients, Walgreen's and FTD developed their identities with Lippincott's assistance. By the mid-20th century, with a consumer culture fully in place, Lippincott thrived in an age of expanding supermarket shelves, working with clients such as Dixie, General Mills, Betty Crocker and Coca-Cola. The firm renamed a number of now-popular brands, too, including the former Cities Service Oil Co. (now CitGo) and U.S. Rubber Company (Uniroyal). In the 1960s, the firm was given a tough challenge: making the Internal Revenue Service seem more friendly and accessible to citizens. To do so, Lippincott helped simplify tax forms, rewrite standard letters from the IRS and redesign logos associated with the unpopular department.

Lippincott saw its reach expanding globally along with its clients', and by the 1970s, companies like Amtrak and American Express had begun adopting the firm's brand identity services.

Joining the MMC fold

In 1986, the firm was acquired by Marsh & McLennan Companies, a powerhouse that owns a number of related firms including Oliver Wyman, Kroll, Guy Carpenter, Marsh and Mercer. In January 2003, Lippincott brought some consultants over to the fold from sister company Mercer Management Consulting, expanding the firm's offerings in brand science and analysis. In November 2005, Lippincott formed an executive committee, made up of Chairman and CEO Ken Roberts, along with COO Suzanne Hogan and Senior Partners Connie Birdsall, Peter Dixon, Richard Wilke and Rick Wise. Lippincott has continued to thrive under the MMC umbrella as a division of Oliver Wyman. Revenue for the specialty consulting group as a whole grew by 19 percent in 2006, to $1.2 billion for the year.

With offices throughout the U.S., Europe, Asia and the Middle East, Lippincott serves a global clientele. Practice areas cover brand strategy, brand science, naming, brand identity, interactive communications, brand environments, brand management, sensory branding and package design. Recent clients include American Express, Aviva, Citigroup, Delta Air Lines, ExxonMobil, Hyatt, IBM, Mashreqbank, McDonald's, Nissan, SK, Samsung and Sprint.

To the Golden Arches and beyond

When McDonald's set out on its first major architectural overhaul of its restaurants since 1969, the fast-food giant turned to Lippincott. The firm was asked to refresh and update the "experience" of the Golden Arches' restaurants, with a focus on design

Visit the Vault Consulting Career Channel at **www.vault.com/consulting** - with insider firm profiles, message boards, the Vault Consulting Job Board and more.

273

elements appealing to young adults, while also satisfying moms and young kids. The firm used a proprietary "customer experience mapping" methodology to express McDonalds' positive attributes from the exterior of each shop all the way through the ordering area, dining room and drive-through. The design was completed for prototyping and testing in 2006, and the remodels continue to roll out with great fanfare throughout the Golden Arches' 31,000 locations.

Lippincott also developed a brand positioning and visual identity for The Bank of New York, and a logo, retail design and sensory identity system for Samsung. Hyatt used Lippincott's services to develop a brand positioning and visual identity for its leading-edge hotel concept Hyatt Place, following its acquisition of AmeriSuites. And when telecom companies Sprint and Nextel merged in 2005, Lippincott developed a new logo that visually conveyed the combined strength of both companies.

And to coincide with Delta Air Lines' emergence from bankruptcy in May 2007, Lippincott created a new brand identity, called Onward and Upward. The updated look appears in advertising, on the airline's web site, and on an increasing number of aircraft. Lippincott's efforts also extended into the planning of one of the most momentous events in Delta's history—one that approximately 5,000 employees attended and thousands of others around the world joined via live satellite feed. After Delta CEO Gerald Grinstein announced that the airline had officially emerged from its Chapter 11 restructuring, the new brand identity—applied to a Boeing 757—was unveiled for employees worldwide.

A sense for branding

For more than 50 years, Lippincott has produced a publication called *Sense*, devoted to design, research, naming and brand strategy. Its consultants produce articles on topics such as "serving the climate-conscious consumer," using strategic branding in mergers and acquisitions, and brand management on the Web. Lippincott has also worked with the publication *Chief Executive* to compile a list of the top-25 brand leaders (Steve Jobs earned the top spot in 2005).

Lippincott remains widely respected in the branding field. In 2006, the firm won an award in the *Chain Store Age* Retail Store of the Year competition for its work on designing a prototype for Infiniti dealerships in Korea. Another prototype, for a new RadioShack store, won the firm honors in the 2005 Institute of Store Planners/Visual Merchandising + Store Design International Store Design Competition. In 2004, the firm was honored by the nonprofit group Save the Children for its work on strengthening and defining the organization's brand.

GETTING HIRED

Seeking brand-savvy candidates

Lippincott doesn't actively recruit at schools, so its web site is a good place to start to find out about available opportunities. Open positions in all six offices are listed online, along with details about requirements for each. The firm says it seeks experienced consultants from a range of creative disciplines, such as brand strategy, naming, identity design, brand management and interactive communications. Candidates are invited to e-mail a resume and cover letter to careers@lm.mmc.com.

Try your hand at design

For juniors, seniors and grad students, the firm offers internships in brand identity and retail practice areas. Students in the fields of architecture, graphic, environmental, industrial, interactive or interior design, or packaging can apply for a 10- to 12-week stint contributing to projects ranging from logo design, packaging conceptualization, retail sign programs and a host of other real-world design projects. The program runs year-round and pays an $18-per-hour stipend. To apply, candidates should submit five to 10 slides of their work, along with a resume and letter to intern@lm.mmc.com.

Lippincott's branding wizards can take credit for some of the most recognizable corporate identities in the world, from the red and white Campbell's soup can to General Mills' big "G."

Visit the Vault Consulting Career Channel at **www.vault.com/consulting** - with insider firm
profiles, message boards, the Vault Consulting Job Board and more.

VAULT CAREER LIBRARY   275

444 Castro Street
Suite 600
Mountain View, CA 94041
Phone: (650) 967-2900
Fax: (650) 967-6367

1050 Winter Street
Suite 3000
Waltham, MA 02451
Phone: (781) 434-1200
Fax: (781) 647-2804
www.prtm.com

LOCATIONS

Chicago, IL • Dallas, TX • Detroit, MI • Mountain View, CA
• New York, NY • Orange County, CA • Waltham, MA •
Washington, DC • Bangalore • Frankfurt • Glasgow •
London • Munich • Paris • Shanghai • Tokyo

PRACTICE AREAS

Business Technology Innovation
Customer Experience Innovation
Operational Strategy
Product Innovation
Supply Chain Innovation

THE STATS

Employer Type: Private Company
Global Managing Director: Scott Hefter
Americas Managing Director: Michael Aghajanian
Europe Managing Director: Dean Gilmore
Asia Managing Director: James So
2007 Employees: 660
2006 Employees: 575

THE BUZZ
WHAT CONSULTANTS AT OTHER FIRMS ARE SAYING ABOUT THIS FIRM

- "Good at their niche"
- "Tedious operations work"
- "Nicest folks in the biz"
- "'One size fits all' approaches/solutions"

RANKING RECAP

Quality of Life
#1 - Relationships with Supervisors
#3 - Interaction with Clients
#4 - Overall Satisfaction
#5 - Firm Culture
#8 - Offices
#9 - Best Firms to Work For
#13 - Work/Life Balance
#17 - Compensation
#20 - Hours in the Office
#20 - Formal Training

Diversity
#5 - Diversity for Minorities
#16 - Diversity for GLBT
#17 - Best Firms for Diversity

UPPERS

- "The types of projects have become much more strategic and interesting"
- Strong mentorship program
- "PRTM works very hard to ensure you will like the people you are working with"
- "You may work twice as hard at PRTM, but you'll advance your career at five times the average rate"

DOWNERS

- Not as many perks as bigger firms
- "No clear career path for women who have children"
- "We are still somewhat of a stealth firm, so we have to work a lot harder to sell to new clients and to recruit"
- "Few social networking events"

EMPLOYMENT CONTACT

Eastern US
Attn: Recruiting
1050 Winter Street
Suite 3000
Waltham, MA 02451
Fax: (781) 466-9521
E-mail: useast@prtm.com

Western US
Attn: Recruiting
444 Castro Street
Suite 600
Mountain View, CA 94041
Fax: (650) 967-6367
E-mail: uswest@prtm.com

Other contact locations available at www.prtm.com

THE SCOOP

"Where innovation operates"

Since the firm's inception in 1976, the catchword at PRTM has been "innovation." The firm makes its mark by helping senior executives make their companies operate more efficiently. The firm focuses on doing that by improving operational strategy, supply chain, product development and customer management processes. Today, the firm has 16 offices worldwide and more than 600 employees in Bangalore, Boston, Chicago, Dallas, Detroit, Frankfurt, Glasgow, London, Munich, New York, Orange County, Paris, Shanghai, Silicon Valley, Tokyo and Washington, D.C.

While the firm may be smaller in size than some of the biggest names in the consulting industry, its reach is wide. Its clients bring problems from every corner of the corporate world, including aerospace and defense, automotive, chemicals and materials, communications and media, consumer goods, electronics and computing, energy, financial services, government, industrial products, life sciences and health care, and software. But no matter the specific industry, PRTM's goal for each engagement is the same: to make bold operational changes that will fundamentally restructure the playing field and deliver value for its clients.

The name of the game ...

Is operational strategy. PRTM believes that too many companies focus on operational improvement—working to become more competent by improving the performance of individual functions like manufacturing or development. But in most cases, says the firm, that's not enough to beat out the competition. Instead, PRTM's professionals help management consider and transform business operations that run across numerous functions, like a supply chain, in order to create shareholder value.

Companies should even think more broadly about how they compete, the firm urges. "Operational innovation," in its broadest sense, says PRTM, "alters the way you compete, creating enduring sources of business value and competitive advantage. It allows you to change the game versus having the game changed on you." PRTM's five tips for changing the game are: transform market forces or challenges into opportunities; find one thing your company can do exceptionally well; think "end-to-end"; think innovatively about your business model, not just business processes; and "execute relentlessly."

Running PRTM's operations

PRTM stands for Theodore Pittiglio, Robert Rabin, Robert Todd and Michael McGrath, the four founding partners who started the company in 1976 in Palo Alto, California. Today, all of PRTM's founding fathers have retired, the last two—Rabin and McGrath—leaving the company in 2002 and 2004, respectively, though they are certainly not forgotten. In 2004, Michael McGrath was awarded the inaugural Lifetime Achievement Award by the Product Development & Management Association. In their stead is a new global management team. Scott Hefter serves in the position of global managing director, while Michael Aghajanian is managing director of the Americas, Dean Gilmore is managing director of Europe and James So is managing director of Asia.

Benchmarking bests

To figure out how a company can improve, PRTM first takes its pulse. That's why one of the first things the firm set out to do was pioneer benchmarking studies to assess clients' product development and supply chain performance. By 1988, PRTM had used those studies to launch PACE® (Product And Cycle-time Excellence), which helps companies, particularly in technology-based industries, to gauge their "stage of process capability." The framework's premise rests on the belief that profitable growth comes from introducing the right products at the right pace. To do that, the best companies are able to upgrade related aspects of their development process at the same time, while managing to transition between different stages of capability quickly. What PACE helps companies do is measure their processes against industrywide benchmarks, such as time-to-market, schedule variance, pipeline throughput, and research and development effectiveness to pinpoint where improvements are needed.

Visit the Vault Consulting Career Channel at www.vault.com/consulting - with insider firm profiles, message boards, the Vault Consulting Job Board and more.

VAULT CAREER LIBRARY   277

In 1996, PRTM created a second tool, the Supply-Chain Operations Reference-model (SCOR), which it developed in conjunction with the Supply-Chain Council. SCOR isolates specific supply chain management processes and matches them against industry-specific best practices and benchmarking performance data so that companies know where and what they should improve. It addresses management issues at the enterprise level, rather than at the functional level, and has typically yielded a 25 to 50 percent reduction in total supply chain costs; a 25 to 60 percent increase in inventory holding; a 25 to 80 percent increase in forecast accuracy; and a 30 to 50 percent improvement in a company's order-fulfillment cycle time.

Carrying on the tradition

In 1998, PRTM rolled these performance measurement tools into a separate business, the Performance Measurement Group LLC. The subsidiary has supplied operational performance benchmarks and services to Fortune 500 manufacturers worldwide for nearly a decade. Its customized solutions encompass supply chain, product lifecycle and customer lifecycle disciplines, and are built upon an extensive collection of corporate performance benchmark databases. Ed Salley, former president of The Salley Consulting Group, joined PRTM to run PMG in March 2005.

Putting it into words

PRTM's consultants are busy people. Not only are they working on business problems for tech giants like Sun Microsystems, Inktomi, Nextel Communications, 3Com, Texas Instruments, Amersham Pharmacia Biotech and Cisco, but they are constantly publishing their ideas and perspectives in books, articles and newsletters. Recently published book titles include *Making Innovation Work: How to Manage It, Measure It, and Profit From It* (2006), *Strategic IT Portfolio Management: Governing Enterprise Transformation* (2005), *Strategic Supply Chain Management: The 5 Disciplines for Top Performance* (2005) and *Next Generation Product Development: How to Increase Productivity, Cut Costs, and Reduce Cycle Times* (2004). For the past 20 years, PRTM has also published a regular newsletter for C-level executives. Called *PRTM Insight*, the quarterly print publication highlights the firm's latest thinking and experience on global issues of concern to the C-suite.

High marks for PRTM

When PRTM execs opened the November/December 2006 issue of *Consulting Magazine*, they probably liked what they saw. That's because their firm ranked along with the likes of Bain & Company, Booz Allen Hamilton, The Boston Consulting Group and McKinsey & Company as one of the 10 Best Firms to Work For. The firm attributes some of its repeat performance in the rankings—having been named to *Consulting Magazine*'s top-10 list for five consecutive years—to its emphasis on maintaining its employees' work/life balance.

One consultant, Brian Kelly, told *Consulting Magazine* that "PRTM is a place where you will work harder than you ever have, learn more than you ever have, deliver more than you ever have and be rewarded in ways you never have." New hires like Kelly can expect to begin their careers at PRTM as consultants, then progress to associate, manager, principal and then partner levels. To make partner, PRTM says prospective employees should be willing to put in seven to nine years, during which employees are required to complete training courses in their areas of expertise.

GETTING HIRED

Seeking top-tier talent

Online, prospective PRTMers can find an application form along with "day in the life" descriptions, a list of MBA and undergrad schools from which the firm recruits and interviewing tips. The firm recruits from most of the top MBA programs, insiders say, and undergrad schools include the Ivies and top state and private universities. One source remarks that "undergraduates should note that it can be extremely difficult to secure a position at PRTM without a master's graduate degree in business, law or public policy." "We are very selective," another consultant confirms. "We look for technical depth, relevant industry experience, a proven track record of exceeding expectations and advancement. In total, we are successful in hiring top-tier talent and people who are interested in growing our business and in doing meaningful work for our clients."

The firm describes its interview process as "straightforward," a description generally echoed by insiders. "Typically there is a phone screening, followed by a phone interview and then a decision-round interview with directors. The emphasis here is on knowledge, skills and experience, not on theoretical case studies," says a source, who adds, "I find this pragmatic approach to be consistent with the way that we do business; we are not just in search of book-smart people here—you have to be able to communicate and to deliver big changes in our clients' organizations (this is true of junior and senior staff)." Since the firm hires with the idea that everyone has the potential to be a director, another source emphasizes that "fit" is critical. As another puts it, "The first interview is a phone interview. Then there is an in-person interview and after that an in-office interview with five different partners. One of the unique features of our process is that only partners interview for the final round, as we hire with the hope that the people we hire will stay for a career."

Get an inside line

Due to the firm's highly selective bent, one source advises that "applicants should first span their network to build a relationship, with a current employee, if possible, as a way to have an internal advocate. Most of the new hires are internal referrals," adding, "Directors are very personable and take sincere interest in applicants' professional experiences, as well as personal interests and hobbies outside of work."

No training for cases

Most sources agree that case questions are rare, if not nonexistent in PRTM interviews. "We are able to get a sense of a candidate's problem-solving abilities and thought processes without them," explains an insider. "Generally, we don't like cases and focus more on experiences and culture fit. Cases can poorly correlate to actual capabilities, particularly since most MBAs and undergrads can train for cases," says another source. "We're not fans of abstract case studies. That said, most interviewers at PRTM will definitely probe a candidate's real-life experience that's relevant to the work we do for our clients. Think of it as a real-life case study ... To be successful in our interviews, the candidate needs to clearly articulate how he's succeeded in solving problems and transforming operations in manners similar to the way we do it," a consultant tells us. Still, a colleague reports, "I was asked a 'soft' case about some initial steps I would take to outsource a pharmaceutical company's manufacturing capability. It didn't involve any numbers and was generally more to test my industry knowledge and understanding of a very real potential client issue."

Some PRTMers report having served as summer associates and going on to become full-fledged consultants. "I was given responsibility based on my experience, which led to a fruitful summer and the acceptance of a full-time job," says a source of his summer associate experience. According to another consultant, "My summer internship at PRTM was the reason that I joined the firm. I was immediately placed on a client project and was expected to contribute. My colleagues, who came from across the United States, were wonderful to work with and helped me come up to speed on consulting."

OUR SURVEY SAYS

A fit with the family

Nice guys (and gals) finish first at PRTM, which boasts a "small, personable culture" where "there is no place for arrogance," insiders say. Since "we view every consultant we hire as a potential partner in the firm," a source explains, "we truly want people to have meaningful careers at the firm." A colleague elaborates: "PRTM's culture is truly unique among management consulting firms. Its cherished family-like environment reflects the fact that most new hires are referrals of current PRTM consultants. At PRTM, the right fit is essential."

Visit the Vault Consulting Career Channel at **www.vault.com/consulting** - with insider firm profiles, message boards, the Vault Consulting Job Board and more.

VAULT CAREER LIBRARY   279

In addition, teamwork is crucial and consultants typically work in small groups with a director on all engagements. "Everyone, regardless of level, is seen as a key contributor and team member—hierarchy is not a focus," and there's a "continual use of 'we' and great support from colleagues at all levels," insiders say. This leads to "the antithesis of a political work environment," along with "great laughs among a group of people who collectively like to get things done and applaud the results achieved," sources exclaim.

The burnout stops here

Many staffers tell us their firm looks out for work/life balance in order to maximize retention. "PRTM directors appreciate that consultants have a life outside of their consulting career and work closely with them to maintain work/life balance. In fact, I have been told in the past to not work so hard because the director group wants me to be at PRTM for the long run and not to burn out," one consultant says. Agrees a co-worker, "With our low consultant-to-director ratio, the burnout model simply wouldn't work."

Another insider mentions, "I still have time for my family, for exercise and for social events," adding, "Another testament to this is the large numbers of our consulting staff who are married and have children. It is critical to have at least some work/life balance to maintain an active family life. The firm definitely takes an interest in staff work/life balance—new parents are staffed close to home, and traveling staff usually have the chance to be home with their families on Thursday nights."

This doesn't mean PRTMers have it easy; in fact, consultants report clocking some brutal workweeks, with one source reporting, "On a regular basis, 15-plus hour days are the norm as you move up in the ranks." With an average workweek of 55 to 70 hours, another insider complains that "too many additional assignments are required in addition to being 100 percent billable to clients. There is talk about limiting chargeability at certain levels, but this does not happen." "I typically spend about 50 hours a week on client work and 10 hours on internal, nonclient work," another source reports.

And while PRTMers are willing to put in the hours, they generally find that they have weekends to themselves. "I only find that it is necessary to work a few weekends a year, usually under special circumstances. On occasions where I've had to put in very heavy workweeks, the directors have allowed me to take a long weekend without using vacation days (as a reward)," a consultant shares. According to a co-worker, "I find that I usually work very hard from Monday to Thursday (14 hours a day), and take it a bit easier on Friday. Weekend work is an exception." Assignment lengths vary, insiders tell us, but a source in the government and public-sector practice notes, "Our projects are longer than those of the average commercial client."

Flying for four

Travel at PRTM is a standard expectation, insiders tell us. "Being at our clients' offices is part of the work that we do. Normally, I travel Monday to Thursday every week," says a source. "In order to effect change for our clients, we need to be on site. This can mean travel, but it will be regional, due to our regional staffing policy," a colleague adds. One consultant remarks that there's "not a lot of forward thinking" at PRTM about travel-easing options like telecommuting or two-day site visits, contending that travel is "not necessarily correlated to client needs, just an assumption that everyone will travel Monday through Thursday."

On the government side, travel tends to be limited to the Greater D.C. area, a source reports, but "international/domestic travel can be requested by consultants in the government practice to foster growth and development. Since PRTM is a global firm, it can make these professional opportunities in the private sector possible."

Satisfactory salaries

PRTM features a compensation structure that's "designed to maximize collaboration and minimize competition within the firm," says an insider, who adds, "Judging from the firm's record of success over the past 30 years, we're on to something—it's an environment where everybody celebrates the firm's successes, and the top performers still receive recognition for their extraordinary contributions." While another source claims that "year-on-year salary increases could be better," he adds, "I'm in this for the quality of the firm and culture, which I highly value, instead of the incremental $10K I'd get each year at other firms with lower-quality people and culture." A colleague offers the bottom line: "My friends at other firms make more money than I do. They don't like their job as much as I do, though." Consultants also benefit from PRTM's profit sharing, which is vested in a 401(k) plan.

As for extras, one source contends that "PRTM isn't particularly perk-laden, but the basics are there: good insurance, vacation and holidays." The source muses, "I suspect that the firm believes that each consultant is the best individual judge of what's best or most highly valued from a prerequisite standpoint. Rather than blow a bunch of money to give everybody the same perks, the firm chooses instead to pay folks as much as it can, and let them decide what to do with the money. That's the best perk of all, from my standpoint." Other perks include full coverage for pursuing an MBA, and several staffers cite PRTM's regional firm retreats, in places like Arizona resorts and Disney World. "We celebrated our 30th anniversary this [past] year with an all-expense-paid weekend at a five-star spa with spouses. In three days, we only had one, three-hour work meeting. Not bad," an insider muses. And PRTMers appreciate the firm's annual gift of a case of fine wine at holiday time.

Paternity benefits are slim, we're told, with no additional time off granted for dads. One source reports, though, that "the firm is almost always able to staff consultants on local projects around the time they are having a child. In addition, consultants are able to take an extended leave of absence if they want to spend extra time at home during this period."

New and improved offices

PRTM's offices are described by one insider as "nice but not over the top, which would not reflect PRTM's values. They are in good locations, good buildings and have the services and space required." A colleague elaborates, "We have nice cubicles for consultants that are set up for hoteling, and small conference rooms used for private meetings. Partners have their own private offices." Several new offices are in the works, sources say, and a consultant reports that "PRTM has invested significantly in upgrading its offices in the last few years, with nearly every office moving and/or receiving significant upgrades. Today's offices are wonderful in their appointments, space and design."

Accessible directors

Because of PRTM's "flat" structure, "directors (partners/owners) are immediately accessible to all staff. They are roll-up-the-sleeves people, and work together on the tough problems side by side with the consultants," an insider observes. Agrees a consultant, "Our low consultant-to-partner ratio (4:1), combined with the fact that our partners spend significant time working on client engagements, allows consultants to interact regularly with partners. There are plenty of opportunities to learn from senior leaders in the firm." "At PRTM, I have never had a bad experience with my superiors," another source chimes in. "My responsible director is heavily involved with my career development, and helps to get me staffed on jobs that will expand my capabilities." And "I was amazed at the level of responsibility I was given soon after joining the firm," recalls a colleague. "PRTM really treats its consultants as full-blown members of the consulting team, not just as analysts. Directors and principals will push you to take on client-facing situations with people all the way up to the C-suite if you prove up to the challenge." Another staffer suggests that "one of the unique aspects of life at PRTM relative to other firms" is the fact that "we hire folks that communicate in a boardroom, as well as in a client project-team meeting. It's challenging, variable and exciting."

"Career yoga"

Because of the immediate access consultants have to top management, "On-the-job training and mentoring are the most common forms of development," an insider reports, adding, "Each consultant is assigned a partner that is responsible for his/her development. Consultants meet regularly (at least quarterly) with these advisors to review career development plans and to discuss any special requests that a consultant may have regarding his/her career path." "We are also staffed strategically to help push our limits and build our experience; my director recently referred to this style as 'career yoga,' which stretches staff in new directions and builds executional muscle," a consultant explains.

As for formal training, "PRTM provides a formal training catalog to support professional development of consultants that ranges from enhancing soft skills critical to a successful consulting career and training focused on building subject matter expertise," a

Visit the Vault Consulting Career Channel at **www.vault.com/consulting** - with insider firm profiles, message boards, the Vault Consulting Job Board and more.

VAULT CAREER LIBRARY   281

source tells us. As another insider puts it, "Training has improved considerably over the past two years. Official training at various consultant levels across the firm is not a bogged down process of full-day, obligatory meetings. Rather, training occurs throughout the year in informal settings and around pertinent topics. Participants attend because they find the content to be worthwhile, and can either attend in person or via conference call."

Mentoring women

When it comes to women at the firm, PRTM is "very receptive in terms of hiring, promoting and mentoring." One insider claims, "There are no flexible policies for women who have children. A number of women have left the firm once they have had kids (but are still working elsewhere)." However, in recent years the firm has implemented practices to help employees maintain balance between personal and professional priorities. Examples include offering flexible schedules, local project assignments, customized professional development programs and extended leaves of absence. A colleague reports that "PRTM is committed to hiring more women and promoting them to leadership positions. A number of women's mentoring programs have been formed to ensure that women have a support system throughout their tenure at PRTM." "The best evidence is the fact that the number of female partners who have progressed through all levels in the firm is substantial and growing," adds an insider.

PRTMers don't have much to say about minorities at their firm, but one insider insists that "PRTM does not differentiate employees in terms of race, religion or sex. To me, this is a higher sign of respect than firms that begin all types of support programs—that just isn't necessary in our environment." Other sources describe the firm as "very international," noting that "staff meetings are like the United Nations: almost an equal mix of Americans, Europeans, Asians, Indians and Hispanics." Generally, sources agree that gay, lesbian, bisexual and transgender issues are "never discussed," but as one insider puts it, "I wouldn't see where it would be a problem."

Community service at PRTM is "typically local office based," but enjoys "overall company support," staffers say. One consultant explains, "We have always been active in our communities and participate in a variety of ways, some at the regional level and others at the office level. Examples include donations to food shelters, Walk for Hunger and cancer research. In 2006, we launched the Make an Impact program to formalize and support all local and international efforts. The results were beyond expectations and so the program will continue to build and strengthen in 2007. Currently, the Boston office is leading an effort to promote renewable energy via carbon offsetting."

"Everyone, regardless of level, is seen as a key contributor and team member— hierarchy is not a focus."

– *PRTM consultant*

Visit the Vault Consulting Career Channel at **www.vault.com/consulting** - with insider firm
profiles, message boards, the Vault Consulting Job Board and more.

VAULT CAREER LIBRARY   283

5 Times Square
New York, NY 10036
Phone: (212) 931-7300
Fax: (212) 931-7310
www.giulianipartners.com

LOCATION

New York, NY (HQ)

PRACTICE AREAS

Corporate Security
Corporate Strategy
Crisis Management
Emergency Preparedness
Financial Management
Private Equity
Public Safety
Risk Assessment & Mitigation

THE STATS

Employer Type: Private Company
Chairman & CEO: Rudolph Giuliani
2006 Employees: 60
2005 Employees: 55

UPPER

• Elite, high-profile firm

DOWNER

• The big guy has bigger plans

EMPLOYMENT CONTACT

Phone: (212) 931-7300
E-mail: info@giulianipartners.com

THE BUZZ
WHAT CONSULTANTS AT OTHER FIRMS ARE SAYING ABOUT THIS FIRM

• "Small and selective"
• "Not all that organized"
• "Great brand, noble mission"
• "Connected, that's all"

THE SCOOP

Yes, that Giuliani

Giuliani Partners doesn't lack name recognition: The New York City-based firm has a branding advantage, thanks to the name of its founder, former two-term NYC Mayor and Republican presidential candidate Rudolph Giuliani. Though the public is familiar with Rudy's rep as a tough politician and attorney, he's also earned his stripes in the consulting arena, having been named *Consulting Magazine*'s Consultant of the Year in 2002, the year of the firm's founding.

Formed through a strategic alliance with Ernst & Young, Giuliani Partners drew on the former mayor's street cred to carve out a niche for itself in the areas of corporate strategy, security, emergency preparedness and crisis management. In late 2004, the firm announced the formation of I-banking subsidiary Giuliani Capital Advisors, along with the acquisition of Ernst & Young's corporate finance division. Said to bring in $4 million a month in revenue, the subsidiary was rumored to be up for sale in early 2007, coinciding with Rudy Giuliani's bid for the Republican presidential nomination.

A powerful crowd

From the start, Giuliani Partners was able to assemble a stable of high-profile experts in security and other lines of business, many of whom boast career ties with the former mayor. Michael D. Hess, who serves as senior managing director and helped found the firm, is an attorney who has represented the U.S. in some major cases, including The Pentagon Papers case against *The New York Times*. Joseph Volpe, who joined the firm in August 2006, served as the director of the Metropolitan Opera for 16 years. In March 2005, Pasquale J. D'Amuro, a 26-year veteran of the FBI and noted counterterrorism expert, was named CEO of the firm's security and safety division. Other heavyweights at Giuliani Partners include Thomas Von Essen, former commissioner of the New York City Fire Department; Richard Sheirer, former Emergency Management commissioner and director of New York City Homeland Security; Daniel Connolly, former special counsel to the Corporation Counsel of the City of New York; Laurence Levy, former deputy counsel to Mayor Giuliani; Maureen Casey, former deputy commissioner of the New York City Police Department; and Christopher Rising, former inspector and counsel to the police commissioner. One notorious name no longer on Giuliani Partners' personnel list is former New York City Police Commissioner Bernard Kerik, who left in December 2004 when a scandal surfaced after he was nominated to head up the Department of Homeland Security.

Rudy's baggage

Giuliani Partners has had to contend with some negative buzz over the years, some of which has been dragged back out into the press, thanks to its founder's presidential bid. A January 2007 Associated Press article argued that a Giuliani candidacy would require him to "revamp the global businesses that bear his name." The article cited Giuliani's ties to the energy and drug industries, along with his sometimes-rocky personal life, noting, "even his baggage has baggage."

One sticky situation for the firm involved Los Angeles-based Applied DNA Sciences, which tapped Giuliani Partners for advice on marketing the company's DNA marking technology. Unfortunately for Giuliani Partners, the company, which created a way to use DNA technology for fraud-protection and anticounterfeit services, had a questionable financial profile, including annual losses, no cash for operations and no customers, according to SEC documents. A March 2005 *USA Today* article raised questions about the firm, noting that Applied DNA had been led by Richard Langley Jr., who had been barred by the SEC from certain types of trading because he had allegedly been involved in a stock scam. Shortly after the article appeared, Giuliani Partners ended its relationship with Applied DNA. Another troubled former client of Giuliani Partners, We the People USA, maker of do-it-yourself legal documents, was notorious for alleged deceptive practices, having been sued numerous times and slapped with a fine by the Federal Trade Commission. Giuliani ended its relationship with We the People in early 2005.

The firm has worked with other publicly unpopular clients, including the Indian Point nuclear power plant in Buchanan, N.Y., and TransCanada Corporation and Shell US Gas & Power Company's Broadwater project, a proposed offshore liquefied natural gas facility on Long Island Sound. In April 2005, the firm published a report, commissioned by the Pharmaceutical Research

Visit the Vault Consulting Career Channel at www.vault.com/consulting - with insider firm profiles, message boards, the Vault Consulting Job Board and more.

VAULT CAREER LIBRARY   285

and Manufacturers of America, calling for an immediate moratorium on drug importation legislation, citing homeland security as a concern.

Cleanup crew

In January 2004, the firm collaborated with Sabre Technical Services, the company that developed technology for anthrax cleanups and provides decontamination services, to form a venture called Bio-ONE, which specializes in biological and chemical preparedness, response and remediation. Through Bio-ONE, the partners rolled out Sabre's chloride dioxide gas delivery technology to kill bio-organisms. The company was hired to scour the anthrax-laced American Media Inc. building in Boca Raton, the first facility found to be contaminated during the bioterrorism threats in 2001. So confident was Giuliani Partners of its process, the firm declared its intention to set up shop in the former AMI building when the process was completed. However, following a contract dispute, another decontamination firm took over the project in 2005, and any plans for a Giuliani Partners tenancy seemed unlikely. Bio-ONE continues to work on other decontamination projects, including the cleanup of some New Orleans buildings after Hurricane Katrina.

Investing in security

In February 2007, online financial site TheStreet.com published an analysis of the portfolio of companies Giuliani Partners has worked with over the years, as part of a larger look at the financial ties of the 2008 presidential contenders. The companies, from a list compiled by another financial site, Stockpickr.com, include those that the firm has "some relationship" with, but is not necessarily a list of its current client base. Among these companies are well-known firms like US Airways, Sprint Nextel and Aon, as well as lower-profile, "small cap" names. The latter list of smaller companies reveals a definite bias toward security issues. One client, Ecosphere Technologies, has developed an advanced water filtration system of interest to homeland security wonks, as it reportedly is capable of decontaminating a water system following a terrorist attack. Other small firms advised by Giuliani Partners include Command Security, which provides security, aviation and support security services to U.S.-based private and governmental clients, and Argyle Security Acquisition, a "blank check company" in the business of buying up security-related firms.

GETTING HIRED

Who do you know?

Giuliani Partners probably isn't going to be setting up card tables at campus recruiting events any time soon. The firm's cast of elite characters is pretty tight—and with no publicly available information on hiring at the firm, it's likely that your best bet of getting in the door is befriending an insider (or wielding plenty of influence on your own).

The New York City-based firm has a branding advantage, thanks to the name of its founder, former two-term NYC Mayor and Republican presidential candidate Rudolph Giuliani.

Visit the Vault Consulting Career Channel at www.vault.com/consulting - with insider firm profiles, message boards, the Vault Consulting Job Board and more.

VAULT CAREER LIBRARY   287

35 LECG

2000 Powell Street
Suite 600
Emeryville, CA 94608
Phone: (510) 985-6700
www.lecg.com

LOCATIONS

Emeryville, CA (HQ)
34 offices in 10 countries

PRACTICE AREAS

Antitrust & Competition Policy
Bankruptcy & Restructuring
Claims Services
Electronic Discovery
Finance, Valuation & Damages
Forensic Accounting
Healthcare & Life Sciences
Intellectual Property
Labor & Employment
Property Insurance Claims
Public Policy
Securities
Strategy & Performance Improvement
Transfer Pricing

THE STATS

Employer Type: Public Company
Ticker Symbol: XPRT (Nasdaq)
Chairman: David J. Teece
2007 Employees: 1,000+
2006 Employees: 810
2006 Revenue: $353.9 million
2005 Revenue: $286.7 million

RANKING RECAP

Practice Area
#5 - Economic Consulting (tie)

UPPER

• "Flexible working hours"

DOWNER

• "Your experience can depend very much on who your manager is"

EMPLOYMENT CONTACT

Go to the careers page of the firm's web site

THE BUZZ
WHAT CONSULTANTS AT OTHER FIRMS ARE SAYING ABOUT THIS FIRM

• "Prestigious economic consulting firm"
• "Significant internal competition"
• "Heady; academic"
• "Siloed"

THE SCOOP

California's know-it-alls

Need some backup in the courtroom? Looking for help in proving your point? Then call on LECG. The Emeryville, Calif.-based firm and its wholly owned subsidiary, LECG, LLC, provide independent expert testimony and analysis and litigation support to a wide range of public and private companies and organizations. Whether their clients are based in Nashville or Auckland, the firm aims to help resolve complex disputes and inform legislative, judicial, regulatory and business decision makers.

LECG's consultants testify on behalf of corporations, law firms, and local, state and federal government agencies in the U.S. and around the world that are involved in a number of different industries like energy, health care or telecommunications. Its consulting services also run the gamut from antitrust and competition policy and bankruptcy issues, to finance and damages, intellectual property, labor and employment, mergers and acquisitions, and securities. LECG experts frequently testify before agencies throughout the world on matters such as antitrust liability, damage assessment and cartel investigations.

When LECG professionals are not in court, they are busy writing in-depth, authoritative studies and providing strategic consulting services for their clients, which include big names like Dow Chemical and New England Power.

Teece time

LECG got its start back in March 1988, when a group of faculty members from the University of California at Berkeley decided to start their own expert advisory firm to help businesses and government agencies resolve commercial disputes. Today, the firm engages with Global Fortune 500 clients in over 30 countries and that small group of researchers and experts has grown to a talent pool of professionals nearly 900-strong. The firm went public on the Nasdaq in 2003.

One of those Berkeley brains was New Zealander Dr. David J. Teece, whom the New Zealand government calls an "economic rock star" and who was recognized in 2002 as one of the United States' Top 50 Business Intellectuals by Accenture for his research in the field of corporate strategy and innovation. In addition to his chairmanship at LECG, Teece wears a number of other important hats. He is the Mitsubishi Bank professor of international business and finance at the University of California at Berkeley's Haas School of Business and director of the Institute of Management, Innovation and Organization. When he's not testifying or teaching, Teece can be found directing the Atlas Family of Mutual Funds. Teece has also been called on to testify before Congress on regulatory policy and competition policy, and has authored over 200 books and articles and edited one of the industry's mainstay publications, *Industry and Corporate Change*.

Teece's mark on innovation

The doctor's big claim to fame? The Teece Model. Known for his studies on corporate strategy and innovation, Teece set about trying to figure out who ultimately profits from an innovation. He found that two factors determine the answer to that question: imitability, or how easily competitors can copy or duplicate the technology or process that underlies an innovation, and complementary assets. One company might come up with an innovative product or service, but if it can't protect its innovation from being duplicated, another competing company may come along with a better set of complementary assets (i.e., a better-known brand name or distribution channels) and walk away with the ultimate benefits of the innovation. So, if imitability is high and complementary assets are easy to find or unimportant, it will be hard to make money off of an innovation.

Six degrees of connection

One of the ways LECG maintains its ties to so many different industries and can testify on so many different subject areas is that it allows its experts to often hold positions with other organizations, such as universities or research labs. Whether they are industry professionals, academics, former senior government officials or consultants, most of LECG's senior professionals—like

Visit the Vault Consulting Career Channel at www.vault.com/consulting - with insider firm profiles, message boards, the Vault Consulting Job Board and more.

VAULT CAREER LIBRARY   289

Teece himself—wear more than one hat. The catch: Compensation is based on performance, so there's no paycheck until the client is happy.

Behind the scenes teams

Most projects LECG consultants deal with—whether they be business, management or litigation projects—often involve market analyses of business options and competition, estimating the financial and pricing impacts of courses of conduct and placing values on unique assets like intellectual property rights. Some examples of projects include studying the impact of a merger, or the effect of financial or environmental damage on another private party or society overall.

Most of the pretrial work at LECG goes on inside LECG's offices in teams. Each team tackling a particular problem is made up of directors and principals—the "experts"—as well as senior staff and researchers, including research analysts and associates. Everyone has their own ingredient to throw into the mix: Directors and principals typically have the most experience, coming from high up in the academic food chain, hailing from government jobs or leading industry and consulting positions. Then there is the senior staff, most of whom hold PhDs, master's degrees or other advanced degrees and certifications. And supporting the team effort is the research staff, with its cumulative expertise in economics, finance, accounting, business, statistics or other areas. The researchers do most of the fact-finding groundwork for each testimony or study, collecting and analyzing trade press, academic research, market intelligence, statistical and economic data, and client records, among other resources.

Doing a little of its own M&A

While its consultants help other firms deal with mergers and acquisitions, LECG has had to do a little of its own merging and acquiring and hiring in recent years. In October 2006, the firm announced the addition of 12 director-level experts, while just two months prior in August, LECG expanded its electronic discovery practice to Europe, installing a new electronic discovery director in its London office. In May 2006, LECG announced plans to acquire nearly all the operating assets of expert services firm BMB Mack Barclay, Inc., and its offices in San Diego and Costa Mesa, Calif., for $13.2 million. The acquisition followed the December 2005 purchases of Beach & Company International, a Houston-based expert services firm, and Lancaster Consulting, which provides business valuation, litigation and management consulting. Together, the two firms set LECG back $2 million.

GETTING HIRED

Strap on your econ gear

When competing for the firm's coveted analyst positions, LECG applicants stomach double doses of interrogation. The first round brings about a basic screening "with a few questions pertaining to economic concepts." In the second half, case studies line the daylong affair, where prospective LECGers encounter "five or six half-hour sessions with different employees"—including research analysts, senior consultants and experts. To adequately prepare for the day's events, applicants should start "by getting super comfortable with case studies and focus on economics," an analyst reports, since the firm requires a timed study "with a written analysis and presentation." Before day's end, interviewees meet with a senior principal or director to gauge fit with LECG's culture.

OUR SURVEY SAYS

Workaholics anonymous

More than anything, staffers describe LECG's culture as "analytically intense" and "intellectually challenging"; the firm is a place where "accuracy is golden" and "errors do not slide," which has analysts working themselves to the bone and their deliverables to perfection. A site for experts, precision and technological savvy, LECG is a "fast-growing firm with lot of advancement opportunities," and encourages teamwork. Analysts have the chance to work on numerous cases, "each developing different skills and introducing you to a different body of knowledge," a facet that makes learning on the job an inherent part of the experience. The company's various practice groups, for the most part, dictate individual pay, hour and promotion timetables, but despite separation, all analysts, working in small teams, gain the "advantage of working next to brilliant people who could be your peers, juniors and especially your supervisors."

Lucky for LECG's busy staffers, "everybody helps out and the atmosphere is really friendly," we're told. The dress code and social culture stay relaxed when possible; insiders enjoy Friday pizza gatherings, monthly events and wine tasting, and the firm's young, culturally diverse co-workers step outside the office for "relatively frequent parties, happy hours, etc." As one source explains, LECG "is a great place to work if you thrive in small, collegial environments." For economics-oriented people looking to work at a consulting firm with "shorter hours and less travel than traditional management consultancies," associates claim that LECG's the champ.

Clocking time

During especially hectic case periods, analysts say "workweeks can spike to 60 or 70 hours a week," often bringing weekends into the picture. Standard office hours vary, "but leaving at 7 p.m. feels early," one source relates, "and leaving after 11 p.m. definitely happens"—10- to 14-hour work stretches aren't daily occurrences, but "everybody works hard, though, so it is not out of place," we're told. While it's not hard for LECGers to fulfill their required 40-hour client billables each week, staffers do claim that the firm's hourly structure can be flexible, providing allowances to work off site or from home, if necessary.

Boost it up

Scoring the firm's salary as "decent," insiders say that "the pay is slightly lower than my peers at LECG's competitors, but not by too much," and bonuses could use a little sprucing. "Year-end bonuses were nearly nonexistent last year," an analyst reports, though stock benefits, quarterly boosts and education allowances help. To further balance out compensation discrepancies, sources note that they work fewer hours and receive more vacation time (three weeks) than their competitors.

Visit the Vault Consulting Career Channel at **www.vault.com/consulting** - with insider firm profiles, message boards, the Vault Consulting Job Board and more.

VAULT CAREER LIBRARY 291

Kurt Salmon Associates

1355 Peachtree Street, NE
Suite 900
Atlanta, GA 30309
Phone: (404) 892-0321
Fax: (404) 898-9590
www.kurtsalmon.com

LOCATIONS

Atlanta, GA (HQ)
25 offices worldwide

PRACTICE AREAS

Consumer Products Division
Business & Brand Growth
Global Sourcing & Manufacturing
Logistics & Distribution
Merchandise Planning
Merchandise Technology
Private Equity
Product Development
Retail Operations
Supply Chain Technology
Health Care Division
Facilities Services
Information Technology Services
Strategy Services
KSA Capital Advisors® — Corporate Finance

THE STATS

Employer Type: Private Company
CEO: William B. Pace
2007 Employees: 600
2006 Employees: 600

RANKING RECAP

Quality of Life
#12 - Work/Life Balance (tie)
#14 - Firm Culture

UPPERS

- "If you are a high performer, they will do as much as they can to retain you"
- Work with well-known clients
- "Flat leverage model ensures daily collaboration with partners"

DOWNERS

- "A rather segmented firm; even entry-level consultants soon specialize in one capability area"
- Very little input on staffing decisions
- "Few processes—always reinventing the wheel"

EMPLOYMENT CONTACT

Americas
www.kurtsalmon.com/content/main/body/careers/
opportunities/body.htm

Asia-Pacific
E-mail: recrAPAC@kurtsalmon.com

Europe
E-mail: recrEU@kurtsalmon.com

THE BUZZ
WHAT CONSULTANTS AT OTHER FIRMS ARE SAYING ABOUT THIS FIRM

- "Specialized, reputable"
- "Very traditional in approach"
- "When it comes to retail, there is no one better"
- "Flying under the radar"

THE SCOOP

The little Salmon that could

It is difficult to imagine that Kurt Salmon, a German immigrant and textile engineer, could have foreseen the modern-day Kurt Salmon Associates when he founded the company in the basement of his Washington, D.C., home in 1935. In the firm's 70-plus-year history, it has grown into a leading provider of retail and health care consulting and corporate financial services, helping clients develop and implement a broad range of solutions. KSA, headquartered in Atlanta, Ga., operates 25 offices throughout North America, Europe and Asia.

Store savvy

KSA boasts an extensive roster of retail clients, from Nike to Nordstrom to grocery chains and seemingly everyone in between. The firm provides five main areas of retail consulting services: business growth, inventory efficiency, margin management, productivity improvement and technology effectiveness. In turn, a typical Kurt Salmon project will simultaneously provide solutions in a number of these areas. For example, in January 2007, the firm guided Nordstrom through the acquisition of the Jeffrey men's clothing shops in Atlanta and New York City. Jeffrey founder Jeffrey Kalinsky was brought onboard as Nordstrom's director of designer merchandising; the deal allowed Kalinsky to remain chief executive of his company and, at the same time, enabled Nordstrom to add a prestigious chain of stores to its list of holdings and make a valuable hire in an area in which it had been performing below expectations.

KSA has been instrumental in the implementation of several technologies in the retail industry. The firm integrates human resources and IT solutions into its practice through strategic alliances with a number of leading HR software companies, including Oracle, SAS and RedPrairie. Additionally, the firm was a vocal proponent of the implementation of radio frequency identification tags, which aid retail clothing and shoe stores by enhancing inventory management and loss prevention capabilities.

A healthy business

KSA's health care business has grown steadily over the last two decades, as the firm acquired Hamilton Associates in 1986, Healthcare Mangement Counselors in 1997 and Space Diagnostics in 2000. In June 2006, the firm merged with Philadelphia-based Katz Consulting Group, and KSA Healthcare now operates from five offices throughout the United States. KSA's health care clients range from large multihospital systems to smaller physician group practices. The firm provides management advisory services in facility planning, strategy and information technology, and boasting over 50 years of experience, the firm advises on everything from the location and design of a new hospital, to inefficiencies in patient care, to marketing initiatives and HR software solutions. Kurt Salmon health care consultants have worked with all of the top-20 hospitals on *U.S. News & World Report*'s America's Best Hospitals list for 2006, and are currently engaged in helping New Jersey hospitals, 51 percent of which are operating at a deficit due to reductions in government funding and Medicare contributions.

Salmon knows shoppers

KSA publishes a wealth of market research analyzing buyer behavior and shopping trends. The firm regularly issues *Soft Goods Outlook*, which highlights the current and future status of the soft goods industry (anything you wear or carry) and also conducts surveys gauging how much and where shoppers plan to spend at a specific time. When the news reports the fiscal results of the annual Black Friday shopping frenzy, for instance, the data is frequently drawn from a Kurt Salmon report. Other publications include *KSA Connections*, which highlights and analyzes the firm's recent work in all areas of its businesses, and *KSA Outlook*, which is designed for leaders in the health care industry. Recent topics have included the management of health care construction projects and the strategic aspects of physician employment at community hospitals.

Visit the Vault Consulting Career Channel at www.vault.com/consulting - with insider firm profiles, message boards, the Vault Consulting Job Board and more.

VAULT CAREER LIBRARY   293

GETTING HIRED

A test-taker's paradise

Before applicants get too excited, the firm's potential superstars should know that their test-taking days aren't over—"KSA requires consultant-level candidates to take and pass two logic tests before first-round interviews," one staffer shares, which disqualify weaklings from moving forward in the undoubtedly rigorous process. For undergrads at institutions like Stanford, Emory, Columbia, Georgia Tech, UVA and UC Berkeley, firm recruiters appear on campus to conduct interviews in pairs with the best and brightest—sessions chock full of case and fit questions. Once through the first round, contenders undergo three to five in-office interviews with senior leadership, which include "a second case, a team skills interview and a case presentation," we're told. And personality matters, too; though "not weighted as highly as the analytical tests," fitting in with Kurt Salmon consultants isn't a component to take lightly.

OUR SURVEY SAYS

Band of brothers (and sisters)

According to consultants, KSA thrives in the culture department. Peers are "tight-knit, friendly, approachable" and, if that's not enough, "the people I work with are some of the most intelligent that I've ever met," an associate gushes. Work takes on a family feel, pulling colleagues together and snuffing out any traces of a cutthroat mentality. As a firm devoted to results and a flat hierarchical structure, one insider boasts of KSA as "the most unique and special working culture I've ever seen," with consultants and principals seamlessly mingling and bonding. This team-oriented model has sources claiming that "the culture is the best part about KSA."

Take what you can carry

Having a buddy system among junior- and senior-level staffers does its share in boosting responsibility at the firm; since "the principals and managers are always willing to share their knowledge and give feedback," consultants have an easier time managing the liability-heavy tasks thrown their way. Staffers work directly with clients regardless of employee level, which helps create substantial "responsibilities very early in your career" with top-tier clients. "I've led client engagements, played a very substantial role in our recruiting and managed significant work streams," an insider shares. And for Kurt Salmon's high performers, we're told, supervisors dole out plenty of praise, which helps cement already collegial relationships.

It's all about proportion

Aside from some excessive workweeks, KSA employees aren't overwhelmed by their office hours. Insiders say the "work hours are great for the most part" and, though toiling often depends on the project and management team, "it also depends on if you take control of your own balance." Despite general satisfaction, several senior staffers warn about bipolar workloads: "Life is either well in or way out of balance, depending on the project and the project manager/principal," one remarks, and another acknowledges "times where work/life balance has spun out of control on certain projects."

Even so, sources say managers keep an eye out to ensure a fair balance for their consultants, and "are very understanding and willing to accommodate your schedule." Taking flexibility into consideration, some peers use KSA's focus on equilibrium to self-manage; as one adds, "I use this flexibility to work half-day Fridays and add the extra time on the weekend."

Lightening the load

At KSA, consultant-level employees are the traveling heavyweights. While practice areas determine client-visiting frequency, staffers are away four days per week, on average, adhering to a Monday through Thursday agenda. For the most part, sources don't seem to mind it too much—"The travel doesn't bother me if the project is interesting and exciting," an insider comments—especially since the firm looks to balance harried travelers. "The staffing coordinator is great at making sure to staff you on a local project if you have been on the road for a while," we're told, and consultants staffed on heavy travel assignments can look forward to a lighter load on the next project round.

The firm also provides consultants with a smattering of training classes during their tenure, but when it comes to client-relevant instruction, there is "very much an apprenticeship model" in place. Sources tell us that when getting settled at KSA, new hires informally learn the ropes from principals, managers and senior consultants, receiving official training only pertaining to soft skills.

Out of the cash box

Regarding compensation, one senior consultant states, "I believe we are slightly below the industry average, but I believe it is partly due to the fact that we have lots of work/life balance." Since KSA staffers don't put in as many crazy hours as other firms are prone to require, few complaints arise about the firm's middling salaries. On top of base salary, employees receive end-of-year bonuses based on seniority and profit-sharing opportunities, along with an invested retirement package, three weeks of vacation and stock options for the consulting upper crust.

On the material end, insiders receive free magazine subscriptions, frequent flier miles, cell phone coverage and "hotel points due to travel, great clients, projects and people."

Competing for charity

While Kurt Salmon participates with organizations like United Way, Habitat for Humanity and Junior Achievement, most community activities manifest in the form of office competitions—like poker nights, sports competitions, company pools—with proceeds donated to volunteer organizations. In addition, during the holidays, the firm encourages associates to send charity donations instead of Christmas cards. Though consultants tend to lead more initiatives than does firm management, sources say KSA "definitely encourages being involved in our community."

A little more variety

With few women in principal-level positions, KSAers claim there are still many women in consultant and management roles. Receptive and willing, the firm says "there is really no difference between men and women at KSA"—everyone receives equal treatment, colleagues report.

The firm has less luck in the ethnic and racial minority area, where, although receptive, little proactive recruiting occurs. "KSA is trying hard, but it doesn't seem to pan out," which may have something to do with a lack of focused hiring initiatives and international sponsorship, consultants suggest. The firm notes that in the past year, more investment has been made in this area by expanding campus efforts and attending events such as the National Black MBA Association and National Society of Black Engineers annual conferences. And, insiders are quick to append that the firm is without bias—"each person is gauged depending on his/her abilities, knowledge and background," comments a senior employee.

Visit the Vault Consulting Career Channel at **www.vault.com/consulting** - with insider firm profiles, message boards, the Vault Consulting Job Board and more.

V/\ULT CAREER LIBRARY   295

1000 El Camino Real
Suite 250
Menlo Park, CA 94025
Phone: (650) 853-1660
Fax: (650) 324-9204

599 Lexington Avenue, 43rd Floor
New York, NY 10022
Phone: (212) 605-5000
Fax: (212) 759-3045
www.cornerstone.com

LOCATIONS

Boston, MA
Los Angeles, CA
Menlo Park, CA
New York, NY
San Francisco, CA
Washington, DC

PRACTICE AREAS

Accounting
Antitrust
Energy
Financial Institutions
Intellectual Property
Securities

THE STATS

Employer Type: Private Company
Chairman: James K. Malernee
CEO & President: Cynthia L. Zollinger
2007 Employees: 400
2006 Employees: 320

RANKING RECAP

Practice Area
#5 - Economic Consulting (tie)

Quality of Life
#1 - Travel Requirements
#2 - Formal Training
#3 - Best Firms to Work For
#4 - Firm Culture
#4 - Offices
#7 - Overall Satisfaction
#9 - Relationships with Supervisors (tie)
#10 - Compensation
#18 - Hours in the Office

Diversity
#2 - Diversity for Women
#5 - Best Firms for Diversity
#7 - Diversity for GLBT
#18 - Diversity for Minorities

UPPERS

- "I can't imagine a more friendly place to work"
- No travel
- "Working on a wide variety of projects, ranging from finance to accounting to economics"
- "Partners that truly care about employees"

DOWNERS

- "Career path is slower than at management consulting firms"
- Lack of international offices
- "Opportunities for analysts to be exposed to the end client are very limited"
- "Variability of busy times; in the litigation world, our schedule is completely driven by the court"

THE BUZZ
WHAT CONSULTANTS AT OTHER FIRMS ARE SAYING ABOUT THIS FIRM

- "High-quality boutique"
- "Very dry work"
- "Broad press exposure"
- "Serious"

EMPLOYMENT CONTACT

www.cornerstone.com

THE SCOOP

Where lawyers go for counsel

For more than two decades, Cornerstone Research has helped attorneys, corporations and government agencies caught up in business litigation and regulatory proceedings by providing financial and economic analysis and expert testimony. The firm's 400-plus staff advises clients from a variety of industries, including financial markets, pharmaceuticals, health care, telecommunications, real estate and high-tech, who are involved in complex litigation dealing with issues like securities, antitrust, intellectual property and "piercing the corporate veil."

Who's in your network?

Cornerstone Research prides itself on its employees' expertise in fields like economics, finance, accounting and marketing research, but the firm is smart enough to know it can't be an expert in everything all the time. And so it often works on cases in partnership with faculty and industry experts. Its network of brains include academics from some of the country's leading business schools, economics departments and law schools who not only help Cornerstone professionals with complex cases but also update the firm on leading academic research in relevant business fields.

Courtroom savvy

In the courtroom, attorneys lean on Cornerstone Research in every phase of the case at hand. In the earliest stages, the firm consults directly with attorneys to pinpoint what key business, economic and financial issues are at stake, outlining areas that require expert testimony and determining what types of experts, data collection and analyses are needed. At this point, Cornerstone consultants will also help clients estimate potential damage claims for shaping case strategies moving forward.

Once the stage is set, Cornerstone Research will work with attorneys to locate expert witnesses, often drawing on the firm's own network of over 200 specialists from institutions like Harvard, Columbia and Stanford. Cornerstone will even help prepare witnesses for deposition and trial and will help attorneys prepare for cross examination of their opponents' expert witnesses. In the meantime, Cornerstone oversees the research efforts in each case, tapping into its financial and economic databases and research capabilities to construct economic, financial and statistical models.

Cleaning up in Cali

Many of the faculty experts on Cornerstone's roster are from Stanford, but that isn't the firm's only connection to the California institution. Cornerstone and Stanford University also co-sponsor the Securities Class Action Clearinghouse, a leading source of data and analytical information on the financial and economic characteristics of securities and class-action litigation.

That kind of research hasn't gone unnoticed, especially at a time when government is coming down hard on companies who don't comply with newly imposed securities regulations. Institutional investors with more than $1.5 trillion in assets under management have signed up for litigation development updates from the Securities Class Action Clearinghouse that could affect investments in their portfolios.

Front-page news

With casework involving a roster of Fortune 500 clients, Cornerstone often finds the outcome on the front page of *The Wall Street Journal*. The firm had a hand in the headlining WorldCom trial, which covered the mishandling of some unlucky WorldCom employees' retirement plans. During the trial, Cornerstone was brought in to advise the Merrill Lynch defense team—and had to prove that Merrill Lynch advised its clients properly and hadn't turned a blind eye to WorldCom's shady dealings. Cornerstone called in one of its expert witnesses, and in February 2005 Merrill Lynch was found not liable. Cornerstone is also involved in major mergers that undergo heavy antitrust scrutiny, such as the Exxon-Mobil megamerger of 1999.

Visit the Vault Consulting Career Channel at www.vault.com/consulting - with insider firm profiles, message boards, the Vault Consulting Job Board and more.

VAULT CAREER LIBRARY   297

Stepping Stone

Most college grads at Cornerstone want to go back to business school and law school, with recent alums headed off to Stanford, Columbia, Wharton and MIT. The firm has brought in admissions counselors from top schools to advise staff on strengthening their applications. In addition, the firm has compiled information from the expanding network of Cornerstone alums who have gone off to various programs, which is shared with analysts considering their next steps. And, to help with the competitive grad program process, analysts have the opportunity to act in leadership roles and get involved in the firm beyond analytical casework, in areas such as recruiting, training and research projects.

GETTING HIRED

Quantitative minds wanted

There's no getting around it—getting into Cornerstone is a "rigorous" process, insiders say. Undergrad newbies to Cornerstone typically start off as analysts, while MBAs and PhDs with backgrounds in economics, finance and the like may come in as associates. Outside of the campus recruiting process, analysts should consult the firm's web site for information on where to send resumes (this varies by region).

The firm also recruits at "most of the top colleges," says an insider, who adds, "We have expanded in the past few years (e.g., in New York it used to be just a few of the local Ivies) as the firm is hiring many more analysts." A source agrees, "As the firm grows, our recruiting targets are raised and the numbers of schools at which we recruit expands."

Eight is your lucky number

"Analyst recruiting is coordinated by analysts at the firm and is overseen by managers. Each office has core schools for recruiting, and first, intermediate and final-round interviews are conducted on campus, as well as by phone and in the office," says another insider. Sources advise candidates to expect at least eight—count 'em, eight—separate interviews over the course of the hiring process, each of which involve some sort of case question. According to one source, "Analysts can expect to interview with up to seven to eight consultants of various experience levels within the firm. Case questions are common with an emphasis on analytical problem solving and data-driven conclusions." The consultant suggests, "Do your research on the firm and economic consulting, in general. The process for associates is similar, but may also include presenting a research paper for PhD applicants."

A chance to shine

An insider reports, "Cornerstone case questions are based on cases we work on and can include any number of our practice areas such as securities, antitrust and intellectual property." But don't fret (too much), says a colleague: "Before coming here I was nervous, as I heard about the number of interviews and the cases they asked. In fact, cases are meant to give the candidate a good idea of what we are working on. I don't think anyone is judged purely on the cases. There is so much more about a person, and Cornerstone recognizes that. Cornerstone is really interested in getting to know the candidate and giving them a chance to shine." Another insider comments, "The best advice I can give regarding how to succeed in the interviews is to have a good grasp of the economic consulting industry and study the theory of commercial and litigation damages. Nearly every case you get will relate to damages and their calculation." "There are no brainteasers or anything like that," a source adds.

Interns in the fray

Cornerstone also offers a few slots for summer analysts and associates, noting that a number of its full-timers started out that way. "Summer staff are included on active project teams and contribute to client work directly, rather than being confined to stylized programs strictly for summer folks. The experience provides good insight into whether the work and the company suit an individual," says a source. Another happy former intern recollects, "Our training was more on the job, and we interacted with everyone in the office. Since there was no distinction between an intern and a full-timer, I knew exactly what I would be doing if I worked as a full-time analyst. Even though the learning curve was steep, the transition was smooth because every intern has a full-time mentor."

OUR SURVEY SAYS

Cornering the market on culture

Cornerstone earns countless raves from insiders for its corporate culture, and it's not just a matter of chance: "The founders of Cornerstone Research have put a lot of thought and time into creating a corporate culture that is very supportive and fun," says a consultant, who adds, "The founders and other senior staff also continue to add resources to preserve the culture as the firm grows." Agrees another source, "Cornerstone not only places a strong emphasis on the culture, but management backs up the words by making substantial investments in time and money to support it." A colleague notes, "I have worked for more than one consulting firm. Cornerstone's culture is unique—it does not feel like an American corporation. Sometimes it is more like a family."

Greater than the sum of its parts

"More than anything," a source chimes in, "it's the type of people that Cornerstone hires that defines its culture." In fact, a colleague notes, "We pride ourselves on hiring smart but also fun and nice people." More bluntly, another insider reports, "Cornerstone has a 'no-jerk' policy that it rigorously enforces from the very top of management, which helps." The benefits of this policy are reflected in the glowing praise Cornerstone insiders heap upon their co-workers. "People are willing to help out and explain concepts to you even when they're busy, and it's not cutthroat or competitive in a negative way," says one source. According to another consultant, "We truly do enjoy working with each other, because everyone has a mutual respect for one another, and we all get along well together. The abundance of social activities and retreats is proof that we all enjoy each other's company, even outside of work." In addition, a source tells us, "It's great to be in a place that understands and facilitates learning and development, rather than one that simply focuses on completing tasks. At Cornerstone, it's all about the people."

Time for dinner parties

Perhaps because they enjoy each other's company so much, Cornerstone consultants don't often grumble about work/life balance. "The firm is very careful about work/life balance," says a source. "There are times where it is unavoidable to work late nights and over the weekends, but after the crunch times the firm is very careful in providing some breathing room. On average, things work out fine, but there are unavoidable spikes every now and then." A colleague affirms that "Cornerstone's case managers meet once a week with each other to balance work demands across consultants." Though "you often work under litigation and court deadlines, and it can be intense around critical report dates," a colleague explains, "management is organized and plans ahead to smooth out workload and often exceeds expectations without increasing hardship on analysts."

And plenty of consultants report having time to pursue their own interests: "In addition to work, I've taken night classes at Harvard, played in two soccer leagues and coached a youth soccer team. I also make it to the gym three days a week and am an avid skier," says one go-getter. Another staffer remarks, "There are times when work gets busy and I have to stay late or work weekends, but most of the time, I have time to throw dinner parties for co-workers and friends and relax on the weekend."

The client is king

Another thing that helps with the balance is a no-face-time policy, insiders report. "If you don't have anything to do, you can leave early and come in late. Also, working long hours is not something to brag about. There is no competition to work the longest hours," says a source. "Cornerstone's target for associates is 50 hours a week: 40 billable hours and 10 non-billable hours," a colleague explains, noting, "I find that, on average, this is the amount I work." Another consultant tells us that "there

Visit the Vault Consulting Career Channel at **www.vault.com/consulting** - with insider firm profiles, message boards, the Vault Consulting Job Board and more.

VAULT CAREER LIBRARY   299

can be high variance in weekly hours worked because of case deadlines," adding, "The firm is open to reduced schedules, at least for its senior consulting staff, although the realities of the job can make such a reduced schedule hard to manage. I have been attempting to work an 80 percent schedule (40 hours a week, on average) but have not been able to maintain that." "Hours can be unpredictable and depend on client requests. If a client needs something urgently and sends an e-mail at 6 p.m., then you will likely be working late," another insider acknowledges. In any case, a co-worker chimes in, "I think that when hours are long, Cornerstone is very understanding of the fact that it is hard and a sacrifice. There is not a macho attitude of 'tough it out.'"

Lengths of assignments at Cornerstone "vary greatly," insiders note. "A case can be as short as a week or two, or can start before you join Cornerstone and still be going on after you leave," says one staffer. A colleague adds, "This is the litigation business. So you can get a settlement or several short or very long extensions at any point in time … An assignment can last two months or three years (on and off)." "Consultants tend to work on two or three assignments at a time," another source reports.

Homebodies

Cornerstone consultants are no road warriors—there's "practically no travel," says a source. According to another insider, "Generally, we meet with our clients over teleconference or video conference calls, or they come into our office. Sometimes when staffed on a cross-office case, some light travel may be involved to other offices, but it is the exception rather than the norm." A colleague suggests that "the amount of travel required is proportional to tenure with the firm. More senior members of the firm travel more than junior members. Travel is typically only required at the beginning of projects, when first meeting the clients, or near the end when presenting final results."

But for those who enjoy traveling, the firm offers a notable perk: "Because the majority of our work can be done on the computer, if I want to visit friends in another city, I can work out of another office as a guest, which is a great way to travel without sacrificing vacation time," says a consultant. As for those who don't have to fly to client meetings, travel is reserved for annual training and company retreats. A consultant notes, "I've traveled exclusively for firm outings, such as our firmwide retreat in Palm Springs or the training sessions in Menlo Park and New York City. The accommodations are always great. We stayed at the W Hotel in New York City for experienced analyst training!"

Hard work pays off

When it comes to salary, "Cornerstone compensates at the high range of comparable firms. The amount is even higher when adjusted for work hours," says a source. A colleague agrees, "I think that our compensation is very competitive, particularly given the average number of hours we work per week." The firm also provides "401(k) matching up to 6 percent of base salary, and a small amount of profit sharing," an insider reports. In addition, a contact says, "Cornerstone also provides an extraordinary hours bonus for people who either work extremely long hours during a single month, or maintain long hours over a span of several months. The bonus is not large enough to be worth it to actively work toward, but it is a nice way of compensating those who are particularly busy."

Cornerstone's many benefits and perks are appreciated by insiders. Some applaud the firm's flexibility: "The company is open to flexible work styles and work hours. You can decrease your working hours (naturally with a corresponding decrease in your salary) or you can work from home for a while," as one source explains. Others cite the firmwide retreat and the regional retreats, both of which take place every three years. An insider adds, "The retreat is for all employees, from the administrative assistants to the analysts, and the associates to the officers. We stay at a resort in Palm Springs where we enjoy lavish dinners, chair massages at breakfast, activities such as golf and hot air ballooning and, at the most recent retreat, a personal fireworks show on the last night." For many consultants, the day-to-day perks are the best, including "lots of free food. We are spoiled with the junk food and drink fridge, as well as the ongoing grocery list. In addition, we will always find reasons to have office lunches or breakfasts." The gym membership reimbursement helps balance out any overindulgence. For new parents, the firm offers generous leave for new moms, 10 days for new dads, and "a large number of employees with children work reduced schedules," a source says. For families, there's an "annual holiday party expressly for the children of employees where Santa pays a visit."

Corporate chic

Unsurprisingly, Cornerstone consultants also cite their offices as perks of working for the firm. "They spared only the most extravagant expenses in outfitting our offices with space and creature comforts," one insider cheers. "The offices are great! I've been to three of the six offices, and they are all conveniently located in their respective cities. Analysts share offices with other analysts, and I think it adds to the fun environment that has made my life at Cornerstone so enjoyable," says a colleague. In Boston, "Our location couldn't be better, right in the heart of the Back Bay. We are constantly outgrowing our office space however, although we are in the process of getting additional space in our current location," a source tells us. Meanwhile, in San Francisco, "the entire office has very high-quality furniture; this office more than the others makes it a point to have really nice furniture and decorations." In the Menlo Park office, where the culture is compared to that of a Silicon Valley tech firm, "polo shirts and khakis are considered appropriate dress attire," and there's a "relaxed and fun working environment," sources say.

Cornerstone coaches

Cornerstone's flat hierarchy is reflected in the positive marks insiders give their supervisors. As one consultant puts it, "There is a large amount of coaching going on. Everyone has an advisor, and a mentor as well. There is always someone to turn to, professionally or personally. They pay attention to analysts not just when they are with Cornerstone, but also after they leave Cornerstone, making sure they carry with them the set of skills that are useful later in life." "I have amazing relationships with some of my managers and great relationships with all of them. I've really appreciated getting to know my managers on a personal, as well as professional level," says a colleague.

Still, another insider comments that "the management quality varies. Some managers are on top of their game and you learn constantly from their equipoise and economic erudition. Other managers can suffer from panic or stress, which negatively affects the ultimate work product. In this way, I am sure the firm is like most others." As another source puts it, "Associates and managers all either have PhDs or MBAs, so they have much to teach analysts. While some managers have had a history of communication problems, most are very open and easily approached."

Back to school

Both formal and informal training have a place at Cornerstone. An insider elaborates, "There is training when you first join Cornerstone; a retreat for all first-year analysts, a retreat for all experienced analysts and individual training sessions for various practice areas during the year. Additionally, Cornerstone will pay for outside classes if they relate to your casework (think finance, economics, accounting, programming, etc.). As for informal mentoring, all the analysts are eager to help one another, and you'll often learn from the more senior analysts working on the same case team as you. Associates and managers are also willing to explain concepts to analysts." Another source reports on "Cornerstone College, which offers real courses like Antitrust or Advanced IO, but in real case contexts. We also have an analyst presentation club, where analysts take turns presenting a paper from some economic journal that has an innovative econometric method or an interesting economic idea. It is a great way to get deep into econ and apply it, and at the same time improve your presentation skills."

Ahead of the gender curve

Gender equality is a no-brainer at Cornerstone, where the "current CEO is a woman, and she was one of the three founders of the firm," an insider comments, adding, "Equality exists not only at the analyst level but all the way up. Additionally, I've seen women have children without any sacrifice to their careers." A colleague agrees, "In an industry that is traditionally male-dominated, the firm is an exception." "Cornerstone is an outlier in that about half of the consulting staff is female. This is true at both the junior and senior levels. Because of the large number of women already in the firm, there are no differences in the hiring, promoting or mentoring between men and women, as everyone is treated with an equal amount of respect and they tend to succeed equally. As an example, in the most recent cycle, 66 percent of the promotions to partner were female," a consultant reports.

Visit the Vault Consulting Career Channel at **www.vault.com/consulting** - with insider firm profiles, message boards, the Vault Consulting Job Board and more.

VAULT CAREER LIBRARY   301

As for minority diversity at the firm, an insider explains, "The consulting staff tends to be Caucasian and Asian, while the support staff is much more diverse. Also, it is worth mentioning that the consulting staff is incredibly diverse in terms of nationalities. While I believe the firm is receptive to minorities, it could probably do better in terms of hiring non-Asian minority consulting staff." Several sources comment on the international flavor of Cornerstone's staff, with one insider summing up, "I think there are seven nationalities from three different continents in one of my case teams." GLBT consultants should find a welcoming environment at the firm, where the "culture is welcoming and respectful of people of all sexual orientations," says a source. A consultant agrees, "We have several openly gay managers and they are treated just the same as any other employee."

Stretching the social conscience

When it comes to community service, "if you have a social conscience, the firm will provide an outlet for it," a source tells us. Explains a colleague, "Each office has a committee called CROP (Cornerstone Research Outreach Program) that organizes community service events for the office to participate in. These include clothing and food drives, Habitat for Humanity builds, servathons, walks and runs for charity, and other such events. The committee is also a great way for analysts to organize events and gain leadership skills." A source adds, "The committee is given a budget, which allows us to participate in larger events." Cornerstone also has a "green team" of staff members who work to reduce the firm's environmental footprint from the use of paper and energy to the selection of items in the kitchen.

"It's great to be in a place that understands and facilitates learning and development, rather than one that simply focuses on completing tasks. At Cornerstone, it's all about the people."

– Cornerstone source

Visit the Vault Consulting Career Channel at **www.vault.com/consulting** - with insider firm profiles, message boards, the Vault Consulting Job Board and more.

VAULT CAREER LIBRARY   303

The Advisory Board Company

2445 M Street, NW
Washington, DC 20037
Phone: (202) 266-5600
Fax: (202) 266-5700
www.advisoryboardcompany.com

LOCATIONS

Washington, DC (HQ)
Mountainview, CA
Portland, OR

PRACTICE AREAS

Executive Briefings
Industry Research
Installation Support
Strategy Research

THE STATS

Employer Type: Public Company
Ticker Symbol: ABCO (Nasdaq)
Chairman & CEO: Frank J. Williams
2007 Employees: 855
2006 Employees: 810
2007 Revenue: $189.8 million
2006 Revenue: $165 million

RANKING RECAP

Practice Area
#7 - Pharmaceutical & Health Care Consulting (tie)

UPPERS

• Great environment for the ambitious
• Research-oriented work

DOWNERS

• High turnover in some roles
• "Young, inexperienced managers"

EMPLOYMENT CONTACT

www.advisoryboardcompany.com/public/
carersabc/home.asp

THE BUZZ
WHAT CONSULTANTS AT OTHER FIRMS ARE SAYING ABOUT THIS FIRM

• "Innovative model; fresh ideas"
• "Fluff"
• "Solid, quality, client-driven research"
• "Hires smart people and burns them out"

THE SCOOP

Experts for health experts

The Advisory Board Company earns its keep by doling out advice to 2,600 of its member-clients in the $2.2 trillion health care industry. Its clients include hospitals, health systems, pharmaceutical and biotech companies, health care insurers and medical device companies. According to *U.S. News & World Report*'s 2006 Best Hospitals honor roll, that membership roster includes 13 of the top-14 hospitals in the country, 90 of the 100-largest health care delivery systems and 20 of the world's largest pharmaceutical and medical device companies.

All of these institutions are drawn to the Advisory Board for its proprietary research, executive briefings, strategy consulting and expertise in implementing new management practices. Big-name members include the Mayo Clinic, Memorial Sloan-Kettering Cancer Center, Amgen, Merck, St. Jude Medical and Kaiser-Permanente.

Subscribe and save

In the Advisory Board's world, the distinction between clients and members is an important one. The firm makes its money via memberships, not on per-project consulting fees, like most consultancies. Members buy annual subscriptions to one or more of the firm's 29 program areas—most of which focus on issues like strategy, operations, benchmarking and management, and include best-practice research studies, seminars, customized reports and decision-support tools. In 2006, four new programs were introduced in the areas of service-line growth strategy, clinical technology assessment, surgery performance and imaging performance. On average, the company estimates that each individual best practice profiled in its research conveys a value of between $250,000 and $1.5 million, far exceeding the average $65,000 membership fee.

With a 92 percent membership renewal rate, it's clear that the Advisory Board's clients feel their membership is well worth the investment. Members share access to the Advisory Board's industry research and the firm takes—at least publicly—a nonexclusionary stance, sharing its findings with all of its members. "Our shared interest is maintaining a permanent board of the world's preeminent institutions, each benefiting from the others' experience across extended periods of time. Our intention is to serve members so fully that there is little question of long-term commitment," the firm states. As of the end of fiscal 2006, the Advisory Board's total contract value equaled $170.5 million.

Roots in research

The Advisory Board believes in the power of ideas and their capacity for changing enterprises. "The great commercial concerns of our time," the company says, "are carried more surely by the force of good ideas than by natural resources, market power and market cunning. Ours is the task to find them." And so the Advisory Board is committed to working in common enterprise with some of the country's leading universities, health systems, corporations and physicians to document the most important advances in medicine. Together, these ideas make up what the firm terms "economies of intellect," which are at the core of what the Advisory Board provides for its members.

Consequently, the firm's research is made up of pretty heady stuff. The average presentation study surveys 2,000 pages of literature and requires 100 or more original interviews. Every year, the Advisory Board's 800-plus professionals publish about 50 major studies and 3,000 customized research briefs, as well as daily and weekly news services, covering management and clinical strategies in health care, highlighting best (and worst) practices.

Finding a niche

The Advisory Board was founded in 1979 on Capitol Hill with one purpose: to conduct research on any question for any company in any industry. But in time, it became apparent that such a wide-ranging objective may be biting off more than the firm could

Visit the Vault Consulting Career Channel at **www.vault.com/consulting** - with insider firm profiles, message boards, the Vault Consulting Job Board and more.

VAULT CAREER LIBRARY   305

chew. Its early projects ranged from topics like the size of the European fountain-pen market to child adoption in South Africa and jet engine sales. The firm needed a focus.

It set about narrowing the field by setting up specialty research divisions. The first was started in 1983, when the Advisory Board began a special strategic research division for the financial services industry. The move met with success—within four years, the firm's membership included every major retail bank in North America. Then, in 1986, it founded another special strategic research division for the health care industry. By 1996, membership surpassed 1,500 preeminent hospitals and health systems. Finally, in 1993, the Advisory Board set up another research unit serving headquarters for the world's largest corporations, which included a roster made up of almost half of the Fortune 500 companies within its first 18 months.

By 1998, the Advisory Board was a consulting force to contend with, employing more than 800 professionals and serving 3,000 enterprises worldwide. To maintain its focus, the firm decided to reorganize again, spinning off its corporate and banking practices in 1999 as a public company, leaving the remaining enterprise and its staff of 400 to concentrate exclusively on the American health care market.

Success stories

The spun-off corporate and banking practices units assumed the name of the Corporate Executive Board, which currently uses the same membership model and has grown by more than $50 million per year since 2002. Today, the firm provides research and consulting services to over 2,400 corporate members around the world and employs 2,200 staff out of its offices in Washington, D.C., and London. The health care services enterprise kept the Advisory Board name and has fared equally as well. Revenue in fiscal 2006 increased 16.5 percent over 2005 to $165 million, and its publicly traded stock has doubled in price since 2002.

Taking action

Since 2000, the Advisory Board has done more than just dish out advice. For the implementation of its ideas, the firm established H*Works in 2000, a program that aims to "install" the management practices uncovered by Advisory Board's research so that member-client hospitals can run their businesses more efficiently. The program's consulting areas include helping hospitals with their emergency department performance, workforce management, revenue management, technology strategies, inpatient and surgical management, nurse staffing, enhancing profit margins and expanding service-line growth. To do this, H*Works uses performance-improvement teams that work with hospital staffers to root out the cause of their problems and find solutions so they can perform as well as their "gold standard," high-performing industry peers.

High-tech benefits

The Advisory Board has made huge investments in its technology services so as to provide members with real-time decision support, data collection and advanced analytical capabilities. Today, more than 200,000 discrete items can be downloaded off of the firm's web pages. In fiscal 2006, more than 82,000 members received online briefings, upwards of 75,000 users accessed the firm's password-protected web sites and more than 8,000 used the various tools and databases housed on the Advisory Board's web site.

The firm's web services were bulked up in 2004 when it partnered with MedeFinance, a California firm that provides revenue cycle analytics based on business intelligence. MedeFinance now serves as the technological backbone of the Advisory Board's Revenue Cycle Performance Program, which provides real-time metrics via the Internet to member hospitals and health systems so they can more easily and efficiently track their financials.

For its technological efforts, the Advisory Board was notified in February 2006 that it had been certified as a Qualified High Technology Company under the New Economy Transformation Act. The classification means the firm will be eligible for Washington, D.C., income tax credits and other benefits, which should make up for the $5.5 million entrance fee it had to pay for the accreditation.

A healthy workplace

As a prominent member of the health care community, the Advisory Board isn't one to neglect the health of its employees. New employees undergo two weeks of orientation training, which includes education on a variety of topics like health care operations and strategy, as well as in-depth skills training for the firm's internal business operations and IT systems. From there, employees have access to an array of professional development and training opportunities; in 2006, employees had 900 hours of training to choose from.

As a result, employee-retention rates are over 85 percent. In 2006, the firm ranked on *Forbes*' list of the 200 Best Small Companies. And prospective employees have taken notice: The firm receives more than 20,000 resumes annually.

GETTING HIRED

Finding your place

To score a spot at the Advisory Board, you should first decide which of the firm's five distinct roles you want to fill: research, executive education, marketing, the firm's H*Works program or internal services. Aspiring consultants will find most of the typical analyst/consulting positions in the research and H*Works sectors of the company, although the executive education and marketing wings have some opportunities as well. On its web site, the firm lists open positions and describes what it's looking for in employees—namely, "force of intellect" and "a spirit of generosity."

The firm's interview process is "straightforward," says an insider. Students can expect one interview round on campus, followed by an "on-site interview day with a writing sample and three interview sessions." Don't worry, the source adds, there's "nothing to put you on the spot," though there is "one broad case study." In addition, the insider says, the "interviewer asked to put me in a few role-playing situations, as if I was soliciting information from research contacts."

Visit the Vault Consulting Career Channel at **www.vault.com/consulting** - with insider firm profiles, message boards, the Vault Consulting Job Board and more.

 **307**

550 West Van Buren
Chicago, IL 60607
Phone: (312) 583-8700
Toll Free: (866) 229-8700
Fax: (312) 583-8701
www.huronconsultinggroup.com

LOCATIONS

Chicago, IL (HQ)
Boston, MA • Charlotte, NC • Houston, TX •
Los Angeles, CA • New York, NY • San Francisco, CA •
Washington, DC • Tokyo

PRACTICE AREAS

Corporate Consulting
Corporate Advisory Services • Operational Consulting •
Strategy/Galt & Company

Health & Education Consulting
Healthcare • Health Plans • Higher Education •
Pharmaceutical & Medical Devices

Legal Financial Consulting
Business Disputes • Economic Consulting • Forensic &
Complex Accounting • Fraud Investigations • Intellectual
Property • Valuation

Legal Operational Consulting
Data Processing • Digital Evidence & Discovery Services •
Document Review • Law Firm Management Services •
Records Management • Strategy & Operational
Improvements

THE STATS

Employer Type: Public Company
Ticker Symbol: HURN (Nasdaq)
Chairman & CEO: Gary E. Holdren
2006 Employees: 1,000+
2005 Employees: 773
2006 Revenue: $288.6 million
2005 Revenue: $207.2 million

THE BUZZ
WHAT CONSULTANTS AT OTHER FIRMS ARE SAYING ABOUT THIS FIRM

- "Up and comer; high growth"
- "Specialized, not global"
- "Very nice small shop with targeted practice areas"
- "Bottom-feeders"

UPPERS

- "High growth means lots of opportunity"
- "It's basically the best of the Big Four without the games"
- Incentive to encourage work/life balance
- "The enthusiasm of our CEO and practice leaders"

DOWNERS

- "The money doesn't seem to trickle down, and there is a lot of it"
- "Increasing bureaucracy as the firm ages"
- Challenges faced by any public firm
- "Everyone is an overachiever, so competition is intense"

EMPLOYMENT CONTACT

www.huronconsultinggroup.com/careers

THE SCOOP

Financial savvy

Huron Consulting Group knows a thing or two about financial operations. The Chicago-based consultancy provides financial and operating consulting services to some of the biggest Fortune 500 companies, often during times of trouble. Its specialty is helping clients—including large- and medium-sized businesses, academic institutions, health care organizations and law firms—that are involved in litigation, disputes, investigations, regulatory compliance, procurement or financial distress. Since its founding in May 2002, the firm has worked on engagements with 39 of the top-40 2006 *American Lawyer* AM LAW 100 law firms, 80 of the top-100 research institutions and academic medical centers, more than 200 general counsels, 50 percent of the nation's largest health care systems and 60 percent of *U.S. News & World Report*'s Honor Roll Medical Centers. Huron Consulting also works with companies and organizations to implement strategic, operational and organizational change.

Huron's clients come from an array of industries, such as consumer products, electronics, energy and utilities, financial services, food and beverage, health care, education, industrial manufacturing, professional services, telecommunications and transportation services.

Andersen breakaways

It's been nearly five years since 213 consultants put in their two weeks' notice at Arthur Andersen to follow Andersen Senior Partner Gary E. Holdren who, with a group of former Andersen partners and with the help of investors from Lake Capital Management LLC, founded Huron Consulting in May 2002. The firm's success is largely due to the same factors that led to the downfall of some of its biggest competitors, like Andersen. Many of the large consultancies that had ties to scandal-ridden firms, like Enron and WorldCom, had companies looking for fresh faces. Huron seemed to be at the right place at the right time.

By 2003, the firm had already hit revenue of more than $100 million and the staff's headcount had more than doubled to over 500 professionals. By October 2004, Huron Consulting had gone public on the Nasdaq. Fast forward to 2006, and the firm had expanded its headcount fivefold and absorbed three consulting firms: Speltz & Weis, a health care turnaround consultancy; Galt & Company, a consultancy focusing on improving shareholder returns; and Aaxis Technologies a document review service provider. In January 2007, two further acquisitions were made—the management consulting firm Wellspring Partners, a leading health care consultancy, and Glass & Associates, a leading turnaround and restructuring firm.

Due recognition

The ride to the top wasn't without some bumps, though. In a 2005 interview with *Entrepreneur* magazine, Holdren recounted that, even after securing the $100 million initial investment in equity commitment from Lake Capital Management, "the phones were not ringing." But once he snagged United Airlines as a client during its bankruptcy, word got out and Huron took off "faster than anticipated."

The consulting industry has recognized Holdren's bold moves since his founding of Huron. Just a year after jumping the Andersen ship, *Consulting Magazine* named him one of the country's most influential consultants of 2003 and 2005, and named Huron one of The Best Firms To Work For in 2006. *Entrepreneur* was also impressed, ranking Huron at the top of its 2005 and 2006 Hot 100 list of the fastest-growing new businesses in America. Most recently, Huron was ranked No. 22 on *BusinessWeek*'s 2007 Hot Growth 100 list.

Wall Street smiles on Huron

Wall Street has been pleased with Huron's progress over the past few years. Since 2004, when the firm went public, the firm's stock price has more than doubled from around $20 to around $70, while its revenue has risen from $101 million at the end of fiscal 2003 to over $207 million at the end of fiscal 2005.

Visit the Vault Consulting Career Channel at **www.vault.com/consulting** - with insider firm profiles, message boards, the Vault Consulting Job Board and more.

VAULT CAREER LIBRARY

309

Its ranks of consultants have grown just as quickly, from a staff of 213 in 2002 to over 1,000 in eight offices just five years later—despite aggressive competition for qualified people across the consulting industry.

Helping out Holdren

To help manage Huron's growth, in February 2007 the company announced the appointments of five vice presidents: Shahzad Bashir, vice president of Huron's legal operational consulting practice; Daniel P. Broadhurst, vice president of operations and business strategy; Joseph J. Floyd, vice president of Huron's legal financial consulting practice; Stanley N. Logan, vice president of the corporate consulting practice; and James H. Roth, vice president of the health and education consulting practice. The firm also announced a five-year renewal of Holdren's contract as chairman and chief executive officer. In May 2007, Daniel P. Broadhurst was appointed chief operating officer and David M. Shade was promoted to vice president of the health care practice.

What makes Huron so popular

Huron Consulting Group's strengths lie in its four service lines. The legal operational consulting service line provides expert guidance on the business challenges that confront today's legal organizations. Huron's team works with corporate law departments, law firms and government agencies to reduce legal spending, enhance client service delivery and increase operational effectiveness to add value in the areas of digital evidence and discovery services, document review, law firm management services, records management, and strategy and operational improvements.

The legal financial consulting service line provides financial and economic analysis to support law firms and corporations in connection with business disputes, lawsuits, and regulatory or internal investigations. Consultants also provide valuation analysis on transactions, litigation or disputes and bankruptcies.

The health and education consulting service line provides consulting services to hospitals, health systems, physicians, managed care organizations, academic medical centers, colleges, universities, and pharmaceutical and medical device manufacturers. Team members help clients effectively address their financial, operational and organizational, research enterprise, strategic, technology and compliance requirements.

And finally, the corporate consulting service line solves complex problems and transforms corporations, leading clients through various stages of transformation that result in sustainable performance improvement. Clients directed toward this group are confronted with stagnate or declining stock price, acquisitions and divestitures, process inefficiency, third-party contracting difficulties, lack of/misaligned performance measurements, margin/cost pressures, performance issues, bank defaults, covenant violations, liquidity issues and negative press.

GETTING HIRED

Huron's hiring

Huron's web site offers some helpful information on the firm's hiring process, including a campus recruiting schedule. It also provides some less helpful "tips," such as, "Be on time." Huron performs "heavy campus recruiting," says a consultant, who also reports that the firm places "a lot of emphasis on experienced hires; especially from individuals with public accounting backgrounds and competitor firms." When it comes to campuses, an insider says, "they seem to put most emphasis on 'good' Midwestern schools, such as University of Illinois, Notre Dame and University of Michigan. They also recruit in the Northeast at Lehigh, Villanova and the University of Massachusetts."

Socially intelligent people need apply

Huron's "subtle but tough and rigorous" hiring process features "much more dependence on fit and behavioral interviewing than other firms," says a source, who adds, "The firm's leaders truly believe that among a group of qualified applicants, the ones that will work best within our organizational culture will do better than candidates that are smarter and more experienced, but lack the necessary fit or social intelligence." "We do significant behavioral hiring because many of us work so independently," agrees a colleague, adding, "I would expect questions that indicate how you performed during a given scenario."

The interview process is markedly different for campus and experienced hires, respondents tell us. "With experienced hires, our practice prefers to do all the interviewing in one day. This means that you may meet with four or five different individuals within the practice in a row. Afterwards, everyone meets and determines your fate," says an insider. A colleague notes that the process for experienced hires may vary by practice.

It's a campus blitz

Although the firm states it's not a standard practice at all schools, one source reports, "We have just switched to a 'blitz' interviewing process on campus and it has gone very well. There are two interviews, back to back, in the first round; then two more the next day if a candidate advances to the second round. The candidate will know if an offer is extended by the night of the second-round interview." Says another insider, "Before second-round interviews, interviewees can attend a pre-night event, which involves dinner and other social activities with Huron employees." The process "can be tough," says a consultant, "but you'll usually know how it went when you walk out the door."

Question marks

Sources suggest that undergrads at Huron don't face traditional case questions. But "case interviews are being used to an increasing extent, especially as we increase recruitment of MBAs," a consultant reports. According to a source, interviewees can expect a "typical case question from real-life engagements," such as "determining how to fix pricing strategy at a heavy equipment manufacturer experiencing sagging profits." On the behavioral tip, sources report questions along the lines of: "Tell me about a time when you spoke up even though it would be easier to go along with a decision or say nothing at all," and "Tell me about a time where you had a team member fail to meet your expectations. How did you address the situation?" Another insider reports being "given a *Wall Street Journal* and told to read and comment on an article on the spot."

The firm offers spots for summer interns. One former summer intern reports, "I was able to travel to the client site and interact with the client as an intern, which was a great experience."

OUR SURVEY SAYS

Culture defined

Huron's culture, according to one insider, is one of the firm's "biggest differentiators." Others say it's still maturing: "The Huron management team is applying considerable resources to encourage staff retention, social networking and ongoing employee communication. There are several 'culture committees' designed to focus firm attention on what Huron believes to be its greatest resource—its people," a source reports. "The culture is still developing, which I like because it allows you to have more of an impact than at a more senior firm," a colleague chimes in. "Virtually everyone is highly educated and/or skilled, but also laid-back and personable," a consultant adds. "When I describe my work environment, people are shocked at the pairing of such positivism with a description of corporate culture." Indeed, "This firm seems to take great care in assessing potential recruits for a culture fit," reports a source, who elaborates, "The internal slogan, penned by the CEO, is 'No Jerks'—and for the most part, especially in certain (nonfinancial and nonstrategic) practices, this policy seems to be supported."

One insider notes that the San Francisco office is "smaller and has a close-knit, family feel," while Huron's Chicago office "is more corporate, as it is much larger." But some worry that a corporate feel is creeping through the entire firm as it grows—"as the firm grows, so does the lack of concern for the individual. Major acquisitions in the last year have diluted Huron's identity and culture," grumbles a source. A colleague agrees, "I think our company has struggled to establish a culture and with new hires and acquisitions, they don't or aren't expected to adapt to the company culture. We end up having a mixture, depending on where

Visit the Vault Consulting Career Channel at **www.vault.com/consulting** - with insider firm profiles, message boards, the Vault Consulting Job Board and more.

VAULT CAREER LIBRARY   311

you work or who you work with." Some insiders complain of "cronyism," arguing that "leadership needs to walk the talk more," and grumble about an "always fire-drill" environment. Another consultant complains about the lack of formal group social events: "When your firm makes over $286 million, don't you think [it] can have more social events so individuals can meet people that are not on their project team?"

A better balance

"For a top consulting firm, the work/life balance at Huron is exceptional," raves a source, who adds, "While there are always exceptions based on responses to client demands and an expectation to exceed client timeframes and expectations, overall there is a focus on enabling Huron consultants to balance work with other priorities." "My division's managing director made a point of encouraging us to balance work and family commitments. You are told to head home if it is a slow day or time. Huron nurtures its employees," a staffer insists. Still, some family guys (and gals) struggle—as one insider tells us, "Between the travel, the uncertain schedule and canceled family vacations (hard to reschedule the kids' spring break at the last minute, for example), and demanding deadlines that put you home after bedtime even when you're not traveling, its hard. But I'm not sure it's any harder or easier here than at the competition. Regardless, it's something that everyone struggles with and talks about in hushed tones."

At Huron, hard work pays off, though, with tangible incentives such as a $750 Amex debit card for every quarter in which consultants spend 25 nights away from home, as well as $25 per month for consultants to spend on spa treatments, gyms and even life-enhancers like cleaning services and dry cleaners (one insider dubs this the "happiness fund"). Sources also appreciate the firm's policy of flexible paid time off with virtually no limit—taking advantage of PTO is "encouraged," an insider happily reports. As one consultant puts it, "Work is sometimes extremely intense, and 90- or 100-hour weeks are not unheard of, but Huron is generally interested in keeping its employees instead of burning them out in three years and sending them to MBA programs or industry. There is no sense of face time."

Racking up miles

But while face time may be minimal, airplane time isn't. "If you want to work here, get your suitcase ready," advises a source. While some insiders report less travel from major markets like New York and Chicago, "The nature of consulting, and specifically in our market, requires us to be on site a great deal of time," says a source. For one consultant, this has amounted to traveling a whopping 50 weeks a year. "We define 'full-time travel' as out on Monday and back home on Thursday afternoon or evening," another insider explains. "Very few people are out of town Monday through Friday, and even fewer are asked to stay over the weekend."

For some Huron employees, the unpredictability of travel is wearying. "This firm needs to improve its communication with the employees," groans a consultant. "Don't tell people you will only need them for two weeks and then they return home eight months later." A colleague adds, "Travel as a consultant is expected. However, it would be nice if more forethought went into the assignments geographically. It is hard for an East Coast associate to manage four clients at all four corners of the country." "Be prepared to be shipped off to anywhere in the U.S," warns an insider. "Once you finish a project, it's pretty much luck of the draw on where you'll be heading next." But one consultant enthuses, "In my practice, we usually always go to the same city each week for a year or more. That gives me the opportunity to learn a new city and really get to know my way around. My other half also gets to accompany me to many of the cities and it works very well for us."

Punching the clock

Huron is big on billable hours (at least 40 per week are expected), causing complaints from some consultants. "Travel hours are not counted toward billable time (even if these hours are not billable to the client, they still should be part of the calculus of an employee's overall work hours per week, given that travel time is, on average, in excess of seven to eight hours—or one full business day—per week)," grouses an insider. Agrees a colleague, "Many of the work-related hours I spend go undocumented, for example, the 'dead-head' time, where I am not charging time but I am away from my family most evenings in another city or at an airport." "I work 60 to 70 hours a week, but only 40 of those are generally chargeable," another source reports, and "Most heads-down work happens from 6 p.m. to 1 a.m. in the hotel room because you are stuck in client meetings all day."

But all those long hours can add up to fatter checks for analysts and associates, who earn overtime for more than 40 billable hours per week. While one associate notes that "the overtime can really be a good bonus if you are consistently billable and working a lot of hours in any given week," a colleague contends that the firm "rarely delivers," adding, "Many times, you will be expected to work overtime but only charge 40 hours."

"Hush-hush" compensation

There's a fair amount of grumbling to be found when it comes to compensation at Huron. A few consultants echo one insider's primary complaint: "For as much money as Huron is making, employees don't share the wealth." Others suspect vast differences between departments when it comes to salary, but no one's really sure, since the firm "doesn't publish pay bands," a source says. "I do not like the 'hush-hush' atmosphere of compensation. I have asked for the salary range in my level so I can get an idea of whether I'm being paid fairly. Unfortunately, I have not been given access to this information," sighs an insider. But a colleague muses, "While my compensation is below norms, the firm rewards more than just utilization, and has systems in place to cover bad years in specific industries so that the risks associated with downturns in a practice area are mitigated."

Sharing the wealth?

As for the extras, insiders laud the firm's 6 percent match on their 401(k)s, but are less impressed with how Huron distributes profits. "When we went public, they did not share equity (options) with nonmanagement-level employees," says a source. Nowadays, "employees have the opportunity to allocate up to 30 percent of their annual bonus to the employee stock purchase plan. Huron matches 25 percent of the allocation," an insider explains. But "bonuses do not seem to relate to the company's performance," a colleague grumbles. As another source puts it, "I am thinking the distribution of equity is not equitable."

In addition to the aforementioned "happiness fund," Huron staffers enjoy other goodies, such as iPods "as presents for a good quarter," a car service for those working late hours, on-the-spot bonuses and reimbursement for the annual Amex rewards fee. Parental leave is described as "pretty standard," though one (male) consultant reports, "They give ridiculous part-time with full compensation deals to all the working moms that they are afraid will leave the company. There is no set policy or program, so every woman is free to negotiate her own deal." Another consultant observes, "they are very flexible with taking maternity/paternity leave and other vacation time, as well as attendance of doctor's appointments both before and after birth. A small present is also sent to each new family."

The cubicle crunch

Huron's office spaces seem to inhabit two extremes—overwhelmingly vast and ridiculously cramped. Surprisingly, the Manhattan office is characterized by insiders as almost too spacious, with a "very spread out" feel leading to "a large lack of communication and socialization between people." In Chicago, on the other hand, sources report "people sitting at card tables." "Desk space is tight and only managing directors have offices, which makes it difficult for managers and directors to have private conversations or to have calls with clients without disruptions," says an insider. "Sitting at cubes with a bunch of managers and directors trying to talk to clients on the phone or meet with staff to review things is embarrassing," a colleague grumbles. "Given that we're told all the time how much money we make, we should have more space. It's important," insists a source. And several insiders bemoan the Chicago office's out-of-the-Loop location, which leads to long commutes and is "not close to any decent restaurants."

Respect for the top

In general, Huron insiders give kudos to their higher-ups. One analyst raves, "Every employee has a coach to act as an advocate and mine is wonderful! Also, I have been impressed with my level of interaction with managing directors at Huron, despite being a newer employee." "Our senior management team are the types of people that you respect in every sense of the word. They

Visit the Vault Consulting Career Channel at **www.vault.com/consulting** - with insider firm profiles, message boards, the Vault Consulting Job Board and more.

VAULT CAREER LIBRARY   313

are successful in business, build great relationships with people and understand the importance of family," another source says. Agrees an insider, "Developing, fostering and growing relationships is a core value of Huron. We have a coaching/mentoring program that is key to our culture and performance management. I have an invaluable relationship with my supervisor, who also serves as a mentor and advocate." According to a consultant, "Huron continues to grow and grow, but it still remains a smaller firm. The positive thing is that you can develop relationships and work closely with top leadership."

However, all's not entirely rosy on the management front, some consultants say. As one insider puts it, "Managers and supervisors are highly variable in both quality and style. I am sure there are types to match everyone; however, one problem I see with this firm is that because it is so young, many of the people in leadership positions, particularly at the manager level, are very young. Their experience is purely the past four to seven years they have spent with Huron, and before that, Arthur Andersen (Huron's predecessor). This breeds a certain exclusion to 'outsiders,' particularly newcomers with additional, more diverse experience and background." A colleague agrees, "Senior management is made of former Andersen partners who are basically promoting people that they know. People that were not part of the clique are left out in the cold."

Still, most Huron employees seem happy about their level of interaction on the client side. "Two years out of school, I was 100 percent responsible for all client management at a Fortune 500 firm," one source says. "Even as an analyst, I worked directly with client CEOs and CFOs, and presented in front of senior executives. I even was allowed to attend a special meeting of a client's board of directors to decide on a restructuring strategy. As an associate, I was placed as an interim director for one client—that type of exposure simply does not exist elsewhere," another insider reports.

Learning by doing

Training at Huron takes the form of "both official training sessions offered by internal departments and external consultants, and unofficial mentoring," as well as "a very good coach and peer mentor system," says a source, adding, "The efficacy of this largely depends on the quality of both the coach and peer." A few insiders report being underwhelmed by the firm's orientation for new hires: "New hire training within the practices is not formalized or coordinated to a proper degree, and doesn't provide enough depth," a source claims. "Much of what I had to learn, I had to figure out for myself. This created some frustration, as I did not know who to call or where the resources were," agrees a colleague. But others report taking part in courses in Chicago and New York through the Huron Academy, as well as "lunch and learn" events and the option for external training, including evening MBA programs and CFA prep courses.

Equal opportunity

At Huron, "we do not have formal programs, but we have an environment that has permitted many women to rise to the top both in management and in the consulting practice," says an insider. "In certain practices and service lines, there is a low presence of women at the higher levels of the organization, resulting in a lack of women role models and mentors," a consultant adds, but "from a hiring standpoint, women appear to be hired as likely as men." Still, a female director contends, "Putting a spotlight on our differences only diminishes the men's view of our capabilities and commitment, and is a waste of time. Be a leader—whether you're a man or woman, and get over the gender issues."

And how about minorities at Huron? Depends who you ask. One insider describes the firm as "overwhelmingly Caucasian," but says, "I don't think it's intentional and employees are generally respectful." "To be honest, I think the glass ceiling is lower for minorities. I have not seem many [minorities] higher up on the food chain," a co-worker opines. But another source remarks, "We seem to hire more minorities than other consulting firms." A consultant sums up, "The firm says it is making an effort in recruiting diverse candidates. It's not a change that can be made overnight, but I do believe it's important to the firm."

Comfortable to be out?

When it comes to sexuality, one gay insider comments, "Right now, I would rate Huron as 'GLBT-tolerant' and not 'GLBT-friendly.' This level of comfort varies between New York and Chicago (less friendly in Chicago). I think there is room for improvement." "I think core Midwestern (read: conservative, traditional) values dominate this firm," says another source.

"Although I have yet to overhear homophobic comments, it's a topic I feel uncomfortable discussing among my co-workers," a gay colleague tells us. But several other insiders report more positive experiences. "The domestic partner benefits are awesome," one insider cheers, and another consultant comments, "This feels like a pretty comfortable place to be out. People bring partners to social functions. I am one of a number of GLBT folks at the MD level—and there are many at all levels."

Hands-on Huron

Huron is gung-ho about community service, largely coordinated through a program known as Huron Helping Hands, staffers say. "There are many opportunities provided throughout the entire year, as well as giving by the company itself. Employees are actively encouraged to participate in charitable organizations in their communities, and Huron employees are active on many nonprofit boards," reports a source. According to another insider, "We have a web-based mechanism for employees to find charitable activities in which to get involved, and we have annual clothing, blood and food drives. Last year, we produced our first annual report on our charitable work." Chicago sources report involvement in food and toy drives, and Boys & Girls Clubs, and providing tax assistance for the needy. In New York, Huron staffers participate in New York Cares Day, the City Harvest food drive, the Revlon Run/Walk and other events.

Visit the Vault Consulting Career Channel at **www.vault.com/consulting** - with insider firm profiles, message boards, the Vault Consulting Job Board and more.

VAULT CAREER LIBRARY   315

VAULT TOP 50

40

PRESTIGE
RANKING

Arthur D. Little

125 High Street
High Street Tower, 28th Floor
Boston, MA 02110
Phone: (617) 532-9550
Fax: (617) 261-6630
www.adlittle-us.com

LOCATIONS

Boston, MA (US HQ)
Paris (HQ)
Houston, TX
New York, NY
30 offices worldwide

PRACTICE AREAS

Automotive & Manufacturing
Chemicals & Healthcare
Energy & Utilities
Financial Services
Operations & Information Management
Strategy & Organization
Sustainability & Risk
Technology & Innovation Management
Telecommunication, Information, Media & Electronics

THE STATS

Employer Type: Subsidiary of Altran Technologies
Ticker Symbol: ALTRAN TECHN (Paris Bourse)
CEO: Michael Träm
2007 Employees: 1,000+
2006 Employees: 1,000+
2005 Revenue: $239 million

THE BUZZ
WHAT CONSULTANTS AT OTHER FIRMS ARE SAYING ABOUT THIS FIRM

- "The granddaddy of them all"
- "Fallen gods"
- "Good niche skills"
- "Weak in US, strong in Asia and Europe"

RANKING RECAP

Quality of Life
#2 - Relationships with Supervisors
#3 - Overall Satisfaction
#4 - Hours in the Office
#6 - Interaction with Clients
#6 - Firm Culture
#7 - Best Firms to Work For
#8 - Formal Training
#9 - Work/Life Balance
#9 - Offices

Diversity
#1 - Diversity for Minorities
#7 - Best Firms for Diversity
#18 - Diversity for Women

UPPERS

- "I feel I'm really a part of a prestigious organization"
- Plenty of opportunities for career growth
- People are "not nearly as artificial and haughty as at other firms"
- "The firm has a history of innovation and of being a 'first mover'"

DOWNERS

- "Politics with regard to ADL and the corporate parent Altran"
- Need more US-based training
- "We don't have the same weight as major firms in the US right now—difficult to get major clients"
- "Sometimes you do not have a choice about which projects you work on"

EMPLOYMENT CONTACT

www.adlittle-us.com/careers

THE SCOOP

The original consultants

Known as the world's first consulting firm, Boston-based Arthur D. Little was founded by chemist and inventor Arthur Dehon Little in 1886. The firm pioneered the development of contracted laboratory research, and in the process helped usher in some of the 20th century's most significant innovations: the word processor, synthetic penicillin, fiberglass and the Nasdaq stock exchange. Today, ADL consults in areas such as environment and risk, information management, operations management, strategy and organization, and technology and innovation—for a roster of largely Fortune 500 clients spread across the automotive, chemical, consumer goods and services, energy, TIME (telecommunications, information technology, media and electronics), private equity, health care, transportation and utilities industries.

A bankruptcy filing in 2002 forced ADL to sell off parts of its business (and reduce its workforce by almost half) to firms eager to buy into the well-known brand, with the French technology and consulting giant Altran Technologies eventually buying the Arthur D. Little name and its core management consulting business. The firm has subsequently become increasingly Euro-centric—in September 2006 the firm's world headquarters were moved to Paris and German-born Michael Träm was named CEO.

New leadership, new markets

Träm succeeded Richard Clarke as Arthur D. Little's CEO. Clarke's tenure was a time of change and rebuilding for the firm, as he guided ADL through the Altran merger and the extended financial ramifications of the 2002 bankruptcy filing. At the same time, Clarke was responsible for expanding ADL's global business in growth markets such as South America, Europe and the Middle East. To this end, Träm seems to be closely following his predecessor's lead; ADL opened a new office in Dubai and New York in early 2007.

With the expansion, in early 2007 ADL hired Markus Lahrkamp as its new managing director of North America. His goal is to expand ADL's North American presence. Today, more than 1,000 ADL associates work in 30 offices around the world, with U.S. consultants working out of offices in Boston, Houston and New York.

Follow my voice

One of Clarke's final steps as CEO was to introduce Arthur D. Little's new slogan—"smart innovation"—which he defined as the "capacity to innovate in order to exploit opportunities associated with complexity." This is a suitably complex concept. ADL consultants work to transform clients into "smart innovators," or companies capable of embracing complex situations to reap economic benefits. For this to occur, clients must first "exploit the complex opportunity"; that is to say, clients must choose whether to eliminate complexity, by streamlining product offerings, for instance, or embrace complexity by recognizing untapped areas of a market that could be exploited through expansion, growth and new business alliances. Clients, too, must master what Clarke termed the "innovation agenda"; they must fully recognize the needs of all concerned stakeholders, and become flexible to adapt instantly and meet the needs of those stakeholders in new ways.

Private equity calling

The firm has also become a player in providing services to private equity firms and their portfolio companies. The New York office has a core group of partners and consultants who are focused on serving private equity and hedge fund clients. Consultants advise equity clients on both their deal due diligence and on operational improvement of portfolio companies. Since 2004, ADL has served over 100 private equity and venture capital clients, including such leading funds as Bain Capital, Carlyle, Apax, Silver Lake and Permira, and also a number of midmarket firms, like Kohlberg & Co., Vestar Capital and Bear Stearns Merchant Banking.

Visit the Vault Consulting Career Channel at www.vault.com/consulting - with insider firm profiles, message boards, the Vault Consulting Job Board and more.

VAULT CAREER LIBRARY   317

Do your research

Consultants at Arthur D. Little lay the groundwork for smart innovation by putting forth exhaustive competitive research. Studies published by the firm in 2006 covered a wide array of issues, from the future of industrial trucking in Europe through 2015, to the viability of 35 British research universities as a resource for contracted independent research, to a comprehensive analysis of the British health care equipment sector. Many of these studies can be requested free-of-charge on ADL's web site.

In each report, the firm's research takes a big-picture approach, analyzing entire industries and geopolitical areas and attempting to influence policy on a broad scale. For instance, an April 2006 report by the firm's TIME unit suggested ways for the British government to create an economic environment in which the private sector would be prepared to make significant investments in the use of energy. Arthur D. Little's client base is of a similarly global scale, comprised largely of governments and the world's largest manufacturing, industrial and high-tech firms.

GETTING HIRED

Independent thinking is a virtue

On its web site, Arthur D. Little indicates a preference for candidates with MBAs or doctorates. It also wants "independent thinking" types with the "ability to put ideas into action." The firm doesn't provide much information about campus recruiting, but since "ADL started from MIT," an insider comments, "MIT is always on the list" of schools from which it recruits. In addition to the usual Ivy League suspects, a colleague notes, "the Boston office recruits at Johns Hopkins, the Houston office recruits at Rice and the New York City office recruits at Columbia and NYU Stern." Sources also list the University of Chicago, Northwestern, Oxford and Tufts as schools where the firm scouts potential candidates.

If you're looking to join ADL, expect a "really selective and demanding recruiting process," says a source, who reports going through nine interviews to get the gig. "Each geographic market has its own hiring process, which ranges from very formal assessment days to interviews with the directors of an office," says another. According to one consultant, "We are looking first for 'intellectual horsepower,' but it must be coupled with good chemistry relative to our culture and team personalities as well."

Express yourself

One insider who was hired straight out of school reports, "[The firm] did not come for a campus interview and I applied online and got an interview. If you are interested in ADL, you should push to express your interest." The source adds, "Before the interview day, I was invited for a one-to-one dinner with one of the senior managers, just to chat!" The following day, says the insider, "I had interviews with five people (a series of behavioral, technical and cases) but never felt [I was] being drilled down. Overall, there is a lot of human interaction in the interview, which you generally don't get with other companies. In short, fit is very important."

According to another staffer, "The firm has extremely high standards. After recruiting events, or online, there's a resume drop. Typically one in 30 resumes makes the cut for a brief phone interview. After the phone interview, there are generally two rounds. However, if you really impress, you can get by with one round, or if there are questions, there might be a third round. Fit with the office is important. Have courage, though—if you are a genuine individual with the necessary drive and talent, it's a very worthwhile process." A colleague adds that the process is "intense and quick," and "you feel proud once you receive the offer."

Expect cases

Insiders advise candidates to "expect at least two cases and some brainteasers." Generally, case questions "come directly from real projects, and are aimed to test how the candidate would have reacted in our same situation." "I had a question involving an operational and marketing assessment of a file folder company," a consultant reports.

For information on summer internship opportunities, it's best to directly contact the office in which you're interested. One insider says the firm's summer internship "was a very rich and rewarding experience. I was able to work on many different projects and learn quickly about the way ADL does projects."

OUR SURVEY SAYS

Shaping the culture

By far, the word ADL consultants use most frequently to describe their firm's culture is "entrepreneurial." "You take part in shaping office culture," says one source, who adds, "it's expected that you are responsible for your work; hence, there is not a lot of telling you exactly what to do—you can be as creative as you can." "The culture promotes independent thought and ideas," agrees a colleague. The firm is also notable for its "open management style," "flat organization," "friendly and professional culture," and a "down-to-earth," "relaxed" environment, insiders tell us.

The international set

ADL consultants enjoy their "collegial and cooperative" co-workers, as well, a source says, noting, "Most ADL people are willing to help in many different situations." Several insiders praise the firm's "international" feel, with one consultant commenting, "International appeal is not given by having many offices in many nations, but by having many nations in one office." In Boston, a source says, "Everyone gets along, there's almost no intra-office politics, and everyone can be themselves. It sounds rather hokey, but it's true. The people here are extremely smart (I feel average here, and was considered significantly above average at Harvard Medical School) but extremely down to earth." A New Yorker consultant chimes in: "The New York office has a great culture. Everyone is entrepreneurial and very respectful of others personal needs. I tend to hang out a lot with people from work by choice, but that's not at all an expectation."

No beach bums here

"Consulting in general isn't a 9-to-5 job, but the hours expected for most ADL offices are reasonable," an insider tells us. ADLers report averaging between 50 and 60 hours a week, and "interesting work makes late nights bearable," a source says. The average length of an assignment can vary widely, from six weeks to more than a year. According to one busy guy, "The director here is known for his ability to sell work; as a result, we rarely have beach time and utilization rates are high. Even as we are finishing up a project, there are usually several other projects he's won and waiting to get free staffers for. In general, a day or two of beach time is all you really need to convince yourself that it's better to be staffed, as you run out of things to do and get bored." The consultant adds, "High utilization also has other trickle-down benefits: better bonuses and higher raises."

Teamwork makes the time fly

Insiders generally agree that "compared to other firms, the work/life balance is respected at ADL." A source reports, "In my experience, working on weekends is the exception, and when we do work on weekends, we pitch in as a team." A colleague elaborates, "Weekend work is rare, and work can usually be done from home. Late nights depend upon project deadlines, but are not a constant. Perhaps most importantly, on the occasion that we do work a weekend or a few long nights, the director will pay for us to take time off." The source adds that "there is no face time culture at ADL—if you're here late, it's because there is a clear need. When things are slower, the job is almost 9 to 5 … That said, if there is a project with tight deadlines, everyone (of their own volition) pitches in to make sure that staffers don't have an excessively long night ahead of them."

Bending over backward for balance

Many staffers praise ADL management for its flexibility when it comes to striking a balance. "The leadership team is very respectful of personal needs, such as attending weddings and family events," a source says. "ADL has an extensive vacation plan

Visit the Vault Consulting Career Channel at www.vault.com/consulting - with insider firm profiles, message boards, the Vault Consulting Job Board and more.

VAULT CAREER LIBRARY   319

that offers 18 days a year plus sick days," adds a colleague, and the "company is flexible to accommodate personal needs." According to another insider, "Whenever there isn't a tight deadline on a project, the work/life balance is fairly good. I can usually get out at a humane hour to live my life." "Our projects are generally carefully aligned in terms of scope, timing and budget expectations, so there's the right amount of time to do the job properly, without running around all night before deadlines as if our hair is on fire (I have had this experience elsewhere and work hard not to replicate it!)," a co-worker agrees.

At ADL, an insider says, "there is a mix of office, local and international assignments," and "it's up to you to decide how much you want to travel." According to another consultant, "For the last two years, I have traveled about one to two days per week every other week. Most project work is done at the home office with occasional travel to the client site for milestone meetings." "Some travel is expected, but I have traveled much less than I did at Booz Allen," an experienced colleague observes. One insider keeps it real: "First off, if you don't like to travel, consulting is not for you. That said, ADL does not have a camp-out-at-the-client mentality like a McKinsey, nor does it chain you to your desk. Moreover you have a say in the amount of traveling you do. A significant amount of the determination is left up to the needs of the project, however." When travel is necessary, "since the firm usually puts you up in upper-end locations … comfort is not an issue," sources say. And "from a work standpoint, on-site work can be very stimulating, due to the fact you are usually interacting with clients and gaining a better understanding of their business," another consultant chimes in.

It pays to negotiate

As for compensation, an insider comments, "Compensation is slightly lower compared to other top-tier global management consulting firms." And while that may be true, some staffers are OK with that. Says one satisfied source, "A few other firms may pay more (e.g., McKinsey), but I also feel that they put in far more hours in the office for the few thousand extra they do make. Several of my friends from Cornell are McKinseyites and are amazed at how rare weekend work is for me." A consultant advises that it "pays off to negotiate your bonus," since they can vary widely, and a colleague reports that a "sign-on bonus was asked for, but not offered." Insiders tell us that the firm's profit-sharing contributions go into a retirement fund, and the firm matches 2 percent of 401(k) contributions.

ADL's perks include fun stuff like karaoke parties and cooking competitions, and "to celebrate special occasions and recognize individual accomplishments, the entire office goes out to lunch or dinner," sources say. There's also paid parking, cell phone coverage and "beer in the fridge." According to one consultant, "In addition to the standard bonuses—vacation time, profit sharing, etc.—we also receive project bonuses and/or gifts partway through and at the end of long projects, and at the end of shorter projects."

Offices get an "A"

When it comes to offices, "the significant investment in adequate, class-A space in a central urban location is well worth the returns in morale and productivity terms," an insider cheers. One consultant applauds the fact that "there is adequate physical space/privacy (thankfully there is no hoteling or hot desk arrangement here!) and natural light for all of our knowledge workers in the office—we can truly focus and be as productive as possible." In New York, "our new office in the Chrysler building needs a bit more furniture and some plants, but it is very spacious and immaculate," an insider says. Up in Boston, "the new offices on High Street are sumptuous and elegant—rated Class AA and overlooking the Boston Harbor." But a colleague down South brags about the "excellent space in the Houston office," adding, "Other offices are not nearly as nice as ours."

ADL consultants also give high marks to their supervisors. One insider says, "Listening to my friends' experiences at other firms, ADL is less hierarchical. Our directors and our managing director are accessible and open to suggestions from all staff." A colleague agrees that supervisors are "very sensible and attentive to the needs of the staff." Says another consultant, "The relationship with management is one if the best aspects of this job. In addition, the exposure to top-level management is unlike any other firm across all levels."

An insider elaborates, "Access both to senior-level supervisors and clients is excellent. While most firms employ a pyramid style, top-down structure, ADL is almost linear. Thus, as a consultant, you are often entrusted with important and often exciting responsibilities, and work directly with directors and senior managers. Additionally, since you are essentially an expert in your case area, you make quite a few presentations to clients' senior management. [Entry levels] here interact and present to all but C-suite clients, and consultants interact, present and facilitate client relationships at the highest levels, particularly after the first year or two."

Nice? How nice!

ADL offers training in some "incredible" locations, including a resort on the French Riviera in Nice, as well as Brussels and Barcelona, sources tell us. A contact explains that the firm's on-the-job training "is provided through interaction with very senior consultants (senior managers, managers and even the director). You get a lot of one-on-one interaction and feedback that I would suspect would be a lot more difficult to achieve at other firms." "The official training is excellent, but needs to be more frequent," one consultant reports, though "informal mechanisms work very well, due to the type of people hired." "I take at least one formal company training course per year offered by ADL. In the past, if I have had an interest in another course outside of ADL, my director has offered to pay for it," another source shares.

Women in the lead

Though sources don't mention any specific programs, "ADL seems like a good place for women to work," an insider opines. "We have excellent representation of women and minorities, and we actively recruit people of all categories," a colleague adds. According to another consultant, the firm employs "numerous women throughout the firm in positions from directors (partners) to analysts." A source sums it up: "I think with any other diversity perspective, ADL is completely unbiased. If you have the talent and the dedication, you will get an offer. Period," adding, "ADL has a roughly equal number of men and women, and perhaps more impressively, [has] women in director roles who can provide strong mentorship."

"I love the diversity" at ADL, a source exclaims, noting, "Many of my colleagues are from different parts of the world." "Being a minority myself, I can attest to the firm's great receptiveness," a colleague remarks. "Diversity is great at ADL Boston. Just about every ethnic background is represented here, and over half of our office are minorities," says another source. The firm states that in the New York office, most of the team members have an international background and all the consultants have had significant international work experience. As another consultant points out, "Diversity is one of the key drivers for our practice. This is where truly great insights come from." And, an insider adds, "I was very pleased to see that the firm is welcoming to members of the gay community."

Quietly charitable

Staffers don't have much to report about ADL's community service initiatives—one consultant puts it (charitably), "I believe our firm would be very open to community involvement in the near future." "Although many of our consultants contribute their own time, we leave that up to the individual," says a co-worker. But another consultant contends, "ADL encourages community involvement and has a long history, particularly in the Boston area, of engaging in quite a bit of anonymous philanthropy."

Visit the Vault Consulting Career Channel at **www.vault.com/consulting** - with insider firm profiles, message boards, the Vault Consulting Job Board and more.

VAULT CAREER LIBRARY   321

Corporate Executive Board

2000 Pennsylvania Avenue, NW
Suite 6000
Washington, DC 20006
Phone: (202) 777-5000
Fax: (202) 777-5100
www.executiveboard.com

LOCATIONS

Washington, DC (HQ)
Chicago, IL
San Francisco, CA
London
New Delhi

PRACTICE AREAS

Corporate Finance
Financial Services
Human Resources
Information Technology
Innovation & Operations
Legal & Governance
Middle Market
Sales, Marketing & Communications
Strategy & Management

THE STATS

Employer Type: Public Company
Ticker Symbol: EXBD (Nasdaq)
Chairman: James J. McGonigle
CEO: Thomas L. Monahan III
2007 Employees: 2,350+
2006 Employees: 2,200
2006 Revenue: $460.6 million
2005 Revenue: $362.2 million

UPPERS

• "Young environment, easy to make friends"
• Lots of happy hours

DOWNERS

• "Too competitive"
• "Getting larger, to the point where bureaucracy is developing"

EMPLOYMENT CONTACT

www.executiveboard.com/Careers + with + us

THE BUZZ
WHAT CONSULTANTS AT OTHER FIRMS ARE SAYING ABOUT THIS FIRM

• "Successful niche player, clear value proposition"
• "Frat boy culture"
• "A great think tank"
• "Chew 'em up, spit 'em out"

THE SCOOP

Learn from the competition

The Corporate Executive Board knows it pays to learn from the best. The executive consulting firm operates on a membership basis, sharing best practices research, analysis and tools with more than 3,700 of its member companies. Its 45 program areas tackle executive challenges in communications, corporate finance, human resources, information technology, legal and governance, innovation and operations, sales and marketing, and strategy and management. The firm also offers seminars, customized research briefs and decision-support tools. With offices in Washington, D.C., London, New Delhi, Chicago and San Francisco, and employing more than 2,300 consulting professionals, CEB counts among its membership over 80 percent of the Fortune 500. In fiscal 2006 alone, the Corporate Executive Board presented its research findings to more than 230,000 executives.

A successful spin-off

The Corporate Executive Board was founded in 1979 as the Research Council of Washington, a name that was changed to the Advisory Board Company in 1983. By 1997, however, the Advisory Board's membership and focus had grown to include programs dedicated to health care, financial services and corporate executives. In order to focus on its core business, health care, the Advisory Board spun off the Corporate Executive Board to focus exclusively on providing support to its financial services and corporate members.

The year CEB opened its doors, it had about 400 staff members and 1,300 member companies. Two years later, it went public, and today employs more than 2,300 people consulting on projects for an impressive 3,700 companies (including Alcoa, BT, the Coca-Cola Company, GM, Shell and Unilever) in 51 countries.

That kind of success evidences on the income statement. Revenue in 2006 was up more than 25 percent from 2005, reaching $460.6 million. Profits have risen annually by 20 percent every year except one, and Wall Street expects earnings to keep growing quickly for the next few years. CEB's optimism got an additional boost when it landed on *Forbes*' 2006 ranking of the 200 Best Small Companies in the World, and 11th on the magazine's list of Hot Shots/Entrepreneurial Companies.

Membership model

The Corporate Executive Board prides itself on being the "largest network of leading executives around the globe"—but just how does that network work? CEB is organized into a selection of stand-alone research programs, each with its own membership network, content archive, dedicated research and service staff. At the end of 2006, CEB had 45 research programs, including the CFO Executive Board, the Procurement Strategy Council, the Sales Executive Council and the General Counsel Roundtable. Member executives subscribe to individual research programs and designate staff within their own organizations to participate in and benefit from CEB's services.

Each company's membership fee, which averages approximately $35,000, allows its employees to access reports relevant to its business, request new research and attend annual meetings with peers at other companies. Members can also tap into CEB's research library and its 25 years' worth of archived case studies and best-practice research.

Middle market

Chairman James McGonigle and CEO Thomas Monahan have plans to continue expanding the firm. In 2005, the firm launched an initiative to tap into the middle market, or companies that have annual revenue between $100 million and $750 million. Previously, CEB only accepted members with a minimum annual revenue of $750 million, but the firm now believes that expanding its customer base to include more than 10,000 companies in North America and Europe could help increase its addressable market to $5 billion—more than 13 times the firm's fiscal 2005 revenue.

Visit the Vault Consulting Career Channel at **www.vault.com/consulting** - with insider firm profiles, message boards, the Vault Consulting Job Board and more.

VAULT CAREER LIBRARY   323

Networking, networking, networking

The Corporate Executive Board has a long list of values, which are central to its business model. Top among these is the "force of ideas," which can "carry an organization forward more surely than can access to superior resources, market power or sheer effort." To help find and implement those ideas, CEB has developed an extensive network of "peer executives" who share their knowledge and experience with each other. CEB—and its members—realize that no one company is the best at everything and that, by sharing information, everyone in the network benefits. In 2005, that network held 511 membership meetings in 61 cities across 18 countries. With a 92 percent membership renewal rate in 2005, it appears that very few of CEB's members have a problem sharing.

Helping in other ways

Outside the office, CEB is dedicated to serving the community through CEB ServiceCorps. The firm promotes and facilitates service opportunities for teams, individuals and the company as a whole. Across the board, all employees are allowed to use 40 hours of daytime leave per year for service-related activities and can also earn extra vacation days by reaching hours of service milestones. In 2006, the Corporate Executive Board's staff contributed over 14,000 charitable hours via tutoring, mentoring, preparing meals and hosting birthday parties for the homeless. The firm also hosts a blood drive every two months and organizes a 'service Saturday' twice each year. For example, in April 2007, hundreds of CEB staff, family and friends spent the day cleaning, landscaping and painting three Washington, D.C., schools. Reflecting the many contributions of the organization and its staff, CEB was recognized by *Washington Business Journal* as No. 9 in the Top 10 Corporate Philanthropists in Greater Washington (ranked by its service hours in 2006).

GETTING HIRED

Dynamic minds wanted

CEB offers a detailed careers section on its web site, with loads of information on career paths, recruiting, and company benefits. While the firm hires a large number of its employees from undergraduate programs, CEB very actively recruits MBA graduates and midcareer professionals for numerous opportunities across the organization.

The hiring process starts with an interview with HR, or "talent management," in firm parlance. According to one insider, the process for research analyst hopefuls incorporates a writing sample and two to three interviews with senior researchers, including case and behavioral questions.

Making a list ...

A colleague reports, "I had one interview over the phone, then I flew out for a full day, which consisted of four interviews (in three different buildings!). The questions were basic interview questions (strengths, weaknesses, how do you prioritize time). Friends who worked at the company had prepped me before to say that I was type A, make lists constantly and hate to leave things undone even if I don't have the time to do them."

OUR SURVEY SAYS

Collegial and collegiate

Corporate Executive Board staffers tend to agree that their firm boasts a "young" and "energetic" corporate culture. Whether this is a good or bad thing depends on who you ask. With "lots of company-sponsored happy hours" and "supportive and nice" co-workers, it's "great for someone straight out of college who doesn't really know what they want to do," theorizes one analyst.

"CEB employs a lot of young people—many just out of college—and there is an enormous drinking culture that CEB condones," a colleague reports. The firm explains that while company-sponsored social events are commonplace, especially in the revenue functions, they are designed to reward and recognize staff for exceptional on-the-job performance, and staff are expected to exhibit appropriate workplace behavior. "Creative people do not do well here. The firm even recognizes (at their firmwide meetings) that CEB has a cultish culture. You either conform and fit their mold, or you leave." And several sources describe CEB as either a "fraternity" or "sorority"—with all the positive and negative connotations those terms convey. As one insider sums up, "While certainly not for everyone, the culture at CEB is quite exhilarating much of the time."

With youth comes less of a need for sleep, and CEB often expects long hours from its lower-level staffers, especially those in the revenue functions. For example, in the marketing and member services departments, "there are several mandatory days per month where you are required to work 7:30 a.m. to 6:30 p.m. without much break time. I think that's too much and it wears people out," one source says. But a more senior insider notes that "generally, you can achieve a healthy balance" between work and life; "I typically work two to three weekends a year, [and] take at least one three-week vacation." "It is very much a 'whatever it takes to get the job done' culture but face time itself has little value, so if you're efficient at your job you need not spend many nights in the office," a staffer explains. As for travel, one source believes that this "varies greatly based on role in the organization, but for research teams it is very manageable."

Parties aplenty

One insider describes CEB compensation as a "weak spot": "Though not noncompetitive, salary is not yet at a McKinsey or BCG level, even though that is the caliber of talent they wish to attract." However, consultants may participate in a stock purchase plan, and reportedly receive 24 vacation days per year. There are also "happy hours and parties" aplenty. Community service is said to be "encouraged and rewarded," and the firm is "highly regarded in the Washington area for its service efforts."

According to a source, there's "lots of diversity across the organization" and "a large international contingent." But the news is mixed for CEB women; insiders observe that it's a "boys' club with lots of very young, impressionable women in the entry-level ranks," and "lots of politically incorrect behavior deemed by management to be in 'good fun.'" The firm challenges this assertion, stating that equal opportunity employment is a strategic priority, and that women comprise much of the senior-level management ranks.

Visit the Vault Consulting Career Channel at **www.vault.com/consulting** - with insider firm
profiles, message boards, the Vault Consulting Job Board and more.

VAULT CAREER LIBRARY   325

90 Park Avenue
New York, NY 10016
Phone: (212) 557-0500
www.fmcg.com

LOCATIONS

New York, NY (HQ)
Seattle, WA
Melbourne

PRACTICE AREAS

Advanced Segmentation
Asset/Liability & Portfolio Management
Business, Product & Customer Profitability
Capital Management & Risk-Adjusted Performance
Corporate & Line of Business Strategy
Cost Structure Management
Credit, Market/Interest Rate & Operational Risk
Customer Acquisition & Retention Programs
Customer Relationship Management
Distribution Strategy
M&A Strategy & Due Diligence
Marketing Effectiveness Assessment
Online & E-Commerce
Operations Strategy
Organizational Design
Pre- & Post-Merger Integration
Product Design & Pricing
Technology Alliances & Outsourcing
Technology Strategy

THE STATS

Employer Type: Private Company
President: James M. McCormick
2007 Employees: 75
2006 Employees: 72

RANKING RECAP

Practice Area
#8 - Financial Consulting

Quality of Life
#1 - Compensation
#4 - Interaction with Clients
#19 - Travel Requirements

UPPERS

- "You actually get to be a consultant at FMCG, as opposed to a data analyst hidden from the client"
- "When we say we interact with C-level clients on their top issues, we really mean it"
- Strong brand in the industry
- "Tremendous intellectual stimulation, coupled with an open-door policy at all levels"

DOWNERS

- "Inadequate social activities and internal communication"
- "Drive for perfection can overkill a problem"
- Administrative support not given adequate resources for high work volume
- "Tedious research work that is necessary because of the small firm size"

EMPLOYMENT CONTACT

www.fmcg.com/careers/overview.htm

THE BUZZ
WHAT CONSULTANTS AT OTHER FIRMS ARE SAYING ABOUT THIS FIRM

- "High-class work"
- "Like working in a straightjacket"
- "Very credible in the financial services space"
- "No growth potential"

THE SCOOP

Going straight to the top

First Manhattan Consulting Group goes for the big guns when it works with the big guys. The New York-based consulting company aims to be the "consulting firm of choice" for higher-ups in the world of financial services." Says the firm, "We begin projects far up the learning curve [so] we can deliver more value and sophistication in less time and for less cost." Since 1980, the firm has worked on 2,500 financial services engagements, including work for 80 percent of the 70-largest U.S. bank-holding companies, insurance carriers, international banks, finance companies, guarantee companies, diversified financial firms, national and regional brokerages, and technology vendors. FMCG scores big on repeat deals, with many of its clients having asked the firm for help on more than 50 different assignments.

Targeted offerings

FMCG's focus on top-line management is clear. Although its engagements are in such diverse locations as Australia, Canada, New Zealand, Mexico and South Africa, its clients all share one quality: They are all senior-level executives at major financial institutions. "We at FMCG have an intentionally narrower focus on high-value added focus," says founder and President James M. McCormick of his firm.

That kind of focus is especially clear when you look at how FMCG categorizes its services. For example, a chief executive officer can go to FMCG for advice on his corporate strategy or merger integration plans. Chief marketing officers can pick FMCG's brains on segmentation, product design and pricing, or customer acquisition programs, while chief risk officers can get help sizing up their company's credit or operational risk. Don't leave out the chief financial officers, who may need help managing their portfolio or cost structure, or the chief information officer, whose technology strategy questions need answering.

Making sense out of cents

Everyone needs a little help; that's what keeps consulting firms like FMCG in business. To keep its edge in a market saturated with advice-givers, however, FMCG has put together a niche mix of strategy, finance, technology, productivity and other skills that helps it to, first and foremost, discover new insights about a company's capacity and increase clients' value. The firm's other goals include helping to develop benchmarks for key lines of business, designing new ways of calculating capital adequacy and capital allocation, and putting into practice its "best practices" for postmerger consolidation and bankwide productivity programs. The firm's final goal is to find concrete ways of helping clients know—and reach—their customers better. One step toward this goal was the introduction of FMCG's trademarked Financial Personality market segment scoring service, launched in November 2006, in conjunction with the Experian Group. The service predicts consumers' attitudes concerning fees and interest rates so that financial services companies know what needs to be done to acquire new customers.

In-house smarts

To work with the level of clients FMCG works with, new hires have to have the know-how to tackle some of the industry's most complex problems. That is why the firm prides itself on its professional development options for the firm's 70-plus employees. Newly hired analysts, for example, travel to two offset sessions when they start at FMCG, which are led by experienced analysts, officers and academics at the firm. The first session focuses on learning and developing the core skills they'll need at FMCG, while during the second, new analysts will go through all the motions of a client engagement in a case study. They are also enrolled in an in-house mentoring program; each consulting staff member with less than two years of experience at FMCG is assigned a mentor who knows the ropes.

On the job, all staffers attend ongoing "knowledge-building sessions" and the firm's industry speaker series. The firm also makes efforts to develop staffers' skills in the areas of meeting and public speaking, coaching and writing. And to make sure everyone's

Visit the Vault Consulting Career Channel at www.vault.com/consulting - with insider firm profiles, message boards, the Vault Consulting Job Board and more.

VAULT CAREER LIBRARY   327

on track, the firm holds regular reviews, whether they be face-to-face or project reviews. Upper management is also routinely reviewed by the employees that support them.

Getting the word out

The nice thing about FMCG is that it doesn't exclusively reserve its advice for clients. The firm regularly publishes articles, and its consultants have been quoted over 500 times in some of the world's biggest publications, including *The Wall Street Journal*, *Forbes*, *The Economist* and the *Financial Times*. Staffers also gives speeches at major investor and industry conferences and for various associations, including the Bank Administration Institute's CFO Roundtable, the Consumer Bankers Association marketing and other industry forums, the RMA Risk Management Forum and North American Asset Liability Association.

FMCG also puts out value-based management white papers, which are available to executives of financial institutions, journalists, bank analysts and educators. They outline the firm's perspectives on a variety of industry trends, like which business measures are the most effective for measuring shareholder returns and banks' organic growth performance, or which retail bank positioning works best with targeted customer groups. Other papers have focused on hot-button industry issues, such as IT outsourcing, franchise retail banking and small-business banking.

For tech-savvy financial services executives, FMCG also started offering an online series of podcasts in November 2006, called *On Banking*, which can be found on BankNet 360 Radio. So far, the series has tackled issues of shareholder performance and cross-selling on customer service calls.

GETTING HIRED

Come one, come all

While FMCG chooses to roam only a select number of college campuses for future firm superstars, determined consulting hopefuls hailing from outside its recruiting sphere should know that there's still hope. "Candidates can apply from anywhere," an analyst explains, but schools like Harvard, Cornell, UPenn, Princeton, Georgetown, Columbia and Dartmouth "are the official recruiting channels, which largely rely on 'recruiting captains' who are respective alumni for their assigned school."

A powwow of epic proportions

No matter where candidates happen to call home, the interview process is tailor-made for one applicant type—endurance specialists. "Hiring for undergraduates consists of two rounds of interviews," we're told, with "the first on campus and the second typically at a Super Saturday in the office." And though the term Super Saturday may clue some in to a somewhat rigorous day of analytical calisthenics, insiders invoke visions of intimate tête-à-têtes with one or two partners: "The second-round interviews themselves consist of four to five individual interviews," a source reports, with potential for more. One managing vice president gives insight into this musical chairs approach, advising interviewees to "just expect to meet more partners than in other firms," because "hiring analysts is the most important thing we do, so we invest a lot of senior folks' time in doing it right."

Cracking the case

During interview sessions, contenders should "expect lots of analytical case questions," insiders say, and should also know that "case studies are verbal and not technically in-depth." A first-year analyst tells all: The "interview format for second rounds is highly structured, with interviewers focusing on different aspects of a desired candidate, such as quantitative skills, interest in consulting, PC skills, willingness to travel, etc." Another new hire advises that although "it is not required of the interviewer to give one," aspirants should prepare for case questions accordingly. In short, FMCG's hiring process is a direct reflection of the firm's meticulous nature. "They are intense," an analyst sums up about interviews, "but so are the people who work here. FMCG has a very good, systematic way of screening and hiring the absolute best candidates available."

OUR SURVEY SAYS

A cultural divide

Although FMCG staffers are described as "incredibly intelligent," "very smart and interesting people," sources say the firm's office culture leaves little room for individual expression. "Everyone from first-year analysts to senior officers are basically good people and most can be classed as 'cool' or 'outgoing,' but have almost no time to let it show in work," an analyst shares. A colleague further compliments his fellow employees, but attests to the suppression consensus, saying that "there is no doubt that the people here are very highly motivated and intelligent; however, the amount of energy this requires leaves something to be desired socially." As a result, the FMCG "culture is pretty intense and can seem icy at times."

But there appears, it seems, to be an exception to the personality censorship present at the firm: Analysts have formed a buddy system all their own. "The culture is not one where people are forced to be together; this is not the FMCG way," a vice president confesses. "However," he continues, "there is a very tight relationship among the analysts—they look out for each other." While veteran employees may feel the burn of stiff individualism, newer hires, who start out as analysts, tend to stick to their kindred counterparts. "The firm is tight-knit," one such staffer reports, adding, "My co-workers are also my friends and teammates."

Hoops and happy hours

For those who complain that "building any form of culture is subjugated to increasing billing hours," as one employee states, fear not—the cavalry is arriving, albeit gradually. Currently, we're told, FMCG is making strides to facilitate more of a social milieu inside and outside its quarters. "There's been more activity lately in spurring more happy hours," a staffer remarks, and FMCG has "recently introduced monthly firm-sponsored events." Shares a managing VP, the firm's communal behavior "has improved tremendously since a few years ago, when there was little collegiality and it was all work and no play." And another agrees that "the tide is shifting" little by little, which may have to do with the firm's recent age reduction. Because "the firm is getting much younger," a source ruminates, "that has a positive effect on the culture here." Along with summer outings added to FMCG's developing social calendar, "also being reinstated is a weekly basketball game, where the firm rents a gym for any who are interested."

Along for the ride

FMCG staffers are definitely working machines, putting in 60 to 80 hours per week on average, but colleagues say that office time is ultimately up to the person in charge. "Hours are highly dependent on the partner you work under. Some have an extremely demanding need for information but no sense of feasibility, and therefore it is easy to have the analysts rack up hours every night," an employee tells us. Another exposes the opposite end of the spectrum, remarking that "other partners, such as mine, give a lot of space to work as you see fit." In either case, analysts say it's common practice to keep plugging away late night: "Some partners will micromanage and stay in constant contact with analysts; this means the analyst is in the office long hours," an insider states. A work-laden colleague goes so far as to declare that "the hours alone will cut my tenure here short."

The good news is that days starting with "S" are usually off limits. "Middle management is very conscious of the work hours put in by analysts and is good in trying not to overwhelm weekends." And a vice president drives the notion home, asserting that "weekend work is a no-no. Vacations and prearranged social plans are off-limits to be disrupted by work." Most sources feel confident that hours will be "getting better in the future with the addition of more staff," since now there are just "not enough analysts to handle all the projects."

Visit the Vault Consulting Career Channel at **www.vault.com/consulting** - with insider firm profiles, message boards, the Vault Consulting Job Board and more.

VAULT CAREER LIBRARY   329

Maximum exposure

On the subject of management, staffers chat positively about their superiors. "Partners take a very active role in analyst development," we're told, and "they are always available for questions if I stop by their offices. Often, a question will result in a longer-than-expected tutorial," an insider chimes in. Though relationships with partners and managers can be "very personality-specific," the general consensus is that "most make it a point to invest a lot of time in making their analysts smarter," even if time is often limited.

FMCG's size is also a factor when it comes to comingling among the ranks; one employee says that "because the firm is small, there is a lot of contact between analysts and officers." Another benefit is client interaction early on in one's tenure. Sources talk of rapid and frequent access to upper-level staff and premium clients, "even for first-year analysts. I think it is the most differentiating aspect of our firm," says a newer hire. Other colleagues mirror these sentiments, valuing their swiftly acquired client exposure and commenting that this "top-level exposure with clients remains very good—better than the industry, in general." One first-year analyst outlines his express-lane scramble up the FMCG ladder: "The first week at FMCG, I was in training. The second week, I was conducting analysis on a project. The third week, I was in a meeting with the executive staff of a major American bank, where my opinions influenced the direction of the conversation."

Because of this early, headfirst plunge into the fast-paced consulting world, FMCG employees are pushed to develop and gain experience much faster than they might at another firm. "At just about every position, you are expected to work several years ahead of yourself," an insider reports. "First-year analysts at other firms need to work more than three years to get the type of experience and exposure you get at FMCG in your first year."

Grow as you go

Because FMCG promises relatively pain-free access to amiable superiors, training for new hires follows suit. Staffers report minimal formal training during introductory stages ("some basics are rushed through in the first two weeks," shares a source), and express an emphasis on "learning by doing, rather than learning by sitting." An insider reports that the available "official training is top notch"—"top professors from universities are brought in to teach accounting and finance sessions"—and the firm even includes a smattering of professional training throughout the year, but "most of the training is on the job and by being thrown into the deep end." Employees say they prefer this informal approach. "Our introductory training is nice, but not very effective in producing useful analysts," a first-year explains, adding that "the on-the-job training, however, is fantastic."

FMCGers also love their proactive coaches, who moonlight as senior partners and management. "Most people learn from officers—who they interact with a great deal—and clients," an insider explains. But this mentor system isn't always fail-safe. "The only problem is that we work in small teams, meaning that whoever you're working with is responsible for your training," states an analyst. "Their strengths and weaknesses are passed on to the analyst, which might be mitigated on a larger team."

Balancing the scale

"If you're allowed to manage your own time, you can fit in a life outside of work," remarks a staffer about the existence of a work/life balance at the firm. Most sources tend to agree that "with a little planning and good communication to both the team and the client, it is manageable," another colleague adds. So enjoying labor-free leisure is not necessarily something FMCGers need to worry about—just as long as they can effectively flex their time-management muscles when it counts.

Still, some analysts do complain of frequently canceled plans ("I have to schedule weeknight dinner with friends on my boss' calendar, which is unacceptable," one vents) but on the whole, employees are willing to make occasional sacrifices if it means more free time later on. Reports one first-year, "My pyramid is not afraid to pull all-nighters, but only when necessary. If there's nothing time-sensitive to be done, there's no pressure to stay at the office." And one analyst candidly spells it all out: "Don't work at any consulting firm if you can't handle more than 40 hours a week. That said, FMCG has very reasonable work commitments across all pyramids. The firm believes happy employees produce award-winning work; the work/life balance here is geared accordingly."

Cha-ching!

FMCG employees may moan about long work hours and a lackluster office culture, but they won't be found grumbling about compensation for their efforts. Boasting of his firm's payout as "the best in the industry—end of story," one newbie describes his cash flow as "enough to appease Croesus." Adding fuel to the fire, "FMCG changed its salary structure drastically in 2006," a VP explains, getting down to business. "The firm has told all employees that it intends to beat or match all major competitors for all professional positions. Overnight, several people had their compensation more than doubled. I believe the firm is now at the top of the list compared with competitors." Suffice it to say that staffers don't worry about going hungry.

Bounteous compensation aside, insiders also mention the firm's profit-sharing plan. Most analysts say they typically aren't in their roles long enough to tell an advantageous profit-sharing tale; "profit sharing vests after three years, so for most analysts it doesn't factor," we're told. But staffers do appreciate FMCG's health benefits, comfortable 401(k) plan, tuition reimbursement program and executive MBA sponsorships. In addition, "the firm offers an interest-free loan when an analyst is hired," a relieved new hire states. Employees also cherish free meals for those who work late, and an insider mentions that "occasionally, partners put Knicks, Yankees and other tickets up for grabs."

Home free

For those who can't bear to leave their Manhattan desk unattended, FMCG may not fare thee well. "Certain domestic projects have recently had extended periods of five-day-per-week travel," insiders say, and "most analysts and consultants travel regularly," though more incessant site-hopping can depend on a staffer's job, group description or managing partner. Opinions of travel are subjective; some glorify it as "a great way to see the world," while others deem it "taxing and less glamorous than it appears. But all seem grateful for the ability to keep their travel points, collected from airlines, car rental, hotels and corporate credit card spending.

But with stringent travel regimens come some downsides. Because flight scheduling is such common practice at FMCG, one insider complains that "international and difficult domestic travel is not rewarded or acknowledged any more than working from the New York City office for extended periods." And for newer hires, this nomadic lifestyle often contributes to rapid exhaustion: "Travel appears to lead to significant burnout among analysts, ranging from quitting to demanding no further international work," says a source. The firm's "five-day-out" policy can cause conflicts as well; while many firms have travelers back in the office on Friday, FMCG's ambassadors "lose their Friday night returning to New York City."

It's better together

"The office is in a great spot—centrally located in Manhattan, on Park Avenue near Grand Central," prides an FMCGer of his firm's physical stationing. When departing from locale considerations, it's true that the excitement fades, but you won't generally find staffers engaged in workspace trash talk. "No complaints here," an employee states, and adds that "analysts are all together in a common room—this was a good recent development." Expanding upon that, one colleague explains that "first-year analysts have been consolidated to cubicle spaces in the library, while more experienced analysts usually have their own or doubled-up offices." Employees also seem satisfied with the amount of space they have, though there a few wistful requests for more windows.

Merit hounds

When it comes to lifestyle diversity, FMCG apparently has it going on. "One senior manager belly dances, one analyst lived in Africa for a time and another analyst won a TV gameshow," boasts a staffer of the firm's "amazing diversity of professional staff." But when reporting on the gender and minority categories, on the other hand, the boasting comes to a halt. "There is a dearth of women working at FMCG, especially beyond the associate level," an employee admits, further elaborating that "there were no female hires in the previous analyst class." As far as reasoning for this shortage, a few theories emerge. One source blames the staggering male/female ratio on "the result of the finance focus of the firm's work," and another on the predominately male-based applicant pool. The fact is, insiders say, FMCG is a "true meritocracy"—"your work dictates your future," we're

Visit the Vault Consulting Career Channel at **www.vault.com/consulting** - with insider firm profiles, message boards, the Vault Consulting Job Board and more.

VAULT CAREER LIBRARY   331

told, and "diversity does not factor for or against hiring someone," a senior analyst explains. "The fact [that there are] fewer women in the ranks and the lack of a mentoring program may make the firm appear less welcoming to women, though this is not intentional." Insiders make comparable remarks on FMCG's race homogeneity; one analyst declares that "hiring is not dependent, at all, on race."

But insiders do tell of an accepting atmosphere with regard to sexual orientation. "There are several openly gay professional staff members at the firm." A consultant informs us that "sexuality is not broadcast, but also is not hidden," and notes that his homosexual co-workers "are treated equally by everyone in the office."

"Because the firm is small, there is a lot of contact between analysts and officers."

– *FMCG staffer*

Visit the Vault Consulting Career Channel at **www.vault.com/consulting** - with insider firm profiles, message boards, the Vault Consulting Job Board and more.

VAULT CAREER LIBRARY

333

Alvarez & Marsal

600 Lexington Avenue, 6th Floor
New York, NY 10022
Phone: (212) 759-4433
Fax: (212) 759-5532
www.alvarezandmarsal.com

LOCATIONS

New York, NY (HQ)
31 offices worldwide

PRACTICE AREAS

Business Consulting
Customer & Channel Solutions • Finance Leadership/CFO
Solutions • Human Resources Solutions • Information
Technology Services • Merger Integration Services •
Strategy & Corporate Solutions • Supply Chain
Management
Corporate Finance
Dispute Analysis & Forensic Services
Healthcare Services
Public Sector Services
Real Estate Advisory
Tax Advisory
Technology Asset Management Services
Transaction Advisory
Turnaround & Restructuring Advisory
Claims Management Services • Debtor & Creditor Advisory
Services • Interim & Crisis Management • Performance
Improvement • Revenue Enhancement • Risk Management
Advisory

THE STATS

Employer Type: Private Company
Co-CEOs: Tony Alvarez II & Bryan Marsal
2007 Employees: 1,100
2006 Employees: 800

THE BUZZ
WHAT CONSULTANTS AT OTHER FIRMS ARE SAYING ABOUT THIS FIRM

- "Good niche reputation"
- "Very localized"
- "Great retention, good salary structure"
- "Churn and burn; aggressive"

RANKING RECAP

Quality of Life
#5 - Hours in the Office
#11 - Compensation
#15 - Work/Life Balance
#17 - Overall Satisfaction
#19 - Interaction with Clients
#20 - Best Firms to Work For

UPPERS

- "Small teams"
- "Each practice is managed locally"
- Given lots of responsibility early on
- "Environment is not competitive in a harmful way"

DOWNERS

- No formal mentoring or training programs in place yet
- "Still some old school types about that make the atmosphere tense"
- "Transaction fatigue"
- "Not enough managers to delegate work to lower-level associates"

EMPLOYMENT CONTACT

E-mail: hr@alvarezandmarsal.com

THE SCOOP

A tactical team

Named for its founders and current directors, Tony Alvarez II and Bryan Marsal, Alvarez & Marsal was founded in 1983. Both Alvarez and Marsal had worked as VPs at large financial firms, and had developed reputations as in-house "Mr. Fix-Its." Over a golf game, the two decided to team up and establish a firm that would challenge "the legions of consultants who got bogged down in details and were afraid to radically change the companies they were trying to save," according to an article in *BusinessWeek*. To this day, the firm describes its approach as "tactical," rather than "strategic," noting, "Our view is from two feet, not 20,000 feet."

A&M's initial foray into consulting focused on helping troubled companies with debt management and advisory services. While the corporate turnaround game is still its main focus, the firm has branched out into operational and strategy consulting as well. The privately held, owner-operated firm doesn't publicize its internal numbers, but reportedly employs around 1,100 consultants worldwide, with offices in North America, Europe, Asia and Latin America.

Recruiting from the big leagues

The firm's business consulting division got its start in 2004, when A&M brought onboard a crew of consulting vets from high-profile positions at BearingPoint, Answerthink, Accenture and other firms. A&M's business consulting services include strategy and corporate solutions, information technology solutions, finance solutions, human resource solutions, supply chain solutions, customer and channel solutions, and merger integration advisory. Through its other divisions, the firm offers services, including turnaround management, interim and crisis management, performance improvement, creditor advisory, corporate finance, transaction advisory, commercial and not-for-profit health care, public sector, dispute analysis and forensics, and real estate and tax advisory. Its experts consult in a wide range of industries, including telecommunications, retail, health care, transportation, apparel, technology, manufacturing, financial services, power and utilities, and the public sector.

Five steps to turnaround

A&M is most well known for its corporate turnaround expertise. The firm's approach to turning around a troubled company involves five steps. During the first step, A&M helps stabilize a client by securing cash where needed and supplementing or supporting the client's management team. To diagnose a client's situation, the firm practices a thorough financial due diligence process—such skills come in handy in the days of increased corporate oversight through regulations like Sarbanes-Oxley. Next, the firm develops a strategic plan, addressing challenges and building on the client's core strengths. Finally, A&M works to forge a consensus among interested parties to implement the plan, and helps the existing management team implement it—or even steps in to provide interim management when needed. The firm profits from making the process work, often receiving "success fees" that are calibrated based on a client's improved value over a period of time.

Helping bread rise

Well-known companies to whom A&M has lent a helping hand include Interstate Bakeries (famous for Wonder Bread and Twinkies), hospital chain HealthSouth and denim giant Levi Strauss. In many cases, A&M's founders themselves step in to take on management roles at the firms they are trying to save. Described as "cocky and intense" in a 2004 *BusinessWeek* profile, Alvarez and Marsal certainly don't shy away from a challenge. At the same time that Alvarez was busy in his role as interim CEO of Interstate, Marsal was finishing up a 15-month stint as chief restructuring officer of HealthSouth, which was flirting with bankruptcy. HealthSouth founder and CEO Richard Scrushy, whose name has joined the ranks of Ken Lay and Jeff Skilling in the annals of corporate malfeasance, left Marsal with quite a mess to clean up, including $3.3 billion in debt. As Alvarez put it, "We come to companies at their worst moments in life, and we save them." In February 2007, the Interstate Bakeries turnaround

Visit the Vault Consulting Career Channel at www.vault.com/consulting - with insider firm profiles, message boards, the Vault Consulting Job Board and more.

VAULT CAREER LIBRARY   335

hit a milestone as Alvarez stepped down from the interim CEO position he had held since 2004, and a bankruptcy judge approved the appointment of Craig D. Jung, formerly head of Panamerican Beverages, to the role.

These takeovers aren't always easy. In July 2006, the firm took over at Hong Kong's troubled Legend Hotel and Casino, formally dismissing its CEO and replacing him with an A&M director. But the CEO didn't go quietly—in fact, according to the firm, he "attempted to incite a number of staff" at the resort to physically eject his A&M replacement, who had to be protected by security escorts. The firm was asked by major stakeholders of the casino's parent company, Legend International Resorts, to clean up the resort's fiscal mess, including debts totaling around $164 million.

For the sake of a catalog

One of A&M's better-known success stories is its work with Spiegel, a retailer covering *Spiegel Catalog*, *Newport News* and Eddie Bauer. By early 2003, the company, saddled with high customer credit card default rates, as well as plummeting sales and high corporate overhead, was forced to file for bankruptcy. A&M consultants took on key roles in Spiegel's management ranks. The firm's turnaround plan included establishing a new credit card program, reducing Spiegel's overhead, closing underperforming stores and improving merchandising. The firm sold off the *Spiegel Catalog* and *Newport News* businesses to outside investors, creating a stand-alone business around Eddie Bauer. By the end of the project, the case was lauded as "almost a perfect poster child of what Chapter 11 is designed to be" by the bankruptcy court judge, and the firm was recognized by the Turnaround Management Association with the Large Company Turnaround of the Year award for its restructuring of the retailer.

More recently, the firm helped video rental giant Movie Gallery Inc. work its way out of the money hole. While the acquisition of rival Hollywood Video helped Movie Gallery secure a place as the nation's second-largest video rental chain, it also left the company over $1 billion in the red. In April 2006, the company hired A&M to help with its turnaround and address liquidity issues; soon thereafter, Movie Gallery successfully refinanced a credit line. The firm also was tasked in December 2006 with restructuring Atlanta's Grady Health System, a regional not-for-profit hospital that had been bleeding millions of dollars since 2000. A&M's work involved providing Grady's board of directors with recommendations and supporting the implementation of a cost reduction and performance improvement program. A&M also stepped in to replace two of the system's VPs with its own consultants in interim management posts. The firm helped identify ways to reduce expenses while improving operations to benefit clinical care over the longer term. This contract concluded in June 2007, when new permanent management was installed to continue the much-needed turnaround effort.

Shaking things up

A&M's "brash" style, as it's been described, sometimes earns the firm criticism in the business arena. The firm's consultants are committed to shaking up the status quo—often, it's these old habits that got troubled companies into trouble in the first place. Some competitors have charged the firm with cozy industry deals, such as hiring six former turnaround specialists from Arthur Andersen at the same time Marsal was helping to dismantle the crumbling accountancy. But A&M actually prides itself on independence and objectivity; in the case of Andersen, Marsal contended, A&M bought out the Andersen staffers' contracts with the board's blessing. Ernst & Young also has accused the firm of brash dealings with its staff, filing a lawsuit contending that A&M had raided its tax and real estate divisions for consultants. A&M denied any wrongdoing, comparing the case to a David and Goliath matchup (with Alvarez & Marsal holding the slingshot).

Growing under pressure

While other firms struggled through a terrible economic slump, A&M ambitiously expanded its reach at home and abroad in the early 2000s—thanks in part to all those struggling companies and the introduction of Sarbanes-Oxley, aimed at curbing fraud and conflicts of interest. In January 2007, A&M expanded its offerings at its Denver office, bringing Senior Director Michael Fink up from Houston to lead the growth of its business consulting practice in the Denver and Phoenix markets. That same month, the firm's transaction advisory group put down additional roots in San Francisco. In November 2006, the firm went north to open an office in Toronto, headed by Douglas R. McIntosh, the former head of KPMG's Canadian restructuring practice. And in

September 2006, the firm announced a strategic affiliation agreement with McGrath Nicol + Partners, an independent corporate advisory and restructuring firm in Australia and New Zealand. Under the agreement, the two companies intend to "serve as preferred resources for each other" in turnaround engagements, allowing A&M to extend its reach Down Under. The McGrath + Nicol alliance is part of the firm's overall strategy to strengthen its presence in the Asia-Pacific region with its own growing offices in Hong Kong, Shanghai and Singapore.

This growth is paying off for employees, too: In January 2007, the firm promoted more than 50 of its consultants to managing director, senior director and director roles. The firm also continues to expand its services; in December 2006, A&M's real estate advisory services division announced the formation of a hospitality asset management team, aimed at providing performance improvement and value enhancement services to developers, capital sources and operators involved in complex real estate projects, like hotel-condominiums.

Public service

A&M's turnaround expertise has been tapped by the public sector. In July 2006, the firm's real estate advisory services branch scored a five-year contract with the U.S. Navy, to serve as the sole advisor for a program related to the leasing of military facilities.

In August 2006, A&M was named the Third Party Fiduciary for the government of the U.S. Virgin Islands, responsible for administering U.S. Department of Education grants aimed at improving the islands' public school system. On this assignment, the firm oversees processes such as purchasing and record keeping related to the grants.

Take out your pencils ...

But the firm is better known for its work with some of the most troubled school districts back on the mainland. In mid-2004, A&M completed an unprecedented turnaround of the near-bankrupt St. Louis Public Schools, a system struggling with operational and financial woes. Under the leadership of A&M Managing Director William Roberti, who served as acting superintendent, the school system instituted dramatic organizational reform, slashing overhead costs and redirecting resources into the classrooms. Reports of the firm's efforts reached New York City in 2006, and Gotham's leaders tapped A&M in a $16 million contract to help improve a number of areas of operation and move control over the budget and resources from the central administration to individual schools.

Getting schooled

Neither the St. Louis nor the New York gigs have been without controversy, however—perhaps unsurprising when it comes to school reform, which is fraught with political turmoil. In a withering op-ed in the *St. Louis Post-Dispatch* in March 2007, columnist Bill McLellan called the A&M team "charlatans" for their work on the school system, arguing that Roberti and his "overbearing, arrogant" team had "made a bad situation worse" for a $5 million price tag. Noting that three years after the fact schools were still facing closure in the system, McLellan suggested suing to recoup the consultancy's fees. Meanwhile, a district teacher, Marilyn Ayres-Salamon, published a book about her experiences working under the Roberti team. The book's title, *A Recipe for Failure: A Year of Reform and Chaos in the St. Louis Public Schools*, gives an idea of the author's slant. "An educational system addressing students from generational poverty cannot be run in the same way as Brooks Brothers," she fumed.

A&M contends that its client disagreed strongly with those sentiments and supports the firm's work vigorously and consistently. Former St. Louis Mayor and School Board Member Vincent Schoemehl wrote in a letter to the editor of *The New York Sun*: "A&M was brought in to salvage an untenable situation. They discovered a $75 million deficit at year-end and a short-term cash shortfall of $99 million—out of a total budget of $450 million. A&M righted the financial house and enabled the St. Louis Public Schools to survive" by getting the district's finances in order, implementing wide-ranging reforms in curriculum and redirected spending from administration to classrooms. In addition, A&M left a five-year operating plan that provided a step-by-step path to continued success—though the firm regrets that the current school board has abandoned this plan. Current Mayor Francis Slay

Visit the Vault Consulting Career Channel at **www.vault.com/consulting** - with insider firm profiles, message boards, the Vault Consulting Job Board and more.

VAULT CAREER LIBRARY   337

added his support in a story in the *St. Louis Post-Dispatch*: "When it comes to education in St. Louis, no one has ever accomplished as much in as little time as Bill Roberti."

Meanwhile, in the Big Apple, the firm came under fire in early 2007 when a botched plan to reroute school bus service in order to cut costs led to mass chaos for commuting city kids in the dead of winter. The firm ended up shouldering much of the blame in the press for the confusion that briefly ensued, thanks in part to inaccurate lists of students who rode the buses. The situation led vocal critics, like Public Advocate Betsy Gotbaum, to demand that Mayor Bloomberg fire A&M, but the mayor and his chancellor seemed determined to stand by the firm, and supported their work publicly.

A new day for New Orleans

But A&M is used to performing under pressure, as evidenced by its work with an even more challenging school reform task in New Orleans. The Crescent City's public school system was already known as the worst in the nation when A&M came onboard, with the firm predicting that the schools would run out of money in September. And that was before the nation's worst natural disaster in decades landed on Louisiana's shores. In the wake of Hurricane Katrina, A&M's job was transformed from securing financing and managing the previously dysfunctional operations for the schools to handling the unusual complications associated with a giant natural disaster, such as setting up payroll funds for more than 7,000 public school employees at Western Union, while trying to track down payroll information from flooded buildings. By early 2006, Roberti's team in New Orleans was showing signs of success—over 10,000 students were back in the 20 schools that were up and running. And the project took a positive turn in February 2007, when the city's new director of recovery had a successful meeting with representatives from A&M and the school district. The director indicated that the city may offer underutilized buildings to the school districts, which are sorely in need of classroom space. As A&M's assignment with the Orleans Parish School Board came to an end, the school system received the first clean audit report it had had in recent memory.

GETTING HIRED

Trolling for talent on campus

A&M's campus recruiting efforts are concentrated in regions near its offices. "College recruiting is heavy," states an insider, adding, "The Houston and Dallas offices recruit from UT Austin, Rice and Texas A&M." Other offices draw graduates from the University of Illinois, Yale, Wharton, Harvard, the University of Michigan and the University of Miami of Ohio, to name a few. On-campus interviews allow candidates to meet "a diverse range of associates through managing directors." A manager explains, "There's a 'super day' by invitation only with intensive questioning on real-work examples, such as, 'How would you audit for fraud in XYZ case,' or 'What can you determine from the following documents?'" An insider notes, "Rather than hypothetical 'McKinsey-type' cases, the cases were based on how you would react to actual A&M engagement scenarios." By contrast, a source in a different office gives a more quant-focused case question that might pop up: "Can you lever a beta? How would you?" Explains a staffer, "The biggest difference is the group case interview. As an interviewee, it allowed me to show the variety of my strengths. On the interviewer side, if a prospect has a weakness, like the inability to work well in a stressful environment or get to the micro and macro of a case, it is crystal clear."

Getting to know you

No matter what sort of case questions the interviewers give, it's not the most important part of the process, according to a manager: "It's more important that we can get along and personalities work, than to test technical knowledge which can be obtained through training." "The hiring process is more focused on personality fit than anything else. I didn't experience any crazy tests or case interview questions. It was simply more of a 'sit down and get to know you' type of interview, to see if your personality will fit in with the go-getter, hardworking, yet relaxed culture of A&M," surmises a colleague. Another consultant agrees that the process felt "laid-back," adding "I had about three or four interviews and it was more of a getting-to-know-you type feeling, not those rigorous, intense interviews like at other firms."

Other than great personality, there are a couple of things that reportedly might give candidates an edge. "Professionalism, follow-up after (yes, send a thank you e-mail within four hours and a written note within 24)," a colleague advises, adding, "Internships are highly sought after and good work will result in offers of employment."

Friends on the inside

Candidates who don't go through campus recruiting might find it more difficult to get an interview, since "jobs aren't advertised." Sources remark that it's "based on relationships," and one associate confirms, "You have to know someone to work here—it makes for a great hiring process." For these candidates, the business consulting interview process is described as "very informal," with "several one-on-one conversations." "The first part is generally a personality and behavioral interview. The second is a live case interview with the other recruits in front of one of our clients," a manager states. One New York staffer calls the process "fast and delightfully unbureaucratic."

OUR SURVEY SAYS

Like a mom and pop shop

A handful of insiders indicate that there are two sides to many aspects of A&M life. "This is very much a work-hard culture, balanced by a strong sense of the importance of family and community," a staffer explains, while a colleague says, "I believe the culture strikes a good balance between being entrepreneurial and meritocratic, while also being nurturing, patient and collaborative." The firm's distinctive "startup nature" means there is "very little red tape for access to higher-ups or to get firmwide decisions made." One source mentions that the close-knit culture seems more like that of a small firm: "In spite of significant growth over the last several years, A&M continues to function as a benevolent patriarchy and retains much of its family-owned company feel."

Insiders cheer about the distinct "family and team atmosphere" and "fun and relaxed environment" at the firm. "I think the culture is one of the strongest points of A&M. Everyone here is very welcoming regardless of their level of experience, and actively works to help you learn and grow with them. Additionally, there is no class system. The top professionals at the firm treat the lower ranking professionals completely as equals," asserts one source. A co-worker boasts that the firm is full of "down-to-earth, smart people," adding, "Very few people have a chip on their shoulder." Another consultant reports, "Nobody is egotistical, and current rank at the firm is rarely discussed." "The culture is truly unique," asserts a source who adds, "The firm's recruiting process is designed to weed out people you wouldn't want to work with." An insider proudly states, "For me, this is what really makes me happy working with A&M. The firm really walks the walk when it comes to their commitment to building the culture of A&M. Whether it's participating in everyone's philanthropic endeavors or attending a firm happy hour or other social event, I always have fun."

Getting chummy

Interaction among all levels is emphasized at A&M. "We work in small teams, so even the lowest level of staff is required and expected to interact with management in a significant way," notes a consultant. Insiders explain that interactions with supervisors are "more of a partnership than a 'boss' relationship." One associate relates, "On my first assignment, when asked a question, I told my director it was his call; he replied, 'This is a democracy.'" "There is a clear organization structure, but we are less bureaucratic than any place I have worked. If you want to talk to the most senior managing partner—including Tony Alvarez or Bryan Marsal—you can give them a call and they will reply," a source attests.

Staffers also give high marks to the amount of client interaction they're granted on engagements. "I would say this is where our firm really excels," claims an insider, stating, "Since our project teams are so lean, I have direct access to the client at all levels." An analyst boasts, "For example, at my last client, despite being just 25 years old, I ended up befriending the CFO and controller

Visit the Vault Consulting Career Channel at **www.vault.com/consulting** - with insider firm profiles, message boards, the Vault Consulting Job Board and more.

VAULT CAREER LIBRARY   339

of a $6 billion company. I currently maintain a strong relationship with both of them via e-mail, as well as over the occasional drink."

It works to their advantage

No one says the work hours aren't intense at this firm, however, insiders seem satisfied that the firm rewards extra time. "We work a lot, but more hours correlates to a better bonus at the end of the year. People can elect to work more or less with the knowledge of how such decisions affect total compensation," explains a source. Week to week, hours are all over the board, but eventually it all evens out, insiders suggest: "You are essentially paid for overtime, so no one complains about working lots of hours. Some of the projects demand a lot of working hours, but generally the work is highly rewarding and the co-workers are great, so I never mind having to put in the extra hours when needed. For each week that might demand 70 to 80 hours, there is a week that might require only 30," a consultant reports

Have job, will travel

These insiders say the travel schedule at A&M makes it "difficult to achieve or maintain a sense or feeling of control over your personal life—everything from personal relationships to paying the bills." Concedes an analyst, "It's not bad, except for the suddenness and inflexibility of it. Nothing like finding out on Monday that you'll be spending Wednesday through Friday in some other city, and once you get there, finding out that you'll be there for three weeks and that you have to stay that weekend to work." And "while the lack of flexibility with travel requirements" is frustrating for many staffers, none of these consultants can claim they weren't warned ahead of time. "The firm makes no effort to hide this from you prior to joining. That is one of the key points they stress to everyone prior to making them an offer: The job requires a good bit of travel," a source declares. "We are traveling consultants. We go to the work and clients. It's understood before day one what you are getting into," agrees a colleague. Even though it's an expected part of the job, a source acknowledges, "The lifestyle is not for everyone, and I would say it's the primary reason anybody leaves A&M."

Choose your office wisely

For some fortunate consultants, working at the client is merely a short drive, rather than a flight, away. "Working out of one of the regional hubs (Houston, New York, etc.) will greatly reduce your travel requirements. Key accounts tend to be located locally to large regional offices and staffing is designed accordingly," hints a staffer. A co-worker explains, "It is mostly local travel. That means you may stay at a hotel, but you don't have to get on a plane. For example, you may be staffed on a project in Philly and living in New York, so you could commute every day, but most people stay in a hotel. Nevertheless, there are no airports, which is a welcome change for some consulting veterans."

"Take what you need"

To balance out the demands of consulting life, insiders claim that A&M grants carte blanche to take personal time as needed. "The restructuring business is as brutal as it gets, with 100 percent travel, 15-plus-hour days and regular weekend work. In between clients, however, A&M has been very good about letting its employees recharge by taking off for as long as they feel is necessary," a source explains. One senior staffer points out, "It is a good balance for the right person. It's not a balance each week. It's a balance overall. If we have to work hard for many months and lose a little balance, we are encouraged to take some time off and get back in balance." Sources appreciate the freedom to determine individually what that requires. "'Take what you need' is our policy. A great example is after finishing a yearlong project recently, I was able to take two full weeks away without opening my computer and simply escaping to the Caribbean. This would not have been possible with my prior firms," avows a manager.

You're on your own

Some sources tell us that at A&M "there is no training," though others claim that formal training is actually evolving. Admits one manager, "It's not a great thing for new consultants just out of school, but we hire very few of them anyway." Another source acknowledges that "this is one area we lack a little in." But "the firm is making headway here," comments a colleague, noting, "There is one set program a year for younger staff and most managing directors are very supportive of any third-party training options surfaced by staff." For some employees, the current system works just fine, however. One staffer remarks, "There is nothing like on-the-job training to learn how the job really gets done."

Make-or-break bonus

Sources divulge that since base salary may "not be quite as high as at top-tier firms," "bonus makes or breaks the year," and as one insider points out, "the trade-off is a better work/life balance." According to the firm, bonuses are somewhat dependent on chargeable hours worked during the year, with a formulaic approach that is adjusted for individual staff. "Bottom line: You are compensated for every hour you work, and the bonus is not as subjective as it is at most firms." One source weighs in, saying, "The bonus structure is attractive. It has accurately compensated me, but I have heard other employees grumble that it does not always accurately compensate."

Where do you put your overhead?

While the New York space is "not very impressive, noisy and uncomfortable," sources in Houston say their office is "new and modern, with the 'open office space' feel." Several associates seem satisfied that spending money on office amenities is not the firm's priority. "I like the fact that our offices are not 'top shelf.' The money for a fancy office goes back into growing the business and funding the bonus pool," a Chicago source opines, while an Atlanta insider adds that the "low overhead" means the firm is able to "maximize the bonus pool available for our people."

Free munchies and massages

A&M offices may be less than impressive, but sources appreciate the loads of munchies available, like "Flavia coffee, tea and cocoa, soft drinks, bottled water, breakfast bars and cereal, yogurt, bagels and English muffins." New Yorkers are reportedly pampered with "free massages and nutrition advice, discounted yoga and pilates classes," and as far as standard health care benefits go, a source says, "I came from another firm and my out-of-pocket contribution went down, and my co-pay is half of what it was." Consultants are also pleased with the "vacation flexibility," and an insider notes that free classes are nice: "They pay for most forms of approved continuing education (i.e., certifications, CPA requirement)."

Growing gender balance

Staffers report there is "not enough balance" between genders at the firm, although one insider remarks that in certain divisions, "Several women have recently been promoted from within to become managing directors." "Women who have an interest in [consulting] seem to be hard to find, though there are more women at this firm then others I am aware of," explains a source. According to employees, the effort to hire and retain women seems to vary by office. A consultant in Houston comments, "We have made a concerted effort to hire more women. A year ago, there was only one female in the consulting group—now there are over a dozen. They have grown much faster than overall hiring." And a co-worker boasts that the number of women at A&M "is great for a consulting firm; we had two women promoted to managing director last year."

On the other end of the spectrum, some insiders feel the firm should take a more proactive approach to hiring and promoting women. Recounts a source, "Of the five groups in the Chicago office, two are rather good at recruiting and retaining women, and three are dreadful." Declares one manager, "[It's] definitely a 'good old boy' firm." And although an associate assures us that "the firm bases hiring and promotion decisions on ability, performance and values alignment," generally, the attitude among insiders is that "more could be done."

Visit the Vault Consulting Career Channel at **www.vault.com/consulting** - with insider firm profiles, message boards, the Vault Consulting Job Board and more.

VAULT CAREER LIBRARY   341

Receptive, not proactive

The same approach seems to apply to the firm's minority diversity efforts. "I think the firm is more or less receptive, just hasn't done anything special in terms of targeting and recruiting," admits one consultant. "I think they hire whoever is best for the job, and race is not an issue. There seems to be a mix of Latin, Asian, Arabic and African-American people that collectively make up about half the workforce. I am actively involved in the recruitment process and would have picked up on any bias—and it would have made me not want to work here. [Your experience] and degree work with grades are what makes the cut here," an insider affirms. Concurs a senior staffer, "Racial or ethnic background play little, if any, role in hiring decisions."

And when it comes to diversity with respect to gays, lesbians and bisexuals, overall, insiders affirm that A&M colleagues promote "a very open and welcoming culture." "I have never heard any comments, positive or negative, related to sexual orientation," states a consultant. A cohort corroborates the story: "Nobody discriminates against anybody. We simply focus on getting our work done as a team and providing the best service that we can for our clients."

Inconsistent efforts

The level of volunteer involvement in the community is different in each A&M office. Explains a source, "Most charity work is initiated by individuals that have a particular interest in something; the firm generally is very supportive of any charities that individuals surface." A Houston associate remarks, "I am participating in the MS 150 with a team of 20 from A&M. The firm has sponsored jerseys and donated money for the first night campout. There is also a group doing the March of Dimes." "Many A&M employees are charity board members and there are a good deal of volunteers," a Denver associate mentions. Another insider reports that "the Atlanta office of A&M is actively involvement in Junior Achievement." However, the Dallas office could reportedly be more involved, according to an insider who declares, "We don't do squat, besides the March of Dimes' Blue Jeans for Babies campaign every spring."

The firm's distinctive "startup nature" means there is "very little red tape for access to higher-ups or to get firmwide decisions made."

– *Alvarez & Marsal associate*

Visit the Vault Consulting Career Channel at **www.vault.com/consulting** - with insider firm profiles, message boards, the Vault Consulting Job Board and more.

VAULT CAREER LIBRARY

343

The Wanamaker Building
100 Penn Square East
Philadelphia, PA 19107
Phone: (215) 861-2000
Fax: (215) 861-2111
www.haygroup.com

LOCATIONS

Philadelphia, PA (HQ)
88 offices worldwide

PRACTICE AREAS

Capability Assessment
Employee & Customer Surveys
HR Effectiveness
Job Evaluation
Leadership Transformation
Managing the Matrix
Mergers & Acquisitions
Organization Effectiveness
Performance Management
Reward Information Services
Reward Strategies
Talent Management

THE STATS

Employer Type: Private Company
Chairman: Chris Matthews
2007 Employees: 2,430
2006 Employees: 2,330
2007 Revenue: $443 million (est.)
2006 Revenue: $372 million

RANKING RECAP

Practice Area
#6 - Human Resources Consulting

UPPERS

- Offers lots of flexibility, great work/life balance
- "Challenging but friendly environment"
- "Ability to chart my own future and growth"

DOWNERS

- "Lack of structure and clearly-defined internal processes"
- "Not much hand-holding or day-to-day support" for new consultants
- Low bonus pool

EMPLOYMENT CONTACT

www.haygroup.com/ww/careers

THE BUZZ
WHAT CONSULTANTS AT OTHER FIRMS ARE SAYING ABOUT THIS FIRM

- "The go-to guys for hiring practices"
- "Narrower HR specialists; data-oriented versus broad consultants"
- "Better work/life balance"
- "Dated"

THE SCOOP

Placing people first

Hay Group knows that even the best technology can't replace good staff to make a company tick. Founded by Edward N. Hay in 1943, the Philadelphia, Pa.-based firm has become one of the biggest names in the human resources consulting field, with more than 2,000 consultants serving over 7,000 clients from 88 offices in 47 countries worldwide. Its specialty: Understanding how work is organized and what causes people to perform at their best. Hay Group applies that understanding by helping its clients—which range from large multinationals like Pfizer and Wal-Mart to government organizations and small startups—develop talent, organize its employee structure, clarify roles and responsibilities, measure the value of various kinds of work and set up performance management processes, among other services.

Hay Group also invests in its own research and benchmarking studies, including employee attitude surveys, leadership assessments, and compensation and benefits studies. Whether they're consulting or researching, Hay Group's professionals are experts in the chemicals, consumer products, education, finance, health care, manufacturing, oil and gas, pharmaceuticals, public sector, retail, technology, telecommunications and utilities industries.

The Hay way

Over the past 60 years, Hay Group has developed a portfolio of services that can be tailored to help each client improve performance. Because the firm recognizes that no two companies have the same exact needs, clients can pick and choose what kind of help they want. As its clients change, Hay Group stays onboard to monitor the companies' development to "help sustain performance."

The firm's services include performance management, which helps business leaders monitor how employees work and respond to feedback and rewards, in addition to the firm's job evaluation methodology, which analyzes organizational structures and evaluates employees and functions. Hay Group professionals also consult on organizational effectiveness, talent management and retention, management searches, leadership development, employee and customer surveys, and employee and executive reward strategies using its trademarked online compensation and benefits portal, Hay Group PayNet.

Knowing your environment

Before approaching a problem, Hay Group consultants gain their footing by taking a look at the business issues each client faces. Today, many of its clients' problems are related to changes in the market, such as a growth or contraction, greater deregulation or privatization of an industry, international competition from challengers like China and India, or technological change. Hay Group first assesses these changes, using its diagnostics to determine what a client really needs, whether that be building a new kind of performance culture, developing a leadership team that can lead the organization through the changes or developing appropriate reward strategies.

The three most common business issues Hay Group helps clients face are mergers and acquisitions, of which only 70 percent deliver their promised value; streamlining organizational matrices, especially when companies try to expand into new markets; and getting HR up to speed so that it can support the organization's changing staffing needs.

Heavy into research

Hay Group's research expertise falls into four main categories: assessment and feedback services, management style and organizational climate studies, reward information surveys and employee surveys. Many of its surveys often hit mainstream news wires. For the past nine years, Hay Group has helped to identify and rank companies for *Fortune*'s Most Admired Companies list and researches best practices for developing leaders for *Chief Executive* magazine. The 2006 *Chief Executive*

Visit the Vault Consulting Career Channel at www.vault.com/consulting - with insider firm profiles, message boards, the Vault Consulting Job Board and more.

VAULT CAREER LIBRARY   345

survey looked at 1,279 companies with at least $8 billion in annual revenue and ranked General Electric, Procter & Gamble and PepsiCo as the top-three companies for leaders.

Another survey that made waves: the findings of Hay Group consultants Scott Spreier, Mary Fontaine and Ruth Malloy, who looked at the long-term productivity of teams led by overachieving leaders. In the beginning, teams led by overachieving leaders move fast, but ultimately, these kinds of leaders end up stifling their workers and bringing down the overall productivity of the firm. In January 2007, it was announced that Hay Group's survey, called "Leadership Run Amok: The Destructive Potential of Overachievers," was the best-selling *Harvard Business Review* article for all of 2006.

Beefing up its own management team

Hay Group has done a little capability assessment of its own offerings and hired a number of managers to head up its business units. One of its major leadership changes came about in December 2006, when David E. Borrebach, an expert in the design and implementation of strategic compensation systems, came over from Mercer Human Resource Consulting to head up Hay Group's job evaluation practice. In October of that year, the firm launched a new board effectiveness practice after it hired former Mercer Delta Consulting Partner Beverly Behan as its worldwide practice managing director.

Funding knowledge

In 2005, Hay Group announced that it was starting a new annual fund for graduate and postgraduate students for study in the field of human motivation, competencies and organizational performance in honor of psychologist David C. McClelland. Every year, through Hay Group's McClelland Center for Research and Innovation, the fellowship awards approximately $40,000.

In July 2006, the McClelland Center announced the recipients of the first annual fellowship to three scholars: Sarah Gervais, a doctoral candidate at Pennsylvania State University studying the antecedents and consequences of subtle sexism; Isabel Ng, a PhD candidate in psychology at the University of Michigan whose dissertation looks at a cross-cultural study of power in China and the United States; and Pranj Mehta, a graduate social and personality psychology student at the University of Texas at Austin researching the effects of hormones and implicit motives on social behaviors.

GETTING HIRED

Bring us your bright

On its web site, Hay Group stresses that there's no one type of personality that's ideal for the firm—rather, the firm seeks all types of "bright and inquisitive" people. Candidates must apply using the firm's online system, which stores application data for a year. The firm isn't big on campus recruiting; when it comes to academic background, "Hay Group looks for good candidates, rather than specific schools," a source says.

Interviewing at Hay Group is "quite a long and involved process," says one consultant, including up to four interviews and a three-hour "behavioral event interview." As an insider describes the process, "I went through various rounds of interviews starting with the hiring manager, the associate consultant and finally the senior consultant, who I later indirectly reported to. The interview process was very typical, asking questions about my past experience and how those might translate to a career in consulting. There were also questions about why I chose to work for an HR consulting firm and what I hoped to get out of it." It's a "disciplined process including interviews and instruments—the same as we do for our clients," another source notes.

In addition, "Hay Group tests for management competencies above certain levels," and "results are shared with individuals and used for personal growth," a consultant shares. "For some positions (mostly client-facing) a panel session (presentation) is also included, with the whole office present. For consultants and senior consultants, a case study is also included at the behavioral event interview stage," insiders tell us.

OUR SURVEY SAYS

Hay, now

Hay Group, an insider reports, is a "collaborative firm with smart people who are willing to share their expertise and develop others." The firm offers a "very friendly," but also "challenging" environment, another source remarks. According to a consultant, Hay Group is "highly collaborative," and everyone is "accessible and on a first-name basis."

"Flexibility is encouraged" at Hay Group, which helps with work/life balance, a staffer notes. The "company is extremely committed to helping employees achieve a balance," agrees a colleague. "I have frequent needs to be at home," reports a consultant, and "Hay Group allows me, within reason, to work at times and places of my choosing." But another insider states that while it's easy to strike a balance, "the work atmosphere is so interesting and challenging that a lot of colleagues decide to devote more time than specified in the contract to their tasks. The workload is not forced on by management; it is a self-[directed] decision, mainly." Workweeks tend to average between 50 and 60 hours, insiders report.

Reasonably demanding

The firm's travel demands are described by one source as "reasonable—we clearly need to work with clients (who pay our salaries), but there is a good balance between client face time and prep/analysis time." "There are many travel possibilities but consultants usually have some say over which opportunities they want to take," another insider tells us. Travel "can be significant," says a colleague, "but with a young family, the firm is supportive of me limiting the nights spent away from home." According to another, "Traveling from time to time (several times per year) is included. Personally, I consider traveling (especially abroad) a small benefit, since corporate standards are rather good with regard to hotel quality and travel expenses."

Hay Group's "good compensation package" includes a profit-sharing "bonus pool for consultants working with key clients," a staffer explains. But another source grumbles that this is a "low bonus pool, therefore low bonuses are only paid at the end of the year." The firm notes that its bonus structure is designed around company profitability, unit performance and individual performance, and adds that it does not reward poor performers well, by design.

Other benefits include generous medical and fitness coverage, as well as four weeks of vacation, tuition reimbursement and a retirement plan, we're told. New parents describe the firm as "accommodating" and "supportive." The firm also gets high marks for its treatment of women—in fact, insiders describe offices that are primarily led by female consultants.

Accessible, within reason

For one Hay Group consultant, an "open and rather friendly relationship with supervisors and clients" is another perk of being at the firm. "Senior management is always accessible (within reason, of course)," adds a colleague. Newer consultants "are expected to be self-starters," so "introductory trainings are not very widely supported," consultants report; however, formal training sessions "are very good with regard to quality and regularity."

Advising NFPs

Hay Group performs "significant pro bono consulting," says an insider, who adds that the firm is "also involved in a major study of leadership in the not-for-profit sector to advance knowledge of this field." Not only do "staff members sit on boards of not-for-profits," but the firm also supports organizations such as United Way and the Hunger Project, insiders tell us.

Visit the Vault Consulting Career Channel at www.vault.com/consulting - with insider firm profiles, message boards, the Vault Consulting Job Board and more.

VAULT CAREER LIBRARY   347

Diamond Management & Technology Consultants, Inc.

John Hancock Center
875 North Michigan Avenue
Suite 3000
Chicago, IL 60611
Phone: (312) 255-5000
Fax: (312) 255-6000
www.diamondconsultants.com

LOCATIONS

Chicago, IL (HQ)
Hartford, CT
New York, NY
Washington, DC
London
Mumbai

PRACTICE AREAS

Growth
 Market Penetration • New Business Development • New Growth
Operations Improvement
 Execution Excellence • Operations Strategy • Profit Improvement • Turnaround Management
Technology
 Architecture Assessment & Strategy • IT Assessment & Strategy • IT Portfolio Assessment & Strategy • Outsourcing Advisory • Security Assessment & Strategy • Technology Program Management

THE STATS*

Employer Type: Public Company
Ticker Symbol: DTPI (Nasdaq)
Chairman: Mel Bergstein
President & CEO: Adam J. Gutstein
2007 Employees: 610
2006 Employees: 554
2007 Revenue: $170 million
2006 Revenue: $145 million

*Diamond is now reporting FY revenue and employee figures only for "continuing operations" in the US, UK and India

THE BUZZ
WHAT CONSULTANTS AT OTHER FIRMS ARE SAYING ABOUT THIS FIRM

- "Best darn technology consultants money can buy"
- "Luster not as bright as it was"
- "Treats employees very well"
- "Not enough strategy work"

RANKING RECAP

Quality of Life
#11 - Offices
#13 - Formal Training
#15 - Compensation
#15 - Interaction with Clients
#15 - Overall Satisfaction
#17 - Relationships with Supervisors
#17 - Firm Culture
#18 - Best Firms to Work For
#18 - Work/Life Balance

Diversity
#13 - Diversity for GLBT (tie)
#20 - Diversity for Minorities

UPPERS

- "The commitment of everyone to work together as one firm"
- A strong mix of technology experts and MBAs/undergrads
- "Commitment to staffing to meet personal/development needs"
- "Entrepreneurial culture recognizes hard workers for their accomplishments"

DOWNERS

- "People still think we are a tech-only firm"
- Heavy travel due to the live-anywhere policy
- "Limited client diversity"
- "Small/young firm—we are still experimenting"

EMPLOYMENT CONTACT

diamondconsultants.com/publicsite/people/careers

THE SCOOP

A downsized Diamond

Diamond Management & Technology Consultants is a strategy and IT consulting firm with operations in North America, the U.K. and India. Formerly DiamondCluster International, the firm cast off the Cluster when it sold a portion of its operations. The firm's services are divided into three categories: growth, operations improvement and technology. Its clients reside in the financial services, logistics, manufacturing, consumer packaged goods, retail and distribution, telecommunications, utilities, health care, insurance and public sectors.

Rocky years

The firm's beginnings go back to 1994, when former CEO and current Chairman Mel Bergstein secured venture capital funding to launch an IT consulting startup. In 2000, a $300 million merger joined the firm with Barcelona-based Cluster Consulting, hence DiamondCluster. The deal added an international client base and gave the firm a global presence. In 2002, the consultancy, like most of its peers, suffered from a slowdown in the tech market that came just as it was still trying to smooth out postmerger bumps. In 2002 and 2003, Diamond was forced to make pay cuts and lay off 36 percent of its staff. CEO Bergstein even forfeited his own pay for six months and encouraged other partners to do the same. An end to the crisis came into view as the firm finally posted revenue growth in 2004.

Polishing the rough spots

A major restructuring for the firm was announced in September 2005, as management aimed to increase performance and cut costs long term. Diamond's offices in Düsseldorf and Lisbon were closed, the Barcelona office was downsized and global headcount was reduced by 6 percent. Revenue for 2005 showed a steady climb, up 25 percent from 2004 to $193.2 million, and improvement seemed to be on the horizon. But at the end of fiscal year 2006, it was clear that the streamlining measures still weren't enough to boost earnings: The firm posted $145 million in revenue, a 25 percent decline for the year. Analyst forecasts for the firm were gloomy, citing slack growth in North America and inability to sell discontinued operations Europe.

In July 2006, Diamond announced an agreement to sell its operations in Continental Europe, South America and the Middle East for about $30 million. Mercer Management Consulting, now the general consulting business of Oliver Wyman, took over the firm's subsidiaries in France, Germany, Spain, Brazil and the United Arab Emirates, and acquired 150 staffers to boot. On August 1, 2006, the firm changed its name to Diamond Management & Technology Consultants, Inc., and began marketing itself under the brand Diamond.

Cut and clarity

With a new name and pared-down structure, the firm announced its sharpened vision for the future: to increase revenue 15 percent, to broaden its client base and to focus on its three core regions: North America, the U.K. and India. The firm also announced new leadership, naming Adam Gutstein—a founding consultant of Diamond Technology Partners—as its new CEO. Mel Bergstein had stepped down from the CEO position in April 2006, but still retains the title of chairman. Gutstein also took over the role of president after former President and Chief Operating Officer Jay Norman left the firm in August 2006.

Diamond typically promotes partners from within its ranks. However, several industry practices at Diamond were boosted with experienced partner hires in recent months. The consumer packaged goods division is strengthened with the addition of Paul J. Upchurch, a 15-year consulting veteran, who joined as partner in November 2006. In October 2006, Julian Sparkes, former CEO of network solutions firm NSC North America, joined as a partner in the enterprise practice. In January 2007, Kevin J. McGilloway, whose experience includes time as chief information officer at Lehman Brothers and Equitable Life Assurance, joined Diamond as a partner in the financial services practice. Retail and consumer goods consulting veteran David Oliver joined Diamond's London office in April 2007.

Visit the Vault Consulting Career Channel at www.vault.com/consulting - with insider firm profiles, message boards, the Vault Consulting Job Board and more.

VAULT CAREER LIBRARY   349

A multifaceted client list

Diamond doesn't advertise its roster of clients or the contracts it wins, but simply claims its engagements involve a wide variety of private- and public-sector companies. The firm's financial services practice has served Goldman Sachs, Visa and the Federal Reserve Bank of Chicago, while the health care practice has worked with Aetna and ActiveHealth Management. Diamond's public-sector practice has worked on a multiyear tech support purchase agreement with the U.S. Department of Justice. One part of the project was to assist with the Department's unified financial management system, which will consolidate multiple financial management and procurement systems departmentwide.

You can't have too much information

According to Diamond's consultants, clients are increasingly asking for more information and data analysis about their businesses. In response, Diamond expanded its information and analytics services in December 2006, and established the Diamond Information & Analytics Center in Mumbai to provide additional expertise to client engagements. The center provides marketing and operational analysis through growth and profitability analytics, business metrics information management and information strategy. The firm also maintains a blog on information and analytics, where readers can access and share current views on a wide range of issues, such as marketing campaign management, process analytics and business intelligence.

The sharpest minds

Since 1997, Diamond has hosted the DiamondExchange, a membership-based, multifaceted senior executive forum that helps business leaders understand where to use technology for competitive advantage—and how to act on that knowledge. The crowd is typically comprised of executives from Fortune 1000 companies and senior government and military officials, who gather at five-star resorts and hotels across the country five times a year to share their insights and perspectives on business strategy. The event often draws big-name speakers—notable past guest contributors have included Jack Greenberg, chairman and retired CEO of McDonald's; Gary Loveman, CEO of Harrah's Entertainment, Inc.; Admiral Mike Mullen, chief of Naval Operations, U.S. Navy; Nicholas Negroponte, founder and director of the MIT Media Laboratory; and General Colin L. Powell, Secretary of State, U.S. Army (retired).

The DiamondExchange has also developed the Diamond Fellows, a network of experts who provide clients with a broad range of perspectives on engagements and interactions throughout the year. Their focused expertise and unbiased opinions serve as a catalyst for launching innovative thought leadership, resulting in breakthrough strategies and solid businesses. Among this brainy group are Gordon Bell, a principal researcher at Microsoft; Alan Kay, one of the earliest pioneers of object-oriented programming, personal computing and graphical user interfaces; and Dan Bricklin, a software designer, best known as the co-creator of VisiCalc, the first electronic spreadsheet.

Trend tracking

Consultants at Diamond have taken a shine to publishing their insights in books, articles and white papers on hot tech trends. The 1998 best seller, *Unleashing the Killer App*, by partner Chunka Mui and e-commerce guru Larry Downes, got a lot of hype in the late 1990s during the dot-com boom. Its popularity endured for quite a while—in October 2005, *The Wall Street Journal* named the title one of the five-best books on business and the Internet. Other titles include 2002's *The Venture Imperative*, co-authored by former Diamond Partner Tim Rohner and *The New Market Leaders: Who's Winning and How in the Battle for Customers*, by Fred Wiersema, in 2001.

Other relevant research is disseminated through *Diamond Perspectives*—articles on business and industry topics. A January 2007 piece, titled "Curing Customer Churn" explores all kinds of theories surrounding "churners," customers who ditch one service provider for another. It advocates ways of finding out who the real at-risk churners are and how to keep from losing their business. Diamond's surveys are another way it keeps up with current issues in global business and technology. Annually, the firm distributes the Global IT Outsourcing Study to collect opinions from buyers and providers of outsourcing services about the current and future state of information technology outsourcing and business process outsourcing. The firm's newest survey is the Digital IQ Study, which asks C-level executives to quantify the ways that technology impacts their particular industry.

A sparkling reputation

Diamond's commitment to flexibility for its employees has earned it a top spot among its consulting peers. In 2006, for the third consecutive year, the firm was ranked by *Consulting Magazine* as one of the 10 best firms to work for. Among 32 consulting firms where employees were polled, Diamond received high marks in the areas of career development, job experience, firm leadership, culture, work/life balance and compensation. To promote work/life balance, the firm offers flexible work arrangements, which allow for part-time work and short-term, no travel or telecommuting options for employees who prefer a nontraditional schedule. Another option, the live-anywhere policy, permits consultants to work out of any place they choose, in order to cater to family needs. In June 2005, the firm was recognized in its hometown by the National Association of Business Resources, as one of 10 elite winners of the Chicago's Best and Brightest Companies to Work For award. In addition, Diamond won kudos from the organization as a "best and brightest" company for its use of innovative HR practices.

GETTING HIRED

Selection time

Information on Diamond's career paths, career profiles, coaching and mentoring, roles and responsibilities, and tips for the interview process are all a click away on the firm's web site. Diamond also provides a listing of job openings for experienced hires and details on campus recruiting events. According to an insider involved with the recruiting process, Diamond's schools of choice include the University of Chicago, University of Michigan, University of Pennsylvania, Northwestern University, Indiana University Kelley School of Business, Duke Fuqua School of Business, Carnegie Mellon, MIT, Columbia, Syracuse and Cornell.

When you come to Diamond, prepare for "an interesting and in-depth interview process [that tests] presentation skills and quick thinking ability," a source says. For campus hires, the process begins with first-round interviews on campus, including one 45-minute behavioral and one 45-minute "situational" (another word for case) interview. For the final round, top picks are flown to Chicago for three 45-minute interviews. An experienced hire says, "The hiring process was quick and to the point. There was a prescreening phone interview by a recruiter. Then that was followed by a domain skills phone interview by a principal-level consultant. If you make the cut, Diamond flies you into Chicago for three more interviews, which consist of two case interviews and a fit interview by a partner."

Popping the question

"Our cases are typically real-life examples of a client situation that we have summarized and shortened for the purposes of the interview. These include technology and strategy alignment and technology strategy questions"—hence the term "situational," an insider explains. Interviewees receive materials for one formal case approximately 48 hours in advance of the interview, during which "candidates have the opportunity to read the case and an industry overview," a source says. "During the first hour of the final round, candidates are given a question/s to prepare on PowerPoint slides. They then present their case to one of the interviewers. Then, they have another behavioral and situational interview," the insider adds. Another consultant notes, "The questions are selected to fit the candidates' strengths and chosen work profile. Thus, the exercise is primarily about how candidates structure and deliver messages to clients."

The good news is, it doesn't take long for Diamond to propose: "The decision process is very quick. For experienced hires, for example, the process from interview day to decision is 48 hours or less, and most often the candidate has a decision the next day," an insider reports.

Visit the Vault Consulting Career Channel at **www.vault.com/consulting** - with insider firm profiles, message boards, the Vault Consulting Job Board and more.

VAULT CAREER LIBRARY   351

The firm offers a few slots for summer interns, a program that provides "excellent exposure to Diamond's type of work and culture" and a "realistic portrayal of life as a full-time employee," an insider reports. One former intern says of his experience as an intern, "I felt very welcome," worked with a "great project and team" and "was challenged with real work and real deliverables."

OUR SURVEY SAYS

SWANS wanted

Diamond enjoys a "unique" culture, insiders say. "Even though we have a virtual model where consultants have a live-anywhere policy, Diamond does a really good job promoting a company culture that focuses on the value of its people," a consultant cheers. Another source frets that the virtual model can make it "hard to get to know others outside your client/project teams," but for the most part, Diamond consultants think their peers are gems. As one insider explains it, the firm "hires SWANS (smart/works hard/analytical/nice)." "The people are as sharp as a tack and nice," agrees a colleague. Diamond is a place where "a sense of humor and the oxymoron of confident humility are common and valued," another source reports.

Insiders also praise the flatness of Diamond's culture. "All levels within the firm are very approachable," says a consultant, adding, "There are no titles on the business cards." "It is a place where the best idea leads," another insider says, and "every single person can contribute to the building of the firm, which makes things exciting." According to a consultant, "Communication is extremely open across all levels of the firm, allowing us to focus on our clients, rather than on rumors of change within our own company." In addition, a source reports, "Strategy and technology consultants all share the same culture and work together as one firm."

Flexibility rules

And Diamond isn't all work and no play, insiders report. "The firm makes time for your personal life. There are times when you have to be head-down and working, but when they can, they enable us to maintain that work/life balance," a consultant explains. Another insider reports that this balance "depends on the partner you work with," but adds that "most partners have a tremendous value for life outside of work and give you personal flexibility." This flexibility plays out in many ways, from the popular live-anywhere policy to alternative working arrangements.

Parents also are able to strike a balance between work and family life at Diamond, we're told. "We recently had our first child, and the partners went out of their way to accommodate me, putting me on a short-term, no travel arrangement that ensured I was at home in the weeks leading up to the birth," says a consultant. "After our son was born, I was given a significant amount of time—in addition to official parental leave—to help out at home. All the partners at Diamond emphasized how important it was for me to do this. I had significantly greater support than friends who've had children at other firms."

Virtual office, real travel

Diamond insiders acknowledge one drawback of living wherever they like: They still have to meet with clients all over the country. A staffer reports that about 25 percent of the firm's consultants live in Chicago or New York, where projects are more local, and this may—but not always—cut down on travel time a bit. But for the rest, a 4:1 travel arrangement is common. There are few complaints about this model: "The firm is pretty accommodating with travel. We stay in good hotels and eat well on the road," says one insider. Being able to work from home on the fifth day also helps, colleagues note. In addition, a consultant reports, "In a small firm like Diamond, it is possible to have some degree of influence on your staffing. I am currently local for at least eight months, due to my proactive effort to influence my staffing."

When it comes to work hours, "There is always some amount of work to do on the weekends and long days are the norm, but this is what is required by the problems we are working on for our clients," says a source, who adds, "I can actually say that I don't mind the long hours and once-in-awhile weekend work because I feel that I am learning a lot and having a direct impact on our clients." Another insider reports that a 55-hour week "is about average, with some peaks and valleys depending on the lifecycle of the project." "I have not worked past midnight on a project in five years," a colleague asserts.

Amassing equity

Diamond's compensation package glitters, insiders say, including "shares of common stock as equity that typically vests over four years." "[The shares] really accumulate quickly. Four years out of MBA, most people have $100K in stock," another source says. Some staffers do grumble about Diamond's bonus structure, however, with one observing that the "bonus needs to match top firms—that is difficult because the firm is public." Another consultant frets that the "bonus level is tied to our performance rating, which leads many to work additional hours to boost their rating to increase the likelihood of a larger bonus, which essentially just equates to working with the hope of being paid for overtime."

Supporting the lifecycle

But you won't hear any complaints about Diamond's 100 percent health care coverage, deemed "best in class" by employees. "The health care [coverage] is amazing," says a consultant, noting, "I've never had to pay for a prescription (and as you get older all the cholesterol drugs and blood pressure drugs get expensive!), and never had to pay for eyeglasses or contacts." Other perks include compensation for home office needs like phone lines and Internet, and a "$10 daily allowance for health clubs when traveling." One insider considers the firm's all-hands approach to meetings a benefit: "We still are a firm that believes in company meetings, which are held in Chicago three times a year. These are tied to a day of education opportunities. We are remote as consultants, but believe in maintaining a close, family-like environment."

On the subject of family, Diamond consultants are pretty happy with their level of maternity ("generous") and paternity (two weeks) leave. The firm also offers flexible work arrangements for new parents. An insider notes that Diamond is "absolutely supportive with any life changes; the firm believes in making sure that one can take care of any family needs and have time to celebrate those events as well."

As for offices, one work-from-home insider says they're rarely used "outside of training, recruiting and client visits, but they are beautiful," and jokes, "My home office where I work on Fridays is very cozy but needs some cleaning!" At headquarters in Chicago on three floors of the John Hancock building, there are "incredible views of the Chicago lake shore and skyline," and "some areas could use some updating, but for the most part the facilities are pretty nice," sources say. The New York, Washington, D.C., and Hartford offices are relatively small, "in support of the virtual office policy," an insider says.

Partners in the trenches

Diamond insiders generally give high marks to their supervisors. "It is nice that my manager sets aside time for each individual on my team to meet for a weekly status meeting. This is a nice way to discuss progress and set future goals," a consultant shares. It's a "smaller firm, so there are definitely good opportunities to interact with upper management," says a source, and "the top-level managers are always available and very responsive to everyone," agrees a colleague.

"Partners are in the trenches at client sites," a consultant tells us. "Everyone has direct interaction with the project engagement partner and clients," attests a source, adding, "Unlike other firms, everyone is invited to meetings with senior executives until they prove that they shouldn't be. In other firms, you need to earn your stripes first." Agrees a co-worker, "Because we're a smaller firm, you're placed into situations where you're interacting with senior-level clients (C-level) much earlier than you would elsewhere. This isn't to say that we take risks with our clients; to get C-level exposure you need to be good, but you will be interacting with high-level clients at a much earlier level than peers at McKinsey, BCG, etc."

The training advantage

Lately, training at Diamond has become "a key focus area for the firm and is at the cusp of becoming a competitive advantage," an insider claims. Other sources agree, praising the firm's "multiple training opportunities, from informal on-the-job, to web-

Visit the Vault Consulting Career Channel at **www.vault.com/consulting** - with insider firm profiles, message boards, the Vault Consulting Job Board and more.

 353

based, industry-specific training, to several types of classroom training." "The firm continuously seeks to find innovative ways in which to better train consultants," a staffer adds. Of course, "the challenge is being able to slip away to attend," notes a colleague. "Partners are always understanding, but it can be hard to escape for more than a week or two each year. One-day and virtual training classes are easier to make it to." Another insider reports that there are "mentoring programs in place, but they are not as structured/effective as they could be." Still, a consultant says, "partners and principals are challenged to coach on the job and actively do this." Speaking of partners, the firm also established a Partner Leadership Academy, which all partners are required to attend annually. In 2007, the partners were immersed in Ken Blanchard's Situational Leadership concepts—a program that is now being rolled out to the entire firm.

Female affinity

Consulting may not always be a girl's best friend, but Diamond takes pains to accommodate and promote women in the workplace, insiders say. "The industry and the firm is still dominated by males, but Diamond has taken several steps to remedy the situation (flexible work arrangements, women's forum affinity group, mentoring programs, etc.)," says a source. Another consultant lauds the firm's "very strong informal mentor network" and "very active Women's Forum that plans educational and social events." "As a woman, I believe women are treated equally and I do not notice a gender gap," says a staffer. Still, an insider observes, "We have good female representation at the partner level, but are weak at the manager/principal levels. This is a high-priority area for us, but it is extremely difficult recruiting women to an environment where there are few women already."

For minorities, the firm offers a "very strong" mentoring program, sources say. "We have many minority consultants and partners, and continue to recruit actively to get more," says a consultant. However, a colleague opines, "We need to continue to push to make minority leaders more visible in the firm."

The firm also features an "established gay and lesbian community with sponsored events and open support," making it "the best consulting firm for members of the GLBT community," insiders claim. "Domestic partnerships are covered by our insurance, and we have prominent gay firm leaders," says a consultant. "We also recruit at the Reaching Out MBA conference annually for full-time candidates," a colleague adds.

Helping locally

According to a consultant, "A dispersed employee base makes it difficult" to organize firmwide community service activities, "but there are periodic events in Chicago and New York where large numbers of individuals live." In addition, "Many non-Chicago personnel are active in their home communities." In fact, an insider reports, it's a "priority for this coming year to do more pro bono work and broader community programs in our local communities." Furthermore, "The firm routinely matches charitable donations for major events (tsunami, Hurricane Katrina)," we're told.

"Even though we have a virtual model where consultants have a live-anywhere policy, Diamond does a really good job promoting a company culture that focuses on the value of its people."

– Diamond employee

Visit the Vault Consulting Career Channel at **www.vault.com/consulting** - with insider firm profiles, message boards, the Vault Consulting Job Board and more.

VAULT CAREER LIBRARY   355

FTI Consulting, Inc.

500 East Pratt Street
Suite 1400
Baltimore, MD 21202
Phone: (410) 951-4800
Fax: (410) 224-8378
www.fticonsulting.com

LOCATIONS

Baltimore, MD (HQ)
40 offices worldwide

PRACTICE AREAS

Corporate Finance
Economic Consulting
Forensic & Litigation Consulting
Strategic Communications
Technology

THE STATS

Employer Type: Public Company
Ticker Symbol: FCN (NYSE)
Chairman: Dennis J. Shaughnessy
President & CEO: Jack B. Dunn IV
2007 Employees: 2,100+
2006 Employees: 1,500+
2007 Revenue: $900 million (est.)
2006 Revenue: $708 million

RANKING RECAP

Quality of Life
#20 - Relationships with Supervisors

UPPERS

- "Few cookie-cutter assignments"
- Flexibility and no micromanagement
- "I have found everyone to be very supportive of my professional development"
- "A tremendous amount of opportunity at the firm as it is continuing to grow organically and through acquisition"

DOWNERS

- "Management's single focus on utilization"
- "No sense of a cohesive effort across the firm"
- "It's a mystery how bonuses are distributed"
- Issues with integration of the continuing acquisition spree

EMPLOYMENT CONTACT

www.fticonsulting.com/web/about/Careers.html

THE BUZZ
WHAT CONSULTANTS AT OTHER FIRMS ARE SAYING ABOUT THIS FIRM

- "Impressive work that flies under the radar"
- "Detailed grunt work"
- "Strong midsized firm"
- "Corporate culture is a mess"

THE SCOOP

Friends in low places

Companies in trouble turn to FTI Consulting to make things right. Since 1982, the consulting firm has worked to dig underperforming companies out from high-stakes investigations and litigation. Whether their clients face charges of fraud, disclosure or malpractice, the Baltimore, Md.-based firm is one of the country's leading providers of forensic accounting and litigation support services.

With the greater regulatory burden companies face under Sarbanes-Oxley, more and more companies are also coming to FTI Consulting for help before problems begin, relying on its services to avert, or at least minimize, future risks. These services include assistance with corporate governance and compliance issues; technology risk assessments; transaction advisory services for acquisitions, divestitures and recapitalizations; interim management; and nonlitigation-related management consulting, such as corporate strategy, transfer pricing and asset optimization.

In 2006, FTI had a total of 2,079 employees providing services for a diverse group of clients, including global Fortune 500 companies, global law firms, global banks and local, state and federal governments and agencies worldwide. The company has operations across 29 U.S. cities, as well as in the U.K., Ireland, France, Russia, Australia, China, Hong Kong, Japan, Singapore, United Arab Emirates and South America.

All in the family

Since a major restructuring of its services in early 2004, FTI Consulting offers its services via five main business segments: corporate finance and restructuring, forensic and litigation consulting, economic consulting, strategic and financial communications, and technology services. The firm's corporate finance and restructuring arm is one of the top-five noninvestment bank restructuring practices in the U.S., and focuses on performance improvement, turnarounds, capital solutions, interim management, creditor advisory and transaction advisory services, among other services. FTI also claims to have one of the country's most experienced forensic and litigation consulting teams, which has been involved in some of the country's most historic high-stakes cases. The economic consulting arm provides law firms, corporations and government agencies with the rigorous economic analyses needed for legal and regulatory proceedings, strategic decisions and public policy debates. And finally, the technology practice collects, analyzes and manages data so that its clients can respond to investigations, make financial restatements, answer regulatory inquiries and deal with large-scale litigation, mergers and acquisitions.

The firm also provides strategic communications services through its subsidiary, Financial Dynamics, one of the world's largest business and financial communications consultancies, which FTI acquired in October 2006. Along with Financial Dynamics, FTI also leans on its wholly owned subsidiary, FTI Capital Advisors, to provide investment banking, M&A, corporate sales and divestiture, private debt and equity placements, and other advisory services. Another subsidiary, FTI Palladium Partners, markets and delivers high-level senior management (CEOs, CFOs, COOs, CIOs and CROs) for companies that are in the midst of a turnaround or are looking for new leadership. FTI also offers marketing strategy services via FTI Helios since acquiring the Helios Consulting Group in 2005.

Born in Baltimore

In 1982, Daniel W. Luczak and Joseph R. Reynolds Jr. founded Forensic Technologies International Corporation to provide forensic engineering and scientific services for clients in the insurance, legal, manufacturing and utility industries. By 1989, the firm had made a name for itself managing a number of major technical investigations and litigation. By 1996, through a series of acquisitions and well-paid projects, the firm was big enough to undergo an initial public offering, and in 1998, changed its name to FTI Consulting. It was also in 1998 that Jack Dunn took his seat as the company's chief executive officer.

Visit the Vault Consulting Career Channel at www.vault.com/consulting - with insider firm profiles, message boards, the Vault Consulting Job Board and more.

VAULT CAREER LIBRARY   357

Since then, FTI has continued to grow via a series of big-name acquisitions, including the purchase of PricewaterhouseCoopers' business recovery services division in 2002, which added an additional 371 professionals and 15 offices to its roster. The sale was financed by the gains FTI made in the aftermath of corporate scandals like Enron and Worldcom.

Growth plan

But even a business full of experts can't avoid a hiccup or two. By 2004, FTI found itself leaking money, not making money— by the end of fiscal 2004, EBITDA had decreased by 18 percent (even though revenue increased by 13 percent from 2003) after fewer and fewer corporations sought restructuring help and whole teams from FTI's corporate finance/restructuring practice jumped ship.

Things have started to look up for FTI since the end of 2005, when it reported a 26.4 percent revenue increase to $539.5 million. Part of the solution to FTI's money crunch was the regulatory environment Sarbanes-Oxley created in the U.S. When it was clear that the Big Four accounting firms could not provide additional consulting services to companies they audited, FTI Consulting stepped in to help them comply with SOX's more stringent governance and conflict-of-interest requirements. "Prior to Sarbanes-Oxley, boards were willing to go down with the ship," said FTI Chairman Dennis Shaughnessy in a December 2005 *Investor's Business Daily* interview. "Now they're not willing to do that, so they're hiring people like ourselves to help solve problems faster." The strategy is still paying off for FTI, which posted revenue of $708 million, a 31 percent increase from 2005.

Wall Street takes a shine to FTI

FTI Consulting has won high marks on Wall Street for its growth potential: By the end of the 2006 calendar year, FTI's shares were only about $1 short of their highest share price of the year, $29.77. What is the Street watching? FTI's revenue potential, for one. The firm said in 2005 that it hopes to achieve revenue of $1 billion by 2009, boosted by an estimated $250 million in gains from acquisitions between 2005 and 2009.

The second big measure of the firm's growth is the number of new hires it has attracted in recent months. In January 2007, former Democratic Majority Leader Dick Gephardt became a consultant for and advisor to the company through an exclusive agreement with his firm, Gephardt & Associates, LLC. In addition, he will serve on the advisory board of Financial Dynamics. In December 2006, FTI hired Daniel L. Rubinfeld and Richard J. Gilbert, both professors of economics at the University of California at Berkeley and former deputy assistant attorneys general at the U.S. Department of Justice's Antitrust Division. In October of that year, another slew of hires joined the fold—Mary G. Barnes, a former partner at KPMG joined as a senior managing director in FTI's forensic and litigation consulting practice; former Deloitte Partner Bruce Burton came on as a senior managing director in intellectual property management services; Mark Weinstein, a former partner in PwC's business recovery services unit, is a senior managing director in FTI's corporate finance practice; and another PwC alumnus Scott Bingham now works in the corporate finance unit. More than a dozen high-level hires preceded these in 2006 alone.

FTI's acquisition strategy is also in full force, which Wall Street has taken as a sign of the company's strength. In January 2007, FTI acquired Holder International, a leading risk mitigation firm serving multinational corporations, regional holding companies, banks, private equity firms and high-net-worth individuals throughout Latin America and the Caribbean, as well as the U.S., Spain and Portugal. In October 2006, FTI purchased Brower, Kriz & Stynchcomb, which, with its experience in the domestic and international construction industry, will boost the firm's forensic and litigation consulting segment. Also added in October was G3 Consulting, whose experience leveraging technology on behalf of clients will further extend the firm's capabilities in the U.K., and also fits well with the needs of the newly-acquired Financial Dynamics client base. In July of that year, the firm bought Hong Kong's International Risk, a risk mitigation consultancy serving blue-chip clients in Asia, India, Russia, the U.S. and Europe. And in January 2006, FTI acquired Competition Policy Associates, a boutique economics consulting firm with offices in Washington, D.C., and San Francisco.

GETTING HIRED

No how-to for hiring

FTI consultants say the firm's hiring process is rather informal and varies from office to office. While some offices exhibit "no structure whatsoever," according to insiders, others interview on campus and then hold a "super day event" that brings in a number of "undergraduate and graduate candidates ... to the office for interviews and lunch." One staffer explains that some offices narrow "the field to a few applicants and then screen them with a phone interview" before inviting candidates to interview in the office where they meet with at least two consultants, while other offices set up interviews with five or six professionals. Sources say experienced candidates usually meet with one or two senior managing directors.

On your best behavior

For the most part, insiders report having gone through "behavioral-based interviews" with "a couple brainteasers." According to one, "If they ask you a case question, it would be rare." A consultant explains that interviews "run the gamut from technical questions designed to test pertinent knowledge to social questions designed to assess interpersonal skills." Questions also vary by practice area, with some groups requiring "financial modeling tests as well as demonstration of specific industry knowledge," sources tell us.

After the interview process, FTI doesn't waste time making up its mind. "In some circumstances, candidates may be asked to come in for additional interviews," says one staffer, but interviewers are usually fairly quick to "deliberate within the office and decide if we want to make an offer." A colleague affirms that "interviewers discuss the candidates, and job offers are extended immediately."

Scouting for talent across the U.S.

FTI recruits on campuses throughout the United States; "It's too many [schools] to name nationwide, but the top schools in each region." Sources explain that some schools are selected for recruiting based on "a strong alumni presence in FTI." And while the firm does engage in significant campus recruiting, we're told that in some offices "most candidates come through referrals or networking."

OUR SURVEY SAYS

Identity crisis

Given FTI's history of acquisitions, sources say the firm "doesn't really have an overall corporate culture," and "there is no sense of common direction for the firm." Several consultants see this problem as stemming from top management, with one director claiming that "senior management and corporate staff have very poor communication skills and do not set a good precedent for the firm." Another gripe with management? One insider remarks, "I would like to see more youth in the firm's leadership. The senior managing director group appears to be too old."

Without a unified front, consultants report that "each office seems to have its own culture," largely defined by the SMDs at the helm of individual offices. That can be good or bad, sources say, depending on the style of the SMDs. One insider explains that "a few SMD-level people have their own culture that many don't like," but on the plus side, "the strongest performers get to select the SMDs they work for and have the best fit with." Those who like to work independently view the atomized culture positively, since, as one consultant puts it, "people and groups have leeway to manage themselves."

Visit the Vault Consulting Career Channel at www.vault.com/consulting - with insider firm profiles, message boards, the Vault Consulting Job Board and more.

VAULT CAREER LIBRARY 359

Open doors, open space

Access to senior management varies between FTI offices just as widely as the corporate culture. A director tells us that "some regions and offices have a great open-door policy where staff can talk to senior management, and others are completely the opposite." While one managing director explains a rather distant relationship with his supervisor—"I do not interact with [my supervisor] on business matters, but generally on reporting requirements for corporate management"—another staffer in Chicago feels differently: "My supervisors go beyond just work colleagues. Being on the road with them allows you to get an intimate understanding of what they are all about." Open-door policies aside, a staffer explains that "there is regular interaction among employees of all levels" because projects are usually staffed with both senior and junior consultants. Affirms one Washington, D.C.-based consultant, "The projects in corporate finance are generally staffed with one or two senior staff members and one or two junior staff members, so there is regular interaction among employees of all levels."

The physical office spaces also vary greatly by office. Consultants in New York report "not enough space" and a "horrible location," while those in Washington, D.C., say they are working in offices that are "new and modern with plenty of space and natural lighting." A Chicagoan notes, "Our company is growing so rapidly that we constantly run out of cube/office space," while one picky staffer in Houston groans that there is too much space, which "makes the office feel empty." A senior manager in New York suggests the perfect fit: "I think a more progressive view toward the work environment as being more like a home environment, with comfortable lounges, etc., would be better."

The good, the bad and the imbalanced

The decentralized culture affects work/life balance as well, making it dependent upon "who you work with, the staffing in the office and your region," says an insider. A consultant notes that "some groups have horrible balance that can be attributable to managers who don't care about staff," while another says that working with other FTI groups "has allowed me to appreciate how well my work group is at maintaining a good work/life balance." One consultant who was lucky in that regard states that she is able to maintain balance "because my office is much friendlier to this than the firm as a whole." Generally, insiders say consultants at FTI gain more control over their schedules "the further you are along in your career," with one director adding the caveat that "this only works based on your project and the senior management that you report to." When faced with SMDs who don't support work/life balance among staffers, sources urge that it's up to "each individual to take control of his own balance." Says one director, "I balance work and life by managing my own time. I put my bonus at risk by taking time off or by working only eight hours a day."

FTI has made some efforts at the corporate level to improve work/life balance and "accommodate people with children, educational aspirations, etc.," we're told. According to some sources, FTI has also recently revised its already generous maternity and paternity leave to be even more accommodating. One staffer says she has been able "to work a 30-hour-per-week flex schedule since returning from my six-month maternity leave!" In addition, the firm lets clients know that "consultants will only be available for four days per week to ensure that they have some balance in their lives."

Counting the hours

When it comes to putting in the time, a number of FTI employees report working several weekends during the year and 50 to 60 hours per week, but some say they stick to a "40-hour week with random overtime as needed." Of course, hourly demands vary based on the project timeline, but according to one insider, there is "no need for face time in the office" and "as long as the work is getting done, when and where is normally not an issue." Still, while getting ahead may not require unnecessary face time, one staffer explains that "most of the successful directors make themselves available 24/7."

Climbing the food chain without chain food

The amount of travel consultants face depends on the practice group, but "everyone is expected to travel sometimes," according to a director, who adds that new staff members are "expected to travel for at least one extended period of time." And insiders seem to accept these travel demands as "just part of the job." A consultant in Chicago explains that "most work is done at the client site, unless relevant documents, data can be brought back a regional office (or your home office)." Life on the road can be difficult, especially since "client and target company locations are not always located in attractive destinations," groans one consultant. Others explain that one of the greatest challenges of constant travel is "maintaining a regular workout and healthy eating," while dealing with "long work hours—[there are] mostly chain restaurants and small fitness centers in many of the hotel chains."

"Business travel in general is not fun, but FTI provides enough flexibility to make it manageable." Consultants appreciate the "free frequent flier miles and hotel points" that they acquire, and another explains FTI's "in-lieu-of travel policy" for employees who are returning to the same client site for consecutive weeks: Staffers can opt to "fly someone to the city in which he/she is working to spend the weekend" or apply the cost of a ticket to their home city toward a flight to another destination for the weekend.

Employees say that with some forethought, "it is usually easy to arrange to take time off or to be in the local office" for commitments and activities outside of work. As one respondent explains, "regular and frequent travel is difficult," but the wear and tear can be "minimized with planning, organization and regular communication with family and friends."

Bewildered by bonuses

Bonuses are a bit more complicated at FTI. Sources tell us the firm has two bonus structures in place: "The first is a quarterly bonus which is based upon employees exceeding an expected monthly utilization percentage (number of hours billed as a percentage of total number of hours available)." According to some sources, this method is problematic because "there is too much focus on utilization rate and not enough focus on the quality of business we are pursuing." A managing director adds, "My base salary is about 10 percent higher than industry standards. But bonus is one-tenth of the industry standard because we do not get bonuses based on the business we bring in. Thus, my total compensation is about 35 to 40 percent lower than my peers in similar organizations."

The second bonus program, we're told, is "an annual bonus paid in accordance with a performance review," and is based on "subjective measures" and "the discretion of the SMDs in one's office." The subjectivity involved in this process leads one staffer to conclude that "there is no way to determine what your bonus compensation will be or why." For some, the structure represents an opportunity for higher bonuses "if people develop key skill sets and become a preferred resource to more SMDs."

Taking stock

In addition to bonuses, employees look forward to other perks, including a "wide variety of snacks and drinks, and lots of free lunches." Others express appreciation for a "monthly ice cream social birthday party," "gym membership," "orthodontia coverage for adults," "dry cleaning" and "great Red Sox tickets," at least for one office. In addition, FTI provides consultants with 401(k) matching with immediate vesting and an employee stock purchasing plan that allows "employees to contribute to the plan throughout the year and purchase the company's stock at a discount semiannually." However, some insiders don't think the program goes far enough and claim that "senior management has little interest in providing long-term compensation (i.e., stock options) to its employees."

Training for newbies

Sources tell us that training at FTI occurs through some official programs, but primarily via on-the-job experience. A senior staffer in Washington, D.C., comments, "There is a formal training program, however the topics covered are primarily beneficial to professionals working on bankruptcy projects." According to a consultant, the firm's "weeklong formal training program" is designed for "employees new to the firm." Reportedly, "official basic training is improving every year." And though "the firm's training opportunities are minimal," notes one director, "they always support and encourage efforts to seek additional training outside the firm."

Visit the Vault Consulting Career Channel at **www.vault.com/consulting** - with insider firm profiles, message boards, the Vault Consulting Job Board and more.

VAULT CAREER LIBRARY   361

Good old boys at the top

Insiders report that FTI is "still a very 'good old boys,'" "male-dominated company from the top levels and board of directors down." According to one managing director, "There are very few women in the higher level positions, but about half in midlevel positions, so this might indicate a changing trend as the women progress in their careers." The firm employs "few minorities," sources say, and for GLBT staffers, FTI provides "same-sex partner benefits, which is a commitment to diversity," asserts one consultant. Regardless of representation, an insider claims, "the firm treats all people with equal respect, regardless of color, sex or religion."

FTI also reaches out to its surrounding communities through "many philanthropic events organized throughout the year." "There are regular announcements for professionals to join groups from the firm for a number of [charitable events]," and the firm sponsors the Cambridge Family and Children's Services holiday gift drive in Boston, while in Nashville, FTI has sponsored the Nashville Conference for Community and Justice of Middle Tennessee for the past three years. A consultant in Chicago notes that "any consultant involved in charity or philanthropy can approach leadership for financial support. We are involved in the United Way, Boys and Girls Club and a whole host of other charities."

"The strongest performers get to select the SMDs they work for and have the best fit with."

– *FTI Consulting source*

Visit the Vault Consulting Career Channel at **www.vault.com/consulting** - with insider firm profiles, message boards, the Vault Consulting Job Board and more.

VAULT CAREER LIBRARY   363

Analysis Group, Inc.

111 Huntington Avenue, 10th Floor
Boston, MA 02199
Phone: (617) 425-8000
Fax: (617) 425-8001
www.analysisgroup.com

LOCATIONS

Boston, MA (HQ)

Chicago, IL • Dallas, TX • Lakewood, CO • Los Angeles, CA
• Menlo Park, CA • New York, NY • San Francisco, CA •
Washington, DC • Montreal

PRACTICE AREAS

Accounting & Litigation Services
Antitrust
Commercial Litigation & Damages
Energy
Entertainment & Media
Environmental Economics
Financial Institutions
Health Care Consulting Services
Innovation Management
Intellectual Property
Labor & Employment
Securities & Financial Instruments
Strategy & Analytics
Telecommunications
Transfer Pricing & Tax
Valuation

THE STATS

Employer Type: Private Company
President & CEO: Martha S. Samuelson
2007 Employees: 375
2006 Employees: 330+

THE BUZZ

WHAT CONSULTANTS AT OTHER FIRMS ARE SAYING ABOUT THIS FIRM

- "Small, friendly"
- "Stiff; serious"
- "Growing, trying to get into every industry"
- "Growth limited because academics get the better assignments"

RANKING RECAP

Practice Area
#4 - Economic Consulting

UPPERS

- "They are casual about the unimportant stuff and strict on the important stuff"
- "Working with top academics"

DOWNERS

- "Billing is a pain"
- "Limited contact with the underlying client"

EMPLOYMENT CONTACT

E-mail: recruiter@analysisgroup.com
www.analysisgroup.com/analysisgroup/careers.aspx

THE SCOOP

Analyze this

For more than 25 years, Analysis Group has been providing economic, financial and business strategy consulting to law firms, corporations and government agencies. Its strong point: providing independent and fact-based assessments to companies embroiled in legal disputes and complex business problems. With 10 offices across the United States—the latest addition being Chicago in 2006—Analysis Group's 375 employees have provided litigation support in litigations for attorneys at more than 500 law firms, including the 25-largest firms in the country, and have helped develop corporate strategies for executives at Fortune 100 companies.

For law firms, Analysis Group offers support with pretrial discovery, development of economic and financial models, preparing testimony and critiquing opposing experts' analyses, among other litigation services. Companies and government agencies call on Analysis Group for financial planning, tax and transfer pricing issues, company and asset valuations, cost-effectiveness analyses, market analyses, and evaluation of mergers and acquisitions. The firm's consultants also help clients create strategies for growth by analyzing market dynamics and organizational capabilities, and pinpointing new market opportunities.

Brains from the beginning

Analysis Group started in April 1981 as a small consultancy based out of Belmont, Mass., a Boston suburb, by former Arthur D. Little consultants Bruce Stangle and Michael Koehn. The meeting of the minds—Stangle has his PhD in applied economics, while Koehn's is in financial economics—aimed to bridge the gap between academia and business litigation by providing economic research. Today, their firm uses economic analysis to solve problems in 16 practice areas, and the ties between business and academia have persevered. Analysis Group's professionals represent 40 countries and 37 languages, and hold advanced degrees in economics, law and business. The firm also regularly partners with academic affiliates, several of whom are Nobel and Draper Prize winners.

As one of its four main operating principles, Analysis Group emphasizes maintaining close ties to experts in academia, industry and government to be able to offer clients full access to the people and ideas they need to solve their problems. The firm also emphasizes strong relationships between its consulting teams and their clients, flexibility to tailor consulting services according to a client's needs and a pragmatic approach to advice-giving that emphasizes applicable solutions.

Their day(s) in court

While Stangle and Koehn's small Massachusetts firm initially consulted on mergers and acquisitions, today Analysis Group's revenue comes mostly from litigation consulting work that has soared, largely in response to the fallout from major business failures such as Enron and WorldCom, and the resulting heightened regulatory scrutiny and increased number of legal actions. Thanks to the growing demand for expert witnesses for testimony on complex business issues, Analysis Group has worked on behalf of big-name clients like the Walt Disney Company, Microsoft, Nike, TiVo, Citibank, Pfizer and Salomon Smith Barney on cases involving antitrust, securities, product liability and intellectual property. In an August 2005 *New York Times* article, Analysis Group's President and CEO Martha S. Samuelson stated that the demand for expert witnesses comes at a time when "business problems that often result in litigation have just become more complicated, harder to understand, and the dollars involved are often very significant."

On the strategy front, Analysis Group consultants use their quantitative skills in combination with management consulting experience. For example, Managing Principal Brian Gorin recently led a team evaluating a multibillion-dollar strategic investment decision for a major commodity enterprise. The team helped the client set an investment strategy and optimal contracting terms and, using real options and analysis techniques, highlighted expected returns and key sources of risk, and then identified approaches to mitigating risk.

Visit the Vault Consulting Career Channel at **www.vault.com/consulting** - with insider firm profiles, message boards, the Vault Consulting Job Board and more.

VAULT CAREER LIBRARY

365

Leading the way

Samuelson joined the Analysis Group in 1992 and became president in 1998. (Bruce Stangle now sits as chairman of the board and Michael Koehn is an academic affiliate and board member.) Over the years, Samuelson has overseen the firm's growth and service diversification, brought in new clients and attracted academic affiliates and new staff. The experience and training she carried with her to Analysis Group has undoubtedly shaped the direction she has taken the firm over the past 10 years. An expert in antitrust, finance and damages analysis, Samuelson is best known for her economic analyses for such large-scale litigations as the Microsoft private antitrust litigations.

At a time when the U.S. Securities and Exchange Commission has examined companies under a regulatory microscope, Samuelson and her colleagues have been busy working with fund companies, boards and regulators in some of the largest settlements addressing market timing and its impact, as well as excessive fee cases. The firm's securities practice has also taken a leading role in cases involving stock options backdating and securities fraud, and has worked on numerous Enron-related litigations in recent years.

Proof positive

There's a reason why clients call on Analysis Group consultants to testify on their behalf: because it works. In January 2007, Analysis Group's client New World TMT won a $2.8 billion default judgment in one of the largest legal victories for a Chinese company in an American court. Managing Principal Bruce Strombom provided damages analysis in this case involving allegations of fraud in technology for video-on-demand cable systems. In September 2006, Analysis Group consulted on a biotech patent infringement case on behalf of Innogenetics against Abbott Laboratories. The jury awarded Innogenetics $7 million in damages, the amount suggested at trial by Analysis Group based on its knowledge of, among other things, industry licensing practices, actual and expected profits, convoyed benefits and the strategic significance of the patent Innogenetics alleged Abbot Laboratories had infringed upon.

Also in September 2006, one of the largest mutual fund excessive fee actions ever filed—Baker v. American Century Investment Management—was voluntarily dismissed by the plaintiffs. Analysis Group and American Century lawyers poked holes in the plaintiffs' allegations that American Century charged excessive management fees to three of its largest mutual funds, totaling more than $1 billion over three years and violating SEC regulations. By the time the trial was set to begin, the plaintiffs conceded that American Century would likely win on most issues and the case was dismissed with prejudice.

And in a widely publicized case in April 2006, a Texas jury found that digital broadcaster EchoStar had violated TiVo's DVR technology patented in 2001, which allows subscribers to play one television while recording another. Analysis Group Managing Principal Keith R. Ugone assessed the economic impact of EchoStar's patent infringement on TiVo, which ended up winning damages of $74 million in the case.

Research repertoire

In addition to helping clients win cases, Analysis Group also publishes regular reports that highlight the range of its areas of expertise. In November 2006, for example, Analysis Group affiliate R. Glenn Hubbard released a report with the Committee on Capital Markets Regulation on the impact of regulations on U.S. financial market competitiveness. Earlier that year, Analysis Group Vice President Genia Long, with academic affiliates Henry Grabowski of Duke University and Iain Cockburn of Boston University, examined the market for "follow-on" biologics, or generic versions of biotech products, in a study published in *Health Affairs*. In February 2007, the firm sponsored an amicus curiae brief submitted to the Supreme Court on behalf of Weyerhaeuser in a major antitrust case. The brief considered economic issues in the case and advocated the reversal of the lower court ruling, and was signed by several prominent Analysis Group academic affiliates, in addition to CEO Samuelson.

Analysis Group consultants are also actively involved in various industry studies. A September 2006 study led by Vice Presidents Howard Birnbaum and Alan White was the first to quantify the cost to society of opioid abuse, while in July of that year, VP Mei Sheng Duh co-authored a paper with Novartis Pharmaceuticals and the Mayo Clinic on breast cancer treatment. And a 2005 study, "Hedge Funds: Risk and Return," continues to garner media attention for its finding that unsuccessful hedge funds stop reporting returns in their final months of operation, leaving the reporting database with only the more successful funds.

GETTING HIRED

Advanced degrees wanted

Analysis Group aims for recruits with quant-heavy backgrounds from "top business schools and PhD programs [for associates], and most selective liberal arts colleges and universities [for analysts]." "Analysts mostly come from backgrounds in economics, business, accounting, math and statistics, while associates are a mix of MBAs and economics PhDs," an insider notes. The interview process typically consists of two rounds. Reveals one source, "For analysts, we do a first round either on campus or over the phone. Then we do a second round, where the candidate faces six to eight interviews."

Love econ?

According to insiders, candidates "may get an informal case," but most interview questions "focus on strong quantitative skills, professionalism and attention to detail." Explains one manager, "Each interviewer has his own style. Some focus on technical questions; others focus on personality. We look for people who actually learned something about economics at school and will be able to fit in." The process is "rigorous, but is mostly trying to get at [the candidate's] interest in the company and in economic consulting, in general."

OUR SURVEY SAYS

Sharpen the intellect

If you love the idea of being a perpetual student, Analysis Group might be a good fit, according to a consultant who states, "Given the academic nature of the work and the firm's ties with leading academics and professors at the nation's top universities, the work environment is very much like working with a professor on a research paper." Another insider describes the culture as "intellectually stimulating, focused on solving complex problems accurately." Consultants are also proud of the often-prominent cases they get to work on. "It is a very talented staff and we have the opportunity to work with many top academics. We also have interesting work—many of our high-profile cases are on the front pages of the financial press." And for those consultants who foresee another degree after a stint in consulting, sources argue that this firm is a good place to prepare. "Most analysts go on to top business, law or PhD programs. Analysis Group's connections with academia help out quite a bit with that process," one manager reports.

Sources claim that despite the studious atmosphere, the firm is "very collegial" and full of "supportive" and "fabulous" colleagues. A staffer remarks, "Even on the most stressful days, I am glad to be here with my team. We find ways of having fun and smiling, even on the occasional all-nighter." "Analysis Group creates a culture that makes it fun to work. The employees are very collaborative and collegial, and they look for opportunities to help each other. The bureaucracy is kept to a minimum," affirms an insider.

Stay-at-home consultants

Associates seem thrilled about the fact that "travel is minimal, usually no more than overnight for a client meeting." Clarifies an insider, "In general there is not a lot of travel. Occasionally there are projects that involve travel, but much of the work and data can be shipped in-house. In general, the higher up you are the more you travel, but even some VPs and principals seldom travel."

Visit the Vault Consulting Career Channel at **www.vault.com/consulting** - with insider firm profiles, message boards, the Vault Consulting Job Board and more.

VAULT CAREER LIBRARY   **367**

Hours are "lumpy"

When it comes to a weekly routine, "work hours can be variable and unpredictable." One source concedes, "The volatility of hours can be a little hard to get used to. Deadlines can change at a moment's notice, forcing some potential work/life balance issues." Overall, though, insiders assure us that hours are usually tolerable and range between 55 and 60 hours a week. A consultant states, "Hours are very lumpy, but typically average out to about 55 a week. The learning curve is steep but tends to flatten out quickly at the analyst level."

Have a job and a life

A number of employees agree that with light travel and "flexible" schedules, the firm makes it possible to maintain a healthy work/life balance. "Although the nature of consulting work sometimes makes work/life balance a challenge, the company and my colleagues go out of their way to try to make things work. I have never had to reschedule a vacation, nor have I known any one else to do that. We just all chip in and get things done," a manager asserts. A colleague notes, "Some people here make their job their life, but the firm recommends having a job and a life."

Insiders claim that they are satisfied with the "competitive" compensation at the firm. One staffer explains, "Bonuses generally make up a higher percentage of total comp than at some of our peer firms." A colleague adds that "401(k) matching is pretty generous, and [we receive] a subsidy to join a gym."

Go your own way

Training is mostly up to the individual since Analysis Group doesn't have an official training program. "It's mostly on the job, but over the past few years we have been working on formalizing training, especially at the analyst level. Each office at Analysis Group does things a little differently," a manager reports, adding, "Employees are encouraged to seek out training for any skill they desire to develop." When it comes to advancement, one source acknowledges that it's "not strictly an up-or-out policy, although the firm hasn't particularly figured out how to deal with the folks who don't go up or out."

Fewer female PhDs

Analysis Group seems to be fairly balanced with respect to gender representation, except at the very top. "We are pretty meritocratic here. If someone deserves to be promoted, they generally are. We have fewer women at the upper levels, but I think that, in part, reflects the fact that fewer woman get PhDs in economics than men. Our CEO is a woman, so I don't view gender as an issue here," explains one consultant.

And while Analysis Group doesn't have focused recruiting initiatives promoting diversity, overall, insiders say the firm has a "very diverse workforce." Explains a source, "We don't treat employees differently based on ethnic background. We have many East Asian and South Asian employees, but we do not seem to get many African-American or Latino candidates." Another analyst agrees that "black Americans are not strongly represented."

With respect to gays and lesbians, staffers admit that there isn't a focus on these groups at the firm. One insider tells us, "I guess we don't actively attempt to recruit gays, lesbians and bisexuals, but we have some on staff and there are no issues as far as I know. Our main goal is finding people who can perform their work adequately."

Informally involved

Analysis Group's community service involvement depends on the individual office, though in general, "pro bono consulting and charity work are all encouraged." Comments a Boston staffer, "There are many opportunities to take part in sponsored charity events." But a colleague in Los Angeles indicates that volunteer work is more of an individual effort than a firmwide initiative: "The firm takes the view that charities are a personal decision. The partners do not want to impose their charities upon the staff, but they encourage people to get involved if they so choose. That being said, some employees work together and volunteer on their own, so there is informal community involvement."

"Most analysts go on to top business, law or PhD programs. Analysis Group's connections with academia help out quite a bit with that process."

– *Analysis Group manager*

Visit the Vault Consulting Career Channel at **www.vault.com/consulting** - with insider firm profiles, message boards, the Vault Consulting Job Board and more.

VAULT CAREER LIBRARY

369

124 Mason Street
Greenwich, CT 06830
Phone: (203) 629-9292
Fax: (203) 629-9432
www.marsandco.com

LOCATIONS

Greenwich, CT
San Francisco, CA
London
Paris
Shanghai
Tokyo

PRACTICE AREAS

"Exclusive" Strategy Consulting

THE STATS

Employer Type: Private Company
CEO: Dominique G. Mars
2006 Employees: 280
2005 Employees: 250

UPPERS

• Exposure to a wide variety of industries
• Strong culture of meritocracy

DOWNERS

• No chance of partnership
• Can be political

EMPLOYMENT CONTACT

124 Mason Street
Greenwich, CT 06830
Phone: (203) 629-9292
Fax: (203) 629-3916
Attn. Francine Even
E-mail: usg.recruiting@marsandco.com

Additional recruiting contacts available at:
www.marsandco.com/index_en.html

THE BUZZ
WHAT CONSULTANTS AT OTHER FIRMS ARE SAYING ABOUT THIS FIRM

• "Smaller, dedicated focus"
• "Arrogant"
• "High integrity""
• "Brain drain, no growth"

THE SCOOP

Exclusively devoted

When Frenchman Dominique Mars founded his company in 1979, his goal was to create the "only high-premium consulting firm that guarantees exclusivity to its clients"—and Mars & Co claims to be just that. A Harvard grad and former director at Boston Consulting Group, Mars was put off by the business model of the larger consultancies. Mainly, he questioned the loyalty of consulting firms that gave the same strategy advice to several clients (often to clients in competition with each other). So he created a small, strategy boutique with a "single-minded" focus: To advise a select number of handpicked clients—each the only one within its industry. The firm asserts that it's the exclusivity of engagements that sets it apart from other consulting boutiques. Though its roster of clients is a closely-guarded secret (even potential hires don't know who they are until late in the process), the firm claims to lend strategy advice to Fortune 100 companies and other international firms of a "sterling nature."

Mars' first location was in Paris, followed by a Greenwich, Conn., office in 1982. A London outpost was established in 1986, then a San Francisco location in 1994. The firm gained a presence in Asia when it opened a Tokyo office in 2000, and later in Shanghai in 2005. Though Mars is a global company, its 280 consultants work under a "one-office" philosophy, meaning every consultant is available for every engagement, no matter the location. Often, engagement teams are comprised of consultants from several Mars offices.

Battle plan

Mars regards clients' businesses like a battlefield, and its own services as essential to "help clients dissect the enemy forces." How does it accomplish this? With three key strategic initiatives: finding out how much profit is "up for grabs" in the client's market, determining what the competitors plan to do and realigning assets to optimize returns. The firm says that its "birthright" is helping clients "delineate the contours of their battlefields" and the positioning of their competitors.

Halfway to the finish line

Mars' founder claims that two things keep him motivated when running his company—helping the firm expand and acting as a mentor to the firm's staffers. As far as Mars' goals for growth, he aims to employ about 400 consultants and to serve between 30 and 40 clients. According to him, the firm is already halfway to that goal "with the wind at its back."

One meritocracy under Mars

Dominique Mars prefers to remain the one in charge at Mars, so partnership isn't part of the deal for consultants. He does claim that the firm is a "meritocracy," with promotion awarded as soon as a consultant proves ready to handle a more demanding role. Employees can advance through eight positions: associate consultant, senior associate consultant, consultant, senior consultant, project manager, vice president, senior vice president and executive vice president. Mars hires at the first three levels, so promotion beyond the consultant level happens only from within. Since promotion is based on accomplishments at the firm, an advanced degree isn't necessary to move up the career ladder, though Mars does seek to hire those with advanced degrees. The firm isn't organized by industry or practice groups, so all consultants work on every type of engagement, honing their skills through exposure to a variety of industries.

Visit the Vault Consulting Career Channel at www.vault.com/consulting - with insider firm profiles, message boards, the Vault Consulting Job Board and more.

VAULT CAREER LIBRARY

371

GETTING HIRED

The Mars mix

The Mars web site outlines a pretty specific wish list for the firm's ideal candidate: One who is well balanced, diverse in background, experience and interests, a team player, a good communicator and enjoys being mobile. Also needed to work for this small, selective group are "strong quantitative skills meshed with creativity," intellectual power and stamina, a sense of humor and the "power of persuasion tempered with humility." If you think you have this very specific mix of qualities, the firm encourages you to apply directly to your office of choice.

Learn from the pros

To find out what life is like on the inside, interested candidates are encouraged to get in touch with members of the staff who are recent graduates—"to get their direct unfettered opinion of life at Mars & Co." Graduates who join the firm with a bachelor's or master's of science degree begin their career as associate consultants, while MBAs enter as consultants. The firm explains that formal training classes are offered, and consultants are also trained via an apprenticeship model, meaning that learning takes place on the job and by working with senior members of the team. The firm notes that there is "no predetermined promotion schedule at any level," but that promotion is completely based on merit; Mars assures that "people are promoted as soon as they can successfully handle a more demanding role." The firm adds that it only promotes from within, providing continuity to its clients and strong growth opportunities to its staff.

Get your passport ready

If you like the idea of hopping continents, the firm affords plenty of opportunities for international travel, depending on client needs and employee preferences. Staffers may take a post at one of Mars' offices for a few months, or they might be assigned to a client location in another country. The firm notes that this sort of travel isn't reserved for top-level execs—associate consultants and other levels of staff are also eligible.

Mars asserts that it's the exclusivity of engagements that sets it apart from other consulting boutiques.

Visit the Vault Consulting Career Channel at **www.vault.com/consulting** - with insider firm profiles, message boards, the Vault Consulting Job Board and more.

VAULT CAREER LIBRARY   373

Aon Consulting Worldwide

VAULT TOP 50
49
PRESTIGE
RANKING

Aon Center
200 East Randolph Street
Chicago, IL 60601
Phone: (312) 381-4844
Fax: (312) 381-0240
www.aon.com/hcc

LOCATIONS

Chicago, IL (HQ)
117 consulting offices worldwide

PRACTICE AREAS

Human Capital Consulting Services
Communication Consulting • Compensation • Global
Benefit Services • Health & Benefits • Management
Consulting • Outsourcing • Research • Retirement • Talent
Management
Specialized Consulting Services
Financial Advisory & Litigation Consulting Services
Management Consulting

THE STATS

Employer Type: Subsidiary of Aon Corporation
Ticker Symbol: AOC (NYSE)
CEO: Andrew M. Appel
2007 Employees: 6,500
2006 Employees: 7,000
2006 Revenue: $1.28 billion
2005 Revenue: $1.25 billion

RANKING RECAP

Practice Area
#10 - Human Resources Consulting

UPPERS

• Flexibility
• Work/life balance achieved

DOWNERS

• "Raises not always tied to individual
performance"
• Lots of downtime

EMPLOYMENT CONTACT

www.aon.com/about/careers.jsp

THE BUZZ
WHAT CONSULTANTS AT OTHER FIRMS ARE SAYING ABOUT THIS FIRM

• "Risk masters"
• "Too diversified; lacking focus"
• "Good name recognition"
• "High pressure"

THE SCOOP

Best in show

Aon Consulting Worldwide, led by McKinsey & Co. veteran Andrew M. Appel, is one of the world's premier human capital and management consulting firms. Operating out of 117 global offices, the company offers consulting, outsourcing and insurance brokerage services, with tailored offerings designed for financial services, government, health care, manufacturing, pharmaceuticals, retail, technology and public-sector companies. In the firm's own words, "We help employers achieve better business results by finding, developing, motivating and rewarding employees in ways that fit with broader financial and business goals to improve employee and business performance."

A business unit of the insurance behemoth Aon Corporation, Aon Consulting's professionals are experts in actuarial science, compensation, employee benefits and compliance, HR information technology, industrial psychology and organizational behavior, leadership development and process improvement design. Beyond conducting research on global human capital issues, the firm also produces customized studies for its clients and works with employers to help improve their employees' health and productivity. In August 2006, the firm won *Business Insurance* magazine's Readers' Choice award for the best employee benefits consulting firm.

Fitting into the big picture

Aon Consulting frequently works hand in hand with its corporate parent, Aon Corporation, whose name means "oneness" in Gaelic. According to *BestWeek Weekly Insurance Newsletter* in April 2007, the company is now the largest insurance brokerage in the world and is the world's leading reinsurance broker, based on brokerage revenue. Founded in 1982 when Combined International Corporation merged with the Ryan Insurance Group, Aon Corporation has since been on an acquisition spree. Its early focus on the insurance industry naturally led it down the path of employee health plans and, later, HR issues. By the mid-1980s, the company split off its consulting business, forming Aon Consulting.

In addition to consulting services, Aon also offers commercial brokerage and consumer insurance underwriting via its 500 offices around the globe. None of its business units are exclusive unto themselves, and Aon likes to keep it that way. As the company states, "Aon companies, wherever their location, operate closely with each other to provide the best resources for our clients' needs, whether they are a multinational or a strictly local business." The firm's goal is to deliver services around the world, but with the local expertise companies need to keep operations running. Today, Aon's clients include multinational companies, small businesses, independent agents or brokers, associations and affinity groups, and individual consumers.

Benefits for all

While the firm's consulting services cover a wide range of human resources issues, the area of employee benefits is where Aon's bread is buttered. The firm has hit upon the realization that there is a constant global-versus-local struggle in multinational corporations, especially when it comes to setting up benefits that befit local environments and still line up with global strategies and policies.

Aon's global benefits management consultants help multinational companies overcome that tension. Once consultants work their magic, the firm says, executives are able to lead their companies' benefits strategy efficiently from their central headquarters, without losing sight of issues and complexities that affect benefits plans locally. Aon's Global Benefit Manager system helps build a framework for centralizing benefits information and a reporting structure for tracking and improving benefits management.

Visit the Vault Consulting Career Channel at **www.vault.com/consulting** - with insider firm profiles, message boards, the Vault Consulting Job Board and more.

VAULT CAREER LIBRARY   375

Other resources for human resources

Helping to design employee benefits isn't Aon Consulting's only strong point. It hosts a cadre of complementary services to help companies attract, retain and reward good employees without breaking the bank. Its HR outsourcing unit helps companies reduce costs and improve workforce effectiveness by streamlining their HR infrastructure, while its research branch conducts best practice research on global human capital issues that can be customizable for each client's needs.

For new employees, Aon's "talent, selection, development and rewards" advice ensures that companies don't over- or underspend on their recruiting and development activities. For employees about to retire, Aon advises companies on the design, administration, funding and communication of a defined benefit and/or defined contribution plan for retirees. And for the all-important issue of executive pay, the firm turns to McLagan Partners, a pay and performance organization, that offers proprietary market studies and consulting services to financial services firms, and Radford Surveys + Consulting for similar information in the technology industry. In addition, Aon offers Benefacts®, a personalized communications service that helps management and HR teams communicate total rewards and other benefits information to employees.

The business of risk

As companies face increasing regulatory scrutiny, consulting firms have been trying to broaden their areas of expertise to help companies avoid trouble. Aon Consulting is no exception. For the past year, it has been funneling resources into its financial advisory and litigation consulting services practice, which offers expertise in forensic accounting, litigation consulting, corporate investigative and IT risk services. Specifically, Aon's IT risk consulting services group, which includes electronic discovery and computer forensic services, helps uncover requests for evidence in lawsuits and regulatory matters that include everything from fraud and identity theft, to theft of trade secrets, unauthorized file access and the inappropriate use of company computers.

The financial advisory and litigation consulting services practice also includes a corporate investigations and security services group, which works with organizations that are undergoing corporate investigations, making sure they adhere to regulatory standards. Clients include law firms, corporations, governmental agencies and not-for-profit organizations that are looking to mitigate risk, involving issues such as due diligence, embezzlement, kickbacks, intellectual property theft, commercial bribery, check fraud, sexual harassment allegations and workplace violence. The unit's team members include former federal and state law-enforcement agents, former attorneys, investigative researchers and threat management professionals.

In January 2007, Aon Consulting announced that it was expanding its corporate investigations and security services group with a new threat management and security services unit to be led by threat management expert Gregory S. Boles, a 25-year veteran of the Los Angeles Police Department. The new unit assists organizations in identifying and mitigating internal and external threats, providing workplace violence response and prevention training, threat assessment, crisis management, executive protection, travel intelligence, risk management and security consulting.

GETTING HIRED

Connecting with students

Aon has an active recruiting program, involving partnerships with 16 universities where it has built relationships with career counselors and faculty. University of North Carolina, Notre Dame, University of Pennsylvania, Howard, Miami University and St. John's are among the schools where Aon's contacts help identify students who might be a match. The firm also has several ways for college seniors to get a taste of consulting before they graduate: the early career development program, rotational development program and the direct development program. Each program allows qualifying students to work on real engagements in different practice areas. Aon welcomes applicants from schools that are not on the recruiting calendar, and encourages any interested candidates to start with the online application, found on its web site.

The firm's site also clarifies the interview process, which consists of a phone interview and office visit. One insider recalls, "I had three interviews. Two of them were group interviews—a very positive experience." Another consultant says that the process was "fairly standard and not overly difficult." Candidates can expect behavioral questions, focusing on past accomplishments and work experiences. Case study questions, which the firm describes as "broad, two-way discussions," are also part of the routine. Interviewers reportedly aren't looking for a specific "right answer." They simply want to understand how well candidates show logical thinking ability when dealing with a problem.

OUR SURVEY SAYS

Take it easy

All around, insiders claim that Aon Consulting is a low pressure workplace, with little of the stress and hard-driving hours found at many consulting firms. An insider reports, "The people are easy to work with. There is little or no office drama." According to one source, it might even be a little too lax: "There are nice people with a rather laid-back attitude—too laid-back to be truly competitive with Mercer or Towers Perrin."

Down on the upper ranks

A number of staffers have a bone to pick with management at the firm. "Due to recent changes in upper management (corporate level), there has been significant turnover, both voluntary and involuntary," explains a source. One consultant complains that there is "almost no business or sales savvy among management," while a co-worker moans, "On average, people are less educated than at other companies I've worked for. Even some members of management don't have bachelor's degrees." "Management is very controlling, micromanages and doesn't communicate much to employees about the direction of the company—and doesn't solicit feedback in any way," laments one associate.

9 to 5

Though the firm's management doesn't win rave reviews, the "flexible scheduling" and reasonable hours sure do. "There is flexibility in terms of just coming in late if you have a doctor's appointment, or leaving early to pick up your kid. In that way, it is family-oriented," a consultant comments. Another source reports, "Expect 40-hour workweeks, 45 hours during very busy times, 50 hours as a max. Many people sneak out early; often there can be downtime with no work to do." Overall, the workload is reportedly light, and so is the travel for most consultants. Declares one insider, "Travel is not a major problem."

It's a trade-off

Though, by and large, Aon consultants aren't stressed about intense work and travel demands, there is a downside to the light hourly load. "The hours are not as long as other benefits consulting firms, but then the pay is not as high. The billable hour target is about to increase, though I'm not sure if the pay will increase accordingly (at least not right away)," a source explains. A colleague, acknowledging the downfalls of compensation, looks at the bright side, stating that "it is a trade-off that is worth it to those who want to enjoy life."

Firmwide, insiders hold disparate opinions on diversity, depending on their location. "There is a fairly diverse set of employees in this office," an East Coast insider reports. However, one source on the West Coast is slightly more skeptical: "Diversity is good in terms of ethnic diversity, but people call the holiday party the 'Christmas party,' and people get two Asian guys confused with each other all the time." And with regard to gender diversity, "There are very few men, though the ratio is more balanced in the management ranks."

Visit the Vault Consulting Career Channel at **www.vault.com/consulting** - with insider firm profiles, message boards, the Vault Consulting Job Board and more.

VAULT CAREER LIBRARY   377

Putnam Associates

25 Burlington Mall Road
Burlington, MA 01803
Phone: (781) 273-5480
Fax: (781) 273-5484
www.putassoc.com

LOCATIONS

Burlington, MA (HQ)
London

PRACTICE AREAS

Economic Analysis
Organizational Strategy
Pharmaceutical & Biotech
Portfolio Management
Product Strategy

THE STATS

Employer Type: Private Company
Managing Partner: Kevin Gorman
2007 Employees: 45
2006 Employees: 45

RANKING RECAP

Quality of Life
#2 - Travel Requirements
#2 - Work/Life Balance
#3 - Relationships with Supervisors
#6 - Best Firms to Work For
#10 - Formal Training (tie)
#11 - Hours in the Office
#12 - Overall Satisfaction
#12 - Firm Culture (tie)
#15 - Offices (tie)

UPPERS

- "A place that truly values personal skill development"
- Management invests time and resources into younger staff
- "No two projects are the same, and each requires innovative thinking"
- "End-of-project evaluations that provide both positive feedback and constructive criticism to help you develop into a well-rounded consultant"

DOWNERS

- "Working in the suburbs"
- Limited exposure to clients
- "Balancing two cases at a time can be a challenge in prioritization and time management"
- "Being confused with Putnam Investments"

EMPLOYMENT CONTACT

www.putassoc.com/careers/index.html

THE BUZZ
WHAT CONSULTANTS AT OTHER FIRMS ARE SAYING ABOUT THIS FIRM

- "Great returns"
- "Lots of turnover"
- "Sophisticated analysis"
- "Niche players, no strategic vision"

THE SCOOP

Health care specialists

Burlington, Mass.-based Putnam Associates is a boutique health care strategy consultancy that offers product strategy, portfolio management, organizational strategy and economic analysis. Founded in 1988, the firm serves pharmaceutical, biotechnology, diagnostics and medical device clients. Its clients include four of the top-five global pharmaceutical firms and three of the five most successful biotech companies. The firm's 45 consultants are primarily located in Burlington, however Putnam also has an office in London. Though mostly under the radar, Putnam won recognition in 2005 as one of the industry's Seven Small Jewels, as designated by *Consulting Magazine*.

The firm's work centers on solving problems involving the "complex integration of patients, prescribers, competitors, payers, economics and government." Typical client engagements include identifying, valuing and prioritizing R&D and commercial growth opportunities; developing pricing, contracting and positioning strategies to maximize product success; and solving key operational or implementation challenges.

There's no hurry

The firm's founder and Managing Partner Kevin Gorman was formerly President Carter's assistant to the Undersecretary of Energy. Gorman and Putnam's three other partners are seasoned health care pros, with an average of 16 years of consulting experience among them. Gorman is responsible for setting the pace of the firm's growth, which is best described as "patient." Since its inception, the firm has sought to make clients long-term customers, rather than pursuing one-off projects. Putnam doesn't release its financial figures, but Gorman asserts that the firm's year-to-year growth rate has been in the high single to low double digits for the past 10 years.

Another part of the firm's overall design is the way it develops consultants. In a 2005 *Consulting Magazine* article, Gorman mentioned, "You get your best people by growing them internally," explaining why he prefers to take on new consultants and polish them to perfection over the years.

Regrouping the troops

Since a key component of most clients' success is understanding their markets, it stands to reason that a number of the firm's engagements focus on market segmentation and customer targeting. Recently, Putnam worked with a company that has a product for a chronic condition that is significantly underdiagnosed. The firm found that low disease awareness was a big barrier, and identified the specific hurdles to patients being diagnosed. The next step was to find the most appropriate patients for the company to target with disease awareness campaigns. Putnam segmented the patient population that should be receiving the client's therapy but is not, and evaluated each segment by potential revenue, difficulty of reaching the segment and patient motivation. Finally, Putnam benchmarked several disease awareness campaigns to help the company refine its own messages and tactics. The client eventually piloted a disease awareness campaign to the patient segments identified by Putnam's study, which resulted in significant sales growth for the client within 12 months.

GETTING HIRED

On the recruiting radar

At Putnam, sources say the recruiting practice is rigorous. Because it's a "medium-sized firm with a lot of time invested to get good people and avoid mistakes," there are "higher standards to make the bar than larger firms," we're told. Recruiting from crème de la crème institutions like Harvard, MIT, Duke, Princeton, Dartmouth, Tufts, Boston College and University of

Visit the Vault Consulting Career Channel at www.vault.com/consulting - with insider firm profiles, message boards, the Vault Consulting Job Board and more.

VAULT CAREER LIBRARY   379

Pennsylvania, Putnam doesn't take candidate-scouring lightly. A staffer reports, "We calculated the other day that 33 percent of us have Ivy League degrees, though MIT and Duke are the two most common alma maters."

The perfect fit

For undergrads in the firm's recruiting rounds, "Expect one to two rounds of interviews with a mix of fit/case questions," shares an associate consultant, while other applicants go through two phone examinations before in-office chats. No matter the communication mode, all first-round candidates spend between 30 and 45 minutes discussing cases and personal background, with case questions popping up in both preliminary interviews. Individuals deemed sharp enough ascend to the next level—on-location dialogues, which include "multiple case questions, problem solving and analytics, background questions and interaction with six to eight employees from the firm, in both formal and informal settings." Interviewees meet with associates at all levels, who also aim conversation toward attitude, team orientation, professional judgment and maturity.

As for case specifics, current staffers say "most of the interviews involve cases, which will be both qualitative and quantitative in nature," though one senior source comments that these are "more like discussions than actual cases." Another insider adds that "case questions were not related or focused in any direct way to the industry the firm serves," with examples including, "How many treadmills are run on a given Saturday in February?" and estimating the "number of cups of coffee sold in the U.S. on a given day."

At the end of the day, Putnam emerges as "very competitive" with regard to hiring, since there are "a lot of interviews for a few spots." As one senior associate sums up, "The process might be a little more involved than at other firms, but that's because, due to our size, we actually end up working with the people we hire, so we really want to ensure a good fit."

OUR SURVEY SAYS

Trust or bust

"Collegial" is the culture keyword at Putnam, where employees are "very open, supportive and demanding from a professional point of view." According to insiders, the firm's open-door policy creates a level playing field, and "working relationships tend to be forged on trust and support, not on competition to impress others." The absent hierarchy also pushes partners and managers together with junior colleagues. Sources say higher-ups "bend over backward to accommodate questions and the development process of those junior to them," perpetuating a tight-knit sense of camaraderie. One senior associate claims to "feel comfortable talking to any of the partners at any time," who are readily accessible to all.

The firm's youth also plays a big hand in the open culture. With a horde of 20-somethings arriving to work each day, we're told, energy escalates and creates "a great balance between strong mentoring and a friendly office environment."

Contact zone

When it comes to career development and client interaction, Putnam peers again flatter their supervisors. "Since we are a relatively small company, you get a chance to interact with the partners of the firm on a daily basis," an insider explains. Rubbing elbows "with the most senior employees is not only possible, but encouraged and necessary for success within the firm," adds a colleague, who cites Putnam's Analyst/Associate Action Committee as a catalyst for junior staffers to bring concerns and ideas to their senior counterparts. "The AAC has directly resulted in the formation of a mentor program, and is currently working on advanced training modules and an 'alumni database,' among other things."

Pertaining to clients, insiders say "contact increases with each year at the firm," though most direct exposure is saved for senior associate consultants and the ranks above. "Partners and senior staff have deep relationships with senior client personnel, providing frequent and meaningful interaction," remarks a partner. And while client site visits normally involve only senior employees—which leaves some junior-level staffers wishing for more exposure—"all team members are typically included in client conference calls, and absent team members are often invited to conference into client presentations as well."

Live long and prosper

As with many consultancies, Putnam staffers report that hours are heavily dependent upon case type, team, workload and deadline. Regardless, "an effort is made to limit the number of weekends people have to work," we're told, with late-night necessities surfacing less frequently than at other firms. Most workweeks run 40 to 60 hours at Putnam, though "several busy weeks a year will push the 70- to 80-hour range."

When after-hour and weekend work does arise, associates say the load is manageable and it's "usually my own initiative around client development or knowledge development," a consultant appends. Other co-workers attest to extracurricular indulgences without last-minute cancellation and frequent dinners at home, along with honored vacation time and flexible, understanding managers who accommodate personal issues. As one partner puts it, "Firm management values employee longevity and tries to manage workloads to promote an environment in which employees can thrive long term." Though a few colleagues gripe about set hours and no flex-time, sources say "Putnam maintains a great work/life balance and that is one of the major advantages of working here."

Infrequent flyers

Face time may not be completely obsolete at the firm, but "the Putnam business model does not center around living at the clients' site," an upper level explains. Putnamites at the senior associate consultant level and above tend to do the traveling, which is reserved mostly for "updates, working sessions and presentations." Trips rarely surpass the one-day mark and occur only a few times per month—a model that one senior associate claims has "absolutely no negative impact" on work/life balance. "There is no travel for the first few years and very minimal travel beyond that," shares an analyst, "which helps maintain a normal life" and a bond with Putnam peers in the office—"a really underrated perk," another adds.

Insiders boast that Putnam's travel model is "one of the key benefits of the firm." Consultants can work as a team, remain at the home office, and avoid taxing and extensive travel schedules required for junior staff at other consultancies. "I'm very happy that I do not travel," comments a relieved analyst, who adds that "it was one of [the] main reasons I chose Putnam." Another associate appreciates Putnam's light travel model, exclaiming, "I have an apartment that I actually live in! While I don't have status on every airline like some of my peers at other companies, I'm just fine with not living out of a suitcase."

No cookie cutters

During their first three weeks at Putnam, newbies are formally trained "with official modules on various topics," but spend the remainder of their time "assigned to a single case to learn on the job and apply the skills from training," we're told. Throughout a consultant's tenure, insiders also cite the "strong offering" of advanced training available, including Access, Excel, secondary research, conceptual frameworks, interviewing techniques and "a practice case, combining all of the above that culminates in a presentation to an associate." In addition, all new, dewy-eyed employees receive mentors from the get-go, and are "encouraged to lean on their peers to teach each other."

Overall, Putnamites say on-the-job learning is most beneficial. "We don't do cookie-cutter projects here, so each case is unique and there is a learning curve for everyone," a senior staffer relates. A new hire commends the ad hoc model as well, remarking that "so much of the office is young and approachable, that the learn-on-the-job mentality really works well."

Greenbacks and Red Sox

Sources at Putnam aren't so candid about salary payouts, though they seem to feel that it's comparable with competitors. One senior consultant notes that compensation "is somewhat above average, from what I hear from classmates." Employees do receive signing bonuses, "great benefits" and 401(k) matching up to 5 percent.

Visit the Vault Consulting Career Channel at **www.vault.com/consulting** - with insider firm profiles, message boards, the Vault Consulting Job Board and more.

VAULT CAREER LIBRARY

381

Putnam presents consultants with an array of company events throughout the year, including Friday wine and cheese parties, bowling and golf outings, annual Halloween and holiday parties, and team events—"usually dinners, but also go-cart racing, paintballing and other fun activities to celebrate the end of each case." Staffers also receive Costco memberships and 20 vacation days after three years with the firm. Most appreciated, however, are the firm's Red Sox season tickets, doled out to colleagues in sets.

'burbs = bland

Putnamites say their recently remodeled work digs are clean, spacious and high-quality, with a gym and cafeteria situated in the building. There is conference space aplenty, and "all consultant-and-above levels get private offices." But regarding the location, Putnam employees pop the perfection bubble. "While the office space is recently renovated and expanded, I would enjoy having an office more centrally located in Boston," shares a consultant. Other co-workers echo the sentiment, lamenting the necessary car commute and presenting the "Burlington = sleepy suburb" equation. However, the firm notes that its Burlington location offers staffers plenty of dining and shopping options, and is a mere 20-minute drive outside of Boston, giving employees the benefit of a reverse commute.

Charity champions

On the community service front, Putnam is big on charitable donations and encouraging staff to pursue independently-initiated activities. One insider explains, "Putnam has begun a tradition of making corporate donations to predetermined charities during the holiday season, with the opportunity for employees to make individual contributions as well." In 2006, the firm matched 100 percent of employee donations to breast cancer, after-school meal programs, homeless and disabled veterans and HIV/AIDS charities. And where corporate involvement stops, individual staffers start. "Many people do community service work on their own," we're told, including Big Brothers Big Sisters participation by younger associates.

Loving but lacking

Sources say "Putnam is very receptive to hiring female employees, but has had difficulty hiring women into more senior positions." When it comes to women at lower levels, the firm's ratio isn't as discouraging, but there are "none in the top-three ranks (consultant, manager, partner)," a fact that senior-level staffers recognize and are attempting to remedy. But "regardless of recruiting and hiring," states an associate, "I believe the office environment is comfortable for individuals of both genders."

Insiders speak of Putnam's receptivity and acceptance of racial and ethnic minorities, too. Though "the firm has very few minority employees and none in the higher ranks," a consultant claims that Putnam is "very open and active in this area." Attesting to this is one senior associate, who affirms Putnam's attention to hiring "individuals of a diverse range of ethnicities and nationalities." She adds, "As a female and minority ethnicity employee, I have been extremely comfortable at Putnam, and I feel the corporate culture is one that is receptive and open."

Concerning sexual orientation, one insider states, "I believe that the firm and our employees would be accepting of anyone intelligent and hardworking, regardless of his or her sexual orientation." Consultants stand by their firm as a "very open, friendly place with liberal-minded people."

THE BEST OF THE REST

TOP 50 CONSULTING FIRMS

Abt Associates Inc.

55 Wheeler Street
Cambridge, MA 02138
Phone: (617) 492-7100
Fax: (617) 492-5219
www.abtassociates.com

LOCATIONS

Cambridge, MA (HQ)
Bethesda, MD (2 locations)
Chicago, IL
Durham, NC
Hadley, MA
Lexington, MA

PRACTICE AREAS

Consulting, Implementation & Technical Assistance
Medical & Life Science
Research & Evaluation
Strategy, Planning & Policy
Survey Data Collection, Management & Analysis

THE STATS

Employer Type: Private Company
Chairman: John A. Shane
2007 Employees: 1,023
2006 Employees: 1,098
2007 Revenue: $199 million
2006 Revenue: $193 million

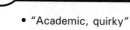

THE BUZZ
WHAT CONSULTANTS AT OTHER FIRMS ARE SAYING ABOUT THIS FIRM

• "Academic, quirky"
• "Old line"
• "Good in health care"
• "Narrow"

THE SCOOP

Social science savvy

Abt Associates is apt to make a difference. The Cambridge, Mass.-based firm is one of the largest for-profit government and business research and consulting firms in the world, specializing in issues in social, economic and health policy, international development, business research and consulting, and clinical trials and registries. Its services include research and evaluation; strategy, planning and policy development; consulting and technical assistance; survey data collection and analysis; and medical and life science research, such as clinical trial design and health research. Clients include the U.S. federal, state and local governments, international organizations, foundations, nonprofit associations and institutions, and businesses.

The firm was founded in January 1965 by Clark Abt, a former engineer and manager of the Advanced Systems and Strategic Studies Departments at defense giant Raytheon Company. In the beginning, Abt Associates started out in a small office above a machine shop in Cambridge with one purpose: to apply interdisciplinary social sciences and systems analysis methods to governmental and industry problems. Today, the firm employs more than 1,000 people in seven corporate offices, maintaining around 40 project sites in 30 countries around the world. By 2005, the firm ranked 18th among the country's top-50 market research firms and 25th among global research firms, according to the American Marketing Association, and was recognized that same year as one of the top-10 work/life balance workplaces in *Consulting Magazine*'s Best Firms to Work For survey.

Not your average Joes

Not just anyone can crunch numbers for Abt Associates—a good thing, since the firm is 99 percent employee-owned. Twenty-seven percent of the firm's 1,000-plus employees carry a PhD, 44 percent have a master's degree and 29 percent have their bachelor's degree in everything from biochemistry to biology, economics to epidemiology, and statistics to software engineering. But the firm's focus on the social sciences is clear when you break down the employees' areas of expertise: 38 percent of Abt Associates' professionals got their degrees in the social sciences; 27 percent in law, medicine and other professional areas; 13 percent in economics; 10 percent in the natural sciences and engineering; 8 percent in management; and 4 percent in the humanities.

A pretty good resume

Since 1965, Abt Associates has stayed true to its founder's vision of a company that could make a difference in the lives of people and nations, mixing research, social sciences and technology to solve problems. The company's first effort toward this end was to find ways to transfer the technology and systems used in the defense industry to civilian use. Abt and his associates eventually found ways to use systems analysis, computer modeling and simulation methods to quantitatively evaluate and improve social programs in the areas of criminal justice, education and housing. By the 1970s, these developments were applied to child care, health care, education and housing in the U.S.

Looking back on its work in the U.S., Abt Associates has played a role in shaping public programs like Medicaid, welfare reform, Head Start, crime reporting and housing experiments. Beyond American borders, the firm has also helped companies move toward market-oriented economies by advising foreign governments and businesses on economic growth and strengthening health systems. Almost 80 percent of its international contracts are doled out by the U.S. Agency for International Development (USAID).

A big deal means big contracts

In March 2006, Abt Associates made it possible to win even bigger contracts from USAID when it acquired IBM's public-sector business consulting unit. The IBM team, which until 2002 had been a subsidiary of PricewaterhouseCoopers, typically won major contracts from USAID, the group's biggest client. (In a March 2006 *Washington Post* interview, Abt Associates CEO Wendell Knox commented that the IBM team's contracts had "very large ceilings.") Adding the IBM group to its consulting

Visit the Vault Consulting Career Channel at **www.vault.com/consulting** - with insider firm profiles, message boards, the Vault Consulting Job Board and more.

VAULT CAREER LIBRARY   385

arsenal meant an immediate revenue boost for Abt Associates, which was already deriving annual revenue of $80 to $85 million from USAID contracts.

For the first time, in fiscal 2005, Abt Associates' international business revenue roughly equaled that from its domestic business, boosted in no small measure by a USAID contract in 2003 to help improve Iraq's ailing health system. As of early 2007, the firm had international project sites in Afghanistan, Azerbaijan, Benin, Botswana, Costa Rica, Dominican Republic, El Salvador, Ethiopia, Georgia, Ghana, Guetemala, Honduras, India, Indonesia, Jordan, Kazakhstan, Kyrgyzstan, Mali, Peru, Senegal, Serbia, South Africa, Tajikistan, Tanzania, Turkmenistan, Ukraine, Uzbekistan, Vietnam, Zambia and Zimbabwe. Its latest USAID project, a contract for $16.7 million, was launched in February 2007 to assist Pakistan's efforts to ensure safe drinking water in 31 selected districts in all four provinces of the country.

Another new relationship

In addition to its acquisition of IBM's consulting unit, in October 2006, Abt Associates announced a new partnership with Outcomes International, a life sciences consultancy based in Basel, Switzerland. Together, the firms plan to offer U.S.- and Europe-based consulting services in health economics, outcomes research and registries, as well as strategic, clinical and market research services. For Abt Associates, the merger strengthens its on-the-ground presence in Europe. As for Outcomes International, piggybacking on Abt Associates' international locations will boost its ability to compete for and work on projects more easily in any part of the world.

Helping out back home

But not all of Abt Associates' engagements are overseas. In November 2006, for example, Abt Associates partnered with the U.S. Office of National Drug Control Policy to restart the Arrestee Drug Abuse Monitoring Program, which originally began in the late 1980s to analyze drug use among recent arrestees. This is not the first time Abt Associates and the Office of National Drug Control Policy have worked together on this issue: In 1997, the firm redesigned what was then called the Drug Use Forecasting system, a data-collection program, which lost its funding in 2003.

In June 2006, the U.S. Department of Housing and Urban Development commissioned an Abt Associates study examining the barriers to Hispanic homeownership. The study found that, as of the fourth quarter of 2005, 76 percent of non-Hispanic whites were homeowners, compared to 50 percent of Hispanics—a homeownership gap of 26 percentage points. That same month, the firm was asked by the U.S. Army Corps of Engineers to assess the human health effects from Hurricane Katrina and to estimate the potential loss of life from future hurricanes of Katrina's magnitude. And in February 2006, a three-and-a-half-year Abt Associates report on the New Visions Self-Sufficiency and Lifelong Learning Project, a community college designed to help adult welfare recipients find better-paying jobs, found that the program was not living up to its expectations. Commissioned by the Administration for Children and Families of the U.S. Department of Health and Human Services, the study has important implications for national welfare policies.

Making waves

Abt Associates' insights have not gone unnoticed. One home-based project spearheaded by three Abt Associates scientists, Drs. Donald McCubbin and Ellen Post, received the U.S. Environmental Protection Agency's Technological Achievement Award in June 2006 for their study on the benefits of enforcing ozone regulations. And in April of that year, Senior Associate Maria Socolof won a gold medal from the agency's Scientific and Technological Achievement Awards program for her four-year study on lead solders.

GETTING HIRED

A well-educated cadre

Candidates who want to work for Abt Associates should head straight to the careers page of the firm's web site, where open positions are listed by location or job title. The site streamlines the whole application process by allowing candidates to paste and send a resume directly through the site. Applicants can also check out profiles of current Abt associates and get a visual of possible career paths, thanks to an online chart.

Judging by the wide range of backgrounds, there's no typical Abt Associates consultant. The firm notes that its ranks are comprised of biochemists, biologists, business strategists, economists, engineers, environmental analysts, epidemiologists, medical scientists, psychologists and statisticians. Not only are consultants a well-educated bunch, but the firm claims it is also "diverse, multidisciplinary, educated and entrepreneurial." Abt Associates also hires individuals without advanced degrees: New graduates with a BA or BS typically start as associate analysts, while those with an MBA join the firm as analysts or senior analysts, depending on their experience.

The interview process is straightforward and simple, according to insiders. "I had one day of interviews. Depending on level and division, it may be a multiday interview schedule with a presentation," a source relates.

OUR SURVEY SAYS

Flexible where it counts

Consultants claim that Abt is all about accommodation when it comes to having a life outside work. Comments one manager, "Abt Associates is flexible. If I need to leave for personal or family matters, I can. I simply shift the work to another time and/or location." A colleague agrees that "there is incredible flexibility in time allocation between work and family."

The firm takes a hands-off approach to training, sources report. "For me, it was minimal formal training—sort of learning on the job with a sink-or-swim attitude," expresses a recent hire, adding, "Fortunately, we tend to hire people that will not sink."

Dive right in!

Sources report that compensation could stand to improve, though most are pleased about the chance to own stock. "We are employee-owned, so we earn shares in the company," a consultant explains. Company benefits include standards such as health care, 401(k) and three weeks of vacation to start, as well as a few extras such as tuition assistance and parental and adoption leave.

Visit the Vault Consulting Career Channel at **www.vault.com/consulting** - with insider firm profiles, message boards, the Vault Consulting Job Board and more.

387

Archstone Consulting

Four Stamford Plaza
107 Elm Street, 6th Floor
Stamford, CT 06902
Phone: (203) 940-8200
Fax: (203) 940-8201
www.archstoneconsulting.com

LOCATIONS

Stamford, CT (HQ)
Chicago, IL
New York, NY
San Francisco, CA
Amsterdam
London
Toronto

PRACTICE AREAS

Brand Innovation
CFO Advisory Services
Consumer Products & Retail
Energy & Utilities
Financial Services
Life Sciences
Manufacturing
Operations
Outsourcing & Information Technology
Strategy

THE STATS

Employer Type: Private Company
CEO & President: Todd D. Lavieri
2007 Employees: 250+
2006 Employees: 250+
2007 Revenue: $74.5 million
2006 Revenue: $60 million

UPPERS

- Flat hierarchy
- Opportunities for international work

DOWNERS

- Low name recognition
- Limited to a few industries/specializations

EMPLOYMENT CONTACT

E-mail: recruiter@archstoneconsulting.com
www.archstoneconsulting.com/careers

THE BUZZ
WHAT CONSULTANTS AT OTHER FIRMS ARE SAYING ABOUT THIS FIRM

- "Emerging brand"
- "Trying, but tiny"
- "Strong heritage"
- "Lacks diversity"

THE SCOOP

Size isn't everything

Archstone Consulting prides itself on being the big guys' little guy. For Stamford, Conn.-based Archstone, it isn't size that matters; experience and having the right skills is what counts. But Archstone Consulting isn't so little anymore. Since its founding in 2003, the firm has almost quadrupled in size to more than 250 employees, setting up additional offices in Amsterdam, Chicago, London, New York, San Francisco and Toronto.

As an independent strategy and operations management consulting, the firm has provided consulting services to 10 of the top Fortune 50 companies, 20 of the top-100 and 52 of the top-500. Its specialty industry areas include consumer products and retail, life sciences, manufacturing, energy and utilities, and service industries like financial services, health care, insurance and telecommunications. And for its clients, Archstone Consulting provides services in CFO advisory, operations, information technology and outsourcing, alliances, mergers and integration, brand innovation, strategic sourcing and procurement, and strategy.

Building up the ranks

Even though it prides itself on offering the tailored services of a small firm, Archstone Consulting is quickly becoming a force to contend with. In June 2006, the firm acquired the Hazelton Group, a research-based brand development consulting firm out of Toronto that focuses on new product and service development, global brand development and brand repositioning. Continuing to operate under the Hazleton Group name, the acquisition provided Archstone Consulting with a Canadian footprint, following its expansion into Europe with the opening of a London office in January 2006 and an office in Amsterdam in late 2005.

The Hazelton acquisition is just the latest in a series of moves Archstone Consulting has made to carve its place into the international consulting landscape. Throughout 2005, the firm focused on expanding its suite of services. In July, it included risk mitigation from "low-cost country sourcing" in its outsourcing services practice. In May of that year, the firm introduced another service—CFO advisory—to walk companies through the challenges facing their global finance organizations. Archstone Consulting's work in this area includes helping CFOs develop an overall business intelligence strategy to achieve significant reporting improvement across their organization. And in March 2005, Archstone Consulting expanded its life sciences practice to include strategies for handling the Medicare Modernization Act of 2003, which affects prescription drug sales across the U.S.

Leading these new specializations are the firm's big-name principals, which Archstone Consulting recruited in 2004, during its first full year. Most of the new talent hailed from well established consultancies like Booz Allen Hamilton, Deloitte, Capgemini, BearingPoint, A.T. Kearney, IBM and Gunn Partners, to name a few, which helped establish Archstone Consulting's new offices in San Francisco, Chicago and New York.

Different is good

Archstone Consulting's founders might have cut their teeth on traditional consulting projects at megafirms like Deloitte & Touche, but today their focus is on offering something "different." Companies are growing disillusioned with consulting firms, Archstone Consulting says, finding them too large, too bureaucratic or too expensive. What makes Archstone Consulting different isn't a new portfolio of never-been-tested strategies, but rather a back-to-basics approach that sells advice, not products, and emphasizes partnering with clients instead of leaving them to implement their new strategies alone.

That said, Archstone Consulting is careful not to overstay its welcome. When the job is done, the consultants are out the door. Todd Lavieri, president and CEO of Archstone Consulting, once said in an interview with *Fortune*: "Clients are terrified that consultants are a modern-day Trojan horse; you let them in the door, they'll take over your company." In addition, the firm does not believe in pushing any specific products or selling anything other than advice, stating, "We will never be compromised by corporate directives to pressure clients into buying proprietary products like software, hardware, financial services or outsourcing."

Visit the Vault Consulting Career Channel at **www.vault.com/consulting** - with insider firm profiles, message boards, the Vault Consulting Job Board and more.

VAULT CAREER LIBRARY

389

Knowing your niche

To grow the way Archstone Consulting has grown since 2003, the advice its consultants dispense had better be good, especially since most of that advice is given straight to corporate executives. That's why the firm's consultants all have backgrounds in specific industries so that the firm can provide its clients with teams that have deep vertical expertise that can be tailored to specific client needs. Each team is replete with experienced professionals, managers, associates and research analysts, most of whom have experience working in a specific industry, either as consultants or industry professionals, before joining Archstone Consulting.

The firm's unique approach to consulting has not gone unnoticed. In September 2006, Archstone Consulting was recognized for its program management and IT consulting services by AMR Research in its report, "An Executive Guide to Selecting BI and Performance Management Service Providers." In 2004, just one year out of the gate, the firm was named of one of "seven small jewels" impacting the consulting industry by *Consulting Magazine*.

Market validation

In April 2007, Archstone Consulting was again featured in *Consulting Magazine*, this time on the cover highlighting the company's strengths and how it differentiates itself in the marketplace. In June, CEO Todd Lavieri made headlines in a Q&A article in *Investor's Business Daily*, which depicted the firm as "on a roll." The article delved into Archstone Consulting's service offerings and approach to client service. Also in June, *The Black Book of Outsourcing* ranked Archstone Consulting the No. 4 boutique outsourcing advisory firm, based on an annual survey of customers.

Reporting the facts

In October 2006, Archstone Consulting released its annual "Holiday Sales Forecast," predicting that the holiday season's sales would be the worst since 2001. Not only was the company right on the mark for the third year in a row, but the business press started taking notice, resulting in coverage in *The Wall Street Journal*, *The New York Times*, Dow Jones News, Bloomberg Business News and CNBC.

Archstone Consulting also made headlines in July 2006 when its study on the challenges of supplier relationship management struck a chord with businesses across the country. The report found that over 90 percent of the 50 American and global companies it surveyed are having problems managing their suppliers in industries ranging from consumer packaged goods to services, retail to manufacturing. "While many companies have conducted strategic sourcing and outsourcing to reduce costs, few have mastered supplier relationship management as a critical part of enhancing their supply chain and reducing overall costs," said Archstone Consulting Principal Ramin Tabibsadeh, a co-author of the study. The survey ended up in the pages of a variety of publications, including *IndustryWeek*, *Supply & Demand Chain Executive* and *Logistics Today*.

Looking ahead

The firm has recently strengthened its divisions with new leadership. In April 2007, Archstone announced the appointment of Mark Simmons to manage its operations practice in Europe. Simmons joined Archstone Consulting with more than 17 years of industry experience and was previously lead partner of Ernst & Young's global sourcing and supplier management practice and a principal at Booz Allen Hamilton. In December 2006, the firm announced that it was expanding its West Coast operations with the appointment of former Deloitte consultant David Fitzpatrick as principal of its West Coast strategy and operations practice based out of Seattle. At Deloitte, Fitzpatrick worked on a number of different projects, including airline maintenance productivity enhancement and postmerger integration strategies. His claim to fame was founding Deloitte's Lean Enterprise and Six Sigma practices.

Earlier in 2006, Archstone Consulting brought on Maryann Gallivan from Monitor Group to serve as head of its global life sciences practice. At Monitor Group, Gallivan had led the firm's strategic advisory practice, focusing on life sciences. Now working out of the Archstone's Stamford headquarters, Gallivan will be looking to expand the firm's strategic service offerings and growth initiatives for the life sciences industry.

GETTING HIRED

Looking to boost its ranks

From the online profiles of Archstone consultants, a few details can be gleaned: they're highly educated (graduates of Wharton, Harvard Business School, Columbia and the like); they're experienced (several report working for larger management consulting firms prior to coming onboard); and they're highly motivated. The firm says it's "actively seeking" candidates at "all levels," and provides an easy-to-use online application tool. But Archstone also draws in analysts and associates through campus recruiting; check with your school to see if they'll be stopping by. The firm says it's especially looking for experienced hires with expertise in their three main areas—strategy, operations and CFO advisory services—and their target industries. More specifically, the firm reports that it has opportunities for candidates with skills in organizational effectiveness, sourcing and procurement, supply chain, IT effectiveness and finance transformation.

Visit the Vault Consulting Career Channel at **www.vault.com/consulting** - with insider firm profiles, message boards, the Vault Consulting Job Board and more.

VAULT CAREER LIBRARY   391

Bates White

1300 Eye Street, NW
Suite 600
Washington, DC 20005
Phone: (202) 408-6110
Fax: (202) 408-7838
www.bateswhite.com

LOCATIONS

Washington, DC (HQ)
San Diego, CA

PRACTICE AREAS

Antitrust
Commercial Litigation
Consumer Finance
Corporate Finance
Energy
Environmental & Product Liability
Health Care
Intellectual Property
International Arbitration
Labor & Employment

THE STATS

Employer Type: Private Company
President & Senior Partner: Charles E. Bates
Managing Partner: Matthew E. Raiff
2007 Employees: 150+
2006 Employees: 150+

THE BUZZ
WHAT CONSULTANTS AT OTHER FIRMS ARE SAYING ABOUT THIS FIRM

- "Academic, smaller but growing aggressively"
- "Crazy hours"
- "Well run, smart, fun"
- "Lack of diversity"

RANKING RECAP

Quality of Life
#5 - Travel Requirements
#7 - Compensation
#10 - Offices
#14 - Best Firms to Work For
#17 - Formal Training

Diversity
#9 - Diversity for GLBT
#12 - Diversity for Minorities
#14 - Best Firms for Diversity

UPPERS

- "Understanding of the diversity of junior consultants' career goals and support for it"
- "Academic bent means partnership is supportive of stopping and taking time to think"
- "High-performing BAs can be promoted to the same level as PhDs"
- "Each paycheck is based on the hours worked"

DOWNERS

- "Repetitive tasks. Repetitive tasks"
- "Social awkwardness that comes from only hiring the very bright"
- "Upper management as a whole provides very little mentorship to managers"
- "Consultants might sometimes feel like they are at the bottom of the food chain"

EMPLOYMENT CONTACT

www.bateswhite.com/careers/careers.htm

THE SCOOP

Business savvy

Founded in 1999 by five entrepreneurs, Bates White offers consulting services in economics, finance and business strategy to the country's biggest law firms, Fortune 500 companies and the government. Based out of Washington, D.C., with a second office in San Diego, the firm's 150-plus employees make up a brainy bunch of economists, econometricians, strategists, financial analysts and information technology specialists. Most of them hold a PhD or master's-level degree in economics, finance, statistics, accounting, information systems or management.

Bates White's full-time professionals and its extensive network of academic and industry experts hail from diverse backgrounds and from all over the world. The firm prides itself on its employee diversity and recruits from a wide range of institutions and a variety of academic fields, including biology, business administration, economics, English, engineering, finance, mathematics, philosophy, physics and statistics. And even though the firm conducts most of its business in the U.S., Bates Whites employees can carry on a conversation in any number of languages, including Bengali, Bulgarian, Mandarin, Croatian, Czech, French, German, Greek, Hindi, Hungarian, Italian, Korean, Polish, Russian, Serbian, Spanish and Turkish. That kind of diversity is in line with the founders' original vision for the firm as a place that would "encourage ingenuity, build an atmosphere of collaboration and continuous learning, and exceed our client's expectations."

Setting a good example

Looking at co-founders Halbert White's and Charles Bates' resumes, it's no wonder that their consulting firm puts such a premium on brain power. White, who currently serves as the firm's chief scientist, is world-renowned for his work in econometrics, predictive modeling and artificial neural networks. In fact, in September 2006, a citation analysis of peer-reviewed economics literature since 1970 found that one of White's papers from 1980 has become the most cited paper in economist literature over the last 35 years, with 4,318 citations. With over 25 years of academic and consulting experience under his belt, he is also a fellow of the American Academy of Arts and Sciences, a Guggenheim Fellow, a fellow of the Econometric Society and has been listed in *Who's Who in the World*. When he's not wearing his consultant hat, White teaches economics at the University of California, San Diego.

The firm's president and senior partner, Charles Bates, has an equally long list of distinctions. Before founding Bates White, he served as a vice president at A.T. Kearney, and before that as a partner in charge of KPMG's economic analysis group. Today, he works as Bates White's senior adviser in charge of economic analysis for the firm's larger, more complex litigation engagements. In 1999, Bates led his firm's team in the largest price-fixing case in U.S. history in In re Vitamins Antitrust Litigation. Bates and his team proved that vitamin manufacturers were colluding throughout the 1990s to set artificially high prices on their products, including vitamins A, C, E, beta-carotene and the B-complex vitamins.

Putting stock in antitrust

Bates White's vitamin antitrust case is just one example of the firm's antitrust services, one of its strongest areas of expertise. Bates White's antitrust team—which boasts over 20 members with PhDs—advises clients on case development and strategy, works alongside clients to measure the strengths and weaknesses of their economic arguments, and provides analysis and advice for determining the best litigation and settlement strategies by applying advanced economic, financial and statistical theory. In the years since its founding, Bates White has consulted on some of the highest-profile antitrust cases in history, addressing issues of monopolization, pricing, market definition, structure and concentration, damages and liability analysis, class certification, competitive effects of exclusive dealing and tying arrangements, mergers and acquisitions, joining venues, efficiencies and failing firm claims.

Because of its industry experience, Bates White's antitrust consultants are often busy publishing and presenting their ideas in journals and at high-brow conferences. Principal Chris Stomberg, for one, published an article on Medicaid's negative effect on

Visit the Vault Consulting Career Channel at **www.vault.com/consulting** - with insider firm profiles, message boards, the Vault Consulting Job Board and more.

 VAULT CAREER LIBRARY   393

generic drugs in the November 2006 *Antitrust Health Care Chronicle*, while his colleague, Dr. Robert C. Marshall, a Bates White partner, spoke at a joint public hearing held by the Federal Trade Commission and the Department of Justice on single-firm conduct and U.S. antitrust law. Bates White also holds a an annual antitrust conference, co-sponsored by the Penn State Center for the Study of Auctions, Procurements and Competition Policy.

Asbestos victims get their due

Growing out of its environmental and product liability services, Bates White boasts a reputation for being an industry leader in asbestos risk assessment. It has estimated and assessed the impact of asbestos liabilities for everything from car parts manufacturers to banks to real estate companies. And in 2005, even Uncle Sam asked Bates White for asbestos help when the American Legislative Exchange Council asked the firm to conduct a study on how much asbestos claims could cost over the next 50 years. The study, commissioned in response to the proposed FAIR (Fairness in Asbestos Injury Resolution) Act, estimated the cost of asbestos claims at $300 to $695 billion, significantly higher than the Congressional Budget Office's proposed amount for compensating asbestos victims. With Bates White's findings in hand, Congress rejected the FAIR Act and the $140 billion budget the CBO had proposed.

The issue of asbestos is a topic Charles Bates has spoken on frequently. In December 2006, he was part of a panel discussion on estimations of asbestos liabilities at Mealey's Asbestos Bankruptcy Conference, and was also a keynote speaker in November 2006 at Mealey's International Asbestos Conference in London. Dr. Charlie Mullin, a partner in Bates White's environmental and product liability practice, has also addressed the issue, speaking at the American Conference Institute's 7th National Asbestos Claims Conference in June 2006.

Big and getting bigger

Things are going well for Bates White—just consider all the new faces in its roster. In August 2006, the firm recruited two new labor economists, Drs. William Carrington and Karl Snow, to join the firm as principals in the labor and employment practice. Both bring with them over 15 years of experience working in academia and as consultants before leaving Bethesda, Md.-based Welch Consulting for Bates White. In July of that year, Bates White expanded its antitrust merger practice when it hired Dr. Keith Waehrer, a former research economist with the U.S. Department of Justice's antitrust division. In March, international economist Dr. Leonardo Giacchino joined the firm's energy practice, while former U.S. Department of Justice antitrust economist T. Scott Thompson came into the antitrust practice in February 2006.

To accommodate all of its new hires, Bates White moved to a larger office on Washington's Eye Street in April 2006. "We have experienced rapid growth across all practice areas," said Managing Partner Matthew E. Raiff. "This new facility enables the firm to support our expansion and continue providing outstanding service to our clients."

GETTING HIRED

Quant qualified

To get this firm's attention, it's helpful to have a background in accounting, computer science, economics, engineering, finance, mathematics, physics or statistics—in short, anything numbers-related. But the firm claims it doesn't completely rule out candidates from other academic fields. Bates White's recruiters scope out grads from top schools, sources say, particularly from "Northwestern, Howard, George Mason, Georgetown, Penn State, Princeton, Duke, George Washington, Berkeley, University of Maryland, Spelman, Stanford and Wellesley."

Insiders tell us that the hiring process consists of one or two rounds of interviews, one of which might take place on campus. For out-of-town candidates, there is always a trip to the office with swank accommodations that, according to insiders, make candidates feel a bit pampered. An insider hired straight out of school reports, "I had two interviews: one on campus (small case question and a behavioral interview) and one at the firm (three behavioral interviews and two cases). They flew me down, put me up at a gorgeous hotel and paid for flights and meals." For some staffers, the entire process takes place at the office in a single day. "I only had one day of interviewing on site, where I had about six interviews—two case, two behavioral and two HR/general interviews," relates a source.

Thorough thinkers only

Bates White is looking for analytical, numbers-savvy candidates who will be able to start solving client problems from the get-go. With that in mind, behavioral questions are involved in the interviews, but there is a much stronger emphasis placed on the cases. According to a consultant, "Cases are tailored to the project work we do. They tend to have a market-sizing part and a computational part." A manager explains that interviewers aren't necessarily looking for a right answer, but rather the ability to think things through. "We are trying to identify people with a natural facility for thinking quantitatively and applying structured logic," explains another manager. Candidates can also expect real-life type questions that examine a client issue, instead of tricky logic questions. "Our case interviews are firm-specific, and are not general 'estimate how many toilets are in Manhattan' types of case interviews. Interviewees are led through a process of identifying important aspects of a specific engagement, asked how these aspects may be confirmed or rejected, and asked to explore alternative approaches to solving problems," a staffer clarifies.

Insiders say that for candidates, the key is being able to walk through the steps of solving a problem and showcase their ability to think analytically. A source recalls, "I faced two cases in the interview. By far the most important thing is the reasoning process, not the specific solution. One of the cases I had to work through in my interview did not have an actual solution yet. They asked me about a hypothetical case based on a real project of the firm. In fact, people at the firm were still discussing which was the best way to face it." The consultant adds, "They liked that I mentioned in my response the main areas to analyze and potential paths to work on and those were, in fact, similar to the internal discussions at that time, even though some of these paths were potentially contradictory."

OUR SURVEY SAYS

"As good as it gets"

Insiders are distinctly positive about the culture at Bates White. According to an associate, "The work environment is as good as it gets, in my opinion. Everyone with whom I work is good at what they do, challenging me to improve daily. Additionally, the personality of the firm is young and friendly." Consultants comment on the "very collegial culture that encourages learning and mentoring," and the "supportive" atmosphere. A source raves, "There is very little to it ... People are just nice, friendly and outgoing, and an environment like this is self-perpetuating." Employees also state that co-workers seem more apt to be supportive than competitive. "There seems to be more collaboration than at other firms. Any competition that exists is strictly a positive-sum game," a staffer claims, adding, "You are rewarded for helping others and supporting their development. I can't think of anything that happens at others' expense."

Several respondents remark that the distinctiveness of the culture comes from working with a group of professors and PhDs. Declares one insider, "The culture is highly collegial. Many times it feels like working in a university." A junior consultant agrees, saying, "The culture at Bates White is very academic. People are always eager to discuss and share ideas, explain theories and connect the dots between research and real-life examples. So far, everyone has been very professional, encouraging and helpful while I've acclimated to a new career." A senior colleague adds, "Nearly all work is team-based. It's very common to have three or more people in a room with a PC and a projector, developing models and writing code together," claims a senior consultant."

Just enough interaction

In addition to collaborative project work, Bates White also provides opportunities to interact outside of the office, but those opportunities are usually optional, we're told. "There are plenty of opportunities for both firm-sponsored and unsponsored social

Visit the Vault Consulting Career Channel at **www.vault.com/consulting** - with insider firm
profiles, message boards, the Vault Consulting Job Board and more.

VAULT CAREER LIBRARY   **395**

interaction with co-workers, but not so much that it's in danger of taking on a cult-like atmosphere, and participation is generally not required," a manager explains.

For all of its collegiality, some staffers feel that the firm's intellectual culture doesn't encourage as much team interaction and socializing as they might like. One insider says, "[Co-workers] are nice and young, but sometimes quiet and conformist." A source agrees, "People should be more cordial around the office. Most other employees will just walk right by me and not even acknowledge my existence." The reason for this behavior, a source remarks, is that "the nature of the work makes the office seem rather solitary."

"Zero call for face time"

Most consultants report that work/life balance is in check, thanks to the fact that the firm generally acknowledges that employees also have personal lives. "People work hard here, but planned time off is respected and the firm is sensitive to workload impact on personal time," claims an insider. Though a minimum of 50 hours a week seems to be standard, staffers indicate that there is a lot of flexibility in terms of when you work those hours. Recounts one manager, "I go kayaking two or three days a week before work, which means that on those days, I often am not in until 10:00 a.m., while a co-worker of mine leaves most days at 5 p.m. on the dot. Both of us make ourselves available at other times during the week to make up for lost time and have developed working relationships with our co-workers that allow us to make these schedules work."

Permission to create a schedule that works for each individual makes most insiders feel that they aren't too overwhelmed by work demands. A source states, "My department does a good job of allowing you to work when you want, such as leaving early on Tuesday and working late on Wednesday." And a colleague notes that the firm's pay scale is conducive to an adjustable schedule: "We have very flexible work schedules. Though busy at times, in the off periods it is very easy to take time to enjoy life. We have an expected number of hours [to be] worked per pay period, rather than a standard hours-per-day requirement, making it easier to take three- or four-day weekends during nonpeak business periods." A consultant adds, "As long as you are getting your work done and willing to work with others to accommodate their needs, there is zero call for face time."

The cycle speaks for itself

During the week, sources insist work hours aren't extremely long, though there are occasional crunch times. "It is widely accepted that there are peaks and valleys, and that some weeks you work 90 hours. Other weeks you don't and, in general, you should average 50," explains a senior consultant. A colleague says, "The job is very cyclical. You will have weeks where you barely fill your 50-hour week, and then there are weeks where you have weeks of all-nighters." But most staffers say those all-nighters are the exception rather than the norm. "Work hours get long only when it is absolutely necessary, given client demands. However, it does not happen too often (on average four times a year). Long hours are appreciated and employees are encouraged to compensate for long work hours by taking days off." A few experienced consultants note that it is really up to the individual to put limits on working hours. "You could easily end up working over 15 hours every day if you wanted to. I force myself to leave most days and learned to know when work can wait," a manager acknowledges.

As for Saturday and Sunday, most insiders claim that the necessity to work on the weekends varies according to the group and the project. Quite a few consultants report working over 25 weekends a year, though the overall average number of worked weekends is closer to 15.

Sticking close to home

Sources claim to be highly satisfied that, unlike most consulting firms, Bates White doesn't put its consultants on the road for engagements. "Consultants may travel occasionally to clients' offices, but most are local clients," explains a staffer, adding that "most projects are based in Washington D.C." For some, an occasional trip may be required, but normally it's recruiting-related, rather than for a client project. "I've only traveled for recruiting. I've traveled four times for recruiting this year, and could have done fewer trips if I had not wanted to," says an insider.

Senior managers and partners might travel a bit more than consultants, but even then travel "does not have a big impact, on average," we're told. As a manager explains, "Travel is confined largely between the San Diego and D.C. offices, with the majority of travel being San Diego-based employees coming to D.C. Very few junior-level staff are ever asked to travel." One employee who's thankful for the limited travel demands appreciates the chance to hang out at the office and get to know his co-workers: "Travel is rare enough that its not a major burden. It's nice coming to work and seeing the same group at the office most days."

Work more, earn more

Sources report that the compensation practice at Bates White is fair to all, thanks to a unique system that pays more for working longer hours. An insider explains, "Everyone below manager level is salaried for a 40-hour workweek, then compensated at the same hourly rate for every hour beyond that (we have 50-hour targets)," adding, "It is nice, because if you feel that you have been required to work more hours than you expected or more than others at the firm, at least you are compensated for it. Likewise, if you work fewer hours for whatever reason, no one resents you for having it light because you are getting paid less." Employees say this system helps keep hours in check, since those in charge of a project are more budget-conscious. "Compensation is based on number of worked hours and is not fixed. This has some advantages because most of the time there is no incentive for a manager to make people stay longer than necessary," a consultant notes.

Judging by employees' reports, the firm seems to be doing a good job in the compensation department. Declares one partner, "A lot of time is dedicated at the firm to making sure we get compensation right. Although the system seems complex, in my experience it tends to get it right at the end of the day."

Working behind the scenes

For consultants starting their career, insiders say there isn't always much client contact in the beginning. A staffer reports, "Client contact is not an integral part of entry-level jobs. If a consultant wants opportunities to interact with clients, he has to seek them out, but they do exist." One source claims it's the nature of the industry that keeps most consultants in the office instead of at the client location: "I have little direct client interaction, but I think that goes with the territory for economic consulting."

Insiders say the firm doesn't prohibit client contact, it just limits those who are put in a position to directly work with clients. One manager explains, "Regarding clients, the organization is very careful about interaction with clients, so they require a lot of experience from the consultants before they are allowed to do so." A colleague adds, "The firm moves quickly to give consultants opportunities for client interaction commensurate with their communication skills and demonstrated professionalism. It's not unusual for very junior people to be leading presentations if they've shown themselves to be up to the task." And one assertive staffer claims, "I have been in contact with partners at various client law firms as well as corporate counsels of Fortune 500 companies."

The caring kind

Though there may be limited client contact for some, sources claim that there is plenty of interaction with management at Bates White. "I consider myself very fortunate to work with my supervisors. Due to the flat hierarchy in the firm, my supervisors go all the way to the president of the firm, with whom I work directly," a consultant states. Echoes a colleague, "The culture is very horizontal, as staff at all levels, including partners, interact with all other staff. Partners and managers frequently seek feedback from junior staff and are generally approachable by anyone in the company."

A number of insiders agree that their supervisors are the kind who get involved with staff. "We have excellent supervisors who really take care to cultivate relationships with the rank-and-file members of our company. But 'rank-and-file' is very misleading because nobody stepping into an entry-level position at Bates White is sectioned off for unimportant tasks," affirms a consultant. An insider who has gotten to know her superiors claims, "My manager has shown that he really does value me as a person. He gives me opportunities to learn skills that will advance my career."

Teaching newbies new tricks

Consultants report that for new hires, there is plenty of opportunity to get up to speed on the way things work through a combination of official and unofficial training. "My first week at Bates White was filled with a range of internally-generated training courses on software and corporate practices. However, I was also assigned a peer coach (another consultant) and a sponsor (a manager) who continue to act as my mentors." Consultants appreciate the formal mentorship program, in which "everybody is assigned a peer coach and a staff sponsor for career and on-the-job development." In the beginning, there is a lot of software training available; a consultant explains, "We have designed extensive formal training for Stata, Excel, PowerPoint, Word, Access, Python, XML and writing." What new staffers seem to appreciate most, however, is the willingness of co-workers to help each other. As one insider puts it, there are "endless resources available in our peers," and a colleague remarks, "Most employees make an effort to teach new consultants assigned to their projects tricks and efficient practices."

Beyond initial formal training, insiders say that most learning happens by absorption. "Most training is unofficial due to the nature of the projects we work on. It is difficult to develop effective, broad-based training for all employees," a source claims. "Individuals get on-the-job training that is more specific to their projects as they progress," expresses a co-worker. Another consultant explains, "There are many PhDs around that are always willing to teach you something, and the firm offers a lot of lunchtime lectures and seminars. In addition, relevant classes taken at nearby colleges are paid for." The firm's mix of "formal training led by internal staff—both PhDs and non-PhDs—and on-the-job training" gets pretty good marks from insiders, but most tend to feel that "the most effective training is on the job."

Representing the pool

According to insiders, women may be underrepresented at Bates White, but that doesn't mean there isn't an effort to promote gender diversity. "We have gone out of our way to hire female consultants, for example, by recruiting at all-female colleges. In terms of promoting and mentoring, females receive equal treatment as compared to males," declares a source. Employees also reveal that there is more gender diversity at the lower levels, while at more senior levels the number of women trickles off. "The male-to-female ratio is probably about 60/40 at the consultant, consultant II and senior consultant levels. It drops off drastically for managers (only two females), and no principals or partners are female," an insider says.

Most insiders tend to agree that the disparity exists because there aren't as many women in the economics-related fields from which Bates White hires. A manager comments, "This is a male-dominated field, but the firm would like to diversify. I think women are treated as well as men; the challenge is in attracting more to the firm." A colleague concurs, "We have fewer women the higher you go in the firm, but I don't think the decrease is due to the firm as much as the characteristics of the pool we are hiring from and the draw of academia. As a woman at the firm, I have felt perfectly satisfied with my treatment with respect to hiring, promoting and mentoring."

Free to be you and me

Insiders express that Bates White is all about encouraging diversity with respect to gay, lesbian and transgender employees. One staffer refers to a recent employee's gender switch: "When one of our male employees decided to become a female, our managing partner sent out a firmwide e-mail in support of her." Sources also claim that while there aren't any affinity groups available, "the firm makes big efforts in being highly inclusive." Affirms a consultant, "This is a nonissue. I can personally say that there are gays and bisexuals at our firm, but only loosely. This has never been an issue, and I get the impression that it's just not important." And another states, "It never occurred to me to keep my orientation a secret here: it's simply a nonissue."

"Seriously meritocratic"

As insiders see it, Bates White is "seriously meritocratic," meaning minorities are given equal consideration when it comes to recruiting and promotion. "They just don't care about color or race; they want smart people who deliver results. And considering the inherent diversity of the economics field, especially at the PhD level, you have to be very open to diversity," claims a manager. Another insider boasts, "We have a very wide range of diversification in our firm with respect to minorities. We have employees from all over the world specializing in various aspects of our consulting business." There is also an official effort to promote minority diversity at the firm, witnesses a senior staffer: "There is a lot of attention to diversity and inclusion, and diversity training was conducted last year."

Still, some point to gaps in the minority ranks. A consultant explains, "We recruit actively at historically black universities. And many of our consultants are not white," though the source looks to the management level and above and sees a serious lack of diversity. A colleague mentions that while the firm has consultants from all over the world, there aren't enough American minorities in client services jobs. "There are many international client services employees, but not many minorities. No special efforts are taken. Most minorities are in nonclient services work, such as office services."

Pingpong and candy—need we say more?

Staffers boast there are a number of nice perks offered at Bates White that help make life just a little more comfortable. The office in D.C. has "an espresso machine, table tennis and a pool table in the staff room." Another consultant mentions "firm-sponsored events, like sailing, baseball and other outings." A few other nice-to-have extras include the "subsidized candy machine, free drinks, and reimbursed dinner and cab home if you have to work late." Employees also note that staying healthy is encouraged with a "health and wellness subsidy of $40 per month—to be put toward anything health related (most often used for gym membership)."

Ergonomic as you like it

It's clear that the employees in D.C. are happier with their offices than those on the West Coast. Says one insider, "Our Washington, D.C., office is brand new and immaculate. It includes an employee lounge area with billiards and table tennis." A colleague elaborates on his lush surroundings: "The office is equipped with numerous work/meeting rooms so that staff can work together in the same room, if necessary. There is a full kitchen and a small cafeteria, as well as several smaller pantries. The firm provides ergonomic chairs to all staff and tries to provide whatever ergonomic resources are needed, within reason," a colleague reports. Sources also brag about the fact that no one at the firm feels cramped in their quarters. Claims an insider, "There is ample office space on our floors, which allows everyone to have their own enclosed office space. Friends have told me that my office is as large as some of the partner's offices at their firm (although lacking the windows)." According to one insider, it might even be a bit too comfortable: "If anything, we spent too much on our new offices. It is not a question of whether they are nice, only a question of whether they are too nice."

But for San Diego insiders, the lack of privacy seems to be an issue. "No doors is not a good idea," grumbles a staffer. Another consultant reports that "the San Diego office is very nice, but not on the same level as the D.C. office. This might change in the near future, however, as we are outgrowing this office."

Connecting with the community

Insiders at Bates White are active in charitable events, many of which are sponsored by the firm. "We have a Community Connection program that supports a lot of activities: the D.C. AIDS walk, Lawyers Have Heart, Bread for the City (cash, food and clothing drives), HAP (mentoring), etc. Basically, the firm is very open to supporting new causes." Reports a consultant, "When the firm upgraded computers, the old computers were given to employees on the condition that $100 was donated to a local charity." Bates White also encourages staffers to get involved by giving them time off to participate in events. "Our firm rewards these efforts, giving high priority to the time commitments, as well as raffle tickets for the year-end holiday party," mentions a respondent.

Aside from supporting a variety of causes, employees are encouraged to come up with their own ideas for ways to give back. Reports a consultant, "There are several initiatives simultaneously. The firm is very involved in community service and it constantly encourages all people to get involved. It also encourages all people to bring new ideas for community projects and it gives serious consideration to them."

Visit the Vault Consulting Career Channel at **www.vault.com/consulting** - with insider firm profiles, message boards, the Vault Consulting Job Board and more.

VAULT CAREER LIBRARY

399

The Brattle Group

44 Brattle Street
Cambridge, MA 02138
Phone: (617) 864-7900
Fax: (617) 864-1576
www.brattle.com

LOCATIONS

Cambridge, MA (HQ)
San Francisco, CA
Washington, DC
Brussels
London

PRACTICE AREAS

Antitrust/Competition
Commercial Damages
Environmental Litigation & Regulation
Forensic Economics
Intellectual Property
International Arbitration
International Trade
Product Liability
Regulatory Finance & Accounting
Risk Management
Securities
Tax
Utility Regulatory Policy & Ratemaking
Valuation

THE STATS

Employer Type: Private Company
Chairman: Peter S. Fox-Penner
2007 Employees: 164
2006 Employees: 172

THE BUZZ
WHAT CONSULTANTS AT OTHER FIRMS ARE SAYING ABOUT THIS FIRM

- "Small but mighty"
- "Very high partner-to-employee ratio; no growth potential for new employees"
- "Academic, solid work"
- "Nerdy"

RANKING RECAP

Quality of Life
#3 - Travel Requirements
#14 - Formal Training (tie)
#17 - Best Firms to Work For (tie)
#18 - Firm Culture
#19 - Overall Satisfaction

Diversity
#12 - Diversity for GLBT
#12 - Diversity for Women
#13 - Best Firms for Diversity

UPPERS

- "The business is doing well"
- "Your input does matter in many ways in this firm"
- "The firm works extremely hard to make the company a pleasant place to work"
- Significant interaction between principals and associates

DOWNERS

- "The pace of economic consulting is tough"
- "A bit ingrown and parochial"
- Career advancement path is not clear
- "Compensation (both base salary and bonus) is below industry average"

EMPLOYMENT CONTACT

www.brattle.com/Careers

THE SCOOP

Going into battle with Brattle

Corporations, law firms, local and international governments and public agencies worldwide have turned to The Brattle Group for its consulting services and expert testimony on economic, finance, regulatory and strategic issues. The firm's 160-plus professionals provide testimony on everything from economic damages, antitrust and competitive analysis, to financial risk, regulatory economics, utility and environmental matters. Headquartered in Cambridge's Harvard Square with offices across the U.S., the U.K. and Belgium, Brattle's main areas of expertise include energy, securities and finance, commercial damages, antitrust, environmental and product liability, and risk management.

The firm prides itself on having in-depth industry expertise in a range of markets, such as airports and airlines, chemicals, electric power, governmental and regulatory bodies, health economics, hydroelectric power, Internet and new economy, insurance, manufacturing and process industries, manufactured gas plants, mining and metals, natural gas, network industries, petroleum, pharmaceuticals, transportation and water.

Bostonians

The Brattle Group started out as a six-person outfit in Harvard Square in 1990. Today, the firm's location isn't its only Harvard connection—Brattle's consultants hold advanced degrees from leading schools, including Harvard, MIT, Berkeley, Stanford, London School of Business, the University of Chicago and Wharton, and exhibit diverse industry experience.

One of the firm's biggest brains, Chairman Peter S. Fox-Penner, holds an advanced degree in engineering and a PhD in economics, and has published a number of books, including the widely-read *Electric Utility Restructuring: A Guide to the Competitive Era*. He has also testified before the U.S. Senate in debates over approval of national energy policies, and previously served as assistant to the deputy secretary at the U.S. Department of Energy. Another Brattle principal, Berkeley Professor Daniel McFadden, was the winner of the 2000 Nobel Prize in Economics, while Principal Robert J. Reynolds was formerly an assistant director for economic policy at the U.S. Department of Justice. Principal Dorothy Robyn was a senior economic adviser to former President Bill Clinton.

Tapping into Brattle's brainpower

The Brattle Group uses its brainpower as its strongest selling point. Most of the time, engagements involve serving as key witnesses in cases where industry players are fighting to defend their business against regulatory decisions, antitrust forces or foreign competition. In the energy industry, for example, Brattle has provided planning advice to electric, gas and other utilities, regulators and governments to help them cope with and explain the shifting energy environment as the industry undergoes "profound restructuring."

Each client's problem is addressed via the firm's "five steps to success" approach. The first step is listening to the client, even if they themselves don't know the root cause of their problems. Then Brattle consultants help clients plan for any unforeseen issues by conducting economic studies of past market structure and performance, valuing assets and business opportunities, and developing business or litigation strategies. The third step: executing assignments while paying attention to analytic detail, and checking and reporting results. Solutions then have to be tested for validity and reproducibility. And finally, the firm transfers project results to clients, government agencies or courtrooms in a professional manner.

Prolific professionals

Since its start in 1990, Brattle's experts have published a library's worth of consulting books and academic papers. Beyond these, the firm also publishes a newsletter series on economic, environmental and energy topics, and its consultants pen articles in magazines, newspapers and journals around the globe.

Visit the Vault Consulting Career Channel at www.vault.com/consulting - with insider firm profiles, message boards, the Vault Consulting Job Board and more.

 401

One report that grabbed media attention was a March 2006 study in which the firm revealed that smaller tobacco companies have managed to grab as much as 8 percent of the tobacco market from Big Tobacco. That's bad news for the 46 state governments that have signed a 25-year agreement with tobacco companies, under which the companies would pay $246 billion in annual payments to taxpayers. Brattle's finding could reduce the annual payments that companies like Philip Morris and RJ Reynolds are forced to pay through 2025 under the Master Tobacco Settlement Agreement. As of April 2006, only $41 billion had been shelled out.

Seeking strength in others

Brattle doesn't just add to the world of advice giving; it supports it through the annually awarded Brattle Prize in Corporate Finance. The award recognizes outstanding papers on corporate finance, selected by the associate editors of *The Journal of Finance*, and awards $10,000 for first prize and $5,000 for second and third place. The 2006 winners were announced in January 2007 at the American Finance Association's annual meeting in Chicago. First prize went to Joshua D. Rauh, an assistant professor of finance at the University of Chicago, for his paper, entitled "Investment and Financing Constraints: Evidence from the Funding of Corporate Pension Plans"—surely a light read.

Brattle also supports internal expertise by awarding the Bill Moss Prize each year to the principal and associate who best demonstrate excellence in mentoring and developing people. These $10,000 awards underscore the firm's commitment to staff development.

Don't forget about the fun and games

With all of its intellectual punch, Brattle ensures that its employees are challenged and their minds stretched, and states, "The Brattle Group's engagements always give our economists, statisticians, technical specialists and researchers a real 'workout.'" Newly hired research analysts, straight out of school, get to work side-by-side with some of the world's most respected economists, thanks to Brattle's "flat" organizational structure that invites and accepts input from Brattle staffers at all levels. And to make sure the intellectual workout doesn't get too strenuous, the firm holds regular "steam-release" parties on Fridays after work, along with regular companywide get-togethers.

It's these team-building initiatives that helped push Brattle into the group of the 25 Best Small Companies to Work for in America, selected by the Great Places to Work Institute and the Society for Human Resource Management in June 2006. The list ranks the top-25 small and top-25 medium-sized companies in America that use strong people management strategies to develop successful organizations with highly productive and satisfied workforces.

GETTING HIRED

Scouting and screening

Brattle's best, says one insider, traditionally come from "hot spots including Emory, Brandeis, Berkeley and MIT and Wellesley," but another remarks that "the firm seems to be more interested in attracting strong candidates and does not have a set list schools." The source adds, though, that "PhD candidates typically come from top-30 programs" in the country. "For associates," says another insider, "the typical hire is a graduating PhD" and "associate hiring is mostly done at the AEA (American Economic Association) meeting in January."

Most newbies go through "an initial screening, usually by phone or on-campus recruiting," says one Boston research analyst. Next, she says, "there is a second-round interview where behavioral and technical questions should be expected. A case study is also given." That second round of on-site interviews includes "meeting with about four to six interviewers," explains one Cambridge principal. "For analysts, this includes a case study, and for associates (who are mostly PhD candidates), it includes a case study and a presentation modeled on an academic job talk, where the candidate presents his own research." One insider from Boston admits that his on-site interview day "was a grueling day, but not painful" and that "the process is being revamped."

OUR SURVEY SAYS

"Kindergarten for brilliant people"

Brattle gets high marks from its employees for its collegial environment: "This is a firm that truly values its culture, [so much so] that it is willing to sacrifice profits to protect it," says one insider. Another agrees, adding, "The firm prides itself on a culture characterized by a good work/life balance, friendliness and excellent learning opportunities." One insider lauds Brattle's "very flexible office culture—casual dress (jeans, T-shirts), headphones, starting time, etc." That kind of culture, according to one research analyst in Boston, makes Brattle feel at times "just like a kindergarten for brilliant people."

A good day's work

Most Brattle professionals say they work anywhere between 45 and 60 hours per week, but "work hours vary depending on your project load," says one research analyst. "The hours can go up and down. As it approaches deadline time, the hours get longer, and you may have to work late nights and weekends." Another insider warns that hours may be longer for research analysts: "Most principals and associates arrive late and work late, which necessitates late hours for research analysts." But as one principal remarks, "Nobody is making me work more than I want to. It's just the amount of time that is necessary in order to be engaged, up-to-date and successful in this business."

Hours per week, however, depend on client projects, which "can vary greatly, from a couple of hours to several years. On average, though, projects last two to six months," according to one insider. Another adds that "work is usually very steady in the utilities practice, with spikes before deadlines. In a given period, I work on two to four engagements at a time."

(Un)pack your bags

"For consulting, the travel is limited" at Brattle Group, says one principal, and it is "required only rarely," adds another insider from Washington. But as one source explains, "Travel varies with position." "Analysts travel fairly little, while principals travel quite a bit" and, "at the research analyst level, there is little to no travel required." Brattle management, acknowledging that travel is part of the business, seems to be in touch with the disruptions that travel imposes. A principal notes that to avoid excessive travel, the firm has installed video conference equipment and many trips are now avoided through its use."

A good balance, with caveats

"The firm promotes itself as having a strong work/life balance, but in reality, the work/life balance is completely dictated by the clients' desires and the partners' preferences," says one research analyst. A colleague takes a slightly different approach: "The firm is flexible about work/life balance; the work often is not. That is, where the deadlines and project commitments permit flexibility, the firm does not get in the way, but often the project demands are substantial." Still, another insider says Brattle does its best to provide "flexible hours and a culture generally supportive of family responsibilities." In the end, says one Brattle employee in San Francisco, "The business of economic consulting is very competitive and the culture is very individualistic. Most, if not all, of the best performers are workaholics."

In recompense

From on high, attitudes toward compensation are positive. "We pay very well at all levels of employment," says one principal from Boston, with a colleague adding, "Compensation is transparent—formulas can be tracked and explained [and there is] very little subjective manipulation involved in compensation. A real plus!" Beyond offering satisfactory base salaries, Brattle "gives profit sharing, which is in the form of a 401(k) contribution," explains one insider, but adds that "there are no matching 401(k) contributions, though, so the profit sharing serves as the company's efforts to aid your retirement savings."

Visit the Vault Consulting Career Channel at **www.vault.com/consulting** - with insider firm profiles, message boards, the Vault Consulting Job Board and more.

 **VAULT** CAREER LIBRARY   **403**

But at lower levels, compensation doesn't come without qualms. "Research analyst salary is slightly below competitors. If one bills sufficient hours, though, bonuses can be fairly big," says one research analyst. And an insider from Boston notes that while "principals are compensated based upon a transparent, formulaic approach that reflects accurately the basic economics of the business, the firm does not raid the compensation pool to feed the bottom line." And with regard to profit sharing, the contributions usually range from 5.5 to 6.5 percent. But a research analyst qualifies, "You only get to keep the money if you stay with the firm for three or more years. Effectively this means that there is no profit sharing for junior-level staff."

Other research analysts regret that "the bonus structure is designed in such a way that it penalizes those individuals who work for partners who do not have a continuous supply of billable work. Unless you are able to bill 85 percent of the possible hours in a year, you do not qualify for an hours-based bonus. In addition, any vacation, sick days or holidays you take negatively affect your hours worked."

It's the little things

Friday night is party night at Brattle: "The Brattle Group has Friday parties every week, giving everyone at the firm a chance to get together at least once a week," a source shares. "We also have an annual summer outing and a holiday party." Another insider adds that there is "a fully-stocked beverage refrigerator and snacks twice a day." There are more substantial perks than just snacks, we're told, such as "excellent medical insurance, including dental and allowances for vision and fitness," according to one Cambridge employee, though another source says that while "benefits are generous, that is standard for this type of consulting."

The overseers

Senior management at Brattle, including associates and principals, "is always willing to help with any questions a research analyst might have and are great in mentoring," says one research analyst from Boston. "Colleagues are genuinely friendly and senior consultants act as mentors," comments another, and a colleague adds that "at the research analyst level, you have plenty of opportunities to interact with the principals in the firm and offer your input into the analysis."

Of course, it always helps if you like who you are working for, another research analyst pipes in: "Like with any job, this is probably hit or miss. I happen to really like my boss. Most of my colleagues happen to like theirs. Obviously there are a few who are unhappy, but they are few and far between."

Training on the job

"There is a combination of official and unofficial training" at Brattle, insiders tell us, including "an annual new employee orientation and a series of new consultant trainings, which teach you the basic skills you'll need to start at Brattle. Additionally, every new research analyst is assigned a mentor, and the senior research analysts are very willing to help you if you have questions."

One principal adds that "the in-house training for junior and midlevel staff is good, [but] all training for partners is at [their] own expense and, therefore, largely nonexistent." Still, another insider says, "An extended training program is being developed," but "plans to implement regular training are often foiled by urgent project work."

Outside of formal training, however, most staffers seem to feel that "by far the most (and most effective) training is informal, because of the nature of the work," a principal explains. A research analyst agrees: "I've learned more through actually engaging in project work than sitting through any presentation about it."

Upholding the glass

When it comes to minority groups at Brattle, "intolerant attitudes are not tolerated in our office," assures one insider in Washington. For women, "there are excellent opportunities. That said, there are substantially more men in senior positions," a male principal from Cambridge points out. "For research analysts," adds a colleague, "the split seems about 50/50. If you are qualified, you will be hired regardless of gender." A principal from San Francisco adds that "women have no barriers, outside of what the clients might impose."

As for minorities, one principal says Brattle is "very receptive" to them, "but we see relatively few qualified and interested minority candidates." A Washingtonian adds that his office typically sees "minority candidates from Eastern Europe, Asia and India, and they are well represented in the firm. We do not see African-American and Latino candidates." That trend may be turning around; the firm notes that in 2007, 70 percent of new hires at the associate and research analyst levels were minorities. One research analyst from Boston says he works "with people from China, Kenya, India, Russia, Mexico, etc. If that makes us diverse, so be it. I've never seen any discrimination."

And regarding gay, lesbian or bisexual candidates, one principal from Cambridge, speaking for the majority, says, "Sexual preference is pretty much a nonissue here." He adds: "I personally subscribe to the 'don't know, don't care' philosophy regarding others' sexual preferences and practices."

Visit the Vault Consulting Career Channel at **www.vault.com/consulting** - with insider firm profiles, message boards, the Vault Consulting Job Board and more.

 **405**

Buck Consultants

One Pennsylvania Plaza
New York, NY 10119
Phone: (212) 330-1000
Fax: (212) 695-4184
www.buckconsultants.com

LOCATIONS

New York, NY (HQ)
More than 40 offices worldwide

PRACTICE AREAS

Communication
Compensation
Global Human Resources
Health & Welfare Benefits
Human Resource Management
Retirement

THE STATS

Employer Type: Independent Consulting Subsidiary of
Affiliated Computer Services
Ticker Symbol: ACS (NYSE)
President & Executive Managing Director: Jan K. Grude
2007 Employees: 1,700
2006 Employees: 2,000

UPPERS

- "Upper management generally leaves us alone"
- Management encourages flexibility and work/life balance

DOWNERS

- "It's like watching *The Office*—except it is real and not very funny!"
- "Instability: In the past nine years, the firm was bought and sold twice"

EMPLOYMENT CONTACT

Go to the "Join our Team" section of the firm's web site

THE BUZZ
WHAT CONSULTANTS AT OTHER FIRMS ARE SAYING ABOUT THIS FIRM

- "Small but smart"
- "Soap opera"
- "Good HR specialists"
- "Poor morale"

THE SCOOP

History of innovation

From its humble 1916 beginnings as a two-person actuarial outfit in New York City, Buck Consultants has grown into a major multinational player in the human resources consulting field, offering solutions for communication, compensation, global human resources, health and welfare benefits, human resource management and retirement. Since its inception, the firm has prided itself on being a constant innovator in human resources consulting. Founder George Buck was one of the first to apply actuarial principles to the management of retirement plans. Subsequently, the firm spearheaded a number of unique HR solutions, including establishing the first global employee stock ownership and cash balance plans, developing the first fully integrated health savings account and introducing Severance Solution, a unique severance package designed to help companies better manage the distribution of severance pay to former employees.

Buck's parent company, Affiliated Computer Systems, specializes in business process outsourcing and information technology solutions. Since acquiring Buck in 2005 (Buck had formerly been held by Mellon Financial from 1997 through 2005, under the name Mellon HR&IS), ACS and Buck have mutually benefited from shared resources and the exchange of expertise in the outsourcing and human resources consulting arenas. Specifically, ACS' reputation and size—the firm is a global Fortune 500 company with over 58,000 employees—have enabled Buck to attract a roster of larger firms and state governments.

Taking matters into their own hands

However, the joining of Buck and ACS was not the ideal marriage for all parties involved. In February 2007, it was announced that two Buck executives, former Senior Managing Director Howard Fine and former Managing Director Christopher Michalak, are being sued by ACS after the two privately sought to sell Buck without the permission of ACS. ACS alleged that Fine and Michalak wished to sell the firm to a venture capital group (that they themselves were stakeholders in) and stated that the two executives encouraged Buck employees to resign if ACS did not agree to sell the company. The case remains under review.

Old people, new business

But on the business side of things, Buck has seen positive growth. As the baby boomer generation collectively ages and moves toward retirement, the issues of employer-provided health care and retirement options loom larger and larger. Buck finds itself well positioned to emerge as a leader in these areas. The firm now services over 200,000 health savings accounts, making it one of the five-largest HSA administrators in the country. HSAs figure to become an increasingly large part of Buck's business, as national enrollment in HSA accounts has increased from 438,000 in 2004 to over 3.2 million today.

Buck continues to add to its roster of retirement service clients as well. In July 2006, the firm announced it would be providing retirement administration services to the Puerto Rico Electric Power Authority. Buck's relationship with PREPA dates back to the 1940s, when George Buck helped form the PREPA's original retirement plan. The firm also recently earned significant contracts with the Illinois Teachers' Retirement System and Employees Retirement System of Texas which, combined, put the retirement plans of 630,000 employees under Buck's supervision. The firm provides similar pension management services for the state of Alaska—in January 2006, Buck announced a four-year contract to manage the state's $6.9 billion pension fund. Buck will be involved with several retirement systems in the state, including the Public Employees', Teachers' and Judicial, as well as the National Guard and Naval Militia Retirement System, encompassing over 98,000 active employees and retirees.

Spot that inefficiency

Buck specializes in helping clients restructure overly costly or inefficient retirement plans. In early 2007, the firm recommended that the age for retirement with full benefits for Vermont employees be raised from 62 to 65 years of age. In January 2007, Buck suggested the liquidation of assets in the NMI Retirement fund in Saigon after the halt of government contributions to the fund left it with unfunded liabilities of $552 million. The firm also determined that same month that the retirement fund for San Diego

Visit the Vault Consulting Career Channel at www.vault.com/consulting - with insider firm profiles, message boards, the Vault Consulting Job Board and more.

VAULT CAREER LIBRARY   407

police officers was wildly underfunded, with officers having to contribute the highest percentage of salary of any municipal employee in the city.

Texas: the actuary state

Since March 2006, Buck has funded an actuarial professorship at the University of Texas at Austin. The Buck Consultants Assistant Director of Actuarial Studies position is the first company-sponsored actuarial professorship in the country, and allows a member of the actuarial faculty to advise students, conduct research and perform administrative duties for the actuarial studies department. The professorship extends Buck's longstanding relationship with the University of Texas, from which the firm has recruited top-tier actuarial graduates for over 20 years.

GETTING HIRED

Recruiting three ways

Buck conducts "extensive recruiting" on campus, as well as through third-party recruiters and its parent company, ACS. One Dallas source reports that the office holds campus recruiting at large Texas schools, such as UT Austin and Texas A&M. The firm also maintains listings of open positions on the careers page of the web site, where jobs are searchable by location or title. Buck makes it easy to submit an application, allowing interested parties to cut and paste a resume directly to its site.

No rush

Interviews consist partly of "testing based on math skills and computer proficiency" through targeted interview questions, and there are usually two or three rounds of interviews for most candidates. The firm is in no hurry to make a decision, according to one source who claims, "It took forever! Four months! I had an interview with my boss, then I was called back the next month to meet with his team, and then I was flown to a different location the following month to meet with the national practice leader. I got an offer two or three weeks later and started three weeks after that." Buck notes that it has brought in new recruiting leadership that has been instrumental in making recruiting a top priority.

OUR SURVEY SAYS

Balanced at Buck

Consultants say that the best thing about working at the firm is its "flexibility." Insiders explain that Buck is open to alternative work scheduling to promote work/life balance; "I have a formal work-at-home arrangement and flextime," shares one associate. Staffers also rate their supervisors highly, and claim to enjoy the independent atmosphere that management allows. "My supervisor is pretty hands-off, so it's up to us to decide when to take days off, when to work from home, etc. We aren't made to feel like we can't do what we need to do to balance our lives," asserts one colleague. Another source notes, "My direct supervisor is very attuned to work/life balance."

Sources are also pleased that work hours aren't too bad—usually ranging from 45 to 55 hours a week. Says a source, "My hours are cyclical. The fall is always insane with annual enrollment. The rest of the year is typically OK." The length of engagements can last from a few weeks to a few years, we're told. "It varies widely, but I'd guess three months from start to finish on an average client project."

Sinking morale

On the downside, insiders complain that "corporate culture has declined since our firm was purchased by ACS in mid-2005." Mourns one insider, "With the purchase of our firm by ACS, the Buck name has been sullied," and a colleague claims that ACS "has the soul of a computer." Another co-worker regrets that there are "no team-building activities, no culture-building, nothing!" Remarks a colleague, "It's like a funeral home in there on some days."

Staying close to home

To the satisfaction of most insiders, travel isn't necessarily part of consultants' day-to-day routine. "I generally travel 10 to 12 times a year for a few days at a time. Travel varies widely among consultants," explains a source. An associate admits, "I rarely travel, and most of my clients are fairly close by," noting, "Actually, I would enjoy traveling more."

One source who does spend time on the road has a few complaints about the less-than-lavish conditions: "Our parent company is cheap, so it makes flying on the airlines I like and staying in the hotels I prefer a challenge from time to time. I'm not expecting to stay at the Four Seasons or fly in first class, but I do expect to stay at a safe, name-brand hotel and fly on a reputable airline I prefer, without making two stopovers to get to my destination."

Compensation clarification

Compensation at the firm gets mixed reviews. One manager states, "I think the comp is generally good," but remarks, "I think the company and our supervisors do a very poor job of explaining to employees what to expect, how the bonus process works and on what factors we're evaluated." As for what is clear about bonus, it's "split out in two payments, one at 25 percent and the remaining to come at the end of our fiscal year." An insider explains that bonus is "largely based on profit goals over which consultants have no control."

But those staffers who aren't satisfied with compensation fear the situation isn't improving. "I have been an employee of this firm for almost 16 years and this is the first time I have contemplated leaving. I feel our corporate parent will only keep chipping away at our compensation and benefits, as it has done since it bought Buck in mid-2005," grumbles one insider. Another source concurs, "Since our firm was purchased by ACS, our annual target bonus, which was always paid by Buck over the past 30 years, is in jeopardy. Thus, our compensation, which used to be competitive when the bonus was included, is not."

Little extras

Benefits at Buck are fairly standard. The firm offers a "very good 401(k), good health plans, dental plans and other nice perks like pet insurance." Buck reports that it also offers a defined benefit pension plan. Comments an analyst, "It's not a perk my company offers, but it's nice that I work six miles from my home—no long commute."

Buck's offices tend to follow a similar pattern. While most sources say Buck's offices offer a "nice, professional office environment," an insider disagrees, complaining that "cubicle space gets smaller with each move, management refuses to fix broken blinds and bathrooms need constant repair."

BCU 101

The firm kicks off training for new hires with "BCU 101, an off-site, multiday session to acquaint new consulting professionals with Buck Consultants and the basics of consulting." Aside from that, training is on-the-job. According to a staffer, "Most is unofficial, but now we're being asked to do goal-setting and attend some sort of training this year."

Mixed on diversity

Gender diversity is fairly balanced at Buck, insiders tell us. "We have plenty of women, including several in director or principal positions," notes one consultant. The same can't be said for minority representation, however. A manager observes, "We have

Visit the Vault Consulting Career Channel at www.vault.com/consulting - with insider firm profiles, message boards, the Vault Consulting Job Board and more.

 409

very few minorities, and of the ones we do have, all but one are in support positions. Only one is a senior consultant/director. It's poor." When it comes to gay and lesbian diversity, an insider tells us, "It's never addressed overtly. I think we have a few gays and lesbians in our workplace, but you'd never know (that's good!)." The source adds, though, that "our parent company never makes it a point to ensure that we're an open, fair organization."

Capco

The Capital Markets Company Inc.
120 Broadway, 29th Floor
New York, NY 10271
Phone: (212) 284-8600
Fax: (212) 284-8601
www.capco.com

LOCATIONS

Antwerp (HQ)
New York, NY
San Francisco, CA
Sunnyvale, CA
Amsterdam
Bangalore
Frankfurt
London
Paris
Toronto

PRACTICE AREAS

Consulting
Asset Management • Capital Markets • Corporate &
Investment Banking • Personal Financial Services
Managed Services
Hedge Fund Services • Reconciliation Services •
Reference Data Services
Technology Solutions

THE STATS

Employer Type: Private Company
Chairman & CEO: Rob Heyvaert
2007 Employees: 500+
2006 Employees: 550+

Visit the Vault Consulting Career Channel at **www.vault.com/consulting** - with insider firm
profiles, message boards, the Vault Consulting Job Board and more.

VAULT CAREER LIBRARY   411

THE SCOOP

Business, Belgian style

Belgian-born consulting firm Capco has a plan and it's sticking to it. For nearly 10 years, the firm has dedicated itself to being the self-regarded "transformation firm" for financial services. With offices around the globe—spanning the U.S., the Netherlands, India, Germany, the U.K., France and Canada—Capco's 500-plus professionals have consulted on projects for some of the biggest names in the financial services industry, including Bank of America, BNP Paribas, JPMorgan Chase, Morgan Stanley and Wachovia.

Capco's areas of expertise lie strictly within the realm of the financial services industry, with specialties in the asset management, retail banking, wholesale banking, market infrastructure and payments industries. It's transformation services include business and technology consulting, processing services and technology solutions.

De Donald

While not everyone in the U.S. has heard of Rob Heyvaert, Capco's founder, chairman and CEO, he's about as popular a boss in Belgium as Donald Trump is in New York. That's because Heyvaert has been busy doling out business advice to young Belgian businesspeople on the country's version of *The Apprentice*, *De Topmanager*, in its 2006 season.

Heyvaert's not a bad person to take advice from—or to win a spot working for, if you're a contestant on *Topmanager*. Before founding Capco in 1998, Heyvaert was CEO and president of Cimad Consultants, a systems integration and professional services firm that he founded in 1989. By the time Heyvaert sold Cimad Consultants to IBM, the firm had grown to be one of the leading consulting and software firms in Europe with over 1,400 people and a $120-million turnover. Until 1998, Heyvaert stayed on at IBM as IBM Global Service's general manager of securities and capital markets, developing the group's overall strategy in these areas.

Heyvaert eventually left IBM and went on to start Capital Markets Company in July 1998, which was rebranded as Capco in 2001. The following year, PriceWaterhouseCooper Consulting's Bill Irving assumed the presidential role at Heyvaert's firm. By that time, Capco had offices in Belgium, London, New York, Frankfurt and Paris, to which facilities in Bangalore and Toronto were added in 2005. The Bangalore office, in particular, has been one of Capco's rising stars. With 100 employees, Capco's Indian operations have gone from being just a service delivery center into a full-fledged consulting outfit, offering consulting services, and technology and managed services to local and international clients.

Transformers

Capco is in the business of transforming companies, ala its tagline, "transformation thinking." The rationale: Average financial services organizations know how to make quick fixes, but great financial services companies will invest in making companywide changes to win in an increasingly competitive market. There is no quick fix for the biggest challenges financial services firms face today, which include securing data management processes in an era of increased regulatory and market scrutiny; improving financial, operational and organizational controls while still being innovative; integrating far-flung businesses as companies keep pace with globalization; getting operations up to speed while managing day-to-day challenges; and raising revenue when margins are tight.

To help companies face these challenges, Capco has developed a set of transformation principles that claim to challenge traditional organizational and technical thinking. Transformation should be "architecture-driven" and implemented continuously; companies should focus on firmwide business services and not break operations up into "organizational silos." According to Capco, even internal business services should be viewed from a competitive commercial perspective. Capco also recommends that firms "embed" enterprise control strategies directly into their core operating processes, streamline and automate workflows, integrate and have companywide access to data, and standardize and centralize organizational infrastructures so that the company and its employees can "digest change" more easily.

Connections count

Over the years, Capco has found friends in high places to help it offer more sophisticated services. Called networked.capco, the firm has developed an industry web of clients, companies, individuals, industry groups and academic partners who connect its clients with the information and business solutions they need. In March 2006, Capco entered into a seven-year agreement with ING Group. As part of the agreement, Capco Reference Data Services will provide managed reference data services to the company through its reference data services division—in a deal that made CRDS the first vendor to provide a managed securities and market reference data service and platform that covers all asset classes and all data types.

The firm also has close relationships with EDS and offshore IT-services companies Wipro and Ness Technologies, to jointly deliver services for clients. In addition, Capco has struck up alliances with service providers, including BEA, Calypso, GL Trade, Microsoft, Omgeo and S.W.I.F.T. to boost its own business savvy and that of its clients.

The Capco Institute

Capco tries to get most of its thoughts on transformation and operational strategy down on paper. The Capco Institute sends out weekly bulletins and in-depth research notes, and regularly publishes its *Journal of Financial Transformation*, "dedicated to the advancement of leading thinking in the field of applied finance." The *Journal* is available online for free to registered users, and has been recognized with an Apex Award for publication excellence. It includes features from some of the world's leading applied finance thinkers from Wharton, IMD International Institute of Management Development, INSEAD, the University of Chicago and the London Business School.

A May 2006 study released by the firm, conducted in conjunction with a research team from the London Business School, found that financial services firms are adopting sourcing lessons from the manufacturing industry, outsourcing and offshoring their operations more and more to increase efficiency. "Financial services … has historically lagged behind manufacturing industries in exploring the opportunities of outsourcing and offshoring—key components of what are known as 'global sourcing models,'" the study reported. It also found that the question in financial services companies' minds is not whether to outsource or offshore their business, but how.

GETTING HIRED

A committed relationship

Capco doesn't hold campus recruiting in the U.S., but rather invites candidates to simply submit resumes through its web site—particularly those who are committed, dedicated and talented, with an interest in capital or global markets. Prospective candidates can peruse the careers pages of the site to search for open positions in eight worldwide offices. Opportunities are organized by location, and candidates are invited to apply online, directly to the office they are most interested in. Applicants who want to get a feel for life at the firm should also take a look at Capital, the firm's online newsletter, which "captures the fun and spirit at the heart of the Capco vision."

Capco stresses that it has an especially diverse group of employees who come from a "rich variety of cultures and languages." The firm asserts that "mutual respect, integrity and commitment" are the common core values that shape its culture.

Visit the Vault Consulting Career Channel at **www.vault.com/consulting** - with insider firm profiles, message boards, the Vault Consulting Job Board and more.

VAULT CAREER LIBRARY   413

Celerant Consulting

45 Hayden Avenue
Lexington, MA 02421
Phone: (781) 674-0400
Fax: (781) 674-0401
www.celerantconsulting.com

LOCATIONS

Lexington, MA (US HQ)
Richmond, UK (Global HQ)
Amsterdam • Brussels • Copenhagen • Düsseldorf • Helsinki
• Oslo • Paris • Stockholm • Toronto • Zurich

PRACTICE AREAS

Asset Management
Business Performance Management
Innovation
Integrated Supply Chain
Organizational Effectiveness
Process Excellence
Revenue Generation

THE STATS

Employer Type: Private Company
CEO: Ian Clarkson
CFO: Malcolm Glyn
President, Celerant Americas: David Henderson
President, Celerant Europe: Eric Guyader
2007 Employees: 600
2006 Employees: 539
2006 Revenue: $145.5 million
2005 Revenue: $133.7 million

UPPER

• "Very satisfying work"

DOWNER

• It can be hard working for a Euro-centric firm

EMPLOYMENT CONTACT

www.celerantconsulting.com/Careers/careers.aspx

THE SCOOP

Operational improvement from the ground up

For 20 years, Celerant has helped companies improve their organizational effectiveness, streamline their business processes, iron out wrinkles in their supply chains, manage their assets and grow revenue. With offices in the U.S., France, Germany, Benelux, the Nordic region, the U.K. and Canada, Celerant is a global management consulting firm specializing in operational improvement, having completed projects in 44 countries since 1987. Over the years, the firm's clients have include BP, Occidental Petroleum, RadioShack, Texas Petrochemicals and Wyeth. Clients come from a wide variety of sectors, including chemicals, energy, consumer goods, insurance, life sciences and health care, manufacturing, metals and mining, pulp and paper, retail, telecommunications and utilities.

Celerant's start

British-born Celerant was founded in 1987 under the nom de guerre Peter Chadwick, the middle names of the firm's two founders. For the next five years, Peter Chadwick grew by more than 50 percent per year and, by the end of the 1990s, the consultancy had expanded, having opened offices across Europe and in the U.S.

In 1997, Peter Chadwick merged with Cambridge Technology Partners, which specialized in technology-based business solutions and was interested in expanding further into Europe. Peter Chadwick changed its name to Cambridge Management Consulting, only to take on the name Celerant Consulting after Cambridge Technology Partners was acquired by software company Novell, Inc., in July 2001 for $266 million in stock.

Life with Novell

Novell's motivation for investing in Cambridge Technology Partners, even if its business was flagging, was to expand its service offerings to include e-business software support, consulting and IT services. For a short while, the deal looked good; revenue rose, thanks in part to the boost from Cambridge Technology Partners and, the following year, due to the acquisition of SUSE Linux. At the same time, any critics of the Cambridge Technology Partners acquisition were quieted by Celerant's revenue increase from $130 million to $150 million in 2004.

But Novell's profitability continued to lag, as the firm still hadn't recovered the market share its NetWare server operating system lost to Microsoft and Linux. In November 2005, the company announced plans to cut costs and return to its core business of open-standards and open-source software. The cuts included the divestiture of Celerant Consulting and its 539 employees, and Novell sold the firm back to Celerant Consulting's management for $77 million in May 2006. The deal was supported by British investment firm Caledonia Investments, which backed the deal with $30 million for a minority stake in the newly independent company.

Getting to know you

Celerant wants to know how its clients really go about their business, meeting them with the right improvements at the right level. It does that by working directly with clients' employees—at both the high and low end of the food chain. "We don't offer any fixed notions or predefined models; we just want to know all about your people, your operations and your business to deliver meaningful, long-term and measurable value."

The close working relationship Celerant fosters with each of its clients is aptly called the Closework® approach. The approach connects technical ideas and solutions with human approaches for engaging employees in improving operational efficiencies across the board. For every engagement, Celerant's consultants first observe how employees go about their work or fix a problem. Then they challenge the management systems with a "thorough yet realistic program of improvement" that includes both technical and tactical changes and builds on existing organizational capabilities.

Visit the Vault Consulting Career Channel at www.vault.com/consulting - with insider firm profiles, message boards, the Vault Consulting Job Board and more.

VAULT CAREER LIBRARY   415

Celerant realizes each engagement is different, however, so its consultants draw on the operational horsepower of its capability and sector centers to provide experienced resources and intellectual property relevant to the client's main operational challenges.

GETTING HIRED

EQ and IQ

Applicants who are interested in working at Celerant should head to the firm's web site to explore available opportunities. Celerant claims to be "expanding rapidly," and therefore is looking to hire qualified individuals. According to the firm, there's no such thing as the "typical Celerant consultant," however recruiters generally look out for experienced consultants who "have EQ (emotional quotient) as well as IQ: the ability to unlock people's potential to do the right thing." Job openings are organized on the site by location and description, and candidates are invited to e-mail a resume and cover letter. A source reports that the hiring process consists of "a phone screening and a minimum of three interviews." Insiders also say that it's a "very fast process with immediate feedback to candidates."

OUR SURVEY SAYS

Stretch your skills

Insiders at Celerant describe a positive working environment, thanks to "the culture, people, can-do attitude and geographical location of offices." Declares a source, "Stretch assignments allow quick personal development. We do very satisfying work. If you like to accomplish things and deliver value to clients, we are a great company to work for." Training also gets high marks from staffers, who say the firm "invests heavily in formal training, both internal and external."

Balance under control

Consultants insist that despite working at least 60 hours a week, there is a reasonable work/life balance at Celerant. "I work hard when on the road, and try to not work during weekends and time with my family," a manager explains. A colleague confirms, "I manage my client commitments and can flex my schedule to allow for a great work/life balance."

The firm gets mediocre ratings for compensation, though, and insiders complain about "weak retirement benefits." But "equity ownership opportunities and special recognition awards" are appreciated perks.

With respect to diversity, Celerant is a place where employees have "extremely diverse backgrounds," though one source admits, "I would like to see more women apply to work for our firm."

Dean & Company

8065 Leesburg Pike, 5th Floor
Vienna, VA 22182
Phone: (703) 506-3900
Fax: (703) 506-3905
www.dean.com

LOCATION

Vienna, VA (HQ)

PRACTICE AREAS

Consumer Products
Energy
Financial Services
Life Sciences
Media & Entertainment
New Technology
Private Equity/M&A Support
Retail Management
Telecommunications

THE STATS

Employer Type: Private Company
Chairman: Dean L. Wilde II
2007 Employees: 70*
2006 Employees: 100

Dean & Company spun off sister firm DC Energy in 2007

RANKING RECAP

Quality of Life
#11 - Travel Requirements

UPPERS

- "Lots of client interaction early on in your career"
- "Generally puts little strain on personal life"
- "They take very good care of their employees"
- Opportunity for rapid salary growth

DOWNERS

- "Longer-term clients means less experiences gained"
- "As a small firm, individual personalities of managers and VPs can come to define your experience on a certain case"
- Many workaholics
- "The IT spending is too low"

EMPLOYMENT CONTACT

www.dean.com/careers/careers.htm

THE BUZZ
WHAT CONSULTANTS AT OTHER FIRMS ARE SAYING ABOUT THIS FIRM

- "Small and innovative"
- "A little socially awkward"
- "Very understanding and kind"
- "Intense and workaholics"

Visit the Vault Consulting Career Channel at **www.vault.com/consulting** - with insider firm profiles, message boards, the Vault Consulting Job Board and more.

VAULT CAREER LIBRARY   417

THE SCOOP

The "value architects"

Dean & Company is in the business of building value. The self-proclaimed "value architects" focus on large companies caught up in changing, turbulent markets such as financial services, life sciences, and telecommunications and wireless, as well as smaller startups that exhibit growth potential. With less than 100 employees, the Vienna, Va.-based firm is small, but its payoff is big. It promises a 15-to-one short-term payback for its clients per engagement, and its consulting projects have realized over $20 billion in cumulative impact since the firm was founded in 1993 by former Mercer Management pros Dean Wilde and James Smist.

Today, Dean's consultants help their clients with pricing, operational effectiveness, mergers and acquisitions, customer targeting and bonding, and with developing new products and delivering them to market. Always on the lookout for new clients, Dean consultants can typically be found scouting out new business in the financial services, life sciences, private equity, telecom, media and entertainment, consumer products, retail management, new technology and energy industries.

Delta details

Co-founder Dean Wilde, his colleagues and MIT Sloan School of Management Professor Arnoldo Hax are the brains behind Dean & Company's brawn. Together, they developed a consulting model in the 1990s that is the cornerstone of the firm's organizing framework: The Delta Model. The concept grew out of the team's belief that the world of business has undergone such significant change that all the old managerial models were incomplete at best, if not obsolete. So said Wilde's and Hax's test group of influential chief executives, who hailed from giant corporations like Saturn, Unilever, Merck and Siemens. At the same time, the team realized it was becoming easier than ever to make contacts and to access information with the advent of the Internet, unlocking previously unimaginable potential for communication and technologies surrounding e-business and e-commerce.

Leaving behind what came before, Wilde, Hax and their cohorts based their consulting model on the core belief that the best way for a company to gain a competitive advantage is not to try to beat out the opposition. Rather, the best way to win is through "bonding," or developing new relationships with customers, suppliers and even competitors.

Breaking it down

The Delta Model can be broken down into four key elements, which Dean & Company promises will make companies more competitive and more successful if implemented together. First, "the triangle" element recommends that a company consider three strategic "positionings" to outperform its competitors: Have the cheapest or most unique product, offer the customer a bigger bang for its buck, and lock in complementary companies or lock out competitors. Second, there are the "adaptive processes," or shaking up a company's core processes so that they are all in sync with the selected "positionings." To make sure everything is going as planned, the third key element is "the metrics," measuring how all of these changes are helping the company. And, not surprisingly, the last element is analyzing those metrics using "experimentation and feedback." Success, the Delta gurus say, "comes not from creating one perfect plan but rather from adapting as the environment changes."

Taking stock in private equity

In 1998, the firm moved to grow its investment advisory services by partnering with Lindsay Goldberg & Bessemer L.P., a New York City-based investment firm with over $5 billion in committed capital. Dean & Company initially just helped to provide Lindsay Goldberg & Bessemer with the insights it needed to carry out due diligence and investment research, but later added business development strategy consulting to its list of services shared in the partnership. Since teaming up with the investment firm, Dean & Company has helped to review over 500 merger and acquisition deals and has achieved historical returns of more than 30 percent. These days, Dean is even investing in startups itself, oftentimes offering consulting services for a combination of fees and equity.

Dean's demands

Only a select few get the chance put The Delta Model into action. Since the firm was founded in 1993, Dean & Company has grown to around 70 employees, with an additional 40 employees in its sister firm, DC Energy, also located in the Vienna, Va., office. It likes to keep its headcount low and its hiring selective; the firm hand-picks candidates with high quantitative aptitude. Almost every analyst or associate that gets through the door probably has a few letters behind his name, too; academic degrees represented at Dean range from undergraduate degrees in biophysics and engineering, to MBAs in strategy and finance, to PhDs in physical chemistry and economics.

But not everyone thinking of applying to Dean & Company has to have a resume full of quantitative/analytical experience. Professionals working at the company have experience in a range of fields, spanning the social sciences, natural and physical sciences, and the humanities.

The employee payback

Dean & Company analysts and associates are regularly reviewed and rewarded for their hard work. The firm prides itself on its collegial and nonhierarchical structure—when someone does a good job they know it. Individuals are promoted purely based on performance, without consideration of seniority. "Promotion is based on a 'speedometer' versus 'odometer' philosophy," the company explains. "It is the individual's skills and drive, rather than tenure, that determine career path." To make sure employees are on the right path, they are regularly reviewed and offered constructive feedback.

GETTING HIRED

Gunning for the big leagues

When it comes to recruiting, Dean & Company doesn't kid around; though the firm does do some local scouting—Wake Forest University, UVA, UNC and Duke are all on its list—graduating Ivies are definitely targeted most, with an especially sharp eye on Princeton, Harvard and Yale. Dean's intimidating list alone makes it perfectly clear that it isn't looking for just anyone to fill consultant shoes.

Despite Dean's choosy nature, though, a Harvard degree and a hefty list of credentials won't get you in the door all too easily; as one consultant says, "Campus recruiting generally involves two rounds of interviews with an emphasis on quantitative case interviews," while another details that the on-campus "hiring process is a single, 30-minute case interview for the first round, and two 45-minute case interviews" for the second.

Brain picking, not teasing

As far as the interviews themselves, many employees comment on Dean & Company's "extremely case-focused" take on the process. One consultant reports that "most cases are based on actual client work, so interviewees shouldn't expect much in the way of brainteasers." Another source recommends that interviewees "expect case interviews that are mathematically and analytically focused." From the get-go, Dean & Company lays out expectations for potential employees, presenting multiple cases that are "more analytical and number-driven than other consulting firms," an employee adds. "Prospective employees are expected to be excellent problem solvers with strong quantitative skills and comfort with numbers."

Hopefuls vying for those coveted positions better prepare themselves for a hard-hitting, whirlwind procedure: All three case interviews are "often over the course of just two days," and "you typically hear back within a week," current analysts say. One staffer adds, "If they like you, they'll fly you up for a sell day"—a day for campus recruits to get to know the firm better.

Visit the Vault Consulting Career Channel at **www.vault.com/consulting** - with insider firm profiles, message boards, the Vault Consulting Job Board and more.

VAULT CAREER LIBRARY   **419**

OUR SURVEY SAYS

A great place to do your TPS reports

Though Dean & Company's recruiting process promises nothing short of rigor and intensity, employees say they feel at ease once inside the firm's doors. Sources gush about an "informal and casual atmosphere," where "90 percent of the doors are open all the time" and where camaraderie thrives. One newbie proudly explains, "We truly do have a very collegial environment in which contributions are valued and used if they are the best, regardless of rank or experience." Staffers are described as "fun," "down to earth" and even lovingly "dorky." Of her colleagues, one analyst says, "I find myself laughing at their jokes and receiving help without complaint."

At Dean & Company, age plays a noteworthy role when it comes to office culture, both inside and outside the firm's walls. "The firm is very young and therefore has a lot of activities geared to young people. We also sometimes go out together on the weekend," reports a first-year employee. A colleague continues, "The analysts are generally a great group of people—there is a large percentage of kids right out of college, which does something to curb the *Office Space* drabness of corporate America."

Gaining access

Dean & Company's environment ranks as young, laid-back and congenial, but how easy is it to approach senior management? One thing is for certain: Rubbing elbows and fostering relationships with senior staff is imperative at the firm, and most sources agree that Dean & Company "has an open-office policy, encouraging easy access to managers, project leaders and VPs." One analyst describes management as "very friendly and open," while a colleague relates, "Experiences vary widely based on who the supervisors are. My experience has been either a 1 or a 10, depending on the person. In general, senior personnel in our firm tend to have extreme personalities, making for excellent or very poor relationships, depending on how compatible those personalities are with junior employees."

The firm's reputation as welcoming, social and close-knit may also have something to do with its smaller size—fewer people means more direct contact with both colleagues and clients. As one first-year analyst shares, the firm "does a good job at giving you client contact when you are ready for it." Another new staffer positively talks up the firm's readiness to push eager rookies into client relationships, saying, "I have had quite a bit of client exposure, which began less than two months after joining the firm. As a first-year analyst, I participate in meetings and communicate with most senior levels of our big pharma client."

Working for the weekend

An open, collegial office environment isn't always enough to keep Dean & Company employees balanced. While most sources agree that "weekend work is typically avoidable," analysts often struggle at first to sustain a gratifying social life outside of work. One insider confides, "Finding time for other activities besides work during the week is much more difficult than I expected. It is almost impossible to attend any regularly scheduled activity, since they're likely to happen between 5 and 9 p.m.—hours that I'm usually working."

Hourly instability for analysts also tends to rupture morale at times. "The real problem," confesses a first-year, "is the unpredictability. Even when the hours are alright, the fact that they can change at any moment is hard to deal with." Staffers report working anywhere from 55 to 75 hours per week, on average, depending on the given project, reporting manager or client relationship. (The firm notes that its long run average has been 55 hours per week over recent history.) "Long workweeks can lead to burnout," a consultant says. Despite the grueling hours, many employees do recognize the firm's attempts to provide balance: "In general, my weekends have been free and one's vacations are respected," an analyst says.

Create your own equilibrium

Because working at a crowned consulting firm like Dean & Company must come with sacrifices, employees concur that "it takes a bit of discipline and planning to prevent work from creeping into your personal life." But, as one analyst reports, separating labor from leisure is not an unattainable fantasy; Dean staffers say they are able to manage some semblance of balance, and "it's certainly possible by establishing work plans that keep certain evenings and weekends free," a consultant states. A co-worker adds, "A lot of your ability to balance work and life depends on your boss and how good you are at knowing when to push back on unrealistic expectations."

Fortunately, Deanies don't need to put travel in the work/life imbalance basket. An insider states, "Travel really depends on the case," but on the whole, staffers are more often office-dwellers than world travelers. "The general balance is toward less travel—the majority of folks are in the office every day," an employee says, while another adds, "A big selling point of the company was the limited amount of travel required."

No training wheels

Though an analyst mentions his one-week training session with the firm, Dean & Company apparently has a loose notion of employee introduction and instruction. We're told that most staffers receive minimal formal training at first—if any at all—and "mostly, you just have to ask for help when learning something new," a consultant explains. While some sources praise this ad hoc prep plan as ultimately effective, others wish for a little more initial guidance. For example, one analyst notes that informal training "is fine for most of the work, but we could use some more programming training," and another chimes in, "Nearly all training is on the job, due to understaffing."

Even if Dean & Company appears short-handed in the formal new-hire coaching department, employees aren't left completely to their own devices. One insider tells us, "They do a good job of mixing official training in once every couple of months, while regularly giving you unofficial training from your co-workers." And sources say that managers make excellent mentors. "I felt that I got a lot of feedback from my manager early on," a staffer reports, and adds, "It was very easy to ask various, more experienced people around the office for help when appropriate."

The good, the bad, the benefits

Despite a few outlying gripes, Dean & Company employees feel adequately compensated for their work. Most analysts report generous signing bonuses and competitive starting salaries. One insider divulges his supreme delight with getting paid even more than his buddies at McKinsey. And the salary transparency in the upper ranks soothes a few first-year nerves, with one insider explaining that "you know what you're working toward." The firm also offers 401(k) and matches 50 percent of up to 8 percent of your salary. But we depart from salary speak, the Deanmobile hits a few potholes. One employee groans about the firm's promotion schedule: "Due to the way our firm schedules career reviews (April/October), you can easily work for one full year without getting a promotion; this leads to a disappointing first-year bonus."

Dean staffers do enjoy an abundance of other company perks. From formally planned, out-of-office proceedings (sporting events, wine tours, ice skating) to more simple affairs (free Friday breakfast and happy hours, expensed dinner if employees stay past 8 p.m., and "nice little social events every month"), the firm plans year-round activities to keep employees upbeat and—we're sure—sane. One analyst shares his enthusiasm for Dean's "extracurricular" planning, with "the highlight being the amazing annual holiday party overlooking the White House."

In the neighborhood

Dean & Company may love to dole out party hats for employees from time to time, but the firm apparently pays little attention to its surrounding communities. Though one insider notes that Dean is "starting to do a charity event each year," sources tell us that community service is conducted primarily on an individual basis. "About 10 analysts volunteer one morning a week at a

Visit the Vault Consulting Career Channel at **www.vault.com/consulting** - with insider firm profiles, message boards, the Vault Consulting Job Board and more.

VAULT CAREER LIBRARY   **421**

local elementary school and no one has any problems with that," an insider reports, but notes that "the firm's feeling on community involvement is that it's fine as long as it doesn't interfere with working."

You stay classy, Dean

Dean staffers have it made when it comes to their working facilities; unlike many offices, they enjoy a cubicle-less universe. "The space is great, and we each have our own office, which we share with another analyst," a first-year says. Another comments, "It is so nice that we actual offices with doors and walls. It is also nice that most of the offices are external with windows. I have a window seat after less than a year of working at the company."

Though the space is "classy and clean," as one analyst reports, staffers do have some beef with the building's geography. "The only negative is that it is in Vienna, not D.C.," says an employee, and it's "a bit isolated—just a bunch of urban sprawl 15 minutes outside of D.C.," another complains. Fortunately, though, employees aren't completely cut off from civilization; Dean is positioned adjacent to a mall, which is a good thing, even if "traffic is terrible, especially around the holidays," according to a source. So those saving their weekends for kick-back can rest assured: "There are a lot of things around the office, so if you need to run errands, you can do them on your lunch break."

Casting call

Championed for its accepting staff and open-door policy, Dean & Company still has work to do when it comes to diversity. As one insider reports, the firm only has "six women out of 40 consulting staff," and another observes that women are "treated as equals, but make up a small percentage of the company." Some sources cite Dean & Company's narrowed scientific and analytical focus as the reason for its male-dominated atmosphere—"it seems to be an uphill battle"—but one first-year expresses a general consensus when he says that "it is not from a lack of trying on the recruiting side." As a female employee remarks, "Dean & Company has good intentions (interviewing and hiring women is a priority)," but she and her colleagues still note the noticeable lack of women in the management ranks.

Similar sentiments are expressed with regard to racial minorities at the firm. "We don't have a single African-American consultant, but I don't think that this is an issue, because the firm would surely extend an offer to a qualified candidate," a consultant asserts. Most staffers agree that when push comes to shove, Dean is ultimately about performance. "They are simply unwilling to change their high standards for an American ideal of diversity," remarks a source.

And while the firm may lack in women and minority staff, colleagues speak optimistically about Dean's openness when it comes to sexual orientation. "We have a number of gay analysts and at least one gay man in management," a staffer shares, while another adds that "one's sexual orientation is irrelevant here."

Deutsche Post World Net Inhouse Consulting

1200 South Pine Island Road
Suite 210
Plantation, FL 33324
Phone: (954) 888-7000
Fax: (954) 424-7763
www.ic.dpwn.com

LOCATIONS

Bonn (HQ)
Ft. Lauderdale, FL
Singapore

PRACTICE AREAS

Benchmarking
Business Strategy & Business Development
Customer Services
Financial Management
Mergers Management
Organizational & Change Management
Process Design & Optimization
Project Management

THE STATS

Employer Type: Subsidiary of Deutsche Post World Net
CEO: Dr. Klaus Zumwinkel
2007 Employees: 140
2006 Employees: 120
2006 Revenue: €60.5 billion (DPWN)
2005 Revenue: €44.6 billion (DPWN)

UPPERS

• Lots of exposure to senior management
• "International culture"

DOWNERS

• "Extremely detail-oriented"
• Very structured environment

EMPLOYMENT CONTACT

Jeane Hah-Garnett
Head of Recruitment—Americas
Phone: (954) 888-7000
E-mail: ic.recruiting@dhl.com

Visit the Vault Consulting Career Channel at **www.vault.com/consulting** - with insider firm profiles, message boards, the Vault Consulting Job Board and more.

VAULT CAREER LIBRARY   423

THE SCOOP

Serving a German giant

When Deutsche Post World Net, the German mail and logistics behemoth, needs consulting help, it doesn't have to look far—it calls on subsidiary DPWN Inhouse Consulting, a group that offers "services that can compete with the best the market has to offer," the firm says. DPWN Inhouse Consulting also acts as a sort of farm team for its giant parent company, helping to "develop future executives for the group" from among its consultant ranks.

Growing strong

Inhouse Consulting has made its mark worldwide within a relatively short timeframe, growing from just three consultants in 1999 to more than 140 in 2007, and taking on more than 50 projects a year. That's just the beginning—DPWN says it aims to grow its staff to about 200. Based in DPWN's German headquarters in Bonn, the group hires about 25 percent of its consultants from elsewhere in the world, and has offices in Ft. Lauderdale, Fla., and Singapore. About 80 consultants work out of the German office. Meanwhile, the Florida office, employing about 20 consultants, focuses on projects for DHL's Americas business, and the Singapore branch, opened in 2006, works on DHL-oriented engagements with a "very international team."

Born from Germany's formerly state-owned postal system, parent company DPWN is a true global giant, employing 500,000 people worldwide. The corporation is made up of three divisions, DHL, Deutsche Post and Postbank, which offers mail, express and logistics, and finance services. The Inhouse Consulting team works directly with management in each of these areas, often working directly on site with clients. The group's services include business strategy and development, organizational and change management, mergers management, process design and optimization, customer services, financial management, benchmarking and project management.

Strategy at work

A typical project for the group involves tackling and streamlining the complex business processes at play in a corporate giant like DPWN. When DPWN acquired shipping company DHL in 2001, it faced the challenge of integrating it with another recently acquired freight company, Danzas. DPWN's air freight divisions were fragmented, with DHL operating a combination of its own and commercial aircraft, and Danzas mostly relying on commercial air. IC was tasked with building a single framework to improve the effectiveness of the corporation's air freight services. The consultants' solution involved forming an airfreight carrier organization with standardized processes and procedures.

In another engagement, the group worked with DHL Express to develop a customer service benchmarking framework. With customer service departments in nearly every country around the world, DHL Express developed a separate customer service group, Key Account Desk, which provides exclusive services to the company's most valuable customers. But demand for these services exceeded capacity, and DHL needed a way to standardize and enlarge its processes worldwide. IC worked with the company to identify best practices, develop benchmarks and come up with a consistent KAD concept, which was then piloted in the U.S.

In late 2006, Inhouse Consulting supported a DPWN-wide quality program called First Choice. IC was responsible for defining the customer experience/touchpoint framework and development; consolidating market research and processing key performance indicators into a scorecard; and implementing continuous process improvement methodology. The IC team has subsequently built a roadmap and a reporting framework, and kicked off 20-plus process improvement initiatives.

GETTING HIRED

Focus on fit

DPWN recruits from a large number of North American business schools, as well as "nonbusiness degree schools (engineering, mathematics/physics/chemistry)." Among the chosen campuses are Georgetown, Thunderbird School of Global Management, Duke, Emory, McGill and Rotman. Sources tell us that the process is "very extensive," beginning with a phone interview and ending with a trip to Germany.

The firm's interview process is a structured routine comprising three stages. A source explains, "There is a phone interview consisting of half-an-hour of resume and half-an-hour of a minor business case. In the second part, there are three one-hour, in-person interviews in Fort Lauderdale—one being more CV-based and two being case-based." Applicants travel to the headquarters for the final interview round. A consultant reports, "The third part is a one-day assessment center in Germany, focusing on team fit, presentation ability, sales skills and degree of structure."

An example of a case question might be: "How does a reduction of speed limit on highways affect the DHL Express business?" And while the questioning is rigorous, interviewers are also interested in a candidate's personality. Reveals an insider, "There is a lot of emphasis on quantitative skills and analytics for junior job levels, and more emphasis on project management and selling skills for more senior job levels. There is extremely high attention to team fit."

OUR SURVEY SAYS

Jump right in

DPWN sources laud the "great team atmosphere" and distinctly "international focus" that characterizes this in-house group of consultants. An insider praises, "We are a small boutique consulting firm that does not make you an anonymous number, but offers you the opportunity to grow with us and our clients' challenges. If you want to work on exciting, international projects, we are the place to be." One junior staffer appreciates the "integration of personal preferences into staffing decisions," while another mentions that consultants are given "responsibility from day one," adding, "It's perfect preparation for a management job."

Being at a small firm also means there is tons of "exposure to senior management," both within the firm and at the client. "There is amazing access to key management—I am directly in contact with the leaders of this organization," declares one associate. And Inhouse Consulting's unique positioning within DPWN gives consultants even more of an opportunity to work with higher-ups. An insider asserts, "Since we are internal consultants, the relationship to the whole management board is very intense and cooperative."

"Culture of learning"

Staffers are pleased with DPWN's "strong culture of learning and personal development." According to respondents, there is a lot of opportunity to gauge individual progress. "The company has a culture strong in direct feedback, constructive criticism and challenge," a manager tells us. A colleague mentions that "each consultant is assigned a personal developer and semiannual personal developer meetings are held to discuss progress and identify improvement areas."

Sources also say that there is a well-rounded program of formal training at IC. "There is good opportunity for training, and formal training is quite good. On-the-job coaching is common, especially at entry levels," explains an insider. Regarding formal training, "We offer 10 days per year [for each] employee, on top of on-the-job training. There are some standard training classes—basic, advanced or experienced consulting skills—a training catalogue and the opportunity for individual training or coaching." Sources note that the emphasis on learning and development is part of an effort to groom leaders from the consulting

Visit the Vault Consulting Career Channel at www.vault.com/consulting - with insider firm profiles, message boards, the Vault Consulting Job Board and more.

VAULT CAREER LIBRARY   425

division for the parent company. "One of our missions is to develop future executives for the group, and we strongly support our leavers to find matching jobs within the group."

Weekends not required—usually

Employees reveal that work hours at the firm are reasonable, and weekends are not part of the deal. A partner says, "I'm working about 45 to 50 hours a week. On weekends I am checking my e-mails occasionally, which will take up to two hours, but I've never worked through a complete day on a weekend." The source adds, "Still, I would like to spend some more time on the tennis court, but I accept that this is consulting."

The firm notes that 50 to 55 hours a week is a fairly accurate average for most consultants. Altogether, insiders find the schedule quite bearable. Suggests one newbie, "The duration and intensity take some getting used to following grad school, but overall there is a good balance, given the kind of fast-track learning that accompanies the position." The majority of projects are in the three- to six-month range, staffers tell us.

"Compared to other consultancies, work/life balance is great at DPWN," one consultant praises, but adds, "Nevertheless, this is not a line function, so from time to time projects require late hours." Even with occasional long days, the consensus is that work/life balance is achievable. "I can balance my work and life and also try to accommodate my team members' needs. Weekends are taboo for me, and I don't expect my team to work on weekends either," expresses a manager. In fact, weekends are off limits for most of these staffers. Remarks a co-worker, "The company discourages weekend work and is good at promoting vacation usage."

You determine the travel

Insiders say that at IC there's an opportunity to travel internationally, but it's not an absolute must. One insider claims, "The amount of travel is dependent on your own willingness. There is always a minimum requirement for travel; however, if you communicate early on that you do not want to travel, project staffing will reflect that as much as possible." Another co-worker mentions, "I only travel when necessary, and many times internationally, which is fun. Many times the client is in the same area where we are because we all work for the same company." Another consultant points out the realities of travel—both positive and negative: "You can only get the exciting projects in Europe and Asia when you travel—it's not possible without. But sometimes, travel makes extra night shifts inevitable."

Take a sabbatical

For a small firm, DPWN is pretty big on perks. One insider mentions the "company car at project manager level," while a co-worker loves the "in-office espresso machine." Then there's the generous tuition policy—"MBA tuition reimbursement up to $40,000 in installments spread over three years" for employees who qualify. Insiders also report that in true European fashion, the firm is liberal about time-off policies. "We can take three months of unpaid leave after one year of working. And we can take a year of sabbatical," explains a consultant.

Staffers are also pumped about the chance for travel to any of the firm's offices around the world. "Our international exposure is outstanding! If you want to work on an engagement in Europe or if you want to be staffed on a project in Asia, the company supports it," a source enthuses. Adds a manager, "The firm offers an assignment to global projects if preferences are communicated early on." Annual trips abroad are another plus for this jet-set group, explains a colleague: "We have the opportunity to attend global strategy conference in Europe each summer."

Sources also give high ratings to compensation at the firm. One insider breaks down the way bonus is calculated, explaining, "Bonus is split in two components: performance (effort and project work) and career development." Compensation is "very performance-driven. And performance-related bonus is as high as 30 percent of total compensation," shares one source.

Waving their flags

Though minority diversity is not a big focus at the firm, insiders report a growing range of cultural diversity at the firm, due to its international roots. "As our consultancy expanded out of Germany 18 months ago, the majority of senior executives are German. However, as most of our new hires are from multiple ethnic backgrounds (our Americas office consists of 16 people from eight different countries), diversity across all job levels is just a matter of time," a source opines. For now, though, "it's a very international group, but some minorities are underrepresented," notes a staffer.

With respect to gender representation, consultants suggest that DPWN is doing a good job. "We have had women on all job levels (including partner), and the share of female employees (estimated at 45 percent) roughly equals the share of female applicants," an employee points out. And a manager states, "There is no quota on minorities. The hiring process focuses on skills and experience much more than on [gender] and race."

Volunteering globally

Consultants at DPWN are active in volunteering efforts, mostly through consulting for humanitarian organizations—"we do pro bono consulting for the United Nations in Indonesia," a source reports. A European colleague says, "All of us (about 130 people) renovated a kindergarten in Eastern Germany last summer," while a colleague mentions "sending footballs to Africa" as another officewide initiative. In addition to the consulting group's efforts, employees have the chance to get involved in the community through their parent company and sister subsidiaries. Comments an associate, "DHL is very active in community relations and involvement. We get a lot of opportunities to volunteer."

Visit the Vault Consulting Career Channel at **www.vault.com/consulting** - with insider firm profiles, message boards, the Vault Consulting Job Board and more.

VAULT CAREER LIBRARY   427

Droege & Comp.

405 Lexington Avenue, 35th Floor
New York, NY 10174
Phone: (212) 557-7616
Fax: (212) 557-6788
www.droegeusa.com

LOCATIONS

Düsseldorf (HQ)
New York, NY
Bucharest
Budapest
Hamburg
London
Lucerne
Moscow
Mumbai
Munich
Paris
Shanghai
Singapore
Vienna
Warsaw

PRACTICE AREAS

Change/Communication
Financial Management
Operational Excellence
Organization/Leadership
Private Equity
Strategy/Portfolio
Turnaround Management

THE STATS

Employer Type: Private Company
Chairman & CEO: Dr. Christian Horn
CFO: Thomas K. Scheffold
2006 Employees: 350
2005 Employees: 325

UPPERS

- "The building is fabulous"
- Opportunity to advance quickly

DOWNERS

- "Sometimes feels like an American 'island' office because all of our corporate collateral is in Germany"
- Very competitive

EMPLOYMENT CONTACT

Droege & Comp.
Attn.: Recruiting
405 Lexington Avenue, 35th Floor
New York, NY 10174
Phone: (212) 557-7616
Fax: (212) 557-6788
E-mail: recruiting_newyork@droegeusa.com
Recruiting Coordinator: Ms. Terri Harris

THE SCOOP

Pragmatic solutions

Founded in 1988 by Walter P.J. Droege, Düsseldorf-headquartered Droege & Comp. currently ranks as Germany's second-largest consulting firm. Droege is an autonomous, globally operated business consultancy and is a subsidiary of the Droege International Group AG, a company group with more than 2,000 employees. The firm operates 15 offices across Asia, Europe and North America, servicing a wide range of top-500 and midsize companies. Droege bills itself as "the pioneer in implementation-oriented top management consulting"; in practice, this means the 245 Droege consultants strive to provide practical solutions, as opposed to relying heavily on theory-based strategy papers. The firm's pragmatic emphasis extends to all areas of the company's business—the firm focuses on helping its clients save money and, instead of billing hourly, offers a results-based fee structure.

Droege offers six main areas of services: change/communication, financial management, operational excellence, organization/leadership, strategy/portfolio and turnaround management. It also engages in private equity by supporting midsize PE funds with due diligence work and value improvement of their portfolio companies. Fifty percent of the firm's clients are industrial, 30 percent are drawn from the financial services sector and the remaining 20 percent are other service-based companies. Many senior consultants have previous management-level experience in one of these sectors before coming to Droege—this industry-based training allows senior Droege consultants to more effectively aid in the on-site implementation of new strategies.

I'll show you the results, you show me the money

Droege was one of the first consulting firms to advocate the increasingly popular results-based method for billing. In a position paper from January 2007, Droege Chairman Dr. Christian Horn touted this fee structure as a "win-win" for clients and consultants alike: Clients benefit from being able to set, in conjunction with the consultant, quantifiable objectives with measurable results. The emphasis on measurable results not only forces the consultant to focus on implementation, as opposed to strategy alone, but also allows the consultant to potentially realize a greater "return on consulting" for successfully meeting objectives.

Midsize firms and private equity

In 2006, Droege continued to expand its services to midlevel private equity and hedge fund clients. North American clients typically hire Droege to conduct in-depth market and strategic due diligence. In December 2006, the firm hosted a symposium on investment opportunities for American companies in distressed European economies. Droege highlighted the numerous opportunities available, particularly in Germany, a market with which Droege is intimately familiar. In May 2007, Droege held another conference in London, together with the London Business School Private Equity Institute and Kirkland & Ellis International LLP, called the Distressed Debt & Turnaround Forum—Prospect for Active Investing in Europe.

The firm places a particular emphasis on helping midsize companies with international growth, and seeks to provide the "experience, networks, market data and temporary concentrated manpower" that midsize firms are typically unable to provide in-house when looking to make a targeted entry into a foreign market. To this end, the firm operates local branch offices in "high-potential regions"—those that aren't yet completely saturated by foreign businesses. Droege is currently expanding into the Central and Eastern European markets with offices in Bucharest and Moscow, and is showing keen interest in developments in Asia as well, with offices in Mumbai, Shanghai and Singapore.

Going global

"Internationalization is no longer the exclusive domain of big business," says Droege. More and more of the consultancy's projects are carrying it overseas and, as a result, its international consulting portfolio has continued to grow, along with its business expertise. Globalization brings with it a whole new set of business problems for Droege to solve, like figuring out

Visit the Vault Consulting Career Channel at www.vault.com/consulting - with insider firm profiles, message boards, the Vault Consulting Job Board and more.

VAULT CAREER LIBRARY   429

market entry and sales strategies for foreign markets, creating value-added strategies involving new partnering business models and maintaining an efficient international corporate structure, as well as restructuring international subsidiaries.

Midsized enterprises have a much harder time going global than larger companies with bigger budgets. They often lack the experience, networks, manpower and readily available market data to target a foreign market. For this reason, Droege markets itself as a "general contractor" for internationalization that can offer regional expertise, global presence, implementation-oriented project design and its integrated business offerings.

International team players

Many new Droege hires will have earned an economics, engineering or science degree from a top-level undergraduate institution, followed up with either an MBA or doctorate degree. As the firm focuses heavily on hands-on implementation, previous work experience is strongly desired, and the Euro-centric nature of Droege's business requires consultants to "move confidently in the international arena." Recent undergrads may join Droege through the firm's fellowship program; fellows are placed on-site for two to three months, during which time the firm evaluates the candidates' performance. Whether joining Droege as an experienced or new hire, it is essential that consultants be comfortable working in close coordination with clients to implement new strategies.

GETTING HIRED

In on the action

Droege's campus recruiting is concentrated at top-10 MBA programs like Wharton, Columbia and NYU. The firm looks for candidates with degrees in economics, engineering or science, especially those individuals with experience working overseas. The firm's fellowship program is a two- to three-month internship for "students fresh from university, as well as career beginners." Fellows are thrust into real consulting engagements, working as part of a consulting team. Interested applicants can find out about upcoming recruiting events and apply for positions online, all through the career pages of the firm's web site.

Interviews are reportedly heavy on the case studies, an associate suggests: "There are case studies, a personality fit and a 20-minute PowerPoint presentation on yourself and your fit with Droege. Case studies typically consist of market sizing, visually representing data, business understanding and others."

OUR SURVEY SAYS

Friendly and fast paced

Droege staffers are a collegial and close-knit group. As an insider expresses, "So far, the U.S. practice still has that small-firm entrepreneurial environment, which is devoid of office politicking typical of big firms." A colleague describes the firm as "a good group of very smart consultants who are committed to doing the best possible work for the client, but also enjoy going out for a beer occasionally—we are a German firm after all." That's not to downplay the serious, "very performance-oriented" side of consultants at the firm, however. Assures an analyst, "[The firm hires] graduates from top MBA programs and alumni of top consulting firms. This makes for very high standards. It's a fast-paced and demanding environment. Only those who agree with this type of scene will fit in well."

They love a challenge

Though it's not exactly a laid-back atmosphere, associates appreciate the "commitment and energy" and "exciting projects" that they find at Droege. "The learning experience is great—we are working with some of the brightest consultants around, and the work is very interesting," asserts one staffer. A colleague echoes the sentiment: "Droege offers an incredibly unique learning experience and greater business exposure than other consulting firms. The hands-on approach to consulting, the generalist model, and performance-based fees make Droege very practical, as well as successful, in this new consulting age."

Sources say that there's a lot to like about Droege, including a "good work/life balance" overall. Insiders note that while it "can be a struggle," the key to maintaining a healthy balance is personal initiative. Explains a consultant, "Accountability is built into the work/life balance choices you make, but no one forces you." "We also have greater independence in managing client expectations so work/life balance issues are easier to control than at traditional general management consultancies," a staffer urges. Another source notes that often, balance is determined by the supervisor: "As with any consulting firm, project demands and work environments are very personality-dependent. The project manager sets the tone, so one's experience can go either way, depending on how one's personality agrees with one's project manager."

Meetings in the Mediterranean

Insiders also appreciate Droege's open-door policy and the "supportive upper management." Aside from that, one analyst is excited that he is "a part of a German company when Germany is such a hot market, especially [in the areas of] private equity and distressed investing." Along with "competitive compensation," sources rave about "great perks, such as company summer summits in the Mediterranean and Christmas parties in Germany, which help us to get to know people from other offices."

Full speed ahead

The ambitious atmosphere at Droege works well for those who want to move up at a rapid pace. "There is no constraint on speed of advancement for talented individuals—it is possible to make principal within only a few years," explains an insider. As far as an up-or-out policy, a colleague reports that "it's left up to the project manager or the consultant to make that final choice." When it comes to moving up the Droege ladder, "expectations are high," a consultant reports. "As a small, elite firm, we don't have the resources to train or coach consultants, so we only hire experienced staff that can contribute from day one and help build business."

As such, Droege's training philosophy seems to suit those comfortable taking matters into their own hands. "There is little training infrastructure in the associate program, however it is growing very steadily. Instead, training takes place on the job with constant advice and critique from management or learning things yourself. New hires are expected to be self-starters and be relatively prepared," one manager expresses. Affirms another source, "Colleagues are always incredibly helpful and are always wanting to help and teach. Most senior hires are expected to have had training from top firms."

Off and on travel

For a number of staffers, "travel is only [required] when it is really needed." One colleague notes, "Some consultants usually do the typical 3-4-5 week," but adds that not all consultants may be required to travel, since there's "plenty of work to be done in the office as well." Staffers who do travel often tell us that it can be disruptive: "The travel schedule, which is fixed and not on an as-needed basis, can make the travel schedule more difficult. Civilian and social life during the week is missed, but that's part of a consultant's life," a source concedes. And for those itching to see more of the world, a co-worker mentions that "there are opportunities to work in other offices, if desired."

Visit the Vault Consulting Career Channel at **www.vault.com/consulting** - with insider firm profiles, message boards, the Vault Consulting Job Board and more.

VAULT CAREER LIBRARY   **431**

Easton Associates, LLC

555 Fifth Avenue, 7th Floor
New York, NY 10017
Phone: (212) 901-0999
Fax: (212) 901-2999
www.eastonassociates.com

LOCATION

New York, NY (HQ)

PRACTICE AREAS

Corporate Development
Due Diligence Analysis
Health Care Industry
Marketing Strategy
Opportunity Assessment
Strategy Development

THE STATS

Employer Type: Private Company
Managing Directors: Robert Friedman, Michelle Hasson,
  Kristine Lowe & Marie Cassese
2007 Employees: 40
2006 Employees: 34

RANKING RECAP

Quality of Life
#7 - Work/Life Balance
#9 - Hours in the Office
#17 - Travel Requirements

Diversity
#3 - Diversity for Women

UPPERS

- "Emphasis on morale"
- "The workload is reasonable and the project topics are extremely interesting"
- Quality of life
- "We're a growing firm with a burgeoning client base, which makes it a really exciting place to be"

DOWNERS

- "Chronically tight resources"
- Hurried knowledge acquisition and inadequate training
- "We could work on marketing ourselves better"
- Insufficient "recognition for excellent work"

EMPLOYMENT CONTACT

www.eastonassociates.com/careers.shtml

THE SCOOP

Health nuts

Easton Associates isn't the biggest kid on the block, but it is one of the most focused. For 20 years, the consultants at Easton Associates have targeted their expertise on the health care industry, advising companies in the pharmaceuticals, biotechnology, diagnostics, and medical supplies, devices and equipment industries. Based in New York City, the firm employs about 40 professionals who take their cues from four managing directors, three of whom were former consultants with The Wilkerson Group, a strategy consulting firm to pharmaceutical, biotech, medical supply and technology device companies.

The firm's typical clients are senior executives in the U.S., Europe and Asia charged with the design, development, manufacture, sale and distribution of medical products, as well as investors interested in the business of medicine. For their money, clients get help searching for opportunities in various health care markets, developing business and marketing strategies, finding potential business partners and performing third-party due diligence for possible acquisitions, alliances or financing projects.

A watchful eye

Easton Associates fills in the business gaps clients may be too busy or too subjective to fill. Since its founding, EA consultants have been surveying the medical market, following developments in the industry via their ongoing projects, staying on top of cutting-edge research and attending high-level conferences, like the Windhover Neuroscience Therapeutic Alliance Series, which the firm co-sponsored in October 2006 with AstraZeneca, Merck and NI Research. The meeting brought together business development and R&D professionals with the goal of facilitating drug commercialization partnerships.

The firm prides itself on long-term client relationships, from which it has managed to develop an extensive network of physicians and clinicians who help EA professionals evaluate new product concepts and medical businesses. The firm's web of medical executives and administrators from the medical device, pharmaceutical, investment banking and medical venture communities also helps pinpoint current trends, unmet needs and upcoming developments in the market.

Changing of the guard

In October 2006, Easton Associates announced that its founder, Robert J. Easton, was stepping down to pursue other interests in the health care industry. For the firm's leadership, Easton's move signaled the end of a very long and close-knit relationship. Three of the firm's four managing directors worked with Easton to build The Wilkerson Group, which was bought out by IBM in 1996 for $20 million. Easton stayed on with IBM for four years as managing director of IBM Healthcare Consulting, but in 2000 decided to found his namesake consultancy, with the help of former Wilkerson staffers and current EA Managing Directors Robert Friedman, Michelle Hasson and Kristine Lowe.

While relinquishing his responsibilities at EA, Easton's reputation continues to loom large over the health care consulting industry. He remains on as a director of CollaGenex Pharmaceuticals and Cepheid, and continues to speak frequently for medical industry and investment groups, even winning the Jerry Goldsmith Award for Excellence from the American Association of Clinical Chemistry and the Diagnostics Marketing Association for his contributions to the diagnostics industry.

New faces at the helm

Managing Directors Friedman, Hasson and Lowe—all Wilkerson alumni—boast strong resumes rife with consulting and industry experience. Friedman was a biotech senior equities analyst on Wall Street before hooking up with Easton. Hasson draws on her experience as a marketing and business development strategist at the United States Surgical Corporation and as a former health care consultant at Deloitte & Touche. And Lowe hails from the medical device industry, having managed The Wilkerson Group's cardiovascular information service for a number of years. Managing Director Marie Cassese draws on her experience as a senior executive in several multihospital systems in New Jersey and Pennsylvania.

Visit the Vault Consulting Career Channel at www.vault.com/consulting - with insider firm profiles, message boards, the Vault Consulting Job Board and more.

VAULT CAREER LIBRARY   433

GETTING HIRED

The one-two punch

Harvard and UPenn seem to be Easton's most championed recruiting campuses for research associate candidates—"they make up the bulk of the staff," we're told—but the firm also likes to pluck candidates from Princeton, Wesleyan, Williams, Columbia, Kellogg, The Johnson School at Cornell and Yale, rounding out an impressive list. When scouting for undergrads and grad students, the screening process first takes shape as a 35-minute on-campus, in-person session, "then we invite a subset of candidates back to our office in New York City for the second round," shares a consultant. During round two, candidates should expect "a series of four to five interviews, each lasting 30 to 45 minutes." And since Easton's headcount just tops 40, the interview process places great emphasis on company fit, "so interviewees meet with many staff members, and an overall assessment is made as to not only the intelligence and capability of doing work, but the likelihood of contributing to the overall culture of the firm," a first-year research associate says.

Do your homework

Easton's unique interview approach is apparent during the case interview segment. Contenders receive the case prior to the office interview and, for this take-home portion, must prepare a PowerPoint presentation. "This is a bit trickier," explains a new hire, "but the key here is to synthesize all of the data points and focus on the strategy aspect of the presentation." Case questions are considered "very straightforward," with particular emphasis on the health care industry. Sources say they have been asked to "assess the market for a new weight-loss drug," predict the future for obesity and bariatric surgery markets, and analyze opportunities for drug therapy. As one Easton principal explains, the firm strives to provide "real-world consulting situations/problems to discuss."

OUR SURVEY SAYS

A very Brady firm

From what employees divulge, Easton's office culture seems more like a *Brady Bunch* episode than one of a hard-hitting consulting firm. One research associate boasts that the firm is "a true family atmosphere," and "there is a lot of EA pride." Easton staffers love to socialize with their "quirky" co-workers, whom they peg as "very interesting and unique people who have a great combination of industry and world insight." This close-knit group helps to foster a relaxed, welcoming environment "with little hierarchy and a real passion for client service." As one first-year proudly concludes, "The people are very intellectual, obsessed by health care and that's it!"

Buffer-free zone

Easton's small-firm advantage also encompasses supervisor interaction, with staffers reporting easy access to their senior counterparts. "There are no buffers between employees and the partners here," a source states, which positions Easton as "not a typical consulting firm in that respect." And having chummy rapport with superiors also allows for speedier trust with clients. "I have the opportunity to work closely with both our management and our clients' top-level managers," an insider reports, while a consultant agrees that his colleagues "are highly encouraged to accept a meaningful part of the client interaction and relationship." Eastonites are allowed to enter into client affiliations during nearly all growth stages with the firm, which one seasoned co-worker believes "offers significant opportunity to demonstrate leadership and take ownership of projects at all levels. Everyone gets a chance to defend the credibility of our work to the most critical audience."

Ditching the premises

Because employees claim that they rarely work more than 60 hours per week, obtaining a work/life balance isn't much of a chore. One associate says the hours are "very reasonable, particularly for New York," and declares that she doesn't "know any New Yorker who works less than nine hours a day." Needless to say, Easton staffers count their blessings. "So long as you're doing good work, nobody is watching the clock," sums up a senior associate consultant.

Though some report feeling the inevitable deadline crunch from time to time, increased office-dwelling rarely rates among consultants as suffocating. "The office is dead by 7 p.m. and on weekends," a source states, citing the firm's flexibility and willingness to let "people complete work from home" and noting that "this is not a firm about unnecessary face time." Employees say the balance they experience is unparalleled in the consulting business, and exists because "much of our work is expertise-based and does not require us to be at the client site," explains a principal. Consultants say weekend work is generally a no-no, and most shake their head at after-hours work, with one experienced consultant affirming that he has done weekend work only a few times over the course of his Easton tenure.

Homeward bound

Also contributing to Easton's balance satisfaction is travel infrequency. Since face-to-face client interaction mainly occurs only "for interim and final meetings or for medical conferences," consultants are normally able to remain homebodies. Insiders say the travel necessity surfaces about once every three to six weeks, and that this "home-based" approach "allows more synergy of ideas among team members." But when client elbow-rubbing needs to happen, "it provides a nice change of pace. It allows you to get out of the office, interact with clients or immerse yourself in an interesting conference," shares a senior consultant. Because employees are not forced to hit the road too often, most say they don't feel the negative effects of travel and can reliably schedule social engagements without untimely disruptions.

See no, speak no, hear no training

Where training is concerned, the compliments come to a halt. Easton staffers gripe about the "see one, do one, teach one" instruction model, and mark it as "one of the downsides of the firm." One source says that "while a few days are set aside in the fall with the incoming class, most training is gained through talking to other employees and learning by doing." And because a structured, formal training program is out of commission, associates report being thrown to the wolves; as one newer hire confesses, "Initial projects are often not staffed appropriately to give new hires a chance to learn." Another newbie notes the laundry list of mistakes made in on-the-job training, contributing to wasted hours struggling to understand project requirements.

On the upside, Easton's noncompetitive nature tends to leverage some stress in the apprenticeship department. As one colleague admits, "This could be viewed as a positive or negative, but I really appreciated being thrown right into a project on my first day—everyone is extremely friendly and willing to help." And since the process is heavily dependent upon helping hands in the office, "a new employee's experience can vary based on who he works with on his project," we're told.

Wealth woes

Compensation at EA doesn't invoke many whoops for joy, either. Associates report a decent benefits package—including comprehensive health insurance, 401(k), eventual share vesting and a pretax flexible spending account—but flinch at in-pocket reimbursement. "One of the biggest issues with this firm is compensation," shares an associate, with a first-year offering a suggestion: "I think more frequent, smaller increases would be better than less frequent, larger increases." In addition, "the promotion track, especially at entry-level, is extremely difficult," we're told, which can put a bit of a damper on morale; one new employee cites the firm's high turnover rate, observing a number of his colleagues walking out over the past six months. The firm notes, however, that it maintains a clear promotion track for consultants: Research associates are promoted to associate consultant in 18 months; senior associate consultants are promoted to consultant in one year; and consultants are promoted to senior consultant in two years. Easton also states that all employees receive an annual review, raise and bonus.

Visit the Vault Consulting Career Channel at **www.vault.com/consulting** - with insider firm profiles, message boards, the Vault Consulting Job Board and more.

 435

But while compensation may not be up to snuff for some, others feel that the trade-off is fair "when taking the work/life balance into account, and considering the fact that I make just a little less than friends who work far, far longer hours," remarks a consultant. Money aside, staff members gladly welcome the extra perks provided, such as holiday parties, summer picnics, "free EA gear (shirts, gym bags, etc.)," a car service and "Monday lunches with outside experts on health care topics," insiders say.

Snacker's paradise

Most Eastoners give credit to the office digs, "conveniently located in the heart of Midtown" Manhattan. We're told that the space "could use new carpeting," but employees appreciate the locale, fresh flowers and plants, and moving room aplenty. One associate praises his work area, exclaiming, "My cubicle is bigger than my bedroom!" And amid raptures over abundant space and pleasant appearance, another staffer extols the "large kitchen, where fruit/snacks/drinks can always be found in abundance— and free of charge," while a colleague gives three cheers to the "endless supply of Girl Scout cookies."

Run your heart out, Easton

While the firm tackles a handful of community service initiatives, Easton staffers say efforts have declined in past years, "especially as one of the motivators in the office has left," an associate explains. Mostly, participation involves events like the Chase Corporate Challenge and the Revlon Run/Walk for Women, along with office food, book and toy drives. Others report concerts, marathons and "participation in an urban professional volleyball league" among Easton's contributions.

Female friendly

Women are more than welcome and accepted at the firm. In fact, sources say "at least half, if not more, of the senior management are women," with further acknowledgement from employees stating that "three of the four managing directors are women." Historically speaking, says one principal, "this has always been a firm with nearly equal numbers of very bright men and women." Easton also prides itself on promoting equal representation with regard to minorities; says one associate, "We have all ethnicities represented."

Exeter Group

One Canal Park
Cambridge, MA 02141
Phone: (617) 494-1600
Fax: (617) 528-5021
www.exeter.com

LOCATIONS

Cambridge, MA (HQ)
Los Angeles, CA
New York, NY
San Francisco, CA
Washington, DC

PRACTICE AREAS

Assessment, Planning & Strategy
Business Intelligence & Data Warehousing
Custom Application Development
Customer Relationship Management
Enterprise Resource Planning
Project & Program Management
Supply Chain Solutions
System Implementation & Integration

THE STATS

Employer Type: Private Company
President: Mark Cullen
2007 Employees: 120
2006 Employees: 120

UPPER

- "Flexible hours, able to work from home"

DOWNER

- Limited brand recognition

EMPLOYMENT CONTACT

Recruitment Coordinator
Exeter Group
One Canal Park
Cambridge, MA 02141
E-mail: careers@exeter.com

Visit the Vault Consulting Career Channel at **www.vault.com/consulting** - with insider firm
profiles, message boards, the Vault Consulting Job Board and more.

VAULT CAREER LIBRARY   437

THE SCOOP

Cambridge roots

Based in the Boston area, Exeter Group offers a suite of services that focus on improving business through better software solutions. But its 120 consultants are more than techies: The firm notes that because its staffers are involved in every stage of a project, including both engineering and interaction with clients, they "aren't just technical gurus, they are also business people." Services include IT-focused assessment, planning and strategy; business intelligence and data warehousing; custom application development; customer relationship management; enterprise resource planning solutions; project and program management; system implementation and integration; and supply chain solutions.

Founded in 1984 by current CEO (and MIT grad) Jonathan Kutchins, Exeter works with clients in a variety of industries, with specific expertise in the higher education, government, health care and finance sectors. In 2002, predicting a growing federal IT budget, the firm founded Exeter Government Services. With more than 60 employees, the division offers management consulting services with a proprietary approach it calls Exeter Insight. The approach involves a portfolio of tools and techniques the firm uses to identify and resolve management issues. Clients have included the U.S. Air Force, Army, Marine Corps, Department of the Interior, the Department of Education, the Department of Health and Human Services, and the Department of Housing and Urban Development.

Helping hand

A privately held company, Exeter doesn't broadcast its client engagements, though its client list includes Fortune 500 companies and more than 100 leading institutions from around the world. The firm helps its clients streamline business processes through IT solutions while reducing costs. The firm has worked with educational institutions, leading public health care organizations and finance organizations in a variety of IT consulting capacities. In the field of education, Exeter works to improve the information technology involved in all aspects of university life, including student systems, financial aid and human resources. According to the firm, solutions can range from conducting business process evaluations to implementing and integrating standard student system packages, and building client-specific applications.

Jumping in to help

Exeter is a supporter of Operation Jump Start III, an annual nonprofit charity event aimed at helping wounded veterans transition to civilian careers. In 2007, the firm also served as a Bronze Corporate Sponsor for the Marine Corps Association, supporting a variety of Marine Corps programs, awards and events.

GETTING HIRED

Students for hire

With recruiting spotlights on Brown, Cornell, Harvard, MIT, Georgia Tech, Northwestern, Williams College and a few others, Exeter pays special attention to students when it comes to filling consulting seats. The most qualified contenders are effective communicators, show brawny technical and analytical skills, boast impressive academic records and are attracted to computing— "regardless of their academic institution," we're told. If captivated, consulting hopefuls can check the firm's web site for places to submit resumes and cover letters.

As for the interview process, qualified applicants can expect a single phone interview and three personal interviews, the third containing exercises addressing how to handle certain situations, e.g., "What would your training strategy be for this particular type of client?"

Fair Isaac Corporation

901 Marquette Avenue
Suite 3200
Minneapolis, MN 55402
Phone: (612) 758-5200
www.fairisaac.com

LOCATIONS

Minneapolis, MN (HQ)
Over 100 offices in 11 countries

PRACTICE AREAS

Business Consulting Services
  Analytic Consulting Services
  Business Strategy & Operations Consulting
  Data Management Services
  Fraud Consulting Services
Enterprise Decision Management (EDM) Applications
Scoring Solutions
  Commercial Credit Scores
  Consumer Credit Education
  FICO Credit Scores
  Insurance Scores
  Marketing & Bankruptcy Scores

THE STATS

Employer Type: Public Company
Ticker Symbol: FIC (NYSE)
CEO: Dr. Mark N. Greene
2007 Employees: 2,700
2006 Employees: 2,850
2006 Revenue: $825.4 million
2005 Revenue: $799 million

RANKING RECAP

Quality of Life
#7 - Hours in the Office (tie)
#8 - Work/Life Balance

UPPERS

- "Small, boutique-like environment, but with the resources of a large company"
- "Extremely high intelligence-to-BS ratio"
- Flexible work arrangements and emphasis on work/life balance and "employee happiness/sanity"
- "We are growing and entrepreneurial as a practice, and that gives one the sense that it is easy to leave a mark on the practice/help build it"

DOWNERS

- "Due to our small size and need, we may not be staffed on projects that we want to work on"
- "We are still developing and streamlining structures and processes for recruiting, training, knowledge management"
- Not much after-work socializing
- "The consulting group is treated like the ugly sister at Fair Isaac"

EMPLOYMENT CONTACT

www.fairisaac.com/Fairisaac/Careers/Opportunities

THE BUZZ
WHAT CONSULTANTS AT OTHER FIRMS ARE SAYING ABOUT THIS FIRM

- "Good at what they do, but not a full service practice"
- "Still transitioning some consulting branches"
- "Reputable"
- "Number crunching"

Visit the Vault Consulting Career Channel at **www.vault.com/consulting** - with insider firm profiles, message boards, the Vault Consulting Job Board and more.

VAULT CAREER LIBRARY   439

THE SCOOP

Keeping score

Fair Isaac has been around since 1956, the result of a partnership between engineer Bill Fair and mathematician Earl Isaac. Although the firm provides consulting services, it's actually known for its pioneering work in analytics and credit scoring. Fair Isaac's statistics-based analytical tools are used widely in the financial and credit industries. Its popular analytical tool, the FICO® credit score, has become the standard way for lenders to calculate credit risk. If you've ever had a credit card or taken out a loan, you've dealt with Fair Isaac, whether you knew it or not. Its consulting services include business strategy and organizational process consulting, in addition to traditional analytic, software and technology support consulting.

Essentially, the firm is focused on helping companies improve the way they make business decisions, from the largest to the most minute. Fair Isaac uses data management and data analysis services to bring more information to decisions in areas such as marketing, customer management, risk and fraud. Clients in the retail, lending, insurance, health care, consumer goods and credit card industries all call on the firm's advanced analytics for help in making decisions. Fair Isaac also counts nine of the top-10 Fortune 500 companies, over 100 telecommunications companies and two-thirds of the top-100 banks in the world as its clients. The firm's almost 3,000 employees are based in 11 countries all over the globe.

Focus on strategy

Fair Isaac's business consulting group is a small segment within the firm that's focused on helping blue-chip Fortune 500 clients transform into more customer-centric organizations to better manage their customers for improved performance. The group's consulting projects are typically focused on marketing, sales and customer care, and can include marketing strategy, customer segmentation and organizational alignment. The team helps clients identify opportunities to improve profitability by better managing their customer relationships, and applies its analytics and business management technology to sustain and extend clients' competitive edge.

Leadership shift

Fair Isaac named Dr. Mark N. Greene as CEO in February 2007. His predecessor, Thomas G. Grudnowski, resigned the previous November after the firm released disappointing results for the fiscal fourth quarter, when earnings fell 38 percent compared with the same period a year ago. For fiscal year 2006, revenue grew just over 3 percent to $825.4 million, but net income declined 23 percent from the previous year. Greene is a 12-year veteran of IBM, where he distinguished himself as a leader in the company's financial services industry segment and software business groups.

Becoming client-centric

In June 2006, Fair Isaac announced a restructuring plan to boost profit and drive growth, partly in response to less-than-exciting financial results. The main goal of the plan is to switch from a "product-centric to a client-centric, go-to-market model." This means clients are regrouped into "integrated client networks," or segments based on needs, a common industry or geographic region. Leadership also aimed to integrate sales and consulting and to use global product development resources more effectively. As might be expected, jobs will be shipped offshore—specifically, quality assurance, maintenance and some engineering jobs will go to Bangalore. The firm will also cut 200 product management, delivery and development staff. If all goes as expected, the restructuring plan is forecasted to shave off $24 million in annual expenses.

Unfair competition

In October 2006, Fair Isaac sued the three major consumer credit bureaus—TransUnion, Experian and Equifax—in an effort to protect its prize product, the FICO score. The firm claims that the three bureaus violated antitrust laws by using unfair competitive practices to market their own product, VantageScore, a credit scoring system that rates consumer credit on a scale of

501 through 990. Allegedly, the three bureaus manipulated the price to promote their product over the FICO score. The three credit reporting agencies are the primary medium through which Fair Isaac's scores are sold to clients, and Fair Isaac claims that with a product in direct competition with FICO, the bureaus could discourage customers from purchasing FICO scores. The agencies, however, argue that VantageScore was created to meet customer demand for a different approach to credit scoring, and that more competition is best for the marketplace.

Ruling the market

Targeted acquisitions have added new technologies to Fair Isaac's portfolio of services over the past few years. In September 2005, the firm beefed up its capabilities in business rule engine software when it bought partial assets of RulesPower, Inc., a provider of high-performance systems that manage business rules. RulesPower was rolled into the firm's own Blaze Advisor, which helps businesses process and execute complex, high-volume business rules faster and more efficiently. In 2007, the latest version of the technology, Blaze Advisor 6.1, which incorporates the Rete III inference engine, was honored with the Intelligent Enterprise Readers' Choice Award for Best Business Rules Engine for the second consecutive year. The firm also ranks as the worldwide revenue leader in the business rules management systems software market, according to IDC.

Global solutions

Fair Isaac continues to rack up deals with businesses worldwide. In fact, in 2006, international sales accounted for about 28 percent of the firm's $825 million revenue. In January 2007, the Raiffeisen Bank S.A. in Bucharest, the Romanian subsidiary of Raiffeisen International Bank-Holding AG, chose Fair Isaac's enterprise origination solution, Capstone, to expand its capabilities. The new solution will automate and streamline the customer application decision process, increase processing capacity and reduce the number of applications that have to be manually reviewed by a credit analyst.

In December 2006, Fair Isaac extended its reach in the Middle East when its TRIAD™ adaptive control system was selected by Arab Financial Services Company B.S.C. Based in Bahrain, AFS will integrate the TRIAD system with its own processing platform to help network issuers manage risk and assist with credit line processes. In May of that year, the firm's enterprise decisions management system was picked by European payment card processor SiNSYS. The Belgian company has a combined portfolio of more than 23 million international payment cards under contract in Belgium, the Czech Republic, Hungary, Italy, Poland, Slovakia and the Netherlands. SiNSYS will integrate Fair Isaac's TRIAD adaptive control system with its own processing platform to efficiently manage lines of credit.

Fraud fighters

Fair Isaac takes credit for preventing all kinds of fraud attempts, including identity theft. In 2007, BBVA Bancomer, S.A.—a leading consumer bank in Mexico—reported that it had experienced an 80 percent reduction in fraud incidents since rolling out the firm's fraud detection analytics to protect its online card transactions. Fair Isaac's system, Falcon Fraud Manager, uses a combination of sophisticated neural network models, account profiling technologies, case management and flexible, user-defined rules to analyze payment card transactions for any sign of fraud.

The firm is continually working on new methods to combat fraud. In March 2007, Fair Isaac teamed up with Aconite, a software and consulting firm for the global payments market, to help banks and transaction processors manage fraud and risk in an offline EMV environment. The companies' combined solutions are designed to help banks adopt a balanced online/offline authorization policy, reduce operational costs, minimize fraud losses and increase revenue through secure approval of more transactions. And when it partnered with telecom solutions provider MACH in January 2006, Fair Isaac came up with a way to fight fraud involving the roaming information associated with wireless devices. In 2005, the firm joined IBM to offer services designed to battle bank fraud. Combining fraud control systems, strategies and services from Fair Isaac and IBM, the initiative came just after the firm relaunched Falcon One, its fraud-fighting software solution.

Visit the Vault Consulting Career Channel at www.vault.com/consulting - with insider firm profiles, message boards, the Vault Consulting Job Board and more.

VAULT CAREER LIBRARY   441

Aiming at Asia

In January 2007, Fair Isaac strengthened its ties to the Asia-Pacific region with a new office in Beijing. The office provides consulting, delivery and implementation support services for enterprise decision management. J.Y. Pook, vice president and managing director of the Asia-Pacific market, will head up the office and will oversee relationships with local clients and strategic partners. The firm already serves local banks in China, as well as international banks that have recently entered the country (such as HSBC). The firm opened its first facility in the Asia-Pacific region in 2004—an analytic consulting and product development center in Bangalore.

GETTING HIRED

Calling all contestants

Fair Isaac's business consulting undergraduate recruitment radar primarily hones in on the top-tier liberal arts campuses, including Harvard and Northwestern, while Kellogg and Yale are among the firm's top MBA pursuits. On campus, applicants can expect a preliminary interview with a partner or senior consultant, "and after that you will be called in for an in-person interview," we're told, in the form of three to four grilling sessions in the office. For candidates who fall outside of Fair Isaac's school radar, one associate says "the process included two phone interviews" to begin with, followed by half-day attendance at the firm's office.

Current staffers say interviews are a "mixture of case studies, personality/fit, interest in consulting and client industries and resume/experience walk-through." One consultant notes the equal division between personal experience questions and case questions, with case studies based "typically around market entry strategy, product launch or market sizing," while others note the emphasis on behavioral matters. And as one associate explains, these "case study questions are frequently used, as well as in-depth questions about projects at previous employers," because "candidates are expected to know and have a perspective on the structure and dynamics of industries they have worked in."

No surprises

Fair Isaac also steers clear of special tests during the interrogation process, keeping inquiries laid-back and based on work coming "directly from previous projects executed by the firm." Among case examples, consultants were asked a variety of questions, from "how would you market a novel cancer drug?" to describing product marketing and visibility considerations for a small office "looking to expand its presence in the locale and increase its visibility." No matter the question, contenders who handle the runaround most effectively will have "both analytical skills, business savvy as well as interpersonal skills," shares an employee.

OUR SURVEY SAYS

The mini firm

Because of Fair Isaac's miniature-sized consulting group, staffers note a cozy, collegial environment where "you get to know everyone." Colleagues are "definitely supportive, not competitive," shares a director, and the office is filled with low-key, "mostly very down-to-earth people," we're told. But familiarity and camaraderie aren't the only elements Fair Isaac wants outsiders to know about the firm's culture—"intellectual curiosity is a must," a lead consultant states. These employees are a hardworking bunch, survivors of recent pivotal shifts in the firm's plate tectonics. But Fair Isaac's consulting group, "embedded in a larger company (Fair Isaac) that we are still more fully integrating into," employees say, has "maintained the positive aspects of the previous firm's culture: a very strong, notable culture of sharing credit and thanking others for contributions to projects, however minor."

Cheers from above

At Fair Isaac, supervisors are accessible motivators who rarely blink before thrusting newbies into the client hustle. "Because of our size, the supervisors and upper management generally know everyone (and their skills and abilities) in our practice," says an insider, while others agree that "everyone is very approachable" and "no one falls through the cracks." Another consultant notes the firm's expectation for newly hired staffers "to work closely with clients from day one," adding that they are "generally expected to present or freely participate in most client meetings—even among higher-level clients." One co-worker notes her surprise when immediately pushed into client contact after signing on with the firm, and is impressed with "how much responsibility I received and how much access I got to people with invaluable advice and experience," she reports.

Fair Isaac employees cite early and continued support from higher ranks as a considerable motivator, because "coaches and project managers take an active interest in one's development, as our growth as a firm depends on it," comments a source. "Relationships are professional yet friendly here, and I feel I can easily seek help with uncertainty about findings or difficulty with clients."

Foresight will set you free

Since most Fair Isaac staffers report working a manageable 50 to 60 hour workweek, the firm's in-office time demands aren't much to groan over, with "little-to-no expectation to work on weekends," a staffer notes. And while "there have been some 80-hour weeks and some 35-hour weeks," consultants say they often have the foresight to predict these peaks and valleys. The amity with supervisors contributes to this leniency, too; "managers respect that you have a life outside of work," comments a second-year source, who adds that "you may be expected to put in extra work right before a project deadline, but managers try to avoid that situation."

Downtime flexibility also makes for a happy team, affording employees the freedom to manage nonwork obligations like doctors appointments and other personal errands. As one source states, "When there is work to be done, you are expected to put in the time and complete your work," but higher-ups do their best to work against grueling late-night labor and accommodate personal issues that may arise. In a firm where individual schedule management—even for first- and second-year consultants—often reigns, insiders say Fair Isaac "understands that better balance leads to employee satisfaction, loyalty and longevity." Along those same lines, says a staffer, management maintains a "low-key environment where hours, travel and balance are very favorable and make consulting an attractive, viable long-term career choice."

Joyful voyagers

Nominal travel requirements tend to swell the work/life balance as well, since "travel has been minimized as much as possible in this environment," an employee states. With much less required client face time than many consulting firms, Fair Isaac employees don't suffer the jet lag blues, especially since "partners try to ensure that consultants get a break from traveling by balancing remote and local projects." One second-year consultant says his travel schedule involves "typically a two- or three-night stay each week," but is quick to remark that "that's more travel than most people here." A partner chimes in, explaining that "we try to manage our client projects so we can work in the office with our case teams. This allows us to manage our lives better and also focus on firm-building activities."

Since "the company does not mandate weekly travel," consultants often catch themselves valuing the time they spend mingling with clients on location. "Travel can be stressful," shares a source, "but when it gives you the chance to immerse yourself in the client's business, it is also enlightening and—dare I say?—fun." And because fostering relationships with clients is the name of the game, Fair Isaac employees acknowledge the significance ascribed to occasionally shifting locale, mainly for project kickoffs, presentations and support-building, and can enjoy the benefits. "The occasional travel improves my work life," a newer employee says, "as I travel often enough to enjoy the change of location and pace, but I don't travel enough for it to wear on me."

Visit the Vault Consulting Career Channel at **www.vault.com/consulting** - with insider firm profiles, message boards, the Vault Consulting Job Board and more.

VAULT CAREER LIBRARY

443

Cash compromise

Staffers tend to shrug when it comes to their earnings. "I would say our salary and bonuses are average," comments a partner, though "they have been trending in a positive direction." Bonuses "below industry standards" strike a few bad chords with insiders as well. On other money planes, however, the firm's doling isn't too shabby, with "multiple opportunities for savings with pretax dollars," substantial stock options with an employee discount purchase plan, 401(k) matching, health/dental/vision and other insured services, and even "free and reduced-price software from Microsoft or other vendors," one consultant reports.

Free Internet, please

"Happy hours, employee-of-the-quarter cash awards, end-of-case team dinners" and other extras help make up what one insider calls the "employee morale fund" at the firm. Co-workers add food, airline miles, lodging, travel expense accounts and hotel discounts to the perk inventory, which a source rates as "nothing unusual and relatively modest, but appreciated nonetheless." And for those with the abode in mind, Fair Isaac has "a very liberal work-from-home policy," with high-speed Internet and mobile phone accommodations provided.

According to the Fair Isaac office occupants, their daytime location offers not only an easy commuting advantage, but convenient access to bars, restaurants and other social pursuits. Inside firm walls, Chicago staffers appreciate that the "industrial loft décor makes it bright and spacious," and other employees note that "most of the consulting offices are sparsely populated and hence very quiet." Though minimal interaction takes place during the day, one consultant mentions, the camaraderie shared among staff creates a gratifying work atmosphere.

Go forth and learn

Though the general consensus among insiders is that "most training is unofficial" at Fair Isaac, they do mention a formal one- to two-week instruction period "for new consultants to introduce core skills, approaches and examples." One lead consultant shares enthusiasm for the dual-leg training he underwent, with the second component "dedicated to a mock assignment where we were broken into teams, given a problem to solve and had a week to gather our thoughts, put together a presentation and present to senior management." A colleague notes the firm's monthly "lunch and learn"—a session that brings company comrades together to discuss projects, strategies and learning garnered from current work. While the firm does endorse its own unofficial training, "reflecting the feeling that people learn best by doing," as one source states, "more formal training plans are in progress to introduce consultants to the portfolio of offerings across the company."

Isolated efforts

Firmwide, Fair Isaac's community involvement seems marginal at best, with "very little formal encouragement," sources say. "We gather shampoos and travel items to give away to those in need," notes a consultant, while others add the firm's $250 corporate donation-matching incentive to the list. Independently, though, employees do what they can to involve themselves in community initiatives, sources say, and the firm usually backs up these individual efforts; "project managers are receptive and frequently adjust work plans," remarks an associate. In projects ranging from local food drives to homeless shelter donations and general volunteer work, one contributor agrees that Fair Isaac is "very understanding and supportive if I want to engage in those things myself."

Making inroads

Female employees are in the minority at Fair Isaac, but the firm seems to have improvements in the works. In Boston, one lead consultant claims, "Of our recent hires, around 65 percent are women," while a New York City source estimates the percentage of women in the firm's total workforce as 40. "We've done a very good job hiring women," an insider says, but adds, "We do, however, need more women at the director level and above." All in all, staffers rate their workplace as "very receptive" to increasing the proportion of women, with a director stating that "people are all treated the same, regardless of gender."

The firm's diversity model echoes with regard to ethnic and racial minorities; colleagues in the Boston office report 50 percent minority hires in the most recent class, and a Chicago brancher notes a "very diverse consulting practice" with "people from different backgrounds." And where voids may still exist, one manager asserts that "this is getting better. We've made great inroads!" Insiders say GLBT co-workers have a place at the firm, too. A consultant attests that Fair Isaac is "definitely diverse in this area as well; our group is getting more well-rounded with each new hire." Word also has it that the firm "performed outreach to university GLBT groups," and that there is gay/lesbian "visibility within upper management."

Visit the Vault Consulting Career Channel at **www.vault.com/consulting** - with insider firm profiles, message boards, the Vault Consulting Job Board and more.

VAULT CAREER LIBRARY   **445**

First Consulting Group

111 West Ocean Boulevard, 4th Floor
Long Beach, CA 90802
Phone: (562) 624-5200
Fax: (562) 432-5774
www.fcg.com

LOCATIONS

Long Beach, CA (HQ)
Alpharetta, GA
Boston, MA
Nashville, TN (2 offices)
Wayne, PA
Antwerp
Bangalore
Frankfurt
Hellerup, Denmark
Ho Chi Minh City (2 offices)
St. Asaph, UK

PRACTICE AREAS

Advisory Services
Applied Research
Implementation & Integration Services
Outsourcing Services
Software Development
Technology-Related Services

THE STATS

Employer Type: Public Company
Ticker Symbol: FCGI (Nasdaq)
CEO: Larry Ferguson
2007 Employees: 2,696
2006 Employees: 2,563
2006 Revenue: $264 million
2005 Revenue: $278 million

UPPERS

- "The ability to command your career and strive for promotions as you want, or to stay at a certain level for your career—it is your choice"
- "A real teamwork environment"
- The ability to live anywhere
- "Exposure to new ideas, implementation styles"

DOWNERS

- "An almost complete turnover in management has caused a feeling of instability within the firm
- In-person interactions and communication are limited in a virtual firm
- "Executive management seems too immersed in their little world"
- "Too much attention to being billable at the cost of improving processes or developing (via training) the staff"

EMPLOYMENT CONTACT

www.fcg.com/Careers/Careers.aspx

THE SCOOP

Making medicine work better

Founded in 1980, First Consulting Group is one of the health industry's leading technology services firms. It provides health care, pharmaceutical, insurance and other life sciences organizations throughout North America, Europe and Asia, the tech help they need to run their businesses more efficiently and cost effectively. Clients include integrated delivery networks, or IDNs, health plans, acute care centers, academic medical centers, physician organizations, governmental agencies, biotech companies, independent software vendors and many of the Fortune 500 pharmaceutical companies. From its headquarters in Long Beach, Calif., and its offices across the U.S., Europe and Asia, FCG's principle services consist of consulting, systems implementation and integration, software development and outsourcing services such as help desk capabilities.

While not the biggest kid on the block—most of FCG's deals fall into the low-millions range—FCG does get around. An April 2006 report by KLAS, an independent heath care consultancy monitoring group, showed that the firm has done more work in implementing computerized physician data entry systems than any other organization. For its hard work, the company was awarded a Best in KLAS award for planning and assessments in 2005. More high praise for FCG came from industry magazine *Healthcare Informatics*, when it ranked the firm No. 25 on its list of the country's 100 leading health care technology companies in 2005.

Breaking it down

FCG organizes its services into six areas: health delivery services, health delivery outsourcing, life sciences, health plans, software services and software products, with so-called "shared service centers" based in India and Vietnam that offer mainly IT services to all of FCG's different business segments.

The health delivery segment offers clinical process improvement, care/disease management, clinical transformation, patient safety and computerized physician order entry, as well as clinical system implementation and integration services to health delivery clients like hospitals, home health care companies and nursing facilities. The health delivery outsourcing wing, meanwhile, provides FCG clients with IT outsourcing services, including hiring staff for its clients and operating a portion or all of their IT operations either on or off site.

FCG applies its FirstDoc® software product to help life sciences companies comply with regulations, reduce costs, improve business processes, increase customer satisfaction and bring products to market faster through its life sciences segment, while its health plans group works with national and regional health plans, as well as Blue Cross and Blue Shield organizations, to improve their operations, processes and technology environments. FCG's software services unit provides offshore software development resources to its client base. And finally, the software products branch assists clients using industry-specific software.

Global connections

Helping FCG support its clients is the FCG software services unit, which until 2005 went under the name FCG Paragon. The group was borne out of the 2003 acquisition of Paragon Solutions, which FCG acquired to improve its "blended shore delivery model" that combines the know-how of both domestic onshore and offshore staff. Today, FCG software services' clients also include some outside of the health care industry, such as independent software vendors for whom FCG provides core product development services through long-term outsourcing projects from offices in Alpharetta, Bangalore and Ho Chi Minh City.

Knowing through knowledge-sharing

It's one thing to have the tools, but it's another to know how to use them. That's why FCG has invested in internal and external research and training programs so that its professionals can have access to information on the top trends in industry and technology. The first of these programs is the emerging practices group, which performs industry research on upcoming trends

Visit the Vault Consulting Career Channel at **www.vault.com/consulting** - with insider firm profiles, message boards, the Vault Consulting Job Board and more.

V/ULT CAREER LIBRARY   447

in the health care and pharmaceutical industries, their implications for the industry and the need for technology support. FCG's employees also have access to 92,000-plus documents on project methodologies, experiences, benchmarks and best practice information from the health care industry as part of its knowledge, information, technology exchange (KITE).

Changes at the top

FCG may have its service systems worked out, but it's had some issues working out its top-level management in recent years. In December 2006, the firm's chief operating officer and executive vice president, Thomas A. Watford, officially took on a third title—chief financial officer. Watford, who had been serving as interim CFO since March 2005, replaced Walter McBride, who resigned from his post for personal reasons. Similarly, current Chief Executive Officer Larry Ferguson took on his role June 2006, succeeding former President Steven Heck, who had been appointed as interim CEO in November 2005 after Luther Nussbaum resigned as the company's chief executive, giving no reason for his departure. In November 2006, Heck also left the company to pursue other interests.

These shake ups haven't taken too much of a toll on FCG's share price, which has risen fairly steadily since 2005. At around $12 per share, however, FCG's stock price is still nowhere near its near-$30 price tag from before the dot-com bust of 2000.

GETTING HIRED

Getting to First

FCG's hiring process is run by a global staffing organization, which conducts initial screenings before hiring managers step in. The firm isn't known for much campus recruiting; in fact, "most of the hiring is through employee referral," an insider reports. The process typically starts with a phone interview, followed by at least one in-person meeting with management.

Interviewees at FCG, we're told, won't encounter many case questions. According to one consultant, "We ask about the toughest project you've worked on and how you anticipated and managed risk." A colleague reports, "I was questioned about how I would respond/react if one of my recommendations turned out to be not the best choice or completely incorrect."

OUR SURVEY SAYS

Changing culture

First Consulting Group boasts a "strong sense of teamwork," along with "very friendly and helpful associates," insiders say. When it comes to corporate culture, however, insiders suggest it's in flux. "Our corporate culture is undergoing change, as new management works to address 'cultural damage' inflicted over the past six years by prior executive leadership," explains a consultant. "The culture has shifted," sighs another source, who adds, "We are no longer focused on people; we are focused on sustained profitability."

Virtually disconnected

The most frequent complaints about FCG's corporate culture come from its "virtual" employees. "The culture within my firm could be developed more and include the virtual employee more actively. Currently, my firm does not have a culture that fosters the environment of a virtual employee," says one consultant. Another insider notes that "as a virtual associate, it's difficult to stay connected to the corporate culture." There's just "not enough personal interaction," a source chimes in.

But when it comes to work/life balance, most insiders agree that the virtual office model has its advantages. "We work hard, but generally, even when we are busy I'm home in the evening with my family and back online later at night. That's very helpful. And I can telecommute whenever I need to, which I do an average of two days per week," a source tells us. A colleague agrees that the option to work from home, while not a cure-all, helps ease the burden: "Due to deadlines, I am often required to work well into the evenings and then am unable to take an equal amount of time off to compensate for the extra hours. However, due to the fact that I work from a home office, there is a bit more flexibility than if I had to commute to a traditional office." Still, late nights seem to be common among FCGers, with another source reporting, "Over the past several years, I have worked extremely long hours during the week with the hopes of having the weekends off to spend with my family." Another associate complains of an increasing amount of recurring evening conference calls.

Sunday flights

Travel requirements vary at FCG, with some consultants serving a local client base and others flying out regularly. One source reports, "Our health care division associates travel extensively," but "I am in the life sciences division where travel is more moderate." "We travel every week as a general rule, but it's part of being a consultant so I don't view it as excessive. They try to have us take reasonable flights, so travel isn't as bad," adds a co-worker.

Favorable travel schedules aren't always guaranteed, though, as an associate complains of "too many projects requiring Sunday night flights out or Friday stay overs, or both." "It's expected that while on a client site you'll be on the road four days a week, but there's the potential based on the assignment for that to be five days a week with only two nights at home," another explains. Even worse, says an insider, "I'm often given assignments were I'm scheduled to be out of town without being asked prior to someone signing an agreement. I have to actively work with my project manager and client to minimize the impact this has on my family."

Workweeks at FCG rarely dip below 50 hours, sources suggest, and telecommuting can lead to an "always on" mentality. "Meetings are scheduled Monday through Friday without realizing [their] impact on home schedules; calls are scheduled from before sunup to well beyond sundown with no regard to time zones," an insider reports.

Bonus blues

FCGers are mostly satisfied with their salary levels, though you'll hear some griping about bonuses. "Our company has a management bonus plan, however it has not paid any significant amounts (above a couple hundred dollars) in years. Recommendations have been made to revamp the program but no action has been taken (or at least been communicated)," says a source. Agrees a colleague, "My firm should consider yearly bonuses based on productivity and accomplishments that make a major impact on our business and reputation." According to another insider, "Since about 2000, there has been a significant disparity between executive leadership compensation and 'rank and file' compensation. It is my understanding that steps are being taken to reduce this disparity." At this point, says a consultant, "Salary and promotions are effectively capped. There is very little upward development."

However, FCG reportedly provides an "excellent 401(k) match" and stock options that fully vest after five years. As for perks, sources say, the firm throws a "great holiday party" with prizes like iPods, consultants can keep travel and hotel miles and points, and there's even an option for pet insurance. In addition, a source says, "If I am unable to leave the client site on the weekend, they will pay to fly my spouse to the client site or they will pay me half of my usual airfare."

Meet the new boss

Like the corporate culture itself, FCG's management has been in a state of transition, tell us. "Our supervisors have changed four times in the 18 months I have been employed here," says one insider. A colleague adds, "Most of the top-level management I have interacted with has recently resigned. I have not met with any of their replacements." And another associate gripes, "I don't speak with my immediate supervisor 'coach' as she doesn't take an interest in my well-being, my relationship with the company or my future growth or goals," but adds that "the top-level management is starting to take interest in other areas and reaching out to the associates."

Visit the Vault Consulting Career Channel at www.vault.com/consulting - with insider firm profiles, message boards, the Vault Consulting Job Board and more.

VAULT CAREER LIBRARY   449

That said, it's possible to find at least some FCGers who are happy with their managers. "I have been very pleased with all my immediate supervisors/project managers," a consultant reports. "Being virtual, exposure to top management is limited, but we do have regular calls and they do visit client sites."

Training at FCG is mainly limited to on-the-job and online opportunities, insiders say. "I would be hard-pressed to report the last time I had formal technical or managerial training," a source says. A colleague agrees, "Since 2000, my employer has severely limited opportunities for employer-paid training, making client-paid training the only material training available." The firm does offer an initial "two-week product training" for new hires and "quality training, which is instructor-led." But beyond that, sources say they usually have "too much work to take the time to train."

Diverse at the core

When it comes to diversity, a consultant says, FCG is "better than average." Another source agrees that the firm "lives up to its core values" in its treatment of women, minorities and GLBT staffers. "All my supervisors have been women, and women outnumber the men on the projects I've been on about 10 to one. I know of several women in very high positions, though the very top positions do seem to be held by men," says a source. Still, one insider complains that the culture is "very male-dominated," while another characterizes it as "still a boys' club." "We have women VPs but not many of them make the 'inner circle,'" adds an insider. One senior manager hypothesizes that this drop-off in women in the uppers ranks is "mostly due to them being of childbearing age and the incompatible travel requirements."

Similarly, insiders report, "We do have minorities in numerous high level positions [but I'm] not aware of any at the VP level." FCG's support for GLBT consultants gets relatively high marks, and staffers report that domestic partner benefits are available.

Giving back, quietly

FCG is also involved in some community service activities, but many insiders aren't very familiar with them, consultants suggest. According to a source, "We allot time off with pay to do community service and we occasionally have a firmwide initiative for charity," and a co-worker adds that "occasionally, corporate apartment equipment purchased by the firm will be donated to a local charity if the project is complete."

Greenwich Associates

8 Greenwich Office Park
Greenwich, CT 06831
Phone: (203) 629-1200
Fax: (203) 629-1229
www.greenwich.com

LOCATIONS

Greenwich, CT (HQ)
London
Tokyo
Toronto

PRACTICE AREAS

Corporate Finance
Equities
Fixed Income
Investment Management
Small Business & Middle-Market Banking
Treasury

THE STATS

Employer Type: Private Company
Senior Managing Director: John (Woody) H. Canaday
2007 Employees: 200
2006 Employees: 185

UPPERS

- "Opportunity to wear many hats"
- The firm is encouraging about finding a position that fits individual interests
- "Professional independence"
- Entrepreneurial—"an individual can still make a difference"

DOWNERS

- "Budget constraints can limit innovation/risk taking"
- "New management structure has added a level of bureaucracy/red tape"
- "Performance reviews are often several months overdue"
- There should be a more evident relationship between hard work and compensation

EMPLOYMENT CONTACT

Jenny O'Donnel
Phone: (203) 625-5430

THE BUZZ
WHAT CONSULTANTS AT OTHER FIRMS ARE SAYING ABOUT THIS FIRM

- "Big name in a narrow sector"
- "People approach is hurting"
- "Very high level"
- "Strong with data; weak with implications"

Visit the Vault Consulting Career Channel at **www.vault.com/consulting** - with insider firm profiles, message boards, the Vault Consulting Job Board and more.

VAULT CAREER LIBRARY   451

THE SCOOP

Focus on finances

Greenwich Associates, launched as a 10-person firm in 1972, has steadily cultivated a reputation as a think tank of sorts for the financial world. As Greenwich sees it, "The buyers and sellers of financial services are engaged in a symbiotic relationship that feeds on the flow of information." The firm's role in this relationship, it says, is to facilitate that flow with independent, credible analysis and advice.

When Charley Ellis founded the firm in its namesake town of Greenwich, Conn., his initial emphasis was on personal trust services, corporate pensions and large corporate banks, with custom services designed to meet client demand. Over time, in response to customer needs, the firm began to cover almost every aspect of financial services for a global client base of banks, securities dealers, investment managers and insurance companies, retaining the customizable aspect of its services. Though the firm doesn't trumpet its engagements, big-name clients have included Merrill Lynch, Goldman Sachs, Morgan Stanley and Fidelity Investments.

Stamford Associates?

Greenwich Associates has stayed close to the world's financial capitals, operating out of offices in Greenwich, London, Tokyo and Toronto. In April 2007, the firm announced a plan to relocate its main operations to neighboring Stamford in the spring of 2008. The firm is helmed by a group of managing directors, led by John (Woody) H. Canaday, a former Bain consultant and J.P. Morgan officer. Canaday took over the top position from Ellis in 2000. Longevity and stability is a hallmark of the firm, with much of its business coming from return clients, and many of its directors boasting more than a decade of experience with the firm.

Customize it!

The firm's consulting practices include corporate finance, equities, fixed income, investment management, small business and middle-market banking, and treasury. In addition to its consulting services, the firm can produce custom research for clients on issues such as strategy formulation, strategy measurement, market trends and customer behavior, and competitive position. Greenwich also offers custom analytics, helping managers, strategists and marketing professionals develop statistical analyses to answer critical business questions; customer satisfaction services, analyzing firms' client satisfaction initiatives with a proprietary solution known as Research Enhanced Strategic Customer Analysis; and real-time strategy management, offering insight on major transactions. Through its subsidiary, CCL, based in Toronto, Greenwich offers large-scale market research. Drawing on CCL's capabilities to conduct large-scale surveys (usually via telephone), Greenwich consultants design and structure custom research for clients. Proprietary tools offered by the firm include the Greenwich Quality Index, Greenwich Information Manager, Greenwich Rankings, Compensation Benchmarks, Market Sizing and Product Demand Analysis.

Straight from the CEOs

Greenwich consultants glean a large portion of their market expertise straight from the source. Using a fleet of "executive interviewers," the firm meets annually with up to 40,000 decision makers in more than 70 countries. Hailing from large corporations, financial services companies and other institutions, these "research partners" provide the firm with up-to-date information on market trends. In exchange for sharing their insights, Greenwich offers its research partners online access to all intelligence gleaned, in any of its survey areas.

The firm produces a steady stream of research and studies on financial services issues and trends. In April 2007, a Greenwich study found that U.S. companies are altering the composition of their equity-based employee compensation plans by adopting and expanding restricted equity award and performance share programs, while scaling back existing stock option plans. Another study, produced in March 2007, showed the U.S. asset management industry "on the brink of revolutionary change." A

November 2006 report compiled interviews of 91 CFOs at large American corporations, and revealed that many of them expected to increase the amount of time spent on investor relations in the coming year.

GETTING HIRED

Where they roam

Sources at Greenwich Associates say the firm's recruitment structure is currently undergoing a bit of a face-lift. "When I joined, recruiting consisted primarily of referrals," a fourth-year associate shares, but we're told that candidate-seekers have recently roved and conducted interviews on campuses such as Colgate, Dartmouth, UConn and Middlebury, and are steadily increasing job fair visits.

Running on the fast track

Applicants should psyche themselves up for a marathon interview procedure. While the beginning stages follow a standard hiring code—prescreening, and perhaps a telephone interview—the in-person sessions for new research associates are another story. "We are following a fast-track hiring model, where a candidate is coming in for a series of interviews one right after another," explains a manager. And to say that the interview process is a bit long would be an understatement; as an insider explains, "There are anywhere from four to eight interviews in one day, along with a case study," while a managing director cites eight to 12 as typical. An associate reports going through "30-minute interviews from 9 a.m. until 2 p.m." with departmental employees (future colleagues and senior consultants).

One team leader says interview protocol can involve "a propriety case study given to candidates. We have an example of what one of our research products looks like, and we ask the candidate to analyze it." Current staffers say "the interviews are straightforward, as is the case study," but contenders should expect more than just case questions. According to insiders, Greenwich conducts "a full personality test to determine cultural compatibility" and personal ethics. And if the firm still isn't sold, or "if there are any questions, the candidate could come back for another three to four interviews."

OUR SURVEY SAYS

A family affair

As a small firm, Greenwich can offer its employees a balanced, welcoming work culture. "People all get to know each other and tend to be very approachable when asked for help or guidance," a satisfied associate remarks, and "the vast majority of people at GA will go out of their way to help out in any way they can," affirms a colleague. Other co-workers boast of the firm's family-oriented nature and tendency to seem a bit paternalistic—but "in a very positive way," one principal assures.

Sources tell us that "GA is also unique in that the senior management is extremely accessible; most of the managing directors (when not on the road) are seated in cubicles among the members they work with, creating an environment that allows for collaboration between members and MDs," as an associate divulges. Because the firm promotes open air between all ranks, insiders declare that "the organization is very flat," encouraging contribution from every level, from research assistants to senior partners. And even though new hires are a young bunch (most fall between 22 and 26 years old), "associates are given considerable responsibility" and are often able to pursue positions relating to their individual interests. "A lot of people are 'GA lifers,' who have been in several different departments and functions, and have progressed upward in an area that interests them," states an employee.

Visit the Vault Consulting Career Channel at **www.vault.com/consulting** - with insider firm profiles, message boards, the Vault Consulting Job Board and more.

VAULT CAREER LIBRARY   453

The corporate clash

But we do hear some clamor about "a dual-class citizen status" between consultants and partners at the firm. "There is a feeling that the members are seen as an expendable commodity and that we should be honored to have the opportunity to work with some of the partners," one source alleges, while another feels that the supervisor/supervisee ratio is too high. Accounting for these gripes may be the firm's adoption of "more of a 'corporate' structure over the last couple of years," explains an associate, "which has slowed down some things that used to happen relatively quickly," such as promotion and performance review schedules.

Punching the clock

Most GAers put in 50 to 60 hours per week, but the numbers can drastically shift depending on the season. "The nature of our business is very cyclical," one senior staffer explains. "When we enter our busy season, it is not uncommon to work weekends for several months on end. This is often compounded by working late nights during the week." And while other employees do report some necessary weekend labor, most say they're not completely bogged down. "I work about one day on most weekends when I do not have specific vacation or recreational plans, but it is quite manageable," a source reports.

Creating symmetry

But acknowledging the tendency toward burnout, insider buzz says Greenwich is attempting to curb work-induced exhaustion. One consultant says the firm has made an effort "to improve the work/life balance over the past year. The result is that people across the firm are working less, on average." Another notes that "the firm has a decent system to allow members to work from home after regular office hours," adding that "many members are also provided with laptops, which makes it possible to work at home outside normal office hours" when needed.

Despite GA's efforts, some admit that balance can still be difficult to maintain, especially during those busy seasons. "Work/life balance during busy times in the schedule is very difficult to maintain. Often, it seems work takes precedent due to deadlines and client demands," says a team leader. And a newer hire vents about high availability assumptions from management, expressing that "it is not uncommon to have a consultant request that work be done after hours or on weekends, and if they do not get an immediate response, they will escalate it as a problem to senior managers." More seasoned employees seem to have a better hold on attaining equilibrium, though. "It is easy to allow it to get out of control if you let it, because there are many who work so hard at the firm," one notes, but "each person is required to determine his own work/life balance and to enforce it for his own sake."

Oiling the training wheels

While Greenwich does have a formal training program in commission, "most training is on the job with a mentor, supplemented by specific courses for time management, presentation skills, sales, etc.," a manager says. One source speaks for many when he states that "this is an effective model, because it provides new members with the basics, and they are prepared to learn hands on." Insiders report that the firm's instruction model is currently in a revamping process, "with recently introduced programs that bring professors into the office for after-work classes in financial topics." Employees also report a good amount of internal training, which focuses on "more business-specific training than general," an associate remarks.

In the pocket

"For members joining right out of college, I believe the firm's starting salary is competitive with other firms," a source says, but as one shimmies up the Greenwich money tree, it looks like the competition wins out and "similarly experienced colleagues are earning more." Another staffer adds, "It seems salaries are capped and bonuses are restricted as well. Those members that provide superior work and effort do not seem to be rewarded for it."

Employee benefits prove to be a saving grace, with a 401(k) starting after just one year and "a profit-sharing plan that has paid up to 15 percent per year, in addition to other forms of compensation." GAers also make use of the firm's tuition reimbursement offerings and health care coverage, and describe most benefits as "top notch."

Trading spaces

At Greenwich Associates, office inhabitants give their work area two thumbs down. Depicted as "adequate, but nothing special," staffers are united in disapproval of the "outdated and cramped" space. But word of a new location in 2008 has staffers optimistic about a less confined future; an associate says they "should be moving sometime in the next year to a larger, better appointed office."

But the condition of the offices isn't a sticking point for most employees, since racking up flyer miles is the norm for consultants at Greenwich. "Consultants are very frequently on the road—as much as every other week, or multiweek trips to Asia," one staffer says, but they "do have a fair degree of control over their travel schedule and are able to make plans several months in advance." The existence of a travel forecast seems to resonate throughout the firm; insiders boast that travel agendas are "more controllable than at many firms, and are typically to interesting places," reports a colleague. And because consultants are frequently on the move, Greenwich offers the luxury of "shorter trips and more nights at home," as opposed to rivaling firms. For nonconsulting staff, infrequent location shifting "is usually limited to the area between Boston and New York," we're told, and there is little pressure to make these trips at all.

Stirring the pot

Though one insider highlights the firm's "strong commitment to balancing the workforce," Greenwich isn't teeming with female employees. "There are very few women in senior positions at GA," observes an associate, which could be "more a result of the industry being more male-oriented than GA's reluctance to promote women." This male/female disparity may start to close up in the years to come, however; insiders say that "women do make up a decent percentage of the management," and "there are a few women on the partner track." With this proportion steadying, employees note a level of camaraderie between existing females in the office, who provide support and help each other reap success. "There also appears to be women's advocate groups within the firm," a first-year female staffer relates, and another associate adds that it "would be great for the more junior female members to have someone to look up to."

Like many firms, Greenwich positions itself as a meritocracy first and foremost—gender, race and sexual orientation aside. "We are pretty good about hiring only those candidates that meet our expectations, no matter male or female," says a manager, and as far as race is concerned, "The firm is a meritocracy where anyone can shine and race is not an issue." Co-workers' all-encompassing attitude extends toward sexual preference, with associates claiming that it's "a nonissue at Greenwich Associates." As one director states, "If anyone is or isn't, everyone appears to be treated the same."

Serving the rest

Among its charitable contributions to the Greenwich community, the firm "is involved in numerous cancer walks, Toys for Tots and other member-sponsored activities." Under the alias G.I.V.E. (Greenwich Internal Volunteer Effort), GA conducts pro bono research and "in 2005, several members formed a group that does pro bono consulting with local nonprofit organizations," sources report.

Visit the Vault Consulting Career Channel at **www.vault.com/consulting** - with insider firm profiles, message boards, the Vault Consulting Job Board and more.

VAULT CAREER LIBRARY   455

Health Advances

9 Riverside Road
Weston, MA 02493
Phone: (781) 647-3435
Fax: (781) 392-1484
www.healthadvances.com

LOCATION

Weston, MA (HQ)

PRACTICE AREAS

Market Assessment & Forecasting
Partnering, Mergers & Acquisitions
Pricing & Reimbursement
Product Positioning & Launch Planning
Sales Force Allocation
Start-Up Planning & Financing
Strategic & Business Planning
Technology Commercialization
Valuation & Financial Analysis

THE STATS

Employer Type: Private Company
Partners: Mark Speers, Paula Ness Speers, Skip Irving & Marie Schiller
2007 Employees: 50
2006 Employees: 45

RANKING RECAP

Quality of Life
#9 - Travel Requirements
#10 - Hours in the Office
#12 - Best Firms to Work For
#14 - Work/Life Balance
#15 - Formal Training
#17 - Interaction with Clients
#18 - Overall Satisfaction (tie)

Diversity
#1 - Diversity for Women
#20 - Best Firms for Diversity

UPPERS

- Lots of opportunity for growth and advancement
- "Relaxed atmosphere relative to other consulting firms"
- "Things can move quickly because there is a small group of people responsible for making decisions"
- "Great client mix, from investors and VC firms to startups and large-cap pharmas"

DOWNERS

- "Going through some growing pains"
- Limitations of working at a small firm; not much name recognition
- "Personal politics seem to play a big role in advancement. Fitting in with the HA culture is important"
- "The lack of public transportation to the office forces the expense and hassle of owning a car"

EMPLOYMENT CONTACT

www.healthadvances.com/joinus.htm

THE SCOOP

A healthy perspective

The name says it all. Health Advances helps health care executives advance beyond business problems like developing and delivering new products, identifying prospective partners, raising capital, conducting clinical trials or developing sales and distribution sales.

Despite its size—the firm employs 50 staffers—the firm's range of expertise is vast. Over the past 14 years, Health Advances has completed over 800 client engagements and its clients hail from every corner of the medical world: biotechnology, pharmaceuticals, medical devices, diagnostics, drug discovery and development, and drug delivery. Even investors and startups come to Health Advances for advice.

Brains behind the brawn

Bain & Company duo Mark Speers and Paula Ness Speers founded Health Advances back in 1992. Together, they had 17 years of health care consulting experience at Bain—Mark as a partner in the health care practice and Paula as head of the firm's research and development practice. As a team, they hoped to provide their hard-earned industry insights to early-stage companies.

To help them reach that goal, in 1997 the Speers added Skip Irving to their leadership team. Before joining Health Advances, Irving had founded and led Arthur D. Little's pharmaceutical consulting practice and, prior to that, consulted on business development and venture investing with the Massachusetts Biotechnology Research Institute. Then, in 2006, Health Advances' leadership was rounded out with the promotion of Marie Schiller to partner. Before joining the firm, Schiller had worked at ArQule, Inc., a cancer treatment research firm, and GelMed, a specialty pharmaceutical company. Helping the managing directors run the Health Advances show is a strong team of industry experts and seasoned consultants. Director Bill McPhee brings with him 25 years of experience in strategy, operations and venture capital consulting, while Vice Presidents Susan Posner and Christophe Marre have extensive industry experience in the pharmaceuticals industry.

A value-driven approach

The Health Advances team puts its best face forward when it engages with clients. The senior consulting group contributes to every project the firm takes on, in hopes of forging a long-lasting relationship with client companies. As part of its values statement, the company also outlines its emphasis on analysis: "We pressure test and triangulate every analysis to ensure our assumptions are solid"—consultant-speak for, "We make doubly sure we're doing the right thing for you." Lastly, the company highlights its capacity to bring its consultants' in-depth industry experience to bear on each case so that its strategies and solutions are effective.

Research, research, research

For each issue Health Advances tackles, it assigns a team of business professionals who set about putting their research skills to work. They don't have to go far: the Health Advances Knowledge Management Center combines internal research, past case histories and external expertise into a formidable research tool for some of the industry's most formidable problems.

Along with records of hundreds of previous projects, the center also offers a "virtual panel" of over 3,500 clinicians, researchers, reimbursement and industry experts whom Health Advances' consultants can ask for help. There is also a searchable library of disease "treatment trees," company profiles, licensing deals and clinical paths collected from industry, clinical and technical literature. On top of all that, Health Advances also internally funds ongoing research projects to stay on top of industry issues, such as regulatory, reimbursement, disease management, technology, business development and competitive trends.

Visit the Vault Consulting Career Channel at www.vault.com/consulting - with insider firm profiles, message boards, the Vault Consulting Job Board and more.

VAULT CAREER LIBRARY   457

Sharing the wealth

Health Advances is known for the medical expertise of its staffers, who are often called upon to share the wealth of knowledge they've amassed over the years. In September 2006, Skip Irving was asked to moderate a workshop at the Licensing Executives Society's annual meeting on drug device product licensing and collaborations. Health Advances executives have also served on panels held by Harvard Business School and numerous other national and international industry associations.

Giving back

It isn't always the health of companies that Health Advances is concerned with. The firm also regularly takes the pulse of its surrounding community. Since its founding, Health Advances staffers have devoted one day per quarter to community service. Organizations the firm has worked with include Community Servings, which offers meals for individuals and families living with AIDS, Waltham Fields Community Farm, which aims to relieve hunger in the Massachusetts area, the Minuteman Arc, a group home for disabled persons, and the Greater Boston Food Bank.

GETTING HIRED

Getting through the interviews

The prospect of as many as two days of one-on-one interviews with senior management would be daunting in most cases, but at Health Advances, the hiring process is a "fairly painless process altogether," says one consultant. Once resumes are collected, the interview process begins with a "phone screen or on-campus interview," a Health Advances veteran explains, which "typically involves a resume walk-through and a simple case question" to determine whether a candidate is a good fit for the company. "I think fit is so important here—you can't get past that," remarks one senior analyst.

If that first interview goes well, "candidates are brought in for one to two full days of interviewing with the senior staff." Says one recruiter, "Everyone will meet at least two of the four partners"—an advantage of applying to a smaller consulting firm— and will be asked case questions. For those being considered for higher-level jobs like senior analyst, there is a "second round of interviews, and then references are checked and offers made."

Real-life cases

Just what are interviewees asked behind closed doors? "Case questions are given at all levels and are focused on actual Health Advances' work, and therefore the business of health care," says one consultant, adding, "Brainteasers and generalist questions are not asked." Not only do real-life cases test a candidate's knowledge of the firm and the industry, "but they also expose you to the type of case work you would actually be doing," affirms another insider.

One consultant notes that his interview "involved a mock interview with an oncologist, and I was supposed to ask questions to determine their treatment pattern for a certain disease and their likelihood to adopt a new therapy." Another was asked, "How would you go about determining the size of the market for a new drug to treat Alzheimer's disease?"

Where Health Advances goes knocking

Health Advances recruits at most top business schools, but the firm has set up "formal analyst recruiting programs at Dartmouth, Harvard and MIT," one senior analyst says. Other schools are also scanned for potential recruits. "Duke and Wellesley are well represented, and candidates from any other schools are considered on a case-by-case basis," adds another source.

OUR SURVEY SAYS

All in the family

Even as Health Advances grows out of its small-firm status, the consultancy's culture remains "very family-oriented" with "an emphasis on camaraderie at all levels," explains one analyst. "The partners have done a tremendous job of trying to maintain a close-knit and family-like environment, even as we continue to grow as a firm," adds a senior analyst. From the "semiweekly poker night, to the occasional Friday Fiestas," where it is not uncommon to see partners or other members of management joining in, "Health Advances makes great effort to promote a collaborative and supporting environment, ensuring that every individual is able to work to their full potential and advance their personal professional development goals," an insider states. "There is an understanding that everyone works hard, and in return we are allowed the freedom and responsibility to keep our schedules flexible when possible and enjoy our time together both in and out of the office," says another insider. As one senior analyst says of her co-workers, "The people are great—fun, hardworking and smart with wicked senses of humor and generally realistic views of the world."

Outside of the office and those Friday Fiestas, Health Advances employees also come together for its "twice-yearly individual pro bono events" to give back to the Weston community. Consultants are "each given two paid days a year to do volunteer work of their choosing," and some also take advantage of the opportunity to take "paid leave to work at your choice of local charities," a source explains. One senior analyst remarks, "The senior people set a great example as they are very involved in community service. Last year a partner worked in an orphanage for her vacation."

No burnout here

While most Health Advances consultants are "usually staffed on two cases at one time, [with] an average case lasting around eight weeks," according to one insider, "the firm's culture is to guard against burnout," a colleague states. "Rather than celebrate someone working over the weekend or late at night, the firm's leadership views these events as anomalies that should be minimized." Health Advances management is, for the most part, "very cognizant about workload and how it affects life outside of work," says one analyst about the work/life balance at the firm. A second source agrees, adding: "They always try to make sure that workloads are evenly balanced between team members, and strongly discourage working extra hours when it's not absolutely necessary." He adds that "instead of giving a pat on the back, management attempts to figure out what went wrong when they hear of employees working above and beyond 50 hours a week."

Work hours "are generally kept under wraps," says one consultant. A "typical workday is 8:30 to 6:30, and people are usually very good about not scheduling meetings and calls outside of these hours." A senior analyst adds, "If there are valuable experts to contact or data that needs to be crunched and work to be done, people are usually quite accommodating." That's different from most consulting firms, claims one analyst, who notes that the "flexibility concerning work hours is much preferred. Some people choose to come in or leave early, while others might opt for a later schedule or prefer to take a break and bring some work home in the evenings, as opposed to working straight through."

Realistically, though, "when it comes down to it, the work has to get done and the company sometimes overpromises on deliverables or agrees to unrealistic timelines," an insider laments. "In those cases, work takes precedence over personal life" but, adds another, "HA does a good job of rewarding employees for that time with comp days, floating holidays and a week off at the holidays without use of personal vacation." Consulting can be demanding, but finding a balance between work and personal life at Health Advances "is easier than at some firms, since our level of travel is pretty low," adds another senior analyst at the firm.

Visit the Vault Consulting Career Channel at www.vault.com/consulting - with insider firm profiles, message boards, the Vault Consulting Job Board and more.

VAULT CAREER LIBRARY   459

Traveling light

Indeed, a factor that sets Health Advances apart from its peers is that "travel is generally only done when necessary," reports a rookie analyst. "Analysts travel less frequently than senior analysts, associates and management, but teams make an effort to have analysts present for the final presentation (if done in person) or other relevant meetings," the source explains.

Typically, "projects are designed around a kick off, interim and final presentation, and these meetings will typically be the three instances of travel per case," states a senior analyst. "Health Advances is located at the epicenter of biotech, pharma and device activity, which means many of our clients are just down the road, contributing to our limited travel requirements," adds the analyst. "I find that there is just enough travel involved that I continue to look forward to (rather than dread) business trips."

The door's always open

Health Advances places a premium on its "pretty strong open-door policy," says an insider, which another consultant attributes to "the moderate size of our office" that "really allows for everyone to interact with senior management." Staffers appreciate their supervisors and, according to an observant source, "supervisors only move up if they are good mentors and coaches; this is a valued skill set."

Compared to her friends at other large consulting firms, one analyst says, "I have had infinitely more contact with the partners, directors and VPs, and [my friends] are always impressed to hear of the opportunities resulting from this experience." From her first days as an analyst, this source says she "felt increasingly comfortable working with my superiors and seeking their advice for case-specific and general professional issues."

Top-down, bottom-up approach

Health Advances' open-door policy especially applies to the firm's newest members. "Team leaders always try to include the entire team in all client meetings whenever possible, and they encourage even new analysts to present and contribute to client meetings," says an analyst. "As a first-year analyst," adds another, "I had the opportunity to spend several days interacting directly with a client here and at their site. While this is not the norm, no one at HA flinched at giving me the opportunity."

Relationships with new employees are also fostered outside the boardroom via Health Advances' mentoring program, "where every employee is paired with a member of upper management," says one insider. "We meet with our mentors every three to six months to receive feedback on our career development."

Getting on the same page

Every new hire is enrolled in "an extensive four- to six-week training process" that "includes dozens of hourlong training modules covering everything from the regulatory process to finance and accounting," an insider reports. "They really try to make sure that everyone starts on the same page and, regardless of your background, they try to ease you into the job as much as possible." Another analyst adds: "Every new employee outside of senior management develops his own training presentation on a unique topic of study that allows a valuable, hands-on introduction to our case methodology."

For new hires as well as analysts who need a refresher course, Health Advances also has "a number of unique and proprietary research and analysis tools that are introduced through training modules and drills, followed up with lunch training presentations and one-on-one support when it is needed," says an analyst. And come time for their first case, where "most of the best training is provided," new hires "will typically shadow someone else at the same level, instead of just being thrust into a case on their own," a manager adds.

Money talks

Analysts at the company say "compensation seems to be in line with other offers," and an insider adds that bonus amounts "may be targeted at a lower level, but they increase with company performance." "Annual bonuses," adds another source, "are calculated based on three factors: personal targets (based on level) as a percent of your annual salary, a company performance multiplier (based on target monthly revenue) and a personal performance multiplier (based on a variety of factors assessed at the individual level)." In 2006, the consultant continues, "bonuses were inflated by 35 percent due to [company] performance."

There is "some sense that at more senior levels, compensation may be less than industry averages," adds one analyst, and a senior analyst agrees: "Salary at my position is typical, although my understanding of raises at Health Advances [compared] to those of other firms is that they are less generous." Still, an associate remarks, "The target [pay] is realistic and the firm is much more open about its finances than other companies I have worked for."

Not your run-of-the-mill health insurance

According to one analyst, "The most interesting perk is probably the medical advice you can receive from your peers or their contacts. From our in-house pediatrician to the firm's knowledge about centers of excellence for different diseases, working here guarantees you quick advice on the best care possible." That's just one of the many perks that HA insiders get excited about. The firm also makes sure that its employees maintain their health by getting an apple a day, plus some other goodies. Many sources appreciate the "range of snacks provided in the kitchen every week," "bagel days once a month" and "monthly birthday parties." And the firm promotes physical fitness by providing health membership reimbursement and maintaining "showers in the bathrooms for those who prefer to run near the office or come straight from the gym."

Consultants also rave about the amount of vacation they get, and are especially appreciative of having "the week off between Christmas and New Year's that does not count toward personal vacation time and allows you to take time away from work and be with family, free of guilt or concern." And when it comes to time off over the course of the year, the firm takes a laid-back approach. A senior analyst says the firm offers "flexible vacations—I have never heard of them turning down a vacation request," and it also allows staffers to take four pro bono days off per year. This flexibility extends to new parents as well. "The company offers both maternity and paternity leave, available from the day you start. In addition, some senior members work reduced hours in order to spend more time with their families," explains an analyst, and a colleague reiterates that "the firm has been very flexible with part-time schedules to allow new parents to ease into their new lives." In addition, "the firm always has a really nice party for the expecting couple and gets the family something special."

Other perks include "a discount program for car and home insurance," limited tuition reimbursement, "a recently renovated quiet reading room offers cozy accommodations for those looking for an escape from their desks," Friday jeans day, "fantastic chairs" and, last but certainly not least, "every year at the company's anniversary party they give out a thoughtful and useful gift."

Destination: Weston, Mass.

"Being in the suburbs, the location could be better," says one insider who warns, "You will definitely need a car to get to work." The plus side: "The reverse commute to and from downtown is only about 15 minutes," the source adds, and "the suburban location allows for more spacious offices and free, covered parking." Another consultant comments: "The work the office does is far more impressive than the space it occupies."

Gender blind

At Health Advances, "two of four partners are women, [and] women comprise more than 50 percent of the management team as a whole," says one analyst. "That said," the source adds, "male representation has risen recently. HA is an amazing example of a firm that actually balances male and female work styles, perspectives and participation. It is a comfortable place for women, but also [for] men like myself who wish to work in an environment that does not discriminate based on gender." Another male staffer feels that "this is perhaps the most female-friendly workplace in America."

Visit the Vault Consulting Career Channel at www.vault.com/consulting - with insider firm profiles, message boards, the Vault Consulting Job Board and more.

VAULT CAREER LIBRARY   461

Making room for new faces

Minorities aren't as well represented at Health Advances, we're told. "HA is heavily focused on the life sciences, and our ethnic balance reflects the field in general," explains one analyst. "While an excellent job has been done in hiring and promoting Asian and Indian employees, we do not have significant representation of blacks and Hispanics." A colleague agrees, stating that Health Advances' ethnic makeup "is a reflection of consulting and society as a whole. We do no better or worse."

As for the gay, lesbian, bisexual and transsexual community at Health Advances, "no one has made this a topic of discussion," a consultant points out, and several respondents claim that they are "not aware of the sexual nature of our staff." Still, "attitudes on the personal level are very strongly encouraging of individual expression and would not discourage a queer employee," reassures one analyst.

IMS Health Incorporated

901 Main Avenue
Suite 612
Norwalk, CT 06851
Phone: (203) 845-5200
www.imshealth.com

LOCATIONS

Norwalk, CT (HQ)
Additional offices in 100 countries worldwide

PRACTICE AREAS

Launch & Brand Management
Portfolio Optimization
Sales Force Effectiveness

THE STATS

Employer Type: Public Company
Ticker Symbol: RX (NYSE)
CEO: David R. Carlucci
2006 Employees: 7,000+
2005 Employees: 6,900
2006 Revenue: $2.0 billion
2005 Revenue: $1.8 billion

RANKING RECAP

Practice Area
#6 - Pharmaceutical & Health Care Consulting

Quality of Life
#8 - Interaction with Clients (tie)
#10 - Travel Requirements
#15 - Firm Culture

Diversity
#1 - Best Firms for Diversity
#4 - Diversity for GLBT
#4 - Diversity for Minorities
#4 - Diversity for Women

UPPERS

- "Lots of global work, including the opportunity to travel to unusual markets"
- "I do not have someone checking up on me to be in exactly at 9"
- Quick career progression
- "People are interested in teaching you, not just in making you do the grunt work"

DOWNERS

- "Growing so fast we are running out of space to seat everyone"
- "Corporate culture is a little conservative and dreary"
- "There seems to be a bit of politics in terms of project placement, hiring and bonuses"
- Sometimes feels too small

EMPLOYMENT CONTACT

www.imshealth.com/careers

Visit the Vault Consulting Career Channel at **www.vault.com/consulting** - with insider firm profiles, message boards, the Vault Consulting Job Board and more.

VAULT CAREER LIBRARY   463

THE SCOOP

Pharma king

When companies like Pfizer or Merck want to know how many prescriptions were written for one of their drugs last month, or to determine the effect of a competing drug on their market share, they call on IMS Health. Established in 1954, IMS has made a name for itself studying the $600 billion dollar pharmaceutical market. The firm has a comprehensive grasp of the prescription drug industry, tracking over one million products and collecting data from 75 percent of all prescriptions written in 100 countries; in the U.S., the firm's data captures 90 percent of all pharmaceutical sales. With the global pharmaceutical market only getting bigger, IMS is aptly poised to get a piece of the pie.

The firm is organized around three business lines with integrated consulting and services capabilities: sales force effectiveness, portfolio optimization, and launch and brand management. IMS' consulting practice works on a range of analytical projects for the health care and pharmaceutical industry. For example, to gauge how to launch a new pharmaceutical product, consultants might assist with developing a marketing strategy through primary research with physicians, pharmacists and regulators, and review past successful launches of similar drugs. The research, combined with hard data, would help guide the pricing, sales activities and overall strategy of a drug launch.

Brains on drugs

The company's structure has a tangled history, beginning with its founding by Ludwig Frohlich and David Dubow, two New York ad agency execs. The pair incorporated IMS—Intercontinental Marketing Services—in 1954, as a European branch of their ad agency, Frohlich Intercon International. In 1957, the pair realized there was a lack of data about drugs on the market, so they created the first market research syndicate for the pharmaceutical industry. The original study published was a drug sales audit of the market in West Germany. The firm then started to expand, covering markets in Australia, Asia, South Africa and Europe, before realizing it had ignored one of the most lucrative markets in the world—the U.S. In 1969, IMS acquired Chicago-based Davee, Koehnlein and Keating, a pharma sales auditing firm that gave IMS a much-needed U.S. presence.

The following year, IMS gained access to Latin America through another acquisition, and continued buying up smaller firms over the next decade. A major coup came in 1974, with its purchase of Pharmatech, a computer data company, which developed what would eventually become an online delivery system for the data IMS collects. Also boosting the firm's future tech capacity was Cambridge Computer, acquired that same year. Cambridge provided information to pharmaceutical sales representatives across several market areas through its drug distribution data product.

Buy and sell frenzy

In 1988, Dun & Bradstreet bought IMS for nearly $1.8 billion, developing its products and information services for the next few years until the company decided to divide. D&B sold the communications division of IMS in 1991 and in 1996, split into three parts, one of which became Cognizant, formed by pooling IMS and Nielsen Media Research, the TV ratings firm. But a subsequent split made IMS independent again in 1998. Through a stock dividend divestiture, IMS was listed on the New York Stock Exchange that year.

Over the next few years, IMS aimed for global expansion. In 1998, the firm purchased Walsh International, a pharmaceutical software company, whose client base was in Europe. It entered markets in Eastern Europe and sub-Saharan Africa, and through acquisitions, gained a healthy presence in Hungary and Switzerland. The firm also introduced localized versions of its products in Brazil and Japan through the acquisition of Sales Technologies, which had sales management tools in local languages. In July 2004, the firm acquired Shanghai-based United Research China, giving it coverage of the prescription and over-the-counter market in Asia. Later that year, IMS and U.K.-based Boots the Chemist signed an agreement giving IMS access to Boots' over-the-counter and health care sales data from its 1,300 retail locations in the U.K.—the first of several similar deals with other

Western European firms. IMS also beefed up its consulting practice in December 2006 by buying out the life sciences practice of Strategic Decisions Group, a Palo Alto-based strategy consultancy focused on pharmaceutical and biotech industries.

Standing on its own two feet

The firm was almost gobbled up by Dutch media firm VNU when it made a pitch for a $6.3-billion merger in July 2005. Two big shareholders at VNU were staunchly opposed to the deal however, and eventually the merger was nixed. Since then, IMS has been on its own, and signs are that it intends to stay that way. Since 2005, the board has authorized several stock repurchases, and by February 2006, the firm had bought back about 10 percent of its total market value.

Staying ahead of the curve

IMS is constantly developing tools that collect new data or ways to help clients look at data differently, mostly in response to marketplace trends. An initiative called New Models, New Metrics was launched in 2006, to address the changes that are constantly springing up in the health care landscape. The market has recently shifted, due to the growing prevalence of specialty pharmaceuticals, managed care, generics and nontraditional distribution channels. To help clients get up to speed on the changes, the firm created Next-Generation Prescription Services™, which analyzes the array of choices in drugs and the various ways in which they are disbursed to patients. The information offered by the program presents a more accurate, complete picture of evolving U.S. prescription trends. In late 2006, IMS announced the launch of another tool designed to integrate anonymized patient-level data (APLD) with information, analytics and consulting. The APLD portfolio details the way a number of factors—such as disease and treatment patterns, patient compliance and persistence, physician practices and cost of care—influence each other over time.

Cost Care, one of IMS' many market intelligence tools, came on the scene in December 2005. This analytical system helps pharmaceutical companies measure the impact of their products on health care costs. Cost Care collects information about patient insights (gathered anonymously) and applies it so drug marketing teams can better appeal to patients and insurance companies. Its main goal is to determine how a drug manufacturer can differentiate a product based on its value, not its cost. For example, the tool would be especially useful in situations where a company is selling a brand name drug facing new competition from generic, lower-priced drugs, or cheaper drugs in the same class.

Disease-specific data

Oncology, expected to become the leading class of drugs by 2010, is seen as a target market for IMS. In October 2006, the firm introduced an expansion of its oncology capabilities, adding market assessment, forecasting and competitive intelligence, pricing, reimbursement, and health economics and outcomes research for the oncology market. IMS also announced a partnership with IntrinsiQ Research, a leading U.S. oncology information provider. IntrinsiQ's patient-level oncology information system will be incorporated into IMS' multicountry oncology tool, Oncology Analyzer®. With all the oncology-focused work the firm has taken on (over 140 engagements in the past two years), IMS has positioned itself to gain an edge in the specialty market.

Taking on meth

In 2007, IMS undertook a study for the U.S. Drug Enforcement Administration to help it combat a national methamphetamine epidemic. Studies were conducted to determine the quantity of ephedrine and pseudoephedrine necessary for legitimate medical usage in America, in response to the U.S. Combat Methamphetamine Epidemic Act of 2005. The firm analyzed sales and use patterns of these chemicals by cross-referencing five separate IMS prescription drug information sources with over-the-counter sales data. The study concluded with naming the exact quantities required to meet the nation's current legitimate patient medical needs for these products.

Visit the Vault Consulting Career Channel at **www.vault.com/consulting** - with insider firm profiles, message boards, the Vault Consulting Job Board and more.

465

In the know

As the firm that tracks who's taking what pill, IMS is often tapped for the inside scoop on the pharmaceutical market. In 2006, *Forbes* published the firm's list of the top-20 drugs sold in the U.S., a list led by cholesterol-reducing blockbuster Lipitor. IMS experts frequently present at conferences around the world on the financial impact of the health care industry. Recently, IMS executives spoke at the JP Morgan Annual Healthcare Conference, the UBS 2007 Global Healthcare Services Conference and the Goldman Sachs Global Healthcare Conference. The firm also offers market intelligence to consumers through Global Insights, its online resource, which offers downloadable reports and studies. Recent studies have examined the economic, political and health dynamics that impact the global pharmaceutical market, as well as new drug compounds to treat obesity.

As an indicator of IMS Health's influence and staying power in the industry, it was named to the 2007 BusinessWeek 50—a list of best-in-class companies from the 10 economic sectors in the S&P 500 that are setting the bar in their respective industries.

GETTING HIRED

Getting IMS to say yes

IMS targets undergrads from the Ivies and other top schools. Specifically, the New York office recruits on campus at Penn, Columbia, Harvard, Brown, Princeton, Northwestern and Cornell. At the senior consultant level, insiders say, MBA students from target schools like Columbia B-school, Wharton, Fuqua and Kellogg receive most of the firm's recruiting attention. IMS has no choice but to focus its searches on the top ranks, sources say, "only because we are small and have limited resources," justifies a senior principal in Manhattan. But that same employee adds, "We encourage applications from individuals, regardless of their school affiliation, and have found some of our best consultants outside of the school recruiting environment."

In general, the interview process involves "one phone case question, one in-person day with two longer cases and a fit interview, and one senior-level interview," says a consultant. Another adds that "cases are focused on traditional business issues, but usually have a health care spin, since our business is health care. Cases are prepared internally by our interviewing team and are meant to provide us with an insight into how people think. Analytical skills are the key thing we look for." Some examples of case questions include, "How many parking tickets are given per day in New York City?" and "How many doors are there on your college campus?" For another stumper, insiders say, be prepared to explain why you're interested in health care consulting.

OUR SURVEY SAYS

Pharma fun

IMS' "focus on pharma/biotech clients and issues" makes the firm a real draw for consultants looking for a medical niche. Like-mindedness also means that "most people feel that their colleagues are also their friends," says one source—a feeling fostered by the firm's "atmosphere of great collaboration," says another. One New York City insider adds that IMS "does a good job screening for personality to make sure everyone meshes properly." Looking for a good fit in new employees is especially important, "given our small size (approximately 50 consultants in the New York office)," according to one consultant, who insists that "everyone knows each other's names, even if they have not worked together on a project."

IMS insiders also describe a laid-back, youthful culture "in which everyone from all levels socializes quite freely. It's almost family-like in feel," says one consultant. Colleagues across the board echo sentiments of the youthful vibrance and friendliness that flow throughout the company; one higher-up, who wouldn't be categorized as "young" himself, states, "The people at IMS make me feel young."

Day-to-day at IMS

Typically, says one senior principal, "work hours are completely manageable and we are flexible in letting people work from home or remote locations to help with work/life balance." An analyst from the New York office says, "You use your autonomy to make your own hours. You can be super-efficient and leave at 6 p.m. every day, or if you prefer to work in the evening, you can come in a little later and stay later into the night. Hours vary tremendously by project and what stage of the project you're in. There is no 'average day.'"

Still, things are changing for IMS consultants, and work demands seem to be getting steeper. "Recently, the company has shifted to a multiple-project model, meaning consultants and senior consultants often work on multiple engagements concurrently. With this shift, the work hours have increased, but not too significantly," reports a source. Another factor that may play a part in this shift is that "the office is staffed lean, which means that people generally don't have a lot of downtime between projects."

Consultants who like to sleep in their own beds

On the whole, IMS employees report minimal travel, but those based in New York have especially low travel demands. In general, says a source, "travel is mainly on the East Coast, and normally day trips to the client site. These occur usually no more than twice a month." Consultants expect a slight increase in travel as they advance to the higher echelons, but not enough to get worked up about. "At the analyst/consultant level," according to one source in New York, "you work the majority of the time in the New York office, traveling only for major client meetings. As you progress up the ladder, you are staffed on multiple projects at once, and therefore will be traveling to more meetings. Overall, you spend 90 percent of your time in the New York office or working from home, if you wish." A more senior consultant attests to this, explaining that "as a project manager, I travel about once a month for about 24 hours or less."

But for those with the travel bug, "you also have the option to work for periods of time on projects overseas." Remarks an analyst, "If international exposure is desired and some level of travel is of interest, there is ample opportunity for that." Travel "to Western Europe, Brazil, China and India is not irregular," adds another. Several consultants also mention that the firm offers the opportunity for top performers to work in the European Union for six months. The bottom line? "If you seek more travel, you can ask for it, but it's not expected."

Balance with borders

Manageable hours and minimal travel seems to add up to a pretty positive work/life balance. Also tipping the scales toward balance are the lack of time required and staffers' ability to manage their own schedule. As one analyst explains, "Our firm holds true to the independent spirit of consulting. Face time is not important. All people care about is getting the job done well. I truly enjoy how the work schedule is very flexible to my life." Agrees a colleague, "It's all about choosing the balance for yourself; we're given a lot of autonomy and it's up to you to decide how to use it." The balance seems to work favorably for parents as well. Explains a senior principal, "I have [a toddler] and have found a way to find time to spend with her as well as deliver on my professional responsibilities. In addition, I was promoted after returning from maternity leave, which, to me, demonstrated the firm's commitment to work/life balance." In addition, says a senior consultant, IMS "allows us to take time off, and is very easy with vacation."

This laid-back culture shouldn't be confused with a lax attitude toward work, and IMS consultants are willing to put in the hours to get the job done. An insider states, "We certainly work weekends at our firm, often because of the type A personalities that are attracted to our industry. There are very few weekends where I put in a full two days, but many weekends will require three to four hours of work." He adds, "We achieve work/life balance by giving people some flexibility to work from home, as needed, and leave when they need to. The only expectations are that we meet our client's needs." One project manager explains how she's been able to incorporate social engagements into her work (or vice versa): "At the project manager level, there is usually a 30-minute e-mail check-in Sunday evenings to prepare for the week. On the extreme end, if a client deliverable is due Monday morning, you will likely work one full day over the weekend. The work schedule is flexible, and I will often leave work at

Visit the Vault Consulting Career Channel at **www.vault.com/consulting** - with insider firm profiles, message boards, the Vault Consulting Job Board and more.

VAULT CAREER LIBRARY   467

6 p.m. to go out for dinner with friends, and then pick up work later in the evening for a couple hours." In the end, "like most firms it can be crazy at times, but overall the balance is reasonable."

Not quite adding up

With all of the quality of life benefits that IMS affords, sources feel that it comes up short in the area of compensation, when compared to other consultancies. Insiders attribute this to the fact that the IMS consulting practice "has a policy of standardized salaries across the board," says a consultant from New York, who adds that "bonus makes up somewhat for that, but not nearly enough." Another source offers her take on the matter: "IMS has historically paid on the lower end of the consulting salary range, partly due to the lower client fees in the health care space, and partly due to its early focus on the lower paying data services side." But, she adds, "In the last year, that gap has closed for analysts as well as senior consultants relative to their peers at other firms." And another optimist asserts, "If you are a top performer, the company will always try to reward you for your effort and performance" in the form of ad hoc financial rewards for excellence.

Perks pay off

Making up for the difference between salaries at IMS and other consulting firms is "a 10 percent discount in the employee stock purchase plan," says one consultant, as well as a "pension, including a small number of stock options." A colleague adds that "stock grants for individuals at the principal level" are also available. Other perks include "discounts on gym membership and full payment of initiation fees; a wellness program that reimburses up to $250 a year; transit card subway cards purchased directly through paychecks; and a 401(k) 50 percent match, up to 6 percent of salary." On top of those, says a source, there is "the other standard fare: corporate credit card, cabs and dinner for late nights, etc." The firm also offers "flexible maternity and paternity leave," with a senior principal explaining, "Our leadership accommodates people to make it fair and to ensure that the transition back is smooth."

Consultants also get excited when mentioning the IMS-organized social events. "We have regular happy hours and social events," explains an insider. "Past social events have included kickball in Central Park, karaoke, a trip to the Hamptons, wine tasting and bowling. During orientation week for new hires, the whole company is involved with training and social activities."

Learning on the job

Another perk: training. New staff "goes through the introductory 'consulting fundamentals' course sometime in their first six months, followed later by a course on writing proposals and running projects," says one insider. But even with this official training regimen, she adds, "most training occurs on the job. Instead of bosses, we each have a development coach who serves as a mentor through the career development and performance review process." And while staffers readily note that co-workers are "dedicated to imparting knowledge gained," they also admit that official training "is somewhat of a weak area for us, since we are fairly small. But we have recently begun implementing many new programs, which are built by the very people for whom they are intended." The firm notes that these programs include monthly "lunch and learns" conducted by consultants on key markets, therapeutic areas, developments, unique projects or any other topic that might be of value or interest to the greater office.

Higher-ups, therefore, play an integral part in setting the stage for the junior-level employees, and are generally appreciated by their analysts. Says one, "Our senior staff are extremely accessible in person, phone or e-mail, and even though they travel a fair amount, most are extremely responsive." Consultants also enjoy the hands-off, yet authoritative presence that managers assume. A source explains, "Our leadership strikes a terrific balance between allowing teams to own their deliverables, but also providing thought leadership and perspectives to help ensure quality deliverables." And, from the mouth of one analyst, "The senior people in the office are amazing: funny, intelligent and social. The firm has become increasingly aware of the value of their junior staff, and through the senior staff, has really reached out in a positive way."

The open-plan offices also help foster communication between the ranks. "Since our office is open, the senior staff does not have offices and often sit next to junior staff members," remarks a consultant. A colleague concurs, describing the offices as "informal and collegiate. [There are] no assigned seats, no cubicles and a lot of white boards—it's brainstorm-friendly. In addition, says a co-worker, "Everyone is exceedingly approachable, and the firm does a good job of reinforcing this by having frequent dinners and happy hours that involve the entire staff."

Working with the man

Newcomers to IMS Health are "exposed and expected to interact with clients very rapidly. This can be anyone from CEO-level down to senior management," says one analyst. In fact, "client interaction is a requirement for all junior team members, not a privilege," adds another. A senior consultant explains that "everyone tries to provide junior members with client face time," and another reiterates that "our junior staff interacts with clients just about as quickly as feasible." Working so closely with the client management is an opportunity rookies should not take for granted, explains an analyst, since "clients are of high caliber, and working with them will greatly result in professional development."

Those who rise to the challenge are able "to take on responsibility as they are ready, and [management] is willing and ready to promote based upon merit, not degree or years of experience," says a senior principal in New York. Along those lines, co-workers add that there are ample "opportunities to take on more responsibility and grow within the company," and there are "significant leadership opportunities at all levels." According to the firm, some of these opportunities include taking on greater client contact and management, presentation creation, and chances to lead and participate in office initiatives for recruiting, social events and training.

The melting pot

At IMS, there is "no question we lead the industry" in terms of women in higher management," says one Manhattan-based consultant, who adds that "two of our most senior professionals are women." Another notes that "the firm is mostly female, and this is consistent at most levels." The same can be said for hiring of minority employees, sources note. In the New York office, "we are generally a melting pot with a range of ethnicities (Asian, Caucasian, black, Indian), nationalities (Indonesian, Ghanaian, Australian) and religions (Hindu, Muslim, Christian, Jewish)," among others. However, an insider comments that while "there are many minorities within the company," there are "not many in higher positions—none above engagement manager, and there are four levels above that."

IMS consultants add that when it comes to hiring gay, lesbian or bisexual candidates, they "would have no trouble feeling comfortable here." In fact, as a New Yorker points out, there are "several openly gay people in the office." An analyst attests, "As a gay man in the office, I can honestly say that it's been an extremely welcoming and unbiased environment."

Visit the Vault Consulting Career Channel at **www.vault.com/consulting** - with insider firm profiles, message boards, the Vault Consulting Job Board and more.

469

Kaiser Associates

1747 Pennsylvania Avenue, NW
Suite 900
Washington, DC 20006
Phone: (202) 454-2000
Fax: (202) 454-2001
www.kaiserassociates.com

LOCATIONS

Washington, DC (Global HQ)
London (Europe HQ)
Cape Town
São Paulo
Toronto

PRACTICE AREAS

Competitor Benchmarking
  In-depth Analysis
  Scenario Development/War Gaming
Go To Market
Growth
  Innovation
  Go to Market
  Mergers, Acquisitions & Divestitures
Operational Effectiveness
  BIC Benchmarking
  Cost Management
  Organizational Design
Strategy Development & Implementation

THE STATS

Employer Type: Private Company
Director, North America: Kevin Dell'Oro
Director, Europe: Luc Deschamps
2007 Employees: 130
2006 Employees: 130

THE BUZZ
WHAT CONSULTANTS AT OTHER FIRMS ARE SAYING ABOUT THIS FIRM

- "Solid firm"
- "Always struggling to get to the next level"
- "Benchmark specialists"
- "Disorganized"

RANKING RECAP

Quality of Life
#1 - Interaction with Clients
#7 - Relationships with Supervisors
#12 - Firm Culture (tie)
#18 - Offices
#18 - Travel Requirements

Diversity
#6 - Diversity for Women
#19 - Best Firms for Diversity
#19 - Diversity for Minorities

UPPERS

- "High degree of client interaction available even to entry-level employees"
- "Quick and transparent promotion process"
- Culturally diverse
- "Boutique consulting firm that operates as a true meritocracy"

DOWNERS

- "Limited control of project assignments in the first couple of years"
- "Lack of recognition of Kaiser name outside the consulting world"
- Resources can be more limited than at larger firms, ie, personnel, IT
- "Relatively low pay at the staff and middle manager levels"

EMPLOYMENT CONTACT

www.kaiserassociates.com/join/consultants.html

THE SCOOP

Just the facts, ma'am

Founded in 1981 by Michael M. Kaiser as a spin-off from Strategic Planning Associates (now Oliver Wyman), Kaiser Associates is a boutique firm with a mission: bringing the facts back to consulting. Kaiser is defined by its fact-based approach, through which it helps clients incorporate externally-driven analysis into its decision making.

The firm's "selective and elite" stable of clients includes five of *Fortune*'s Global 10 Most Admired Corporations; six of the top-10 in *BusinessWeek*'s Global 1000; and seven of the EuroSTOXX 50. Return clients make up more than 80 percent of the firm's engagements. Industries served by the firm include aerospace and defense, chemicals, communications, consumer products, energy/oil and gas, financial services, health care, high tech and electronics, industrial, media and entertainment, and private equity.

On the bench

A hallmark of Kaiser's fact-based approach is benchmarking. The firm has been a trailblazer in the field, publishing the first book on the topic, *Beating the Competition: A Practical Guide to Benchmarking*, in the 1980s. Completing more than 200 benchmarking studies between 1982 and 1985, the firm established itself as a leader in the field; so far, the consultancy has completed more than 3,000 benchmarking engagements across every major industry and function. To produce reports tailored to clients' needs, Kaiser helps its customers select the companies they want to be measured against before providing the research and data for comparison.

In fact, the ability to establish ground and build expertise in niche markets and methods is one of Kaiser's specialties. The firm has expanded to offer go-to-market, M&A, economic development, divestiture, white space identification, organizational effectiveness and supply chain consulting services. An April 2006 *BusinessWeek* article highlighted the firm's expertise in performance metrics, noting that Kaiser is forging a new path in developing tools to measure the business impact of innovation. The firm's approach to "innovation performance" is relatively new, using a complex set of rules, metrics and definitions to analyze the value of new ideas. "Unlike financial performance indicators such as ROI or ROA, innovation lacks a common set of rules around what's included and what isn't," a problem now being addressed by Kaiser, the article explained.

The international jet set

The firm's Washington office serves as its global headquarters, and also covers its business throughout the U.S. as well as Mexico, the Caribbean and Central America, and Asia. Through an active exchange program, consultants are given the opportunity to transfer to other Kaiser offices worldwide. The firm's London office serves Kaiser's European and Asian businesses, drawing on an international staff of consultants for projects such as helping a consumer goods manufacturer develop market entry strategies for Eastern Europe, working with the government of Dubai on strategy and feasibility analysis for a major trade infrastructure project, and working with a specialty chemicals manufacturer in Germany on strengthening supply chain operations. In Latin America, the firm serves clients through an office in São Paulo, opened in 1997. Clients in the region include energy, communications and pharmaceuticals firms, and Kaiser's economic development practice also works with regional governments. In addition, consultants from the São Paulo office regularly participate in knowledge and personnel exchanges with the firm's other branches. The Toronto office serves clients in a host of industries such as aerospace, financial services, consumer products, natural resources, communications and utilities.

Into Africa

With the opening of the South African office in 1997, it became clear that the firm's strategy expertise could make a valuable contribution to the challenges of economic development. In response to the growing need for these services and the unique requirements of delivering this work, Kaiser established a dedicated economic development practice in 1998. The practice was

Visit the Vault Consulting Career Channel at **www.vault.com/consulting** - with insider firm profiles, message boards, the Vault Consulting Job Board and more.

V/\ULT CAREER LIBRARY   471

initially aimed at enhancing economic and social development in southern Africa through services such as small business development, job creation, black economic empowerment and export growth. These days, Kaiser performs EDP work outside of Africa as well, working with clients such as the governments of Dubai and Punjab.

From its Cape Town facility, Kaiser focuses on developing industries, export abilities, national branding and developing policy in the surrounding region. The firm was tapped in 2001 by the National Economic Development and Labor Council to develop a strategy and business plan for the Proudly South African campaign. The campaign's goal was to stimulate economic growth and create jobs through an increased demand for the region's products and services. In addition, the country's Fund for Research into Industrial Development, Growth and Equity asked Kaiser to help South African businesses assess their procurement practices, and develop strategies to use procurement to boost socioeconomic development. Other regional clients have included the South African Department of Trade & Industry, which engaged the firm to come up with an export strategy for the country's electronics sector, and the local jewelry trade association, which called on Kaiser to help it create a sustainable jewelry export industry.

Quick ride to the top

Hard workers can get ahead pretty swiftly at Kaiser, the firm suggests. Upon joining the firm at the ground floor, new Kaiserites spend about 30 months as consultants. The first half of this period is spent mastering research, writing and project delivery. During the second half, most associates earn a promotion to senior consultant, with promotion to managing consultant possible for outstanding performers within just 25 months. Managing consultants are invited to join practice teams led by one of the firm's senior VPs.

GETTING HIRED

Reeling them in

At college recruiting time, Kaiser North America tends to fish from the East Coast pond, with a special lookout for the liberal arts school variety—Middlebury, Williams, Swarthmore, Haverford and Bowdoin are high on the list. Depending on candidate locale, HR representatives and consultants conduct an initial interview on campus or by phone, which is "a typical one-hour discussion regarding an applicant's work experience and interests," mostly to gauge fit with the firm. Once past the stage-one hurdle, Kaiser flies contenders out to its D.C. office for a second-round Super Day, a "daylong, in-person interview that contained a writing test, a quantitative case, an analytical case and more general interviews," a staffer recollects. Other colleagues say the procedure's "unique components include a qualitative research study that focuses on research resourcefulness, original thought and storytelling," and gives competitors "a good feel for the personality of the firm."

Current Kaiser insiders throw out a few sample case questions: "If GE came out with a light bulb that never died, what do you think they should price it at?" one associate contributes, while another offers, "How many gas stations are in Maine?" and "How many planes leave Dulles on a given day?" Departing from purely quantitative questions, one consultant notes that "one of the more analytical case questions was about a North American beverage company expanding into Latin America."

OUR SURVEY SAYS

Kick back and relax

Sources at Kaiser praise their "very young, energetic and highly ambitious" co-workers, who are both "extremely entrepreneurial and collegial." At work and after hours, staffers say they get ample opportunities to get to know each other, whether it's through project work or frequent happy hours. "Kaiser's culture is why I chose this firm," an insider shares, while a colleague adds that "there is very little in the way of internal politicking, and overall it's been my experience that it is a very open and collaborative place." With Casual Fridays and an endless supply of employee birthday cake on hand, sources are comfortable within the Kaiser sphere, and are also rewarded for talent and diligence. "Many firms claim to be a meritocracy," remarks a senior consultant, "but Kaiser actually is." And though hardworking, associates don't take their down-to-earth office pals for granted. Concludes a source, "Everyone has tough weeks, but on the whole, the office is both fairly happy and relaxed, given the amount of work we all have."

Go get 'em

As for access to upper ranks, "this is where Kaiser shines," a staffer shares, continuing, "I get daily exposure to managers who are typically top-level MBAs with years of wisdom and experience." Consultants note their firm's nonhierarchical structure, which affords them "the opportunity to work closely with the senior leaders of the firm almost immediately," and perpetuates an open-door atmosphere where even the newest hires can contact their superiors without jumping through hoops. In fact, "supervisors do a great job of meeting with consultants early in each engagement to understand what the consultant hopes to get out of the project, from a developmental perspective," a source adds.

Loosening the leash

Intimate interaction with bigwigs transfers over to client relations, too. Kaiserites report unique, high-interface opportunities with the firm's patrons, which supervisors encourage. "Your VPs and managers at Kaiser will give you as much responsibility and client time as you can adequately handle," we're told, with staff "given extremely long leashes to pursue opportunities." Employees all note the swift client access as a "sharp contrast" to other firms in the industry; one associate shares, "In my first three projects, I became well acquainted with my clients, to the point that they would direct research questions at me during meetings." Another expresses similar sentiments, reporting, "As an entry-level consultant, I was able to present and discuss with C-level executives at Fortune 500 companies." According to insiders, the trust passed on to newbies is unparalled: "Being straight out of college and advising VPs of Fortune 500 companies either face-to-face or over the phone is a very unique opportunity that I'm grateful for," boasts a source.

Accommodating agendas

"As at most major firms, the workload is cyclical," an associate explains of the firm's varied agenda. "Some weeks you'll have a very easily manageable workweek, and others, you'll have to put in 15-hour days, as well as weekends." But largely, most employees don't have much to complain about when it comes to Kaiser's hourly demands. "Although the hours can be long, the firm is flexible and understanding of our personal needs and other obligations," says a source, and others agree. "The firm supports good balance," we're told, so "when you are on the bench or are done with your work, you are encouraged to go home and not stick around."

At Kaiser, "the VPs realize you work hard." Staffers acknowledge the firm's focus on work/life balance and say management pushes for an accommodating schedule, even providing "coaching on how to manage the balance better." Furthermore, those wishing for less time at the office are given some freedom to flex their consulting skills from home, if needed. As one insider clarifies, "If your schedule permits it, you are more than welcome to work from home and structure/schedule your hours based on what is most convenient for you," an option that Kaiser staffers more than appreciate. In addition, employees recovering from drawn-out, marathon-esque projects with clients are cut a little slack: "If you've just finished a particularly tough engagement or week, they'll usually work with you to get you scheduled so that you can have some time to relax and regroup," states a consultant. A co-worker attests to the perk, describing a recent project, "where for two weeks I worked, on average, 12-hour days plus weekends," he says, and "in return for my hard work, my VP gave me a day off when the project was done."

Stick around

For consulting hopefuls looking to remain geographically stationary, Kaiser may be just the place. "Most work is done from the office, with travel only as needed to client sites," employees report, usually making one to two client-locale stints per job for

Visit the Vault Consulting Career Channel at **www.vault.com/consulting** - with insider firm profiles, message boards, the Vault Consulting Job Board and more.

473

project kickoffs and closings, unless extenuating circumstances apply. "Firm management strives to minimize unnecessary travel by the engagement, to the benefit of the client and the consultant," a relieving facet to many staffers who say that the heftiest travel burdens are reserved for vice presidents. Since Kaiser performs its services heavily over the phone, staffers don't mind occasional trips. As one first-year associate shares, "Travel is limited enough that it provides an interesting diversion and a break from office life." This sentiment resonates among other colleagues, who say that "the infrequent travel is generally much more enjoyable," "mitigates employee burnout" and, most importantly, "doesn't disrupt your life."

Education by example

According to Kaiser sources, the firm's official training wheels could use some oiling. "Training is outdated," a managing consultant admits, and a co-worker says it's "the weakest part of the firm, by far." Word has it, though, that change is in the air. "The firm is working on making the training program more systematic," employees say, "which will hopefully improve the depth." For the time being, Kaiser associates report a formal one- to two-week training period—a "series of PowerPoint modules and group working sessions led by different subject matter experts within the firm"—that is only marginally helpful. "It was a good opportunity to meet the older consultants and start to understand how things are done here at Kaiser," a newer hire explains, but admits to learning more "on-the-fly" over the course of engagements. Even with a new model on the rise, staffers claim they learn the most from the informal guidance received from co-workers. Plus, "mentors act as an advocate during performance reviews, and also do a great job of making themselves available for everyday questions."

Elevator to the top

Consultant cash flow at Kaiser is up to par, sources indicate. According to one senior manager, "Kaiser tends to pay less at the staff and junior management levels," and a colleague agrees, stating, "I think that the compensation is about average for the industry, but when you factor in the superior work/life balance that Kaiser offers, you are actually being paid more for your time." Another insider notes that compensation "was almost exactly the same as my other offers," but adds, "We understand that if we master the skills needed, we can earn rapid promotion here." "Getting to that senior management level happens a lot quicker than it does at the big firms," we're told. And that rapid advancement offers more than just heady titles, sources say— compensation "gets extremely attractive as you move up through the ranks to VP and senior VP," positions that receive supplementary funds derived from premium performance. "Officers (VPs and SVPs) are provided additional compensation based upon their business development (revenue generating) performance," staffers explain. In addition, a consultant notes, "People are awarded for performance in a number of ways, including biannual bonuses, promotions every one to two years and increasing levels of responsibility."

I'll take iPod for free, Alex

A fast promotion track isn't the only incentive motivating Kaiser employees to be meticulous workers. Among company trips to baseball and hockey games, free Starbucks and a stocked refrigerator as part of a healthy snacks program, "we just got a new foosball table to ease the stress on late nights and over lunch," an associate gloats. Sources also exalt golf tournaments, gym memberships, cab fare for late-night laborers, a respectable expense policy and break room televisions in D.C.—"we all watch *Jeopardy* during lunch," a senior employee says. Also offered to employees are "revenue challenges" to sustain both efficiency and morale, along with "special opportunities to people who earn the top rating in their six-month reviews." Client teams raking in the most profit from engagements receive cash prizes (which one insider says accounts for the office foosball table), and when Kaiser arrived at its revenue goal, "we all received iPod shuffles," a consultant adds.

Divided they stand

D.C.-based Kaiser consultants are situated in two downtown D.C. offices, right across the street from one another, and sources agree that "one is much nicer and better appointed than the other." Kaiserites depict one office's interior as "functional, clean and well lit," but grumble that "too many of us have cubicles. Even long-tenured managers remain in cubes until they reach VP level." Some have been fortunate enough to move into the new facility across the street, which has a little more to offer. "The office boasts a roof deck with vistas over every major D.C. monument and the mall," associates gush, and note that "the interior is newly spacious, and offices and huddle rooms are now plentiful." The new digs are also home to "a nice kitchen that is frequently filled with complimentary snacks, comfortable conference rooms" and the infamous, aforementioned foosball table. Regardless of what perks lie within, though, consultants from both offices get excited when thinking about their location: "Our two D.C. offices are less than a block from the White House, across the street from the World Bank and easily accessible to the nicest residential neighborhoods in D.C." Another adds, "The location is pristine and easily one of the key points of attraction for consultants."

Where women rule

"Women have a strong voice at Kaiser and can be found at all levels of leadership," sources indicate, and estimate a 40 percent female presence in the ranks. Employees position the firm as "a champion for the development of female consultants," and though the bulk of women are low- to midlevel workers, they say Kaiser does boast a female co-owner and two vice presidents. Overall, the firm "seems to be very strong in terms of hiring, promoting and including women."

While internationally diverse—one associate reports "more than 15 foreign languages spoken"—Kaiser comes up short in the staffing department with respect to racial minorities. As one senior consultant shares, "Racial minorities are present, but not enough to call the firm diverse. However," the source continues, "I am a minority and feel absolutely comfortable." Staffers do note the firm's "open, liberal and inclusive" attitude extended toward sexual orientation as well, though one colleague admits, "I'm not sure how large the GLBT community is at Kaiser."

Arms open wide

One managing staffer says that "opportunities abound" at Kaiser when it comes to getting involved in its neighboring communities. "Kaiser works with the local Boys and Girls Club on a variety of projects, and also 'adopts' a number of families each holiday season," an employee explains, with further resources devoted to participation in gift drives, charity walks, tutoring/mentoring events and other volunteer initiatives by Kaiser's own community service committee. Piloting four to five yearly events, staffers say that "participation is encouraged at all levels of the firm," with many younger associates contributing frequently to Kaiser's causes.

Visit the Vault Consulting Career Channel at **www.vault.com/consulting** - with insider firm profiles, message boards, the Vault Consulting Job Board and more.

VAULT CAREER LIBRARY   475

The Lewin Group

3130 Fairview Park Drive
Suite 800
Falls Church, VA 22042
Phone: (703) 269-5500
Fax: (703) 269-5501
www.lewin.com

LOCATION

Falls Church, VA (HQ)

PRACTICE AREAS

Analytic Modeling
Health Care Strategy
Health & Human Services Policy Research
Management Consulting
Program Evaluation

THE STATS

Employer Type: Independent, Wholly Owned Subsidiary of
  Ingenix, Inc.
Executive VP: Ron Johnson
2007 Employees: 175
2006 Employees: 140

UPPER

• Casual and collaborative culture

DOWNER

• Little known outside of health care circles

EMPLOYMENT CONTACT

www.lewin.com/Careers

THE BUZZ
WHAT CONSULTANTS AT OTHER FIRMS ARE SAYING ABOUT THIS FIRM

- "Health care specialists"
- "Good policy, but always outdated by the time it is
  published"
- "Good research"
- "Lost too much autonomy with Quintiles merger"

THE SCOOP

Health wonks

In business for more than 36 years, The Lewin Group serves clients in the public, nonprofit and commercial markets providing health care and human services. Its client offerings include empirical research and data analysis, strategic and business planning, actuarial analysis and capitation rate-setting, program design, surveys, and evaluations of public programs and demonstration projects. Over the years, Lewin had developed and refined a number of proprietary analytic modeling tools such as the Health Benefits Simulation Model.

Based in Falls Church, Va., The Lewin Group employs about 150 consultants, many of whom come from high-ranking positions in government, academia and the health care industry. The firm is owned by Ingenix, Inc., a health care IT and consulting company, which purchased Lewin in June 2007 from its previous owner, Quintiles Transnational Corp. Ingenix is a subsidiary of United Health Group, the largest health insurer in the world.

In August 2006, one of the Quintiles execs took over the lead role at Lewin. Ron Johnson, who held senior positions at the Food and Drug Administration before serving as executive VP at Quintiles since 1997, was named executive vice president of the firm. Lewin gained other high-profile VPs that year—former America Institutes for Research strategist Margo Edmunds, former AARP Services exec Roberta Milman and former Ernst & Young Senior Director of Providers David Bender.

On-demand research

Lewin's consultants are often tapped to pen reports on health policy issues for clients. A September 2006 report, commissioned by the trade group Pharmaceutical Research and Manufacturers of America, analyzed the new choices available to beneficiaries under Medicare Part D. "A Report to Congress," published in May 2006 at the behest of the Department of Health and Human Services, studied the supply and demand for critical care physicians. The firm also has produced reports on Medicaid and long-term care trends for state governments, including those of Pennsylvania and Mississippi. In addition, the firm publishes an e-newsletter, Lewin Insight.

A healthy interest in politics

Lewin isn't shy about getting involved in politics—it conducts studies for various interested parties—but aggressively insists upon its objectivity and independence in doing so. In March 2007, one of its VPs, health care economist John Sheils testified before the Senate Finance Committee Hearing on the future course of health care reform. Sheils discussed the country's rising health care costs and the consequent impact on uninsured Americans. During the 2004 presidential race, Sheils presented a comparative analysis of the health policies in candidates Bush's and Kerry's respective platforms, which was picked up by the media and noted for its objectivity. Since then, he has conducted additional analyses of President Bush's health care reform proposal as well as Senator Ron Wyden's sponsored legislation, the Healthy Americans Act.

Lewin's work for the federal government has earned the firm accolades. In 2006, Lewin was named an Outstanding Contractor by the U.S. DHHS' Administration for Children and Families for its work on the Healthy Marriage Initiative. Lewin assisted 45 recipients of Healthy Marriage grants—primarily in the African-American and Hispanic communities—with implementing programs, strategic planning, establishing performance measures and developing management information systems.

Visit the Vault Consulting Career Channel at **www.vault.com/consulting** - with insider firm profiles, message boards, the Vault Consulting Job Board and more.

477

GETTING HIRED

From health care and beyond

Though it's a niche firm, The Lewin Group welcomes applicants from fields other than health care. The firm claims its consultants come from a diverse range of backgrounds, from government to academia. The best way to find out about available positions is by searching its web site, where open jobs are listed by location and category. Candidates can also create an online profile, and the firm will send e-mail alerts when a position that matches their skills and interests becomes available.

OUR SURVEY SAYS

Laid-back Lewin

If you're looking for an easygoing place to work, where people appreciate their colleagues, insiders say Lewin might be the place for you. A source comments, "The working environment is very flexible—you can work at home, depending on the budget." In addition, we're told, "Dress style is casual and jeans [on Fridays] is fine." Staffers enjoy the firm's "collaborative culture," and "the people are very down-to-earth and seriously smart," a senior associate boasts, adding, "It's definitely not a Big Five, but it builds its brands in the industry."

Mercator Partners LLC

30 Monument Square
Suite 155
Concord, MA 01742
Phone: (978) 287-7500
Fax: (978) 287-7600
www.mercatorpartners.com

LOCATIONS

Boston, MA (Global HQ)
Washington, DC

PRACTICE AREAS

Business Development Support
Business Unit Strategy
Campaign Mapping & Program Management
Corporate Strategy
Investment Evaluation
Marketing & Sales
New Opportunity Assessment
Organizational Design
Partnerships & Alliances
Product & Service Design
Strategic Planning Processes

THE STATS

Employer Type: Private Company
CEO: Charles Gildehaus
2007 Employees: 25
2006 Employees: 25

UPPERS

- Opportunities for advancement
- "Obsessive dedication to excellence"

DOWNERS

- "Work/life balance is a bit blurry"
- "Lack of resources of a big firm"

EMPLOYMENT CONTACT

Lisa Burkholder, Recruiting Coordinator
E-mail: careers@mercatorpartners.com

Visit the Vault Consulting Career Channel at **www.vault.com/consulting** - with insider firm profiles, message boards, the Vault Consulting Job Board and more.

VAULT CAREER LIBRARY   479

THE SCOOP

Mercator calling

Mercator Partners, founded in 1998, specializes in the mobile, broadband and convergence markets. The firm is focused on the communications, technology and media sectors, with a mission to assist senior management teams solve strategic, operational and organizational issues. It serves high-profile clients like Sprint Nextel, AT&T, XM Satellite Radio, Comcast, Sony Ericsson and Verizon.

With just 25 consultants in its ranks, Mercator has offices near Boston and Washington, D.C. Its narrow focus means its consultants are able to dig deep into the markets it serves. The firm has developed its own data sets on mobile devices, converged products and services, and customer needs, which it leverages in its engagements for clients. Recent projects have included overall convergence product strategy and creating a roadmap for a major converged service provider; a mobile device strategy and portfolio planning system for a major U.S. wireless carrier; and assisting with a major cable operator's acquisition and integration process.

Kings of convergence

Mercator's partners all boast years of hands-on experience within the sectors they serve. Co-founder Charles Gildehaus, who serves as CEO, has more than 20 years of experience in strategy, finance and law, and has launched and serves on the board of several successful mobile startups. Senior Partner Chuck Ennis served as CEO for Telepad and Roku technologies (both mobile data specialists) before signing on with Mercator, and Advisor Tom Wheeler was CEO of the Cellular Telecommunications & Internet Association (CTIA) from 1992 to 2003. Senior Advisor John Stenbit previously served as assistant secretary of defense, reporting directly to former Secretary of Defense Donald Rumsfeld in the capacity of chief information officer. His main focus was mobile and networkable data systems.

In March 2007, the firm announced the addition of two new partners, Tony Abate, a former engagement manager at McKinsey, and Moe Kelley, whose prior experience was in the cable industry.

Mercator enjoys close ties with the CTIA, which co-sponsors the annual convergence study. The study interviews over 30 executives from four key service provider groups in the broadband sector to create an evolving picture of where the convergence market is headed. In the past, Mercator's view has been that as technologies continue to merge, disparate voice and data networks will become indistinguishable to end users. Accordingly, the firm says, companies in the wireless business must be prepared to compete in their market space with a variety of broadband players.

GETTING HIRED

The Mercator projection

If you have an undergraduate degree and less than two years of industry experience, you may be able to join Mercator as an associate—or an "executive consultant in training"—according to the firm's web site. Consultants join at the next level up, with experience or, in some cases, a non-MBA graduate degree. Managers must come equipped with "significant" industry experience and/or an MBA; then it's on to principal and partner.

The firm's site also offers a handy list of recommended reading for prospective applicants, along with addresses (both e-mail and snail-mail) to which to send resumes. An insider reports that Mercator recruits from Dartmouth, Brown, Smith, Harvard, MIT, and Amherst and "via the Web at other top schools."

Getting screened

An insider reports that after an "initial screening interview (usually by phone)," candidates can expect "several interviews on one day, then follow-up interviews if the firm is on the edge," during which "all candidates are interviewed by the top executives." The "typical hire will interview with five to six people," says another source.

For interns, a source reports, the "summer experience is no different than full time. I worked on a series of due diligence engagements looking at telecom investments for global name-brand investors. It was high profile, intellectually challenging, interesting work."

OUR SURVEY SAYS

Getting exposed

Mercator, according to an insider, offers "strong collaboration" and a "team atmosphere" in which "most junior people work closely with partners and clients and everyone's ideas are valued," which results in "great opportunities for learning." The "great exposure early on" allows for building "great working relationships and a global network in the telecom industry." A colleague agrees that there are "lots of one-on-one working sessions with managers, partners and clients," along with "amiable co-workers."

Hours, travel and work/life balance are variable at Mercator, sources suggest. While hours are "all driven by client work and deliverables, not by face time," a source says, "often there are late nights or weekends before major deliverables." And according to an insider, "some travel is great—you get in front of the client and see the world. I've had a mostly good travel experience with project work taking me to London, Madrid, Japan, Paris, Sweden, Amsterdam, Denver, Atlanta and D.C."

Learning as you go

While "training is mostly informal, on-the-job mentoring," a source comments that this approach "is effective, particularly on longer-term projects." And Mercator offers "very fast advancement for individuals who prove themselves capable," says a colleague.

While gender diversity is not one of the firm's strong points at this time, an insider tells us that Mercator "is actively seeking to improve our ratio of women to men and is generally very receptive. This is not a 'boys' club'; on the other hand, recruiting women is particularly difficult at a boutique." With regard to ethnic diversity, the source adds, "We have had a wide variety of people from diverse backgrounds, races and nationalities."

Visit the Vault Consulting Career Channel at **www.vault.com/consulting** - with insider firm profiles, message boards, the Vault Consulting Job Board and more.

 VAULT CAREER LIBRARY   481

Milliman, Inc.

1301 Fifth Avenue
Suite 3800
Seattle, WA 98101
Phone: (206) 624-7940
Fax: (206) 340-1380
www.milliman.com

LOCATIONS

Seattle, WA (HQ)
Offices in 33 US cities and 14 offices abroad

PRACTICE AREAS

Health Consulting Services
Life & Financial Consulting Services
Pension, Employee Benefits, Investment & Compensation
 Consulting Services
Property/Casualty Consulting Services

THE STATS

Employer Type: Private Company
President & CEO: Patrick J. Grannan
2007 Employees: 2,000
2006 Employees: 1,900
2006 Revenue: $472 million
2005 Revenue: $435 million

RANKING RECAP

Quality of Life
#4 - Compensation
#11 - Best Firms to Work For
#12 - Interaction with Clients
#12 - Relationships with Supervisors
#13 - Overall Satisfaction
#13 - Travel Requirements
#16 - Offices
#17 - Hours in the Office

Diversity
#7 - Diversity for Women
#8 - Best Firms for Diversity
#11 - Diversity for Minorities
#15 - Diversity for GLBT

UPPERS

- Flexibility to make your own schedule and choose your assignments
- "Retention is high"
- "Flexibility in running a local consulting practice while still having the resources of a larger firm"
- "Ability to get equity ownership"

DOWNERS

- "The stress of being an entrepreneur can get to me"
- "Being privately held, we have more capital limitations than other firms"
- "Shrinking market means the good days are probably behind us"
- "Sometimes the work is slower than I'd like it"

EMPLOYMENT CONTACT

www.milliman.com/careers/careers_at_milliman.php

THE SCOOP

Actuarially speaking

Milliman employs more than 2,000 staffers, about 900 of whom are professionally credentialed consultants. Its practice areas include pension, employee benefits, investment and compensation consulting; health consulting; life insurance and financial consulting; and property and casualty insurance consulting. Founded in Seattle in 1947, the firm operates out of 33 U.S. cities, plus 14 offices in major cities overseas. The firm is owned and managed by approximately 270 principals, and reported revenue of $435 million in 2005. A founding member of Milliman Global—an international organization of consulting firms serving insurance, employee benefits and health care clients worldwide—Milliman Inc. and its related member firms provide actuarial and management advice from locations in principal cities around the world.

Milliman tends to keep quiet about its client engagements, but a few come to light from time to time. In March 2007, the firm reported the completion of an extensive consulting project for Fitch Ratings. Milliman helped the global ratings organization design and build a new model known as Matrix, aimed at helping financial guarantors keep up with an evolving risk profile. Among the firm's public-sector clients is the state of New Jersey, which calls on Milliman to serve as the actuary for its Teachers' Pension and Annuity Fund. And in 2006, American International Group (better known as AIG) tapped Milliman to review the loss reserves for its property and casualty business. The firm was asked to conduct a thorough independent study of the business' asbestos and other environmental exposures. Based on the findings, AIG decided to increase its loss reserves.

Health plans with a Latin beat

In January 2007, the firm acquired Acser, an actuarial company focusing on health care in Brazil. The company provides consulting services to approximately 100 health plans in the region. In August 2006, Milliman agreed to buy the business of Lawrence Johnson & Associates, a full-service retirement and employee benefits consulting firm based in Oakland.

Holding the Mayo

Milliman landed a big client in September 2006, when the Mayo Clinic licensed several of the firm's evidence-based clinical guideline products. Known as *Milliman Care Guidelines* and written by doctors and other clinicians, the products are used to help health care providers address specific patient conditions with appropriate levels of care. In May 2006, the *Guidelines'* editor in chief, James M. Schibanoff, MD, was named among the nation's 50 Most Powerful Physician Executives by *Modern Physician* and *Modern Healthcare* magazines.

In September 2006, Milliman announced the hiring of Gregory A. Ray as research director for its health care practice, overseeing the group's data and research strategy. Ray previously worked with Humana and Wellpoint, helping to develop and execute electronic data systems.

Keeping them satisfied

In 2006, for the second year running, Milliman placed first in overall client satisfaction among plan sponsors in Boston Research Group's ranking of defined contribution providers. The study gathers responses from nearly 2,000 401(k) plan sponsors, rating defined contribution record keepers on the services they provide to their clients.

And Milliman's also no slouch when it comes to keeping its own employees happy. In November 2004, *Consulting Magazine* ranked Milliman, one of the 10-best consulting firms to work for.

Pondering pensions

Milliman produces regular reports of interest to the actuarial crowd, including an annual pension funding study. In addition, the firm offers specialized publications, such as the quarterly *Insight*, addressing topics such as "Life After Work: The Future of

Visit the Vault Consulting Career Channel at **www.vault.com/consulting** - with insider firm profiles, message boards, the Vault Consulting Job Board and more.

 VAULT CAREER LIBRARY   483

Retirement Security." Milliman's online publications include the Multiemployer Review, Medical Professional Liability News Briefs and the Benefits Information Bulletin. The firm also occasionally appears in the popular and business press; in April 2007, *The Wall Street Journal* interviewed Milliman Principal Dan McCarthy on strategies small employers can use to lower health coverage costs.

Milliman also offers proprietary tools of use to its specialized clients. In October 2006, the firm teamed with health information underwriter Hooper Holmes to introduce Hooper IntelliScript, a web-based prescription history service for insurers in the life insurance industry.

GETTING HIRED

Local flavor

Recruiting at Milliman is conducted on a local level, so each office decides when to hire new applicants. Most offices report that there's no formal recruiting program, but each office has contacts at regional schools from which applicants are drawn each year. Sources say the firm doesn't recruit on campus, since it typically looks for experienced staff but, we're told, new graduates are sometimes considered, depending on the needs of the office. A source lists "Tufts University, MIT, Bentley College and a few other New England schools," and a colleague mentions "NYU, Penn, Hofstra and Columbia" as schools where the firm looks for entry-level candidates.

Because recruiting is carried out regionally, the process varies widely, though in general, "the number of interviews is related to the level of the candidate," a source notes. Comments an insider in Hartford, "We look for the best candidates whenever we have an opening. Interviews include all levels of employees: co-workers, supervisors and managers. In many hires, we look for actuarial exam success." A Chicago staffer explains, "For our particular group, the candidate will meet with all of the managers as well as other staff members. We take time to ensure that the candidate not only meets our technical requirements but will be a good fit within the company's overall culture and our local group's dynamics." A consultant in Atlanta reports, "Interviewees come in, meet with their contact for 15 minutes, then have three or four rounds of 30 minutes each, with one or two employees. Afterward, if the candidate is an out-of-town guest, he is taken to lunch by his contact and possibly a few more employees." But in other offices, the process can be more succinct; for example, according to a manager in Phoenix, the hiring process consists of "two interviews. Both are with the final decision maker."

Can you cite code?

While interview experiences vary across offices, Milliman employees say that across the board, candidates are asked general questions based on experience and knowledge, rather than case questions. "Questions focus on ability to connect with clients and amenability to variable schedule inherent in consulting," a manager notes. "It's typical to have a minimum of two interviews. We do screen for technical knowledge by using a special test," an associate shares. For instance, "We might ask about IRS code references, and have the applicant explain everything they know about the topic."

A consultant recounts his experience: "My first interview was on the phone. It was with my current manager. It took about 20 minutes and was very succinct. For my second interview, they flew me down to Atlanta and I talked with five different people, each for about 30 minutes. Mostly, we talked about health care in general, what they do, who they work with and some examples of projects they do. There were very few canned interview questions. Then, three of us went to lunch (interview continued, obviously) and it was over by 1 p.m. I sent a follow-up e-mail the next morning. Two days later, my recruiter called and told me I had an offer."

According to insiders, interviewing isn't the most difficult part of getting hired at Milliman—it's landing an interview that's tough. Admits a staffer, "It's hard to get the interview with my firm, but if you can accomplish that, the interview process is not bad at all."

OUR SURVEY SAYS

Go-getters

The consensus is that Milliman's culture is decidedly entrepreneurial and supports those who want to run their own show. "Milliman is all about freedom and entrepreneurship. The culture here nurtures success," remarks an insider. Agrees a source, "If they are so inclined, Milliman consultants have the same opportunity as any of their peers to become a Milliman principal and owner." And another manager confirms, "If you are driven to do something to make a difference, we can provide the opportunity to make that happen."

Staffers also say that part of the appeal of the job is the creativity and freedom they're granted. Claims one associate, "The freedom in which we work allows for creative problem solving. Our culture embraces creativity and finding new ways to satisfy client needs that often require custom solutions." In addition to individual freedom, each office operates on an independent basis—a status that employees appreciate. "Our culture is very decentralized and allows for many decisions to be made locally. Since we have a profit center structure, we are the direct beneficiaries of these decisions. We love this freedom," boasts a consultant. That decentralized structure also means that culture will vary depending on the location. An East Coast insider notes, "Office culture for this firm is exceptional. Each office is managed independently and is a reflection of the managing partner." Being a part of an independently owned company is also a boon to insiders: "Most of my college friends with similar occupations are envious that I found this job," boasts a source. "The majority of them plan on switching companies within a few years. There's just no comparison with publicly traded companies."

A nice bunch of folks

Sources also comment that "smart," "friendly and helpful" co-workers are another plus to working at Milliman. "We all get along. Everyone is knowledgeable, and most people just have the willingness to help out and get the job done," comments one associate. "The standards and expectations are high, but the atmosphere is relaxed. Everyone seems to be genuinely nice and supportive of each other." Another happy insider lauds the firm's concurrent values of teamwork and individualism: "The atmosphere is very collegial and people are valued for who they are. And, diversity is both up and down the hallway."

Employees also seem pleased with the amount of interaction they have with firm management. "My supervisor gives me significant discretion to work with my clients. He is available and accessible as needed," a consultant states. "The culture is very flat; it is not difficult to ask questions," claims an insider, while another source adds, "I can tell that my boss really does care about his employees."

Look to the valleys

Most insiders claim that work/life balance exists at Milliman, thanks to reasonable hours and an easygoing pace, but they do acknowledge that there are peaks and valleys in the work demands, just like at any consulting firm. "The hours need to be worked during crunch time but there are sufficient times when work is not overly demanding that you can accomplish nonwork-related goals and objectives," explains a principal. Sources claim that 50 to 60 hour weeks are about average, with a few weeks in the 80- to 90-hour range. A consultant explains that "overtime and weekend work is expected at this firm. Usually, the hours are not oppressive (outside of our busiest time of the year) and the weekend work is usually less than two to three hours." An insider confirms, "There are some busy times when your personal life may be restricted, but for the most part, it is a relaxed atmosphere and there is a comfortable balance." So outside of the usual consulting crunch-time woes, staffers assert that it's possible to maintain a satisfactory personal life outside of the office.

Recognizing that long hours will inevitably be a part of their experience at Milliman, sources advise that it's necessary to take initiative in balancing your own work and life. A senior employee states, "I tend to work quite a bit by choice. What is nice about Milliman's culture is that there is no up-or-out mentality. Rather, for each person within the firm, you are given an opportunity to succeed and be rewarded at the highest levels." He continues, "Like many things in life, you get what you put

Visit the Vault Consulting Career Channel at www.vault.com/consulting - with insider firm profiles, message boards, the Vault Consulting Job Board and more.

VAULT CAREER LIBRARY   485

into it. Everyone within Milliman draws their own lines with respect to personal and work commitments, without pressure to forsake one for the other." From the opposite end of the totem pole, an associate, after having worked at Milliman just under two years remarks, "Thus far, I have had no trouble balancing my work with the rest of my life. Managers and co-workers are very respectful and practical when I have other commitments."

Get it done—on your own time

So how do they keep work/life balance at a healthy level? Flexibility is key, according to a colleague: "I can have balance to the extent that I want. Working at home on evenings and weekends instead of normal business hours is always an option. Rule No. 1 is: Get the work that we promised done on time, on budget and of the highest quality. Rule No. 2 is to be flexible about everything except Rule No. 1." Sources also indicate that it's easier for consultants with less responsibility to take advantage of flexibility than for those in management. Mentions an insider, "With respect to our employees, we have been very flexible in our office about telecommuting and part-time work. However, I am an equity principal and, as such, the balancing act is more difficult."

But those who are able to take advantage of the firm's flexibility relish the benefits. "The ability to work at home has lessened the need to stay late at the office or go to the office on weekends," mentions a source. Other employees choose to work longer hours during the week so that they can protect valuable weekend time. Relates an analyst, "My manager believes in not having to work weekends since he has four children. It's very helpful that he understands the importance of family time."

Traveling up the Milliman ladder

Milliman insiders report that travel "varies widely from time to time, depending on client needs," practice and position. For many consultants, having local clients means that no long-distance travel is necessary. "Most of the client work is local. The majority of travel is for corporate and professional business," explains a source in New York. Another staffer claims, "Travel is expected and the feeling is that if you turn it down, you won't be around very long. I'd say it decreases one's happiness of a work/life balance." Others agree that travel is a necessary part of advancement at the firm and indicate that travel frequency increases with greater responsibility. "There is lots of travel for principals but virtually none for everyone else," comments a consultant, while a co-worker adds, "There are minimal requirements. The travel question really relates to how much or little you put into your career at Milliman and the clients you attract and maintain."

Fortunately for some consultants with families, the firm has made exceptions to reduce travel demands. A Midwesterner comments, "My position requires considerable travel; unfortunately, this does result in being away from home more than I would like. One of my balances has been a two-week vacation with my wife and other family members each winter." A colleague shares his experience: "I was gone for two months at a time (coming home on weekends), but it was taking a toll on the family, and the firm adjusted to relieve that added pressure." Another insider affirms, "The opportunity to travel is there if you want it, but they do consider your family situation before shipping you off."

Paid for peak performance

Insiders at this firm don't seem to have many complaints about compensation and bonus. "I feel I am adequately compensated and more so than I would be at another company. Milliman does not have a standardized ladder to the top, but rather compensation and growth is highly based on performance. This is a good thing," assures a manager. A colleague declares, "Once you prove yourself, the salary gets competitive. We've had a problem with new employees coming in at higher levels than existing employees, but I think changes have been put in place to remedy that." Consultants also indicate that since compensation is performance-based, it largely depends on how hard each individual wants to work. "My compensation is lower than most consultants in my position because I spend far more time playing than most. There are several consultants with annual incomes at the $1 million or more mark," a longtime employee attests.

Employees ranging from the consultant to associate actuarial level report that bonuses might range from $5,000 to $28,000 annually. For principals, bonus is higher, unless they buy into the firm's equity profit-sharing plan. Details one principal, "My current salary is low because I'm deferring compensation by buying into a $4 million practice. When I retire (about eight years from now), I will sell the $4 million practice to my successor and receive $250,000 to $300,000 per year for the 10-year period following retirement. We also have a generous profit-sharing plan that contributes 15 percent of pay up to IRS maximums."

"From one person's brain to another"

Milliman insiders claim that the firm's formal training could use a face-lift. "Training is unofficial, although our office has gotten more proactive about official training this year. Our people work in teams and learn from each other," notes a staffer. An East Coast employee reports, "Training is almost entirely on the job. There is some written documentation, but the primary method is transfer from one person's brain to another." A colleague confirms, "Training is pretty minimal. You learn by asking and finding." Still others maintain that the current training system in place is sufficient for these independent-minded consultants. Asserts an associate, "Training is almost exclusively unofficial, but in a way that puts the burden of learning on the individual, which I support."

Some offices reportedly offer more formal training opportunities than others, we're told, since training offerings are decentralized, and coordinated for each office on the local level. A Hartford-based consultant details, "There is a blend of official and unofficial. Technical meetings for all consultants are held each year. Attendance at industry and professional meetings is encouraged, and on-the-job training is always taking place." Explains a manager in Minneapolis, "We have formal and informal opportunities with the firm for different types of training, including raise/bonus programs for continued education and designation attainment." "Training is coordinated on a national level when it makes sense to do that. But for the most part, training is on the job at the local level," a principal clarifies.

Just enough to keep them happy

Not every office at Milliman is decked out with fancy perks, but sources seem satisfied with things like "flexible leave time" and "equity ownership of your clients." According to one insider, "The perks vary by practice. In my practice, we offer whatever accommodations we need to keep good people. There are staff working from home, from another state (due to a spousal move), working part time, etc., as the situation warrants." Occasionally, employees receive "tickets to sporting events where our families may attend, or that we can provide to clients or co-workers as rewards," a consultant shares. A colleague mentions that he appreciates the "subsidized bus passes—it's not real flashy, but I think it really encourages people to use public transportation more."

But a few Milliman offices don't hold back when it comes to doling out extras. An Atlanta staffer says, "We have Million Dollar Weekend—a getaway weekend once a year for you and your family to a nice resort. It's a fun time to hang out with co-workers, relax and do some fun activities." In Minneapolis, there are "monthly birthday lunches, free sodas, very solid profit-sharing contributions and three or four colleague gatherings per year, like picnics, bowling parties and Christmas parties." A colleague in New York notes, "We get free drinks—whatever we want. I got a new office computer and they let me keep my old one." And according to one source, simply being thanked by the boss means the most: "The principals of our practice in Atlanta are very kind and generous, showing appreciation to employees every time they get the chance, and that is the biggest perk!"

Equality for all

Milliman insiders describe the firm as "very equal opportunity" when it comes to gender mix. "Several of our senior consultants are women. Half of my staff is women, including several of the key employees and leaders," attests a manager. A source relates, "I am a woman who has worked for our firm for more than 20 years. Gender is not an issue in terms of hiring, promoting or mentoring. The individual has the freedom to succeed regardless of gender."

Sources boast about gender equality, but add that the firm doesn't have an official initiative to hire women. "At some firms, there are special programs to recruit and advance women. There is no such program here, as it happens naturally. There are many women throughout all levels of the company," one associate explains. Milliman also gets high marks for its policies toward

Visit the Vault Consulting Career Channel at www.vault.com/consulting - with insider firm profiles, message boards, the Vault Consulting Job Board and more.

VAULT CAREER LIBRARY   487

family-minded women at the firm. "I am a woman, and I was elected principal while I was a part-time employee on three months' maternity leave," an insider shares.

Minorities at Milliman

Though there is also no official policy regarding minority hiring, either, respondents claim that Milliman has strong minority representation. "There are no barriers to hiring and promotion of minorities, but we are not attempting to be proactive about diversifying. We take people as they come and judge them on their merits, that's all," declares a principal. "Milliman's diverse culture is our core strength. The firm is very receptive to minorities," a colleague expresses. Some sources claim there are too few minorities in the firm's ranks, but not because of the firm's hiring policies. Says one insider, "There are not a lot of minorities, but that may be due to the nature of the business. The ones I know of are in the senior levels of management and enjoy working for the firm. I'm also white, but again, I believe we recognize passion and ability above any other personal characteristics." A principal sums up the firm's philosophy: "It's all about the work—not the gender or ethnic background or other personal affiliations … If you're qualified, you're getting hired."

According to insiders, the firm takes a similar approach when it comes to hiring gay and lesbian employees. "In our office we have numerous members of the GLBT community," a source states. "I do not believe sexual orientation is an issue whatsoever in hiring or promoting," affirms another consultant. A staffer based in the South was overjoyed at the firm's openness, given the cultural predisposition of the region, and exclaims, "Nobody here gives a damn—that's kind of unexpected, being from another part of the country and living in the South. Here, if you can do the job, who cares about your preference?"

Personally involved

Milliman doesn't loudly promote its efforts in the community, but employees assert that the firm supports efforts to get involved in charity work on a local level. "We sponsor foster children and children in need throughout the year. We provide clothes and school supplies and gifts during the holidays," relates a Minneapolis staffer, while a Boston insider notes, "Our local office does this. Usually we provide labor like painting or landscaping for local schools or nonprofits. The firm as a whole does not have an official program for this." A San Francisco-based employee says, "We do periodic work with a local charity where all employees take the day off to do a project together." On occasion, the firm does come together nationally; "with no fanfare, Milliman corporate paid for more than 50 volunteers to go to New Orleans for post-Katrina cleanup work," an associate proudly reports.

Mitchell Madison Group LLC

17 State Street, 22nd Floor
New York, NY 10004
Phone: (646) 873-4100
Fax: (212) 742-9719
www.mitchellmadison.com

LOCATIONS

New York, NY (Global HQ)
London (European HQ)
Los Angeles, CA
Manila
Munich

PRACTICE AREAS

Best Practices Benchmarking
Capital Efficiency
Credit, Market & Operational Risk
Pricing Optimization & Cost
Process Reengineering
Sales & Revenue Growth
Strategy Consulting
Technology Management

THE STATS

Employer Type: Private Company
CEO: Rolf Thrane
2007 Employees: 170
2006 Employees: 127

RANKING RECAP

Quality of Life
#3 - Compensation
#15 - Offices (tie)

Diversity
#1 - Diversity for GLBT
#2 - Diversity for Minorities
#6 - Best Firms for Diversity

UPPERS

- "The aura of being at a firm that is growing at lightning speed and raking in money is exciting"
- "Almost a startup culture"
- "Immediate opportunities to work with partners and clients"
- Flexibility and freedom to think outside the box

DOWNERS

- "Managers and partners give very little feedback/acknowledgment"
- "Lack of structure—it can seem disorganized"
- "Not very welcoming at the beginning; you really have to stick your neck out and ask questions"
- Little formal training

EMPLOYMENT CONTACT

Jim Quallen
E-mail: careers@mitchellmadison.com

A calendar of campus visits and interviews is available at:
www.mitchellmadison.com/careerssub2.html

THE BUZZ
WHAT CONSULTANTS AT OTHER FIRMS ARE SAYING ABOUT THIS FIRM

- "Very hands-on and entrepreneurial"
- "Good people, bad brand"
- "Solid in financial services"
- "A vestige of a once-great society"

Visit the Vault Consulting Career Channel at **www.vault.com/consulting** - with insider firm profiles, message boards, the Vault Consulting Job Board and more.

VAULT CAREER LIBRARY   489

THE SCOOP

Idealistic inception

The original Mitchell Madison Group was started in 1991 by a group of McKinsey veterans recruited by rival A.T. Kearney to form a strategy consulting division. In its early years, the firm was led by Tom Steiner, who fled McKinsey and took with him a few entrepreneurial-minded consultants reportedly frustrated with the structure and goals of McKinsey. Steiner aimed to create a less hierarchical firm based on freedom and creativity. The name represents the junction of two important points in the firm's history: Mitchell Street in New York, the home of the bar where Steiner made the decision to leave McKinsey, and Madison Avenue, the firm's first location.

Too big, too fast

For the next five years, business boomed as MMG expanded to 800 employees and 14 offices on four continents. By 1999, revenue had hit the $200 million mark, and MMG was a top pick among new MBA grads. Though impressive, the rapid growth had actually put the firm in a cash crunch and the lack of funding had also caused division within the leadership ranks. As a result, five of the firm's founding partners and directors departed. After MMG laid off 10 percent of its staff and rescinded job offers to graduates, the board started looking for a buyer. In September 1999, a promising offer came from USWeb/CKS Corporation, an Internet marketing company. The acquisition, valued at over $300 million, looked like it would perfectly round out USWeb's capabilities, enabling the firm to offer strategy along with Internet advertising.

Death march

In December 1999, however, after encountering financial problems of its own, USWeb merged with Whittman-Hart, an IT solutions company, in an ambitious attempt to consolidate IT consulting. Industry observers were skeptical, however, and the $8 billion deal sent both companies' stock prices plunging. The new firm, marchFIRST, was named for the day of the fateful merger in 2000. But marchFIRST wasn't able to withstand the dot-com bubble burst that followed, and barely stayed in business one year. In March 2001, the holding company that distributed marchFIRST stock to MMG shareholders was declared insolvent. The firm finally filed for bankruptcy in April 2001, after the stock price had plunged to $0.31 per share.

Encore!

It might have looked like the end for MMG, but its history tells the tale of a company that just wouldn't die. In 2003, a few MMG founders, along with now-CEO Rolf Thrane, rallied to bring it back. They bought the rights to the name and relaunched the consultancy, intent on doing things differently. Over the past five years, the firm has grown steadily, expanding from four to 170 employees. Headquartered in New York, MMG now has a global presence, with offices in Los Angeles, London, Manila and Munich. And the firm got an extra boost when, in 2007, Thrane was named one of the top-25 consultants by *Consulting Magazine*.

New and improved

Today, MMG focuses mainly on strategy and cost optimization for companies in a variety of industries. Though most engagements involve those core services, the firm also has capabilities in credit, market and operational risk, process reengineering, pricing optimization, capital efficiency, technology management, best practices benchmarking, and sales and revenue growth. Consultants aim to use strategic sourcing and outsourcing skills, combined with reengineering and business strategy services to strengthen clients' performance. MMG also employs an unconventional pay structure, with part of the firm's compensation based on results achieved for the client. Retaining one quality of the original group, the firm still claims to be "exceptionally free of hierarchy."

GETTING HIRED

The few, the brainy

Insiders at Mitchell Madison say the firm "seems to prefer brainy types," which may account for its primary recruiting efforts at Columbia, Brown, Caltech, Harvard and Stanford, among others. But applicants beware: Hailing from one of MMG's favored institutions doesn't guarantee entry. "We get a flood of resumes from our target schools—over 300 for 52 interview slots at Columbia, for example," a new hire shares, "so demonstrating some sort of client work experience, entrepreneurial spirit or just plain math smarts is very helpful." Candidates can expect to strut their stuff in the form of two to three interviews, with the first round conducted as "pretty much a personality/brain check" to ensure fit with the firm, explains a business analyst. "Personality is big," we're told. Whether conducted on campus or at Mitchell Madison's office, round-two interviews are "much more challenging, with brainteasers and case questions" posed to gauge an applicant's analytical and quantitative skills.

Tailor-made

While current employees regard interview questions as "pretty standard," associates, managers and partners tailor questions to the individual. As one source remarks, "Many case questions are made up on the spot" to account for a person's particular strengths or weaknesses. "Since we are a quantitative-heavy firm, candidates who are not obviously numbers-proficient should expect a numbers-heavy case, and should maintain their confidence and not get flustered when given a situation outside their expertise," a source advises. And though MMG steers clear of special tests during the process, one staffer says candidates possessing superb writing skills are looked upon favorably.

For hopefuls curious about their odds of landing a spot at MMG, look no further: "Generally, about a third of interview candidates get invitations to second rounds," a rookie analyst confides, with two to six offers awarded per school within the firm's recruiting network.

OUR SURVEY SAYS

Look out, Bain

According to one associate who's had experience at numerous consulting firms, "Bain has nothing on these guys" when it comes to culture. An absent hierarchy throughout MMG allows colleagues to "easily work or hang out with associates, managers and partners" without butting heads, and insiders talk up their "brilliant and sociable" co-workers, with whom they communicate openly about "everything under the sun." Employee camaraderie extends beyond the work sphere: "Work stress may take its toll," relates an analyst, but staffers still enjoy each other's company after the office is locked up. And Mitchell Madison's meritocracy also has sources raving. Says one MMGer, "I can rely on my colleagues to be smart and competent, and they rely on my intelligence as well." A colleague agrees, noting that "people are very open-minded and there isn't much hierarchy across positions—analysts can easily work or hang out with associates, managers and partners."

All business from above

Even though associates say that "the CEO plays guitar and used to box," and another senior partner "helps run magazines and a clothing line in his spare time," not all supervisors are about fun and games. "Managers are 100 percent bottom-line oriented and move as fast as they can to plow through issues," we're told, which can cause occasional grief for employees at the bottom of the totem pole. While they do offer some guidance, partners and managers are usually pressed for time and thus overworked. "The partners are all very smart, but not particularly nice people," adds a first-year analyst.

Nice or not, a self-propelled consultant can prove invaluable in the eyes of top-level staffers. "If you show the initiative and capability to move up, MMG will take that and promotions/increases in responsibility happen very fast," comments a source.

Visit the Vault Consulting Career Channel at www.vault.com/consulting - with insider firm profiles, message boards, the Vault Consulting Job Board and more.

VAULT CAREER LIBRARY   491

The ability to hobnob with senior clientele mostly depends on the project at hand, however. One newbie boasts "a good deal of client interaction" after less than two years with the firm, while another gripes, "I'm working for a company with many billions in annual revenue and I have not interacted directly with the client's top-level management yet." A co-worker credits the wishy-washy opportunities to the firm's project distinctions: "I would say the firm does two very distinct projects—those with a strategy focus and those with a turnaround feel. I have spent my time working with and interacting with our partners that work the strategy projects, and find myself interacting exclusively with the senior management of firms."

Sink or swim, and that's OK

At MMG, the formal training isn't so plentiful; though a single week of official training and one to two "mini-training" sessions exist per year, managers expect rookies to be sharp, quick learners. "Sometimes the stress comes from being thrown into things without feeling completely prepared or knowledgeable of what exactly you're doing," an insider shares of his experience, but appends, "My opinion, though, is that classroom training doesn't really stick unless you've applied it, so I prefer on-the-job" training. This sink-or-swim mentality resounds among co-workers, who say Mitchell Madison's informal approach, though daunting at first, contributes to swifter knowledge acquisition in the long run. Sources say that "supervisors do a good job of providing you with the emotional support and coaching" one on one, and that everyone pitches in to the process. Though "serious attempts have been made to formalize a few things key to our profession," we're told that MMG's open culture provides the necessary, "very brief and efficient" guidance. Included in the support system is a mentoring program to ensure that employees can share concerns related to their current work and overall career progression.

Busy day at the beach

With the "problem of having more business than there are employees to staff on them," MMG consultants see their fair share of heavy workloads and late nights. As one manager grumbles, "Unplanned, last-minute client 'fire drills' often cause employees to drop everything they are doing," which frequently results in pileups and weekend work. "You will be busy even if you are on the beach," a staffer adds. On the other hand, insiders laud the lax office policy. MMGers put in protracted hours, but the firm "is very output-oriented, so working from home or scheduling work around errands is not that big of a deal—as long as you hand in your deliverable on time," colleagues note. Insiders say they have the ability to take vacation time and extended weekends, with some associates taking nearly two weeks for winter festivities.

Catching Zs

At Mitchell Madison, efficiency dictates the work/life equilibrium. In conjunction with an unarguably intense workload, "there is ample opportunity to structure your own agenda," a seasoned consultant asserts. A co-worker expresses his personal preference to "devote at least a couple hours each weekend," since "the choices are really either going on four hours of sleep a night from Monday to Friday, or sleeping but working a bit over the weekend." During the first few years at the firm, consultants say achieving a work/life balance is tough—MMGers are often at manager/partner mercy. "Sixteen- to 18-hour days are not uncommon on certain teams," shares an analyst, with understaffed projects definitely calling for extra hours. In a word, staffers say MMG is "driving," which means that "if you work efficiently, you sleep more, too."

Far and away

As a small firm with international operations and a client base spread across the U.S. and Europe, associates have a tendency to rack up frequent flyer miles. One MMG newbie reports a 50 to 75 percent chance for travel each week, with a standard three-night away, four-night at home schedule. "Historically, we hardly have any New York-based clients," a junior employee states, so short-leashed travel is rare.

Insiders don't hesitate to highlight the negative aspects of travel. Since voyagers are on site with clients during the week, "all your chores and little to-do items have to be done on the weekend," gripes a source, and he's quick to mention the amount of

MMG work already reserved for weekends. For some consultants, "traveling means longer hours and less sleep," though for others, the time away from home can be fun and productive.

"I enjoy the experience, and having an occasional free weekend in Europe is great," a first-year analyst comments. Along with delight emanating from experiences abroad, decent accommodations also relax a few tense shoulders. "Being away from home all week is difficult," admits an insider, "but at least we are well taken care of when we travel, with fair expense policies."

Earn your pay

There are a few mumbled complaints about compensation arising from associates, but according to a junior-level employee, "Being a small firm, your contributions are more identifiable, and promotions/increases come as often as you can prove/show that you've earned one." On a similar front, a colleague reports receiving a considerable salary boost and a two-week vacation after only three months with the firm. Another consultant laments the void of a signing bonus, and others indicate a performance-based compensation structure for partners and managers that is more limited for analysts and associates. The firm explains that while a manager's bonus can range from zero to 100 percent, depending on performance, analyst and associate bonuses range from zero to 30 percent.

Party hats

Intermittent grievances aside, MMGers revel in the firm's doled-out perks. Staffers chat about team dinners, flexible expense policies, weekly happy hours, dinner vouchers and free transportation for post-8 p.m. office work, travel points and even "a CEO with a penchant for private plane flying." One analyst draws a portrait of an elaborate holiday party at a rented "swank nightclub in New York City's Meatpacking District," where colleagues hung out with colleagues until dawn. Employees appreciate that the "HR folk know that human resources wear down and some partying is necessary."

Sprouting community roots

Even as a young firm in the industry, MMG is committed to putting community involvement on its firmwide agenda. "Now that we're more 'stable,' I do know this is something the partners want to start getting into," remarks an associate. MMG has started working with Children for Children to provide mentoring to students at public schools in Manhattan. "A few self-organized teams participate in things like City Year or JPMorgan's Corporate Challenge," insiders report, and a group of new analysts and associates in New York has a pro bono project in the works, pending partner support. Along with contributions to charities and arts events, one honor recently instituted was the Humanitarian of the Year Award, which is a "community service award to recognize consultants who are taking on community service roles in their spare time." The honoree in 2006 founded a charity to help raise funds for needy children of Kathmandu, Nepal.

Office digs

From the Big Apple, sources tote MMG's window perch as "one of the best views in New York City," with Battery Park and the Statue of Liberty in sight. As far as the interior, a few moans emerge with regard to tight space, especially on Fridays, when all hands are back from their travels. On those days, "the space gets a little cramped for desks, and some people end up in conference rooms all day," we're told. In Los Angeles, employees report smaller quarters, due to a much heftier travel schedule—"the L.A.-based staff almost never works from the home office," an associate explains.

Minority as majority

Racial and ethnic diversity at MMG "is practically unmatched," insiders report. Continues a staffer, "I would guess that we have more international than American-born consultants, even in our American offices." Asian, South Asian/Indian, Eastern European, Middle Eastern and African employees make up the majority of MMG's minority groups, which creates a "very

Visit the Vault Consulting Career Channel at **www.vault.com/consulting** - with insider firm profiles, message boards, the Vault Consulting Job Board and more.

V/\ULT CAREER LIBRARY   **493**

diverse, very accepting" place to work, according to colleagues. Amongst the ranks, we're told, 23 languages are spoken. "The minority is the majority here," an analyst comments.

Just as welcomed at the firm are gay, lesbian and bisexual employees, at whom "no one really bats an eyelash." Co-workers say "there are several gay people in the firm, and the topic is not taboo at all." One gay associate says MMG "takes the cake" where open-mindedness and tolerance are concerned: "There is no formal program, but you feel absolutely able to discuss your personal life in the same breath as others discuss their personal life."

Women wanted

MMGers talk about "a large effort to increase the hiring of women over the past year," since female numbers pale in comparison to male employees. "They are doing a better job of hiring analyst and associate women," sources report, "but managers and partners are all pretty much men," which some attribute to the consulting industry's tendency toward male domination. Women are definitely in the minority, but according to one consultant, "the women who are at MMG seem to do very well in terms of promotions and opportunities."

Novantas LLC

485 Lexington Avenue
New York, NY 10017
Phone: (212) 953-4444
Fax: (212) 972-4602
www.novantas.com

LOCATIONS

New York, NY (HQ)
Chicago, IL
Burlington, Ontario
Madrid

PRACTICE AREAS

Brokerage & Wealth Management
Cards & Payments
Information Services
Insurance
Retail & Commercial Banking
Sourcing
Telecommunications
Travel & Leisure

THE STATS

Employer Type: Private Company
Managing Partners: Rick Spitler & Dave Kaytes
2007 Employees: 120
2006 Employees: 100

RANKING RECAP

Quality of Life
#1 - Work/Life Balance
#2 - Firm Culture
#2 - Hours in the Office
#5 - Relationships with Supervisors
#5 - Best Firms to Work For
#9 - Overall Satisfaction
#14 - Interaction with Clients
#19 - Compensation
#19 - Formal Training

Diversity
#14 - Diversity for GLBT
#15 - Best Firms for Diversity
#15 - Diversity for Minorities
#19 - Diversity for Women

UPPERS

- Incredibly close-knit, fun-loving group
- "Working closely with senior partners and gaining from their incredible experience and abilities"
- Lots of fun outings

DOWNERS

- "Potential to get 'tracked' into a practice area very early on in your career"
- "Unstructured promotion process"
- "The work is heavily quantitative, so if they tell you otherwise, don't believe it"

EMPLOYMENT CONTACT

www.novantas.com/careers_who.shtml

Visit the Vault Consulting Career Channel at **www.vault.com/consulting** - with insider firm profiles, message boards, the Vault Consulting Job Board and more.

VAULT CAREER LIBRARY   495

THE SCOOP

Solutions, not studies

Novantas was conceived in the mid-1990s when a few practice leaders from Booz Allen Hamilton, Bain and First Manhattan Consulting Group met to strategize about shaking things up in the industry. While discussing what clients disliked about traditional consulting firms—like inexperienced staff, overpriced work and studies that didn't actually help the client—the group decided to start its own firm. The founders determined that the new consultancy would give clients what they wanted: pragmatic and tangible results from their advisors. Though this privately held company doesn't publicize its revenue figures, it claims revenue has grown at an average of 35 percent annually since its inception.

Novantas is dedicated to the financial services industry, and structures its practice teams around the industry's sectors. Its clients are primarily in retail banking, corporate banking, cards and payments, brokerage and insurance, although Novantas serves other industries as well. Among the firm's customers are Citibank, Merrill Lynch & Co., Barclays Bank PLC, AXA Financial, Microsoft Corp. and United Airlines Corp. Novantas also serves 20 of the top-30 U.S. banks and four of the top-10 global banks. The bulk of the firm's clients are in North America and Western Europe, but it is occasionally called upon to assist institutions in Eastern Europe, Southeast Asia, Latin America and the Middle East.

Fully engaged

Novantas' operative strategy is to keep engagement teams relatively small—three to six consultants and one or two managing directors. The firm also stresses that teams are led by "engaged senior professionals" who spend time actually working on projects, instead of just selling the work. Typical engagements include advising on customer segmentation, product design, pricing strategy, and improving the ability of sales and service representatives to interact with customers. Another major strength is customer interface (especially voice and Internet customer support systems).

Science-driven

Revenue strategy (or as the firm terms it, "customer science") is at the core of the firm's consulting services. The firm studies branding, market mix management, segmentation, product design, pricing, distribution management and sales execution effectiveness—in short, anything that can be done to increase revenue-building capabilities. Novantas places strong emphasis on analytical rigor and, as such, makes heavy use of advanced analytics. Consultants utilize a scientific approach, and aim to leave clients with analytical tools that they can continue using once the engagement is completed.

Run the numbers

Novantas' patented proprietary tools are at the core of its scientific method. One tool, PriceTek, was developed because a large portion of Novantas' work focuses on understanding how pricing affects individual consumer behavior. PriceTek, an application service provider, continuously analyzes a bank's customer and prospect responses relative to bank pricing. MindSwift is another web-based platform that facilitates customer interaction through a test-and-learn process and is used at major call centers. Apex is the firm's database-driven tool that provides local market performance metrics and helps banks learn to sell more successfully. And StratShop assesses branch sales and service behaviors, offering guidance for training, coaching and management purposes.

In January 2006, Novantas' network of consultants added another patent to their credit. Bruce Weiner, an exec at Novantas subsidiary LogicSourcing, was granted a patent for an online system that handles the distribution of commercial insurance products extensively used in the United States. Weiner was among four patent designees for innovations featured in the "Methods and Apparatus for Selecting an Insurance Carrier for an Online Insurance Policy Purchase," a system currently used by over 2,500 insurance agencies.

Benchmarking buffs

Novantas' benchmarking tools are pretty popular in the banking industry—they've been used by the majority of the top-30 U.S. banking companies. The firm's benchmarking services cover small business, consumer, loan and deposit banking products within the branch trade area, in major markets and at the regional level. In 2005, Novantas launched an information services subsidiary, Qualytix, which provides customer-related revenue performance benchmarks for retail and small business banking. Recently, the firm was chosen by the Bank Administrative Institute and Corporate Executive Board to manage the twice-yearly, nationwide banking revenue benchmarking program—the most comprehensive analysis of comparative performance in the banking industry.

A Connecticut crowd

To add to its service capabilities, in recent years Novantas has been acquiring smaller companies. It just so happens that most of these strategic targets have all been based in Connecticut. In December 2005, PriMetriq, an information services company in Greenwich, was added to the Novantas family. PriMetriq provides sophisticated information tools that help financial institutions market and sell their services to small businesses. It also provides benchmarking information for bank branch networks. In November 2005, Novantas announced the acquisition of Wallace & Mackenzie Inc., a Darien-based management consultancy focused on wealth management and private banking. And in 2004, Novantas purchased Westport-based NBW Consulting Group, a consulting firm with expertise in branch sales performance improvement, which was responsible for developing the proprietary StratShop tool.

Novantas also made strides in the Midwest when it acquired the Jackson LaSalle Group in March 2007. Based in Chicago, Jackson LaSalle is a financial services consultancy that focuses on commercial banking, payments, investment services and insurance clients. Its main strength is helping firms improve performance by analyzing customer behavior.

Seen and heard

Banking industry pros at Novantas are frequently published in such journals as *Banking Strategies*, *American Banker* and *US Banker*. In a 2007 *American Banker* article, Novantas consultants examined how banks can improve pricing and advertising effectiveness in branch networks. In a recent issue of *Commercial Lending Review*, two Novantas execs penned an article looking at ways commercial banks can sustain client relationships in the face of tough competition. Managing directors also pop up around the world at banking conferences to teach or give presentations. Rick Spitler, a managing director, spoke on managing complexity at BAI's 2006 Retail Delivery Conference, and managing director Les Dinkin was featured at the *American Banker* Small Business Banking Conference in 2006.

GETTING HIRED

Career news you can use

Smarts, analytical and people skills, motivation and team spirit—sure, these are important attributes. But, Novantas observes, they've become mere "platitudes" in the recruiting world. "Who wants unmotivated, antisocial morons?" the firm scoffs. On its web site, the firm goes on to present a laundry list of attributes that define the best candidates, including a "high 'get-it' quotient"; what it calls "clock-speed" ("how fast are you smart?"); "comfort in the absence of structure"; "social grace, self-assurance and diverse interests"; and many more. Novantas offers a wealth of other information for consulting hopefuls on its career web pages, including practice case resources and a discussion of the interview process. (In fact, the firm's frank take on interviewing and case tips are well worth checking out when preparing for any consulting interview, even if you've decided Novantas itself isn't for you.)

The firm holds regular campus recruiting events at a handful of big-league schools, including Harvard, Yale, Columbia, Cornell and Penn, although "we are expanding to a range of different schools," including Duke, Carnegie Mellon, Northwestern and the

Visit the Vault Consulting Career Channel at www.vault.com/consulting - with insider firm profiles, message boards, the Vault Consulting Job Board and more.

 497

University of Chicago, sources say. Associates are typically plucked straight from undergrad, while the firm hires MBAs and experienced professionals as consultants. For students, the firm offers some summer internship opportunities. One former intern tells us, "My internship experience was amazing; I was sent to London for three weeks with a great, intimate team and given real responsibilities. My deliverables were used by the COO of my client. I had great opportunities to ask questions and tremendous ownership of my work."

High intensity

Make no mistake, the interview process at Novantas is "very intense," insiders agree. "Being extremely smart and quick on your feet alone won't cut it; we are looking for people who also have a social charisma," cautions this source. Typically, the selection process "funnels resume submissions down to offers at about a 1:50 ratio," estimates another insider.

According to this staffer, "First-round interviews are typically conducted on school campuses, and they involve both quantitative exercises and case questions. If the candidate makes it to the second and final round, he is brought into the firm's New York office to be interviewed by directors and managers." "If you make it to the second round, they'll put you up in a hotel in Midtown Manhattan and entertain you for the day after the interview (and make you think it's like that all the time)," preps a colleague.

Quant-jocks? Not necessarily

"There are generally two first-round interviews and two final-round interviews in the office," a Novantas consultant tells us. "All the interviews will likely involve some mathematical brainteasers. We tend to be a quantitative firm, though we're not looking exclusively for quant-jocks. My own experience is that if you enjoy an empirical approach to problem solving, you'll do well in the interview, even if you can't do every math problem under the sun."

According to another insider, "As one who does the interviewing, I can say that we have a very hands-on process where candidates go through several interviews with different levels of staff, up to and including partners. We care very much about the identity of the firm and try to find those that aren't just smart but also fit within our culture." This is reflected in the experience of another source, who says, "Throughout the process, I felt that the firm really cared about each individual recruit, and took the time to make sure we had all of our questions/concerns answered."

OUR SURVEY SAYS

Go Team Novantas!

Novantas, describes this source, is "truly a close-knit, talented and fun group of people with a solid track record in one of the city's volleyball leagues." That about sums it up—numerous consultants rave about the closeness of the Novantas team, which works and plays hard together in equal measure. "One of my favorite things about coming back from a long-term engagement is being back in the office," an insider shares, adding, "I have never worked in a place with so many smart and engaging people who have such varied backgrounds. Groups from the office usually go out together at least once a week, and many Novantas associates have actually chosen to become roommates." "It's a great place to work because it still has a collegial feel," a colleague chimes in. "I never feel like I'm just a worker drone; in fact, I do get excited very often, just going to work and getting to see all of my co-workers."

Of course, this means Novantas isn't the place for loners, one insider suggests: "It's a tough culture to get into if you're not the 'rah-rah, make-your-co-workers-your-life' type. No matter how pleasant the people can be, there's a large internal politics machine, and you can tell that people are constantly keeping score of you and your participation in firm events."

Still, most consultants we heard from are gung-ho about Novantas' "positive energy." "It's like we're all on the same mission, and each person goes all out to help everyone else because it helps the mission," one insider cheers. "The firm attracts and encourages people who are friendly, intelligent and ambitious, without being overly competitive," says another source. A consultant comments, "As a young company, we lack the rigid structure and rules that more established organizations have."

Getting involved

With such a tight group, the line between work and life can be fuzzy. But as far as work/life balance goes, you won't hear too many complaints, with several sources reporting bustling lives outside the office. "Novantas partners are very good at trying to accommodate personal needs; they understand that unhappy and stressed employees are going to be less productive employees," explains an insider, who adds, "I'm involved in a number of different organizations throughout the city, and not only do the partners do their best to make sure that I can participate regularly, some have even chosen to get involved as well!" "Having small children at home, I'm able to spend time with them in the evenings. If work needs to be done I can spend the evening with the kids and get back to work later on," says another source. A colleague adds, "Many of us are travelers by nature and so we take off for weekend trips frequently. I have been able to take off on earlier trains/buses [so long as] I continue to work and get whatever I need to get out on time." As an insider sums up, "While there are often late nights and sometimes weekend days to work, there are just as many times that I can take three-day weekends without any problem, or leave early for personal things."

That's not to say the hours are always predictable, sources suggest. "While hours tend not to be as bad as other firms, I'm a little unhappy about the all-too-inconsistent workflow: working lightly all week and then having to work all weekend," one source complains. Another insider tells us that hours vary "from client to client," but on average, workweeks range from 60 to 80 hours. "Most of the time, you can get your work done by 7 p.m. or so. There will obviously be those nights where you need to work late or the occasional weekend, but that's to be expected, especially in the consulting industry," says a colleague. As another consultant puts it, "I have had 90-hour weeks and 30-hour weeks. This is not a place where face time is required, or even encouraged—you just get the work done. I'm pretty good at working at home, and no one cares if I do that sometimes. You have to be in for the team meetings, but otherwise I'm in the office because I like being here—it's where my friends and colleagues are, and it's where I get energized to do my best work." Engagement lengths also vary, but as one source puts it, "My average assignment has been about three months. A few people I know have had assignments up to a year long, but for the most part, three to six months is average for everyone."

Third time's a charm

One source breaks it down: "About a third [of projects] require weekly travel or long-term, on-site presence; a third require travel to the client one to two times per month for a few days; and a third require no travel outside of New York City" because so many of the firm's clients are based in New York. And those who do travel don't adhere to a rigorous schedule—"Novantas is not dogmatic about having an on-site presence, and lets the specifics of the project and the client dictate travel requirements," says a source. "We try to balance travel. Those that like to travel can put their hand up, those that don't can indicate their preference. While it's not always possible to respect the wishes, given client demands, we make every effort to do our best," a colleague reports. According to another insider, "Travel can be great if you are in an interesting location (i.e., Los Angeles, Europe) or not so glamorous if you are in a rural location (i.e., South Carolina, Maine)." Farther afield, cities like London, Dubai and Barcelona are mentioned as international client destinations.

Bonus bonanza

As one insider describes it, "Compensation is competitive, well-thought-through and quite transparent." The firm "tends to be very generous with bonuses," says a colleague, and throws in a 6 percent 401(k) match and donations to a tax-free health savings account. One consultant describes compensation as "very bonus-weighted, ranging up to 100 percent or more of salary. However, nearly everyone gets at or near the maximum each year, and a few get above. Total compensation is above what my friends at other consulting firms make, but behind those in private equity or I-banking."

Visit the Vault Consulting Career Channel at **www.vault.com/consulting** - with insider firm profiles, message boards, the Vault Consulting Job Board and more.

VAULT CAREER LIBRARY   499

Give my regards to Broadway

Novantas offers plenty of perks, but most notable are the lengths the firm goes to encourage socializing among its consultants. One insider affirms, "Novantas wants us to be a close-knit team, so the firm pays for nights out together among associates and senior associates. Whether it's going out to clubs or days off together for boat rides around Manhattan, the company will pay for it as long as we are together as a team." Adds a colleague, "There are in-office activities, such as 80s Day and luaus. During the summer while our interns are here, we have activities every other week. These include a whitewater rafting trip, Coney Island, a trip to the Belmont Park Racetrack and a Broadway show (*Avenue Q*). And of course, countless sponsored happy hours." As another insider puts it, "In addition to everyone being very smart, the people who work here also have a social charm"—and it helps that "we also have a large number of people who are surprisingly attractive."

Other benefits and perks include a company-paid cell phone and home Internet access, summer hours (early closing) on Fridays, and dinner and car service home for late nights. Consultants who are traveling can choose a "travel in lieu of" perk, where they can fly to another destination or import a companion instead of flying home for the weekend.

No pyramid scheme

When it comes to supervisors, an insider says, "The best thing about this place is the interaction with senior partners and clients. There is no dreaded pyramid of midlevel managers between you and the senior people. I work directly with the most senior partners in the firm, and can sit together and debate the best way to do things based on the facts. When I describe this to my friends at other firms, they plainly don't believe it. Most of them haven't seen the senior partner since being recruited. I'm in my senior partner's office each day, sharing my work and getting pointers on how to improve my consulting abilities. It's really amazing when I think about it."

Another source is less buoyant, however, griping that "top-level management varies wildly in their style and willingness to engage with peons like us." But most insiders tend to agree that supervisors are "approachable." "People here want to see you succeed. We don't get pushed out in a few years, so it's not like we're all competing for a limited number of spots. Supervisors are always trying to help you improve whenever they can," says one consultant. Another insider loves "working closely with senior partners and gaining from their incredible experience and abilities. It's like the difference in college between sitting in a big lecture hall (which is what I imagine is what it's like working for a big consulting firm) and doing research side by side with a world-renowned professor (which is what it's like here)." In addition, says a source, "As a first-year associate, I was given the opportunity to present to the CEO of a major credit card institution."

Training at Novantas is a blend of formal and informal, though a few insiders say training for new hires isn't quite there yet. As one source puts it, "Training was inadequate at best, and reflected a very genuine lack of skill-building that would be useful to clients immediately after training. What shocks me is that so many of us new associates spent so much time on the beach in the first few months, but they only scheduled one week of training. Why not one month if we're not going to be doing anything else?" "The first week of work is a crash course on pretty much everything our firm does. Most in-depth training after that occurs on the job," agrees a colleague, who adds, "However, we also have a fabulous training program that keeps everyone up to date on topics that range from trends in the retail banking industry to a new statistical program that someone in the firm has developed and how to use it. These occur about once every two weeks." Another insider comments, "There is a great support network of associates, senior associates and managers available to help build your analyst's toolkit." In addition, says a source, "We just started new monthly lunch training sessions regarding trends in the business, direction of the firm, intellectual capital material, etc."

"The only thing that is not tolerated is bad behavior"

When it comes to gender balance at Novantas, an insider confesses, "We're doing much better, but still have a way to go." Another source reports that there is "one senior woman, several with considerable experience (but not yet partners) and most relatively junior but advancing well. Numbers are way up and this has been a big improvement in the last 18 months." A female consultant tells us, "As a woman working at the firm, I feel the culture is welcoming toward women." But a colleague thinks that "a lot of women are turned off by the buddy-buddy atmosphere of the firm and the lack of women in upper management (there's one female director out of 12)."

And while there's "no active discrimination" against minorities at Novantas, insiders say the firm could do better, with one consultant describing the situation as "abysmal. Just abysmal," adding, "We have no professional-level minorities (all Asian and white). That's not to say that they wouldn't be treated equally, but the recruitment just isn't there." "We are ethnically diverse in all areas but in the number of African-Americans," agrees a colleague. As for diversity in sexual orientation, at Novantas "there are gays at every level of the firm, and most employees are very accepting—it's virtually a nonissue," says a source. But a colleague reports, "The fact that there are gay people here is no question, in fact there's a good number of them. But quite a few are closeted about it, and there are no benefits for partners or gay spouses provided. What's more, whether it's true or not, I think people feel like many managing directors are not particularly eager to be open about gay people." Still, "partners are welcome at the holiday party and other firm events," another consultant pipes in. As an insider sums up, "The only thing that is not tolerated here is bad behavior—putting people down for any reason, or sexual harassment. Recently, at a recruiting event, a candidate made a crude remark to another candidate. He was talked to." Based on that event, he elected to withdraw his candidacy. According to sources, the partners allowed the recruiting team to intercede "and supported us 100 percent."

Informal service

Though the firm participates in a few community service events around New York each year, one insider grumbles, "It's kind of pathetic that in 2007, at a company this size, there aren't any formal community service programs." Another source reports, however, that "as we grow, we are looking to expand our program to tutoring and educational outreach to the underserved communities." "We participate in New York Cares Day as well as many other charity events throughout the year," contributes another staffer, who adds, "In general, our employees are very involved—from volunteering at animal shelters, to being big brothers or big sisters to organizing toy drives for underprivileged children around the holidays." In addition, observes a consultant, "Most of the partners have significant community involvement" via service on nonprofit boards.

Visit the Vault Consulting Career Channel at **www.vault.com/consulting** - with insider firm profiles, message boards, the Vault Consulting Job Board and more.

VAULT CAREER LIBRARY   501

OC&C Strategy Consultants

244 Madison Avenue, 4th Floor
New York, NY 10016
Phone: (646) 479-7127
www.occstrategy.com

LOCATIONS

New York, NY
San Francisco, CA
Abu Dhabi
Brussels
Delhi
Dubai
Düsseldorf
Hamburg
Hong Kong
London
Mumbai
Muscat
Paris
Rotterdam
Shanghai

PRACTICE AREAS

Group Strategy
M&A & Transaction Support
Operational Excellence
Organization & Change
Product/Market/Channel Strategy

THE STATS

Employer Type: Private Company
Worldwide Managing Partner: Michael Jary
2007 Employees: 350+
2006 Employees: 350

UPPERS

- Internationalism; "international training week each year"
- Meritocratic

DOWNERS

- "Small size of the US offices"
- Not enough organization—still in startup mode

EMPLOYMENT CONTACT

www.occstrategy.com/recruiting

THE SCOOP

Centered on strategy

OC&C is a small, global consulting firm with a distinct strategy focus. The firm's founder, Christ Outram, first set up shop in in London in 1987. While he served as the chairman for 18 years, the firm grew to 10 offices in Europe, the U.S. and China. OC&C also developed affiliate partnerships with associates in Italy, South America and the Middle East. Outram resigned in February 2005, and Michael Jary was elected worldwide managing partner. Jary, an ex-Booz Allen Hamilton consultant, has been with the firm since its inception. OC&C offers a range of services from its international locations, including group strategy, product and channel strategy, organization and change, operational excellence, and mergers and acquisitions support. Though it is best known for retail, consumer goods and private equity consulting, it also serves telecommunications, technology, travel and financial services companies.

Recently, the firm tapped into the Middle East market through its affiliation with Middle East Strategy Advisors (MESA), a strategy consulting, change management and investment advisory firm. Announced in early 2007, the partnership will allow OC&C to take advantage of MESA's client network and regional experience, while OC&C's expertise and resources will expand opportunities for the firm.

Quality over quantity

Despite OC&C's growth over the years, the firm insists that expansion isn't the goal; rather, it aims to be the "preferred strategy consultancy for a select number of prestigious clients." The firm employs over 350 strategy consultants in 15 offices and is led by a small group of partners. It aims to help clients boost shareholder value and increase sales through strategies that aren't just "radical" but also "practical, cost effective and action-oriented." The firm boasts that its creative solutions come from an out-of-the-box approach to solving problems.

The goods

Though OC&C's capabilities span several industries, consumer goods is one of its core sectors. A number of the firm's consumer goods engagements focus on the food and beverage industry. Issues like building a trade strategy for globalization, improving the profitability of promotions or prioritizing investments are examples of services clients often need. For 20 consecutive years, OC&C has published the annual "Grocer Index," a well-known report on the food industry. The report gives an annual ranking of food industry players and an exposé on new trends in the marketplace. In 2005, OC&C also published an inaugural "Food Sector Study," which put forth opinions of senior execs in the European food industry regarding trends, major issues facing the industry and future strategies.

OC&C's "2006 Christmas Trading Index" was another industry-specific report, published in U.K. trade magazine *Retail Week*. The "Christmas Trading Index" is a "festive" evaluation of the most and least successful consumer goods retailers of the Christmas season. The report divides retailers into "crackers," retailers who raked it in, and "turkeys," those whose sales fell sadly short.

Equity edge

OC&C claims to be one of the leading players in the European private equity market. Managing Partner Jary brought his experience in the area to his leadership position, having advised private equity houses on over 50 major retail transactions. Though the firm keeps the particulars of its client work strictly confidential, an example of the kind of work it might undertake in this sector has involved a national manufacturing company facing a buyout, unless it could accomplish a quick turnaround. OC&C's role was to assess the company's sales prospects for the next few years and determine how to increase the client's performance across its two brands. Consultants honed in on what was driving profitability and evaluated what kinds of

Visit the Vault Consulting Career Channel at www.vault.com/consulting - with insider firm profiles, message boards, the Vault Consulting Job Board and more.

VAULT CAREER LIBRARY   503

partnerships might add value. As a result, the client implemented changes in distribution and formed partnerships to widen its sales channels, resulting in a sizeable climb in earnings over the next three years.

OC&C also disseminates its private equity insight in its publication *Boardroom Matters*. A recent issue, entitled "Applying Private Equity Principles to Public Companies" examined why private equity companies are often more successful than public companies in turning around acquired companies.

"Soft on people"

In May 2006, London's *Financial Times* listed OC&C's Rotterdam office as one of the 100 Best Workplaces in Europe for the second consecutive year. The Best Workplaces study is conducted by the Great Places to Work Institute and is based partly on a survey of employees and partly on the institute's "culture audit" of the firms—an analysis of HR policies, culture and corporate values. The Rotterdam office claims to be "hard on skills, soft on people," and with perks like customized training, ski trips and annual Christmas dinners where each employee gets to invite eight friends, who can argue? The firm won another bit of acclaim in May 2007, when its Düsseldorf office made the 100 Best Workplaces in Europe list.

See what it's like

College undergrads can try out their strategy skills at OC&C's annual International Strategy Workshop, held in international cities like Barcelona and Istanbul. The four-day course allows students to work on an actual case study supervised by senior staff and the client. The workshop serves as a chance for students to get to know the firm better, and as a venue for the firm to recruit stellar performers. Team players, who are "capable of combining analytical thinking with creative and interpersonal skills" are invited to apply. Out of the 2005 group of attendees, six of the 26 participants received a job offer after going through the recruiting process. Interested students can check out photos from past workshops and learn how to apply online at www.weknowyoucan.com.

GETTING HIRED

99 bottles of beer on the wall ...

OC&C is looking for "highly motivated, analytically rigorous and very creative" applicants, with a "broad range of extracurricular activities and interests." The firm is less Ivy League-enamored than some of its consulting competitors, recruiting "primarily at UC Berkeley, CalTech, Columbia and NYU." Other favored schools include "Stanford, Michigan, Cornell and MIT," as well as Penn and Johns Hopkins. New graduates enter OC&C as associate consultants, while those with MBAs join up as consultants; based on relevant experience, non-MBA applicants can enter at either level. Typically, associates spend three years at the AC level before promotion to consultant.

Explains a source in New York, "We have a pretty standard hiring process, including numeracy tests and case study interviews." Elaborates a colleague, "There are two rounds of interviews for associate consultants. The first round is generally with two consultants. The second round is with the directors and managers." This second round incorporates "both case and behavioral questions," and is "unique in that it involves a group case presentation, which tests a number of important qualities: ability to work within a team, ability to work under pressure/time constraints, presentation skills, etc." In terms of cases, one staffer muses, "I had one that involved providing a recommendation to a supermarket chain about whether to open a new store in a certain location or not. The market information was given in a number of slides." A colleague recalls being asked, "How would you estimate the annual value of sales of beer through 'off trade' (i.e., liquor stores, grocers)?"

OUR SURVEY SAYS

It's a small world after all

For many OC&C staffers, the firm's small size has distinct appeal. As a consultant in San Francisco reports, "OC&C U.S. is extremely collaborative—the small, team environment fosters a lot of camaraderie and teamwork." Seconds a colleague in the same office, "The small-team feel really suits my personality and work preference. You get to know your colleagues well and you are able to command significant responsibility right from the start." Affirms this New Yorker, "I have never worked in such a meritocratic and supportive environment. Insight and input are valued from the outset, and team support and on-the-job training are exceptional." Another appreciates that "a lot of responsibility is given even to newcomers." And this associate gets satisfaction in building the office up: "It's nice to be a part of growth in the U.S. business." But counterbalancing the company's relatively narrow U.S. presence is its internationalism, an aspect that staffers relish. Remarks this associate, "The international nature of the company is a huge plus. All my projects so far have involved partnering with the foreign offices, and have enabled travel to some great locations. I know that some of my colleagues at other firms have little to no exposure to international business environments, and this is a point of jealousy for them."

The firm's size and "startup nature," do have drawbacks, though. The type of work is a bit circumscribed—as a New Yorker pouts, OC&C is just "not big enough yet in the U.S. to take on very big projects." And the back-office could use some love and attention. "Given that this is still a small operation, OC&C U.S. is a bit behind other firms in terms of support services," a San Francisco staffer notes. "But this should be addressed in the near term and isn't a significant issue anyway." Confesses a New York associate, "Not everything is organized," while a colleague on the opposite coast cautions that new hires "need to be ready for an unstructured environment."

I can drive 65

Consultants at OC&C spend about 55 to 65 hours per week on the job, though this number can skyrocket at the close of a major assignment or while "on a private equity due diligence (which can be 100-plus hours per week)." Observes one staffer, "Like other firms of which I am aware, there is heavy focus on high-quality client delivery. The extent to which work/life balance is achieved depends on the project/client and the partner/manager." Naturally, it also "depends very much on project locale and type," and is "harder when a lot of traveling is involved." Agrees this pragmatic associate, "Consulting is not a 9 to 5 job, but there is enough time in the week when we're not at work to fulfill all our hobbies and interests." A staffer in San Francisco has this to say: "Balancing work and life at a consulting firm is always a challenge. However, I think this is an area OC&C is conscientious of. They want to promote balance for their employees."

As for travel, "OC&C is particularly adept at identifying when this is required and is very supportive in ensuring that timings are convenient." One staffer feels that "the type of work OC&C performs is conducive to time in the home office, so it is easy to see when travel is necessary and valuable (as opposed to maintaining a presence at a client site for its own sake)." According to another, "We travel less than most firms (I've traveled four months in two years), which makes it easier to make plans during the weeks. There are times when working hours can be intense, but if that carries on for more than a few days, you are often given extra vacation days." Confirms one New York source, "Travel has been very manageable thus far. It has enabled me to work with colleagues from other offices, and to see three international cities I haven't seen before, which is a real treat." Yup, affirms a colleague—"great locations so far, including international destinations (Asia, Europe)." Beams one newbie, "As someone who is young and unattached, traveling for work has been great—no expenses, comfortable hotels." The firm's flexibility makes travel demands much easier, too, we're told: "Travel requirements are flexible around individuals' personal lives, and we're always back home on the weekends (and usually Friday), unless the individual chooses to stay out in the new location."

Partnering up

"Partner interaction is a big determinant for the quality of work life at a consulting firm," states a San Francisco associate. "That said, the U.S. partners are fantastic. They are tremendously impressive and command some amazing client networks, but they

Visit the Vault Consulting Career Channel at **www.vault.com/consulting** - with insider firm profiles, message boards, the Vault Consulting Job Board and more.

 VAULT CAREER LIBRARY   505

are also very down-to-earth and extremely easy to work with. They have a great vision for the company in the United States, and it will be a pleasure to be a part of realizing it." Adds an East Coast colleague, "We are a meritocratic company that believes in supporting capability and not seniority. As a consequence, if you show prowess and skills early on, you will have excellent access to very senior management. I have presented directly to CEOs and chairmen of billion-dollar organizations, and have led client meetings with similar audiences."

Foreign exchange

OC&C has its training routine down. Enthuses one New York source, "The training program is pretty well prescribed. There is a series of courses delivered upon joining, as well as an international training week each year. For the ITW, the firm gathers off site somewhere, and you take classes with members of your peer group from around the world. Classes cover consulting skills, finance, economics, writing, leadership, etc." There is also a "U.S. officewide, off-site training session every year. It is similar to the ITW, but at a great U.S. location and for a long weekend." And as for mentoring and learning by doing, a colleague adds, "Personally, I am amazed by the informal training, i.e., on the job. This is testament to the friendly and supportive environment that we work in."

To Africa, with love

Community involvement for the New York office includes pro bono consulting; the firm also "tends to support programs in which OC&C employees are involved." The San Francisco outpost "supports Operation Access (a San Francisco-based charity) and Junior Achievement of the Bay Area," consultants say, and is currently "setting up a charity to bring used computers to Africa." Internationally, the London office "works with the Impetus Trust to help other charities."

Group dynamics

In terms of employee diversity, one San Franciscan insists, "We are meritocratic. If you're capable and skilled, you will be hired and progress." Still, a colleague in the same office notes that "women are represented, but like all consulting firms, they could be better represented here." An East Coast insider remarks, "Female employees don't stay long with firm," and the female presence slims down at the top, others add. There is, however, "great ethnic diversity at OC&C, especially within the U.S. offices." Well, qualifies one stickler, "If 'minorities' mean blacks or Hispanics, then there aren't any."

OC&C, take me away!

Among staffers' favorite perks is the aforementioned "companywide training session for one week every year, usually in a European city. It's a great chance to meet colleagues, share knowledge and experiences, and visit great international cultures." Oh, and there's that New Economy-style "four weeks of paid vacation" and the "nice company trips and parties." One New York staffer notes, "I have been able to benefit from a personal development budget, which provides me with funds to follow hobbies of particular interest to me." And how's this for a disclaimer? "There is a stipulation that the hobbies/interests must not be work-related." Well, if you insist …

Opera Solutions

100 Park Avenue, 9th Floor
New York, NY 10017
Phone: (646) 437-2100
Fax: (646) 437-2101
www.operasolutions.com

LOCATIONS

New York, NY (Global HQ)
London
New Delhi
Paris
Shanghai

PRACTICE AREAS

Collaborative Reengineering
Customer Loyalty & Product Innovation
Growth Analytics
Investment Governance
Outsourcing & Offshoring
Procurement Optimization

THE STATS

Employer Type: Private Company
Chief Operating Officer: Peter Cummings
2007 Employees: 250
2006 Employees: 130

RANKING RECAP

Quality of Life
#11 - Interaction with Clients
#14 - Compensation
#18 - Overall Satisfaction (tie)

Diversity
#3 - Diversity for Minorities

UPPERS

- "Building a firm where you see yourself leading"
- Open-door policy at all levels
- "High potential for promotions, given how fast the firm is growing"

DOWNERS

- "No partnership structure like traditional consulting firms"
- Lack of brand recognition
- "Has had some growing pains and sometimes comes off as disorganized"

EMPLOYMENT CONTACT

See the company's web site for job openings, and send your resume to:

Maria Pugliese
Opera Solutions
100 Park Avenue, 9th Floor
New York, NY 10017
E-mail: mpugliese@operasolutions.com

THE BUZZ
WHAT CONSULTANTS AT OTHER FIRMS ARE SAYING ABOUT THIS FIRM

- "Up and coming"
- "Watered-down MMG spin-off"
- "They look like cool people"
- "Small client base"

Visit the Vault Consulting Career Channel at **www.vault.com/consulting** - with insider firm profiles, message boards, the Vault Consulting Job Board and more.

VAULT CAREER LIBRARY   507

THE SCOOP

12-month turnarounds

Opera Solutions has a need for speed—the firm says it's focused on delivering "substantial and sustainable bottom-line impact to clients within 12 months." With 250 consultants in New York, London, Shanghai, Paris and New Delhi, Opera sees itself as an entrepreneurial firm, characterized by a collaborative and results-driven work environment. Much of this entrepreneurial spirit derives from the firm's founders, who previously started Mitchell Madison Group. But the firm's focus isn't "growth at all costs," Opera says; rather, its aim is "selective growth to do the kind of work we like to do, and where we can make the greatest impact."

From data to action

Through its growth analytics practice, Opera helps clients convert data into actionable strategies, helping companies with customer acquisition, risk management, behavioral modeling, fraud, collection and recovery, and rewards, loyalty and attrition. The firm's global talent pool is comprised of scientists, engineers and mathematicians who perform advanced analytics. Its investment governance practice aims to help Fortune 1000 companies apply the same rigor and scrutiny to their annual investment portfolios as private equity firms do to increase returns. Other services include customer innovation and loyalty, global technology and operations, and procurement optimization and collaborative reengineering.

Opera's clients include Fortune 1000 and midsize corporations across a variety of industries. Its leadership team has worked on more than 900 projects worldwide for clients in the automotive, retail, corporate and investment banking, credit cards, insurance, media and entertainment, publishing and telecommunications industries.

Opera's stars

The firm is headed by Chief Operating Officer Peter Cummings, an entrepreneur who founded The Cummings Group, a firm focused on acquiring underperforming companies in the mining and communications industries. Opera's global technology and operations practice is led by the appropriately named Thomas Cash, an innovator in the outsourcing arena who worked for American Express for more than three decades. Paul ter Weeme, the firm's procurement optimization head, formerly held executive positions at Zeborg and Fair Isaac. Growth analytics practice leader Don Yan helped found the pricing and product design practice at Mitchell Madison Group. And Stuart Ellis, who heads up the investment rationalization practice, earned his consulting stripes at Bain.

In the news

The firm's consultants are often quoted in specialty business publications such as *CardLine*, where Yan commented on the acceptance of the Discover Card in Japan; *InfoWorld*, where Managing Director Peter Nag talked about outsourcing; and *DM Review*, in which Ajay Pillai, principal of the growth analytics practice, commented on event-based analytics. In a May 2006 report from TCM.net, COO Cummings explained that Opera helps companies in their postmerger phases by analyzing investments and standardizing purchasing across business units.

Operating under a "one firm" model, Opera continuously exchanges consultants across its offices worldwide. Consultants start out as business analysts/associates, then become senior associates and work their way up to engagement managers and senior managers before becoming principals.

GETTING HIRED

Global enlisting

When snagging undergrad applicants, Opera Solutions looks to best-of-the-best schools like Cornell, Dartmouth, MIT, Harvard and Columbia, then probes further into those institutions via their MBA program for senior associates. The firm also extends recruiting arms internationally to INSEAD (France and Singapore) and to Indian technology and management institutions in Bangalore, Calcutta, Ahmedabad, Bombay and Delhi.

No funny business

Once behind closed doors, interviewees should expect "typical consulting case interviews, usually consisting of two rounds with two case interviews per round, with some personal fit questions squeezed in," foretells a manager. Three to six interviews is the norm for the process, with first-rounds conducted by senior associates and managers, and second-round chats with principals. Insiders say sessions are propelled solely by interview, so candidates shouldn't lose sleep over special tests springing from the woodwork. Worried about case questions? "Estimate the number of traffic lights in Manhattan," one staffer offers as a possible scenario, while another adds, "What is the price of a panda on loan to the San Diego Zoo for two years?"

OUR SURVEY SAYS

Opera around the world

Opera proudly celebrates its "incredibly diverse consulting staff" through multiple firm-sponsored initiatives and programs designed to "make the culture fun," sources say. From funded soccer, tennis, volleyball and basketball teams to photography and private investing interest groups, "everyone tries to build the firm culture to make it coherent and unique," comments a senior associate. Since the firm counts "representatives from nearly every major geographic region/country" in the world among its workforce, Opera's prime directive is making everyone feel at home. With its "well-grounded but interesting" employees, one staffer says the firm runs a "monthly Opera Around the World program, in which consultants share information on their own background and country of origin." And because Opera actively promotes this cultural cohesion, colleagues declare that their workplace initiatives "build a greater sense of camaraderie amongst our consultants."

Full contact

Opera insiders sketch their superiors as "very down-to-earth" and "easy to build relationships with," and though demanding, these chief overseers are known to "take care of their team when the team is in need." Because of the firm's petite size, colleagues note an open-door policy with upper ranks, along with speedy access to top-tier client executives. "Almost immediately," one employee relates, "new business analysts, associates and senior associates are put in client-facing roles." A co-worker echoes the sentiment, appreciating the "opportunity to interact with clients at the director and VP level regularly," stating, "I am very happy with the exposure I get and the relationships I am building."

Getting (and keeping) a life

Work hours at Opera don't have staffers gasping for breath; some 70- to 80-hour weeks, all-nighters and weekend toiling may surface when dealing with demanding clients, but "that's on a project-by-project basis," we're told. By and large, employees evade unending, arduous hours at the office, and "most managers and principals give enough flexibility to manage one's time," sources say, as long as consultants promise to put in the necessary time and effort on a project.

Visit the Vault Consulting Career Channel at www.vault.com/consulting - with insider firm profiles, message boards, the Vault Consulting Job Board and more.

509

When after-hours work is unavoidable, it's "usually about five to six hours of work spread over the two weekend days," remarks a senior associate, claiming, "I have come only once to the office on a weekend." And according to co-workers, "Opera encourages life outside the firm" and "respects previous commitments and/or planned vacations." One analyst says the work/life equilibrium was a crucial factor in his choice to join Opera; weekdays are for business, he explains, but "weekends are for relaxing and rejuvenation."

Jamaica, here we come!

Opera insiders welcome the "reasonable and fair" salary structure the firm offers. "In fact," comments a manager, "compensation is equivalent to the top-three consulting firms," with a year-end bonus described as "very, very generous." Since the firm totes an absolute compensation system, insiders cheer, "salary and bonuses (sign-on, year-end) all add up to a number determined by your yearly review."

Only principals enjoy profit sharing, but sources list tax counseling, 100 percent insurance and health coverage, and 401(k) opportunities as appreciated benefits. We're told that "expense policies are very accommodating," the firm is lenient with leaves of absence and complimentary seats at sporting events aren't too uncommon. Additionally, international employees value Opera's green card dispensation. A senior associate speaks elatedly about one specific perk: "When projects end with a high client impact, the team gets an all-expenses-paid trip to any place in the world," with expense caps in mind. "My team went to Jamaica last December, and two of us even took our significant others along."

Do it yourself

"Training for all levels is pretty bare bones," admits an Opera manager; after a three-day instruction period for new hires and those recently promoted, most learning comes in the way of mentoring. Boasts one source, "Mentoring is very important at Opera and works very well. All the managers and principals are always available for on-the-job training." Though the firm defends its learn-as-you-go training model, some formalization is in the works. "There has been an attempt to improve training and have manager training as well," an associate says, but at Opera, it's understood that you "mostly need to learn on your projects."

Travel? Yes, please

A few Opera staffers note that they are not required to travel much, but many others note frequent trekking exhaustion. "While some of our clients are located in New York," an insider explains, "we have a good number of clients scattered around the U.S., and since we don't have any other offices [in the U.S.], travel five days per week is a prerequisite for those engagements." Off site, sources report a four- or five-day stay at client locations, which can make work life "a bit more hectic and difficult." And since the firm is adding more offices overseas, meeting cross-continental patrons will put a greater strain on a labor and social equilibrium.

While some staffers complain about frequent trips, travel is a coveted entity for others. "Traveling to these places makes it more fun," comments an analyst. "I think this is one aspect of my job that gives me a kick." And with offices in London, Delhi, Paris and Shanghai, one associate insists that "travel is usually a sought-after item" for those itching to see the world. Opera does, however, influence its team to be office-bound from time to time, since staying part of a cohesive machine is in the firm's blood. "The firm organizes special events one Friday per month, which encourages most of the consultants to be in the office at least one day of the month."

Uprooting

Opera staffers in the New York office say they could use a little more space for their firm's rapidly budding family. As one manager shares, the headcount has increased "from 70 to 250 employees in a span of 18 months," and the tight working quarters just aren't cutting it anymore. Colleagues say "the offices are not very nice and inviting," but the company "intends to move soon to accommodate all the new hires" by year's end to an office that associates deem "a much nicer place."

And outside of its own walls, reaching out to its surrounding communities is a vital firm initiative, insiders tell us. From park cleanups and coat drives to "activities with New York Cares and other nonprofits," Opera makes sure to help out in the neighborhood. Employees note participation in "various charities as well as city government initiatives," along with renovating public school buildings and other community service efforts "about once a quarter."

Opera sings (diversity) praises

Since Opera Solutions employs "individuals from all parts of the world," ethnic and racial minorities are prevalent at the firm. One senior associate claims he doesn't "know of any firm, consulting or otherwise, that is more diverse than Opera," while a colleague agrees, toting Opera as "one of the most international, diverse firms you will ever find." But where diverse heritage flourishes, the male/female ratio withers. "There aren't many women in our firm," reports a source. "Of the 20-plus principals, only one or two are women."

Visit the Vault Consulting Career Channel at **www.vault.com/consulting** - with insider firm profiles, message boards, the Vault Consulting Job Board and more.

VAULT CAREER LIBRARY   511

PA Consulting Group

4601 North Fairfax Drive
Suite 600
Arlington, VA 22203
Phone: (571) 227-9000
Fax: (571) 227-9001

123 Buckingham Palace Road
London SW1W 9SR
United Kingdom
Phone: +44 (0)20 7730 9000
Fax: +44 (0)20 7333 5050
www.paconsulting.com

LOCATIONS

Arlington, VA (North American HQ)
London (Global HQ)
Offices in more than 35 countries throughout Europe, North
America, Latin America, Asia and Oceania

PRACTICE AREAS

Business Operations Consulting
Decision Sciences
Information Technology & Systems Integration
Market Analytics
People & Organizational Change
Program & Project Management
Sourcing for Value
Strategy & Marketing
Technology & Innovation—Product & Process Development

THE STATS

Employer Type: Private Company
CEO: Alan Middleton (effective September 2007)
2007 Employees: 3,400
2006 Employees: 3,000
2007 Revenue: £362 million
2006 Revenue: £317 million

THE BUZZ
WHAT CONSULTANTS AT OTHER FIRMS ARE SAYING ABOUT THIS FIRM

- "Global, smart"
- "Really scientists, not strategists"
- "Very specialized"
- "Past its prime"

RANKING RECAP

Quality of Life
#16 - Formal Training

UPPERS

- "Go-getters get very far very quickly"
- "Balanced lifestyle"
- "Carte blanche if you are billable"
- Share plan and bonus

DOWNERS

- "Relatively unknown in the US"
- "'Old boys' club"
- UK-centric culture takes adjustment
- "Travel expectations are massive"

EMPLOYMENT CONTACT

www.paconsulting.com/join_pa

THE SCOOP

The greatest generation

Based in London, PA Consulting Group is one of the largest strategy firms in Europe, serving clients in the financial services, government, energy, life sciences and telecommunications industries. Founded in 1943 as Personnel Administration, PA was established with the aim of helping companies improve their productivity as Britain engaged in the war effort. To that end, PA employed the relatively new theories of "time and motion" management. One of its notable early efforts was helping to train women in the assembly of British bombing aircraft. Once the war ended, the firm expanded along with a rise in demand for civilian goods and an influx of veterans into the workforce.

By the 1970s, PA had become one of the world's largest consultancies, with offices around the world. The firm lost some market share to rivals like McKinsey through the 1970s and 1980s, but also took an early lead in developing a technology consulting practice. PA's fortunes dimmed along with the consulting industry's in the early 1990s, and during that period the firm found itself on the losing end of a battle for staff with aggressive recruiters like IBM and EDS. The firm managed to recover by the middle of the decade.

In it together

More recently, the firm has enjoyed year after year of record growth, thanks to some hefty contracts and savvy investments by its venture capital wing. And this growth can only be good news for PA's associates, who each own a piece of the firm in a broad partnership. The firm prides itself on its independence and impartiality, and a salary structure weighted heavily toward bonuses means members will "respect each other and work to make each other successful, rather than seeking to be hailed as lone heroes," PA says.

Resilience boosters

The firm's practice areas include strategic management, innovation and technology, IT, operational improvement, human resources and complex program delivery. Attention-getting engagements have included helping to build a new strategic innovation unit for Novo Nordisk, aiding Lloyds TSB Bank with a postmerger integration strategy and helping to negotiate an outsourcing contract between Sabre Holdings and EDS.

One of PA's recent areas of focus is corporate resilience counseling. Through this service, which PA defines as a broader concept than just "business continuity," the firm helps clients deal with unexpected events—both negative and positive—that have unknowable consequences. With resilience built into its operations, an organization can seize opportunities and innovate more readily, the firm argues. In June 2006, PA boosted its health care consulting profile with the acquisition of London International Healthcare, a consultancy with 10 years of experience working with governments, aid agencies and private-sector clients in over 20 countries in Europe, the Middle East, Africa and Asia.

Executive shifts

In March 2007, the firm announced the promotion of Alan Middleton, current head of its IT strategy business, to the position of CEO. Middleton is slated to take over the position from 30-year PA veteran Bruce Tindale following Tindale's retirement in September 2007. In other appointments, Martin Stapleton was named the firm's new head of ventures in January 2007; Chris Poole, a former Procter & Gamble exec, joined PA in December 2006 as a member of the management team; and General Sir Mike Jackson, a former chief of the General Staff in the U.K., was named a senior advisor to the firm that same month.

Visit the Vault Consulting Career Channel at www.vault.com/consulting - with insider firm profiles, message boards, the Vault Consulting Job Board and more.

 VAULT CAREER LIBRARY   513

Start me up

PA's dedication to its startup ventures differentiates it from many of its peers. One of its current ventures, Aegate, serves the pharmaceutical industry, helping drug manufacturers develop a database and software to tackle the complicated challenge of illegal drug counterfeiting. In April 2006, Aegate, along with investment firm 3i, won the Venture Capital Deal of the Year award at the 2006 Private Equity Awards for forming, developing and selling UbiNetics, a supplier of software and other materials to the wireless industry.

Despite its entrepreneurial leanings—which PA sees as a natural extension and expression of its dedication to strategy—the firm plans to keep its focus on management consulting. PA prides itself on being a "real consultancy," as opposed to a firm whose bread and butter is creating and selling companies, outsourcing or software implementation. As outsourcing continues to heat up worldwide, "sourcing"—the act of linking clients who need to outsource with appropriate outsourcing vendors—is also becoming a necessary service. A May 2006 report from Forrester Research identified PA as a "solid option" for sourcing services, for clients who wanted alternatives to more well-known companies in the area such as McKinsey, Accenture and IBM. The analysts particularly recommended PA for North American firms with large European operations, and cited PA's independence as an asset when it comes to impartial advice on technologies.

PA in the U.S.A.

PA has about 430 staffers in the U.S., and its strongest presence is in the energy sector, with a new focus in the oil and gas sector. In January 2007, *The Sunday Times* reported that PA planned to open a new technology development center in Bangalore, noting that the firm is also "keen" to expand in the U.S., possibly through acquisitions. In August 2005, *Government Executive* magazine named PA one of the top-200 contractors for the U.S. government in fiscal 2004, with contracts totaling $2.2 million that year.

Into infrastructure

PA is the only international consultancy to hold three infrastructure-related contracts with the U.S. Agency for International Development. Retained by the agency, PA has worked jointly with government agencies and donors in the Americas, Europe, Asia and Africa to support local governments, sustain the environment, carry out energy reforms and eliminate poverty. These projects have taken PA out of the comfort zone of everyday strategy consulting. In the impoverished nation of Georgia, for instance, the firm was tasked by USAID with turning around the state-owned electric utility, UEDC.

When PA took on the project in 2003, UEDC's distribution system couldn't handle delivering more than three or four hours of electricity a day, all the while battling criminals who were stealing wattage along with poles and wires. Multimillion-dollar debts and poor collection rates, along with ongoing political tensions with Russia, compounded the utility's woes—and the utility's rampant internal corruption didn't help matters. A November 2006 *Financial Times* article, "Mission Improbable," described how PA "risked its reputation" by agreeing to such a daunting task, including a contract with no performance-based incentives and limited external funding. Among the challenges PA faced were a "mysterious" fire that destroyed internal records shortly before PA came to Tbilisi, egregious cases of overstaffing (one office boasted 42 drivers and just two vehicles), hostile company officials and even a knife fight between members of rival clans. And that was all before the layoffs PA was forced to make, which resulted in one former employee abandoning a baby at a UEDC office. These days, thanks to PA's reforms, Georgians are becoming accustomed to seeing electricity as a service that must be paid for, and the country is enjoying uninterrupted electricity supplies for the first time in 15 years.

The firm's Georgian adventure earned PA the platinum prize of Overall Winner for the best consulting assignment of the year at the April 2006 Management Consultancies Association Management Awards. The award was among six of the 19 top prizes the firm took home at the ceremony that year.

Tracking tickets

PA consultants are often published and quoted in high-profile periodicals such as the *Financial Times*, as well as specialty publications like *Electric Light & Power*. It's not every day that a strategy firm can make Hollywood sit up and take notice, but PA managed to do just that with a survey published in January 2007. The survey found that consumers are increasingly dissatisfied with the moviegoing experience, and will continue to spend less on going out to see new releases as the opportunities for home entertainment (such as DVDs) grow. The survey, which polled both American and European respondents, focused on Hollywood's share of consumers' entertainment budgets, rather than on the content the industry is producing.

Avatars welcomed

In October 2006, the firm broke new ground—virtually, anyway—by becoming one of the first consultancies to establish a presence in the online alternate world *Second Life*. PA's office in *Second Life* allows the firm to meet and discuss issues with new and existing clients, and to inform and woo tech-savvy candidates, the firm explains. The virtual world may even serve as a space for consulting itself, said PA Partner Claus Nehmzow: "We can now work with clients to build 3D 'immersive' environments that can be used to collect customer feedback, involve customers in design, and eventually use this medium as a customer service and interaction channel." In a March 2007 profile of the initiative in *Consulting Magazine*, the firm described how it hired a grad student following a chat session with his online avatar. The new recruit reported being impressed with the firm's innovative approach to high tech, as well as the chance to interact with a wide variety of PA staffers in an informal atmosphere.

GETTING HIRED

Generally more than generalists

PA recruits experienced consultants and also taps Ivy League and other top schools located near the cities in which it has offices. Favored schools include Babson, Boston University, Colorado University, Columbia, Cornell, Duke, Harvard, MIT, NYU, Princeton, UCLA, USC and Yale.

As for PA's hiring procedures, sources offer a range of opinions: Some view the process as "stringent," "quite tough" and "laborious," while others deem it "fairly average" or a "very good process overall." Prospective candidates will "interview in individual and team settings to determine the proper fit technically, consultatively and culturally," explains a Boston source. Depending on the position level, prospects can face as many as "eight to 10 interviews," but "the standard process for anyone at the consultant rank or below is a phone interview, an interview day and then a partner interview," states a New York insider. Expect "a numerical test, a verbal reasoning test and a team exercise," advises an East Coast colleague. On the day of the in-person assessment, prospects are given case histories, behavioral tests, "technical assessments and numerous interviews with members of the practice." These are followed by final-round interviews that "typically include screening by the partner" and a team case study exercise. PA managers are looking to "determine which practice and role you fit best in," explains a consultant, adding that a serious prospect will "not be just a generalist" but will possess "excellent knowledge of his or her own area."

Luckily, the firm has a reputation for a "very quick turnaround"; according to a New York-based staffer, it was "two weeks from my first conversation to the offer letter." "The process was fast and smooth," one newbie relates, while another beams that "even as a recruit with one year of work experience, the firm covered all of my travel expenses—and the burden of booking travel—for my interview." On the downside, advises a source based in Washington, D.C., "If you want the job, you have to follow up, as it is easy to get lost in the shuffle."

Visit the Vault Consulting Career Channel at www.vault.com/consulting - with insider firm profiles, message boards, the Vault Consulting Job Board and more.

VAULT CAREER LIBRARY   515

OUR SURVEY SAYS

Flat as a pancake

PA consultants give high marks to their company's corporate culture. The firm is full of "very friendly and down-to-earth people," nods an insider. A Washington, D.C., source sees the culture as being "collaborative and collegial," while New Yorkers term it "very entrepreneurial and self driven, empowering" and "a fun place to be." As for hierarchy, reports one consultant, "The structure is very flat, which means you regularly get to interact with very senior partners." Indeed, adds a colleague, PA provides an "open working culture. Partners and assignment managers are very approachable."

Still, sources tell us that there is always room for improvement. A source in Houston is less happy that the firm is shifting away from an entrepreneurial "to a massive delivery model"; as a result, this Los Angeles consultant feels that "the admin requirements are onerous." A source in D.C. also feels that the "overhead of activities from the U.K.-based corporate office is cumbersome." And while agreeing that "there is a bit of U.K.-centricity to operations," this insider predicts that "this will change as other geographies gain maturity and profitability."

The glass is either half full ...

On the topic of work/life balance, PA consultants are divided: Some claim that they are able to maintain a healthy balance "very well," while others are adamant that they cannot. A D.C. source believes that he is able to achieve a "good work/life balance for the most part," acknowledging that yes, "There is extensive travel, but given the nature of the business, that is to be expected. The interview process makes it very clear that significant travel is expected of consultants." Others in the glass-half-full camp cite PA's flexibility in occasionally working from home as key to maintaining balance. "Working time is flexible and working from home is OK," explains one source. "I'm able to work from home when some matter needs to be dealt with. There is no pressure to work long hours," agrees another Washington consultant. And "because they allow for partner travel," some sources feel that PA's travel policy helps alleviate the strain.

... or half empty

Meanwhile, there are those who say they find it difficult, if not impossible, to achieve that healthy balance, primarily due to long hours and heavy travel. "There is no time to pursue leisure activities or have a social life outside of your immediate circle of work colleagues," complains one New Yorker, while another claims that due to PA's "emphasis is on being as flexible as possible to meet the needs of our consultants," he struggles to find time for an outside life. A Washington, D.C., source adds that he is only "somewhat" able to achieve balance, as the "U.K.-based corporation has very little understanding of the expectations for travel in the U.S. and hasn't adjusted goals accordingly." Another colleague in the same office asserts, "They say there is work/life balance but you are rewarded based on utilization. Therefore, the more you work, the better." Still others cite seniority as their primary challenge. Reports one source, "The higher I get in the company, the harder it is to maintain a work/life balance," while another in Denver affirms, "As you progress, more and more time is eaten up with nonconsulting business. However, the expectation is that you have to contribute to all aspects of the business: recruiting, conferences, sales and consulting full time. No time is given to allow this." One source in Houston is adamant that the long hours limit any sort of balance: "We are required to be on call 24/7. We average 50 hour billable work weeks with another 24 hours for admin, and squeeze in marketing when available. The pace is too intense and most staff is too fatigued to have a life."

Time after time

PA sources average about 55 hours per week, though some consultants' workweeks run as high as 65 to 70 hours. "I don't mind working the long hours that this job requires," a source in New York asserts. "Not being on a client assignment is difficult, though, and affects your bonus." A colleague in the same office tabulates, "I spend 60 hours per week in the office. If I wanted to spend less time, I could—it is my decision!"

On the flip side, a Houston source believes that continuous long hours point to larger problems. "Twelve- to 16-hour days are common, not the exception," he states. "Eight-hour weekends are compulsory. There is constant crisis. The firm should be working toward better leverage. If too many people are working 65-hour weeks, it points to poor leadership and project management." A colleague in Los Angeles adds, "It's a struggle; the internal requirements often require working off-hours and weekends to keep up." Regarding weekend work, a Boston source admits that he usually works Saturdays and Sundays—"sometimes it's a challenge and the weekend is often used to catch up on a busy week." Contributes a New York consultant, "I check e-mail nearly 24/7 and often respond on weekends. But I seldom, if ever, spend the majority of my weekend working." Conversely, a San Francisco source relates that he works "every Sunday," while an East Coaster says he has "worked almost every weekend so far this year."

On the road again (and again, and again)

This consultant speaks for many: Travel is just "part of the job, one goes where the client and work are." At PA, travel requirements can vary widely. Offers a Princeton consultant, "Travel varies a lot; it depends on your client location and the type of work you're doing." Cautions a New York source, "That may mean spending very significant periods of time away from home."

The PA travel model is typically 3-4-5: "Three nights away from home, four days at client and five days' work per week," a consultant elucidates. "If you're not traveling internationally or to the East Coast from Los Angeles, it doesn't take much of a toll on work/life balance," a Los Angeles source relates. Others concur, including one lower-level consultant in New York who testifies that he has had no travel thus far—"all my jobs have been based out of my home office." Adds a Princeton consultant, "I have developed a number of local accounts, so my travel is minimal. The balance is quite nice. It doesn't affect me much right now, as I do not have kids and my husband accompanies me most weekends (and his job is extremely flexible)."

Others aren't so fortunate, or so content. "All travel all the time equals no work/life balance during the week," fumes a D.C. source who averages five days a week on the road. "It is too consuming," agrees a Houston staffer, who travels to "three to five cities a week because we cut across so many projects. This is on top of 65-hour workweeks." "Having a young family and having to travel for work can be hard to manage," adds another insider, while still another has this to say about the effects of travel on his life: "I would have gotten a divorce if I had not cut back on my travel, which had been averaging four days per week out of country for the first two years of my marriage. But there are obvious professional consequences for cutting back."

Give me some higher love

A New Jersey source reports that there is a "360-degree peer review for each assignment," and that the "overall review process [is] excellent." Access to supervisors also rates well; a junior consultant in Los Angeles reports, "We're a small group of about 45 in the U.S., so I've worked directly with our U.S. practice lead." And while this Houston source rates the PA upper echelon as "great leaders, mostly," in the experience of this New York insider, "Partners seem to reap most of the benefits and claim credit for work of staff."

On the client side, some PA sources do feel that they have ample opportunity for client interaction. "PA strongly encourages client networking," a New York source asserts. "The firm is very self-driven. If you have the capabilities, PA generally doesn't get in the way." Still, notes a colleague in the same office, "We don't really operate at the top-level management tier of our client organizations."

Supersize my salary

PA's pay scale is competitive, though sources feel it could be higher. "Compensation is fair but not outstanding," admits a Washington, D.C., consultant, while another believes that "salaries are not market." Company administrators must be listening to employee grumbles, according to a source in Cambridge: "PA is rerationalizing salaries this year to ensure they are well above the mean in total compensation." While salary may be a little under average, "performance bonuses can be very lucrative for top performers." As PA is wholly owned by its employees, bonus monies can also come in the form of company shares, which are

Visit the Vault Consulting Career Channel at **www.vault.com/consulting** - with insider firm profiles, message boards, the Vault Consulting Job Board and more.

V/ULT CAREER LIBRARY   **517**

allocated based on individual performance. "Shares can be in the range of 30 percent of bonus," explains a source in New York. And as a Cambridge staffer points out, "These returns have been tremendous over the past 20 years, with 20 percent annual growth for the last 10 years." Shares in company-owned ventures" are also offered as part of the firm's total compensation package, as is a 6 percent company-matched 401(k) plan.

Additionally, PA offers its employees "good health care," a "long-term care policy," "partner travel," "eight holidays and 10 sick days," and "standard 22 days vacation, although this extends to 27 days after 10 years of service." The firm notes that eight days of vacation carries over until April 30th of the next year, pending manager approval. PA also offers employees the option to take a "six-month unpaid sabbatical after three years."

Top-shelf training

PA offers "fantastic training opportunities throughout the year for all ranks," confirms a New York source. "All new joiners are required to go to the U.K. for at least a week of introductory training." Adds a colleague in the same office, "PA offers a more extensive training program with more choices and options than I have seen at other firms such as PwC or KPMG. The firm puts an abnormally large emphasis on training, including mandating that the most senior members of the firm teach a significant number of specialized courses."

Ramping up for more community efforts

PA employees tell us that their firm engages in community service-related activities like "pro bono consulting, charity work and event sponsorship," but that at the moment these efforts are "minimal." "The Giving Back Initiative has been piloted," notes a source on the East Coast. "There are significant efforts to popularize and encourage consultants to give back to the society. The rollout has been a bit Euro-centric for the time being, but it will catch on in other geographies." However, consultants are able to devote "three pro bono days for your own charity with approval," and they can also "donate in a pretax way." Furthermore, contributes a New York source, PA "gives a portion of the firmwide bonus pot to a charity."

All for one, one for all

"PA is very internationally diverse—far more internationally diverse that any other firm I have seen," a New York consultant believes. Insiders report that "there is a formal support community" as well as "an ongoing program in place to ensure that we continue to diversify ourselves." But there are staffers who feel that the firm needs to do more work on the ethnic diversity front. "The firm is white male, IT/engineer, U.K.-centric. There are very few minorities apart from admin and accounting," observes this source. And a Washington, D.C., consultant feels that there is less attention paid to minority issues and "more on women and work/life balance. Minority advancement could use more focus." Regarding sexual orientation, one source comments, "As a gay male I can say that PA is supportive and sets the right policy and direction. In reality, however, there is less GLBT diversity than might be expected." Still, adds a Denver source, "No one I know in the workplace assigns any value to a person's sexual preference. It's a nonfactor."

Pearl Meyer & Partners

445 Park Avenue
New York, NY 10022
Phone: (212) 644-2300
www.pearlmeyer.com

LOCATIONS

New York, NY (HQ)
Atlanta, GA
Boston, MA
Charlotte, NC
Chicago, IL
Houston, TX
Los Angeles, CA

PRACTICE AREAS

Compensation Surveys
Director Compensation
Employee Compensation
Executive Compensation

THE STATS

Employer Type: Private Company
President: David N. Swinford
2007 Employees: 100+
2006 Employees: 80+

EMPLOYMENT CONTACT

www.pearlmeyer.com/firm/careers/index.shtml

Visit the Vault Consulting Career Channel at **www.vault.com/consulting** - with insider firm profiles, message boards, the Vault Consulting Job Board and more.

VAULT CAREER LIBRARY   519

THE SCOOP

Pay-day professionals

Since 1989, Pearl Meyer & Partners has provided boards and senior management with advice on what they should pay their employees and how. More than 1,000 clients, ranging from Fortune 500 to emerging high-growth companies to not-for-profits, pay PM&P to help them align rewards with their long-term business goals and to create compensation programs to attract, retain, motivate and reward executives, employees and directors.

With headquarters in New York and six offices across the country, the firm's 100-plus professionals offer a comprehensive approach to compensation planning that includes board compensation programs, salary programs, annual incentives, value creation and performance measurement systems, long-term performance incentives, stock options programs, executive stock purchase arrangements, sales incentives, retirement and executive benefits, among other services. PM&P also conducts compensation surveys to provide clients with perspective on total compensation for broad groups of employees.

Flying solo

Until recently, PM&P was a subsidiary of 40-year-old consulting giant Clark Consulting. In March 2007, Clark was acquired by a U.S. subsidiary of AEGON N.V., a Netherlands-based life insurance and pension group, in a $293 million deal that placed a 32 percent premium on Clark's closing share price at the time of the November 2006 merger announcement. As a result of the merger, other Clark assets, including PM&P, were sold to Clark Wamberg LLC, an investment group formed by Clark Consulting Chairman and CEO Tom Wamberg and CEO Jim Benson of Clark Benson, for $55.5 million.

Knowing how to dole out the goods

Despite the top-down changes Pearl Meyer & Partners has dealt with over the past year, it continues to do what it does best: compensation consulting. The firm is best known for its executive and employee compensation consulting services, which include helping clients create a compensation philosophy and guiding principles, plan documentation and disclosure requirements, analyze what competitors are paying their executives, design incentive programs, dole out benefits, draw up employment contracts and severance agreements, and implement "special situation" programs such as retention plans or carried interest plans.

For companies with boards of directors or advisers, PM&P also offers director compensation services. This group helps clients decide what kind of guidance and assistance directors should be given and how they should be compensated for their services—that means helping companies decide how much information they should disclose to their boards, how they should set up their committee charters, policies and procedures, and what they need to do to ensure that their board structure is in compliance with regulations.

Survey says

Beyond offering advice and helping companies set up their employee pay structures, PM&P also conducts industrywide compensation surveys to paint a broader picture of what goes into how companies pay and reward their employees. In addition to industrywide data, the firm offers custom-made survey reports by request, using its own real-time Survey Online System. The firm also offers the CHiPS family of surveys, composed of six compensation surveys that cover every employee level within an organization, from new graduates to executive and senior management. The surveys are designed to give a complete overview of total compensation. On top of that, the firm provides managed surveys, including the research and development survey, the systems integration and outsourcing survey, and the national engineering and construction salary survey.

PM&P professionals also produce regular research reports, articles and white papers, and give presentations and write articles on corporate governance and compensation issues. The firm's consultants are often quoted in the news for their thoughts on compensation issues, in publications such as *The New York Times*, *Forbes*, *BusinessWeek*, *CFO Magazine*, *Entrepreneur* and *The Wall Street Journal*, and on the Dow Jones newswire.

GETTING HIRED

Getting to know you

Sources report that Pearl Meyer recruits at several schools on both coasts, including Claremont, USC and UCLA on the West Coast; Brandeis, Bentley, Northeastern and other Boston-area schools; and Cornell, the University of Rochester and other top-100 schools around the country. Candidates coming out of college can "expect multiple rounds, meeting both the folks you'll be working for and the folks you'll be working with," according to one insider.

Staffers say the initial interview lasts about half an hour, often a "phone interview with HR," and the second is with a panel of analysts, consultants and managing directors. Others report that candidates must "interview with anyone that you are likely going to work under" and that sometimes the process includes "several interviews spread over a long period of time." With more experienced candidates, we're told that PM&P may identify potential employees by using a search firm. One VP who was contacted this way interviewed with his "boss, the president of the firm and several managing directors either in person or by telephone."

Goals and spreadsheets

Insiders say the interview includes "all behavior questions," most of which are focused on "expectations and goals." Sources note that there are case questions and that analyst- and associate-level candidates must take "Excel tests on formulas that we use every day at work." One staffer noted that a writing sample was also requested.

OUR SURVEY SAYS

Great expectations

Pearl Meyer "attempts to create a family atmosphere," as one analyst notes, but it can sometimes feel like a family of workaholics. The office has "lots of competitive personalities," says one consultant, while another explains that, depending "on where your priorities are, if work is No. 1, then you will find it easy to balance." Well sure, working "some weekends may sound like a lot, but it is self-imposed," one hardworking managing director admits, adding, "I work from home some days, as I have the ability to manage my own schedule. For me, it's simply a terrific environment." Insiders say consulting projects can last anywhere from two weeks to over a year, and consultants "work on several clients at a time." All in all, says one source, "the firm (or, at the very least, my manager) is very good in allowing our schedules to be flexible as long as the work gets done."

A travel leg up

Travel demands are pretty light for PM&P consultants, especially in an industry not much known for staying put. Sources generally agree that "most of the work is done in the office via e-mail and by phone," with site visits consisting of "primarily day trips." That's not to say that you can't travel if you don't want to. "I travel a fair bit, but it's partially by choice," one consultant explains. "I could travel a bit less if I desired."

The work hours aren't particularly light, though. We're told that the average workweek is about 50 hours, with "some highs and some 40s, but nothing below." Hours "vary wildly depending on the client and my personal level of participation in the project," a staffer shares. Certain projects can make it "hard to leave the office at a reasonable hour," another source remarks, but adds that "the payoff at bonus time helps ease the pain."

Visit the Vault Consulting Career Channel at **www.vault.com/consulting** - with insider firm profiles, message boards, the Vault Consulting Job Board and more.

VAULT CAREER LIBRARY   521

The bonus bonanza

Overall, Pearl Meyer employees say they feel "very well compensated" for the work they put in. One insider reports that the annual bonus is "about 15 to 20 percent of base salary," and a colleague notes that along with cash bonuses, consultants can receive "gifts of various forms based on individual and company performance." As a colleague gleefully testifies, "We just had an outstanding month and we all received iPods, iTunes gift certificates and online gift certificates."

Working in Candyland

The benefits aren't bad, either. Along with a 401(k) match and "great health coverage," PM&P offers "gym membership reimbursement," sources tell us. That might come in handy, since the firm also supplies its offices with "free coffee, candy, drinks" and a "fully-stocked fridge." An analyst characterizes it as "low-end food (which is always appreciated)," and a consultant gushes about "free breakfast on Mondays" and "weekly fresh flowers for my office."

As for their offices, employees seem more than pleased. The firm intended each office to reflect its marketplace: Los Angeles' office is on the 54th floor of the tallest building downtown, which is ultramodern with great views, and New York's is on Park Avenue. And the Boston office is "just below resort quality," one insider notes approvingly, while a co-worker waxes poetic about "artwork on loan from nearby museums and an 18-hole executive putt-putt course." Managers are generous when it comes to the party department, too. "In the past few months, we've had an overnight holiday party at the Four Seasons," a consultant reports. Consultants also recently enjoyed a three-day professional development meeting at the Chatham Bars Inn on Cape Cod.

Of managers and mentors

PM&P managers get generally high marks, though there doesn't seem to be a uniform management style. One consultant says that there's a "very hands-off management style, which matches senior consultants' expectations," but another comments approvingly, "My boss is very involved in our engagements and views every situation as a learning opportunity for subordinates. He is a true mentor." All in all, an insider says, there are "lots of opportunities for recognition, with immediate feedback."

Train at your leisure

Staffers generally agree that training is mostly unofficial and on-the-job, through informal mentoring. As one consultant puts it, "Managing directors are committed to providing (and creating) 'stretch' opportunities to expand your skill set." But Pearl Meyer will pony up for formal training if you make a good enough proposal, we're told. The firm is "open to any reasonable training, networking, etc., opportunities," a consultant says, while a colleague reports that "the company will reimburse you for most outside industry training and certification courses."

The available in-house training receives mixed reviews. One managing director says that "for a smaller firm, a good deal of attention is paid to training, particularly at entry- and midlevels." However, a newer hire complains that "training was largely in the form of a binder of past projects (which were out of date in every way imaginable and some ways that weren't imaginable). All in all, it would have been better not to have." On second thought, the source concedes, "At least there was training—some training is always better than none."

Things aren't so different

PM&P gets pretty high marks as a place for women, minorities, and gays and lesbians to work, although staffers note that the firm only has about 20 percent minorities. Women, however, have a large footprint. The firm states that about 37 percent of its female contingent is at the VP and managing director level. "There are more women than men at this establishment," one consultant declares, and "they are at all levels within the firm." Another insider clarifies, "Although there are more women hired at the lower levels, there are few at the top managing director level."

Fair share of giving

PM&P has a consistent record of encouraging its employees to give a little something to those in need, especially when December rolls around. "During the winter, we did a version of the Toys for Tots charity," an analyst recalls. "We each chose a child and bought them a present."

But charitable efforts aren't limited to "holiday gifts for the needy." The firm also supports "local projects" like food pantries and charity runs. "Last year, the Los Angeles office did the Climb to the Top for the YMCA of Downtown L.A.," a California staffer says. "We raised money for the YMCA and climbed 65 flights of stairs to the top of the U.S. Bank building (where our offices are)."

Visit the Vault Consulting Career Channel at **www.vault.com/consulting** - with insider firm profiles, message boards, the Vault Consulting Job Board and more.

VAULT CAREER LIBRARY 523

Protiviti Inc.

2884 Sand Hill Road
Menlo Park, CA 94025
Phone: (650) 234-6000
Fax: (650) 234-6998
www.protiviti.com

LOCATIONS

Menlo Park, CA (HQ)
59 offices throughout the Americas, Asia-Pacific and Europe

PRACTICE AREAS

Business Risk Management
Internal Audit
Technology Risk Management

THE STATS

Employer Type: Wholly Owned Subsidiary of Robert Half International Inc.
Ticker Symbol: RHI (NYSE)
CEO, Robert Half International: Harold M. Messmer Jr.
2007 Employees: 2,900 +
2006 Employees: 2,200 +
2006 Revenue: $543 million
2005 Revenue: $479 million

UPPERS

- The environment encourages you to do your personal best
- Gender diversity is strong at all levels

DOWNERS

- Company is still formalizing its internal processes
- Not enough brand recognition

EMPLOYMENT CONTACT

See the careers section of www.protiviti.com for information on job opportunities and contact information

THE BUZZ
WHAT CONSULTANTS AT OTHER FIRMS ARE SAYING ABOUT THIS FIRM

- "SOX experts"
- "Small, specific IT solutions"
- "Fast-growing company; feels like a winner"
- "Boring"

THE SCOOP

Keeping companies in check

Since its founding in May 2002, Protiviti has been dedicated to helping companies navigate the stricter corporate regulations that resulted from the passage of the Sarbanes-Oxley Act, and assisting companies in identifying, assessing, managing and monitoring business- and technology-related risks encountered in their industries. The Menlo Park, Calif.-based company's more than 2,900 professionals also offer a full spectrum of internal audit services to assist management and directors with their internal audit functions, including full outsourcing, co-sourcing, technology and tool implementation, and quality assessment and readiness reviews. Protiviti has 59 offices across the Americas, Asia-Pacific and Europe. Along with its three core practices, Protiviti also offers specialization in more than 20 industries, ranging from financial services to energy, and offers proprietary technology tools to support a given internal audit or risk consulting engagement.

Protiviti's clients include more than 35 percent of all Fortune 100 companies, more than a quarter of all Fortune 500 companies and more than 20 percent of the Fortune 1,000. For each, Protiviti has developed competencies and methodologies in an array of industries, including communications, consumer products, distribution, education, energy, financial services, government, health care, hospitality, insurance, life sciences, manufacturing, media, nonprofit, real estate, retail, professional services, technology, transportation and utilities.

Turning risk into profitability

Protiviti professionals know a thing or two about following the rules. Many of the company's staff, including managing directors, used to work for the internal audit and business and technology risk consulting practices of Arthur Andersen LLP; these practices operated separately from Andersen's external audit and attestation services. In June 2002, Andersen was convicted of obstruction of justice for shredding documents related to its audit of scandal-ridden Enron. The company surrendered its licenses and its right to practice before the Securities and Exchange Commission. Though the U.S. Supreme Court later overturned the verdict, the event resulted in 28,000 Andersen employees losing their jobs.

Before Andersen's dust had settled, however, a multibillion-dollar specialized staffing company—Robert Half International Inc.—saw its opportunity. In May 2002, the company hired more than 650 Andersen internal audit and risk consulting partners and professionals (none of whom had been involved with the Enron scandal) and quickly rebranded the newly formed group as Protiviti. Today, the firm remains a wholly owned subsidiary of RHI, a public firm listed on the New York Stock Exchange and a member of the S&P 500 index.

Quick to success

Protiviti performed well right out of the gate by capitalizing on the heightened regulatory environment that emerged from infamous misfortunes of Wall Street heavies like Enron, Global Crossing, Tyco and WorldCom. As a June 2005 article from The Institute of Internal Auditors states, "Let's hear it for Enron. If it weren't for such spectacular corporate meltdowns—and the federal crackdown that followed—many fewer college graduates would be making good money as auditors. Internal auditing is the hot field these days."

Protiviti, under the umbrella of $4 billion RHI, has been able to quickly and effectively meet the huge surge in demand for regulatory compliance assistance post-Sarbanes-Oxley, and its bottom line ballooned along with its client portfolio. In the calendar year 2006, the company brought in $543 million in revenue, up from just $133 million in 2003. In September 2006, *BusinessWeek* ranked four-year-old Protiviti as one of the Best Places to Launch a Career. In addition, various Protiviti offices in the U.S. have received recognition as best places to work in publications in their local markets, such as Tampa, Houston and Dallas.

Visit the Vault Consulting Career Channel at www.vault.com/consulting - with insider firm profiles, message boards, the Vault Consulting Job Board and more.

525

What risk consulting means

Protiviti's risk consulting practice helps clients identify and manage business- and technology-related risks that might rear their heads during times of upheaval or change (e.g., reorganization, new regulations, mergers or divestitures), but many risks (e.g., competition, records management, fraud, IT security, identity management) occur and must be managed on a daily basis as part of normal business activities. Business risk may have to do with regulatory concerns, supply chain capacity, financial reporting reliability, human resources availability or customer relationship integrity. Technology risks, such as lax IT security, insufficient continuity planning or poor project management, can be equally pervasive and equally damaging. In both cases, sloppy systems and poor controls slow a company down and place it at a competitive disadvantage.

To help ensure that its clients' businesses are snag-free, Protiviti professionals are experts in outsourced and co-sourced internal audits, business operations controls and effectiveness, technology security and continuity best practices, technology infrastructure and resources management, and fraud risk management, among many others. The company also advises boards of directors on the latest corporate governance issues, on enterprise risk management strategies and on the internal audit function.

Tools of the trade

To help clients get the most out of their Protiviti engagements, the company offers a suite of technology solutions that support the consulting process. The SarbOx Portal™, for example, is a web-based process and knowledge management solution that serves as a centralized repository for all internal control documentation, evaluation and testing related to a Sarbanes-Oxley compliance program. Another tool, the Self-Assessor, allows companies to see if their employees are complying with internal controls and alerts management if they are not. Protiviti's web-enabled Operational Risk Management (ORM) Portal™ provides an integrated solution for enabling compliance with certain Basel II, Sarbanes-Oxley, FDICIA and other regulatory requirements. In addition, since 2002, Protiviti has partnered with a number of companies to complement its risk management offerings, including software makers Oracle (in June 2006) and SAP (in May 2006).

Hedging its bets

Of late, industry watchers have speculated that, as more and more companies grow accustomed to Sarbanes-Oxley regulations, there will be less need for companies like Protiviti. Protiviti's parent company even noted during its fourth-quarter report that the consulting company's future success cannot depend solely on ongoing demand for Sarbanes-Oxley or other regulatory compliance services.

For this reason, Protiviti continues to offer consulting services in numerous other areas of business risk, including anti-money laundering programs and litigation consulting services. In March 2006, for example, the company acquired P.G. Lewis & Associates, which provides data forensic investigations and litigation support in civil and criminal matters involving digital evidence. Protitivi has also attracted attention for its expertise in enterprise risk management. In November 2005, it was named one of the four leaders in the enterprise risk management sector by market research company Forrester Research. And, in June 2007, Forrester again recognized Protiviti as a leader in risk consulting services.

Over the long term, Protiviti has shown a commitment to product diversification. In fact, the company works with its Sarbanes-Oxley compliance clients to build and implement an approach that will enable them to fulfill reporting requirements primarily with in-house resources and processes—thus reducing reliance on companies like Protiviti for these projects. In turn, the company continues to make strides in expanding practice areas such as internal audit, business continuity, fraud and financial investigation, credit risk, and IT security and privacy, among others.

Overseas opportunities

Other countries are watching the U.S. market and implementing similar corporate governance standards, which has resulted in a global demand for the kinds of skills Protiviti provides in the U.S. One such area is India; in October 2006, Protiviti set up two new offices in Mumbai and New Delhi to help organizations cope with the fast-paced growth of South Asian financial markets. The Indian offices operate as Protiviti Consulting Private Limited, a wholly owned subsidiary of Protiviti.

The India announcement followed an expansion into São Paulo, Brazil, in September 2006. In May of that year, the company expanded its European operations with two offices in Germany—in Frankfurt and Düsseldorf—preceded in January 2006 by the opening of an office in Mexico City.

Continuing to expand

So far, demand remains strong for the company's governance, risk and compliance services, which were ranked among the country's best by Forrester Research in April 2006. In addition, Robert Half International reported at the end of January 2007 that in the fourth quarter, Protiviti continued to experience double-digit revenue growth on a year-over-year basis.

Whatever lies ahead for Protiviti in terms of its Sarbanes-Oxley services, the company is presently taking advantage of its success by continuing to expand its business offerings. In December 2006, after acquiring Enspier Technologies, Inc., the company spun off its public-sector operations into a wholly owned subsidiary, Protiviti Government Services, Inc. The new subsidiary delivers Protiviti's internal audit and risk management expertise to federal, state, local and international governments, and draws upon Enspier's technology and management consulting expertise.

In March 2006, the company partnered with enterprise contract management software company diCarta to shore up its contract management compliance solution. Going forward, the partnership will help companies manage their contracting risks. Only a month earlier, Protiviti announced the acquisitions of Creative Options and Radius, two Canadian companies that specialize in loss prevention and risk management for the retail sector. In addition, in April 2007, Protiviti acquired PENTA Advisory Services, LLC, which provides restructuring and insolvency services, litigation services, and bankruptcy-related tax, accounting and administrative services.

GETTING HIRED

Straight to the source

At the entry level, Protiviti recruits from more than 65 colleges and universities across the United States. Though these campuses are heavily represented, the company says they "also encourage and interview candidates from nontarget schools." For undergrad contenders, the interview race begins on campus, with questions about an applicant's resume, school and study program, and behavior.

On your mark, get set ...

Once at the Protiviti office, the process continues in three acts, conducted respectively by human resources managers, practice area managers and directors. The "HR manager asks the typical behavior-based questions," a staffer shares. "As long as you are prepared, you shouldn't have any problems with this round." During the second installment, managers and directors pose technical inquiries; the process closes with a meeting with an office leader or managing director. For this last short leg, staffers encourage applicants to "show your interests in consulting and Protiviti." Primarily, insiders claim, the company is "currently focused on behavioral interviewing, but is looking to move to some case-based interviewing."

Interview questions may run along the lines of "How much do you know about Sarbanes-Oxley?" or, for the IT practice area, requesting your insight into the "kinds of technology risks an IT shop typically faces." At the end of the day, candidates are often given an opportunity to ask questions—a perfect window for company-specific queries.

Visit the Vault Consulting Career Channel at **www.vault.com/consulting** - with insider firm profiles, message boards, the Vault Consulting Job Board and more.

VAULT CAREER LIBRARY   527

OUR SURVEY SAYS

Busy bees

"Corporate culture is definitely where Protiviti excels," an associate remarks. Full of "friendly, hardworking, proactive people," the company boasts "a higher number of females in all levels, a number of internationals and a lot of different backgrounds." Insiders also tell us that the company drives its consultants to "perform one level above their current level." Since "most of the managing directors are approachable and open to recommendations," Protiviti's environment encourages immediate responsibility and professional development; as one consultant drives home, "Where else do you get to speak and work with the founding members of such a successful company? Nowhere!" Supervisors also act as mentors—they "will let you know what is acceptable and also give you good career advice." "Many interns and consultants right off campus get the chance to interview C-level clients," comments a source, "while their fellow grads [at other firms] are stuck on the bench waiting on opportunities with Big Four companies."

Sources also tell us that they work fewer hours than their Big Four counterparts. Office hours are generally 8:30 to 5:30, though consultants stress the importance of vocalizing scheduling preferences. "This is a company that is new and still ironing out details," one insider advises. "But if you are willing to speak up, people are there and will listen."

All about the bonuses

Employees are relatively silent on the salary front, but gush about Protiviti's benefits packages. Performance-based bonuses, ranging from 4 to 20 percent, keep Protiviti consultants happy. As one staffer reports, "If you sell past your targets or work more hours than target, your bonus is potentially unlimited." Also lauded are the company's health care options, 401(k) and Roth IRA availability, RHI stock grants and "generous per diem when out of office." For travelers, Protiviti offers 20 days off per year— three days added for every three years—and closes the deal with nine paid holidays.

Right Management

1818 Market Street, 33rd Floor
Philadelphia, PA 19103
Phone: (215) 988-1588
Fax: (215) 988-9112
www.right.com

LOCATIONS

Philadelphia, PA (HQ)
300 offices worldwide

PRACTICE AREAS

Attract & Assess
Develop
Engage & Align
Transition

THE STATS

Employer Type: Subsidiary of Manpower Inc.
Ticker Symbol: MAN (NYSE)
CEO: Owen Sullivan
President & COO: Doug Matthews
2007 Employees: 3,100
2006 Employees: 3,000
2006 Revenue: $414 million
2005 Revenue: $406 million

UPPER

• No extreme hours

DOWNER

• Variable business and workload volume

EMPLOYMENT CONTACT

E-mail: contactus@right.com

Visit the Vault Consulting Career Channel at **www.vault.com/consulting** - with insider firm
profiles, message boards, the Vault Consulting Job Board and more.

 VAULT CAREER LIBRARY   529

THE SCOOP

Opportunities ahead

Right Management consultants may be the only people who don't dread pink slips. That's because layoffs mean big business for Right Management, a subsidiary of staffing services company Manpower since 2004, which steps in to help its clients manage the full scope of their workforce needs—from hiring through transitioning. The firm specializes in organizations undergoing change and experiencing layoffs to ensure that processes are managed effectively and productively for both the company and the individuals who are affected. Right Management's professionals are skilled in assisting employees in transition land on their feet successfully—and as quickly as possible. In addition to outplacement services, the firm's 3,100 professionals help organizations attract and assess new managerial talent and skilled workers, develop current employees' leadership and professional skills, and help engage and align them with the company's goals and strategies.

With more than 300 service locations in 50 countries, Right Management works hard at keeping its own workforce engaged and aligned. And so far, so good: The Philadelphia-based consultancy's client portfolio includes 80 percent of the Fortune 500 and half of the Global 1000 firms.

Booming after the bust

Right Management, a human capital services consulting firm, was founded in December 1980 by Frank Louchheim, Larry Evans, Rob Fish and Boardman Thompson, who first dubbed the firm Right Associates. Back then, the company had only three offices—its headquarters in Philadelphia and two locations in New York and Stamford, Conn. Organic growth, coupled with a strategic acquisition plan, enabled Right Management to expand each year since its founding. In 1992, Rich Pinola was named president and CEO. Under his leadership, Right Management developed an organizational consulting business in addition to its outplacement business.

With the fallout of the dot-com bubble in 2000 and the ensuing waves of layoffs, the firm really picked up steam. Within four years, Right Management was a hot commodity—in January 2004, it had an unsolicited bid for its stock from Manpower, Inc., an $18 billion global provider of employment services. The company swept up Right Management in a stock deal worth almost $500 million, and merged its own consulting wing into Right Management.

More on Manpower

The 2004 acquisition of Right Management was one of many deals Manpower has made since 2000. The company has been through a growth spurt, adding 700 offices to its worldwide roster since 2000, financed by fast-paced revenue growth from $10 billion in 2001 to $17.6 billion by the end of fiscal 2006. With 4,400 offices in 73 countries and 400,000 clients, Right Management's parent company is one of the country's largest, ranking at No. 136 on the Fortune 500. And, in 2006, Manpower made it onto the pages of *Fortune* magazine, when it was named America's Most Admired Staffing Company for the fourth year in a row, based on the quality of its products and services, innovativeness, quality of management, employee talent, social responsibility, financial soundness, long-term investment value and its use of corporate assets. In addition to Right Management, the company's other brands include Manpower Professional, Elan and Jefferson Wells.

Right-on focus

Right Management's consulting services fall into four main practice areas that cover the full employment lifecyle. The "attract and assess" area focuses on bringing in the top talent in a client's market, assessing for competencies to ensure the right people are in the right roles. The "develop" practice area focuses on leaders already within the company, offering them coaching, leadership development and professional skill development services. This helps to hone the effectiveness of leaders and ensures a strong pipeline of future talent to fill the anticipated gaps organizations face as baby boomers begin retiring. The "engage and align" practice area connects employees with an organization's strategy, vision and purpose to achieve better organizational performance.

But the bulk of Right Management's business has to do with its fourth practice area—outplacement services—which it now terms transition services. For the companies doing the letting go (due to events like restructuring, new strategy implementation, new technology introductions, deregulation or a merger or acquisition) the firm offers organizational transition planning and implementation. For client employees that have been let go, Right Management offers career transition and career management services. The firm has also developed RightChoice™, an outplacement solution that provides displaced employees with support. RightChoice supports the individual with personal, one-on-one coaching, connections to marketplace resources, job search skills training, and in-office and at-home web-based solutions to stay connected with the individual until he or she has achieved success.

Confidence counts

Annually, the career experts at Right Management take the pulse of full-time workers around the world to measure career confidence. In phone interviews with thousands of full-timers in 18 countries in Europe, the Americas and Asia, Right Management's professionals ask employees two questions: whether they feel they will be laid off from their job in the next year and how easy or difficult it would be for the average person just laid off from his job to find a similar job at the same pay.

A November 2006 survey showed that career confidence had risen to an all-time high of 58.6 out of a possible 100, with worker confidence levels rising in 15 of the 18 countries surveyed. November's score is the highest global Career Confidence Index level in the four years that Right has been conducting the survey. In the United States, 80.8 percent of workers said they didn't expect to lose their jobs in the coming year, and a record number of survey respondents—22.8 percent—felt it would be easy to find a similar job at the same pay if they were laid off.

A new face at the top

In January 2007, Right Management CEO Owen Sullivan got a helping hand when the firm named Douglas Matthews its new president and chief operating officer. Formerly executive vice president of Right Management's global operations, Matthews, long-tenured and well respected in the industry, is now in charge of the firm's global operations, business development, product management, finance and marketing.

A new hot market

Where better to look for new work opportunities and skilled workers than India? That's what Right Management was likely thinking when, in December 2006, it acquired Grow Talent Company Limited, an organizational and individual consulting firm with offices in Guragaon, Mumbai and Bangalore. CEO Sullivan explained at the time that the acquisition was part of the company's overall plans to expand its service delivery network abroad, especially in India.

GETTING HIRED

Searching for opportunities

Easily accessible career information for prospective Right Management candidates is hard to come by. An insider advises that the best way to get in the door is by networking. As for this source's interview, "I don't remember specific questions but do remember questions relating to working with diverse individuals, experience with training and facilitation, and experience within the outplacement and career transition industries." Another insider who applied for an associate position reports, "There was a request for a writing sample and two examinations: one for position fit and the other for energy level to see if I was compatible with the culture." For an organizational consultant role, the source adds, "There would be a need for several phone screens, face-to-face interviews, completion of at least two online assessments and a presentation on a topic of your choice. It's a very vigorous process, but it ensures fit."

Visit the Vault Consulting Career Channel at **www.vault.com/consulting** - with insider firm profiles, message boards, the Vault Consulting Job Board and more.

VAULT CAREER LIBRARY   531

The Segal Company

One Park Avenue
New York, NY 10016
Phone: (212) 251-5000
Fax: (212) 251-5490
www.segalco.com
www.segaladvisors.com
www.segalmgc.com
www.sibson.com

LOCATIONS

New York, NY (HQ)
Offices in the US and Canada

PRACTICE AREAS

Benefits Consulting
Communications Consulting
Investment Consulting
Strategic Human Resources Consulting

THE STATS

Employer Type: Private Company
President & CEO: Joseph A. LoCicero
2006 Employees: 900+
2005 Employees: 900+
2006 Revenue: $180 million
2005 Revenue: $178.3 million

UPPER

- The firm tries to ensure work/life balance for its consultants

DOWNER

- Top-down communication needs improvement

EMPLOYMENT CONTACT

www.segalco.com/careers/index.html

THE BUZZ
WHAT CONSULTANTS AT OTHER FIRMS ARE SAYING ABOUT THIS FIRM

- "Laid-back"
- "Too specialized"
- "Multiemployer plan experts"
- "Expertise in public sector is diminishing"

THE SCOOP

Starters' advantage

The Segal Company was one of the first consultancies established to help companies help their people. Founded in 1939 and headquartered in New York City, the employee-owned firm focuses on benefit, compensation and human resources consulting, drawing on the expertise of more than 900 employees working in offices throughout the U.S. and Canada. In the 68 years since Martin E. Segal founded the firm, The Segal Company has conceived and designed benefits programs that are now widely accepted, from the first supplemental benefits programs to the first PPOs (networks of preferred health care providers).

Clients are located throughout the United States and Canada, as well as in Puerto Rico, the Virgin Islands, the Bahamas and Europe, and range in size from several hundred employees to more than 400,000 employees. Segal clients include corporations, nonprofit organizations, professional service firms, state and local governments and joint boards of trustees administering pension and health and welfare plans, all of which are serviced by one of Segal's distinct practices—corporate consulting (which includes nonprofit consulting), public-sector consulting and multiemployer plan consulting.

Creativity through competition

While The Segal Company was one of the first to enter the HR and benefits plans consulting market, these days it certainly isn't alone. To gain competitive advantage, the firm has created a network of subsidiaries, each with their own expertise. In 1969, The Segal Company established its first subsidiary, Segal Advisors Inc., an investment consulting affiliate that offers independent investment consulting services to more than 225 clients with approximately $73.6 billion in assets. In November 2006, Segal Advisors was ranked as one of the top-25 consultancies by *Pensions & Investments*.

In 2001, Segal created a second affiliate, Segal/MGC Communications, via its acquisition of New York-based Marjorie Gross & Company. The merged company advises on strategy and tactics, education, marketing, training, research, benefits programs, human resources and organizational communications. Clients include some of the most widely-recognized Fortune 500 companies.

In January 2002, Segal bought compensation consultancy Sibson Consulting from Nextera Enterprises for $16 million; in February 2007, it combined Sibson's human capital consulting division with its own corporate benefits and actuarial practice to create Sibson Consulting. Today, the division specializes in strategic human resources consulting, which maximizes the performance, efficiency and motivation of clients' employees. Sibson Consulting's services—which include talent management, benefits, organization design, sales effectiveness and change management—are used by many Fortune 500 companies.

The old standbys

The Segal Company still serves as an umbrella for a number of in-house practice divisions. Its public-sector unit offers employee benefits, actuarial, compensation and human resources advice to state and local governments, statewide retirement systems and health plans and federal government agencies. Meanwhile, Segal's multiemployer unit services more multiemployer benefit plans than any other firm.

Climbing up the ivory tower

The American higher-education market has never been more competitive, and The Segal Company and Sibson Consulting are there to help these educational institutions run more like businesses as they race to keep up. University leadership is turning over, teaching models are changing and universities are facing never-before-seen competition from well-funded distance learning and for-profit institutions. To keep talented employees onboard and to manage change, universities need strong human resources departments, and Segal and Sibson help educational institutions develop rewards strategies, benefits programs, absence management programs, compensation plans, performance management measures and human resources assessments.

Visit the Vault Consulting Career Channel at **www.vault.com/consulting** - with insider firm profiles, message boards, the Vault Consulting Job Board and more.

VAULT CAREER LIBRARY   533

Publishing perspectives

Segal regularly shares its findings with the general public, publishing papers on issues that concern clients of its consulting, public-sector and multiemployer practices. It also publishes two online newsletters: Capital Checkup, which summarizes health care news from Washington, and Compliance Alert, which looks at important developments affecting benefits plan compliance issues. Sibson publishes Perspectives a quarterly e-zine.

GETTING HIRED

Nice to meet you

Those gunning for a job at Segal must be creative thinkers, excellent communicators, team players and achievement-oriented. Insiders admit that the three-round process is "long," but believe that it's "good for both candidates and the company." One analyst recalls meeting with a human resources representative and two business analysts, and being asked basic questions focusing on analytical skills and situational cases. A vice president remembers that he "met with many individuals who were as eager to know more about me as they were to answer my questions."

OUR SURVEY SAYS

Give and take

"In some respects," this consultant shares, "the company feels like a mix between academia, family and a successful (if somewhat nontraditional) business." Staffers do take the initiative to look after both the business and their peers, "partly because it is employee owned, and partly because people genuinely care about one another." Sources also tout the firm as perfect for lifelong learners, and cite Segal as a surefire pick for those "looking to work for a socially progressive benefits consulting firm." And, consultants appreciate that Segal "will work with you to ensure that you have a fulfilling experience working at this firm."

Still, as some insiders divulge, Segal's administration could use a little fine tuning. "The management does not always utilize good communication about issues within the firm," reports an associate, especially when it comes to clarifying job titles and functions. And though the firm does remarkably well with staff retention, such high levels of retention can also "create some barriers to embracing change."

Cashing out

Segal insiders rate their salary as "solid, though not spectacular," but take a dimmer view of their bonuses, describing them as "a mystery," with "no direct link between behavior/accomplishments and incentive pay." The firm notes, however, that bonus plans changed in 2006. On the upside, and as befitting a firm that specializes in HR consulting, benefits are comprehensive and allotted generously, and include a pension, 401(k) plan, medical coverage, a maximum of four weeks' vacation, a sabbatical policy and a tuition reimbursement plan.

Simon-Kucher & Partners

One Canal Park
Cambridge, MA 02141
Phone: (617) 231-4500
Fax: (617) 576-2751
www.simon-kucher.com

LOCATIONS

Boston, MA (US HQ)
Bonn (World HQ)
New York, NY
San Francisco, CA
Cologne
Frankfurt
London
Milan
Munich
Paris
Tokyo
Toronto
Vienna
Warsaw
Zurich

PRACTICE AREAS

Marketing & Sales Optimization
Marketing Strategy
Price Management
Setting Prices

THE STATS

Employer Type: Private Company
Chairman & CEO: Hermann Simon, PhD
2007 Employees: 365
2006 Employees: 300
2006 Revenue: $76 million
2005 Revenue: $66 million

RANKING RECAP

Quality of Life
#11 - Work/Life Balance
#12 - Travel Requirements
#16 - Relationships with Supervisors (tie)
#16 - Firm Culture
#18 - Formal Training
#19 - Hours in the Office

Diversity
#5 - Diversity for GLBT
#6 - Diversity for Minorities
#12 - Best Firms for Diversity

UPPERS

- "Office-based consulting model versus on-site model"
- Entrepreneurial and laid-back spirit
- "A lot of opportunities and responsibilities for young/new consultants"
- "Large enough to have an international footprint, and small enough to have consistent access to all partners"

DOWNERS

- "Lacks a middle layer that can provide guidance and be role models to up-and-coming consultants"
- "Low level of professionalism with regard to internal issues"
- "Increase in growth is slightly changing the culture of the firm"
- Lower compensation than other top firms

EMPLOYMENT CONTACT

Attn: Recruiting Team
One Canal Park
Cambridge, MA 02141
E-mail: recruit-usa@simon-kucher.com

Visit the Vault Consulting Career Channel at **www.vault.com/consulting** - with insider firm profiles, message boards, the Vault Consulting Job Board and more.

VAULT CAREER LIBRARY   535

THE SCOOP

Pricing pros

Simon-Kucher & Partners is known as the world's largest consulting practice dedicated to pricing. The Bonn-based firm was conceived in 1985, when Hermann Simon, a professor at a German management school, and two of his former PhD students launched a business as a natural expansion of their empirical research. Their goal: To offer strategy consulting with a numbers-based bent. *BusinessWeek* has referred to SKP as "a world leader in giving advice to companies on how to price their products." Though pricing is its forte, SKP also "covers the whole value chain" for clients in the areas of marketing and strategy. That means consultants will work on everything from analysis, marketing and strategy development to implementation and monitoring. However, the firm insists it is not a general management consultancy, and even goes so far as to turn down projects that don't fall within its narrow range of expertise.

Today, SKP has over 365 consultants working in 15 offices in 10 countries around the world. Its consultants cover a broad range of industries, including pharma, financial services, telecom, media, software, construction, and nonprofit organizations. The majority of SKP's clients are Fortune 500 firms, such as BMW, Barclay's, Coca-Cola, Dresdner Bank and Royal Dutch Shell. It also has served most of the big-name pharmaceutical clients, among them Johnson & Johnson, Novartis, Eli Lilly and GlaxoSmithKline.

No wining and dining here

The firm indicates that it works with clients on a meritocratic basis, boasting that it earns repeat business based on its quality of work, not by "wining and dining" them. It prides itself on not exactly being a "relationship firm," but rather a product firm— one that wins clients because of its expert knowledge in a specific product area. SKP keeps a low profile on project specifics, though it does reveal examples of the types of client issues it deals with. For example, the firm recently helped a bank improve profit through expanding its cross-selling. To get the job done, consultants investigated the products that could be grouped together, the optimal prices of each package and determined the effects on volume and returns.

Steady expansion

Those strategies seem to be getting the job done. In 2006, SKP posted $76 million in revenue, up 15 percent from the previous year. And SKP has lofty ambitions for growth: The firm says its goal is to keep up its pace of the past decade and grow at 20 percent per year, and expects that international expansion will make that happen. To better serve its clients, SKP opened four new offices in 2007, in New York, Toronto, Cologne and Vienna. As part of its growth plan, SKP has also been steadily augmenting its leadership with new partners. In December 2006, the firm named eight new partners to its management team, all of whom will work in SKP offices outside of Germany.

The firm claims that as a global operation, international orientation is a big part of its culture. It also notes that consultants of many nationalities often work in one office as a team. Employees are encouraged to spend three months to a year abroad—or for those extra-ambitious associates, the chance to open a brand new office in a developing area.

SKP front man

Founder Dr. Hermann Simon is an eminent management thought leader and one of the best-known pricing experts. In 2005, he was voted the second-most influential management thinker in Germany after his friend, the late Peter Drucker. Simon is a permanent visiting professor at the London Business School, and has been a visiting professor at Stanford Business School, MIT Sloan Business School, the Universities of Mainz and Bielefeld, INSEAD and Keio. He is also the author of over 30 books in 15 languages, including best-selling titles *Hidden Champions* and *Power Pricing*.

Simon's most recent book, *Manage for Profit, Not for Market Share*, published in 2006, questions the management focus on market share and advises managers to concentrate on profit increases through pricing. Co-authors Frank F. Bilstein and Frank Luby collaborated to lay out strategies for managers to differentiate their products, raise prices, conduct promotional campaigns and better grasp the preferences and behavior of consumers. In 2006, Simon made a whirlwind tour lecturing on the topic at conferences in Barcelona, Leon, Lisbon, Milan, Shanghai, Rome and Madrid.

Training the troops

SKP claims to be "in the knowledge business" and, as such, puts a lot of emphasis on learning and education for its consultants. Upon joining the firm, staffers take part in STEPS (Strategic Training for Employee Professional Success), a training course in Bonn that breaks consultants in by having them work on simulated projects. It sounds pretty serious, but consultants assert that classwork is broken up by regular trips to Bonn beer gardens in the evening. Trainees also hear lectures from experts within and outside of the firm. Consultants in the U.S. also go through a week of training specific to their first divisional assignment, which introduces them to particular industry dynamics and key strategy challenges. Presentations and educational talks remain part of life at SKP throughout an employee's career, as the firm regularly invites speakers to weigh in on relevant topics and sponsors internal presentations, known as SKP Universities.

GETTING HIRED

Jumping through the hoops

Scouts for Simon-Kucher head to Harvard, MIT, Yale, Brown, Tufts, Dartmouth, Penn, Columbia, Amherst, Williams, Stanford and Berkeley in search of high-achieving undergraduate candidates, while Sloan, Fuqua, Wharton, Tuck, HBS, Stern and Columbia remain prime targets for MBA all-stars. These fresh-faced recruits go through preliminary interviews on campus, while outside applicants undergo telephone grilling sessions. It is not unusual to face two preliminary on-campus or telephone rounds, complete with behavioral and case questions. The last step is coming face-to-face with SKP consultants for a full-day interview cycle in your preferred office.

Mental mathletes

During in-office interviews, contenders "meet with a variety of people at all different levels" within the firm, and associates emphasize that "case studies are important"—a mediocre case performance generally sends a hopeful applicant packing. But depending on the business area, "some interviewers focus solely on interest and fit, while others focus on cases," an employee reveals. And since SKP leads the world in pricing expertise, the firm also puts high value on quantitative skills, requiring a short, basic math test for finalists—so "be prepared to do math in your head," insiders warn.

OUR SURVEY SAYS

Simon solidarity

At SKP, "the people make the company, which makes working here that much more enjoyable," we're told. Co-workers "are a friendly, helpful, energetic bunch" and like to get together after work—"so interactions are not limited to the office setting," a source adds. This camaraderie spills over from a solid in-office rapport, with roots in a merit-based and hierarchy-free model. Bureaucracy takes a backseat, offering each employee an all-access pass to the firm's various levels, where someone will always be willing to answer questions and "discuss project experiences, career development or any other topic."

Insiders also note the thriving cross-continental culture that permeates the firm. Remarks a senior staffer, "Our projects are generally international in scope, and we work on international project teams to match that scope. However," he continues, "the

Visit the Vault Consulting Career Channel at **www.vault.com/consulting** - with insider firm profiles, message boards, the Vault Consulting Job Board and more.

VAULT CAREER LIBRARY   **537**

company is able to extend its small-firm feel across offices" by bringing globally sprawling teammates together for meet-and-greet sessions, which tie up loose ends and foster worldwide Simon-Kucher cordiality.

Put your heads together

Due to the firm's "relatively flat organizational structure," SKP associates hit the jackpot when it comes to tracking down supervisors. Insiders say superiors "leave their doors open and are always open to questions," which applies to partners as well—"they are always involved in project work, not just acquisition," according to a senior consultant. When it's time to work alongside SKP's top dogs, we're told, "partners have very different working styles," so "satisfaction is really dependent on who you happen to be working with."

Differences aside, consultants can't deny junior- and senior-level magnetism; explains an insider, "even as an entry-level consultant, I have been able to work closely with partners on projects and business development." And at SKP, the word "exposure" extends beyond the firm's ranking structure; newbies are given as much responsibility as they can handle, and manage "a significant amount of interaction with clients both on site and by phone and e-mail," a first-year shares.

Hours ahead of the pack

Hailing from the core of consulting hustle and bustle, SKP staffers know about work hour fluctuations. Luckily, though occasionally prone to late-night work for project deadlines, sources say they usually leave by 6:30 or 7 p.m. The firm notes that efficiency is rewarded over face time at all levels, and consultants report that SKP head-honchos do their part to "structure the week's workload so that there is no weekend work involved." One staffer admits that this isn't always doable, "but their attitude about a five-day workweek with a two-day break (as opposed to the 'we work around the clock' mentality) is critical to ensure a productive work/life balance." Other colleagues agree, acknowledging SKP's leniency with consultants and efforts "to ensure that the staff isn't stretched too thin." Employees file in, do their diligent duties and still have time for family dinners, home relaxation, weekend ski trips—whatever strikes their fancies—because "colleagues value the importance of ending work at some point in the day, and not just when we have to fall asleep to recharge for work the next day."

With work/life balance at an ostensible apex, insiders are quick to acknowledge a decline in the past year. "In 2006, working late nights and weekends was much more common," an associate shares, mostly because the firm's business is starting to outgrow its staff. "As the company continues to grow faster than they can hire and train new employees," a colleague remarks, "I think they will need to keep an eye on working conditions to make sure that we don't adopt the same work hours as our competitors." But in this cautionary tale still lies some silver lining: "Nevertheless, we are still miles ahead of the rest of the industry," assures a source.

Pain-free travel

When it comes to travel, SKPers aren't the type to complain. Since most work stays within the firm's walls, consultants don't spend too much time exploring other shores, and usually trek out just for meetings and presentations. Coming and going at short intervals, staffers maintain that travel rarely puts a damper on time allotted for family and friends. Says a senior colleague, "We try to minimize travel so that we have day or one-night trips to the clients, rather than extended stays," which associates agree helps immensely with work/life equilibrium.

For the most part, Simon-Kucher consultants view travel as a "nice variation," and as one director states, the rate is "just enough to be interesting without being so much that it is a pain." As it stands, partners tend to shoulder most of the flight and jet lag burden, though according to one senior staffer, "I still think I travel less than partners at other consultancies."

Taking the training abroad

Whether taught formally or informally, SKP insiders feel adequately trained and undoubtedly, the most exciting aspect for newbies just entering the consulting ranks is the trip to Bonn, Germany, where "they are introduced to our methodologies, our divisions and our project approach," explains a senior consultant. During the one-week international induction, new hires from the firm's global offices tackle mock projects, schmooze with peers and attend company events. Once back in their hometown, trainees undergo the second one-week leg of the new hire training program—a divisional affair. To keep employees on the ball, the firm throws in additional training sessions throughout the year, including SKP Universities, where consultants gather to share lessons learned and experiences gained.

Diving into cases with rolled-up sleeves makes the most difference, sources say, regardless of formal training. Though official guidance can be valuable, "most of what you're learning is from being involved in the projects and talking to fellow co-workers, project managers and mentors," we're told. As one consultant comments, the STEPS program offered to new consultants "does not teach much, other than to help integrate you," so "the actual knowledge comes from on-the-job experience," a colleague adds. With teamwork, mentoring and direct project work, peers conclude that "unofficial training seems to be more successful at bringing people up to speed."

Dollars and incentives

Simon-Kucher consultants are satisfied with their somewhat competitive salaries, but the firm's raise and bonus configurations have them griping about lost dollars and cents. Moans one first-year, "The bonus at my level is much lower than at other top consulting firms"—a bonus that, depending on an associate's level, creates a 3 to 6 percent pay bump. Other insiders claim that SKP's "bonus structure gives us no incentive to work toward hitting the firm's revenue growth targets," nor are they fond of the promotion-only raise schedule.

Partner profit sharing, 3 percent 401(k) matching, health care and dependent care flexible spending accounts, equity ownership and tuition incentives make up some of the other monetary perks at the firm.

To Germany with love

On the nonmonetary side of things, sources prize their happy hours, paid parking, company cars, free public transit and "opportunities for all levels to rotate in foreign offices for three to six months." But all pale in comparison to the annual world meeting and three-day holiday extravaganza in Bonn, where staffers and their significant others congregate at the company's expense. "The holiday party in Germany is, to put it mildly, special," a consultant chirps. Co-workers spend a day discussing global company strategy, and then on Saturday night get gussied up for an "impeccable black-tie event," which all adds up to a "luxurious setting, exceptional food, dancing until dawn and a long flight home to catch up on sleep."

Landing a room with a view isn't an uncommon concept at SKP's Boston location, which has consultants settling into individual offices within one to one-and-a-half years' tenure. That said, associates could use a bit more legroom; the accommodations are "somewhat space-crunched at the moment," colleagues report. Another bullet on the "cons" list goes to location. The offices are not in the heart of downtown Boston or San Francisco (though the firm notes that they are accessible by public transportation) but few complaints arise with regard to the office's interior.

Service and support

An SKP-sponsored community service day brings the firm closer to its neighboring communities. Recent projects have included helping out Habitat for Humanity and local food banks. Aside from this annual occurrence, the firm contributes sporadically to food drives and charity collections, but most involvement is left to individual initiatives. "We have various people who bring their personal interests into the office, so they'll collect cans and food around the holidays," says one associate. "People in the firm are involved in other types of charities and solicit support, but there is no firm support for those other activities—no discouragement, either, just no encouragement."

Visit the Vault Consulting Career Channel at **www.vault.com/consulting** - with insider firm profiles, message boards, the Vault Consulting Job Board and more.

 **VAULT** CAREER LIBRARY **539**

Thinning at the top

"I believe women now outnumber men in the Boston office," one senior consultant boasts, a claim uncontested by colleagues. The firm explains that there are significant fluctuations in the composition of the incoming class from year to year. Last year, for example, "we hired more women than men," an insider reports, but then addresses the catch—"as you move up the ladder, positions become more male-heavy." As sources disclose, though there are "several women working at SKP as directors and senior consultants," only one out of the 30 global partners is female, a fact that has the firm considering more proactive efforts to retain women. "Women partners and role models are sorely needed," we're told.

Much like the female conundrum, racial and ethnic minorities at the firm thin out in the higher ranks. "We probably hire more minorities than nonminorities," according to consultants, "but as you move up the ladder, again it is flipped." This inequality, as with women, has little to do with the firm's receptivity; insiders attest to the firm's openness, but admit that diversity programs and initiatives are lacking.

The atmosphere is the same for GLBT employees; sexual orientation has no bearing on respect at SKP. According to a Boston-based consultant, "The [U.S. offices are] small with good people, so GLBT colleagues are not afraid to talk about their sexual orientation or bring their spouses/significant others along to company events."

Stern Stewart & Co.

111 Broadway
Suite 1402
New York, NY 10006
Phone: (212) 261-0600
Fax: (212) 581-6420
www.sternstewart.com

LOCATIONS

New York, NY (HQ)
Bangkok
Johannesburg
London
Melbourne
Milan
Mumbai
Munich
São Paulo
Shanghai
Singapore
Tokyo
Vienna
Zurich

PRACTICE AREAS

Corporate Financial Policy
EVA-Based Solutions

THE STATS

Employer Type: Private Company
Chairman & CEO: Joel M. Stern

UPPERS

- Top destination for finance consulting
- New consultants are quickly exposed to clients' top executives

DOWNERS

- No formal training program for new hires
- Squabbling for projects

EMPLOYMENT CONTACT

E-mail: careers@sternstewart.com

THE BUZZ
WHAT CONSULTANTS AT OTHER FIRMS ARE SAYING ABOUT THIS FIRM

- "If you need finance help ... go here"
- "One-dimensional"
- "Solid niche player"
- "Repackaging basic concepts"

Visit the Vault Consulting Career Channel at **www.vault.com/consulting** - with insider firm profiles, message boards, the Vault Consulting Job Board and more.

VAULT CAREER LIBRARY   541

THE SCOOP

New meaning to value-added

Everyone in business is looking to get more value for their money. The consultants at Stern Stewart & Co. specialize in showing their clients how. The New York City-based financial consulting firm hangs its hat on its ability to increase clients' shareholder value and to drive up their share price. And with additional offices in London, Munich, Johannesburg, Melbourne, Mumbai, São Paulo, Singapore and Bangkok, it isn't much of a surprise that 300 companies around the world—including big shots like Goldman Sachs and Credit Suisse First Boston—now employ Stern Stewart's trademarked value-added approach themselves to increase the value of their businesses. Clients include virtually every type of company, both public and private, from banks to heavy manufacturers to government agencies like the U.S. Postal Service.

Founded in 1982 by current Chairman and CEO Joel M. Stern and G. Bennett Stewart III, now a senior adviser at Stern Stewart, the firm consults with both large and middle-market companies, walking them through the minutiae of corporate financial policy so that they get the most out of restructurings and recapitalizations, share repurchases, acquisitions and divestitures, and financial strategy. Stern Stewart also advises clients on raising capital, incentive plans and litigation support, among other traditional financial consulting services. But the lens through which Stern Stewart sees all its services is through its proprietary management concept and measurement tool EVA, or economic value added.

The ABCs of EVA

In consultant-speak, EVA "is an estimate of true 'economic' profit, or the amount by which earnings exceed or fall short of the required minimum rate of return shareholders and lenders could get by investing in other securities of comparable risk." In plain language, EVA standardizes how value is measured in a company by recalculating how businesses traditionally assess their value by looking at things from a shareholder's perspective. It calculates how much value a corporate financial policy brings to a company after accounting for the cost of executing it—in both debt and equity—and the opportunity cost of what else could have been done while the company put that policy into place.

According to the firm, EVA is the clearest measure of the total real costs involved in any business venture. It prevents companies from the usual pitfalls of appearing profitable when they are not, usually because they haven't fully accounted for certain costs or have inconsistent standards for measuring financial goals and objectives. Instead, EVA uses a single financial measure by associating all business processes with improving EVA. When Stern Stewart works its magic, EVA provides a "common language" that allows all management decisions to be modeled, monitored, communicated and compensated in a manner consistent with the goal of adding shareholder value so that investors continue to invest in the firm.

Case in point

Still confused? Here's an example of how EVA is different from the more standard profit measure of net income, which subtracts costs from total sales. Say Company X earned $100,000 on a total capital base of $1 million. Normally, Company X's finance team would say their bosses did a good job, offering a return on capital of 10 percent. But Company X is a new company in a risky market. Its shareholders are only willing to continue investing in Company X if they can get a 13 percent return on their money.

So even though Company X made $100,000, it lost 3 percent for its shareholders. So, if Company X's capital is $100 million (which includes debt and shareholder equity) and the cost of using its $100 million in capital is $13 million per year (to finance interest on its debt and the cost of underwriting the equity), Company X's shareholders will only get what they expect when Company X's profits are more than $13 million per year. If Company X has a spectacular year and profits $17 million next year, its EVA will be $4 million. The calculation is: EVA equals the net operating profit after taxes (NOPAT), minus a company's capital multiplied by the cost of that capital.

EVA EVerywhere

If EVA were that simple, however, Stern Stewart would be out of business. If the firm's 300 EVA acolytes—which include Bausch & Lomb, Best Buy, Coca-Cola, JC Penney and Toys R Us—could figure out EVA for themselves, they would. For forking over their consulting fees, however, Stern Stewart shows evidence that companies who use EVA to measure their financial well-being significantly outperform other companies in their industries. And in July 2006, Stern Stewart established EVA Dimensions, LLC, whose sole purpose is to manage the firm's EVA data and investment research and hedge fund management services.

In fact, Stern Stewart's metric has become so popular, it has had to fend off copycats along the way as more and more companies began treating EVA as public property and not as Stern Stewart's proprietary methodology. Stern Stewart really became incensed in 1995, when KPMG, which was auditing Stern Stewart's books at the time, created its own consulting service based on a tool called Economic Value Management that was too close to EVA for comfort. KPMG also hired away three Stern Stewart employees to set up the new consulting practice and peddle the new service. Stern Stewart promptly filed a lawsuit against KPMG, attempting to prove that EVA was a proprietary concept, and in August 1997, a judge ruled that KPMG had abused its relationship with Stern Stewart.

Healthy skepticism

But even though EVA is now an accepted standard performance metric, due in no small part to Stern Stewart's own marketing efforts, the technique has its critics. The first, and most basic, criticism is that it is risky to depend on a single metric for taking a company's financial pulse. In 1997, for example, business expert Gary Hamel said, "No one measure can capture all the dynamics of corporate performance."

But more importantly, with so many high-growth, high-tech markets springing up since the late 1990s, many EVA critics (using Hamel as their starting point) lament that the measure doesn't accurately account for intangibles like investments in innovation and knowledge capital. That explains why so many high-tech and other startup companies that spend big bucks on research and development without reaping an immediate return, are loathe to adopt EVA as their standard form of performance measurement. One 2002 article in *General Management Review*, based out of India, worried that too much reliance of EVA may be "anti-growth and anti-risk."

Joining the EVA ranks

Companies that want to join the ranks of EVA fans first meet with Stern Stewart consultants. The board and senior management are versed and trained in how the metric is applied both theoretically and practically within the context of the company. Once the company has signed on, Stern Stewart works with a cross-functional team of staff and executives to find practical ways of implementing EVA so that it meets the company's information needs, existing accounting data, organization and management. EVA-based incentives are then built into the new framework and the rest of the company's employees are trained in EVA basics so that they are cognizant of how their day-to-day decisions affect shareholder value. To do this, Stern Stewart draws on its arsenal of software-based EVA tools, like EVA Game, which demonstrates the difference between EVA analysis and conventional accounting-based decisions. Finally, Stern Stewart follows up with clients to make sure they are properly realigning their business according to the EVA system.

The beat goes on

Stern Stewart isn't just good at adding shareholder value. It's also good at reminding companies that it's good at adding shareholder value. Its biggest marketing tool: Chairman and CEO Joel Stern, who constantly publishes articles, gives interviews and sits on panels extolling the benefits of EVA. In November 2006, Stern Stewart held a forum for local companies in Bazil, led by none other than Joel Stern, on how to align value creation with corporate management, processes and customer approaches. In October 2006, Stern sat on a similar panel in Israel as a key speaker at a *Forbes* conference. That same month,

Visit the Vault Consulting Career Channel at **www.vault.com/consulting** - with insider firm profiles, message boards, the Vault Consulting Job Board and more.

VAULT CAREER LIBRARY   543

University of Pennsylvania's Wharton School of Business' 2006 Finance Conference featured Stern as a keynote speaker. The theme of the conference: creating value in a global economy.

GETTING HIRED

Very calculating

Stern Stewart's web site isn't forthcoming about career information. Sources tell us that the firm tends to draw primarily from the University of Chicago, University of Rochester and Columbia, though candidates from Michigan, NYU, MIT and UVA have made the cut in the past.

A solid grasp of applied corporate finance theory and corporate accounting is a must for establishing a career at Stern Stewart. Most associates at the firm have backgrounds in these areas, and MBAs hoping to join up are advised to focus their studies on valuation and financial management.

Value added

The hiring process includes two rounds of interviews, according to sources. The first may take place over the phone or on campus, after which there's a daylong round at one of the firm's offices. For campus interviews, insiders say, the cases are "simplified," but expect to give your brain a technical workout, just in case. Examples include, "If you had to value a company, what would be the different valuation methods you'd use?" and assessing "debt versus equity—when to use convertible debt or the cost of financial distress."

Stockamp & Associates, Inc.

6000 SW Meadows Road
Suite 300
Lake Oswego, OR 97035
Phone: (503) 303-1200
Fax: (503) 303-1224
www.stockamp.com

LOCATIONS

Lake Oswego, OR (HQ)
20 locations nationwide

PRACTICE AREAS

Patient Progression: Inpatient Flow
Patient Progression: Surgical Flow
Revenue Cycle Solution

THE STATS

Employer Type: Private Company
CEO: Dale Stockamp
2007 Employees: 400
2006 Employees: 385

RANKING RECAP

Quality of Life
#10 - Interaction with Clients
#12 - Formal Training
#16 - Relationships with Supervisors (tie)

Diversity
#9 - Diversity for Women
#13 - Diversity for GLBT (tie)
#16 - Best Firms for Diversity

UPPERS

- "Focused on personal development"
- Corporate apartments and travel perks
- "I love the value we provide to clients due to actual implementation"
- "Immediate and consistent client interaction"

DOWNERS

- "Fairly strict promotion timeline that focuses heavily on time and grade"
- "A tendency to stretch human resources"
- Only a few service lines—"job can feel repetitive"
- "Strict adherence to methodology"

EMPLOYMENT CONTACT

E-mail: career_info@stockamp.com

Go to the careers section of the company's web site for more information

.

Visit the Vault Consulting Career Channel at **www.vault.com/consulting** - with insider firm profiles, message boards, the Vault Consulting Job Board and more.

VAULT CAREER LIBRARY   545

THE SCOOP

Putting stock in Stockamp

Since Dale Stockamp opened his doors in 1990, some of the country's most successful hospitals have turned to Stockamp & Associates to keep their bottom lines from flatlining. The Lake Oswego, Ore.-based health care consultancy works with major hospitals and health systems to improve their financial and patient care operations with the goal of boosting revenue. After working with St. Luke's Episcopal Health System in Houston from June 2004 to May 2005, for example, Stockamp helped increase the hospital's overall capacity by 5.1 percent, an $8.5 million increase in annual revenue opportunities.

Judging from Stockamp's client list, the firm has had some pretty happy customers. Over the past 17 years, it has worked with more than 80 clients, totaling more than 100 engagements.

Stockamp's bread and butter

In consulting, reputation is everything and Stockamp has a reputation for revving up hospitals' revenue with its revenue cycle solution. For each client, Stockamp's proprietary solution looks at a client's revenue cycle—from the moment an appointment is made until payment is received—as an integrated core process. It then looks for holistic ways to make comprehensive, end-to-end changes to that cycle, and promises to produce initial financial benefits in 30 to 60 days. Within five years, hospitals are told they can expect a cash benefit of $50 to $100 million or more for investing in Stockamp's revenue cycle solution.

The firm's 400 employees must be living up to their promises; Stockamp won the 2006 Best in KLAS Award for its revenue cycle consulting services. KLAS, a provider of independent research and vendor performance rankings to the health care industry, also ranked Stockamp as the top overall professional services firm.

Patient and surgical care

In addition to the revenue cycle solution, Stockamp's two other main areas of focus are helping hospitals streamline patient operations and surgical care coordination. The firm's patient progression solution, for one, looks at patient discharge delays, housekeeping bed turnaround time and the accuracy of predicted discharges, as well as other factors, to figure out what is limiting a hospital's capacity for improving patient flow without adding new beds. The patient progression solution promises to both bring in more money for hospitals and increase patient satisfaction.

Stockamp's surgical care coordination solution also works to improve patient flow, but in operating rooms, not waiting rooms. Stockamp professionals assigned to surgical care clients work to streamline the surgical process from operating room scheduling to postsurgical patient transfer and billing. On average, the firm promises that if hospitals follow its advice, they can expect to see a 1 to 3 percent annual increase in net patient revenue and improved patient and physician satisfaction.

From June through December 2005, Chicago's Children's Memorial Hospital, which performs more than 15,000 surgical procedures annually, worked with Stockamp to improve patient flow. By the end of the engagement, the hospital had eliminated a backlog of 450 surgery reservations, improved operating room utilization by more than 5 percent, improved efficiency with a 45 percent decrease in turnaround time between surgeries and made it possible for more than 350 additional children to have surgeries at the hospital each year, providing the hospital with an estimated $1 to $2 million in additional annual net revenue.

Praise over the airwaves

Stockamp keeps a very low profile, and doesn't seek out press or industry newsletters to publicize its findings. But it found a fan in ex-Steelers quarterback Terry Bradshaw. For his *Pick of the Week* business broadcast on CNBC in November 2004, Bradshaw chose Stockamp for its work with Stanford Hospital & Clinics. Stanford Hospital CEO Martha Marsh had nothing but good things to say about Stockamp on the air, which she claims boosted her hospital's bottom line by $8 million and its balance sheet by $40 million—"double what we expected."

GETTING HIRED

Not just business majors

Stockamp has an extensive campus recruiting system. University of Michigan, Georgia Institute of Technology, Howard University, Pennsylvania State University and UNC Chapel Hill are just a few of the schools where the firm's representatives conduct interviews. Stockamp accepts applicants from diverse academic backgrounds, but sets the GPA requirement at 3.0. Assures a consultant, "We hire all majors and all degrees, which adds a lot of diversity to our firm. You won't be working with just a bunch of business majors or engineers—it's a cross section of those plus liberal arts folks." A source notes, "There is a lot of great information on the Stockamp web site that reviews the kinds of questions that candidates can expect during the recruiting process, and it is a great resource for anyone going into the hiring process with Stockamp."

How to get a thumbs-up

The rigorous selection process puts candidates through three rounds of interviews, consisting of behavioral and case questions, as well as "a basic test to make sure that you can do simple math." An insider explains, "Our recruiting process is extremely competitive at all levels and is very selective. Experienced candidates complete behavioral, case and site visit interviews as well." For campus candidates, the first and second interviews are usually held on campus with a combination of recruiting staff and field management. For noncampus candidates, a source tells us, the interviews are "usually on site at a project with a manager and senior manager, which includes a math problem, case study and more behavioral interview questions." Indicates a staffer, "The first two interviews can be intense, but they are intended to see if you can think on your feet and solve problems that you are not familiar with." "The third [interview] is a site visit to a current project where the applicant meets a variety of people on the project team and learns about the different aspects of the project and project life. The third round closes with a final interview with a member of a project management team," explains another source. According to a manager, the key is to make a good impression on all the interviewers: "Everyone has to give a thumbs-up, or the candidate is not extended an offer."

"Why Stockamp?"

Candidates who make it to the second round of Stockamp interviews are well advised to brush up on practical knowledge about operating medical facilities, since most case questions are "specifically related to health care." The purpose of the case interview, the firm explains, is to walk through a problem-solving scenario with the interviewer to assess critical thinking skills. In addition to the case, candidates are asked to complete a basic math question to assess their quantitative abilities. Beyond wowing the interviewers with case study solutions, candidates need to show enthusiasm about the firm, hints a colleague. "They've got to be able to talk about 'why Stockamp.' If they can't do that, they won't receive an offer."

OUR SURVEY SAYS

How young is too young?

"Supportive," "fun" and "achievement-oriented" are just some of the ways insiders describe the Stockamp culture. One source states, "The culture is one of the things that keeps me here after four years. I have the opportunity to work with amazing people who are motivated to work hard to achieve results for our clients. We work well together and celebrate our successes together." "The culture is defined by intelligent, young, active people that strive to achieve great things," boasts one manager. Another insider agrees, raving that it's a "young, progressive culture focused on personal development."

Most insiders claim the firm's culture is "strong, consistent and welcoming," but a few acknowledge that it might not be for everyone. "Stockamp has a very strong corporate culture. For those who enjoy it, it's rewarding. For those who do not, it can be isolating." "I think that this is an asset, but it is sometimes difficult for experienced people to come in and assimilate into that

Visit the Vault Consulting Career Channel at **www.vault.com/consulting** - with insider firm profiles, message boards, the Vault Consulting Job Board and more.

V/\ULT CAREER LIBRARY   547

culture," explains a respondent. A colleague clarifies, "The company culture can be a little repressive, if you don't fill the 'ideal' associate mold, then you will get feedback about it."

Good times

Insiders praise their "dynamic" and "talented" co-workers, asserting that they are the kind of people they enjoy spending time with—even after hours. "My project teams become my social network when I am working in a city other than my home living location, and it makes all the difference in a positive working experience." Another source attests, "The culture here is laid-back and extremely fun. Everyone pranks each other while we work hard all day." When asked about the best thing at the firm, one happy camper confirms it's "the people—this is the most amazing, bright and talented group of people I have ever worked with."

Working "hand in hand"

Respondents give supervisors high marks for being "supportive" and "readily available." One analyst says, "We have the ability to interact regularly, sometimes daily, with our top management; directors and owners are accessible to staff at all levels." "My supervisor is very aware of my development and cares deeply about my career," insists a colleague. Insiders seem to appreciate that consultants and managers alike "work hand in hand in a peer-like setting for most of the project."

Staffers also praise the "very high level of client interaction" afforded at the firm. "It would be impossible to have more interaction with the client than a consultant has at Stockamp. As a new consultant, you are pushed to the ledge of the pier, but not over. Two months after I started, I was responsible for 10 client staff members," one associate tells us. Another source agrees, "[There is] great client contact at all levels. Our entry-level associates are given client contact from day one. You don't see that in many other consulting firms."

Cyclical hours

Staffers say the hours at Stockamp aren't necessarily overwhelming, though "it depends upon the stage of the project." A source explains that weeks can range "anywhere from 50 to 65 hours during the assessment and implementation phases at the beginning, to 40 toward the end of the project." Discloses one insider. "I have worked 80 hours in a week and 20 hours in a week. Stockamp does not charge clients based on billable hours, which relieves a lot of pressure on its consultants." Most staffers say that hours are doable, but allow time for little else. In the words of one insider, "I realize I am at the age where I can devote more time to my career. I appreciate the professional challenge and level of responsibility, but for the long term, I would like a job that allows for more personal time during the week."

Home away from home

The firm's travel requirements are well defined and understood by all: "100 percent travel is a part of the job." Insiders claim that it's one of the most difficult aspects of life at Stockamp. Explains a consultant, "You can expect to receive short notice for upcoming assignments, and you are expected to respond appropriately as the company's resource." Despite the difficulty, the firm tries to make it as comfortable as possible for employees to be away from home. "We get apartments at the client site, so there's no living out of a suitcase," says a source, while a colleague adds that these corporate apartments "allow you to feel as though you are living in a home away from home, which is a good feeling and provides some stability in your daily workweek."

At least traveling all the time allows for a few cool perks, sources admit. "It's hard, but in order to do the work I love, I have to travel, so I accept it and make it work for me. I take full advantage of all the travel perks, fly-ins and fly-outs, airline miles and Amex points," a staffer explains. A colleague raves, "The opportunity to fly elsewhere for the weekend (taxable airfare) has afforded me getaways I never would have taken otherwise. I get to visit family and friends, which helps me maintain those relationships."

Balance in question

Being constantly on the road, it's no wonder sources say work/life balance is a "very serious concern" at Stockamp. "Work/life balance, hours and travel are the worst things about working for Stockamp," declares a consultant, adding, "We're often staffed very thinly, so it's a challenge to maintain work/life balance. The firm seems to rely on the same core group of people to do all major initiatives and we risk burnout."

Insiders say management has taken notice of the issue and has made some much-needed changes. "I feel as though Stockamp has really made an effort in the last year to increase the work/life balance benefits. The Monday morning and Thursday/Friday flight policies have been changed to allow for more time in your living location. Employees are given a floating holiday to use whenever they would like, and there have been some changes to the work-at-home policy to allow for more flexibility when traveling to locations other than your living location," a source points out. A co-worker explains, "Travel is an obvious constraint, and you simply must be prepared to devote your workweek to the job. However, our company leadership is quick to accommodate special requests and we're now able to work on Fridays from anywhere in the country without taking the day off." Another respondent remarks, "Given the nature of travel in this industry, I think it's the best it can be. I find that balance is really 'owned' by the individual and is achievable if it is a priority for that person."

Another way the firm promotes balance is by accommodating consultants who decide to step off the traditional career path to work fewer hours. "I work part time and average 30 to 35 hours per week. Stockamp has provided me with the flexibility to adjust my schedule when I have wanted a change in my family life," attests one manager.

Sunday is fun-day

Insiders also appreciate the fact that "working weekends is discouraged at Stockamp." "I have a lot of flexibility in terms of how/when I get my work done, so I am easily able to get everything done during the week, leaving my weekends free for personal time," reports a staffer. A director explains, "Every project differs. Some are better than others and some managers work hard to help people support work/life balance more than others. We do try hard to ensure that our people are not working weekends."

Working hard for the money

Insiders are rather ho-hum about compensation at the firm. Admits a source, "The benefits package is excellent, but salaries are not always as lucrative as you might find at other firms. We typically stick to the market average for salaries." A colleague states, "Pay is good at manager level and above because loyalty is rewarded, but associate- and senior associate-level salaries are average for the consulting industry." The firm offers an annual performance bonus program in which all senior associate and management personnel are eligible to participate; according to the firm, bonuses can range from 10 to 35 percent of an employee's salary, depending on level and performance. In addition, Stockamp's profit-sharing program kicks in after two years, and is "paid out at 10 percent of base salary."

One manager acknowledges that there needs to be some adjustment: "We are in the process of reevaluating our salary structure, especially at our senior associate and above range, as we feel we may not be as competitive as we need to be. We are also reevaluating our overall bonus plan and we expect to make changes to it this year as well." According to the firm, the first result of this reevaluation was an increase to base salaries for the majority of consulting staff in June 2007.

"Surprise bonuses"

The firm is strong on standard benefits, says one insider who mentions that "vision, dental and preventive insurance (for physicals, other wellness items) are only a few dollars a month." One insider enthusiastically declares that the "work-at-home policy is a great perk." The firm claims associates and senior associates work from home an average of three Fridays per month. "We also are offered one full week of working at home on each project," details a staffer. Occasionally, management doles out "surprise financial bonuses" and "extra holidays" as rewards for hard work. The only thing lacking, according to insiders, is

Visit the Vault Consulting Career Channel at **www.vault.com/consulting** - with insider firm profiles, message boards, the Vault Consulting Job Board and more.

 **V∧ULT** CAREER LIBRARY   **549**

benefits for new parents. Complains one source, "This is not a strength of Stockamp. The company does not have a maternity benefits program."

Stepping up training

Stockamp offers new hires a four-week formal training course. In addition, all associates receive about "two weeks of formalized training each year, between company conferences and available training courses." Other than that, insiders reveal that "informal training and mentoring occurs constantly throughout engagements." One associate concedes, "I feel that the training for new employees and less experienced employees is well above average. However, we need to continue to develop our executive development plan, which is below par." The firm has a new program in the works, according to one manager who states, "Our training is good, and I think with some of the innovations currently being discussed, it could become great."

First female owner

Insiders are proud to say that Stockamp has recently done an excellent job of naming women to leadership positions. "We promoted our first female owner/partner within the company in 2006, and three new female directors were also promoted," recounts one source. A colleague points out, "Every project I've been on (four total) has had a woman in a leadership position (senior manager and above)." Still, employees acknowledge that at the top levels, there isn't yet an equal gender balance—a fact they attribute to "lifestyle choices (like having kids) instead of a lack of opportunities." Explains a senior manager, "Women are as capable and able to be an owner at Stockamp as men. Many choose to not be an owner if they have families because of the extensive travel."

"Actively seeking diversity"

Though Stockamp's minority representation isn't quite up to par, insiders say the firm is working on it. "There is a concentrated effort to improve racial diversity in our company, but it is still in its beginning stages," an employee states. A manager avows, Stockamp is "actively seeking diversity" through its hiring policies—"we have made concerted efforts to recruit at schools with larger minority populations," asserts a source. Colleagues agree that minority diversity is "getting much better and is recognized as a priority."

As far as GLBT diversity goes, the firm is reportedly "very open to alternative lifestyles." Stresses a staffer, "We have a strong contingent of gays and lesbians in our workforce. This is evidenced by commitment announcements on our company intranet and introduction of domestic partner benefits."

Volunteer wherever you are

Being away from home all the time doesn't keep these consultants from pitching in to worthy community causes. Associates tell us that teams select a nearby charity where they devote time and resources, and an analyst explains, "Each team is given a select budget to spend on charity programs near each client." "Every year, the firm chooses a theme and each project team spends two days doing a charity project in their project's community. For example, during my last project we spent a day creating a movie room at a local Ronald MacDonald house, complete with freshly painted walls, new chairs, a movie projector and screen, and a popcorn maker," an insider shares. "The company also sponsors Habitat for Humanity International projects for employees, and I have been a participant in a recent project in El Salvador," notes another consultant. In addition, the firm's "matching package for philanthropic endeavors" is popular among employees. "Stockamp will match up to $1,000 for any charity to which an individual wants to donate."

Strategic Decisions Group

735 Emerson Street
Palo Alto, CA 94301
Phone: (650) 475-4400
Fax: (650) 475-4401
www.sdg.com

LOCATIONS

Palo Alto, CA (HQ)
Boston, MA
Houston, TX
New York, NY
London
Mumbai
New Delhi

PRACTICE AREAS

Executive Education
India Strategy & Development
Middle East Strategy & Development
North America Strategy & Organizational Transformation
Oil & Gas
Power
Technology & Communication

THE STATS

Employer Type: Private Company
CEO: Carl Spetzler
2007 Employees: 75
2006 Employees: 100

UPPER

- Vacations are "sacred"

DOWNER

- Narrow industry focus

EMPLOYMENT CONTACT

www.sdg.com/home.nsf/sdg/Careers—Home

THE BUZZ
WHAT CONSULTANTS AT OTHER FIRMS ARE SAYING ABOUT THIS FIRM

- "Great analysis"
- "Too formulaic"
- "Academic"
- "Overly idiosyncratic culture"

Visit the Vault Consulting Career Channel at **www.vault.com/consulting** - with insider firm profiles, message boards, the Vault Consulting Job Board and more.

 VAULT CAREER LIBRARY   551

THE SCOOP

Fortune 500 fallback

Strategic Decisions Group is where some of the country's biggest companies turn when they need to deal with business uncertainty and improve shareholder value. The Palo Alto, Calif.-based consultancy works with key decision makers, such as boards of directors and senior managers, during times of rapid change when uncertainty and risk are as high as the potential for creating value. SDG helps these businesses clarify their organizational and business values, develop alternative strategies, quantify both the risk and value of considered alternatives and then build the organizational commitment to act.

SDG's clients come mostly from the oil and gas, power, technology, transportation, commodities, engineering and infrastructure and chemicals sectors. Its consultants are also proficient in the issues and trends endemic to the financial services, real estate, private equity, consumer products, forest products, and media and entertainment industries. The firm counts Dow Chemical, DuPont, Bayer, British Petroleum, Chevron, Pfizer and Philips Electronics on its roster of clients.

Saying goodbye to life sciences

Up until December 2006, one of SDG's top areas of expertise was the life sciences industry, which the firm broke down into pharmaceuticals, biotechnology and devices, and diagnostics companies. Its life sciences practice had won the firm high praise in the industry: In August 2006, Jerry Cacciotti, head of the life sciences practice, was named by the readers of *PharmaVOICE* as one of the industry's 100 most inspiring people.

But on December 14, 2006, the life sciences practice was acquired by IMS Health, a publicly traded $1.8 billion health care information company based in Norwalk, Conn. Neither company revealed the terms of the deal. SDG's education and advisory services, as well as its management consulting services to the oil and gas, power, technology, transportation and other nonpharmaceutical industries, were not involved in the merger.

Four guys and an idea

SDG began in 1981 in Menlo Park, Calif., when Ronald Howard, Carl Spetzler, James Matheson and Jeff Foran set out to create a consultancy that combined the best of academia and business, targeting big problems, solving them with rigorous processes, stressing continuous learning, collegiality, individual accountability "and—perhaps most important—fun." The guiding concept for the founding four was the process of "decision analysis," a term first coined in 1963 by co-founder Howard when he was teaching at Stanford University. Howard had been studying how to measure the reliability of data on which decisions are based, while also looking for ways to automate and take some of the guesswork out of decision making, breaking the process down into component parts and comprehensively listing all options available.

In its most basic form, decision analysis is a structured, statistical way of thinking about how any given action could lead to a result. To consider how an action might play out, decision analysts will look at three features of a situation: the decision to be made, the chance and impact of known or unknown events that can affect the result, and the result itself. It may sound like pretty basic stuff, but think again—the brain that thought up decision analysis also earned itself a bachelor's, master's and doctorate in electric engineering.

Some sound advice

Today, SDG has offices in Boston, Houston, London, New York and Palo Alto, as well as offices in India. After some tweaking of the decisional analysis concept, the firm now uses its business savvy to offer clients clear assessments and sound insights into ways they can reach and sustain higher levels of success. Often, SDG solutions will include realigning and prioritizing a company's existing businesses or business portfolios, and optimizing its investments in research and development technologies, intellectual property, products or other assets. SDG might also tell clients to look into new business areas via mergers or acquisitions or, conversely, to divest some of its low-potential businesses.

Old-fashioned consulting

SDG and its executives have been in the consulting field for almost 30 years and know a fad when they see one. The firm prefers to stick to the tried-and-true basics: create sound alternatives, use a dialogue-based decision process, offer proven, powerful techniques for addressing uncertainty and remain committed to resolute action. Every client relationship with SDG is a reflection of these principles. Engagements are collaborative, with "significant involvement" of client teams. These teams, which are integrated and complemented by SDG consultants, directly involve corporate decision makers, line executives, business and technical experts, and cross-functional teams so that a project with SDG "creates capabilities, not dependencies," according to the firm.

Clients seem to be happy with SDG's staid strategies. In fact, 85 to 90 percent of its revenue is brought in by long-term relationships with its clients. Many of the firm's client relationships last for more than six years, with the average relationship lasting for almost three years.

GETTING HIRED

For the long haul

At SDG, careers begin at the consultant or business analyst level. The former typically have MBAs or other graduate degrees, while analysts need only be armed with a bachelor's-level degree. Recruiting takes place at several universities at both the undergraduate and graduate levels, with Dartmouth, Stanford and INSEAD being popular pickup spots.

20 questions (or more)

Due to the smallish nature of the firm, SDG is very selective, sources tell us. Insiders say SDG hopefuls can expect three rounds of interviews, with the first consisting of one fit and one business interview. The ante is upped in the second round with an analytic interview, a case study and another fit-oriented discussion. During the final session, interviewees will meet with partners, who will continue to gauge their interpersonal skills, consultants report. An insider notes that interviewers may take a "teach-me-something" approach, asking for a detailed explanation of a subject. The depth of questioning, we're told, is due to the fact that partners take a long-term outlook when it comes to junior hires—they want someone who will make it all the way to partner level.

Visit the Vault Consulting Career Channel at **www.vault.com/consulting** - with insider firm profiles, message boards, the Vault Consulting Job Board and more.

553

Strategos

820 West Jackson Boulevard
Suite 525
Chicago, IL 60607
Phone: (312) 655-0826
Fax: (312) 655-8334
www.strategos.com

LOCATIONS

Chicago, IL (HQ)
Lisbon
London

PRACTICE AREAS

Enterprise Innovation Capability
Growth Strategy
Leadership & Organization
Management Innovation
New Market & Product Development

THE STATS

Employer Type: Private Company
CEO: Peter Skarzynski
2007 Employees: 31
2006 Employees: 31

RANKING RECAP

Quality of Life
#8 - Hours in the Office
#10 - Overall Satisfaction
#13 - Firm Culture
#13 - Interaction with Clients
#17 - Best Firms to Work For (tie)
#18 - Compensation
#19 - Relationships with Supervisors

UPPERS

- "Ability to work closely with senior clients as both a coach and a consultant"
- Variety of clients and projects
- "Low-stress work environment"
- Cutting-edge strategic innovation

DOWNERS

- "Small size of firm can restrict the variety of engagements and locations"
- "Keeping up with the pace of client demand for our services"
- "Slow evolution of the offering—not enough bandwidth to radically change it very often"
- Limited career advancement opportunities

EMPLOYMENT CONTACT

Go to the "Join Us" section on the firm's web site

THE BUZZ
WHAT CONSULTANTS AT OTHER FIRMS ARE SAYING ABOUT THIS FIRM

- "Good strategy"
- "Gary Hamel vehicle"
- "Strong innovation players"
- "Too niche"

THE SCOOP

Buzzword: innovation

Strategos likes to think its place in the consulting world is as unique and different as its name. The Chicago, Ill.-based consultancy counsels clients from nearly every business sector, including consumer products, health care, manufacturing, financial services, energy and high tech, showing them how to "instill innovation into the core of the organization." Some of Wall Street's biggest names take their place on Strategos' 100-client-strong roster, including Microsoft, Best Buy, Whirlpool, Clorox, Nestle, Nokia, Shell and Roche.

Innovation Czars

Peter Skarzynski, Gary Hamel, Pierre Loewe and Jim Scholes founded Strategos back in 1995 because they were tired of the old consulting approaches to increasing profitability. They are all seasoned professionals—*The Economist* has gone so far as to label Hamel "the world's reigning strategy guru"—and their focus on innovation sets Strategos apart from other, more traditional consultancies. The core of the firm's consulting advice today stems from the innovation model developed by the founders, which offers methods and tools for finding strategic opportunities, improving organizational capabilities and sustaining those changes.

In a June 2006 *Crain's Chicago Business* interview, Skarzynski said the biggest mistake companies make is not making innovation an integral part of their business' day-to-day operations. "Many companies isolate innovation, either in a department or team, believing it doesn't have to be part of the senior management's agenda," he said. "But if [innovation] is going to be meaningful, it has to impact the core business. To do that, companies need a disciplined process that connects their isolated islands of ideas, capital and resources."

Hamel paves the way

It's worth mentioning a few highlights of co-founder Hamel's resume. His name won't be unfamiliar to business school grads; Hamel's best sellers, *Leading the Revolution* and *Competing for the Future*, have appeared on every management best-seller list and have been translated into more than 20 languages. For those in the know, Hamel has also been listed as one of the 20th century's 25 most influential business thinkers by the *Journal of Business Strategy*, right alongside business legends Henry Ford and Bill Gates.

Everything Hamel does and says as a professional consultant leads back to innovation. In a November 2006 interview with *Business Innovation Insider*, Hamel stated that companies can try to create wealth by offshoring and outsourcing, but in the long run, "there are no substitutes to innovation." And, innovation only really counts when management is 100 percent onboard: "Management research—fundamental advances in the way companies allocate capital, motivate employees, organize activities, create strategies and set priorities—has the most potential to create long-lasting competitive advantage."

Today, Hamel serves as a member of Strategos' board of directors and works with a community of thought leaders to solve the world's toughest business problem: how to help large institutions become capable of continuous, crisis-free growth. He also continues to teach strategic and international management at the London Business School, where he has been a faculty member since 1983.

Hands-on engagements

Strategos is a different kind of company, right down to the way it works with clients. From the get-go, Strategos' client engagements are participatory, pairing its senior-level consultants with both client executives and broadly-based client teams. Additionally, the combined client-Strategos team will often reach out to the broader client organization and beyond to gather insights and ideas on client needs, emerging industry trends and identifying growth opportunities through multiday "innovation labs" and "action labs," where the client's employees can get their creative juices flowing. Together with its clients, Strategos

Visit the Vault Consulting Career Channel at www.vault.com/consulting - with insider firm profiles, message boards, the Vault Consulting Job Board and more.

VAULT CAREER LIBRARY   555

promises to accelerate and improve new product development processes, create and act on game-changing strategies, identify and develop new segments and markets, tackle innovation challenges and critical business issues, build leadership skills for innovation and capitalize on competencies.

That all sounds like typical consultant jargon, but there's nothing typical about this: Strategos consultants once took a team of Nokia employees to Venice Beach and to Tokyo nightclubs to give them a first-hand view of what's trendy and stylish. Other Strategos consultants have guided their clients through American Girl stores to show clients how to attract customers beyond their normal demographic, or through Amish communities to demonstrate how overwhelming and frustrating new technology can be for the less tech-savvy.

The firm stands behind its unorthodox methodologies, stating that since client team members play an integral role in the process from day one, they develop a deep understanding of the growth opportunities and strategic initiatives that are critical for their firm's future success. More importantly, they became the key enablers as their firms look to implement various innovations.

Success!

Strategos' marketing materials are littered with highly-placed executives from big brands singing the company's praise, but a few case studies stand out. One engagement with Whirlpool, as reported in *BusinessWeek* in March 2006 and the subject of a Harvard Business School case, started in 2000 when management realized that coming up with bigger and better appliances wouldn't be enough to keep its top position in the market. It needed to think hard and find new ways to massage the market. Strategos worked with Whirlpool leadership and project teams to develop new points of view on the industry, create new growth products and platforms to take to market, and incorporate sustainable innovation capabilities for the company.

Two years after bringing in Strategos consultants, Whirlpool had an "innovation pipeline" with 100 business ideas in the concept stage, 40 concepts at the experiment stage and over 25 new products being prototyped. By the time Strategos exited the company, innovation was ingrained into Whirlpool's working environment. "I-consultants," who were charged with encouraging Whirlpool individuals, groups or business units to come up with new ideas are spread out through the company with hundreds of "I-mentors" who help the "I-consultants" push innovative ideas in their workplace. By 2005, Whirlpool generated revenue of around $3 billion from its innovation efforts, up from $1.3 billion in 2003.

GETTING HIRED

No experience, no chance

Even though Strategos keeps tabs on alumni offices at Northwestern, Stanford, University of Chicago and University of Michigan, the firm doesn't spend time scanning campuses for recruits. Instead of hiring starry-eyed college seniors, "we typically look for alumni with several years of post-MBA experience under their belts," shares a principal. Recruiters seek "experienced consultants or industry managers" to join the Strategos ranks, many of whom come through a talent search firm.

Hey smarty pants!

Staffers say the interviewing process "usually starts with either a phone screening or an in-person screening," followed by several interview rounds to test for "critical thinking skills, fit and client-facing capabilities," which make up the perfect-hire trifecta. Interviewees can expect to chew the fat with five to eight consultants during the whole process, who each cover separate topic areas and reportedly "hire with a bias toward smarts and real-world experience."

During case evaluations, candidates may tackle questions such as, "How much do consumers spend annually on gasoline purchases in the U.S.?" or "How would you address the situation I am currently facing at client X?" These are classes of problems faced by Strategos consultants, so they're examining the "skills and helpful frameworks for attacking the issue" from applicants. As one director comments, the interview structure probes an individual's knowledge and expertise, "not whether she or he can come up with the 'right answer.'"

OUR SURVEY SAYS

A place to chill out

"Pleasant, friendly and accommodating" are characteristics frequently linked to Strategos, according to employees. "The culture is about delivering results," an associate explains, which "simplifies politics and aligns the members of the firm rather well." Achievement-driven yet relaxed, insiders say "colleagues take their work and their clients very seriously, but not themselves," a feature that allows consultants to remain supportive and less concerned with racking up hours or face time.

Recipe for rapport

Informal peer relations continue with top-level staffers at Strategos. As one veteran source relates, the "relationship with the managing director of the firm is very open and accessible." Other consultants also boast chummy superiors, referring to them as "outstanding individuals" with whom they love to work.

Client interaction at the lower ranks isn't unheard of, either. Strategos associates cite "lots of senior client interaction at all levels in the firm," which provides kindling for sparking loyal relationships. One director points to the "good mix of autonomy and support" present within these affiliations, since the firm's clientele spans "from CEOs to truck drivers." Because Strategos covers ground across all company levels and staff titles, sources say patrons flock to the firm and "are enthusiastic about the project, and the project is about growth—perfect ingredients for good relationships."

Take it easy

At Strategos, no one runs around dictating work hours. Consultants have freedom to build their own schedules, within reason, and "it's a personal choice as to how much you want to put into the firm, to advance the firm and your own career prospects within the firm," we're told. With a strategy model focused on output and meticulous results, one director notes that "each individual is free to organize his time as he sees fit—subject to client needs." Working at one's own discretion means duty-free weekends and time to squeeze in personal commitments without stressing out. "Nobody is telling me to work harder," adds a colleague.

Strategic placement

Scenery changes are expected at Strategos, but the client and case determine the frequency. "The firm's policy is that you travel when the client needs you to be there, and work in the office when the work calls for it," an associate lays out. Along with case variance, your home base has a considerable impact on travel regularity, since "working with local clients can reduce the travel load significantly," indicates a source.

When it comes to travel, Strategos employees sing the typical consulting firm blues: The "downside of travel is that it is generally impossible to plan ongoing, nonwork activities outside of the weekend because you never know when you will be on the road," states one director. Staffers also mention the firm's effort to "mix and match" consultants across projects, because while traveling teams develop strong bonds, always traveling with the same people "makes it more difficult to keep up with the other teams."

Ask and you shall receive

Given its size, Strategos applies an "ask, ask, ask" policy to its training model, which insiders say is chiefly unofficial. "Formal training takes place during preparations to start a new project," an associate explains. "We simulate the whole project over a few days and therefore cover all the tools and processes we will use," he adds, but for most other times, consultants learn through on-

Visit the Vault Consulting Career Channel at **www.vault.com/consulting** - with insider firm profiles, message boards, the Vault Consulting Job Board and more.

V\ULT CAREER LIBRARY   **557**

the-job instruction. Since the informal approach "doesn't always appeal to those we may be recruiting," the firm is reportedly working on its training and mentoring consistency.

Happy campers

Strategos reimburses its big shots accordingly, we're told. Says one consultant, "We have a generous compensation system for nondirectors, partly because our offering requires high talent for effective delivery." In addition to salaries on par with the market rates, consultants receive frequent boosts for first-class performance, with profit-sharing opportunities fluffing up the year-end cash sum. Amid bonus pools, stock options, company-funded health savings accounts, 401(k) contributions and substantial health benefits, staffers seem satisfied with their earnings.

While one consulting director values the firm's maternity leave and "generous vacation and holiday packages for all employees," a colleague rates the wine, beer and Dove bars in the freezer as indisputable Strategos perks. Other colleagues put annual holiday gifts and sabbatical prospects on the list as well.

To each his own

As for community involvement, co-workers say the firm lives vicariously through its staffers, "who then bring the opportunities to the firm for involvement/sponsorship." On its own, Strategos performs occasional pro bono work, along with "episodic community involvement and clothing drives," a director shares, adding that most community service is ad hoc at best, though the firm does consistently match up to $3,000 in organizational donations per associate.

Mostly male

Sources at Strategos say they're receptive to bringing in more women to the consulting frontline, but currently the firm's makeup is chiefly male. "There are few women at the firm, but this has nothing to do with any policies," remarks a principal, who suggests that the female-recruiting trouble comes with heavy travel schedules required for the job. One consultant promises that female-focused recruiting attempts are under way, and in the meantime, "we do everything we can to bring women to the interview pipeline; otherwise, everyone benefits from the same mentoring and talent development processes," an associate concludes.

On the race and ethnic minority front, insiders say the firm is diverse for its small stature. "I don't think we have formal programs," comments a staffer, "but there seems to be a decent amount of diversity, given our size." As with women, co-workers concur with the hard-to-locate reasoning, reflecting that "it is much tougher to find minorities for interviewing." With regard to gay, lesbian and bisexual receptivity, Strategos colleagues say sexual orientation is "not a criteria or consideration in hiring," and conclude that sexual orientation isn't brought to anyone's attention. "We simply hire every qualified person," consultants state. A co-worker closes up the discussion by asserting that the "only thing that matters is talent and results—gender, race, sexual orientation, etc., are totally irrelevant, as they should be."

Trinity Partners, LLC

Prospect Place
230 Third Avenue
Waltham, MA 02451
Phone: (781) 487-7300
Fax: (781) 487-7301
www.trinitypartners.com
www.trinitypharmasolutions.com
www.akutacorp.com

LOCATIONS

Waltham, MA (HQ)
New York, NY

PRACTICE AREAS

Brand Strategy
Commercialization Strategy
Custom Data Solutions
Forecasting
Licensing & Acquisition
Market Assessment & Sizing
Portfolio Prioritization
Statistics

THE STATS

Employer Type: Private Company
Managing Partner: John E. Corcoran
2007 Employees: 65
2006 Employees: 60

RANKING RECAP

Quality of Life
#1 - Best Firms to Work For
#2 - Overall Satisfaction
#2 - Interaction with Clients
#3 - Work/Life Balance
#6 - Hours in the Office
#7 - Travel Requirements
#8 - Compensation
#9 - Firm Culture

UPPERS

- "Work is fun, exciting and always changing"
- Access to client management, project management and senior-level client executives early in one's career
- "You learn not only from your managers but also from your associates"
- "Knowing that you will be fairly compensated, praised and promoted at every turn"

DOWNERS

- Lack of clarity around bonus/compensation and career progression
- "Workload can be excessive"
- "Politics between principals and partners"
- "Still developing as a company, so it's a learning experience on how to recruit, develop our talent and manage all our clients"

EMPLOYMENT CONTACT

E-mail: careers@trinitypartners.com

Visit the Vault Consulting Career Channel at **www.vault.com/consulting** - with insider firm profiles, message boards, the Vault Consulting Job Board and more.

VAULT CAREER LIBRARY   559

THE SCOOP

Pharmaceutically minded

Trinity is a boutique consultancy that specializes in health care strategy for pharmaceutical, biotech and life sciences firms. The firm's 65 consultants serve clients through two practices—consulting services and data services. The consulting group offers forecasting, licensing and acquisition, new product commercialization, therapeutic area landscapes, strategic planning, patient flow modeling and statistical analysis. Founded in 1996, the firm is based outside of Boston in Waltham, Mass., home to a cluster of biotech and pharmaceutical firms in nearby Cambridge.

The firm is led by a small group of executives, headed up by founder and Managing Partner John E. Corcoran. A Harvard grad, Corcoran has over 15 years of health care consulting experience under his belt. Aside from Trinity, he also founded Akuta Labs, a New York-based company that sells software to pharmaceutical and biotech firms. Two other partners and six principals—all of whom have extensive pharma industry experience—round out the management team.

Data intensive

Trinity operates around the philosophy that product lifecycles are "relics of the past," and claims that these days, it's facts and data that give clients an edge. The firm distinguishes itself from peers by its heavily quantitative approach to solving problems for clients. Claiming proficiency in strategy and data management, Trinity uses copious amounts of collected data to create market models and commercial and launch strategies. Consultants generally act as information managers, meaning that a large part of their time is spent running the numbers and getting deep into the data to come up with competitive strategies. Clients, in turn, benefit from the firm's "pragmatic, bottom-line driven and data-tested analytic orientation."

L&A strategies

With the heightened competition in the pharmaceutical market, one way drug companies look to increase sales and profit is by licensing their products to other firms, or by acquiring a license to sell another manufacturer's drug. Trinity consultants offer assistance to companies exploring licensing and acquisition opportunities around the globe. In fact, Trinity annually underakes over 100 assessments in multiple therapeutic areas, including oncology, central nervous system, cardiovascular, anti-infective and pain. The firm deals with drugs in the phase II, phase III and launch stages to determine if a licensing deal will work for a particular client.

Pharmaceutical companies have also had to focus attention to the way they conduct sales efforts. Recognizing a need for more sales support systems on the IT side, the firm spun off Trinity Pharma Solutions in 2004 to focus on building systems that support drug marketing. TPS builds databases and data warehouses, and provides security, maintenance and archiving services for IT systems related to sales. The subsidiary is closely affiliated with its parent, and is often called on to implement IT projects on Trinity Partners' engagements.

Checking up on patients

Beyond licensing and sales, the firm offers an array of analytical services for clients like Johnson & Johnson, Pfizer and Novartis. In the compliance strategies area, the firm recently helped a client determine why a surprisingly high number of patients were discontinuing their medication, an injectable therapy for autoimmune disease. Consultants gathered data from patients to determine exactly which patients were likely to stop treatment and why. The data showed that the main reasons patients quit complying was because physicians didn't encourage them to continue taking the drugs. As a result, Trinity consultants advised the client to create patient-directed programs to educate them about the long-term benefits of continuing therapy.

Spot on

In 2005, Trinity's data subsidiary entered into a partnership with Spotfire, an applications and services provider, to boost its capabilities in data analysis. Spotfire specializes in making complex data user-friendly by creating a visual interface. Trinity also acquired a license to DecisionSite, Spotfire's proprietary data mining software, which makes data analysis "quicker and more intuitive through its visual and interactive capabilities." Through the partnership, the firm aims to apply the kind of in-depth data analysis that is available to R&D scientists to its own sales and management analysts. DecisionSite made a splash in the industry when *IT Week* named it one of the top-50 technology innovations of 2005.

A niche within a specialty

When the firm developed proprietary software of its own in 2006, it launched another subsidiary, Akuta Corporation. Akuta's pinpoint focus is on the market of medical science liaison teams (MSLs) hired by pharmaceutical and biotech companies. The software provides web communication and forecasting technology on a platform that is "as easy as e-mail." mslConnect is one of the company's tools for communicating, sharing resources and reporting, allowing MSLs to link up with each other and with headquarters. Industry organization InPharm recently recognized mslConnect as the top MSL software program.

GETTING HIRED

Applicants, start your engines

For Dartmouth, Harvard and Princeton undergrads considering a stay in consulting, be on the lookout for Trinity reps on campus—according to insiders, these institutions make up the bulk of the firm's on-campus undergraduate recruiting network, but there are many exceptions. Current Trinity staffers include alums from MIT, Wellesley and Ohio State, among others.

"Undergraduate applicants undergo a standard set of two on-campus interviews," we're told, which both have a case and fit component. Once through the first two hoops, successful candidates jump into the "extremely competitive" third round, arriving on site at Trinity's office for back-to-back quiz sessions. "Applicants need to prove their quantitative and analytical skills, especially in the case interviews," a consultant reports, which focus heavily on health care industry issues. "What do you think peak sales of this (psoriasis, diabetes, etc.) drug will be?" and other strategy and market-sizing inquiries are common topics, designed not as brainteasers, but to test interviewees on listening and insightful questioning abilities. A principal advises that "reading the headlines from the industry for the few days before your interview would definitely give you a step up on candidates who are not so prepared."

Get smart

Because of the firm's limited headcount, fitting in with the Trinity team isn't a laughing matter. "Interviewees must show quantitative skill and ability to think outside of the box," explains an associate, "but fit with the Trinity culture is also highly stressed. The most successful candidates are outgoing, smart, curious, fun and independent." One partner continues, sizing up the firm's favorites as "people who can listen, show analytic rigor and do simple math in their head."

OUR SURVEY SAYS

Who could ask for anything more?

Choosing a vibrant image to characterize Trinity's culture, one associate consultant shares that "many of our employees have substituted their office chair for a yoga ball, indicating how fun and open the environment is." Sources describe intelligent,

Visit the Vault Consulting Career Channel at **www.vault.com/consulting** - with insider firm profiles, message boards, the Vault Consulting Job Board and more.

V/\ULT CAREER LIBRARY   561

young and sociable peers who "often get together on the weekends for outdoor activities, sporting events and BBQs," a facet that "carries into the working environment and creates a very collegial corporate culture."

Despite a laid-back dress code and casual culture, staffers don't fool around when it comes to work. Says one principal, "We are very collegial and relaxed most of the time, but we know when to buckle down as well." The firm's youthful, outgoing makeup also creates a competitive environment, colleagues report, but "good ideas are welcomed, regardless of the seniority of the source." And according to a co-worker, "Trinity focuses on extremely high-quality work, but how you get that high-caliber work is up to you." Insiders appreciate the praise they receive for a job well done, and most are even willing to stay late to help out colleagues with a heavy workload. As one consultant sums up, "The company is young, smart and growing. What more can a kid out of college want?"

Boss buddies

At Trinity, supervisors aren't looming ominously over subordinates, expecting failure. In fact, consultants say they're more like chums and family members, maintaining an equal playing field. "My boss is my best friend," admits a principal, adding, "That's what makes coming to work every day so livable." Other insiders count Trinity superiors among their closest friends as well, nothing that they "are always available to talk or answer questions, and they always give credit where credit is due."

These senior staffers aren't letting associates sit idly on the sidelines, either. "Trinity management is extremely knowledgeable, approachable and friendly, but also able to delegate. You are immediately given responsibility upon your start at Trinity," a newer hire contributes. Across all firm levels, employees are involved in client meetings and able to interact with top-tier clientele. "Everyone gets good exposure to the clients from their first year. We have second-year associates as project managers with primary client management responsibilities," a co-worker boasts. "This speaks to our ability to let talented young people take the reins on project management right from the start."

Elastic hours

"Trinity's hours are fantastic compared to other firms," gushes an associate. Most staffers say they work between 50 and 60 hours per week and, "when I am finished with my work, my superiors encourage me to leave," a peer chimes in. With a focus on productivity, efficiency and no face time requirement, "nothing is excessive," according to a source, "and [how much time is spent at work] really depends on the motivation of the person." As long as consultants give their workloads plenty of TLC, hourly schedules are flexible. "We produce high-quality work, and if we stay late one or two nights one week, we can be flexible the next day and come in a bit later or work from home for a few hours," explains a colleague.

A stretchy agenda creates more space for extracurricular action, too. Staffers claim to rarely work weekends, and "generally, we think it's a good day if we can do all three of the daily essentials: work, workout and go out," relates a principal. Another associate adds, "Trinity demands a work/life balance for all employees," who are involved in numerous outside activities. Declares a principal, "We make a conscious effort to find time to stay healthy, including exercising before or after work. We even do triathlons together!" "My manager has been very understanding of any issues (especially emergencies) in my personal life that may require me to completely stop doing what I am working on," one insider shares.

Quick trips

"We are not believers in the 'live at the client' consulting mentality," an insider says about Trinity's travel model. At the associate level, staffers average one to two travel days per month, though "this ramps up as you get higher in the firm," we're told, though higher-up folks travel little more than one to two days each week. "Travel is usually domestic and quick," a co-worker explains, and "tends to be early-morning departures and evening arrivals." With these whirlwind journeys, sources say they rarely reach a breaking point. Instead of shadowing clients through all phases, "we generally travel for a kickoff meeting, an interim meeting and a final presentation," remarks an associate, adding that weekend trips are never required.

Since the firm keeps travel to a minimum, consultants are more eager to jump on an opportunity to change scenery. As one newbie puts it, "It is a fun way to mix up the office life and allows you to interact one-on-one with clients, but is in no way daunting." And because most assignments save staffers from hotel stays, Trinity's travel schedules don't put much stress on work/life balance, we're told. "It is significantly more manageable than most consulting firms, where consultants are on site with their clients part of every week," a second-year adds. "Compared to most of my peers in consulting or similar careers, my travel schedule can't be beat."

Where learning never stops

New hires at Trinity Partners undergo a two-week structured training program, comprised of team projects, Boston outings and getting-to-know-you exercises with colleagues. "There are multiple presentations each morning, and the afternoon is used to begin learning about client work and the role you will play," a source explains. And "because we are a small firm," she continues, "each person is constantly working to improve his own skills, and we are strongly encouraged to share new findings or skills with our colleagues." Since peers are always sharing knowledge, unofficial instruction is where all the magic happens. Says one co-worker, "Informal training for new associates is overly abundant, through lunch meetings, etc., where they are able to ask questions in a less structured atmosphere."

Following initial training, too, is "a three- to six-month mentor-based, hands-on training program," remarks a consultant, "thereby enabling a smooth transition between classroom-based learning to a more real-life learning process." Staffers report that more official guidance models are in the works as well. "Being so young, we are always looking for more training," employees say. "We're working on improving our formalized training, but still have a ways to go."

Copious compensation

Consultants at Trinity Partners aren't sore over their earnings. Shares an insider, "Trinity's compensation is extremely generous—when our team does well, it flows down to all levels and that is well known." Other staffers pipe in, citing the firm's competitive salaries and even larger bonuses. "Bonuses are well above industry average," comments a principal, which "are more in line with the investment industry than the consulting industry, as far as I know." The better the firm performs, the more money staffers pocket, creating an "everyone wins" camaraderie. Sums up an associate, "People are very willing to work hard because they know they will be fairly recognized, both financially and professionally, in the form of career advancement."

In addition to generous payouts, Trinity offers a health and dental package, 401(k) matching plan and profit-sharing program for partners. Insiders are also pleased that everone starts at three weeks' paid vacation.

Trips and triathlons

According to insiders, Trinity is all about building and bonding. The firm offers a multitude of extracurricular activities, including team dinners, summer barbeques, ski trips, picnics and a holiday party—"a full night of dinner and dancing at a really fancy venue in downtown Boston." In 2006, Trinity shipped several consultants to Puerto Rico for a four-day off-site meeting, which one staffer says "proved to be an added bonus." Additionally, colleagues relish their casual dress code, untracked hours and athletic peers. "Last year, about 10 people from the office did two to three triathlons," comments an associate. "We got team jerseys, and more people from the office came to cheer on the group. It was great team-building and really nice that we were sponsored for jerseys." Aside from triathlons, the company sponsors an intramural soccer team and puts on "the most competitive volleyball games at the summer picnic." And when rivalry surfaces and escalates in the office, one peer claims that "we can settle disputes/arguments amongst one another on the putting green in our building."

Love the scenery

As for office accommodations, Trinity employees give the interior design an underwhelming thumbs-up. Consultants appreciate the layout, free gym and "more office, less cube" atmosphere, adding only a few complaints like "the nonergonomically correct chairs," for one. Most save their praise for outside perks. "Externally, the office building has a great view, and the nearby area

Visit the Vault Consulting Career Channel at **www.vault.com/consulting** - with insider firm profiles, message boards, the Vault Consulting Job Board and more.

 **563**

is very nature-friendly," with bike trails, ponds, mountains and more, according to a staffer. Building on the scenery excitement is a principal who gushes about "easy access to running/biking/swimming so we can train for triathlons together!"

Taking care of the rest

Of Trinity's dedication to service, "there isn't an anti-community ethic, but there isn't any specific community involvement," confesses a senior consultant. That said, insiders are open to neighborly contribution and "would welcome someone driving this in the firm." And with such a well-rounded bunch—"top of their class, athletes, musicians"—individual community initiatives aren't lacking. "People at Trinity do not need encouragement for community involvement," states a co-worker, as many take time to give back on their own.

Need a little balance

When it comes to the male/female ratio, Trinity tries to balance the scale. "We are about 50/50 in terms of gender across the firm," states a principal, while another co-worker adds, "Half of my class is women, and three-fourths of last year's class is women." Females at the firm may balance out in the lower ranks, but even with four of the last seven promotions granted to women, "there are fewer women in upper-level positions," employees report. "While there doesn't seem to be a bias against women, I would definitely like to see more women in leadership positions."

Despite some imbalance, staffers say they've "never seen any indication that gender has even been a factor in hiring, project assignment or career advancement," and tote the firm as an equal playing field. As one associate relates, "I am female and I am extremely pleased with Trinity and its hiring practices. I was actively involved in recruiting last year."

Ethnic and racial minority representation, while welcomed at the firm, is limited. "No senior management are minorities, and hiring and recruiting for minorities could be enhanced," shares a senior consultant. But insiders do want to emphasize Trinity's equal opportunity outlook, regardless of minority status. "I myself am one," a staffer shares, "and from personal experience, I can definitely say that it does not matter what background you come from, as long as you can perform well." And consultants agree that inside the firm's open culture, "no one receives preferential treatment."

Sentiments repeat for sexual orientation, which consultants dub a "nonissue." One employee says that "Trinity is extremely welcoming. I have never seen anything to indicate that sexual orientation is a factor in any decision process." Echoing recruitment efforts extended to women and minorities, a senior-level source emphasizes that "we hire the best people, regardless of their orientation."

Vantage Partners

Brighton Landing West
10 Guest Street, 3rd Floor
Boston, MA 02135
Phone: (617) 354-6090
Fax: (617) 354-4685
www.vantagepartners.com

LOCATIONS

Boston, MA (HQ)
Los Angeles, CA

PRACTICE AREAS

Alliance Management
Key Customer Relationships
Outsourcing Management
Sourcing & Supplier Management

THE STATS

Employer Type: Private Company
Directors: Danny Ertel, Mark Gordon, Jonathan Hughes, Stuart Kliman, Bruce Patton, Larraine Segil (Emeritus) & Jeff Weiss
2007 Employees: 70
2006 Employees: 70

UPPERS

- "Given a lot of room to innovate and do new things"
- "You're no cog in a wheel here—we all really matter"
- Young, developing firm

DOWNERS

- "Given how young we are, there's still plenty of ambiguity"
- "Not great at sending tough messages when someone's performance isn't up to snuff, which can make for some awkwardness occasionally"
- Getting time from busy partners

EMPLOYMENT CONTACT

E-mail: hr_recruiting@vantagepartners.com
www.vantagepartners.com/aboutus/career.cfm?

Visit the Vault Consulting Career Channel at **www.vault.com/consulting** - with insider firm profiles, message boards, the Vault Consulting Job Board and more.

VAULT CAREER LIBRARY   565

THE SCOOP

Crimson ties

Vantage Partners, founded in 1997, traces its roots back to the Harvard Negotiation Project, an interdisciplinary research center focused on negotiation in world conflict that was started at Harvard Law School in 1979. Though the HNP was initially designed to facilitate more effective international relations, its members soon realized that the same principles used to engage in successful diplomatic relations could also be applied to the business world. Thus, Vantage Partners was born.

With offices in Boston and Los Angeles, Vantage Partners helps companies such as Johnson & Johnson, IBM and Microsoft manage partnerships and organizational conflict. The firm offers four main areas of consulting services: alliance management, key customer relationships, outsourcing management, and sourcing and supplier management. And the Vantage-Harvard connection lives on—every current Vantage director attended Harvard College and/or Harvard Law School.

Let's talk it out

A fundamental principal at Vantage is that "between 50 and 70 percent of business relationships fail to meet their objectives, and that the primary cause of this failure is poor or damaged working relationships between partners." Through its consulting services and corporate education products, Vantage works with a broad spectrum of clients across the information technology, financial services, pharmaceutical, telecommunications, entertainment, petroleum and minerals, professional services and manufacturing industries to help form lasting and more productive strategic alliances. In February 2007, Vantage announced a new Virtual Seminar Series, which explores crucial aspects of managing key alliance, supplier, outsourcing, customer and internal relationships.

Taking relationships high tech

In October 2006, Vantage Technologies, the software solutions arm of Vantage Partners, merged with Ann Arbor-based Janeeva, a provider of outsourcing relationship management software. Janeeva CEO Vinay Gupta remained head of the combined units, while Vantage Director Danny Ertel was named chairman of the Janeeva board of directors. According to Janeeva, the combined expertise of Janeeva and Vantage Technologies will serve to make the new company the foremost global provider of ORM software.

The pen is mightier

Aside from their work as consultants, many Vantage staffers are prolific writers, public speakers and educators. *Getting to YES: Negotiating Agreement Without Giving In*, originally published in 1983 and now in its second edition, is easily the firm's most recognized publication, and serves as the basis for much of Vantage's work. *Getting to YES* serves as a guide to negotiating personal and professional disputes and has sold over three million copies translated into 23 languages. *Negotiating and Managing Key Supplier Relationships: A Cross-Industry Study of 20 Best Practices*, co-authored by Vantage Directors Mark Gordon and Jonathan Hughes in 2004, addresses relationship management practices with key suppliers across six areas: evaluation and selection, negotiation, post-deal relationship management, performance monitoring, termination, and portfolio governance and management.

And there's promise for more insightful business tomes—in July 2006, Vantage announced an alliance with Harvard Business School Publishing, in which the two companies will produce a suite of leadership development products designed to enhance negotiation, communication and relationship management.

In our free time, we like to negotiate world peace

In addition to the Harvard Negotiation Project, several senior members at Vantage are aligned with the nonprofit Conflict Management Group. Founded in 1985, CMG served as a think tank for troubled regions around the world and merged with Mercy Corps in 2004. Though international diplomacy is not a specific focus of Vantage's business, Vantage consultants have served as mediators during constitutional negotiations in an apartheid-free South Africa and as support personnel for talks between the PLO and Israel.

GETTING HIRED

The endurance test

At one time, Vantage scouted undergrads at Harvard and Wellesley, but these days it resorts to a campus-free hiring model. After a heavy phase of resume screening, the firm sets up 45-minute phone interviews with its chosen few. The strongest contenders ascend to the next level: Interview Day, a series of one-on-one and group sessions with consultants and partners in the firm's office. Throughout the daylong marathon, candidates go through up to 10 interviews, each lasting 30 to 35 minutes, including case studies and a group, mock negotiation exercise. Wedged into the affair is a presentation about Vantage and information about the actual consulting position, along with a Q&A period. As a whole, this insider states, "The process is pretty rigorous. But by the end of the day, not only do we know the candidates well, but the candidates get to know us well, too, so that they can make a good choice for themselves, should they be given an offer."

OUR SURVEY SAYS

Closing the consultant/partner divide

Vantage's "petite frame" can be credited for the firm's "friendly, social, supportive atmosphere," where the consultant/partner divide is bridged by collegiality. As one source shares, "A small firm allows close relationships and increased responsibility," so "there's a real push for rigorous thinking and lots of open communication." Staffers say their superiors foster a family atmosphere, and are careful to ensure that Vantage "is a good place to work, that people are recognized and supported, and that people enjoy each other and the work environment."

Since Vantage touts its flat hierarchical structure, "consultants are given a lot of responsibility and, as a result, ample opportunity to interact with top management in client organizations." Partners care about their junior staff, treating "each consultant as an individual" and leaving their doors open for any question or feedback session that a staffer might initiate.

Ready, steady

When it comes to workload, Vantage staffers tell us that their firm's flexibility certainly helps. "The demands of consulting can make it difficult to achieve a realistic balance," remarks a consultant, "but the firm is understanding and supportive of people taking time for life outside of work." Compared to most consultancies, sources insist that Vantage emphasizes the importance of having an outside life—"I specifically came here for the work/life balance," one states. Aside from the occasional late-night and weekend work stretch, there are few time barriers to developing and maintaining an outside life. Firm higher-ups acknowledge and honor outside priorities and, according to staffers, personal plans are accommodated as much as possible—a flexibility that comes "coupled with a requirement that consultants use it wisely and judiciously." As one insider comments, "Hours are flexible; you need to be available to your clients and colleagues, but there are no rules about face time."

Taking days off is okay, too: "They expect you to take vacation days," consultants stress. Others chime in, asserting that "vacations are sacred, so we can actually plan ahead and know that client demands won't always trump personal plans." And as one's tenure lengthens, project timelines get a bit more wiggle room.

Visit the Vault Consulting Career Channel at www.vault.com/consulting - with insider firm profiles, message boards, the Vault Consulting Job Board and more.

VAULT CAREER LIBRARY   567

Movers and shakers

Because travel schedules vary by project, travel patterns are a little hard to pin down. "My projects have required minimal travel," one consultant reports, while another notes that "traveling two to three days per week certainly beats being away from the home office full time." Whatever the frequency, Vantage sources claim they "don't typically work on site with clients for extended periods, which makes travel much more bearable."

Under construction

Aside from assigning partner "coaches" to new hires, Vantage doesn't offer much in the way of formal training. "It's nearly all learn-as-you-go, with the support and coaching of colleagues and supervisors," a system that co-workers don't seem to mind. And coming soon to a Vantage office near you is a new professional development program, partnered with a consultant-led committee and more focused training efforts.

The payout equalizer

Consultants may claim to receive a lower compensation package than competitors, but they do so without much rancor, factoring in Vantage's "generous" bonuses, reasonable work hours and "great culture and lifestyle" as explanation for a less competitive salary. All things considered, the pay "seems to be right about average with the consulting industry," one source notes.

In other money news, the word "generous" pops up again with regard to Vantage's 401(k) matching and profit-sharing programs, though the vesting period for profit sharing is three years.

Vantage advantages

Vantage staffers keep busy, but they are all about taking necessary breathers every once in awhile. Every Thursday afternoon, consultants congregate for a firm-sponsored "snack time," where co-workers take turns bringing munchies and have a chance to catch up with each other. In addition, insiders cut the workday to 3 p.m. before long weekends, attend consultant learning days and party together around various holidays. The most anticipated event is the summer Fun Day, when "our office closes for a day each summer and we all go for a surprise day of fun activities," a source reports. Staffers say they've "gone sailing, roller skating and on a vineyard tour"—and no matter the affair, "it's always a blast." To round off the day of revelry, one Vantage partner hosts a company party in the evening.

What's all the racket?

Vantage's office space has its inhabitants wishing for a bit more life and décor, but once the office's renovation process ceases, bringing an end to the noise and dust, sources will be much happier with their surroundings. Regardless, "It is generally a clean, well-lit place," we're told, though "individual project rooms/team rooms are sometimes at a premium."

Say yes to service

When it comes to helping the community, Vantage has more than one iron in the fire. The firm's service committee, Vantage Volunteers, organizes volunteer activities with area nonprofits, typically one-day stints each quarter. Associates aren't strangers to pro bono consulting, either, "and are looking to create a new pro bono initiative, whereby our consultants donate their time to nonprofit organizations under the supervision of more senior people in the firm." Individually, many staffers dip into other projects outside work, "where they volunteer or raise funds for organizations they care about."

Beefing up diversity

Females are definitely welcome at Vantage. "Most of the office is comprised of women," co-workers say; of 14 consultants, 10 are female, though women are completely absent at the partner level. According to peers, "The firm is very good at hiring women, and just rolled out a career path that will hopefully allow women to have more senior roles in the firm." It's racial and ethnic minorities who are few and far between, but consultants are quick to say that "this appears to be by coincidence and not design." Due to the firm's small size, there aren't any specific minority recruiting initiatives in place, and though one seasoned insider notes that Vantage offers "a highly accepting and welcoming environment," he admits that it "could do a better job of attracting quality minority candidates for consulting roles."

Visit the Vault Consulting Career Channel at **www.vault.com/consulting** - with insider firm profiles, message boards, the Vault Consulting Job Board and more.

569

Vivaldi Partners

125 Park Avenue, 15th Floor
New York, NY 10017
Phone: (212) 965-0900
Fax: (212) 965-0992
www.vivaldipartners.com

LOCATIONS

New York, NY (HQ)
Los Angeles, CA
Amsterdam
Buenos Aires
Düsseldorf
Hamburg
London
Munich
Shanghai
Zurich

PRACTICE AREAS

Branding
Innovation
Marketing
Strategy
Supporting Capabilities
  Creative Services
  Marketing Analytics

THE STATS

Employer Type: Private Company
CEO: Dr. Erich Joachimsthaler
2007 Employees: 87
2006 Employees: 72

UPPERS

- Entrepreneurial spirit
- "People interact in a more personal way; you are not constantly on guard as it is with the larger strategy firms"
- "Access to our CEO"

DOWNERS

- "Company is still figuring itself out—in every way"
- "Salary is not entirely competitive"
- "Workload shifts can be huge because there are very few professionals to spread the load"

EMPLOYMENT CONTACT

E-mail: recruiting@vivaldipartners.com

THE SCOOP

The customer comes first

Vivaldi Partners is a global consulting firm with a focus on marketing, strategy, branding and innovation. Former Professor Dr. Erich Joachimsthaler founded the firm in 1999, with the main objective to "find growth opportunities from a customer-first perspective for clients." Since its inception, the firm has grown to include 10 offices and a number of joint ventures, with a presence in seven countries. Its clients are in the automotive, consumer products, energy, oil and gas, financial services, food and beverages, IT, telecommunications, media, not-for-profit, pharmaceuticals, retail, health care, professional services, and travel and leisure industries.

DIG it

Vivaldi claims that what separates it from other strategy consultancies is its demand-first approach; that means, instead of finding customers to match with products, services or brands, the firm seeks out certain products, services, solutions or experiences to match with consumers. To come up with breakthrough strategies for creating strong brands, innovations and businesses, the firm has devised its own method called the demand first innovation and growth (DIG) model. Consultants work with clients to design and develop a product concept, devise a business model, create a brand and implement a brand-building program—basically guiding clients from start to finish in the marketing strategy process.

The firm boasts that its most valuable expertise is being able to uncover consumers' desires before they are even aware of them. Recently, the firm worked with a snack food manufacturer to discover what drove consumption of snacks. Consultants studied the "unarticulated" demands of consumers by immersing themselves in the lives of consumers for 30 days. They mapped every daily activity around food consumption by reconstructing days and using diaries. Through this "immersion strategy," consultants were able to develop growth platforms and new product concepts based on actual consumer demand.

Expand the brand

Though growth hasn't been the driving force at Vivaldi, gradual expansion has come about as a result of the firm's broadening base of clients all over the world. In November 2006, the firm opened an office in Zurich to serve European clients. In April 2007, Vivaldi entered the West Coast market in the U.S., with an office in Los Angeles that works in partnership with its New York headquarters and regional offices to serve established and new clients. Silke Meixner, who has worked with consumer packaged goods, e-commerce and professional services clients leads the California outpost.

The brains behind its own brand

CEO Joachimsthaler, has not only guided Vivaldi's operative strategy, but has emerged as a thought leader in branding. Joachimsthaler holds master's degrees from universities in the U.S. and Germany, and completed his education with a postdoctorate fellowship at Harvard Business School. He previously spent 15 years in academia, holding posts at IESE in Barcelona and the University of Southern California. In 2007, Joachimsthaler published *Hidden in Plain Sight: How to Find and Execute Your Company's Next Big Growth Strategy*, and his 2000 title, *Brand Leadership*, co-written with David A. Aaker, which examined ways companies can change their organizational structures, systems and cultures. Joachimsthaler has also authored a number of articles and case studies, and published in academic and business journals, including the *Harvard Business Review*, *Sloan Management Review* and *BusinessWeek*. While still getting involved in consulting projects at the firm, he also spends time leading executive-level conferences and workshops internationally.

Visit the Vault Consulting Career Channel at **www.vault.com/consulting** - with insider firm profiles, message boards, the Vault Consulting Job Board and more.

VAULT CAREER LIBRARY   571

GETTING HIRED

Round 'em up

Described as "typical strategy consulting processes," Vivaldi's hiring constituent packs several interview rounds into its practice, including informational and formal components. With NYU, Columbia, Cornell, Yale and Harvard under its campus recruiting belt, insiders say the ordeal "usually begins with a phone screen, then two rounds of in-person interviews, with three to four consultants each time." Staffers advise applicants to expect resume evaluations and discussions focused on "knowledge of marketing, interest in the company, skills and fit with company culture," along with creative and problem-solving abilities. "If everything goes well," an associate shares, "the second interview may be the final one where you meet with a managing director and HR director."

Preparing for case questions is a given, but sources deny that any special tests and brainteasers are thrown into the equation. Common topics include market-sizing and brand-related queries, such as "What are some of your favorite brands and why?"

OUR SURVEY SAYS

Culture carving

Vivaldi's mini-firm stature gives way to a "down-to-earth, approachable and hardworking" bunch who value collaboration, entrepreneurship and professional development. These "bright, intellectually-driven consultants" are also able to skip over the bureaucracy and hierarchy associated with larger firms and concentrate on culture evolution, which is "great if you are the type of person who is motivated by shaping the culture of the environment you are in," according to a senior-level employee.

With collaborative co-workers come interactive supervisors, who promote an open-door policy at the firm: "Our CEO is a great source of ideas," states a director. In addition, insiders report ample exposure and work with senior clients and client teams.

No pressure, no problem

At Vivaldi, hours spent at the office often fluctuate with the project at hand, but even so, staffers don't complain much about the schedule—"we work hard; not crazy, but hard," relates an engagement manager—and possess the flexibility to self-manage. When it comes to achieving work/life balance, "I don't think the firm actively assists, but I have no trouble doing this on my own," a consultant shares. And where personal management stops, the firm's management steps in, recognizing "that consultants need to be rewarded with downtime after stressful projects," explains a source. Another consultant affirms Vivaldi's leeway for balance, which she obtained through a four-day workweek contract.

Just the bare necessities

Vivaldi consultants leave home mostly for client meetings and research, and "don't do the Monday through Thursday client site routine." For those not too keen on extensive suitcase-toting, this arrangement may seem ideal, since co-workers aren't bogged down by globe-trotting, even when it's mandatory. Some insiders do warn about project specifics, which can require more travel from time to time. "At times in the past, travel has been more important," remarks a director, and continues, "Currently, I am on New York-based clients and don't travel." But a colleague values the firm's travel model: "I have been able to see the world and understand new cultures, thanks to Vivaldi."

Training takes a DIY approach at Vivaldi, where instruction is ad hoc at best. When they need a little extra help, consultants report that they "need to seek it out personally" and at their own expense. "A lot of attention is placed on creating individual development plans," we're told, which allows staffers to focus on personal progress, but forces on-the-job learning. Sources do suggest, though, that the lack of official training is only a pothole, and note that a program "is being developed currently."

On the plus side

Vivaldi staffers aren't too vocal about salary satisfaction, but when it comes to perks, insiders tell us they receive medical and dental insurance, life insurance, 401(k), 11 paid holidays and two weeks' paid vacation each year, as well as a competitive maternity and paternity leave policy. Aside from the official benefits package, one consultant cites "free breakfast every Monday during our Monday get-togethers" as an added bonus, along with free espresso and coffee in the office. The firm also pays year-end bonuses.

As for the office itself, sources describe the lodgings as conveniently located, "spacious, clean and quiet," though one seasoned colleague says the "cubes are very corporate" and "not as fun as the open space we used to have."

Respectable representation

Considering its limited staff numbers, insiders say there is "no bias for or against women," and claim to have "amazing representation" in terms of diversity at the firm. "Many nationalities and ethnicities are represented," a source states.

When community involvement comes into play, associates aren't certain of any firm initiatives, aside from some "consulting engagements for nonprofits at reduced rates," we're told.

Visit the Vault Consulting Career Channel at **www.vault.com/consulting** - with insider firm profiles, message boards, the Vault Consulting Job Board and more.

VAULT CAREER LIBRARY   573

VAULT
THE MOST TRUSTED NAME IN CAREER INFORMATION

Vault guides and employer profiles have been published since 1997 and are the premier source of insider information on careers.

Each year, Vault surveys and interviews thousands of employees to give readers the inside scoop on industries and specific employers to help them get the jobs they want.

VAULT

TOP

50

APPENDIX

CONSULTING

FIRMS

Index of Firms

Visit the Vault Consulting Career Channel at www.vault.com/consulting - with insider firm
profiles, message boards, the Vault Consulting Job Board and more.

CAREER
LIBRARY   577

Visit the Vault Consulting Career Channel at www.vault.com/consulting - with insider firm
profiles, message boards, the Vault Consulting Job Board and more.

CAREER
LIBRARY   579

About the Editor

Naomi Newman

Naomi Newman is the Global Consulting Editor at Vault. She graduated with a BA in American Studies from Barnard College, with a concentration in Economics.

Visit the Vault Consulting Career Channel at **www.vault.com/consulting** - with insider firm profiles, message boards, the Vault Consulting Job Board and more.

VAULT CAREER LIBRARY   581

Use the Internet's
MOST TARGETED
job search tools.

Vault Job Board

Target your search by industry, function, and experience level,
and find the job openings that you want.

VaultMatch Resume Database

Vault takes match-making to the next level: post your resume
and customize your search by industry, function, experience
and more. We'll match job listings with your interests and
criteria and e-mail them directly to your in-box.

VAULT
> the most trusted name in career information™